Due Return

LITERARY CRITICISM

in England,

1660–1800

THE BORZOI SERIES
in Eighteenth-Century Literature

English Poetry of the Mid and Late Eighteenth Century
EDITED BY Ricardo Quintana and Alvin Whitley
both of The University of Wisconsin

Political Writers of Eighteenth-Century England
EDITED BY Jeffrey Hart
Dartmouth College

Literary Criticism in England, 1660–1800
EDITED BY Gerald Wester Chapman
University of Denver

IN PREPARATION

*English Poetry of the Restoration
and Early Eighteenth Century*
EDITED BY H. T. Swedenberg, Jr.
University of California at Los Angeles

LITERARY
CRITICISM
in England,
1660–1800

Edited with Introductions by

Gerald Wester Chapman

UNIVERSITY OF DENVER

NEW YORK 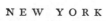 *Alfred·A·Knopf*

1966

To Robin and Wes

PR
1365
C57

THE AUTHOR AND PUBLISHER GRATEFULLY ACKNOWLEDGE:

Material from *The Critical Works of John Dennis*, Edward Niles Hooker, ed.,
reprinted by permission of The Johns Hopkins Press.

Material from *Essays of John Dryden*, W. P. Ker, ed., reprinted by permission
of the Clarendon Press, Oxford.

Material from *The Critical Works of Thomas Rymer*, Curt A. Zimansky, ed.,
reprinted by permission of Yale University Press. Copyright 1956 by Yale
University Press.

Preface

Eighteenth-century critics expressed themselves in lengthy treatises, and in spacious, leisurely prose. To sample them representatively is very hard. Even masterpieces may have to be cut, and masterly critics may have to be omitted. To omit Pope, Fielding, and Goldsmith, for example, certainly risks distortion, but such are the exigencies of space in a volume already overcrowded: furthermore, all three are likely to be read anyhow, and in larger samplings than this text could possibly include. It seemed wiser to include minor writers not easily accessible and whose criticism helps to round out a consecutive development. Many of them, such as Barrow, Blackmore, Morris, Morgann, and Price, have never been anthologized; others such as Hutcheson, Blackwell, Gerard, Alison, and Whiter are available in Elledge's comprehensive two-volume *Eighteenth-Century Critical Essays,* but nowhere else. Still others, such as Davenant, Hobbes, Locke, Rymer, Burke, Young, parts of Kames, Hurd, and Reynolds, are omitted from Elledge. Some mangling and foreshortening of texts has seemed a reasonable price to pay for inclusion and juxtaposition.

Most texts come from authoritative early editions; for Dryden, Rymer, Dennis, Shaftesbury, Morris, and Morgann, later scholarly editions or facsimiles were used. In every case, however, the texts are "modernized." Once the principle of modernizing is admitted, there is no agreed stopping-place, and every sentence calls for an editorial judgment. I have altered punctuation, spelling, capitalization, and italicizing as I saw fit. Such matters are not always so external as one might suppose: many critics, such as Hurd, italicized and capitalized to emphasize distinctions and balances of thought, and to level his entire text would be a serious loss. Yet, to keep everything in every text would be pedantic in an anthology meant for general use; it leads to historical clutter which annoys more readers than it gains, and hence a forbidding exterior conceals the substance of live thought. In general, I have leaned toward mercy, and have kept as much of the original mechanics as I could see cause for keeping. Scholars and research students will go to the full original texts anyhow as soon as they can.

For footnotes I am indebted to a hundred scholars who have beat the field ahead of me; but I have checked their findings. The introductions are more nearly my own, but hardly a sentence is without obligation of some kind to some one. I have tried to condense as much as possible of what others have discovered into short compass, mix it with my own thinking, and hope for the best. Translations from Latin, Greek, Italian, and French are mine, but in every case I have checked my translations against those of authorities.

I wish I could be content with what is done, but I am not. There are all the interesting small points in every text and every critic which had to be ignored; and there are doubtless many significant large points which I simply failed to see, or blurred in the expression, or forgot to mention. And then, there is the vast stretch of the unincluded. If I have missed reading a piece of eighteenth-century criticism in preparation for this collection, I am sorry, for it is good reading—open, learned, suggestive, full of rewards and surprises. It would be dishonest to say that this collection or juxtaposition of texts has any sort of fixed virtue: it is only one of several thousand permutations, selections, and arrangements which would be interesting. It intends to be interesting and useful.

Contents

LITERARY CRITICISM
in England,
1660–1800

INTRODUCTION

"Till of late years," wrote Rymer in 1674, "England was as free from critics as it is from *wolves.*" A few years before, in his preface to *The Sullen Lovers,* Shadwell had noticed "this very critical age, when every man pretends to be a judge." In 1677 Dryden felt himself to live in "an age of illiterate, censorious, and detracting people, who, thus qualified, set up for critics." During the Restoration criticism started to become in England what it presently is, a distinct office in the commonwealth of letters, competing in pride, if not in value, with literature itself—half profession, half public sport, almost a way of life. Less than a century later, in 1754, Thomas Warton noticed, with mixed feelings of worry and wonder, that "critical taste is universally diffused"; and by that date English criticism was, on the whole, the most advanced in Europe, vigorously individualistic and competitive, intent upon particulars and upon discovery. By 1800, when English critics had started once more to look abroad for inspiration, they were accustomed to ideas which to Rymer, or indeed to Dryden, would have seemed strangely off-center, almost unintelligible. Between 1650 and 1800, English criticism witnessed its first great age, its first movement of consolidation and originality in modern times: it matured as a discipline, if not a public industry, found a language and an audience, both in England and on the continent, and produced a continuous tradition of critical advances. Indeed, not until the twentieth century, when American criticism forged into prominence, was criticism in English again so obviously in the lead.

To be sure, England had a rich miscellany of critical writing stretching back into the Renaissance, and on the whole it was written by the same classes of writers as during the Restoration and much of the eighteenth century—gentlemen-amateurs, preface-minded poets, playwrights, translators, rhetoristic academicians and scholars, here and there an ecclesiastical moralist or a philosopher on holiday. It may very well be that the most deeply governing ideas of English criticism before 1800 were articulated somewhere, in some manner, before the death of Bacon in 1626 or Ben Jonson in 1637. The qualification "in some manner" is crucial, however. The eighteenth century imported order and clarity into criticism, a sense of progress in a cooperative enterprise and of participation in "the civility of Europe," a consecutive precision in language, a standard of scholarship, a public voice and concern. Gentlemen-amateurs soon found themselves environed by a growing crowd of journalists, commentators, editors, dialoguists, essayists, treatise makers, "letter" writers, and pamphleteers, soon to be joined, as the century wore on, by periodical reviewers, anthologists, conjectural discoursers, prosodists, lexicographers, biographers, historians, philosophical inquirers, and aestheticians. According to Swift, "it is grown a word of course"—that is, a commonplace—"to say this 'critical age' as divines say this 'sinful age.'" Cassandra-cries of warning continued throughout the eighteenth century—by Pope, Addison, Fielding, the Wartons, Johnson, Goldsmith, to mention only a few—and were a symptom of disturbed foundations. All felt that, somehow, they lived in an age of critic-learning; all had doubts about its healthiness, and all kept writing criticism as spontaneously as breathing.

To a remarkable degree, poetry, fiction, and drama of the period, the very best and the very worst, were penetrated by critical self-consciousness. Learned standards or theories fed more directly into the creative process and governed the forms of work, if only in some cases by stirring up a belligerent anti-learning. Criticism or a critical concept was sometimes the subject of serious poems, as many titles suggest: "Of Wit," "An Essay on Poetry," "Upon the Earl of Roscommon's Translation of Horace," "On Mr. Milton's Paradise Lost," "An Essay on Criticism," "The Pleasures of Imagination," "Taste," "The Progress of Poesy," "Ode on the Poetical Character," "Ode to Fancy." Satire of critics and the critical trade was everywhere, often half-concealed in the convention of the "learned fool":

Butler's *Hudibras*, for example, Swift's *Tale of a Tub* and *Battle of the Books*, Pope's *Dunciad* and Gay's farces, Fielding's *Tom Thumb* and *Tom Jones*, Sterne's *Tristram Shandy*, in Johnson's essays, Sheridan's comedies, even Burke's political speeches and Gibbon's history, and in countless minor writers from Waller to Churchill to the Anti-Jacobins. The ambition to be a critic—a connoisseur or man of taste—became as widespread as the ambition to be a gentleman.

Here, as in all other matters humanistic, causes are much more obscure than results. No doubt the whole course of eighteenth-century "enlightenment" in England, and of social, economic, and political development, made the movement possible. Much impetus came from France, whose critical tradition was older. The diaspora of English courtiers during the civil wars exposed them to French neoclassicism during its formative period; they returned with French ideas and tastes. The Restoration coincided with the brilliant, if despotic, reign of Louis XIV; and it was natural in England, as in other parts of Europe, to emulate the accomplishment of French men of letters, or more accurately, to define oneself against their standards. As French neoclassicism was in its own way an affirmation of order after anarchy, so its appeal to Englishmen tired of civil slaughter was more than theoretical. Indeed, the sudden flowering of English criticism after the Restoration is hard to imagine apart from the war: an interrupted tradition had somehow to be recovered, renewed, and redirected. Criticism, then as now, becomes necessary as experience is complicated by alternatives. Both motifs, the French precedent and the need for national continuity, thread through Dryden's great *Essay of Dramatic Poesy* (1668), and are still strong almost a century later in Johnson's Preface to the *Dictionary*. Still another, and perhaps profounder, cause of criticism was the Baconian tradition of "the advancement of learning." Almost every critic in this volume, from Hobbes to Reynolds, alludes at one time or another to Bacon, who figured in eighteenth-century eyes as the progenitor of a natively English, suitably compromising philosophy of experience, practical reform, and progress. Whatever the causes, the result by 1800 was a relatively sudden and complete redirection of European critical thought—a victory for the Moderns won very often by critics who were anxious to restate or support or reclaim some part of orthodoxy. Similar changes occurred in France and Germany, but England (and Scotland) was the seed-bed.

The story of eighteenth-century criticism requires a converging double plot, in which eroding orthodoxy passes almost imperceptibly into constrained revolution; in which ancient code, which has always to be rediscovered and restated, acts as a civilizing, complicating brake upon new codes, which have painfully to be invented. Following recent convention, I have used the word *neoclassic* as an omnibus term for European orthodoxy at any given moment from c.1500 to the close of the eighteenth century, though I am aware that it may conceal as much as it explains. It assumes that European critical theory, and much of its practice, had internal developing order during three centuries. Vida, Scaliger, Ben Jonson, Boileau, and Samuel Johnson, to pick examples at random, were agreed on fundamentals, would have had only family quarrels, and even in quarreling would have appealed to many of the same authorities in similar language to discuss much the same issues. Neoclassicism was a self-conscious *traductio studii* from "classical" Greece and Rome to baroque Renaissance Italy to regular seventeenth-century France to the individualistic melting pot of eighteenth-century England. *Après cela, le déluge.* I am aware, however, that several centuries of European thinking about literature are by no means simple and uniform; that what is called neoclassicism was kept alive by the efforts of each critic to think through his own problems, and that it is still relevant. The same language does not always have the same meaning, the same beliefs are not given the same order of importance, the same conclusions are not always drawn from the same premises; what may be considered part of orthodoxy in one country at one time might be ridiculed or unheard of in another country at the same time. What is understood is not always stated, and what is stated often disguises what is understood; finally, what one values most in a critic may be perceptions hardly at all related to his prevailing neoclassicism. There are at least two ways of reading criticism, as history and as intelligence, and perhaps neither is entirely separable from the other, even in criticism written this morning. One may see in it ideas particular to the times or to a systematic fashion, and largely limited by the fashion; or more openly, one may see its ideas with analogous imagination, as potent with second life and truth. The following collection has tried to anticipate and encourage both ways of seeing.

Neoclassicism has been studied in depth many times, and it would be quixotic in the brevity of an introduction to attempt the whole ground again. Introductions to individual critics touch on major premises as they become relevant. Generally, every critic in this volume assumes, in some degree or other, the authority of the classics: the literature and criticism (indeed the whole humanistic culture) of ancient Greece and Rome is an initial basis, and *mutatis mutandis* a continuing standard for all subsequent literary culture in the Western world. Hence they assume an order of timeless masterworks, beginning with Homer, which any worthwhile criticism must judge and explain; and they assume likewise a tradition of critics—chiefly Aristotle, "the father of criticism," Horace, Quintilian, Cicero, and, during the eighteenth century, Longinus. The Ancients are considered a vast fund of wisdom to be tapped, a system of precedents sifted from "natural" experience and tested through the ages, in Dryden's phrase, by "the general consent of the most civilized parts of the world." Neoclassic criticism is, at bottom, the Roman enterprise of abstracting from the Ancients a body of critical jurisprudence which will "regulate taste" as civil law does conduct, which will civilize taste, or, that failing, will domesticate it. At the same time, however, an appeal is left open to fresh experience that may accrue to Moderns (for example, from Christianity or from science), and hence Modern writers, if they aspire to the standard, take their place in a continuous tradition. Critics from Aristotle to the present are envisioned as part of a common enterprise—in Johnson's phrase, "the collective labor of a thousand intellects."

At bottom, authority of the classics rests upon the idea of unchanging regularity in Nature, including human nature, which permeates neoclassic criticism at every turn. For example, Dryden's appeal to "general consent," the *consensus gentium,* implies it. Almost every critic in this volume assumes that art imitates Nature, that is, it re-"presents" objective realities, whether those realities are understood as the world revealed by the senses, the world grasped by cognitive intellect or by educated feeling, the typical or probable norms of human action and character, the ideal, or some combination of them. The first preoccupation of a neoclassical critic is the relation of art to reality or "truth," including moral truth. Most of his adverse criticism is directed against distortions or falsifications, and most of his theory hovers round the question of how art "imitates" or should "imitate." He assumes that the laws of Nature can be grasped by reason—that is, reality is an objective rational order which it is human dignity to know—and his main goal is a comprehensive statement of the laws which govern art and distinguish it from other ways of dealing with Nature, such as philosophy, history, or science. In the idea of Nature all arts have a common ground, that is, they tend to the same "end" of instruction and pleasure by different mediums. Hence the neoclassical critic often interests himself in the laws which are "proper" to different mediums, and in the interrelationship of poetry and painting, or poetry and music, architecture, gardening, and sculpture. Within a given medium, art is ranked "naturally" in a hierarchy of kinds (forms, genres), each with its "proper" laws to be discovered, its varying "rules" of subject, structure, style, and emotional effect. In literary criticism, epic is considered the most dignified, difficult, and comprehensive form of poetry—the highest achievement of the human mind—though its rank is sometimes disputed by tragedy, followed by the ode. Other forms, such as comedy, satire, or epigram, are ranked according to their degree of seriousness and dramatic fullness; the art of prose is little regarded. The neoclassical critic is concerned with the power of art to rouse and educate the emotions, and ranks literary forms partly by the kind and dignity of emotional effect, or "pleasure," which is characteristic of each—cathartic pity and fear, for example, heroic wonder, or satiric indignation. Finally, he is concerned with the laws governing the poet himself, his qualities of individual character and genius, and his education.

In the early seventeenth century, neoclassicism was still avant-garde; by the nineteenth century it seemed obsolete, or at least could be taken for granted; in the twentieth century it has reawakened as a rich historic alternative, inadequate to all the facts but asking right questions; in the period covered by this anthology, from 1650 to 1800, it was a status quo leaning into change, sometimes awkwardly and unwillingly. One of the fascinations of eighteenth-century criticism, especially in England, is the vigor with which it assimilated old and new, held in solution sharp opposites, and without abandoning ideal standards or examples of past greatness, faced head-on into "modern" experience. In critic after critic, neoclassicism collided with contradictions and innovations, and yet so far from being destroyed, was enlarged and strengthened for new collisions, until gradually and quietly it ceased to be neoclassicism at all as it had once been understood.

Classical Nature, say in Cicero, was fundamentally idealistic and ethical, centering in the dignity of man and the full development of his "reason" in a static world order. But during the seventeenth and eighteenth centuries, the growth of English empirical science imposed new ideas of Nature and Reason, more mechanistic, material, and at the same time more dynamically open and more in-

terested in the investigation of particulars in the "real" world.
Nature in the new empiricism was based on analogies with the
physical world and the induced laws of change. Wherever the new
ideas penetrated, they subtly colored and shifted the foundations
of criticism. At the same time that English empiricism, as in Locke
and Hobbes, directed attention away from metaphysical norms, it
turned inward to investigate the structure and workings of the
human mind, and the limits of its experience. As Kant says somewhere, British philosophy, and one may add British criticism, assumed a fiction called "the mind," then constructed endless working
models of it. One may think of a Gothic cathedral patiently reared
generation after generation, by innumerable additions and repeti-
tions, in the service of an unseen faith. One result was to turn the
search for laws of art into study of the laws of subjective response
to it, and the laws of its origin in subjectivity. Hence the vogue of
psychological criticism—questions of "taste" (how people actually
respond to a work, or experience it) of "imagination" and "emotion" and their interworkings with the rest of the mind, of "genius"
(the originating force of creativity), of "sympathy" (the mental
origin of moral concern for others). Analyzing the "effects" of art
upon the mind led also to the classification of effects into aesthetic
categories such as the "sublime," "beautiful," "picturesque,"
"Gothic" or "romantic," "magical" and "faery," "pathetic," and since
art imitates Nature, to analysis of what qualities of "objects" in
Nature produce certain effects in art. Aesthetics was virtually created
as a branch of philosophy in eighteenth-century England. The profound and widespread shift to emotionalism and subjectivity had
numerous causes in that century, and can by no means be attributed
to empirical philosophy alone, which after all was a philosophy of
reason. Yet it gave philosophical underpinning to the movement
by turning inquiry back upon the experiencing mind in individual
men, and limiting knowledge to, presumably, what can be known.

At the same time, English critics faced the problem of their own
national literature. They prepared editions of Chaucer, Spenser,
Shakespeare, and Milton, among others, and struggled to assimilate
their values to the neoclassic system. In doing so, they subjected
neoclassic criticism to unprecedented strains, which forced it to
enlarge. Shakespeare especially became a focus of transvaluing experience: at almost every point he contradicted, or seemed to contradict, neoclassic canons of dramatic structure, characterization,
and language. English critics had either to deny Shakespeare,

which was unthinkably dishonest, or to deny classical standards, which was equally unthinkable, or, the course which they chose, evolve a compromised, reformed neoclassicism.

Finally, English critics gradually became aware of history as a vast continuous process, at every moment concrete and "different," and they extended their idea of Nature to comprehend it. The first history of English poetry was written in 1774, but even before that time antiquarian researches had discovered new information about the classical world, the medieval world, and "primitive" cultures. A sense of history was perhaps more developed in England than in the rest of Europe even during the Renaissance. Furthermore, English empiricism, once more, by anchoring the individual mind in "experience" of a changing world, implied history. Perhaps it is no accident that both Bacon and Hume ventured into historical writing.

Empirical science and psychology, national tradition, sense of history—the collision of such forceful ideas, and their corollaries, with the neoclassic system was liberalizing and energizing. The following collection samples some of the more interesting results, whose reverberations are still felt.

NEW PHILOSOPHY:

Thomas Hobbes *1588–1679*

and

John Locke *1632–1704*

AT THE Restoration, Hobbes was a witty hardheaded sage of seventy-two, who had almost two decades yet to live. His reputation was growingly international—"among the deepest minds of the century," Leibnitz said; to Hazlitt, more than a century later, Hobbes seemed "the father of modern philosophy." In Restoration England, however, he was hounded from all sides. Churchmen feared his cogently argued materialism, despite his lifelong conformity to the Anglican Church. *Leviathan* (1651) was burned at Oxford after his death. To many Royalists he seemed a traitor for abandoning exile in Paris and making his private peace with Cromwellian England, though in fact he was simply a pacifist tired of bloodshed, and a patriot tired of national divisions. Still others disliked his pessimistic view of human nature: he saw the human animal as aggressively egotistical, enslaved by imagination-driven appetites, and forced, for the sake of civilization, if not survival, to cede many "natural" liberties to the state. As Charles II's former tutor (in mathematics), he had free entry at court when he wanted it, where his sharp tongue scandalized the sober as much as it delighted a merry gang of wits who for a time took up "Hobbism" fashionably. To the post-war young—Etherege, Buckingham, Mulgrave, Rochester, Wycherley—he seemed for a while, as in some respects he still is, a tough iconoclastic blast of fresh air, and at the same time a link with the pre-war past. Cowley praised his spirit of bold Baconian modernism, and, according to Aubrey's *Lives*, Dryden was at one time "his great admirer, and oftentimes makes use of his doctrine in his plays—from Mr. Dryden himself." As a critic, he has national importance for having articulated, as it were with his left hand, the spirit of a new aesthetic dawning in Restoration England—a simplifying Gallic spirit of *vraisemblance* and utility, a rationalistic tightening. But he has European importance for switching neoclassic criticism onto the track of psychological inquiry. As Professor Thorpe remarked, Hobbes "brought the whole creative process indoors." [1]

Born the year of the Spanish Armada, he became a favorite private secretary of Bacon, and in 1629 published (with a preface) the first complete translation in English of Thucydides, whose hardheaded realism was congenial to him. He knew Ben Jonson, and in later years Gassendi, Descartes, and Galileo. He mastered a prose style of remarkable piquancy (his similes are famous). Only a few years before his death at ninety-one he translated (because, as he said, he had nothing better to do) the *Iliad* and *Odyssey*, prefacing the latter with a formal essay on epic poetry.[2] His most succinct essay in criticism, however, first published in 1650 during his Parisian exile, was an "answer" to Sir William Davenant's preface to the heroic poem *Gondibert*.

To be grasped, this essay should be read in the context of *Leviathan*, for at first glance its bold novelty may not be apparent. Hobbes was restating time-honored commonplaces of heroic theory. Poets, like painters, imitate Nature (represent human manners) by an art of fiction which obeys certain decorums, and is expressed in delightful and measured lines with the purpose of averting men from vice and inclining them to virtuous action. Verse is superior to prose, and poetry is neither history nor philosophic precept. Epic poetry, like that of Homer and Virgil, is the presiding standard of all poetry. Its characters, who should be consistent, are "princes and men of conspicuous power"; its language should be lofty. Comedy and tragedy should never be mixed: "great men" have no leisure to laugh; furthermore, they cannot be supposed acquainted with "mean conversation" or "humble and evil arts." Apparently, his inquiry into "the nature and differences of poesy" intended no assault upon commonplaces, despite his contempt for those who "take not the laws of art from any reason of their own, but from

---

[1] *The Aesthetic Theory of Thomas Hobbes* (1940), p. 294.
[2] Reprinted in Spingarn.

the fashion of precedent times." If anything, his etiology of literary genres from the rigid class structure of seventeenth-century society was ultraconservative in its strictness. At the time, however, formal analysis of a poem according to the rules of its genre, whether epic or pastoral or ode, was new in English criticism: together with Davenant, he imported a French method of analysis which in time was assimilated by critics from Dryden to Addison to Johnson. His breakdown into *argument* or *subject, characters,* and *expression* was the prototype of that into *fable, characters, sentiments,* and *diction,* which, following Aristotle and the French critic Le Bossu, governed epic discussion until the end of the eighteenth century. And far more important, a fully worked-out and toughly reasoned philosophy lay behind his remarks: Hobbes poured modernistic wine into old constraints: the content of terms like *imitation, reason, nature,* and *decorum* was radically colored by the new empiricist model of the mind which he had constructed.

The moving present, Hobbes believed, is absolute in experience, and from the train of sense-experiences all the rest of man's mind is built up: "the present only has being in nature." (The same was true, one should remember, for Homer as for a Restoration gentleman.) Every man, including the poet, knows of nature—that is, matter mechanically in motion—only what his memory stores up in finite sense-impressions as he lives along, and what he deduces, by a high geometry, from impressions long decayed or decaying. The poet's fiction, then, edging toward the rationalistic and representational, cannot transcend his final loneliness, though it may be improved by what he learns from other men, past or contemporary. As reason is only a combination of "names" into propositions, so to create is only to combine remembered "images" of matter. For imagination, the source of fiction, is only decaying sense, a mode of memory, and though it can always make chimerical combinations of "images"—Cyclops or Centaurs—they are meaningless and dishonest in modern society. The ancients, who knew no better because of their religion, may be primitively, even delightfully indulged in their "superstitions," but not the modern heroic poet like Davenant. "Beyond the actual works of nature a poet may now go" (that is, he is not a mere reporter, he invents) "but beyond the conceived possibility of nature, never." Hobbes's exposition of how experience of a present world tyrannizes over imagination is perhaps his main contribution to aesthetics.

At the same time, however, he bequeathed more problems than he solved—e.g., reduction of nature to matter, isolation of the poet, inhibitions on the creative act by modern "philosophy" and hence an unbridgeable gulf between ancient and modern poetry, rigid division between *imagination* and *truth* and gift to *truth* of final dominion over works. Hobbes was himself near enough an earlier age to keep a heroic freedom and openness, as one can see in his celebration of Fancy (see p. 24). But later critics were not.

His psychology further assumed that all "discourse of mind" is a "train of thoughts" as mechanical in its motions as the outer world of matter, except under the guidance of *sagacitas* or passionate "design"—an active seeking out of human ends found by experience to be life-enhancing, as high poetry is life-enhancing and stirs a "delightful appetite of knowledge." Thus, he sketched the first of two major theories of associationism (the other was Locke's) which, by the end of the eighteenth century, had pervaded critical thinking in England. He helped to anchor neoclassicism in mechanistic theory. No major critic or writer pronounced himself a follower of Hobbes, unless perhaps Hume; his influence was more subtle and affirmed as often as not by negation, by the readiness of a critic to deny Hobbesian premises (e.g., Shaftesbury, Addison, Hutcheson, Hurd) or to burlesque them (e.g., Swift). Yet, the mechano-materialistic philosophy which Hobbes represents was *mutatis mutandis* the quietly menacing background against which eighteenth-century liberal criticism was carried out.

In 1690 John Locke published the first version of *An Essay Concerning Human Understanding*, and it is on Locke's model of the mind, which in numerous ways is more practical, that most later psychological criticism is based. Technically speaking, Locke wrote no literary criticism at all, but without some awareness of his thought, much in eighteenth-century criticism—indeed, the whole of eighteenth-century intellectual life—will be unintelligible. Deductions from Locke in literary theory posed problems similar to those from Hobbes (*cf.* p. 184, on wit), but Locke thought of the mind less as an appetitive mechanism built up passively from outside than as a complex self-governing activity with a wide range of rational freedoms in its healthy or normal state: it can respond positively to its environment and even remake it, within limits, according to an ascertainable moral law.

The most interesting part of Locke's psychology for later criticism is his chapter "Of the Association of Ideas," which was not added to his *Essay* until the edition of 1700. By "association" Locke does not mean the whole "train of ideas," which for Hobbes constitutes all mental activity, but only abnormal and irrational linkages—

ideas falsely joined by chance, education, or custom, especially in childhood, and thereafter "keeping company," "ganging," "associating" together outside rational consciousness. "One no sooner at any time comes into the understanding but its associate appears with it, and if they are more than two which are thus united, the whole gang, always inseparable, show themselves together." Such associations are a disease, a degree of madness which "universally infects mankind," and as much as possible should be prevented and cured. One may see here the beginnings of a concept of "unconscious" mind. Off and on through the eighteenth century, wherever Locke's associationism is understood, one meets a growing sense of irrational, quasi-"unconscious" depths in human character, e.g., Pope's *Moral Essay* I, Sterne's *Tristram Shandy*, Johnson's *Rambler* essays, Burke's analyses of the English state. And as Professor Tuveson has explained at length, by the end of the eighteenth century it had become rather fully articulate in literary criticism (*cf*. Morgann, p. 565; Whiter, p. 586).

If reason and imagination are different, and if association is unlike reason, then it is a short step to explain imagination as the associating faculty, a way of putting experience together which is outside or beyond reason. Gradually, but very gradually, association came to be considered not as a disease, but as a source of creativity (*cf*. Addison, p. 239), meaning in language (*cf*. Burke, p. 331), individual genius (*cf*. Gerard, p. 276), and finally the condition of all aesthetic experience (*cf*. Alison, p. 557).

Literary criticism is not philosophy; in fact, philosophers are often if not usually bad critics. But it is always written in a philosophic climate or context whose presuppositions are effective. Certainly, English criticism between 1660 and 1800 cannot be divorced from the context of English empiricism as it developed from Bacon through Hobbes, Locke, Berkeley, Hume, and into the nineteenth century, or from English empirical science as represented by Newton, Harvey, Boyle, and the Royal Society. Much criticism of the period was written in the exhilarating light, or else the strongly felt shadow, of a scientific world-view and its growing successes.

* * * *

THOMAS HOBBES
FROM
The Leviathan [1651]

FROM PART I, CHAPTER 2
Of Imagination

When a body is once in motion, it moveth, unless something else hinder it, eternally; and whatsoever hindereth it cannot in an instant, but in time and by degrees quite extinguish it; and as we see in the water, though the wind cease, the waves give not over rolling for a long time after, so also it happeneth in that motion which is made in the internal parts of a man, then, when he sees, dreams, etc. For after the object is removed or the eye shut, we still retain an image of the thing seen, though more obscure than when we see it. And this is it the Latins call *imagination* from the image made in seeing, and apply the same, though improperly, to all the other senses. But the Greeks call it *fancy*, which signifies "appearance" and is as proper to one sense as to another. *Imagination* therefore is nothing but *decaying sense*, and is found in men and many other living creatures as well sleeping as waking.

The decay of sense in men waking is not the decay of the motion made in sense but an obscuring of it, in such manner as the light of the sun obscureth the light of the stars, which stars do no less exercise their virtue, by which they are visible, in the day than in the night. But because amongst many strokes which our eyes, ears, and other organs receive from external bodies, the predominant only is sensible, therefore, the light of the sun being predominant, we are not affected with the action of the stars. And any object being removed from our eyes, though the impression it made in us remain, yet other objects more present succeeding and working on us, the imagination of the past is obscured and made weak as the voice of a man is in the noise of the day. From whence it followeth that the longer the time is after the sight or sense of any object, the weaker is the imagination. For the continual change of man's body destroys in time the parts which in sense were moved, so that distance of time and of place hath one and the same effect on us. For as at a great distance of place, that which we look at appears dim and without distinction of the smaller parts, and as voices grow weak and inarticulate, so also, after great distance of time, our imagination of the past is weak, and we lose, for example, of cities we have seen, many particular streets, and of actions, many particular circumstances. This decaying sense, when we would express the thing itself, I mean fancy itself, we call *imagination*, as I said before, but when we would express the decay and signify that the sense is fading, old, and past, it is called *memory*. So that imagination and memory are but one thing, which for divers considerations have divers names.

Much memory, or memory of many things, is called *experience*. . . .

The imagination that is raised in man or any other creature indued with the faculty of imagining, by words or other voluntary signs, is that we generally call *understanding*, and is common to man and beast. For a dog by custom will understand the call or the rating of his master, and so will many other beasts. That understanding which is peculiar to man is the understanding not only his will but his conceptions and thoughts, by the sequel and contexture of the names of things into affirmations, negations, and other forms of speech, and of this kind of understanding I shall speak hereafter.

FROM PART I, CHAPTER 3

Of the Consequence or Train of Imaginations

By *consequence* or *train* of thoughts, I understand that succession of one thought to another which is called, to distinguish it from discourse in words, *mental discourse*.

When a man thinketh on anything whatsoever, his next thought after is not altogether so casual as it seems to be. Not every thought to every thought succeeds indifferently. But as we have no imagination whereof we have not formerly had sense, in whole or in parts, so we have no transition from one imagination to another whereof we never had the like before in our senses. The reason whereof is this: all fancies are motions within us, relics of those made in the sense; and those motions that immediately succeeded one another in the sense continue also together after sense, insomuch as, the former coming again to take place and be predominant, the latter followeth by coherence of the matter moved in such manner as water upon a plane table is drawn which way any one part of it is guided by the finger. But because in sense, to one and the same thing perceived, sometimes one thing, sometimes another succeedeth, it comes to pass in time that in the imagining of anything there is no certainty what we shall imagine next. Only this is certain: it shall be something that succeeded the same before at one time or another.

This train of thoughts, or mental discourse, is of two sorts. The first is unguided, without design, and inconstant, wherein there is no passionate thought to govern and direct those that follow to itself as the end and scope of some desire or other passion, in which case the thoughts are said to wander, and seem impertinent one to another as in a dream. Such are commonly the thoughts of men that are not only without company but also without care of anything, though even then their thoughts are as busy as at other times, but without harmony, as the sound which a lute out of tune would yield to any man, or in tune to one that could not play. And yet in this wild ranging of the mind, a man may ofttimes perceive the way of it and the dependence of one thought upon another. . . .

The train of regulated thoughts is of two kinds: one, when of an effect imagined we seek the causes or means that produce it, and this is common to man and beast. The other is when, imagining anything whatsoever, we seek all the possible effects that can by it be produced, that is to say, we imagine what we can do with it when we have it. Of which I have not at any time seen any sign but in man only, for this is a curiosity hardly incident to the nature of any living creature that has no other passion but sensual, such as are hunger, thirst, lust, and anger. In sum, the discourse of the mind when it is governed by design is nothing but seeking or the faculty of invention, which the Latins called *sagacitas* and *solertia*—a hunting out of the causes of some effect, present or past, or of the effects of some present or past cause. Sometimes a man seeks what he hath lost; and from that place and time wherein he misses it, his mind runs back from place to place and time to time to find where and when he had it, that is to say, to find some certain and limited time and place in which to begin a method of seeking. Again, from thence his thoughts run over the same places and times to find what action or other occasion might make him lose it. This we call *remembrance* or calling to mind; the Latins call it *reminiscentia*, as it were, a "re-conning" of our former actions.

Sometimes a man knows a place determinate within the compass whereof he is to seek, and then his thoughts run over all the parts thereof in the same manner as one would sweep a room to find a jewel, or as a spaniel ranges the field till he find a scent,[1] or as a man should run over the alphabet to start a rhyme.

Sometimes a man desires to know the event of an action; and then he thinketh of some like action past and the events thereof one after another, supposing like events will show like actions, as he that foresees what will become of a criminal re-cons what he has seen follow on the like crime before, having this order of thoughts— the crime, the officer, the prison, the judge, and the gallows. Which kind of thoughts is called *foresight*, and *prudence*, or *providence*, and sometimes *wisdom*, though such conjecture, through the difficulty of observing all circumstances, be very fallacious. But this is certain: by how much one man has more experience of things past than another, by so much also he is more prudent and his expectations the seldomer fail him. The present only has being in nature; things past have a being in the memory only; but things to come have no being at all, the future being but a fiction of the mind, applying the sequels of actions past to the actions that are present, which with most certainty is done by him that has most experience, but not with certainty enough. And though it be called prudence when the event answereth our expectation, yet in its own nature it is but presumption. For the foresight of things to come, which is providence, belongs only to Him by Whose will they are to come. . . .

There is no other act of man's mind that I can remember naturally planted in him so as to need no other thing to the exercise of it but to be born a man and live with the use of his five senses. Those other faculties of which I shall speak by and by, and which seem proper to man only, are acquired and increased by study and industry, and of most men learned by instruction and discipline, and proceed all from the invention of words and speech. For besides sense, and thoughts, and the train of thoughts, the mind of man has no other motion, though by the help of speech and method the same faculties may be improved to such a height as to distinguish men from all other living creatures.

Whatsoever we imagine is finite. Therefore there is no idea or conception of anything we call *infinite*. No man can have in his mind an image of infinite magnitude, nor conceive infinite swiftness, infinite time, or infinite force, or infinite power. When we

---

[1] *Cf.* Dryden on *wit*, p. 169.

say anything is infinite, we signify only that we are not able to conceive the ends, the bounds of the things named, having no conception of the thing but of our own inability.

* * * *

THOMAS HOBBES

FROM

The Answer of Mr. Hobbes to Sir William Davenant's Preface before Gondibert [1650]

SIR,

If to commend your poem, I should only say in general terms that in the choice of your argument, the disposition of the parts, the maintenance of the characters of your persons, the dignity and vigor of your expression, you have performed all the parts of various experience, ready memory, clear judgment, swift and well-governed fancy, though it were enough for the truth, it were too little for the weight and credit of my testimony. For I lie open to two exceptions, one of an incompetent, the other of a corrupted witness. Incompetent, because I am not a poet, and corrupted, with the honor done me by your preface. The former obliges me to say something, by the way, of the nature and differences of poesy.

As philosophers have divided the universe, their subject, into three regions—*celestial, aerial,* and *terrestial*—so the poets, whose work it is by imitating human life in delightful and measured lines, to avert men from vice and incline them to virtuous and honorable actions, have lodged themselves in the three regions of mankind—*court, city,* and *country*—correspondent in some proportion to those three regions of the world. For there is in princes and men of conspicuous power, anciently called heroes, a luster and influence upon the rest of men resembling that of the heavens; and an insincereness, inconstancy, and troublesome humor in those that dwell in populous cities, like the mobility, blustering, and impurity of the air; and a plainness, and though dull, yet a nutritive faculty, in rural people that endures a comparison with the earth they labor.

From hence have proceeded three sorts of poesy, *heroic, scommatic,*[1] and *pastoral.* Every one of these is distinguished again in

---

[1] gibing, derisive.

the manner of representation, which sometimes is narrative, wherein the poet himself relateth, and sometimes dramatic, as when the persons are every one adorned and brought upon the theater to speak and act their own parts. There is therefore neither more nor less than six sorts of poesy. For the heroic poem narrative, such as is yours, is called an *epic* poem; the heroic poem dramatic is *tragedy*. The scommatic narrative is *satire*, dramatic is *comedy*. The pastoral narrative is called simply *pastoral*, anciently *bucolic*; the same dramatic, *pastoral comedy*. The figure therefore of an epic poem, and of a tragedy, ought to be the same, for they differ no more but in that they are pronounced by one or many persons; which I insert to justify the figure of yours, consisting of five books divided into songs or cantos, as five acts divided into scenes has ever been the approved figure of a tragedy.

They that take for poesy whatsover is writ in verse will think this division imperfect, and call in sonnets, epigrams, eclogues, and the like pieces which are but essays[2] and parts of an entire poem; and reckon Empedocles and Lucretius, natural philosophers, for poets; and the moral precepts of Phocylides,[3] Theognis,[4] and the quatrains of Pybrach,[5] and the history of Lucan, and others of that kind, amongst poems: bestowing on such writers, for honor, the name of poets rather than of historians or philosophers. But the subject of a poem is the manners of men, not natural causes; manners presented, not dictated; and manners feigned, as the name of poesy imports,[6] not found in men. They that give entrance to fictions writ in prose err not so much, but they err. For prose requireth delightfulness, not only of fiction but of style, in which, if prose contend with verse, it is with disadvantage and, as it were, on foot against the strength and wings of Pegasus.

For verse amongst the Greeks was appropriated anciently to the service of their gods and was the holy style—the style of the oracles, the style of the laws, and the style of the men that publicly recommended to their gods the vows and thanks of the people, which was done in their holy songs called hymns; and the composers of them

---

[2] sketchy beginnings.

[3] A gnomic poet of Miletus (c. 540 B.C.).

[4] A contemporary of Phocylides who wrote elegies full of apothegms to an aristocratic youth. Later, in Athens, they were extracted and turned into a handbook of morality for the guidance of young people.

[5] Gui du Faur, Sieur de Pibrac (1529–84), a French jurist and author of quatrains on marriage. Their early seventeenth-century translation by Sylvester used the *Gondibert* stanza.

[6] poesy derives from Gr. ποιεῖν, "to make, create."

were called prophets and priests, before the name of poet was known. When afterwards the majesty of that style was observed, the poets chose it as best becoming their high invention. . . .

There is, besides the grace of style, another cause why the ancient poets chose to write in measured language, which is this: their poems were made at first with intention to have them sung, as well epic as dramatic (which custom hath been long time laid aside, but began to be revived in part, of late years, in Italy),[7] and could not be made commensurable to the voice, or instruments, in prose, the ways and motions whereof are so uncertain and undistinguished, like the way and motion of a ship in the sea, as not only to discompose the best composers but also to disappoint sometimes the most attentive reader, and put him to hunt counter[8] for the sense. It was therefore necessary for poets in those times to write in verse.

The verse which the Greeks and Latins, considering the nature of their own languages, found by experience most grave, and for an epic poem most decent, was their hexameter, a verse limited not only in the length of the line but also in the quantity of the syllables. Instead of which we use the line of ten syllables, recompensing the neglect of their quantity with the diligence of rhyme. And this measure is so proper to a heroic poem as, without some loss of gravity or dignity, it was never changed. A longer is not far from ill prose, and a shorter is a kind of whisking, you know, like the unlacing rather than the singing of a muse. In an epigram or a sonnet, a man may vary his measures, and seek glory from a needless difficulty, as he[9] that contrived verses into the forms of an organ, a hatchet, an egg, an altar, and a pair of wings; but in so great and noble a work as is an epic poem, for a man to obstruct his own way with unprofitable difficulties is great imprudence. So likewise, to choose a needless and difficult correspondence of rhyme is but a difficult toy, and forces a man sometimes, for the stopping of a chink, to say somewhat he did never think. I cannot therefore but very much approve your stanza, wherein the syllables in every verse are ten, and the rhyme alternate.

For the choice of your subject you have sufficiently justified yourself in your preface. But because I have observed in Virgil that the honor done to Aeneas and his companions has so bright a reflection upon Augustus Caesar, and other great Romans of that time, as a man may suspect him not constantly possessed with the noble

---

[7] I.e., in operas.
[8] hunt in the wrong direction.
[9] George Herbert.

spirit of those his heroes—and I believe you are not acquainted with any great man of the race of Gondibert—I add to your justification the purity of your purpose, in having no other motives of your labor but to adorn virtue and procure her lovers, than which there cannot be a worthier design, and more becoming noble poesy.

In that you make so small account of the example of almost all the approved poets, ancient and modern, who thought fit in the beginning, and sometimes also in the progress of their poems, to invoke a Muse, or some other deity that should dictate to them or assist them in their writings—they that take not the laws of art from any reason of their own, but from the fashion of precedent times, will perhaps accuse your singularity. For my part, I neither subscribe to their accusation not yet condemn that heathen custom, otherwise than as accessory to their false religion. For their poets were their divines; had the name of prophets; exercised amongst the people a kind of spiritual authority; would be thought to speak by a divine spirit; have their works which they writ in verse (the divine style) pass for the word of God, and not of man, and to be hearkened to with reverence. Do not the divines, excepting the style, do the same, and by us that are of the same religion cannot justly be reprehended for it? Besides, in the use of the spiritual calling of divines, there is danger sometimes to be feared from want of skill, such as is reported of unskillful conjurers that, mistaking the rites and ceremonious points of their art, call up such spirits as they cannot at their pleasure allay again, by whom storms are raised that overthrow buildings and are the cause of miserable wrecks at sea. Unskillful divines do oftentimes the like, for when they call unseasonably for *zeal*, there appears a spirit of *cruelty*, and by the like error, instead of *truth* they raise *discord*, instead of *wisdom*, *fraud*, instead of *reformation*, *tumult*, and *controversy* instead of *religion*. Whereas in the heathen poets, at least in those whose works have lasted to the time we are in, there are none of those indiscretions to be found that tended to the subversion or disturbance of the commonwealths wherein they lived. But why a Christian should think it an ornament to his poem either to profane the true God or invoke a false one, I can imagine no cause but a reasonless imitation of custom, of a foolish custom, by which a man enabled to speak wisely from the principles of nature, and his own meditation, loves rather to be thought to speak by inspiration, like a bagpipe.[1]

---

[1] "Enthusiastic" Puritans were likened to bagpipes (e.g., in Butler and Swift) because Scotland was a center of Presbyterianism and because they spoke with a nasal drone.

Time and education beget experience; experience begets memory; memory begets judgment and fancy; judgment begets the strength and structure, and fancy begets the ornaments of a poem.[2] The ancients therefore fabled not absurdly in making Memory the mother of the Muses. For memory is the world, though not really, yet so as in a looking glass, in which the Judgment, the severer sister, busieth herself in a grave and rigid examination of all the parts of nature, and in registering by letters their order, causes, uses, differences, and resemblances; whereby the Fancy, when any work of art is to be performed, finds her materials at hand and prepared for use, and needs no more than a swift motion over them, that what she wants, and is there to be had, may not lie too long unespied. So that when she seemeth to fly from one Indies to the other, and from heaven to earth, and to penetrate into the hardest matter and obscurest places, into the future, and into herself, and all this in a point of time, the voyage is not very great, herself being all she seeks.[3] And her wonderful celerity consisteth not so much in motion as in copious imagery discreetly ordered and perfectly registered in the memory; which most men, under the name of philosophy, have a glimpse of, and is pretended to by many that, grossly mistaking her, embrace contention in her place. But so far forth as the fancy of man has traced the ways of true philosophy, so far it hath produced very marvellous effects to the benefit of mankind. All that is beautiful or defensible in building, or marvellous in engines and instruments of motion; whatsoever commodity[4] men receive from the observations of the heavens, from the description of the earth, from the account of time, from walking on the seas;[5] and whatsoever distinguisheth the civility of Europe from the barbarity of the American savages, is the workmanship of fancy, but guided by the precepts of true philosophy. But where these precepts fail, as they have hitherto failed in the doctrine of moral virtue, there the archi-

---

[2] Here judgment and fancy seem opposed, one cognitive and constructive, the other merely ornamental. But in the remainder of the paragraph, the creative power of fancy (imagination) is glowingly celebrated. Fancy and judgment are components of "wit" whose true opposite is dullness. Hobbes's distinction implies, however, a rationalistic distrust of unregulated fancy and therefore a limit on what ought to be created. See p. 168.

[3] Cf. Davenant's preface (Spingarn, II, 20–1), as also Swift's spider in The Battle of the Books: "[Wit] is a web consisting of the subtlest threads, and like that of the spider is considerately woven out of our selves."

[4] advantage.

[5] The allusion to Christ's walking on the waters, as a product of fancy, would seem playful irreverence.

tect Fancy must take the philosopher's part upon herself.[6] He therefore who undertakes a heroic poem, which is to exhibit a venerable
and amiable image of heroic virtue, must not only be the poet, to
place and connect, but also the philosopher, to furnish and square
his matter, that is, to make both body and soul, color and shadow
of his poem, out of his own store; which, how well you have performed, I am now considering.

Observing how few the persons be you introduce in the beginning, and how in the course of the actions of these, the number
increasing, after several confluences they run all at last into the two
principal streams of your poem, Gondibert and Oswald, methinks
the fable is not much unlike the theatre. . . . But when I considered that also the actions of men, which singly are inconsiderable,
after many conjunctures grow, at last, either into one great protect-
ing power or into two destroying factions, I could not but approve
the structure of your poem, which ought to be no other than such
as an imitation of human life requireth.

In the streams themselves I find nothing but settled valor, clean
honor, calm counsel, learned diversion, and pure love, save only a
torrent or two of ambition which, though a fault, has somewhat
heroic in it and therefore must have place in a heroic poem. To
show the reader in what place he shall find every excellent picture
of virtue you have drawn is too long. And to show him one is to
prejudice the rest; yet I cannot forbear to point him to the description of love in the person of Bertha, in the seventh canto of the
second book. There has nothing been said of that subject, neither
by the ancient nor modern poets, comparable to it. Poets are painters. I would fain see another painter draw so true, perfect, and natural a love to the life, and make use of nothing but pure lines, without the help of any the least uncomely shadow, as you have done.
But let it be read as a piece by itself, for in the almost equal height
of the whole, the eminence of parts is lost.

There are some that are not pleased with fiction unless it be bold
not only to exceed the *work*, but also the *possibility* of nature: they
would have impenetrable armors, enchanted castles, invulnerable
bodies, iron men, flying horses, and a thousand other such things,
which are easily feigned by them that dare. Against such I defend
you, without assenting to those that condemn either Homer or

---

[6] Hobbes believed that no philosopher had succeeded in reducing ethics to a
science. He was ambitious to be first, but his epistemology implied a relativism
which he could not escape. With logical honesty, he must allow the poet to
"make" his own moral judgments.

Virgil, by dissenting only from those that think the beauty of a poem consisteth in the exorbitancy of the fiction. For as truth is the bound of historical, so the resemblance of truth is the utmost limit of poetical liberty. In old time amongst the heathen, such strange fictions and metamorphoses were not so remote from the articles of their faith as they are now from ours, and therefore were not so unpleasant. Beyond the actual works of nature a poet may now go, but beyond the conceived possibility of nature, never. . . .

There remains now no more to be considered but the expression, in which consisteth the countenance and color of a beautiful Muse, and is given her by the poet out of his own provision, or is borrowed from others. That which he hath of his own is nothing but experience and knowledge of nature, and specially human nature, and is the true and natural color. But that which is taken out of books (the ordinary boxes of counterfeit complexion) shows well or ill as it hath more or less resemblance with the natural, and are not to be used without examination unadvisedly. For in him that professes the imitation of nature, as all poets do, what greater fault can there be than to betray an ignorance of nature in his poem, especially having a liberty allowed him, if he meet with anything he cannot master, to leave it out?

That which giveth a poem the true and natural color consisteth in two things, which are to know well, that is, to have images of nature in the memory distinct and clear, and to know much. A sign of the first is perspicuity, propriety, and decency, which delight all sorts of men, either by instructing the ignorant or soothing the learned in their knowledge. A sign of the latter is novelty of expression, and pleaseth by excitation of the mind, for novelty causeth admiration,[7] and admiration curiosity, which is a delightful appetite of knowledge.

There be so many words in use at this day in the English tongue that, though of magnific sound, yet like the windy blisters of troubled waters, have no sense at all, and so many others that lose their meaning by being ill coupled, that it is a hard matter to avoid them; for having been obtruded upon youth in the schools by such as make it, I think, their business there, as it is expressed by the best poet,

With terms to charm the weak and pose the wise,[8]

they grow up with them, and, gaining reputation with the ignorant, are not easily shaken off.

---

[7] wonder.
[8] *Gondibert,* II, v, 44.

To this palpable darkness, I may also add the ambitious obscurity of expressing more than is perfectly conceived, or perfect conception in fewer words than it requires. Which expressions, though they have had the honor to be called "strong lines," [9] are indeed no better than riddles, and not only to the reader, but also after a little time to the writer himself, dark and troublesome.

To the property of expression I refer that clearness of memory by which a poet, when he hath once introduced any person whatsoever speaking in his poem, maintaineth in him to the end the same character he gave him in the beginning. The variation whereof is a change of pace that argues the poet tired.

Of the indecencies[1] of a heroic poem, the most remarkable are those that show disproportion either between the persons and their actions, or between the manners of the poet and the poem. Of the first kind is the uncomeliness of representing in great persons the inhuman vice of cruelty or the sordid vices of lust and drunkenness. To such parts as those, the ancient approved poets thought it fit to suborn not the persons of men, but of monsters and beastly giants, such as Polyphemus, Cacus, and the Centaurs. For it is supposed [that] a Muse, when she is invoked to sing a song of that nature, should maidenly advise the poet to set such persons to sing their own vices upon the stage, for it is not so unseemly in a tragedy. Of the same kind it is to represent scurrility or any action or language that moveth much laughter. The delight of an epic poem consisteth not in mirth, but admiration. Mirth and laughter are proper to comedy and satire. Great persons, that have their minds employed on great designs, have not leisure enough to laugh, and are pleased with the contemplation of their own power and virtues, so as they need not the infirmities and vices of other men to recommend themselves to their own favor by comparison, as all men do when they laugh.[2]

---

[9] "Strong" was a common adjective during the seventeenth century for what is now termed "metaphysical" conceit.

[1] indecorums.

[2] *Cf. Leviathan*, I, vi; and *Treatise of Human Nature*, ix, 13: "I may therefore conclude that the passion of laughter is nothing else but sudden glory, arising from sudden conception of some eminency in ourselves by comparison with the infirmity of others or with our own formerly; for men laugh at the follies of themselves past when they come suddenly to remembrance, except they bring with them any present dishonor. It is no wonder therefore that men take heinously to be laughed at or derided, that is, triumphed over. Laughter without offense must be at absurdities and infirmities abstracted from persons, and when all the company may laugh together, for laughing to oneself putteth all the rest into jealousy and examination of themselves." The later and numerous critics of this famous theory of egoistic laughter often slurred over the possibilities of the last sentence.

Of the second kind, where the disproportion is between the poet and the persons of his poem, one is in the dialect of the inferior sort of people, which is always different from the language of the court. Another is to derive the illustration of anything from such metaphors or comparisons as cannot come into men's thoughts but by mean conversation and experience of humble or evil arts, which the person of an epic poem cannot be thought acquainted with.[3]

From *knowing much* proceedeth the admirable variety and novelty of metaphors and similitudes, which are not possible to be lighted on in the compass of a narrow knowledge. And the want whereof compelleth a writer to expressions that are either defaced by time or sullied with vulgar or long use. For the phrases of poesy, as the airs of music, with often hearing become insipid, the reader having no more sense of their force than our flesh is sensible of the bones that sustain it. As the sense we have of bodies consisteth in change and variety of impression, so also does the sense of language in the variety and changeable use of words. I mean not in the affectation of words newly brought home from travel, but in new (and withal significant) translation to our purposes of those that be already received, and in far-fetched (but withal apt, instructive, and comely) similitudes. . . .

Having thus made way for the admission of my testimony, I give it briefly thus: I never yet saw poem that had so much shape of art, health of morality, and vigor and beauty of expression as this of yours. And but for the clamor of the multitude that hide their envy of the present under a reverence of antiquity, I should say further that it would last as long as either the *Aeneid* or *Iliad* but for one disadvantage, and the disadvantage is this: the languages of the Greeks and Romans, by their colonies and conquests, have put off flesh and blood and are become immutable, which none of the modern tongues are like to be. I honor antiquity, but that which is commonly called *old time* is *young time*.[4] The glory of antiquity is due not to the dead, but to the aged. . . .

I believe, Sir, you have seen a curious kind of perspective[5] where he that looks through a short hollow pipe, upon a picture contain-

---

[3] Hobbes is disagreeing with Davenant on the propriety of technical terms in heroic poetry. His purism anticipates the final position of Dryden who in the early Preface to *Annus Mirabilis* (1667) had defended experiments with them.

[4] *Cf.* Bacon, *Novum Organum*, I, lxxxiv.

[5] optical glass.

ing divers figures, sees none of those that are there painted, but some one person made up of their parts, conveyed to the eye by the artificial cutting of a glass. I find in my imagination an effect not unlike it from your poem. The virtues you distribute there amongst so many noble persons represent, in the reading, the image but of one man's virtue to my fancy, which is your own, and that so deeply imprinted as to stay forever there, and govern all the rest of my thoughts and affections in the way of honoring and serving you to the utmost of my power, that am,

Sir,

Your most humble and obedient servant,

THOMAS HOBBES.

Paris, Jan. 10, 1650.

* * * *

JOHN LOCKE

FROM

An Essay Concerning Human Understanding [1690]

FROM BOOK II, CHAPTER XXXIII

Of the Association of Ideas [1700]

1. *Something unreasonable in most men.* There is scarce anyone that does not observe something that seems odd to him, and is in itself really extravagant, in the opinions, reasonings, and actions of other men. The least flaw of this kind, if at all different from his own, everyone is quicksighted enough to espy in another, and will by the authority of reason forwardly condemn, though he be guilty of much greater unreasonableness in his own tenets and conduct, which he never perceives and will very hardly, if at all, be convinced of.

2. *Not wholly from self-love.*—This proceeds not wholly from self-love, though that has often a great hand in it. Men of fair minds, and not given up to the overweening of self-flattery, are frequently guilty of it; and in many cases one with amazement hears the arguings, and is astonished at the obstinacy, of a worthy man

who yields not to the evidence of reason, though laid before him as clear as daylight.

3. *Nor from education.* This sort of unreasonableness is usually imputed to education and prejudice, and for the most part truly enough, though that reaches not the bottom of the disease, nor shows distinctly enough whence it rises or wherein it lies. Education is often rightly assigned for the cause, and prejudice is a good general name for the thing itself; but yet, I think he ought to look a little farther who would trace this sort of madness to the root it springs from, and so explain it as to show whence this flaw has its original in very sober and rational minds, and wherein it consists.

4. *A degree of madness.* I shall be pardoned for calling it by so harsh a name as "madness" when it is considered that opposition to reason deserves that name, and is really madness; and there is scarce a man so free from it but that if he should always, on all occasions, argue or do as in some cases he constantly does, would not be thought fitter for Bedlam than civil conversation. I do not here mean when he is under the power of an unruly passion, but in the steady calm course of his life. That which will yet more apologize for this harsh name and ungrateful imputation on the greatest part of mankind is that, inquiring a little by the by into the nature of madness [Book II, Chapter XI, Section 13], I found it to spring from the very same root, and to depend on the very same cause we are here speaking of. This consideration of the thing itself, at a time when I thought not the least on the subject which I am now treating of, suggested it to me. And if this be a weakness to which all men are so liable, if this be a taint which so universally infects mankind, the greater care should be taken to lay it open under its due name, thereby to excite the greater care in its prevention and cure.

5. *From a wrong connection of "ideas."* Some of our *ideas* have a natural correspondence and connection, one with another. It is the office and excellency of our reason to trace these, and hold them together in that union and correspondence which is founded in their peculiar beings. Besides this, there is another connection of *ideas* wholly owing to chance or custom. *Ideas* that in themselves are not at all of kin come to be so united in some men's minds that 'tis very hard to separate them; they always keep in company, and the one no sooner at any times comes into the understanding but its associate appears with it; and if they are more than two which are thus united, the whole gang, always inseparable, show themselves together.

6. *This connection, how made.* This strong combination of *ideas*, not allied by nature, the mind makes in itself either voluntarily or by chance; and hence it comes in different men to be very different, according to their different inclinations, educations, interests, etc. Custom settles habits of thinking in the understanding, as well as of determining in the will and of motions in the body; all which seem to be but trains of motion in the animal spirits, which, once set a going, continue in the same steps they have been used to, which, by often treading, are worn into a smooth path, and the motion in it becomes easy and, as it were, natural. As far as we can comprehend thinking, thus *ideas* seem to be produced in our minds; or if they are not, this may serve to explain their following one another in a habitual train, when once they are put into that track, as well as it does to explain such motions of the body. A musician used to any tune will find that, let it but once begin in his head, the *ideas* of the several notes of it will follow one another orderly in his understanding, without any care or attention, as regularly as his fingers move orderly over the keys of the organ to play out the tune he has begun, though his unattentive thoughts be elsewhere a wandering. Whether the natural cause of these *ideas*, as well as that regular dancing of his fingers, be the motion of his animal spirits, I will not determine, how probable soever by this instance it appears to be so. But this may help us a little to conceive of intellectual habits and of the tying together of *ideas.*

7. *Some antipathies and effect of it.* That there are such associations of them made by custom in the minds of most men, I think nobody will question who has well considered himself or others; and to this perhaps might be justly attributed most of the sympathies and antipathies observable in men, which work as strongly and produce as regular effects as if they were natural, and are therefore called so, though they at first had no other original but the accidental connection of two *ideas;* which either the strength of the first impression or future indulgence so united that they always afterwards kept company together in the man's mind, as if they were but one *idea.* I say most of the antipathies—I do not say all—for some of them are truly natural, depend upon our original constitution, and are born with us; but a great part of those which are counted natural would have been known to be from unheeded, though perhaps early impressions or wanton fancies at first, which would have been acknowledged the original of them if they had been warily observed. A grown person surfeiting with honey no sooner hears the name of it but his fancy immediately carries sick-

ness and qualms to his stomach, and he cannot bear the very *idea* of it; other *ideas* of dislike and sickness and vomiting presently accompany it, and he is disturbed; but he knows from whence to date this weakness, and can tell how he got this indisposition. Had this happened to him by an overdose of honey when a child, all the same effects would have followed, but the cause would have been mistaken, and the antipathy counted natural.

8. I mention this not out of any great necessity there is, in this present argument, to distinguish nicely between natural and acquired antipathies; but I take notice of it for another purpose, *viz.*, that those who have children or the charge of their education would think it worth their while diligently to watch and carefully to prevent the undue connection of *ideas* in the minds of young people. This is the time most susceptible of lasting impressions; and though those relating to the health of the body are by discreet people minded and fenced against, yet I am apt to doubt that those which relate more peculiarly to the mind, and terminate in the understanding or passions, have been much less heeded than the thing deserves. Nay, those relating purely to the understanding have, as I suspect, been by most men wholly overlooked.

9. *A great cause of errors.* This wrong connection in our minds of *ideas*, in themselves loose and independent one of another, has such an influence, and is of so great force to set us awry in our actions (as well moral as natural), passions, reasonings, and notions themselves, that perhaps there is not any one thing that deserves more to be looked after.

10. *Instances.* The *ideas* of "goblins" and "sprites" have really no more to do with darkness than light; yet let a foolish maid inculcate these often on the mind of a child, and raise them there together, possibly he shall never be able to separate them again so long as he lives. But darkness shall ever afterwards bring with it those frightful *ideas*, and they shall be so joined that he can no more bear the one than the other.

11. A man receives a sensible injury from another, thinks on the man and that action over and over, and by ruminating on them strongly or much in his mind, so cements those two *ideas* together that he makes them almost one; never thinks on the man but the pain and displeasure he suffered comes into his mind with it, so that he scarce distinguishes them, but has as much an aversion for the one as the other. Thus hatreds are often begotten from slight and almost innocent occasions, and quarrels propagated and continued in the world.

12. A man has suffered pain or sickness in any place—he saw his friend die in such a room: though these have in nature nothing to do with one another, yet when the *idea* of the place occurs to his mind, it brings (the impression being once made) that of the pain and displeasure with it; he confounds them in his mind, and can as little bear the one as the other.

13. *Why time cures some disorders of the mind which reason cannot*. When this combination is settled, and whilst it lasts, it is not in the power of reason to help us and relieve us from the effects of it. *Ideas* in our minds, when they are there, will operate according to their natures and circumstances; and here we see the cause why time cures certain affections which reason, though in the right and allowed to be so, has not power over, nor is able against them to prevail with those who are apt to hearken to it in other cases. The death of a child that was the daily delight of his mother's eyes and joy of her soul rends from her heart the whole comfort of her life, and gives her all the torment imaginable. Use the consolations of reason in this case, and you were as good preach ease to one on the rack, and hope to allay, by rational discourses, the pain of his joints tearing asunder. Till time has by disuse separated the sense of that enjoyment and its loss from the *idea* of the child returning to her memory, all representations, though ever so reasonable, are in vain; and therefore, some in whom the union between these *ideas* is never dissolved spend their lives in mourning, and carry an incurable sorrow to their graves.

14. *Farther instances of the effects of the association of ideas*. A friend of mine knew one perfectly cured of madness by a very harsh and offensive operation. The gentleman who was thus recovered, with great sense of gratitude and acknowledgement, owned the cure all his life after, as the greatest obligation he could have received; but whatever gratitude and reason suggested to him, he could never bear the sight of the operator. That image brought back with it the *idea* of that agony which he suffered from his hands, which was too mighty and intolerable for him to endure.

15. Many children, imputing the pain they endured at school to their books they were corrected for, so join these *ideas* together that a book becomes their aversion, and they are never reconciled to the study and use of them all their lives after; and thus reading becomes a torment to them, which otherwise possibly they might have made the great pleasure of their lives. There are rooms convenient enough that some men cannot study in, and fashions of vessels which, though ever so clean and commodious, they cannot drink

out of, and that by reason of some accidental *ideas* which are annexed to them, and make them offensive. And who is there that hath not observed some man to flag at the appearance or in the company of some certain person not otherwise superior to him, but because having once on some occasion got the ascendant, the *idea* of authority and distance goes along with that of the person, and he that has been thus subjected is not able to separate them?

16. Instances of this kind are so plentiful everywhere that if I add one more, it is only for the pleasant oddness of it. It is of a young gentleman who, having learned to dance, and that to great perfection, there happened to stand an old trunk in the room where he learned. The *idea* of this remarkable piece of household stuff had so mixed itself with the turns and steps of all his dances that, though in that chamber he could dance excellently well, yet it was only whilst that trunk was there, nor could he perform well in any other place unless that or some such other trunk had its due position in the room. If this story shall be suspected to be dressed up with some comical circumstances a little beyond precise Nature, I answer for myself that I had it some years since from a very sober and worthy man, upon his own knowledge, as I report it; and I dare say there are very few inquisitive persons who read this who have not met with accounts, if not examples, of this nature, that may parallel or at least justify this.

17. *Its influence on intellectual habits.* Intellectual habits and defects this way contracted are not less frequent and powerful, though less observed. Let the *ideas* of being and matter be strongly joined either by education or much thought; whilst these are still combined in the mind, what notions, what reasonings will there be about separate spirits? Let custom from the very childhood have joined figure and shape to the *idea* of God, and what absurdities will that mind be liable to about the Deity?

Let the *idea* of infallibility be inseparably joined to any person, and these two constantly together possess the mind; and then one body in two places at once shall, unexamined, be swallowed for a certain truth, by an implicit faith, whenever that imagined infallible person dictates and demands assent without inquiry.

18. *Observable in different sects.* Some such wrong and unnatural combinations of *ideas* will be found to establish the irreconcilable opposition between different sects of philosophy and religion; for we cannot imagine every one of their followers to impose willfully on himself, and knowingly refuse Truth offered by plain reason.

Interest, though it does a great deal in the case, yet cannot be thought to work whole societies of men to so universal a perverseness as that every one of them, to a man, should knowingly maintain falsehood. Some at least must be allowed to do what all pretend to, i.e., to pursue Truth sincerely; and therefore there must be something that blinds their understandings, and makes them not see the falsehood of what they embrace for real Truth. That which thus captivates their reasons, and leads men of sincerity blindfold from common sense, will, when examined, be found to be what we are speaking of: some independent *ideas*, of no alliance to one another, are by education, custom, and the constant din of their party, so coupled in their minds that they always appear there together; and they can no more separate them in their thoughts than if they were but one *idea*, and they operate as if they were so. This gives sense to "jargon," demonstrations to absurdities, and consistency to nonsense, and is the foundation of the greatest, I had almost said of all the errors in the world. Or, if it does not reach so far, it is at least the most dangerous one, since, so far as it obtains, it hinders men from seeing and examining. When two things, in themselves disjoined, appear to the sight constantly united; if the eye sees these things riveted which are loose, where will you begin to rectify the mistakes that follow, in two *ideas* that they have been accustomed so to join in their minds as to substitute one for the other, and, as I am apt to think, often without perceiving it themselves? This, whilst they are under the deceit of it, makes them incapable of conviction, and they applaud themselves as zealous champions for Truth when indeed they are contending for Error; and the confusion of two different *ideas*, which a customary connection of them in their minds hath to them made in effect but one, fills their heads with false views, and their reasonings with false consequences.

19. *Conclusion.* Having thus given an account of the original, sorts, and extent of our *ideas*, with several other considerations about these (I know not whether I may say) instruments or materials of our knowledge, the method I at first proposed to myself would now require that I should immediately proceed to show what use the understanding makes of them, and what knowledge we have by them. This was that which, in the first general view I had of this subject, was all that I thought I should have to do. But upon a nearer approach, I find that there is so close a connection between *ideas* and words, and our abstract *ideas* and general words

have so constant a relation one to another, that it is impossible to speak clearly and distinctly of our knowledge, which all consists in propositions, without considering first the nature, use, and signification of language; which therefore must be the business of the next book.

—◦◦❧❀❧◦◦—

John Dryden

1631–1700

—◦◦❧❀❧◦◦—

WITHOUT THE Janus-figure of Dryden, the classical tradition in England might have splintered off and died of narrowness and irrelevance. He kept alive, if precariously, a concept of nature as ethical order and of creation as an act of the whole mind. His notorious changes of position signal an honest pilgrimage of renewal which was more than personal.

Dryden came of age in the shattered if vigorous culture of late civil-war England, whose heritage of contradictions—religious, philosophical, literary, social—he and his generation never entirely escaped. A lost past had somehow to be understood and present divisions healed, and yet there was no going back: a new but conserving order must be built.

> *Youth, that with joys had unacquainted been,*
> *Envied gray hairs that once good days had seen:*
> *We thought our sires, not with their own content,*
> *Had, ere we came to age, our portion spent.*

So he reflected in 1660, in "Astraea Redux." In 1700, the year of his death, he turned his back on the whole seventeenth century in the oracular style of "The Secular Masque":

> *All, all of a piece throughout:*
> *Thy chase had a beast in view;*

> Thy wars brought nothing about;
> Thy lovers were all untrue.
> 'Tis well an old age is out,
> And time to begin a new.

In the forty-year interval, groping for personal order, he helped cod-
ify a neoclassic compromise with the post-war English situation
which would remain viable until late in the eighteenth century.
Starting as a late metaphysical poet, he adopted "new classicism"
at the Restoration and shared its vision of rational civility, its brac-
ing, almost apocalyptic hope for a more "natural" order in society,
philosophy, language, and the arts. But from the start, Dryden had
also a religion-based skepticism about human hopes, a poet's openness, and a satirist's sense of fact. "Mankind," he knew, "is ever the
same, and nothing lost out of Nature, though everything is altered."
He became, accordingly and by choice, a "common-sense" critic.
"Common sense," he said in 1700, "is a rule in everything but matters of faith and revelation." Understanding the sophisticated complexity of what he meant by common sense may be the most rigorous practical test of one's understanding of Dryden.

Throughout the Restoration and eighteenth century, from Rymer
to Johnson, from Locke to Burke, critics, philosophers, and poets of
very different visions appealed to common sense as a standard, often
with conflicting aims. Historically, the term reached back to Stoical
ethics, the *notitiae communes* of conscience which are a sufficient
guide to virtuous action; it implied the availability of practical truth
in a world of inescapably suffered confusion and change. In Elizabethan psychology, common sense was the mediating faculty
between sense, imagination, and intellect, and in Dryden's lifetime
became increasingly determined by the new psychology of empiricism, in which no man can "understand" any idea that is not
rooted in his own "experience," especially experience of an outer
world of verifiable facts "common" to others. At the other extreme,
however, it could also imply the neoclassical premise of *consensus
gentium*, the community of insight and taste which links rational,
educated men in all ages and nations. Hence the origin, according
to Spingarn, of the "common sense school"—or, as it might better
be called, the "no-nonsense school"—which began in English criticism with Thomas Rymer and with Buckingham's *The Rehearsal*
(1671). Rationalists like the latter distrusted imagination, because
it is so often self-loving and capricious, and insisted that works of
imagination withstand the scrutiny of plain-minded men who are
trained in the classics and who know a phony when they see one.

At its most negative, such no-nonsense criticism, then as now, could issue in narrow, cold-blooded judgments rationalizing prejudice or blindness, for looking to common rule, it retreated from complications to the static safety of what was "obvious" at a given time and place. Yet what distinguished the common sense of Dryden was his very openness to complications—his power to live with a great variety of conflicting facts of value without becoming paralyzed, to have practical insight into excellence of every character wherever he found it, to affirm the limited value of anything just as he experienced pleasure in it, and progressively to look at all the several sides of a matter, even at the risk of a skeptical dead end.

As one might predict, his statements of formal theory are mostly restatements, exploratory footnotes to Aristotle, Horace and the Roman rhetoricians, their Renaissance commentators, and French critics from Corneille to Boileau. Dryden re-examined time-honored problems such as the meaning of imitation, the relative superiority of genres, the function of rhetoric, and recent derivatives such as the propriety of supernatural machinery in epic and of rhyme in drama. He struggled to reconcile conventional antitheses of nature and art, pleasure and truth. "The soul is but half satisfied when there is not truth in the foundation" of a poem or play, but pleasure is "the chief, if not the only end of poesy: instruction can be admitted but in the second place, for poesy only instructs as it delights." [1] People are not always pleased with good poems and plays, nor are those which please them always good, but "generally to have pleased, and through all ages, must bear the force of universal tradition." "Those things which delight all ages must have been an imitation of Nature." Increasingly after the 1670's he drew on the laissez-faire impressionism of Longinus, whom he discovered in middle age. Longinus's enthusiasm, his interest in the genius and character of the poet, in "flashes" of beauty within a unified whole, in "imaging," in "effluences" from great writers of the past, in the utility of literature to an "age" of society, in letting every man "cherish the view which pleases him best"—all these gave classical sanction to a pre-existing taste.

But Dryden snatched ideas from any source, from new science and the Royal Society as well as from his reading in scholasticism, Neo-Platonism, and the Church fathers, from Hobbes as well as from Cicero, from Rymer as well as from Ben Jonson; and with the mind of a poet, he assimilated them so thoroughly to one another

[1] "A Defense of An Essay of Dramatic Poesy" (1668).

that very often one is at a loss to disentangle the derivative from the earned insight, the traditional from the original. "The poet who borrows nothing from others is yet to be born." [2] To be sure, his criticism is shot through with hasty or dated judgments; sometimes he wrote calculated rhetoric for hire, to flatter a patron or an audience. "I confess my chief endeavors are to delight the age in which I live." [3] Sometimes careless, affected, or entangled in his own sophistries, he overvalued whatever work was immediately in hand, as pioneers will, or whatever opinion he had most recently discovered. But even at his most commercial or most pedantic, Dryden never closed his mind to exceptions, though he might mask his awareness of them in ironic reserve. At his most conservative, he can still be seen sifting and revaluing in the light of his age and his growing insight into his craft. As Dr. Johnson remarked, Dryden formulated principles by "experience perpetually increasing" and "a habit of reflection that suffered nothing useful to be lost."

His prose is the perfect vehicle of his sense, at once majestic and nonchalant, guided by decorums but freely associative, "never wholly out of the way, nor in it" after the practice of "honest Montaigne." It is the mixed manner of heightened conversation, or a "loose, epistolary style": Dryden *talks* his criticism, is now digressive, now minutely argumentative, sometimes abrupt or ungrammatical as if he were thinking aloud or suddenly remembering. But his mind is always full. He is at his best when, gradually gaining on a principle—"sailing with some side-wind or other toward the point"—he feels his way allusively through particular authors, works, and bye-considerations. "With Dryden," Johnson said, "we are wandering in quest of Truth, whom we find, if we find her at all, dressed in the graces of elegance, and if we miss her, the labor of the pursuit rewards itself."

The formal premise which most often recurs in his criticism is "propriety" (the rules, *decorum*, τὸ πρεπον, proportion, means of perfection, correctness) which always implies propriety to nature, and is a rhetorical corollary of the theory of imitation. "If nature is to be imitated, then there is a rule for imitating nature rightly; otherwise there may be an end and no means conducing to it." [4] Propriety includes all the "rules"—that is, principles or practical means— whereby a work of art becomes as excellent as possible so as to effect the pleasure of its kind. It is therefore a principle of "finish," of re-

---

[2] "Dedication to the Aeneis" (1697).
[3] "Defense," *op. cit.*
[4] *Ibid.*

fined development and completion—that which calls forth into co-developed wholeness all the possibilities of the subject matter which are capable of "natural" development with one another. And hence it implies also selection, retrenchment or superfluities, co-adaptation of parts.

Propriety encompasses whatever aspects of literary creation can be analyzed: the genre or kind of poetry, the form or construction of an individual poem, the character of the poet, his language, and his audience. The neoclassic genres, each with its latent principles, are "natural" forms, timelessly proper to the nature of man. "Nothing can be improved beyond its own species, or farther than its original nature will allow." [5] In single works, propriety refers to a blended economy of means which, without excrescence, keeps the beauty of the work entire. Each element, for example of a play, should be ordered proportionately to all others in a single effect: plot or "design" is the foundation, all elements should be subservient to one significant and single action; characters come next, each with manners appropriate to his "age, quality, country, dignity, etc.," [6] and no character should be included which is not necessary to the plot, understood by the poet, credible, consistent, and freshly observed. (For example, each of *The Canterbury Tales* is proper to the character who tells it, while the character himself is individually distinct and proper to the fourteenth century.) Each character has thought "which arises naturally from the subject or which the poet adapts to it";[7] and finally, the diction of a play should fit the spirit of the whole work.

The poet must obey his own proprieties. He is "not to write all he can, but only all he ought." [8] He has a particular nature or latent character, a genius, which he must discover and exploit; rhyme, for example, was improper to Ben Jonson's sparely intellectual and allusive genius. And he must also fit himself to the audience at a particular moment in history. Dryden's insights into the "character" of Shakespeare, Jonson, Chaucer, Juvenal, Lucretius, Horace, Virgil, Ovid, are among the glories of his criticism, as also his frank discussion of his own self-discoveries and his grasp of what was "proper" to English poetry in his time. The propriety of a language, abstractly speaking, is its "significancy," its having stored in itself intelligence equal to the ends of civilized experience and use. Near

[5] "Preface to Albion and Albanius" (1685).
[6] "Preface to Troilus and Cressida" (1679).
[7] "Albion," *op. cit.*
[8] "Preface to Fables Ancient and Modern" (1700).

death Dryden described himself as "a man who has done my best
to improve the language," and he consistently affirmed "improvement" of the language as a poet's first duty. Within given poems,
however, the propriety of language is to exploit all the possibilities
for beauty and meaning consistent with the specific pleasure of the
poem. Hence Dryden's justification of rhyme: historically it is
"proper" to all modern European vernaculars because it has evolved
within them, but also rhyme is an extra pleasure if so "properly"
part of a poem as never to mislead the sense.

Dryden tried his hand at almost every official genre—tragedy,
comedy, satire, ode and panegyric, epistle, elegy, epigram, song—
and at late Renaissance hybrids such as opera, masque, tragicomedy,
historical poem, and, finally, heroic play, which he justified as "an
imitation, in little, of a heroic poem," that is, of epic. He confessed
puzzlement that many men should be "shocked at the name of
rules as if they were a kind of magisterial prescription upon poets" [9]
instead of helps to more refined practice. But as he humorously admitted, he never "strictly observed those rules myself, which I can
teach others." He laughed at little decencies and punctilios "which
a master of ceremonies may decide." [1] "Better a mechanic rule were
stretched or broken than a great beauty were omitted." [2] Yet in theory no antinomy exists between rules and beauty, critical reason and
imagination. "Imagination in a man or reasonable creature is supposed to participate of reason." [3]

He wrote criticism from inside his craft, rarely on a genre which
he had not practiced. Almost all his criticism was thrown out occasionally—responsive to cases and occasions—by way of appendage
to works in hand or recently finished, when insight was fresh. Even
his famous "character" of Chaucer followed upon his modernizing
translations from The Canterbury Tales; "Of Heroic Plays" (1672)
and the "Author's Apology for Heroic Poetry" (1677) followed
upon his efforts in the genre; "The Grounds of Criticism in Tragedy" (1679) followed his first five experiments in tragedy. After
writing an opera, he reflected on opera; during his years of translations, he reflected on translation. "Poets themselves," he remarked,
"are the most proper, though I conclude not the only critics," [4] and
accordingly, as Johnson observed, his was "the criticism of a poet,

---

[9] "Troilus," op. cit.
[1] "Preface to All for Love" (1678).
[2] "Dedication," op. cit.
[3] "Defense," op. cit.
[4] "All for Love," op. cit.

not a dull collection of theorems, nor a rude detection of faults."
"His observations were framed rather for those that were learning
to write than for those that read only to talk." He cared most about
poetry as poetry, about theory only as it fitted or enhanced the practice—or the sale—of poetry.

For example, the *Discourse Concerning Satire* (1693), written
after his great decade of satiric poetry, though rambling, syco-
phantic, secondhand in scholarship, is still a major document of
insight. Groping for a tradition of serious philosophic parody, mock-
heroic, and ironic encomium, Dryden illuminates his own art even
as he throws a forward light on Swift, Pope, and others yet to come.
Its genetic formalism is Aristotelian: satire originated in a natural
human instinct for invective and mocking, and expressed itself variously, as in parts of *Job* and Aristophanic comedy, Greek satyr plays,
Mcnippean or Varronian epistles and dialogues. But having passed
through many changes, it found its natural form in a tradition of
Roman poetry, in a "genius and particular way of thinking" which
evolved, by stages, into the art of Horace, Juvenal, and Persius.
Dryden brilliantly analyzes the "character" of the three Roman
satirists, compares their practice, and judges of their relative excellence in the form. But throughout, his governing concern is not so
much the history of satire as "how a modern satire should be made,"
the principles of "hidden beauty" in the classics which a modern
satirist can reapply or develop.

In sheer volume of criticism Dryden outwrote all English predecessors; at the same time, no one before him analyzed such a variety
of genres, works, and styles from so many national literatures, or
brought so many unlike writers to the test of comparison. Indeed,
in the early, great set-piece of his career, *An Essay of Dramatic
Poesy* (1668), he virtually created the structural-analytic and comparative method in English. Its dialogue form is "skeptical, according to that way of reasoning which was used by Socrates, Plato, and
all the Academics of old, which Tully and the rest of the ancients
followed, and which is imitated by the modest inquisitions of the
Royal Society." [5] Socrates *and* the Royal Society! The four speakers
argue conflicting dimensions of his awareness, classical and modern,
English and continental, each having its advantage, its degree of
"probable" gain on perfection, but each implicitly defective in
some way. Neander's defense of English "variety" and imaginative
freedom reaches forward to much else in Dryden's later critical

---

[5] "Defense," *op. cit.*

writing. By measuring English writers against the standard of
Europe and reinterpreting Europe by English writers—Chaucer,
Spenser, "the divine Shakespeare," Jonson, Donne, Milton, and
many others— Dryden extended the range of the whole critical enterprise in his time, which had yet to assimilate English "irregularity," had yet therefore to become fully European, as increasingly it
would during the next century. From his late seventeenth-century
vantage he could grasp the emergence of English literature as a
national tradition, with a historic continuity and identity of its
own. Indeed, the feeling for "traditions" in literature, orders of
value and work developing impersonally in a given language—
within the larger tradition of classical-Christian Europe, itself
gradually developing the limits of Nature—all this is increasingly
precise in Dryden's thought as he grows older. It is no wonder that
T. S. Eliot has felt attracted to him in this century.

* * * *

FROM

An Essay of Dramatic Poesy [1668]

TO THE READER

The drift of the ensuing discourse was chiefly to vindicate the
honor of our English writers from the censure of those who unjustly prefer the French before them. This I intimate lest any
should think me so exceeding vain as to teach others an art which
they understand much better than myself. But if this incorrect
essay, written in the country without the help of books or advice
of friends,[1] shall find any acceptance in the world, I promise to
myself a better success of the second part, wherein the virtues
and faults of the English poets who have written either in this,
the epic, or the lyric way, will be more fully treated of and their
several styles impartially imitated.[2]

It was that memorable day,[3] in the first summer of the late war,
when our navy engaged the Dutch, a day wherein the two most
mighty and best appointed fleets which any age had ever seen, dis-

---

[1] Theatres were closed on June 5, 1665, during the Great Plague. Dryden
retired to the country home of his father-in-law. The "second part" was never
written.
[2] Imitation of style—parody, in the broadest sense—is a critical act?
[3] June 3, 1665.

puted the command of the greater half of the globe, the commerce of nations, and the riches of the universe. While these vast floating bodies, on either side, moved against each other in parallel lines, and our countrymen, under the happy conduct of his Royal Highness, went breaking by little and little into the line of the enemies, the noise of the cannon from both navies reached our ears about the city, so that all men being alarmed with it, and in a dreadful suspense of the event which they knew was then deciding, every one went following the sound as his fancy led him; and leaving the town almost empty, some took towards the park, some cross the river, others down it, all seeking the noise in the depth of silence.

Among the rest, it was the fortune of Eugenius,[4] Crites,[5] Lisideius,[6] and Neander,[7] to be in company together, three of them persons whom their wit and quality[8] have made known to all the town, and whom I have chose to hide under these borrowed names, that they may not suffer by so ill a relation as I am going to make of their discourse.

Taking then a barge, which a servant of Lisideius had provided for them, they made haste to shoot the bridge,[9] and left behind them that great fall of waters which hindered them from hearing what they desired. After which, having disengaged themselves from many vessels which rode at anchor in the Thames and almost blocked up the passage towards Greenwich, they ordered the watermen to let fall their oars more gently; and then, every one favoring his own curiosity with a strict silence, it was not long ere they perceived the air to break about them, like the noise of distant thunder, or of swallows in a chimney; those little undulations of

---

[4] "nobly born, generous." Charles Sackville, Earl of Dorset (1638–1706), at this time Lord Buckhurst and in service with the fleet whose victory is recounted. A gay favorite at court, he left accomplished *vers de société* and became Dryden's patron. Loosely he sides with Moderns in the argument.

[5] "discerner, judge," with perhaps an allusion to Critias the somewhat harshstyled Athenian poet and tragedian. Sir Robert Howard (1626–98), Dryden's brother-in-law with whom he collaborated in *The Indian Queen* but disagreed in critical theory. He speaks for the Ancients.

[6] Latinized anagram for Sedley, with perhaps a punning allusion to *Le Cid*. Sir Charles Sedley (1639–1701), another gay courtier, notoriously dissolute, who wrote tragedies, comedies in imitation of Molière, and amatory songs. He speaks for French drama.

[7] "new man." Dryden himself, who alone among the participants in the dialogue was not born to the nobility. He speaks for a new point of view in behalf of English drama.

[8] rank.

[9] The piers of London Bridge, by narrowing the river channel, created a rapids at ebb tide.

sound, though almost vanishing before they reached them, yet still seeming to retain somewhat of their first horror which they had betwixt the fleets. After they had attentively listened, till such time as the sound by little and little went from them, Eugenius, lifting up his head and taking notice of it, was the first who congratulated to the rest that happy omen of our nation's victory, adding that we had but this to desire in confirmation of it, that we might hear no more of that noise which was now leaving the English coast. When the rest had concurred in the same opinion, Crites, a person of a sharp judgment and somewhat too delicate a taste in wit, which the world have mistaken in him for ill-nature, said, smiling to us, that if the concernment[1] of this battle had not been so exceeding great, he could scarce have wished the victory at the price he knew he must pay for it, in being subject to the reading and hearing of so many ill verses as he was sure would be made on that subject. Adding, that no argument could scape some of those eternal rhymers, who watch a battle with more diligence than the ravens and birds of prey, and the worst of them surest to be first in upon the quarry; while the better able either, out of modesty, writ not at all, or set that due value upon their poems as to let them be often desired and long expected. "There are some of those impertinent people of whom you speak," answered Lisideius, "who to my knowledge are already so provided, either way, that they can produce not only a Panegyric upon the victory but, if need be, a Funeral Elegy on the Duke; wherein, after they have crowned his valor with many laurels, they will at last deplore the odds under which he fell, concluding that his courage deserved a better destiny." All the company smiled at the conceit[2] of Lisideius. But Crites, more eager than before, began to make particular exceptions[3] against some writers, and said the public magistrate ought to send betimes[4] to forbid them, and that it concerned the peace and quiet of all honest people that ill poets should be as well silenced as seditious preachers.[5] "In my opinion," replied Eugenius, "you pursue your

---

[1] importance. Dryden elsewhere uses the term *concernment* technically to mean the emotional involvement of an audience in a play or of a reader in a poem. Its introduction is part of the delicate art of the dialogue as a whole, whose backdrop of war among great nations and of English victory reinforces the argument.

[2] witty thought.

[3] complaints—a legal term.

[4] speedily and early.

[5] Alluding to three recent acts of Parliament against religious dissent and sedition: Act of Uniformity (1662), Conventicle Act (1664), and Five Mile Act (1665).

point too far, for as to my own particular, I am so great a lover of
poesy that I could wish them all rewarded who attempt but to do
well. At least I would not have them worse used than one of their
brethren was by Sulla the Dictator: *Quem in concione vidimus*
(says Tully), *cum ei libellum malus poeta de populo subjecisset,
quod epigramma in eum fecisset tantummodo alternis versibus
longiusculis, statim ex iis rebus quas tunc vendebat jubere ei prae-
mium tribui, sub ea conditione ne quid postea scriberet.*[6] "I
could wish with all my heart," replied Crites, "that many whom we
know were as bountifully thanked upon the same condition—that
they would never trouble us again. For, amongst others, I have a
mortal apprehension of two poets[7] whom this victory, with the help
of both her wings,[8] will never be able to escape." " 'Tis easy to guess
whom you intend," said Lisideius; "and without naming them, I
ask you if one of them does not perpetually pay us with clenches[9]
upon words and a certain clownish kind of raillery? if now and then
he does not offer at a catachresis or Clevelandism,[1] wresting and
torturing a word into another meaning: in fine, if he be not one
of those whom the French would call *un mauvais buffon?* one who
is so much a well-willer to the satire that he intends at least to
spare no man, and though he cannot strike a blow to hurt any, yet
he ought to be punished for the malice of the action, as our witches
are justly hanged because they think themselves to be such, and
suffer deservedly for believing they did mischief, because they
meant it." "You have described him," said Crites, "so exactly that
I am afraid to come after you with my other extremity of poetry.
He is one of those who, having had some advantage of education
and converse, knows better than the other what a poet should be,
but puts it into practice more unluckily than any man. His style and
matter are everywhere alike: he is the most calm, peaceable writer
you ever read: he never disquiets your passions with the least concernment, but still leaves you in as even a temper as he found you.

---

[6] Cicero, *Pro Archia*, x, 25: "We may note that in a public gathering once,
when from among the people a bad poet handed up to Sulla a little book of
epigrams about him, although in rather long elegiac verse, immediately Sulla
ordered that the poet be given a reward from what was then being sold [the
spoils of conquest] on one condition, that afterwards the poet write nothing
else."

[7] Robert Wild and Richard Flecknoe.

[8] The goddess Victory, Roman and Greek, was represented with wings.

[9] puns, plays on words.

[1] John Cleveland (1613–58) was a Cavalier poet who in 1656 published a
volume of thirty-six poems notorious for their far-fetched conceits.

He is a very Leveller[2] in poetry. He creeps along with ten little words in every line, and helps out his numbers with "for to" and "unto" and all the pretty expletives he can find, till he drags them to the end of another line, while the sense is left tired half way behind it. He doubly starves all his verses, first for want of thought, and then of expression; his poetry neither has wit in it nor seems to have it; like in Martial,

Pauper videri Cinna vult, et est pauper.[3]

"He affects plainness, to cover his want of imagination. When he writes the serious way, the highest flight of his fancy is some miserable antithesis or seeming contradiction, and in the comic he is still reaching at some thin conceit, the ghost of a jest, and that too flies before him, never to be caught. These swallows which we see before us on the Thames are the just resemblance of his wit. You may observe how near the water they stoop, how many proffers they make to dip, and yet how seldom they touch it; and when they do, it is but the surface. They skim over it but to catch a gnat, and then mount into the air and leave it."

"Well, gentlemen," said Eugenius, "you may speak your pleasure of these authors, but though I and some few more about the town may give you a peaceable hearing, yet assure yourselves there are multitudes who would think you malicious and them injured. Especially him[4] whom you first described. He is the very Withers[5] of the city: they have bought more editions of his works than would serve to lay under all their pies at the Lord Mayor's Christmas. When his famous poem first came out in the year 1660, I have seen them reading it in the midst of 'Change time; nay, so vehement they were at it that they lost their bargain by the candles' ends.[6] But what will you say if he has been received amongst great persons? I can assure you he is this day the envy of one who is lord in the art of quibbling, and who does not take it well that any man should intrude so far into his province." "All I would wish," replied Crites,

---

[2] A Puritan party under Cromwell that aimed to level social ranks.

[3] Epigrams, viii, 19: "Cinna wishes to appear a pauper, and a pauper he is."

[4] Wild, whose Iter Boreale (1660) on the subject of the march of General Monk and the end of civil war was popular among middle-class readers.

[5] George Withers (1588–1667), a prolific writer of satires, pastorals, and religious verse, a major-general in Cromwell's army, imprisoned 1661–63 on suspicion of satirizing the 1661 Parliament. Among Augustans, his name became a byword for duncical scribbler.

[6] During bargaining-time on the Royal Exchange, goods up for auction were sold to the last bidder when a candle had burned down to one inch.

"is that they who love his writings may still admire him and his fellow poet: *Qui Bavium non odit, etc.*,[7] is curse sufficient." "And farther," added Lisideius, "I believe there is no man who writes well but would think he had hard measure if their admirers should praise anything of his: *Nam quos contemnimus, eorum quoque laudes contemnimus.*"[8] "There are so few who write well in this age," says Crites, "that methinks any praises should be welcome. They neither rise to the dignity of the last age nor to any of the Ancients, and we may cry out of the writers of this time, with more reason than Petronius of his, *Pace vestra liceat dixisse, primi omnium eloquentiam perdidistis:*[9] You have debauched the true old poetry so far that Nature, which is the soul of it, is not in any of your writings."

"If your quarrel," said Eugenius, "to those who now write be grounded only on your reverence to antiquity, there is no man more ready to adore those great Greeks and Romans than I am. But on the other side, I cannot think so contemptibly of the age in which I live, or so dishonorably of my own country, as not to judge we equal the Ancients in most kinds of poesy, and in some surpass them; neither know I any reason why I may not be as zealous for the reputation of our age as we find the Ancients themselves were in reference to those who lived before them. For you hear your Horace saying,

Indignor quidquam reprehendi, non quia crasse
Compositum, illepideve putetur, sed quia nuper.[1]

And after:

Si meliora dies, ut vina, poemata reddit,
Scire velim, pretim chartis quotus arroget annus?[2]

"But I see I am engaging in a wide dispute, where the arguments are not like to reach close on either side, for poesy is of so large an extent, and so many both of the Ancients and Moderns have done well in all kinds of it, that in citing one against the other we shall

---

[7] Virgil, *Eclogues*, III, 90: "Who does not hate Bavius, [let him love thy songs.]"
[8] "For we despise those whose praises we also despise."
[9] *Satyricon*, 2: "By your good leave, let me say that more than anyone else you have ruined eloquence."
[1] *Epistles*, II, i, 76: "I am displeased when any work is condemned, not because it is thought coarse or ungraceful, but because it is modern."
[2] *Ibid.*, 34: "If time improves poems, as it does wine, I should like to know how many years must pass before writings become valuable?"

take up more time this evening than each man's occasions will allow him. Therefore I would ask Crites to what part of poesy he would confine his arguments, and whether he would defend the general cause of the Ancients against the Moderns, or oppose any age of the Moderns against this of ours?"

Crites, a little while considering upon this demand, told Eugenius that, if he pleased, he would limit their dispute to dramatic poesy, in which he thought it not difficult to prove either that the Ancients were superior to the Moderns, or the last age to this of ours.

Eugenius was somewhat surprised when he heard Crites make choice of that subject. "For ought I see," said he, "I have undertaken a harder province than I imagined, for though I never judged the plays of the Greek or Roman poets comparable to ours, yet, on the other side, those we now see acted come short of many which were written in the last age. But my comfort is, if we are overcome, it will be only by our own countrymen. And if we yield to them in this one part of poesy, we more surpass them in all the other, for in the epic or lyric way, it will be hard for them to show us one such amongst them as we have many now living, or who lately were. They can produce nothing so courtly writ, or which expresses so much the conversation of a gentleman, as Sir John Suckling; nothing so even, sweet, and flowing as Mr. Waller; nothing so majestic, so correct as Sir John Denham; nothing so elevated, so copious, and full of spirit as Mr. Cowley. As for the Italian, French, and Spanish plays, I can make it evident that those who now write surpass them, and that the drama is wholly ours."

All of them were thus far of Eugenius his opinion that the sweetness of English verse was never understood or practiced by our fathers. Even Crites himself did not much oppose it. And every one was willing to acknowledge how much our poesy is improved by the happiness of some writers yet living, who first taught us to mold our thoughts into easy and significant words, to retrench the superfluities of expression, and to make our rhyme so properly a part of the verse that it should never mislead the sense, but itself be led and governed by it.

Eugenius was going to continue this discourse when Lisideius told him that it was necessary, before they proceeded further, to take a standing measure[3] of their controversy, for how was it possible to be decided who writ the best plays before we know what a play should be? But this once agreed on by both parties, each might

---

[3] to set a standard; hence, to define terms.

have recourse to it, either to prove his own advantages or to discover the failings of his adversary.

He had no sooner said this but all desired the favor of him to give the definition of a play, and they were the more importunate because neither Aristotle, nor Horace, nor any other who had writ of that subject had ever done it.

Lisideius, after some modest denials, at last confessed he had a rude notion of it, indeed rather a description than a definition, but which served to guide him in his private thoughts when he was to make a judgment of what others writ: that he conceived a play ought to be, A *just and lively image of human nature, representing its passions and humors, and the changes of fortune to which it is subject, for the delight and instruction of mankind.*

This definition, though Crites raised a logical objection against it—that it was only *a genere et fine*[4] and so not altogether perfect— was yet well received by the rest; and after they had given order to the watermen to turn their barge and row softly, that they might take the cool of the evening in their return, Crites, being desired by the company to begin, spoke on behalf of the Ancients, in this manner:

"If confidence presage a victory, Eugenius, in his own opinion, has already triumphed over the Ancients. Nothing seems more easy to him than to overcome those whom it is our greatest praise to have imitated well; for we do not only build upon their foundations, but by their models. Dramatic poesy had time enough, reckoning from Thespis (who first invented it) to Aristophanes, to be born, to grow up, and to flourish in maturity. It has been observed of arts and sciences that in one and the same century they have arrived to great perfection; and no wonder, since every age has a kind of universal genius which inclines those that live in it to some particular studies: the work then, being pushed on by many hands, must of necessity go forward.

"Is it not evident in these last hundred years (when the study of philosophy has been the business of all the virtuosi[5] in Christendom) that almost a new nature has been revealed to us? that more errors of the school have been detected, more useful experiments in philosophy have been made, more noble secrets in optics, medicine, anatomy, astronomy discovered, than in all those credulous and doting ages from Aristotle to us? So true it is that nothing spreads more fast than science when rightly and generally cultivated.

---

[4] It states the *genus* (general class) and *finis* (purpose) but omits *differentia.*
[5] See Shaftesbury, p. 210, n. 6.

"Add to this the more than common emulation that was in those times of writing well; which though it be found in all ages and all persons that pretend to the same reputation, yet poesy, being then in more esteem than now it is, had greater honors decreed to the professors of it, and consequently the rivalship was more high between them. They had judges ordained to decide their merit, and prizes to reward it; and historians have been diligent to record of Aeschylus, Euripides, Sophocles, Lycophron,[6] and the rest of them, both who they were that vanquished in these wars of the theatre, and how often they were crowned; while the Asian kings and Grecian commonwealths scarce afforded them a nobler subject than the unmanly luxuries of a debauched court or giddy intrigues of a factious city. *Alit aemulatio ingenia* (says Paterculus), *et nunc invidia, nunc admiratio incitationem accendit:*[7] emulation is the spur of wit, and sometimes envy, sometimes admiration quickens our endeavors.

"But now, since the rewards of honor are taken away, that virtuous emulation is turned into direct malice, yet so slothful that it contents itself to condemn and cry down others without attempting to do better: it is a reputation too unprofitable, to take the necessary pains for it; yet, wishing they had it, that desire is incitement enough to hinder others from it. And this, in short, Eugenius, is the reason why you have now so few good poets and so many severe judges. Certainly, to imitate the Ancients well, much labor and long study is required, which pains, I have already shown, our poets would want encouragement to take if yet they had ability to go through the work. Those Ancients have been faithful imitators and wise observers of that Nature which is so torn and ill represented in our plays; they have handed down to us a perfect resemblance of her, which we, like ill copiers, neglecting to look on, have rendered monstrous and disfigured. But, that you may know how much you are indebted to those your masters and be ashamed to have so ill requited them, I must remember you that all the rules by which we practice the drama at this day (either such as relate to the justness and symmetry of the plot, or the episodical ornaments such as descriptions, narrations, and other beauties which are not

---

⁶ Lycophron (fl. first half of 3rd century B.C.), a librarian at Alexandria who wrote a lost work on Greek comedy, and because of his (lost) tragedies was one of the "Pleiad," the seven tragedians under Ptolemy Philadelphus who were considered the equals of their Athenian predecessors.

⁷ Velleius Paterculus (c. 19 B.C.—c. 30 A.D.), *Historiae Romae*, I, 17. Often quoted in Dryden's essay, Paterculus wrote in a spirit of court adulation.

essential to the play) were delivered to us from the observations which Aristotle made of those poets who either lived before him or were his contemporaries. We have added nothing of our own, except we have the confidence to say our wit is better; of which none boast in this our age but such as understand not theirs. Of that book which Aristotle has left us περὶ τῆς Ποιηκῆς, Horace his *Art of Poetry* is an excellent comment, and, I believe, restores to us that second book of his concerning comedy,[8] which is wanting in him.

"Out of these two have been extracted the famous rules, which the French call *des trois unités*, or, the three unities, which ought to be observed in every regular play; namely, of time, place, and action.

"The unity of time they comprehend in twenty-four hours, the compass of a natural day, or as near as it can be contrived; and the reason of it is obvious to everyone—that the time of the feigned action or fable of the play should be proportioned as near as can be to the duration of that time in which it is represented. Since, therefore, all plays are acted on the theatre in the space of time much within the compass of twenty-four hours, that play is to be thought the nearest imitation of nature whose plot or action is confined within that time. And by the same rule which concludes this general proportion of time, it follows that all the parts of it are (as near as may be) to be equally subdivided; namely, that one act take not up the supposed time of half a day—which is out of proportion to the rest, since the other four are then to be straitened within the compass of the remaining half—for it is unnatural that one act, which being spoke or written is not longer than the rest, should be supposed longer by the audience. It is therefore the poet's duty to take care that no act should be imagined to exceed the time in which it is represented on the stage, and that the intervals and inequalities of time be supposed to fall out between the acts.

"This rule of time, how well it has been observed by the Ancients, most of their plays will witness. You see them in their tragedies (wherein to follow this rule is certainly most difficult) from the very beginning of their plays, falling close into that part of the story which they intend for the action or principal object of it, leaving the former part to be delivered by narration. So that they set the audience, as it were, at the post where the race is to be concluded; and saving them the tedious expectation of seeing the

---

[8] Aristotle's treatise on comedy, which is lost.

poet set out and ride the beginning of the course, they suffer you not to behold him till he is in sight of the goal and just upon you.[9]

"For the second unity, which is that of place, the Ancients meant by it that the scene ought to be continued through the play in the same place where it was laid in the beginning. For the stage on which it is represented being but one and the same place, it is unnatural to conceive it many, and those far distant from one another. I will not deny but, by the variation of painted scenes,[1] the fancy, which in these cases will contribute to its own deceit, may sometimes imagine it several places with some appearance of probability. Yet it still carries the greater likelihood of truth if those places be supposed so near each other as in the same town or city, which may all be comprehended under the larger denomination of one place, for a greater distance will bear no proportion to the shortness of time which is allotted, in the acting, to pass from one of them to another. For the observation of this, next to the Ancients, the French are to be most commended. They tie themselves so strictly to the unity of place that you never see in any of their plays a scene changed in the middle of an act: if the act begins in a garden, a street, or chamber, 'tis ended in the same place. And that you may know it to be the same, the stage is so supplied with persons that it is never empty all the time: he who enters second has business with him who was on before, and before the second quits the stage, a third appears who has business with him. This Corneille[2] calls *la liaison des scènes*, the continuity or joining of the scenes; and 'tis a good mark of a well-contrived play when all the persons are known to each other, and every one of them has some affairs with all the rest.

"As for the third unity, which is that of action, the Ancients meant no other by it than what the logicians do by their *finis*, the end or scope of any action, that which is the first in intention and last in execution. Now the poet is to aim at one great and com-

---

[9] Crites enunciates the extreme neoclassic doctrine of literal representation, as in Castelvetro, and its structural corollary of centering the play at a crisis.

[1] Popularized on the Restoration stage by Davenant.

[2] The criticism of Pierre Corneille (1606–84), the great seventeenth-century French playwright, consists of three *discours*—on the moral purpose of tragedy, on tragic catharsis, and on the unities—plus the *examens* (analytical discussions) of his own plays. They were published in 1660, partly in defense against members of the *Académie Française* who blamed his irregularities. Corneille claims to revere and obey Aristotle's rules, but insists that allowances be made for the modern stage and for cultural changes since ancient Greece. His influence on Dryden's essay is pervasive.

plete action, to the carrying on of which all things in his play, even the very obstacles, are to be subservient; and the reason of this is as evident as any of the former. For two actions, equally labored and driven on by the writer, would destroy the unity of the poem; it would be no longer one play but two. Not but that there may be many actions in a play, as Ben Jonson has observed in his *Discoveries*.[3] But they must be all subservient to the great one, which our language happily expresses in the name of *under-plots*, such as in Terence's *Eunuch* is the difference and reconcilement of Thais and and Phaedria, which is not the chief business of the play, but promotes the marriage of Chaerea and Chremes's sister, principally intended by the poet. There ought to be but one action, says Corneille, that is, one complete action, which leaves the mind of the audience in a full repose; but this cannot be brought to pass but by many other imperfect actions which conduce to it, and hold the audience in a delightful suspense of what will be.

"If by these rules (to omit many others drawn from the precepts and practice of the Ancients) we should judge our modern plays, 'tis probable that few of them would endure the trial. That which should be the business of the day takes up in some of them an age; instead of one action, they are the epitomes of a man's life; and for one spot of ground, which the stage should represent, we are sometimes in more countries than the map can show us.

"But if we allow the Ancients to have contrived well, we must acknowledge them to have written better. Questionless we are deprived of a great stock of wit in the loss of Menander[4] among the Greek poets, and of Caecilius, Afranius, and Varius[5] among the Romans; we may guess at Menander's excellency by the plays of Terence, who translated some of his, and yet wanted so much of him that he was called by C. Caesar the half-Menander,[6] and may judge of Varius by the testimonies of Horace, Martial, and Velleius Paterculus. 'Tis probable that these, could they be recovered, would decide the controversy; but so long as Aristophanes and Plautus are

---

[3] *Timber, or Discoveries,* a notebook of quotations and miscellaneous remarks, the chief remains of Jonson's prose criticism, not published until 1640. Dryden alludes to the fourth section from the end.

[4] Founder of Greek "New Comedy" (c. 343–291 B.C.). A 1328-line fragment was discovered in 1906, and in 1957 a complete comedy *Dyskolos,* "The Peevish Man."

[5] Caecilius (d. 166 B.C.) and Afranius (fl. 100 B.C.) were imitators of Menander; only titles of their work survive. Varius (d. 12 B.C.) was a friend of Horace and Virgil, and famous for epic and tragedy; fragments only remain.

[6] See Suetonius, *Vita Terenti,* v.

extant, while the tragedies of Euripides, Sophocles, and Seneca are in our hands, I can never see one of those plays which are now written but it increases my admiration of the Ancients. And yet I must acknowledge further that to admire them as we ought, we should understand them better than we do. Doubtless many things appear flat to us, the wit of which depended on some custom or story which never came to our knowledge, or perhaps on some criticism in their language which, being so long dead and only remaining in their books, 'tis not possible they should make us understand perfectly. To read Macrobius[7] explaining the propriety and elegancy of many words in Virgil, which I had before passed over without consideration as common things, is enough to assure me that I ought to think the same of Terence, and that in the purity of his style (which Tully so much valued that he ever carried his works about him) there is yet left in him great room for admiration, if I knew but where to place it. In the meantime, I must desire you to take notice that the greatest man of the last age (Ben Jonson) was willing to give place to them in all things. He was not only a professed imitator of Horace, but a learned plagiary of all the others; you track him everywhere in their snow; if Horace, Lucan, Petronius Arbiter, Seneca, and Juvenal had their own from him, there are few serious thoughts which are new in him. You will pardon me, therefore, if I presume he loved their fashion when he wore their clothes. But since I have otherwise a great veneration for him, and you, Eugenius, prefer him above all other poets, I will use no farther argument to you than his example: I will produce before you Father Ben, dressed in all the ornaments and colors of the Ancients. You will need no other guide to our party if you follow him, and whether you consider the bad plays of our age or regard the good plays of the last, both the best and worst of the modern poets will equally instruct you to admire the Ancients."

Crites had no sooner left speaking but Eugenius, who had waited with some impatience for it, thus began:

"I have observed in your speech that the former part of it is convincing as to what the Moderns have profited by the rules of the Ancients, but in the latter you are careful to conceal how much they have excelled them. We own all the helps we have from them, and want neither veneration nor gratitude while we acknowledge that, to overcome them, we must make use of the advantages we

---

[7] Neo-Platonist antiquarian of the 5th century A.D. whose *Convivia Saturnalia*, seven books of table talk, mingle critical remarks with masses of information on miscellaneous subjects.

have received from them; but to these assistances we have joined our own industry. For had we sat down with a dull imitation of them, we might then have lost somewhat of the old perfection but never acquired any that was new. We draw not therefore after their lines, but those of Nature; and having the life before us, besides the experience of all they knew, it is no wonder if we hit some airs and features which they have missed. I deny not what you urge of arts and sciences, that they have flourished in some ages more than others; but your instance in philosophy makes for me. For if natural causes be more known now than in the time of Aristotle, because more studied, it follows that poesy and other arts may, with the same pains, arrive still nearer to perfection. And that granted, it will rest for you to prove that they wrought more perfect images of human life than we; which seeing in your discourse you have avoided to make good, it shall now be my task to show you some part of their defects and some few excellencies of the Moderns. And I think there is none among us can imagine I do it enviously, or with purpose to detract from them, for what interest of fame or profit can the living lose by the reputation of the dead? On the other side, it is a great truth which Velleius Paterculus affirms: *Audita visis libentius laudamus; et praesentia invidia, praeterita admiratione prosequimur; et his nos obrui, illis instrui credimus:*[8] that praise or censure is certainly the most sincere which unbribed posterity shall give us.

"Be pleased then, in the first place, to take notice that the Greek poesy, which Crites has affirmed to have arrived to perfection in the reign of the Old Comedy, was so far from it that the distinction of it into acts was not known to them, or if it were, it is yet so darkly delivered to us that we cannot make it out.

"All we know of it is from the singing of their Chorus, and that too is so uncertain that in some of their plays we have reason to conjecture they sung more than five times. Aristotle indeed divides the integral parts of a play into four.[9] First, the *protasis* or entrance, which gives light only to the characters of the persons, and proceeds very little into any part of the action. Secondly, the *epitasis* or

---

[8] *Historiae Romae*, II, 92: "Things heard we praise more freely than things seen; and we accompany envy for things present with admiration for things past; and by the former we believe ourselves overwhelmed, by the latter readied for battle."

[9] The division is not Aristotle's but that of Julius Caesar Scaliger (1484–1558) in his *Poetics* (1561), I, 9, one of the major Renaissance statements of neoclassicism.

working up of the plot, where the play grows warmer: the design or action of it is drawing on, and you see something promising that it will come to pass. Thirdly, the *catastasis*, called by the Romans *status*, the height and full growth of the play. We may call it properly the counterturn, which destroys that expectation, imbroils the action in new difficulties, and leaves you far distant from that hope in which it found you; as you may have observed in a violent stream resisted by a narrow passage, it runs round to an eddy, and carries back the waters with more swiftness than it brought them on. Lastly, the *catastrophe*, which the Grecians called λύσις, the French *le dénouement*, and we the discovery or unravelling of the plot: there you see all things settling again upon their first foundations; and, the obstacles which hindered the design or action of the play once removed, it ends with that resemblance of truth and nature that the audience are satisfied with the conduct of it. Thus this great man delivered to us the image of a play; and I must confess it is so lively that from thence much light has been derived to the forming it more perfectly into acts and scenes. But what poet first limited to five the number of the acts, I know not; only we see it so firmly established in the time of Horace that he gives it for a rule in comedy: *Neu brevior quinto, neu sit productior actu.*[1] So that you see the Grecians cannot be said to have consummated this art, writing rather by entrances than by acts, and having rather a general indigested notion of a play than knowing how and where to bestow the particular graces of it.

"But since the Spaniards at this day allow but three acts, which they call *jornadas*, to a play, and the Italians in many of theirs follow them, when I condemn the Ancients, I declare it is not altogether because they have not five acts to every play, but because they have not confined themselves to one certain number. It is building a house without a model; and when they succeeded in such undertakings, they ought to have sacrificed to Fortune, not to the Muses.

"Next, for the plot, which Aristotle called τό μύθος and often τῶν πραγμάτων σύνθεσις,[2] and from him the Romans *fabula*: it has already been judiciously observed by a late writer[3] that in their tragedies it was only some tale derived from Thebes or Troy, or at least some-

---

[1] *Ars Poetica*, 189 (misquoted): "Let it be neither shorter nor more prolonged than five acts."
[2] *Poetics*, VI, 5.
[3] Sir Robert Howard (Crites) himself, in his Preface to *Four New Plays* (1665), in Spingarn, II, 99.

thing that happened in those two ages; which was worn so thread-bare by the pens of all the epic poets, and even by tradition itself of the talkative Greeklings (as Ben Jonson calls them), that before it came upon the stage it was already known to all the audience. And the people, so soon as ever they heard the name of Oedipus, knew as well as the poet that he had killed his father by a mistake, and committed incest with his mother before the play; that they were now to hear of a great plague, an oracle, and the ghost of Laius; so that they sat with a yawning kind of expectation, till he was to come with his eyes pulled out, and speak a hundred or more verses in a tragic tone, in complaint of his misfortunes. But one Oedipus, Hercules, or Medea had been tolerable. Poor people, they escaped not so good cheap: they had still the *chapon bouillé*[4] set before them till their appetites were cloyed with the same dish, and the novelty being gone, the pleasure vanished; so that one main end of dramatic poesy in its definition, which was to cause delight, was of consequence destroyed.

"In their comedies, the Romans generally borrowed their plots from the Greek poets; and theirs was commonly a little girl stolen or wandered from her parents, brought back unknown to the city, there got with child by some lewd young fellow, who, by the help of his servant, cheats his father; and when her time comes to cry *Juno Lucina, fer opem*,[5] one or other sees a little box or cabinet which was carried away with her, and so discovers her to her friends, if some god do not prevent it by coming down in a machine and taking the thanks of it to himself.

"By the plot you may guess much of the characters of the persons. An old father who would willingly, before he dies, see his son well married; his debauched son, kind in his nature to his mistress, but miserably in want of money; a servant or slave who has so much wit to strike in with him and help to dupe his father; a braggadocio captain, a parasite, and a lady of pleasure.

"As for the poor honest maid on whom the story is built, and who ought to be one of the principal actors in the play, she is commonly a mute in it: she has the breeding of the old Elizabeth way, which was for maids to be seen and not to be heard, and it is enough you know she is willing to be married when the fifth act requires it.

"These are plots built after the Italian mode of houses: you see

---

[4] Fr. "boiled capon."
[5] Terence, *Andria*, III, 473: "O Juno, goddess of childbirth, help me."

through them all at once. The characters are indeed the imitation of Nature, but so narrow as if they had imitated only an eye or a hand, and did not dare to venture on the lines of a face or the proportion of a body.

"But in how strait a compass soever they have bounded their plots and characters, we will pass it by if they have regularly pursued them, and perfectly observed those three unities of time, place, and action, the knowledge of which you say is derived to us from them. But in the first place, give me leave to tell you that the unity of place, however it might be practiced by them, was never any of their rules. We neither find it in Aristotle, Horace, or any who have written of it, till in our age the French poets first made it a precept of the stage. The unity of time, even Terence himself, who was the best and most regular of them, has neglected: his *Heauton-timorumenos* or "Self-Punisher" takes up visibly two days, says Scaliger,[6] the two first acts concluding the first day, the three last the day ensuing. And Euripides, in tying himself to one day, has committed an absurdity never to be forgiven him, for in one of his tragedies[7] he has made Theseus go from Athens to Thebes, which was about forty English miles, under the walls of it to give battle, and appear victorious in the next act; and yet, from the time of his departure to the return of the Nuntius,[8] who gives the relation of his victory, Aethra and the Chorus have but thirty-six verses; which is not for every mile a verse.

"The like error is as evident in Terence his *Eunuch*, when Laches, the old man, enters by mistake into the house of Thais, where, betwixt his exit and the entrance of Pythias, who comes to give ample relation of the disorders he has raised within, Parmeno, who was left upon the stage, has not above five lines to speak. *C'est bien employer un temps si court* says the French poet,[9] who furnished me with one of the observations. And almost all their tragedies will afford us examples of the like nature.

"It is true they have kept the continuity, or as you called it *liaison des scènes*, somewhat better: two do not perpetually come in together, talk, and go out together, and other two succeed them, and do the same throughout the act, which the English call by the name of single scenes; but the reason is because they have seldom above two or three scenes, properly so called, in every act; for

---

[6] *Poetics*, VI, 3.
[7] *The Suppliants*. Dryden is borrowing from Corneille.
[8] messenger.
[9] Corneille, *Discours III*: "Fast work!"

it is to be accounted a new scene, not only every time the stage is empty, but every person who enters, though to others, makes it so; because he introduces a new business. Now the plots of their plays being narrow and the persons few, one of their acts was written in a less compass than one of our well-wrought scenes; and yet they are often deficient even in this. To go no further than Terence: you find in the *Eunuch* Antipho entering single in the midst of the third act, after Chremes and Pythias were gone off; in the same play you have likewise Dorias beginning the fourth act alone; and after she had made a relation of what was done at the Soldier's entertainment (which by the way was very inartificial,[1] because she was presumed to speak directly to the audience and to acquaint them with what was necessary to be known, but yet should have been so contrived by the poet as to have been told by persons of the drama to one another and so by them to have come to the knowledge of the people), she quits the stage, and Phaedria enters next, alone likewise. He also gives you an account of himself, and of his returning from the country, in monologue; to which unnatural way of narration Terence is subject in all his plays. In his *Adelphi* or "Brothers," Syrus and Demea enter after the scene was broken by the departure of Sostrata, Geta, and Canthara; and indeed you can scarce look unto any of his comedies where you will not presently discover the same interruption.

"But as they have failed both in laying of their plots and in the management, swerving from the rules of their own art, by misrepresenting Nature to us, in which they have ill satisfied one intention of a play, which was delight; so in the instructive part they have erred worse. Instead of punishing vice and rewarding virtue, they have often shown a prosperous wickedness and an unhappy piety: they have set before us a bloody image of revenge in Medea, and given her dragons to convey her safe from punishment; a Priam and Astyanax murdered, and Cassandra ravished, and the lust and murder ending in the victory of him who acted them. In short, there is no indecorum in any of our modern plays which, if I would excuse, I could not shadow with some authority from the Ancients.

"And one farther note of them let me leave you: tragedies and comedies were not writ then as they are now, promiscuously, by the same person; but he who found his genius bending to the one never attempted the other way. This is so plain that I need not instance to you that Aristophanes, Plautus, Terence, never any of them writ

---

[1] lacking in art.

a tragedy; Aeschylus, Euripides, Sophocles, and Seneca never meddled with comedy; the sock and buskin were not worn by the same poet. Having then so much care to excel in one kind, very little is to be pardoned them if they miscarried in it; and this would lead me to the consideration of their wit, had not Crites given me sufficient warning not to be too bold in my judgment of it; because, the languages being dead, and many of the customs and little acci-dents on which it depended lost to us, we are not competent judges of it. But though I grant that here and there we may miss the application of a proverb or a custom, yet a thing well said will be wit in all languages; and though it may lose something in the translation, yet to him who reads it in the original, 'tis still the same: he has an idea of its excellency, though it cannot pass from his mind into any other expression or words than those in which he finds it. When Phaedria, in the *Eunuch*, had a command from his mistress to be absent two days, and, encouraging himself to go through with it, said, *Tandem ego non illa caream, si sit opus, vel totum triduum?*[2]—Parmeno, to mock the softness of his master, lifting up his hands and eyes, cries out, as it were in admiration, *Hui! universum triduum!* [3] the elegancy of which *universum*, though it cannot be rendered in our language, yet leaves an impression on our souls. But this happens seldom in him; in Plautus oftener, who is infinitely too bold in his metaphors and coining words, out of which many times his wit is nothing; which questionless was one reason why Horace falls upon him so severely in those verses:

> Sed proavi nostri Plautinos et numeros et
> Laudavere sales, nimium patienter utrumque.
> Ne dicam stolide.[4]

For Horace himself was cautious to obtrude a new word on his readers, and makes custom and common use the best measure of receiving it into our writings:

> Multa renascentur quae nunc cecidere, cadentque
> Quae nunc sunt in honore vocabula, si volet usus,
> Quem penes arbitrium est, et jus, et norma loquendi.[5]

---

[2] Terence, *Eunuchus*, 223–24: "Pray then, shall I not do without her, if there is need, even for three days?"

[3] *Ibid.*: "O my! the *all* of three days!"

[4] *Ars Poetica*, 270–72 (misquoted): "But our ancestors praised both the versification and the jests of Plautus, much too patiently, not to say stupidly."

[5] *Ibid.*, 70–72: "Many words shall flourish again which now have fallen away, and many shall fall which are now in their glory, if usage so decides, for in it is the judgment, and the right and rule of speech."

"The not observing this rule is that which the world has blamed in our satirist Cleveland: to express a thing hard and unnaturally is his new way of elocution. 'Tis true, no poet but may sometimes use a catachresis. Virgil does it—

> Mistaque ridenti colocasia fundet acantho[6]—

in his eclogue of Pollio, and in his 7th *Aeneid:*

> mirantur et undae,
> Miratur nemus insuetum fulgentia longe
> Scuta virum fluvio pictasque innare carinas.[7]

And Ovid once so modestly that he asks leave to do it—

> quem, si verbo audacia detur,
> Haud metuam summi dixisse Palatia caeli[8]—

calling the court of Jupiter by the name of Augustus his palace, though in another place he is more bold where he says *et longas visent Capitolia pompas.*[9] But to do this always, and never be able to write a line without it, though it may be admired by some few pedants, will not pass upon those who know that wit is best conveyed to us in the most easy language, and is most to be admired when a great thought comes dressed in words so commonly received that it is understood by the meanest apprehensions, as the best meat is the most easily digested. But we cannot read a verse of Cleveland's without making a face at it, as if every word were a pill to swallow: he gives us many times a hard nut to break our teeth, without a kernel for our pains. So that there is this difference betwixt his satires and Doctor Donne's, that the one gives us deep thoughts in common language, though rough cadence; the other gives us common thoughts in abstruse words. 'Tis true, in some places his[1] wit is independent of his words, as in that of *The Rebel Scot:*

> *Had Cain been Scot, God would have chang'd his doom;*
> *Not forc'd him wander, but confin'd him home.*[2]

---

[6] *Eclogues,* IV, 20: "[The earth] shall pour forth colocasiums, mingled with the laughing acanthus."

[7] Actually *Aeneid,* VIII, 91–93: "The waves and unaccustomed woods are astonished by the distant-gleaming shields of soldiers and the painted ships floating on the stream."

[8] *Metamorphoses,* I, 175–76: "which, if I may be allowed an audacious phrase, I shall scarcely fear to call the Palatia of the highest heaven."

[9] *Ibid.,* 561: "and the temples of Jupiter shall see long processionals."

[1] Cleveland's.

[2] ll. 63–64.

"*Si sic omnia dixisset!*[3] This is wit in all languages. It is like Mercury, never to be lost or killed; and so that other—

> *For beauty, like white powder,*[4] *makes no noise,*
> *And yet the silent hypocrite destroys.*[5]

You see the last line is highly metaphorical, but it is so soft and gentle that it does not shock us as we read it.

"But to return, from whence I have digressed, to the consideration of the Ancients' writing and their wit (of which by this time you will grant us in some measure to be fit judges). Though I see many excellent thoughts in Seneca, yet he of them who had a genius most proper for the stage was Ovid; he had a way of writing so fit to stir up a pleasing admiration and concernment, which are the objects of a tragedy, and to show the various movements of a soul combating betwixt two different passions, that, had he lived in our age, or in his own could have writ with our advantages, no man but must have yielded to him; and therefore I am confident the *Medea* is none of his, for, though I esteem it for the gravity and sententiousness of it, which he himself concludes to be suitable to a tragedy—*Omne genus scripti gravitate tragaedia vincit*[6]—yet it moves not my soul enough to judge that he, who in the epic way wrote things so near the drama as the story of Myrrha, of Caunus and Biblis, and the rest, should stir up no more concernment where he most endeavored it. The masterpiece of Seneca I hold to be that scene in the *Troades* where Ulysses is seeking for Astyanax to kill him: there you see the tenderness of a mother so represented in Andromache that it raises compassion to a high degree in the reader, and bears the nearest resemblance of anything in the tragedies of the Ancients to the excellent scenes of passion in Shakespeare or in Fletcher. For love-scenes, you will find few among them; their tragic poets dealt not with that soft passion, but with lust, cruelty, revenge, ambition, and those bloody actions they produced, which were more capable of raising horror than compassion in an audience; leaving love untouched, whose gentleness would have tempered them, which is the most frequent of all the passions, and which, being the private concernment of every person, is soothed by viewing its own image in a public entertainment.

---

[3] Juvenal, *Satires*, X, 123: "If only he had spoken all things thus!"
[4] A gunpowder supposed to explode without noise.
[5] Cleveland, *Rupertismus*, 39–40.
[6] *Tristia*, II, 381: "Tragedy surpasses every kind of writing in seriousness."

"Among their comedies, we find a scene or two of tenderness, and that where you would least expect it, in Plautus; but to speak generally, their lovers say little when they see each other but *anima mea vita meu; Ζωὴ καὶ ψυχή*,[7] as the women in Juvenal's time used to cry out in the fury of their kindness. Any sudden gust of passion (as an ecstasy of love in an unexpected meeting) cannot better be expressed than in a word and a sigh, breaking one another. Nature is dumb on such occasions, and to make her speak would be to represent her unlike herself. But there are a thousand other concernments of lovers, as jealousies, complaints, contrivances, and the like, where not to open their minds at large to each other were to be wanting to their own love; and to the expectation of the audience, who watch the movements of their minds as much as the changes of their fortunes. For the imaging of the first is properly the work of a poet;[8] the latter he borrows from the historian."

Eugenius was proceeding in that part of his discourse when Crites interrupted him. "I sec," said he, "Eugenius and I are never like to have this question decided betwixt us, for he maintains the Moderns have acquired a new perfection in writing; I can only grant they have altered the mode of it. Homer described his heroes men of great appetites, lovers of beef broiled upon the coals, and good fellows, contrary to the practice of the French romances, whose heroes neither eat nor drink nor sleep, for love. Virgil makes Aeneas a bold avower of his own virtues:

> *Sum pius Aeneas, fama super aethera notus;*[9]

which in the civility of our poets is the character of a fanfaron[1] or Hector,[2] for with us the knight takes occasion to walk out, or sleep, to avoid the vanity of telling his own story, which the trusty squire is ever to perform for him. So in their love-scenes, of which Eugenius spoke last, the Ancients were more hearty, were more talkative: they writ love as it was then the mode to make it; and I will grant this much to Eugenius, that perhaps one of their poets, had he lived in our age—*si foret hoc nostrum fato delapsus in*

---

[7] Juvenal, *Satires*, VI, 195: "My soul, my life." The Latin and Greek mean the same.
[8] The modernist Eugenius is interested in psychological portraiture, not in plot.
[9] *Aeneid*, I, 378–79: "I am dutiful Aeneas, famed even among the heavens."
[1] braggart.
[2] scolding bully.

aevum,[3] as Horace says of Lucilius—he had altered many things; not that they were not natural before, but that he might accommodate himself to the age in which he lived. Yet in the meantime, we are not to conclude anything rashly against those great men, but preserve to them the dignity of masters, and give that honor to their memories (*quos Libitina sacravit*[4]), part of which we expect may be paid to us in future times."

This moderation of Crites, as it was pleasing to all the company, so it put an end to that dispute, which Eugenius, who seemed to have the better of the argument, would urge no farther. But Lisideius, after he had acknowledged himself of Eugenius his opinion concerning the Ancients, yet told him he had forborne, till his discourse were ended, to ask him why he preferred the English plays above those of other nations? and whether we ought not to submit our stage to the exactness of our next neighbors?

"Though," said Eugenius, "I am at all times ready to defend the honor of my country against the French, and to maintain we are as well able to vanquish them with our pens as our ancestors have been with their swords, yet, if you please," added he, looking upon Neander, "I will commit this cause to my friend's management. His opinion of our plays is the same with mine, and besides, there is no reason that Crites and I, who have now left the stage, should reenter so suddenly upon it; which is against the laws of comedy."

"If the question had been stated," replied Lisideius, "who had writ best, the French or English forty years ago, I should have been of your opinion, and adjudged the honor to our own nation; but since that time," said he, turning towards Neander, "we have been so long together bad Englishmen[5] that we had not leisure to be good poets. Beaumont, Fletcher, and Jonson (who were only capable of bringing us to that degree of perfection which we have) were just then leaving the world, as if in an age of so much horror, wit and those milder studies of humanity had no farther business among us. But the Muses, who ever follow peace, went to plant in another country. It was then that the great Cardinal Richelieu[6] began to

---

[3] *Satires*, I, x, 68: "if by fate he had dropped into our age."
[4] Horace, *Epistles*, II, i, 49: "which the goddess of funerals has hallowed."
[5] During the civil war.
[6] Armand Jean Duplessis, Cardinal, Duc de Richelieu (1585–1642), minister of Louis XIII; while suppressing popular liberties in France, he nevertheless built it into the leading military and cultural power on the continent. He founded the *Académie Française*.

take them into his protection and that, by his encouragement,
Corneille and some other Frenchmen reformed their theatre,
which before was as much below ours as it now surpasses it and the
rest of Europe. But because Crites in his discourse for the Ancients
has prevented[7] me, by observing many rules of the stage which the
Moderns have borrowed from them, I shall only, in short, demand
of you whether you are not convinced that of all nations the
French have best observed them? In the unity of time you find
them so scrupulous that it yet remains a dispute among their poets
whether the artificial day of twelve hours, more or less, be not
meant by Aristotle, rather than the natural one of twenty-four, and
consequently, whether all plays ought not to be reduced into that
compass. This I can testify, that in all their dramas writ within
these last twenty years and upwards, I have not observed any that
have extended the time to thirty hours. In the unity of place they
are full as scrupulous, for many of their critics limit it to that very
spot of ground where the play is supposed to begin; none of them
exceed the compass of the same town or city. The unity of action
in all plays is yet more conspicuous, for they do not burden them
with underplots, as the English do; which is the reason why many
scenes of our tragi-comedians carry on a design that is nothing of
kin to the main plot, and that we see two distinct webs in a play,
like those in ill-wrought stuffs,[8] and two actions, that is, two plays,
carried on together to the confounding of the audience; who, before
they are warm in their concernments for one part, are diverted to
another, and by that means espouse the interest of neither. From
hence likewise it arises that the one half of our actors are not known
to the other. They keep their distances, as if they were Montagues
and Capulets, and seldom begin an acquaintance till the last
scene of the fifth act, when they are all to meet upon the stage.
There is no theatre in the world has anything so absurd as the English tragi-comedy; 'tis a drama of our own invention, and the fashion
of it is enough to proclaim it so; here a course of mirth, there another of sadness and passion, and a third of honor and a duel; thus,
in two hours and a half, we run through all the fits of Bedlam.[9] The
French affords you as much variety on the same day, but they do it
not so unseasonably or *mal à propos* as we. Our poets present you

---

[7] anticipated.
[8] fabrics.
[9] St. Mary of Bethlehem, the London hospital for lunatics.

the play and the farce together, and our stages still retain somewhat of the original civility of the Red Bull:[1]

Atque ursum et pugiles media inter carmina poscunt.[2]

The end[3] of tragedies or serious plays, says Aristotle, is to beget admiration, compassion, or concernment; but are not mirth and compassion things incompatible? and is it not evident that the poet must of necessity destroy the former by intermingling of the latter? That is, he must ruin the sole end and object of his tragedy, to introduce somewhat that is forced into it, and is not of the body of it. Would you not think that physician mad who, having prescribed a purge, should immediately order you to take restringents?

"But to leave our plays and return to theirs. I have noted one great advantage they have had in the plotting of their tragedies; that is, they are always grounded upon some known history, according to that of Horace, *Ex noto fictum carmen sequar*,[4] and in that they have so imitated the Ancients that they have surpassed them. For the Ancients, as was observed before, took for the foundation of their plays some poetical fiction such as under that consideration could move but little concernment in the audience, because they already knew the event of it. But the French goes farther:

Atque ita mentitur, sic veris falsa remiscet
Primo ne medium, medio ne discrepet imum.[5]

He so interweaves truth with probable fiction that he puts a pleasing fallacy upon us, mends the intrigues of fate, and dispenses with the severity of history, to reward that virtue which has been rendered to us there unfortunate. Sometimes the story has left the success[6] so doubtful that the writer is free, by the privilege of a poet, to take that which of two or more relations will best suit with his design: as for example, in the death of Cyrus, whom Justin and some others report to have perished in the Scythian war, but

---

[1] Popular Jacobean playhouse, used during the Commonwealth period for performance of drolls. By the Restoration it was dacayed and soon demolished.
[2] Horace, *Epistles*, II, i, 185: "in the middle of poetic speeches, they call for a bear or for boxers."
[3] fulfilling purpose.
[4] *Ars Poetica*, 240: "I should use familiar material in my poem."
[5] Horace, *Ars Poetica*, 151–52: "And he lies so skillfully, so mingles the false and the true, that the beginning is not inconsistent with the middle or the middle with the end."
[6] outcome.

Xenophon affirms[7] to have died in his bed of extreme old age. Nay more, when the event is past dispute, even then we are willing to be deceived; and the poet, if he contrives it with appearance of truth, has all the audience of his party, at least during the time his play is acting: so naturally we are kind to virtue, when our own interest is not in question, that we take it up as a general concernment of mankind. On the other side, if you consider the historical plays of Shakespeare, they are rather so many chronicles of kings, or the business many times of thirty or forty years cramped into a representation of two hours and a half, which is not to imitate or paint Nature, but rather to draw her in miniature, to take her in little, to look upon her through the wrong end of a perspective,[8] and receive her images not only much less, but infinitely more imperfect than the life. This, instead of making a play delightful, renders it ridiculous:

Quodcunque ostendis mihi sic, incredulus odi.[9]

For the spirit of man cannot be satisfied but with truth, or at least versimility; and a poem is to contain, if not τὰ ἔτυμα, yet ἐτύμοισιν ὁμοῖα,[1] as one of the Greek poets has expressed it.

"Another thing in which the French differ from us and from the Spaniards is that they do not embarrass or cumber themselves with too much plot; they only represent so much of a story as will constitute one whole and great action sufficient for a play. We, who undertake more, do but multiply adventures, which, not being produced from one another as effects from causes, but rarely following, constitute many actions in the drama, and consequently make it many plays.

"But by pursuing closely one argument, which is not cloyed with many turns, the French have gained more liberty for verse, in which they write; they have leisure to dwell on a subject which deserves it, and to represent the passions (which we have acknowledged to be the poet's work) without being hurried from one thing to another, as we are in the plays of Calderón,[2] which we have seen lately upon our theatres under the name of Spanish plots. I have

---

[7] In the *Cyropaedia.*
[8] telescope.
[9] Horace, *Ars Poetica,* 188: "Unbelieving, I am disgusted by whatever you show me of this sort."
[1] Homer, *Odyssey,* XIX, 203: "true things." Hesiod, *Theogonia,* 27: "things like the truth."
[2] Pedro Calderón de la Barca (1600–81), the great Spanish playwright.

taken notice but of one tragedy of ours whose plot has that
uniformity and unity of design in it which I have commended in
the French, and that is *Rollo*,[3] or rather, under the name of Rollo,
the story of Bassianus and Geta in Herodian.[4] There indeed the
plot is neither large nor intricate, but just enough to fill the minds
of the audience, not to cloy them. Besides, you see it founded upon
the truth of history. Only, the time of the action is not reduceable
to the strictness of the rules; and you see in some places a little
farce mingled, which is below the dignity of the other parts; and
in this all our poets are extremely peccant. Even Ben Jonson
himself, in *Sejanus* and *Catiline*, has given us this oleo of a play,
this unnatural mixture of comedy and tragedy, which to me sounds
just as ridiculously as the history of David with the merry humors
of Golias. In *Sejanus* you may take notice of the scene betwixt
Livia and the physician, which is a pleasant satire upon the artificial
helps of beauty; in *Catiline* you may see the parliament of women,
the little envies of them to one another, and all that passes betwixt
Curio and Fulvia—scenes admirable in their kind but of an ill
mingle with the rest.

"But I return again to the French writers, who, as I have said, do
not burden themselves too much with plot, which has been reproached to them by an *ingenious person*[5] of our nation as a fault;
for, he says, they commonly make but one person considerable in a
play; they dwell on him and his concernments while the rest of the
persons are only subservient to set him off. If he intends this by it,
that there is one person in the play who is of greater dignity than
the rest, he must tax not only theirs but those of the Ancients and,
which he would be loth to do, the best of ours; for it is impossible
but that one person must be more conspicuous in it than any other,
and consequently the greatest share in the action must devolve on
him. We see it so in the management of all affairs; even in the most
equal aristocracy, the balance cannot be so justly poised but some
one will be superior to the rest, either in parts, fortune, interest, or

---

[3] Fletcher, *The Bloody Brother, or Rollo, Duke of Normandy* (1619?), mentioned by Rymer as among "the choicest and most applauded English tragedies
of this last age."
[4] Greek historian (c. 170–240 A.D.) who wrote a history of the Roman emperors during his lifetime.
[5] Thomas Sprat in *Observations on M. de Sorbier's "Voyage into England"*
(1665). The attack on English science, theatre, and religion by the Frenchman
Samuel Sorbière, *Relation d'un Voyage en Angleterre* (1664), lies in the background of Dryden's essay.

the consideration of some glorious exploit; which will reduce the greatest part of business into his hands.

"But if he would have us to imagine that in exalting one character the rest of them are neglected, and that all of them have not some share or other in the action of the play, I desire him to produce any of Corneille's tragedies wherein every person, like so many servants in a well-governed family, has not some employment, and who is not necessary to the carrying on of the plot or at least to your understanding it.

"There are indeed some protatic[6] persons in the Ancients, whom they make use of in their plays either to hear or give the relation, but the French avoid this with great address, making their narrations only to or by such who are some way interested in the main design. And now I am speaking of relations, I cannot take a fitter opportunity to add this in favor of the French, that they often use them with better judgment and more à propos than the English do. Not that I commend narrations in general, but there are two sorts of them. One, of those things which are antecedent to the play, and are related to make the conduct of it more clear to us. But 'tis a fault to choose such subjects for the stage as will force us on that rock, because we see they are seldom listened to by the audience, and that is many times the ruin of the play; for, being once let pass without attention, the audience can never recover themselves to understand the play. And indeed it is somewhat unreasonable that they should be put to so much trouble, as that, to comprehend what passes in their sight, they must have recourse to what was done perhaps ten or twenty years ago.

"But there is another sort of relations, that is, of things happening in the action of the play and supposed to be done behind the scenes, and this is many times both convenient and beautiful; for by it the French avoid the tumult to which we are subject in England by representing duels, battles, and the like; which renders our stage too like the theatres where they fight prizes. For what is more ridiculous than to represent an army with a drum and five men behind it, all which the hero of the other side is to drive in before him, or to see a duel fought, and one slain with two or three thrusts of the foils, which we know are so blunted that we might give a man an hour to kill another in good earnest with them.

---

[6] belonging to the *protasis*; extended by Corneille to include all characters merely expository and not essential to the action.

"I have observed that in all our tragedies, the audience cannot forbear laughing when the actors are to die; it is the most comic part of the whole play. All *passions* may be lively represented on the stage, if to the well writing of them the actor supplies a good commanded voice, and limbs that move easily and without stiffness; but there are many *actions* which can never be imitated to a just height. Dying, especially, is a thing which none but a Roman gladiator could naturally perform on the stage, when he did not imitate or represent, but do it; and therefore it is better to omit the representation of it.

"The words of a good writer, which describe it lively, will make a deeper impression of belief in us than all the actor can insinuate into us, when he seems to fall dead before us, as a poet in the description of a beautiful garden or a meadow will please our imagination more than the place itself can please our sight. When we see death represented, we are convinced it is but fiction; but when we hear it related, our eyes, the strongest witnesses, are wanting, which might have undeceived us; and we are all willing to favor the sleight when the poet does not too grossly impose on us. They therefore who imagine these relations would make no concernment in the audience are deceived, by confounding them with the other, which are of things antecedent to the play: those are made often in cold blood, as I may say, to the audience, but these are warmed with our concernments, which were before awakened in the play. What the philosophers say of motion, that when it is once begun, it continues of itself and will do so to eternity, without some stop put to it, is clearly true on this occasion: the soul being already moved with the characters and fortunes of those imaginary persons, continues going of its own accord; and we are no more weary to hear what becomes of them when they are not on the stage, than we are to listen to the news of an absent mistress. But it is objected that if one part of the play may be related, then why not all? I answer, some parts of the action are more fit to be represented, some to be related. Corneille says judiciously that the poet is not obliged to expose to view all particular actions which conduce to the principal: he ought to select such of them to be seen which will appear with the greatest beauty, either by the magnificence of the show, or the vehemence of passions which they produce, or some other charm which they have in them; and let the rest arrive to the audience by narration. 'Tis a great mistake in us to believe the French present no part of the action on the stage; every alteration or crossing of a design, every new-sprung passion and turn of it, is a part of the action, and much the noblest, except we conceive nothing to be action till the players come to blows; as if the painting of the hero's mind were not more properly the poet's work than the strength of his body. Nor does this anything contradict the opinion of Horace where he tells us,

> *Segnius irritant animos demissa per aurem,*
> *Quam quae sunt oculis subjecta fidelibus.*[7]

For he says immediately after,

> *Non tamen intus*
> *Digna geri promes in scenam; multaq; tolles*
> *Ex oculis, quae mox narret facundia praesens.*

Among which many he recounts some:

> *Nec pueros coram populo Medea trucidet,*
> *Aut in avem Progne mutetur, Cadmus in anguem, etc.*

That is, those actions which by reason of their cruelty will cause aversion in us, or by reason of their impossibility, unbelief, ought either wholly to be avoided by a poet or only delivered by narration. To which we may have leave to add such as, to avoid tumult (as was before hinted), or to reduce the plot into a more reasonable compass of time, or for defect of beauty in them, are rather to be related than presented to the eye. Examples of all these kinds are frequent, not only among all the Ancients but in the best received of our English poets. We find Ben Jonson using them in his *Magnetic Lady,*[8] where one comes out from dinner and relates the quarrels and disorders of it, to save the undecent appearance of them on the stage and to abbreviate the story; and this in express imitation of Terence, who had done the same before him in his *Eunuch,* where Pythias makes the like relation of what had happened within at the Soldier's entertainment. The relations likewise of Sejanus's death, and the prodigies before it, are remarkable, the one of which was hid from sight to avoid the horror and tumult of the representation, the other to shun the introduction of things impossible to

---

[7] *Ars Poetica*, 180–87: "Things heard stir the mind more sluggishly than things placed before our trusty eyes." He continues: "Things properly kept off stage should not be brought forth upon it; and you will keep from sight many things which in time an actor will narrate in our presence." "Medea should not carve up her children in front of the audience, nor should Procne be changed into a bird, or Cadmus into a snake."
[8] II, ii.

be believed. In that excellent play *The King and no King*, Fletcher goes yet farther; for the whole unravelling of the plot is done by narration in the fifth act, after the manner of the Ancients; and it moves great concernment in the audience, though it be only a relation of what was done many years before the play. I could multiply other instances, but these are sufficient to prove that there is no error in choosing a subject which requires this sort of narrations; in the ill management of them, there may.

"But I find I have been too long in this discourse, since the French have many other excellencies not common to us; as that you never see any of their plays end with a conversion or simple change of will, which is the ordinary way which our poets use to end theirs. It shows little art in the conclusion of a dramatic poem, when they who have hindered the felicity during the four acts, desist from it in the fifth, without some powerful cause to take them off their design; and though I deny not but such reasons may be found, yet it is a path that is cautiously to be trod, and the poet is to be sure he convinces the audience that the motive is strong enough. As for example, the conversion of the Usurer in *The Scornful Lady*[9] seems to me a little forced; for, being a Usurer, which implies a lover of money to the highest degree of covetousness—and such the poet has represented him—the account he gives for the sudden change is that he has been duped by the wild young fellow, which in reason might render him more wary another time, and make him punish himself with harder fare and coarser clothes, to get up again what he had lost; but that he should look on it as a judgment, and so repent, we may expect to hear in a sermon, but I should never endure it in a play.

"I pass by this. Neither will I insist on the care they take that no person after his first entrance shall ever appear but the business which brings him upon the stage shall be evident; which rule, if observed, must needs render all the events in the play more natural; for there you see the probability of every accident in the cause that produced it; and that which appears change in the play will seem so reasonable to you that you will there find it almost necessary; so that in the exit of the actor you have a clear account of his purpose and design in the next entrance (though if the scene be well wrought, the event will commonly deceive you); for there is nothing so absurd, says Corneille, as for an actor to leave the stage only because he has no more to say.

---

[9] By Beaumont and Fletcher (c. 1613).

"I should now speak of the beauty of their rhyme, and the just reason I have to prefer that way of writing in tragedies before ours in blank verse, but because it is partly received by us, and therefore not altogether peculiar to them, I will say no more of it in relation to their plays. For our own, I doubt not but it will exceedingly beautify them, and I can see but one reason why it should not generally obtain, that is, because our poets write so ill in it. This indeed may prove a more prevailing argument than all others which are used to destroy it; and therefore I am only troubled when great and judicious poets, and those who are acknowledged such, have writ or spoke against it. As for others they are to be answered by that one sentence of an ancient author: *Sed ut primo ad consequendos eos quos priores ducimus, accendimur, ita ubi aut proeteriri, aut aequari eos posse desperavimus, studium cum spe senescit: quod, scilicet, assequi non potest, sequi desinit; . . . praeteritoque eo in quo eminere non possumus, aliquid in quo nitamur, conquirimus."* [1]

Lisideius concluded in this manner; and Neander, after a little pause, thus answered him:

"I shall grant Lisideius, without much dispute, a great part of what he has urged against us; for I acknowledge that the French contrive their plots more regularly, and observe the laws of comedy, and decorum of the stage (to speak generally), with more exactness than the English. Farther, I deny not but he has taxed us justly in some irregularities of ours which he has mentioned; yet, after all, I am of opinion that neither our faults nor their virtues are considerable enough to place them above us.

"For the lively imitation of Nature being in the definition of a play, those which best fulfill that law ought to be esteemed superior to the others. 'Tis true, those beauties of the French poesy are such as will raise perfection higher where it is, but are not sufficient to give it where it is not; they are indeed the beauties of a statue, but not of a man, because not animated with the soul of Poesy, which is imitation of humor and passions. And this Lisideius himself or any other, however biassed to their party, cannot but acknowledge, if he will either compare the humors of our comedies, or the characters of our serious plays, with theirs. He who will look upon theirs which have been written till these last ten years, or

---

[1] Velleius Paterculus, *Historiae Romae*, I, 17 (previously quoted): "But as we are inflamed to follow those whom we think foremost, so if we despair either of surpassing or equalling them, our zeal flags along with our hope; for indeed if it cannot keep up, it ceases to follow. . . . When that is past in which we cannot be eminent, we seek for something for which to strive."

thereabouts, will find it a hard matter to pick out two or three passable humors amongst them. Corneille himself, their arch-poet, what has he produced except *The Liar*, and you know how it was cried up in France; but when it came upon the English stage, though well translated, and that part of Dorant acted to so much advantage by Mr. Harte[2] as I am confident it never received in its own country, the most favorable to it would not put it in competition with many of Fletcher's or Ben Jonson's. In the rest of Corneille's comedies you have little humor; he tells you himself [3] his way is, first, to show two lovers in good intelligence[4] with each other, in the working up of the play to embroil them by some mistake, and in the latter end to clear it and reconcile them.

"But of late years Molière, the younger Corneille,[5] Quinault,[6] and some others have been imitating afar off the quick turns and graces of the English stage. They have mixed their serious plays with mirth, like our tragi-comedies, since the death of Cardinal Richelieu; which Lisideius and many others not observing, have commended that in them for a virtue which they themselves no longer practice. Most of their new plays are, like some of ours, derived from the Spanish novels. There is scarce one of them without a veil and a trusty Diego,[7] who drolls much after the rate of *The Adventures*.[8] But their humors, if I may grace them with that name, are so thin-sown that never above one of them comes up in any play. I dare take upon me to find more variety of them in some one play of Ben Jonson's than in all theirs together; as he who has seen *The Alchemist*, *The Silent Woman*, or *Bartholomew-Fair*, cannot but acknowledge with me.

"I grant the French have performed what was possible on the groundwork of the Spanish plays; what was pleasant before, they have made regular. But there is not above one good play to be writ on all those plots; they are too much alike to please often; which we need not the experience of our own stage to justify. As for their new way of mingling mirth with serious plot, I do not, with Lisi-

---

[2] Charles Harte, great-nephew of Shakespeare and a leading actor during the Restoration.
[3] *Discours I*.
[4] understanding.
[5] Thomas Corneille (1625–1709), brother of Pierre, tragedian, translator of Ovid, and member of the *Académie Française*.
[6] Phillippe Quinault (1635–88), writer of comedies and of librettos for the operas of Lully.
[7] Type-name for a comic servant.
[8] *The Adventures of Five Hours* (1662) by Sir Samuel Tuke.

deius, condemn the thing, though I cannot approve their manner of doing it. He tells us, we cannot so speedily recollect ourselves after a scene of great passion and concernment as to pass to another of mirth and humor, and to enjoy it with any relish. But why should he imagine the soul of man more heavy than his senses? Does not the eye pass from an unpleasant object to a pleasant in a much shorter time than is required to this? and does not the unpleasantness of the first commend the beauty of the latter? The old rule of logic might have convinced him, that contraries, when placed near, set off each other. A continued gravity keeps the spirit too much bent; we must refresh it sometimes, as we bait[9] in a journey that we may go on with greater ease. A scene of mirth, mixed with tragedy, has the same effect upon us which our music has betwixt the acts; which we find a relief to us from the best plots and language of the stage, if the discourses have been long. I must therefore have stronger arguments ere I am convinced that compassion and mirth in the same subject destroy each other; and in the meantime cannot but conclude, to the honor of our nation, that we have invented, increased, and perfected a more pleasant way of writing for the stage than was ever known to the Ancients or Moderns of any nation, which is tragi-comedy.

"And this leads me to wonder why Lisideius and many others should cry up the barrenness of the French plots above the variety and copiousness of the English. Their plots are single; they carry on one design, which is pushed forward by all the actors, every scene in the play contributing and moving towards it. Our plays, besides the main design, have under-plots or by-concernments, of less considerable persons and intrigues, which are carried on with the motion of the main plot, as they say the orb of the fixed stars and those of the planets, though they have motions of their own, are whirled about by the motion of the *primum mobile*,[1] in which they are contained. That similitude expresses much of the English stage; for if contrary motions may be found in nature to agree, if a planet can go east and west at the same time—one way by virtue of its own motion, the other by the force of the First Mover—it will not be difficult to imagine how the under-plot, which is only different, not contrary to the great design, may naturally be conducted along with it.

"Eugenius has already shown us, from the confession of the

---

[9] halt, as for food or rest.
[1] The tenth, outermost sphere in Ptolemaic astronomy, the "first mover" which controls movement of the other spheres.

French poets, that the unity of action is sufficiently preserved if all the imperfect actions of the play are conducing to the main design; but when those petty intrigues of a play are so ill ordered that they have no coherence with the other, I must grant that Lisideius has reason to tax that want of due connection; for co-ordination in a play is as dangerous and unnatural as in a state. In the meantime he must acknowledge, our variety, if well ordered,[2] will afford a greater pleasure to the audience.

"As for his other argument, that by pursuing one single theme they gain an advantage to express and work up the passions, I wish any example he could bring from them would make it good; for I confess their verses are to me the coldest I have ever read. Neither, indeed, is it possible for them, in the way they take, so to express passion as that the effects of it should appear in the concernment of an audience, their speeches being so many declamations, which tire us with the length; so that instead of persuading us to grieve for their imaginary heroes, we are concerned for our own trouble as we are in tedious visits of bad company: we are in pain till they are gone. When the French stage came to be reformed by Cardinal Richelieu, those long harangues were introduced to comply with the gravity of a churchman. Look upon the *Cinna* and the *Pompey*: they are not so properly to be called plays as long discourses of reason of state, and *Polieucte* in matters of religion is as solemn as the long stops upon our organs.[3] Since that time it is grown into a custom, and their actors speak by the hour-glass, like our parsons;[4] nay, they account it the grace of their parts, and think themselves disparaged by the poet if they may not twice or thrice in a play entertain the audience with a speech of a hundred lines. I deny not but this may suit well enough with the French; for as we, who are a more sullen people, come to be diverted at our plays, so they, who are of an airy and gay temper, come thither to make themselves more serious; and this I conceive to be one reason why comedies are more pleasing to us and tragedies to them. But to speak generally, it cannot be denied that short speeches and replies are more apt to move the passions and beget concernment in us, than the

---

[2] "Variety" like "humor" has nationalistic associations with English liberty to be individualistic. But Dryden also anticipates later aesthetic theorists—e.g., Hutcheson and Hogarth—who locate the source of aesthetic pleasure in the unification of variety.

[3] Corneille, *Cinna, ou La Clémence d'Auguste* (1639); *La Mort de Pompeé* (1641); *Polyeucte, Martyr, tragédie chrétienne* (1640).

[4] Each pulpit was equipped with an hourglass. Cf. *Hudibras*, I, iii, 1061 ff.

other; for it is unnatural for any one in a gust of passion to speak long together, or for another in the same condition to suffer him without interruption. Grief and passion are like floods raised in little brooks by a sudden rain: they are quickly up; and if the concernment be poured unexpectedly in upon us, it overflows us; but a long sober shower gives them leisure to run out as they came in, without troubling the ordinary current. As for comedy, repartee is one of its chiefest graces; the greatest pleasure of the audience is a chase of wit, kept up on both sides and swiftly managed. And this our forefathers, if not we, have had in Fletcher's plays to a much higher degree of perfection than the French poets can reasonably hope to reach.

"There is another part of Lisideius his discourse in which he rather excused our neighbors than commended them, that is, for aiming only to make one person considerable in their plays. 'Tis very true what he has urged, that one character in all plays, even without the poet's care, will have advantage of all the others, and that the design of the whole drama will chiefly depend on it. But this hinders not that there may be more shining characters in the play—many persons of a second magnitude, nay, some so very near, so almost equal to the first, that greatness may be opposed to greatness, and all the persons be made considerable, not only by their quality but their action. 'Tis evident that the more the persons are, the greater will be the variety of the plot. If then the parts are managed so regularly that the beauty of the whole be kept entire, and that the variety become not a perplexed and confused mass of accidents, you will find it infinitely pleasing to be led in a labyrinth of design, where you see some of your way before you, yet discern not the end till you arrive at it. And that all this is practicable, I can produce for examples many of our English plays, as *The Maid's Tragedy*,[5] *The Alchemist, The Silent Woman*. I was going to have named *The Fox*[6] but that the unity of design seems not exactly observed in it; for there appear two actions in the play, the first naturally ending with the fourth act, the second forced from it in the fifth; which yet is the less to be condemned in him, because the disguise of Volpone, though it suited not with his character as a crafty or covetous person, agreed well enough with that of a voluptuary, and by it the poet gained the end at which he aimed, the punishment of vice and the reward of virtue, both which that dis-

---

[5] By Beaumont and Fletcher (c. 1610).
[6] That is, *Volpone*.

guise produced. So that to judge equally of it, it was an excellent fifth act, but not so naturally proceeding from the former.

"But to leave this, and pass to the latter part of Lisideius his discourse, which concerns relations: I must acknowledge with him that the French have reason to hide that part of the action which would occasion too much tumult on the stage, and to choose rather to have it made known by narration to the audience. Farther, I think it very convenient, for the reasons he has given, that all incredible actions were removed. But whether custom has so insinuated itself into our countrymen, or nature has so formed them to fierceness, I know not, but they will scarcely suffer combats and other objects of horror to be taken from them. And indeed, the indecency of tumults is all which can be objected against fighting, for why may not our imagination as well suffer itself to be deluded with the probability of it as with any other thing in the play? For my part, I can with as great ease persuade myself that the blows are given in good earnest, as I can that they who strike them are kings or princes, or those persons which they represent. For objects of incredibility, I would be satisfied from Lisideius whether we have any so removed from all appearance of truth as are those of Corneille's *Andromede*, a play which has been frequented the most of any he has writ. If the Perseus, or the son of a heathen god, the Pegasus, and the Monster were not capable to choke a strong belief, let him blame any representation of ours hereafter. Those indeed were objects of delight; yet the reason is the same as to the probability; for he makes it not a ballette[7] or masque, but a play, which is to resemble truth. But for death, that it ought not to be represented, I have, besides the arguments alleged by Lisideius, the authority of Ben Jonson, who has forborne it in his tragedies; for both the death of Sejanus and Catiline are related; though in the latter I cannot but observe one irregularity of that great poet: he has removed the scene in the same act from Rome to Catiline's army, and from thence again to Rome; and besides has allowed a very inconsiderable time after Catiline's speech for the striking of the battle and the return of Petreius, who is to relate the event of it to the senate; which I should not animadvert on him, who was otherwise a painful observer of τὸ πρέπον, or the *decorum* of the stage, if he had not used extreme severity in his judgment on the incomparable Shakespeare for the same fault. To conclude on this subject of relations: if we are to be blamed for

---

[7] Any theatrical dance, often in pantomime fancifully staged.

showing too much of the action, the French are as faulty for discovering too little of it. A mean betwixt both should be observed by every judicious writer, so as the audience may neither be left unsatisfied by not seeing what is beautiful, or shocked by beholding what is either incredible or undecent.

"I hope I have already proved in this discourse, that though we are not altogether so punctual as the French in observing the laws of comedy, yet our errors are so few and little, and those things wherein we excel them so considerable, that we ought of right to be preferred before them. But what will Lisideius say if they themselves acknowledge they are too strictly bounded by those laws, for breaking which he has blamed the English? I will allege Corneille's words as I find them in the end of his discourse of the three unities: *Il est facile aux spéculatifs d'estre sévères, etc.* ' 'Tis easy for speculative persons to judge severely; but if they would produce to public view ten or twelve pieces of this nature, they would perhaps give more latitude to the rules than I have done, when by experience they had known how much we are limited and constrained by them, and how many beauties of the stage they banished from it.' To illustrate a little what he has said: by their servile observations of the unities of time and place, and integrity of scenes, they have brought on themselves that dearth of plot and narrowness of imagination which may be observed in all their plays. How many beautiful accidents might naturally happen in two or three days, which cannot arrive with any probability in the compass of twenty-four hours? There is time to be allowed also for maturity of design, which, amongst great and prudent persons such as are often represented in tragedy, cannot, with any likelihood of truth, be brought to pass at so short a warning. Farther, by tying themselves strictly to the unity of place and unbroken scenes, they are forced many times to omit some beauties which cannot be shown where the act began; but might, if the scene were interrupted, and the stage cleared for the persons to enter in another place; and therefore the French poets are often forced upon absurdities; for if the act begins in a chamber, all the persons in the play must have some business or other to come thither, or else they are not to be shown in the act; and sometimes their characters are very unfitting to appear there—as, suppose it were the king's bed-chamber—yet the meanest man in the tragedy must come and dispatch his business there rather than in the lobby or courtyard (which is fitter for him), for fear the stage should be cleared and the scenes broken. Many times they fall by it in a greater inconvenience; for they keep their scenes unbroken and yet change the place, as in one of their newest plays,[8] where the act begins in the street. There a gentleman is to meet his friend; he sees him with his man, coming out from his father's house; they talk together, and the first goes out. The second, who is a lover, has made an appointment with his mistress; she appears at the window, and then we are to imagine the scene lies under it. This gentleman is called away, and leaves his servant with his mistress; presently her father is heard from within; the young lady is afraid the serving-man should be discovered, and thrusts him into a place of safety, which is supposed to be her closet. After this, the father enters to the daughter, and now the scene is in a house; for he is seeking from one room to another for this poor Philipin[9] or French Diego, who is heard from within, drolling and breaking many a miserable conceit on the subject of his sad condition. In this ridiculous manner the play goes forward, the stage being never empty all the while; so that the street, the window, the houses, and the closet are made to walk about, and the persons to stand still. Now what, I beseech you, is more easy than to write a regular French play, or more difficult than to write an irregular English one like those of Fletcher or of Shakespeare?

"If they content themselves, as Corneille did, with some flat design which, like an ill riddle, is found out ere it be half proposed, such plots we can make every way regular as easily as they; but whenever they endeavor to rise to any quick turns and counterturns of plot, as some of them have attempted since Corneille's plays have been less in vogue, you see they write as irregularly as we, though they cover it more speciously. Hence the reason is perspicuous why no French plays, when translated, have or ever can succeed on the English stage. For if you consider the plots, our own are fuller of variety; if the writing, ours are more quick and fuller of spirit; and therefore 'tis a strange mistake in those who decry the way of writing plays in verse, as if the English therein imitated the French. We have borrowed nothing from them; our plots are weaved in English looms: we endeavor therein to follow the variety and greatness of characters which are derived to us from Shakespeare and Fletcher; the copiousness and well-knitting of the intrigues we have from Jonson; and for the verse itself, we have

---

[8] *L'Amour à la Mode* (1651) by Thomas Corneille.
[9] Comic servant in Quinault's *L'Amant Indiscret*. The latter has a similar scene which, as Ker notes, Dryden confuses with Corneille's.

English precedents of elder date than any of Corneille's plays. Not to name our old comedies before Shakespeare, which were all writ in verse of six feet, or Alexandrines, such as the French now use, I can show in Shakespeare many scenes of rhyme together, and the like in Ben Jonson's tragedies: in *Catiline* and *Sejanus* sometimes thirty or forty lines, I mean besides the Chorus or the monologues; which, by the way, showed Ben no enemy to this way of writing, especially if you read his *Sad Shepherd*, which goes sometimes on rhyme, sometimes on blank verse, like a horse who eases himself on trot and amble. You find him likewise commending Fletcher's pastoral of *The Faithful Shepherdess*, which is for the most part rhyme, though not refined to that purity to which it hath since been brought. And these examples are enough to clear us from a servile imitation of the French.

"But to return whence I have digressed, I dare boldly affirm these two things of the English drama: first, that we have many plays of ours as regular as any of theirs, and which, besides, have more variety of plot and characters; and secondly, that in most of the irregular plays of Shakespeare or Fletcher (for Ben Jonson's are for the most part regular) there is a more masculine fancy, and greater spirit in the writing, than there is in any of the French. I could produce, even in Shakespeare's and Fletcher's works, some plays which are almost exactly formed, as *The Merry Wives of Windsor* and *The Scornful Lady*. But because (generally speaking) Shakespeare, who writ first, did not perfectly observe the laws of comedy, and Fletcher, who came nearer to perfection, yet through carelessness made many faults, I will take the pattern of a perfect play from Ben Jonson, who was a careful and learned observer of the dramatic laws; and from all his comedies I shall select *The Silent Woman*, of which I will make a short examen according to those rules which the French observe."

As Neander was beginning to examine *The Silent Woman*, Eugenius earnestly regarding him: "I beseech you, Neander," said he, "gratify the company, and me in particular, so far, as before you speak of the play, to give us a character of the author, and tell us frankly your opinion, whether you do not think all writers, both French and English, ought to give place to him."

"I fear," replied Neander, "that in obeying your commands I shall draw some envy[1] on myself. Besides, in performing them, it will be first necessary to speak somewhat of Shakespeare and

---

[1] spite, bad feeling.

Fletcher, his rivals in poesy, and one of them, in my opinion, at least his equal, perhaps his superior.

"To begin, then, with Shakespeare. He was the man who of all Modern, and perhaps Ancient poets, had the largest and most comprehensive soul. All the images of Nature were still present to him, and he drew them not laboriously, but luckily;[2] when he describes anything, you more than see it, you feel it too. Those who accuse him to have wanted learning give him the greater commendation: he was naturally learned; he needed not the spectacles of books to read Nature; he looked inwards and found her there. I cannot say he is everywhere alike; were he so, I should do him injury to compare him with the greatest of mankind. He is many times flat, insipid; his comic wit degenerating into clenches, his serious swelling into bombast. But he is always great when some great occasion is presented to him; no man can say he ever had a fit subject for his wit and did not then raise himself as high above the rest of poets,

Quantum lenta solent inter viburna cupressi.[3]

The consideration of this made Mr. Hales of Eton[4] say that there was no subject of which any poet ever writ but he would produce it much better done in Shakespeare; and however others are now generally preferred before him, yet the age wherein he lived, which had contemporaries with him Fletcher and Jonson, never equalled them to him in their esteem; and in the last king's court, when Ben's reputation was at highest, Sir John Suckling, and with him the greater part of the courtiers, set our Shakespeare far above him.

"Beaumont and Fletcher, of whom I am next to speak, had, with the advantage of Shakespeare's wit, which was their precedent, great natural gifts improved by study; Beaumont especially being so accurate a judge of plays that Ben Jonson, while he lived, submitted all his writings to his censure, and, 'tis thought, used his judgment in correcting, if not contriving all his plots. What value he had for him appears by the verses he writ to him, and therefore I need speak no farther of it. The first play that brought Fletcher and him in esteem was their *Philaster*; for before that they had written two or three very unsuccessfully, as the like is reported of Ben Jonson before he writ *Every Man in his Humour*. Their plots were generally more

---

[2] not by planning, but as he chanced upon them.
[3] Virgil, *Eclogues*, I, 26: "as cypresses usually do among trees that bend."
[4] John Hales (1584–1656), English divine, fellow of Eton, and of course easily a member of Shakespeare's audience. His remark was made to Sir John Suckling.

regular than Shakespeare's, especially those which were made before Beaumont's death; and they understood and imitated the conversation of gentlemen much better; whose wild debaucheries and quickness of wit in repartees no poet before them could paint as they have done. Humor, which Ben Jonson derived from particular persons, they made it not their business to describe: they represented all the passions very lively, but above all, love. I am apt to believe the English language in them arrived to its highest perfection: what words have since been taken in are rather superfluous than ornamental. Their plays are now the most pleasant and frequent entertainments of the stage, two of theirs being acted through the year for one of Shakespeare's or Jonson's. The reason is because there is a certain gaiety in their comedies, and pathos in their more serious plays, which suit generally with all men's humors. Shakespeare's language is likewise a little obsolete, and Ben Jonson's wit comes short of theirs.

"As for Jonson, to whose character I am now arrived, if we look upon him while he was himself (for his last plays were but his dotages), I think him the most learned and judicious writer which any theatre ever had. He was a most severe judge of himself as well as others. One cannot say he wanted wit, but rather that he was frugal of it. In his works you find little to retrench or alter. Wit and language, and humor also in some measure, we had before him; but something of art was wanting to the drama till he came. He managed his strength to more advantage than any who preceded him. You seldom find him making love in any of his scenes, or endeavoring to move the passions; his genius was too sullen and saturnine to do it gracefully, especially when he knew he came after those who had performed both to such an height. Humor was his proper sphere, and in that he delighted most to represent mechanic people.[5] He was deeply conversant in the Ancients, both Greek and Latin, and he borrowed boldly from them: there is scarce a poet or historian among the Roman authors of those times whom he has not translated in *Sejanus* and *Cataline*. But he has done his robberies so openly that one may see he fears not to be taxed by any law. He invades authors like a monarch, and what would be theft in other poets is only victory in him. With the spoils of these writers, he so represents old Rome to us, in its rites, ceremonies, and customs, that if one of their poets had written either of his tragedies, we had seen less of it than in him. If there was any fault in his language, 'twas

---

[5] working people, tradesmen.

that he weaved it too closely and laboriously, in his comedies especially. Perhaps, too, he did a little too much Romanize our tongue, leaving the words which he translated almost as much Latin as he found them; wherein, though he learnedly followed their language, he did not enough comply with the idiom of ours. If I would compare him with Shakespeare, I must acknowledge him the more correct poet, but Shakespeare the greater wit. Shakespeare was the Homer, or father of our dramatic poets; Jonson was the Virgil, the pattern of elaborate writing; I admire him, but I love Shakespeare. To conclude of him: as he has given us the most correct plays, so in the precepts which he has laid down in his *Discoveries*, we have as many and profitable rules for perfecting the stage as any wherewith the French can furnish us.

"Having thus spoken of the author, I proceed to the examination of his comedy *The Silent Woman*.

EXAMEN OF THE SILENT WOMAN

"To begin first with the length of the action: it is so far from exceeding the compass of a natural day that it takes not up an artificial one.[6] 'Tis all included in the limits of three hours and a half, which is no more than is required for the presentment on the stage —a beauty perhaps not much observed; if it had, we should not have looked on the Spanish translation of *Five Hours* with so much wonder. The scene of it is laid in London; the latitude of place is almost as little as you can imagine, for it lies all within the compass of two houses, and after the first act, in one. The continuity of scenes is observed more than in any of our plays except his own *Fox* and *Alchemist*. They are not broken above twice or thrice at most in the whole comedy; and in the two best of Corneille's plays, the *Cid* and *Cinna*, they are interrupted once. The action of the play is entirely one, the end or aim of which is the settling Morose's estate on Dauphine. The intrigue of it is the greatest and most noble of any pure unmixed comedy in any language; you see in it many persons of various characters and humors, and all delightful. As first, Morose, or an old man to whom all noise but his own talking is offensive. Some who would be thought critics say this humor of his is forced; but to remove that objection, we may consider him first to be naturally of a delicate hearing, as many are to whom all sharp sounds are unpleasant; and secondly, we may attribute much of it to the peevishness of his age, or the wayward authority of an old

---

[6] twelve hours.

man in his own house, where he may make himself obeyed; and to this the poet seems to allude in his name Morose. Besides this, I am assured from divers persons that Ben Jonson was actually acquainted with such a man, one altogether as ridiculous as he is here represented. Others say, it is not enough to find one man of such an humor; it must be common to more, and the more common the more natural. To prove this, they instance in the best of comical characters, Falstaff. There are many men resembling him—old, fat, merry, cowardly, drunken, amorous, vain, and lying. But to convince these people, I need but tell them that humor is the ridiculous extravagance of conversation[7] wherein one man differs from all others. If then it be common or communicated to many, how differs it from other men's? or what indeed causes it to be ridiculous so much as the singularity of it? As for Falstaff, he is not properly one humor, but a miscellany of humors or images, drawn from so many several men. That wherein he is singular is his wit, or those things he says *praeter expectatum*, unexpected by the audience; his quick evasions when you imagine him surprised, which, as they are extremely diverting of themselves, so receive a great addition from his person; for the very sight of such an unwieldy old debauched fellow is a comedy alone. And here, having a place so proper for it, I cannot but enlarge somewhat upon this subject of humor into which I am fallen. The ancients had little of it in their comedies, for the τὸ γελοῖον[8] of the Old Comedy, of which Aristophanes was chief, was not so much to imitate a man as to make the people laugh at some odd conceit, which had commonly somewhat of unnatural or obscene in it. Thus, when you see Socrates brought upon the stage, you are not to imagine him made ridiculous by the imitation of his actions, but rather by making him perform something very unlike himself, something so childish and absurd as by comparing it with the gravity of the true Socrates, makes a ridiculous object for the spectators. In their New Comedy which succeeded, the poets sought indeed to express the ἦθος, as in their tragedies the πάθος of mankind.[9] But this ἦθος contained only the general characters of men and manners; as old men, lovers, serving-men, courtesans, parasites, and such other persons as we see in their comedies; all which they made alike, that is, one old man or father, one lover, one courtesan, so like another as if the first of them had begot the rest of every sort. *Ex*

---

[7] conduct, manner of life.

[8] the laughable, ridicule; see below, the *ridiculum*.

[9] The terms occur in Aristotle's *Poetics*: ἦθος, "character, actual distinguishing quality": πάθος, "suffering, passive emotion."

homine hunc natum dicas.[1] The same custom they observed likewise in their tragedies. As for the French, though they have the word *humeur* among them, yet they have small use of it in their comedies or farces, they being but ill imitations of the *ridiculum*, or that which stirred up laughter in the Old Comedy. But among the English 'tis otherwise, where by humor is meant some extravagant habit, passion, or affection, particular (as I said before) to some one person, by the oddness of which he is immediately distinguished from the rest of men; which being lively and naturally represented, most frequently begets that malicious pleasure in the audience which is testified by laughter, as all things which are deviations from customs are ever the aptest to produce it: though by the way this laughter is only accidental, as the person represented is fantastic or bizarre; but pleasure is essential to it as the imitation of what is natural. The description of these humors, drawn from the knowledge and observation of particular persons, was the peculiar genius and talent of Ben Jonson, to whose play I now return.

"Besides Morose, there are at least nine or ten different characters and humors in *The Silent Woman*; all which persons have several concernments of their own, yet are all used by the poet to the conducting of the main design to perfection. I shall not waste time in commending the writing of this play; but I will give you my opinion that there is more wit and acuteness of fancy in it than in any of Ben Jonson's. Besides that, he has here described the conversation of gentlemen in the persons of True-wit and his friends, with more gaiety, air, and freedom than in the rest of his comedies. For the contrivance of the plot, 'tis extreme, elaborate, and yet withal easy; for the λύσις[2] or untying of it, 'tis so admirable that when it is done, no one of the audience would think the poet could have missed it; and yet it was concealed so much before the last scene, that any other way would sooner have entered into your thoughts. But I dare not take upon me to commend the fabric of it, because it is altogether so full of art that I must unravel every scene in it to commend it as I ought. And this excellent contrivance is still the more to be admired because 'tis comedy, where the persons are only of common rank, and their business private, not elevated by passions or high concernments, as in serious plays. Here every one is a proper judge of all he sees, nothing is represented but that with which he daily converses; so that by consequence all faults lie open to dis-

---

[1] Terence, *Eunuchus*, 460: "You might say that this man was a born image of that one."
[2] Aristotle, *Poetics*, XVIII, 1.

covery, and few are pardonable. 'Tis this which Horace has judiciously observed:

> Creditur, ex medio quia res arcessit, habere
> Sudoris minimum; sed habet Comedia tanto
> Plus oneris, quanto veniae minus.[3]

"But our poet, who was not ignorant of these difficulties, has made use of all advantages, as he who designs a large leap takes his rise from the highest ground. One of these advantages is that which Corneille has laid down as the greatest which can arrive to any poem, and which he himself could never compass above thrice in all his plays, viz., the making choice of some signal and long-expected day whereon the action of the play is to depend. This day was that designed by Dauphine for the settling of his uncle's estate upon him; which to compass, he contrives to marry him. That the marriage had been plotted by him long beforehand is made evident by what he tells True-wit in the second act, that in one moment he had destroyed what he had been raising many months.

"There is another artifice of the poet which I cannot here omit, because by the frequent practice of it in his comedies, he has left it to us almost as a rule; that is, when he has any character or humor wherein he would show a *coup de maistre,*[4] or his highest skill, he recommends it to your observation by a pleasant description of it before the person first appears. Thus, in *Bartholomew-Fair* he gives you the pictures of Numps and Cokes, and in this those of Daw, Lafoole, Morose, and the Collegiate Ladies, all which you hear described before you see them. So that before they come upon the stage, you have a longing expectation of them, which prepares you to receive them favorably; and when they are there, even from their first appearance you are so far acquainted with them that nothing of their humor is lost to you.

"I will observe yet one thing further of this admirable plot: the business of it rises in every act. The second is greater than the first, the third than the second, and so forward to the fifth. There too you see, till the very last scene, new difficulties arising to obstruct the action of the play, and when the audience is brought into despair that the business can naturally be effected, then, and not before, the discovery is made. But that the poet might entertain you

---

[3] *Epistles*, II, i, 168: "It is believed that to write comedy requires a minimum of sweat because it fetches its subjects from ordinary life, but it takes just so much more labor as its faults are less indulged."

[4] master-stroke, a term from fencing.

with more variety all this while, he reserves some new characters to show you, which he opens not till the second and third act; in the second Morose, Daw, the Barber, and Otter; in the third the Collegiate Ladies, all which he moves afterwards in by-walks or under-plots, as diversions to the main design, lest it should grow tedious, though they are still naturally joined with it, and somewhere or other subservient to it. Thus, like a skilful chess-player, by little and little he draws out his men, and makes his pawns of use to his greater persons.

"If this comedy and some others of his were translated into French prose (which would now be no wonder to them, since Molière has lately given them plays out of verse, which have not displeased them), I believe the controversy would soon be decided betwixt the two nations, even making them judges. But we need not call our heroes to our aid. Be it spoken to the honor of the English, our nation can never want in any age such who are able to dispute the empire of wit with any people in the universe. And though the fury of a civil war, and power for twenty years together abandoned to a barbarous race of men, enemies of all good learning, had buried the muses under the ruins of monarchy; yet, with the restoration of our happiness, we see revived poesy lifting up its head, and already shaking off the rubbish which lay so heavy on it. We have seen since his Majesty's return many dramatic poems which yield not to those of any foreign nation, and which deserve all laurels but the English. I will set aside flattery and envy: it cannot be denied but we have had some little blemish either in the plot or writing of all those plays which have been made within these seven years; and perhaps there is no nation in the world so quick to discern them, or so difficult to pardon them, as ours; yet if we can persuade ourselves to use the candor of that poet who, though the most severe of critics, has left us this caution by which to moderate our censures—

> *ubi plura nitent in carmine, non ego paucis*
> *Offendar maculis;*[5]—

if, in consideration of their many and great beauties, we can wink at some slight and little imperfections, if we, I say, can be thus equal to ourselves, I ask no favor from the French. And if I do not venture upon any particular judgment of our late plays, 'tis out of the con-

---

[5] Horace, *Ars Poetica*, 351: "When many things shine in a poem, I am not offended at little blemishes."

sideration which an ancient writer gives me: *vivorum, ut magna admiratio, ita censura difficilis:*[6] betwixt the extremes of admiration and malice, 'tis hard to judge uprightly of the living. Only I think it may permitted me to say that as it is no lessening to us to yield to some plays, and those not many, of our own nation in the last age, so can it be no addition to pronounce of our present poets that they have far surpassed all the Ancients and the Modern writers of other countries.[7] . . .

"And this, Sir, calls to my remembrance the beginning of your discourse, where you told us we should never find the audience favorable to this kind of writing [rhymed drama] till we could produce as good plays in rhyme as Ben Jonson, Fletcher, and Shakespeare had writ out of it. But it is to raise envy to the living, to compare them with the dead. They are honored and almost adored by us, as they deserve; neither do I know any so presumptuous of themselves as to contend with them. Yet give me leave to say thus much, without injury to their ashes, that not only we shall never equal them, but they could never equal themselves were they to rise and write again. We acknowledge them our fathers in wit, but they have ruined their estates themselves before they came to their children's hands. There is scarce a humor, a character, or any kind of plot which they have not used. All comes sullied or wasted to us, and were they to entertain this age, they could not now make so plenteous treatments out of such decayed fortunes. This therefore will be a good argument to us either not to write at all or to attempt some other way. There is no bays to be expected in their walks: *tentanda via est, qua me quoque possum tollere humo.*[8]

"This way of writing in verse they have only left free to us; our age is arrived to a perfection in it which they never knew and which (if we may guess by what of theirs we have seen in verse, as *The Faithful Shepherdess*[9] and *Sad Shepherd* [1]) 'tis probable they never could have reached. For the genius of every age is different; and though ours excel in this, I deny not but to imitate Nature in that perfection which they did in prose is a greater commendation than to write in verse exactly. As for what you have added, that the peo-

---

[6] Velleius Paterculus, *Historiae Romae*, II, 36: "As admiration of the living is great, so to criticize them is difficult."
[7] In the omitted portion, Dryden discusses rhyme in drama.
[8] Virgil, *Georgics*, III, 8: "New ways I must attempt, my grov'ling name/To raise aloft." [Dryden's translation.]
[9] By Fletcher.
[1] By Jonson.

ple are not generally inclined to like this way: if it were true, it would be no wonder, that betwixt the shaking off an old habit and the introducing of a new, there should be difficulty. Do we not see them stick to Hopkins' and Sternhold's psalms[2] and forsake those of David, I mean Sandys[3] his translation of them? If by the people you understand the multitude, the οἱ πολλοί, 'tis no matter what they think; they are sometimes in the right, sometimes in the wrong: their judgment is a mere lottery. *Est ubi plebs recte putat, est ubi peccat.*[4] Horace says it of the vulgar, judging poesy. But if you mean the mixed audience of the populace and the noblesse, I dare confidently affirm that a great part of the latter sort are already favorable to verse and that no serious plays written since the King's return have been more kindly received by them than *The Siege of Rhodes,* the *Mustapha,*[5] *The Indian Queen,*[6] and *Indian Emperor.*" [7] . . .

Neander was pursuing this discourse so eagerly that Eugenius had called to him twice or thrice ere he took notice that the barge stood still, and that they were at the foot of Somerset-stairs,[8] where they had appointed it to land. The company were all sorry to separate so soon, though a great part of the evening was already spent; and stood awhile looking back on the water, upon which the moonbeams played, and made it appear like floating quicksilver. At last they went up through a crowd of French people, who were merrily dancing in the open air, and nothing concerned for the noise of the guns which had alarmed the town that afternoon. Walking thence together to the Piazze,[9] they parted there; Eugenius and Lisideius to some pleasant appointment they had made, and Crites and Neander to their several lodgings.

---

[2] The metrical versions by Thomas Sternhold (1500–49) and John Hopkins (d. 1570) which were the standard hymnody of the Church of England until the eighteenth century.

[3] George Sandys (1578–1644), otherwise known for his translation of Ovid's *Metamorphoses,* made during a ten-year tenure as a colonial agent in Virginia, and for his travels in the Near East. Cultured readers were likely to prefer his more elegant version of the Psalms.

[4] Cf. Horace, *Epistles,* II, i, 63: "There are times when the people think rightly, times when they go astray."

[5] *Mustapha, Son of Solyman the Magnificent* (1664) by Roger Boyle, Earl of Orrey (1621–79).

[6] By Dryden and Howard (1664).

[7] Sequel to *The Indian Queen,* by Dryden (1665). All the forementioned are heroic plays.

[8] A noted landing-place, often to get water, near Old Somerset House.

[9] An open arcade recently designed by Inigo Jones in Covent Garden, center of London's night life.

* * * *

FROM

The Author's Apology for Heroic Poetry and Poetic License, Prefixed to The State of Innocence and Fall of Man, an Opera [1677]

I cannot without injury to the deceased author of *Paradise Lost* but acknowledge that this poem has received its entire foundation, part of the design, and many of the ornaments from him. What I have borrowed will be so easily discerned from my mean productions that I shall not need to point the reader to the places; and truly I should be sorry, for my own sake, that any one should take the pains to compare them together, the original being undoubtedly one of the greatest, most noble, and most sublime poems which either this age or nation has produced. . . . [But] we are fallen into an age of illiterate, censorious, and detracting people who, thus qualified, set up for critics.

In the first place, I must take leave to tell them that they wholly mistake the nature of criticism who think its business is principally to find fault. Criticism, as it was first instituted by Aristotle, was meant a standard of judging well, the chiefest part of which is to observe those excellencies which should delight a reasonable reader. If the design, the conduct, the thoughts, and the expressions of a poem be generally such as proceed from a true genius of poetry, the critic ought to pass his judgment in favor of the author. 'Tis malicious and unmanly to snarl at the little lapses of a pen, from which Virgil himself stands not exempted. Horace acknowledges that honest Homer nods sometimes.[1] . . . And Longinus, who was undoubtedly, after Aristotle, the greatest critic amongst the Greeks, in his twenty-seventh chapter περὶ ὕψους, has judiciously preferred the sublime genius that sometimes errs, to the middling or indifferent one which makes few faults, but seldom or never rises to any excellence. . . . This kind of genius writes indeed correctly. A wary man he is in grammar, very nice[2] as to solecism or barbarism, judges to a hair of little decencies,[3] knows better than any man what is not

---

[1] *Ars Poetica*, 359.
[2] finical.
[3] decorums.

to be written, and never hazards himself so far as to fall, but plods
on deliberately, and as a grave man ought, is sure to put his staff
before him: in short, he sets his heart upon it, and with wonderful
care makes his business sure, that is, in plain English, neither to be
blamed nor praised. . . .

'Tis worth our consideration a little to examine how much these
hypercritics of English poetry differ from the opinion of the Greek
and Latin judges of antiquity, from the Italians and French who
have succeeded them, and indeed from the general taste and approbation of all ages. Heroic poetry, which they contemn, has ever
been esteemed, and ever will be, the greatest work of human nature;
in that rank has Aristotle placed it; and Longinus is so full of the
like expressions that he abundantly confirms the other's testimony.
Horace as plainly delivers his opinion, and particularly praises
Homer in these verses:

> *Trojani belli scriptorem, Maxime Lolli,*
> *Dum tu declamas Romae, Praeneste relegi:*
> *Qui quid sit pulchrum, quid turpe, quid utile, quid non,*
> *Plenius ac melius Chrysippo et Crantore dicit.*[4]

And in another place, modestly excluding himself from the number of poets, because he only wrote odes and satires, he tells you a
poet is such a one,

> *cui mens divinior, atque os*
> *Magna sonaturum.*[5]

Quotations are superfluous in an established truth; otherwise I
could reckon up, amongst the Moderns, all the Italian commentators on Aristotle's book *Of Poetry*,[6] and amongst the French, the
greatest of this age Boileau[7] and Rapin,[8] the latter of which is alone

---

[4] *Epistles*, II, i, 1–4: "While you study declamation at Rome, Lollius Maxi-
mus, I have been at Praeneste reading the writer of the Trojan War, who,
more clearly and better than Chrysippus or Crantor, teaches us what is beautiful, what is foul, what is useful and what is not."

[5] *Satires*, I, iv, 43–44: "to whom is given a divine understanding, and a tongue
of majestic utterance."

[6] Dryden refers to the remarkable, mixed group of critics, such as Vida (*De
Arte Poetica*, 1527), Daniello (*La Poetica*, 1536), Minturno (*L'Arte Poetica*,
1564), Castelvetro (*Poetica*, 1570), and others, who are founders of Renaissance neoclassic doctrine.

[7] Nicolas Boileau-Despréaux (1636–1711), poet and critic, whose *Réflexions*
on Longinus and translation of him (1674) initiated the vogue of *Peri Hupsous*
in eighteenth-century criticism. His other most influential critical work was
L'Art poétique (1674), the Horatian prototype of Pope's *Essay on Criticism*.

[8] René Rapin (1621–87), most influential by his *Réflexions sur la poétique*

sufficient, were all other critics lost, to teach anew the rules of writing. Any man who will seriously consider the nature of an epic poem, how it agrees with that of poetry in general, which is to instruct and to delight; what actions it describes, and what persons they are chiefly whom it informs; will find it a work which indeed is full of difficulty in the attempt, but admirable when 'tis well performed. I write not this with the least intention to undervalue the other parts of poetry; for comedy is both excellently instructive and extremely pleasant; satire lashes vice into reformation, and humor represents folly so as to render it ridiculous. Many of our present writers are eminent in both these kinds; and particularly, the author of *The Plain Dealer*,[9] whom I am proud to call my friend, has obliged all honest and virtuous men by one of the most bold, most general, and most useful satires which has ever been presented on the English theatre. I do not dispute the preference of tragedy: let every man enjoy his taste; but 'tis unjust that they who have not the least notion of heroic writing should therefore condemn the pleasure which others receive from it, because they cannot comprehend it. Let them please their appetites in eating what they like, but let them not force their dish on all the table. They who would combat general authority with particular opinion must first establish themselves a reputation of understanding better than other men. Are all the flights of heroic poetry to be concluded bombast, unnatural, and mere madness, because they are not affected with their excellences? It is just as reasonable as to conclude there is no day because a blind man cannot distinguish of light and colors. Ought they not rather, in modesty, to doubt of their own judgments, when they think this or that expression in Homer, Virgil, Tasso, or Milton's *Paradise* to be too far strained, than positively to conclude that 'tis all fustian and mere nonsense? . . . But I will presume for once to tell them that the boldest strokes of poetry, when they are managed artfully, are those which most delight the reader.

Virgil and Horace, the severest writers of the severest age, have made frequent use of the hardest metaphors and of the strongest hyperboles; and in this case, the best authority is the best argument, for generally to have pleased, and through all ages, must bear the force of universal tradition. And if you would appeal from thence

---

d'*Aristote et sur les ouvrages des poètes anciens et modernes* (1674), translated the same year, with a preface, by Rymer. Among other works, his discourse on pastorals (1684) was widely studied.

9 Wycherley.

to right reason, you will gain no more by it in effect than, first, to set up your reason against those authors; and, secondly, against all those who have admired them. You must prove why that ought not to have pleased which has pleased the most learned and the most judicious; and, to be thought knowing, you must first put the fool upon all mankind. If you can enter more deeply than they have done into the causes and resorts of that which moves pleasure in a reader, the field is open, you may be heard; but those springs of human nature are not so easily discovered by every superficial judge. It requires philosophy as well as poetry to sound the depth of all the passions, what they are in themselves, and how they are to be provoked;[1] and in this science the best poets have excelled. Aristotle raised the fabric of his *Poetry* from observation of those things in which Euripides, Sophocles, and Aeschylus pleased; he considered how they raised the passions, and thence has drawn rules for our imitation. From hence have sprung the tropes and figures for which they wanted[2] a name who first practiced them and succeeded in them. Thus I grant you that the knowledge of Nature was the original rule, and that all poets ought to study her as well as Aristotle and Horace, her interpreters. But then this also undeniably follows, that those things which delight all ages must have been an imitation of Nature; which is all I contend. Therefore is rhetoric made an art; therefore the names of so many tropes and figures were invented, because it was observed they had such and such effect upon the audience. Therefore catachreses and hyperboles have found their place amongst them, not that they were to be avoided, but to be used judiciously, and placed in poetry as heightenings and shadows are in painting, to make the figure bolder, and cause it to stand off to sight. . . .

'Tis true, the boldness of the figures is to be hidden sometimes by the address[3] of the poet, that they may work their effect upon the mind without discovering the art which caused it. And therefore they are principally to be used in passion, when we speak more warmly and with more precipitation than at other times, for then *si vis me flere, dolendum est primum ipsi tibi:*[4] the poet must put on the passion he endeavors to represent; a man in such an occasion

---

[1] Dryden anticipates here the "philosophical inquiries" of later critics, though the premise may be traced into classical antiquity—e.g., Cicero, *De Oratore.*
[2] lacked.
[3] skill.
[4] Horace, *Ars Poetica,* 102: "if you want me to cry, you must first feel grief yourself."

is not cool enough either to reason rightly or to talk calmly. Aggravations[5] are then in their proper places; interrogations, exclamations, hyperbata,[6] or a disordered connection of discourse, are graceful there because they are natural. The sum of all depends on what before I hinted, that this boldness of expression is not to be blamed if it be managed by the coolness and discretion which is necessary to a poet.

Yet before I leave this subject, I cannot but take notice how disingenuous our adversaries appear: all that is dull, insipid, languishing, and without sinews in a poem, they call an imitation of Nature. . . .

What fustian, as they call it, have I heard these gentlemen find out in Mr. Cowley's *Odes?* I acknowledge myself unworthy to defend so excellent an author, neither have I room to do it here; only in general I will say that nothing can appear more beautiful to me than the strength of those images which they condemn.

Imaging is, in itself, the very height and life of poetry. 'Tis, as Longinus describes it, a discourse which, by a kind of enthusiasm or extraordinary emotion of the soul, makes it seem to us that we behold those things which the poet paints so as to be pleased with them and to admire them.

If poetry be imitation, that part of it must needs be best which describes most lively our actions and passions, our virtues and our vices, our follies and our humors; for neither is comedy without its part of imaging; and they who do it best are certainly the most excellent in their kind. This is too plainly proved to be denied. But how are poetical fictions, how are hippocentaurs and chimeras, or how are angels and immaterial substances to be imaged; which, some of them, are things quite out of nature, others such whereof we can have no notion? This is the last refuge of our adversaries, and more than any of them have yet had the wit to object against us. The answer is easy to the first part of it: the fiction of some beings which are not in nature ("second notions" as the logicians call them) has been founded on the conjunction of two natures which have a real separate being. So hippocentaurs were imaged by joining the natures of a man and horse together, as Lucretius tells us, who has used this word of *image* oftener than any of the poets.[7] . . .

The same reason may also be alleged for chimeras and the rest. And poets may be allowed the like liberty for describing things

---

[5] exaggerations.
[6] inversions of normal word-order.
[7] Dryden quotes *De rerum natura,* IV, 739–42, in which *imago* appears twice.

which really exist not, if they are founded on popular belief. Of this nature are fairies, pigmies, and the extraordinary effects of magic; for 'tis still an imitation, though of other men's fancies; and thus are Shakespeare's *Tempest*, his *Midsummer Night's Dream*, and Ben Jonson's *Masque of Witches* to be defended.[8] For immaterial substances, we are authorized by Scripture in their description; and herein the test accommodates itself to vulgar apprehension in giving angels the likeness of beautiful young men. Thus, after the pagan divinity has Homer drawn his gods with human faces; and thus we have notions of things above us by describing them like other beings more within our knowledge. . . .

From that which has been said, it may be collected that the definition of Wit (which has been so often attempted and ever unsuccessfully by many poets) is only this: that it is a propriety of thoughts and words, or, in other terms, thoughts and words elegantly adapted to the subject.[9] If our critics will join issue on this definition that we may *convenire in aliquo tertio*;[1] if they will take it as a granted principle, 'twill be easy to put an end to this dispute. No man will disagree from another's judgment concerning the dignity of style in heroic poetry; but all reasonable men will conclude it necessary that sublime subjects ought to be adorned with the sublimest and (consequently often) with the most figurative expressions. In the meantime, I will not run into their fault of imposing my opinions on other men any more than I would my writings on their taste; I have only laid down, and that superficially enough, my present thoughts, and shall be glad to be taught better by those who pretend to reform our poetry.

---

[8] *Cf.* "Of Heroic Plays" (1672); in the Preface to *Troilus and Cressida* Dryden praises Caliban as the creation of a person "not in Nature"; the example became a commonplace in later criticism.

[9] Later critics of Dryden, even into the present century, have tended to stress the word *elegantly*, but Dryden intended stress to lie on *propriety* or *adapted to the subject* and therefore on the interacting, "natural" unity of imagination, language, and subject so as to create the "delight" proper to poetry.

[1] come together in some third term, compromise.

* * * *

FROM

A Discourse concerning the Original
and Progress of Satire [1693]

If we take *satire* in the general signification of the word, as it is used in all modern languages, for an invective, it is certain that it is almost as old as verse; and though hymns, which are praises of God, may be allowed to have been before it, yet the defamation of others was not long after it. After God had cursed Adam and Eve in Paradise, the husband and wife excused themselves by laying the blame on one another, and gave a beginning to those conjugal dialogues in prose which the poets have perfected in verse. The third chapter of *Job* is one of the first instances of this poem in Holy Scripture, unless we will take it higher from the latter end of the second [chapter] where his wife advises him to curse his Maker.

This original, I confess, is not much to the honor of satire; but here it was nature, and that depraved; when it became an art, it bore better fruit. Only, we have learnt thus much already, that scoffs and revilings are of the growth of all nations, and, consequently, that neither the Greek poets borrowed from other people their art of railing, neither needed the Romans to take it from them. But considering satire as a species of poetry, here the war begins amongst the critics. Scaliger, the father,[1] will have it descend from Greece to Rome; and derives the word *satire* from *satyrus*, that mixed kind of animal or, as the ancients thought him, rural god, made up betwixt a man and a goat, with a human head, hooked nose, pouting lips, a bunch or *struma*[2] under the chin, pricked ears, and upright horns, the body shagged with hair, especially from the waist, and ending in a goat, with the legs and feet of that creature. But Casaubon[3] with his followers, with reason, condemn this der-

---

[1] Julius Caesar Scaliger in his *Poetics* (1561) as distinct from his son Joseph Justus, the great classical scholar and founder of modern textual methods of editing.

[2] goiter, swelling.

[3] Isaac Casaubon (1559–1614), French Protestant humanist and Greek scholar. Dryden alludes to *De satyrica Graecorum poesi et Romanorum satira* (1605).

ivation, and prove that from *satyrus* the word *satira*, as it signifies a poem, cannot possibly descend. For *satira* is not properly a substantive but an adjective, to which the word *lanx* (in English, a charger or large platter) is understood; so that the Greek poem, made according to the manners of a satyr and expressing his qualities,[4] must properly be called satyrical and not satire. And thus far 'tis allowed that the Grecians had such poems, but that they were wholly different *in specie* from that to which the Romans gave the name of satire. . . .

The Grecians, beside these satyric tragedies,[5] had another kind of poem which they called *silli*, which were more of kin to the Roman satire. Those *silli* were indeed invective poems, but of a different species from the Roman poems of Ennius, Pacuvius, Lucilius, Horace, and the rest of their successors.[6] They were so called, says Casaubon in one place, from Silenus,[7] the foster-father of Bacchus; but in another place, bethinking himself better, he derives their name ἀπὸ τοῦ σιλλαίνειν, from their scoffing and petulancy. From some fragments of the *silli* written by Timon,[8] we may find that they were satyric poems full of parodies, that is, of verses patched up from great poets and turned into another sense than their author intended them. Such amongst the Romans is the famous *Cento* of Ausonius;[9] where the words are Virgil's, but by applying them to another sense, they are made a relation of a wedding night, and the

---

[4] The generally received idea of satire in Elizabethan and Jacobean England. See Alvin Kernan, *The Cankered Muse: Satire of the English Renaissance* (New Haven: Yale University Press, 1959).

[5] That is, satyr-plays were performed as afterpieces to tragic trilogies, often burlesquing tragic subjects. Pope jokingly speaks of *The Dunciad* as "satyric tragedy."

[6] The line of development in Roman satire, as Dryden saw it. Ennius (239–170 B.C.), a Hellenizing epic poet and tragedian who introduced the Greek hexameter, also wrote saturae or miscellanies which Dryden believed to be refinements of Fescennine verses and the spirit of Aristophanic comedy lately imitated on the Roman stage by Andronicus. Pacuvius (c. 220–130 B.C.) was a tragedian about whom little is known. Lucilius (c. 180–103 B.C.) wrote thirty books of satires of which fragments survive. Horace considered Lucilius the founder of satire and modeled his own works after him.

[7] The most famous of the satyrs, snub-nosed, bald, and drunken, who enters the history of satire in Plato's *Symposium*, where Alcibiades describes Socrates as a Silenus, ugly and farcical on the outside but divine within. *Cf.* "The Author's Prologue" to Rabelais's *Gargantua*.

[8] Greek skeptic and poet (c. 320–230 B.C.), known as the Sillographer for his *Silloi*, three books of mock-epic hexameters whose character Dryden describes. Only fragments survive.

[9] Late Latin poet (c. 309–92 A.D.), lawyer, professor of rhetoric, and consul of Gaul.

act of consummation fulsomely described in the very words of the most modest amongst all poets. Of the same manner are our songs which are turned into burlesque, and the serious words of the author perverted into a ridiculous meaning. Thus in Timon's *Silloi* the words are generally those of Homer and the tragic poets, but he applies them satirically to some customs and kinds of philosophy which he arraigns. But the Romans not using any of these parodies in their satires—sometimes, indeed, repeating verses of other men, as Persius cites some of Nero's, but not turning them into another meaning—the *silli* cannot be supposed to be the original of Roman satire. To these *silli*, consisting of parodies, we may properly add the satires which were written against particular persons, such as were the iambics of Archilochus[1] against Lycambes, which Horace undoubtedly imitated in some of his *Odes* and *Epodes*,[2] whose titles bear sufficient witness of it. I might also name the invective of Ovid against *Ibis*, and many others; but these are the underwood of satire rather than the timber-trees: they are not of general extension, as reaching only to some individual person. And Horace seems to have purged himself from those splenetic reflections[3] in his *Odes* and *Epodes* before he undertook the noble work of *Satires*, which were properly so called.

Thus, my Lord,[4] I have at length disengaged myself from those antiquities of Greece, and have proved, I hope, from the best critics, that the Roman satire was not borrowed from thence, but of their own manufacture. . . .

[Casaubon's] opinion is grounded on sure authority, that satire was derived from *satura*, a Roman word which signifies full and abundant, and full also of variety, in which nothing is wanting to its due perfection. It is thus, says Dacier,[5] that we say "a full color," when the wool has taken the whole tincture, and drunk in as much of the dye as it can receive. . . . *Satura*, as I have formerly noted, is an adjective, and relates to the word *lanx*, which is understood; and this *lanx*, in English a charger or large platter, was yearly filled

---

[1] (Fl. 714–676 B.C.) often regarded as the first lyric poet and ranked by the ancients along with Homer, Pindar, and Sophocles. He introduced iambic verse; but was also famous for lampoons so effective that Lycambes hanged himself and his family for shame.

[2] Horace's *Epodes* imitate the iambs of Archilochus.

[3] reproaches.

[4] The essay is addressed to Charles Sackville, Earl of Dorset (Eugenius) and flatters him fulsomely, at length.

[5] André Dacier, French critic, from whose essay on satire (1687), appended to his translation of Horace, Dryden borrows much of his information.

with all sorts of fruits, which were offered to the gods at their festivals, as the *premices*[6] or first gatherings. . . . The word *satura* has been afterwards applied to many other sorts of mixtures, as Festus calls it a kind of *olla*, or hotchpotch, made of several sorts of meats. Laws were also called *leges saturae* when they were of several heads and titles, like our tacked bills[7] of Parliament. . . . From hence it may probably be conjectured that the *Discourses* or *Satires* of Ennius, Lucilius, and Horace, as we now call them, took their name because they are full of various matters, and are also written on various subjects, as Porphyrius says. But Dacier affirms that it is not immediately from thence that these satires are so called, for that name had been used formerly for other things, which bore a nearer resemblance to those discourses of Horace.[8] . . .

Having thus brought down the history of satire from its original to the times of Horace, and shown the several changes of it, I should here discover some of those graces which Horace added to it, but that I think it will be more proper to defer that undertaking till I make the comparison betwixt him and Juvenal. In the meanwhile, following the order of time, it will be necessary to say somewhat of another kind of satire which also was descended from the Ancients: 'tis that which we call the Varronian satire (but which Varro[9] himself calls the Menippean) because Varro, the most learned of the Romans, was the first author of it; who imitated in his works the manner of Menippus the Gardarenian, who professed the philosophy of the Cynics.

This sort of satire was not only composed of several sorts of verse, like those of Ennius, but was also mixed with prose, and Greek was sprinkled amongst the Latin. . . .

Tully in his *Academics*[1] introduces Varro himself giving us some light concerning the scope and design of these works. Wherein, after he had shown his reasons why he did not *ex professo*[2] write of philosophy, he adds what follows: "Notwithstanding," says he,

---

[6] Fr. "first-fruits."

[7] bills to which riders are tacked on.

[8] At this point Dryden discusses the Fescennine (or Saturnian) verses "which, says Dacier, we cannot better represent than by imagining a company of clowns on a holiday, dancing lubberly and upbraiding one another, in *ex tempore* doggerel, with their defects and vices and the stories that were told of them in bakehouses and barbers' shops."

[9] Marcus Terentius Varro (116–27 B.C.) who wrote over seventy different works on agriculture, language, history, philosophy, and other subjects. His *Saturae Menippeae* ran to 150 books.

[1] Cicero, *Academica*, I, 2.

[2] openly and publicly.

"that those pieces of mine wherein I have imitated Menippus, though I have not translated him, are sprinkled with a kind of mirth and gaiety, yet many things are there inserted which are drawn from the very entrails of philosophy; and many things severely argued, which I have mingled with pleasantries on purpose, that they may more easily go down with the common sort of unlearned readers." . . . Thus it appears that Varro was one of those writers whom they called σπουδογέλοιοι, "studious of laughter," and that, as learned as he was, his business was more to divert his reader than to teach him; and he entitled his own satires Menippean, not that Menippus had written any satires (for his were either dialogues or epistles) but that Varro imitated his style, his manner, and his facetiousness.[3] All that we know further of Menippus and his writings, which are wholly lost, is that by some he is esteemed, as amongst the rest by Varro; by others he is noted of cynical impudence and obscenity; that he was much given to those parodies which I have already mentioned; that is, he often quoted the verses of Homer and the tragic poets and turned their serious meaning into something that was ridiculous; whereas Varro's satires are by Tully called absolute, and most elegant and various[4] poems. Lucian, who was emulous of this Menippus, seems to have imitated both his manners and his style in many of his dialogues, where Menippus himself is often introduced as a speaker in them and as a perpetual buffoon; particularly his character is expressed in the beginning of that dialogue which is called Νεκυομαντεία. But Varro, in imitating him, avoids his impudence and filthiness, and only expresses his witty pleasantry.

This we may believe for certain: that as his subjects were various, so most of them were tales or stories of his own invention. Which is also manifest from antiquity by those authors who are acknowledged to have written Varronian satires in imitation of his; of whom the chief is Petronius Arbiter, whose satire, they say, is now printed in Holland, wholly recovered and made complete; when 'tis made public, it will easily be seen by any one sentence whether it be supposititious or genuine.[5] Many of Lucian's dialogues may also properly be called Varronian satires, particularly his *True His-*

---

[3] For a contemporary definition of Menippean satire and its relation to the novel, see Northrop Frye, "The Four Forms of Prose Fiction," *Hudson Review*, II (1950), 582–95.

[4] As would be proper to a satire, by definition, but perhaps with a pun on Varro. See first sentence of the next paragraph.

[5] Only chapters 15 and 16 remain of his comic romance the *Satyricon*, plus fragments. The most famous part is the Banquet of Trimalchio.

tory; and consequently the *Golden Ass* of Apuleius, which is taken from him. Of the same stamp is the mock deification of Claudius,[6] by Seneca; and the *Symposium or Caesars* of Julian the Emperor.[7] Amongst the moderns we may reckon the *Encomium Moriae* of Erasmus, Barclay's *Euphormio*,[8] and a volume of German authors[9] which my ingenious friend Mr. Charles Killigrew once lent me. In the English, I remember none which are mixed with prose, as Varro's were; but of the same kind[1] is *Mother Hubbard's Tale* in Spenser, and (if it be not too vain to mention anything of my own) the poems of *Absalom* and *MacFlecknoe*.

This is what I have to say in general of satire; only, as Dacier has observed before me, we may take notice that the word *satire* is of a more general signification in Latin than in French or English. For amongst the Romans it was not only used for those discourses which decried vice or exposed folly, but for others also where virtue was recommended. But in our modern languages we apply it only to invective poems, where the very name of satire is formidable to those persons who would appear to the world what they are not in themselves. . . .

I beg leave to take notice of this sentence where Holyday[2] says, "A perpetual grin, like that of Horace, rather angers than amends a man." I cannot give him up the manner of Horace in low satire so easily. Let the chastisement of Juvenal be never so necessary for his new kind of satire; let him declaim as wittily and sharply as he pleases; yet still the nicest[3] and most delicate touches of satire con-

---

[6] Roman emperor (10 B.C.–54 A.D.). Seneca's satire on his death, mingling verse and prose, is entitled *Apocolocyntosis*, which means, roughly, "pumpkinification."

[7] Roman emperor (c. 331–63 A.D.) called "the Apostate." See Gibbon's *Decline and Fall*, chs. 22–24. His *Symposium*, an imitation of Varro, ridiculed other emperors from Caesar downwards.

[8] John Barclay (1582–1621), Scottish writer, born in France, whose Petronian *Euphormionis Lusinini Satyricon* (1603–7) was dedicated to James I. Dryden elsewhere quotes his essays (Ker, I, 6) *Icon Animorum* (1614). His most famous work, throughout Europe, was *Argenis* (1621), a politico-satirical romance still being read in the late eighteenth century when translated by Clara Reeve as *The Phoenix* (1772). Both Cowper and Coleridge praised it.

[9] Probably, as Ker notes, the *Epistolae obscurorum virorum* (1515), forty-one anonymous "letters of obscure men," a neo-Latin humanistic attack on monastics, an early example of *Dunciad*-literature.

[1] The common denominator of the "kind" is not as clear as one might wish, though apparently Dryden is driving toward the mock-heroic (ridicule in a noble or grand style) as distinct from mere burlesque.

[2] Barten Holyday (1593–1661), archdeacon of Oxford, who translated Juvenal (1673), with commentary.

[3] most refined.

sist in fine raillery. This, my Lord, is your particular talent, to which even Juvenal could not arrive. 'Tis not reading, 'tis not imitation of an author, which can produce this fineness;[4] it must be inborn; it must proceed from a genius and particular way of thinking which is not to be taught; and therefore not to be imitated by him who has it not from nature. How easy is it to call rogue and villain, and that wittily! But how hard to make a man appear a fool, a blockhead, or a knave, without using any of those opprobrious terms! To spare the grossness of the names, and to do the thing yet more severely, is to draw a full face, and to make the nose and cheeks stand out, and yet not to employ any depth of shadowing. This is the mystery of that noble trade which yet no master can teach to his apprentice; he may give the rules, but the scholar is never the nearer in his practice. Neither is it true that this fineness of raillery is offensive. A witty man is tickled while he is hurt in this manner, and a fool feels it not. The occasion of an offense may possibly be given, but he cannot take it. If it be granted that in effect this way does more mischief, that a man is secretly wounded, and though he be not sensible himself, yet the malicious world will find it out for him; yet there is still a vast difference betwixt the slovenly butchering of a man, and the fineness of a stroke that separates the head from the body, and leaves it standing in its place. A man may be capable, as Jack Ketch's[5] wife said of his servant, of a plain piece of work, a bare hanging, but to make a malefactor die sweetly was only belonging to her husband. I wish I could apply it to myself, if the reader would be kind enough to think it belongs to me. The character of Zimri in my *Absalom* is, in my opinion, worth the whole poem; it is not bloody, but it is ridiculous enough; and he for whom it was intended [6] was too witty to resent it as an injury. If I had railed, I might have suffered for it justly; but I managed my own work more happily, perhaps more dexterously. I avoided the mention of great crimes, and applied myself to the representing of blind sides and little extravagances, to which, the wittier a man is, he is generally the more obnoxious.[7] It succeeded as I wished; the jest went round; and he was laughed at in his turn who began the frolic.[8]

---

[4] finish.

[5] Famous Restoration hangman and headsman (d. 1686) whose name became a byword.

[6] George Villiers, Duke of Buckingham.

[7] vulnerable.

[8] Buckingham had satirized Dryden in *The Rehearsal*.

And thus, my Lord, you see I have preferred the manner of Horace, and of your Lordship, in this kind of satire, to that of Juvenal, and, I think, reasonably. . . . Let the *Manes*[9] of Juvenal forgive me if I say that this way of Horace was the best for amending manners, as it is the most difficult. His was an *ense rescindendum*,[1] but that of Horace was a pleasant cure with all the limbs preserved entire, and, as our mountebanks tell us in their bills,[2] without keeping the patient withindoors for a day. What they promise only, Horace has effectually performed; yet I contradict not the proposition which I formerly advanced.[3] Juvenal's times required a more painful kind of operation; but if he had lived in the age of Horace, I must needs affirm that he had it not about him. He took the method which was prescribed him by his own genius, which was sharp and eager; he could not rally, but he could declaim; and as his provocations were great, he has revenged them tragically. This notwithstanding, I am to say another word which, as true as it is, will yet displease the partial admirers of our Horace. I have hinted it before, but it is time for me now to speak more plainly.

This manner of Horace is indeed the best, but Horace has not executed it altogether so happily, at least not often. The manner of Juvenal is confessed to be inferior to the former, but Juvenal has excelled him in his performance. Juvenal has railed more wittily than Horace has rallied. Horace means to make his readers laugh, but he is not sure of his experiment. Juvenal always intends to move your indignation, and he always brings about his purpose. Horace, for aught I know, might have tickled the people of his age, but amongst the moderns he is not so successful. . . . Upon the one half of the merits, that is, pleasure, I cannot but conclude that Juvenal was the better satirist. . . .

'Tis but necessary that after so much has been said of satire, some definition of it should be given. Heinsius,[4] in his dissertations on Horace, makes it for me, in these words: "Satire is a kind of poetry, without a series of action,[5] invented for the purging of our minds; in which human vices, ignorance, and errors, and all things

---

[9] Roman name for spirits of the dead.
[1] tearing or cutting away with a sword.
[2] as quacks say in their advertisements.
[3] "Juvenal is of a more vigorous and masculine wit; he gives me as much pleasure as I can bear"; and so, "granting Horace to be the more general philosopher, we cannot deny that Juvenal was the greater poet, I mean in satire."
[4] Daniel Heinsius (1580–1655), Dutch professor of classics at Leyden. Dryden alludes to his essay on satire appended to his edition of Horace (1612).
[5] That is, non-narrative.

besides which are produced from them in every man, are severely reprehended; partly dramatically, partly simply,[6] and sometimes in both kinds of speaking, but, for the most part, figuratively and occultly;[7] consisting in a low familiar way,[8] chiefly in a sharp and pungent manner of speech, but partly also in a facetious and civil way of jesting; by which either hatred or laughter or indignation is moved." Where I cannot but observe that this obscure and perplexed definition, or rather description, of satire is wholly accommodated to the Horatian way, and excluding the works of Juvenal and Persius as foreign from that kind of poem. . . . Is the *grande sophos*[9] of Persius and the sublimity of Juvenal to be circumscribed with the meanness of words and vulgarity of expression? If Horace refused the pains of numbers and the loftiness of figures, are they bound to follow so ill a precedent? Let him walk afoot, with his pad[1] in his hand, for his own pleasure; but let not them be accounted no poets who choose to mount and show their horsemanship. . . . Would not Donne's *Satires*, which abound with so much wit, appear more charming if he had taken care of his words and of his numbers? But he followed Horace so very close that of necessity he must fall with him; and I may safely say it of this present age that if we are not so great wits as Donne, yet certainly we are better poets.

But I have said enough, and it may be too much, on this subject. Will your Lordship be pleased to prolong my audience[2] only so far till I tell you my own trivial thoughts how a modern satire should be made? I will not deviate in the least from the precepts and examples of the Ancients, who were always our best masters. I will only illustrate them and discover some of the hidden beauties in their designs, that we thereby may form our own in imitation of them. Will you please but to observe that Persius, the least in dignity of all the three, has notwithstanding been the first who has discovered to us this important secret in the designing of a perfect satire—that it ought only to treat of one subject, to be confined to one particular theme or at least to one principally. If other vices occur in the management of the chief, they should only be transiently lashed, and not be insisted on so as to make the design

---

[6] straightforwardly.
[7] by concealment and indirection.
[8] This part of the definition Dryden rejects, insisting in satire upon the value of the grand style and (mock-) heroic manner.
[9] lofty "bravo!"
[1] saddle.
[2] interview, hearing.

double. As in a play of the English fashion which we call a tragi-comedy, there is to be but one main design; and though there be an underplot, or second walk, of comical characters and adventures, yet they are subservient to the chief fable, carried along under it and helping to it, so that the drama may not seem a monster with two heads. . . . I know it may be urged in defense of Horace that this unity is not necessary, because the very word *satura* signifies a dish plentifully stored with all variety of fruit and grains. Yet Juvenal, who calls his poems a *farrago*, which is a word of the same signification with *satura*, has chosen to follow the same method of Persius and not of Horace; and Boileau, whose example alone is a sufficient authority, has wholly confined himself in all his *Satires*[3] to this unity of design. That variety which is not to be found in any one satire is, at least, in many written on several occasions. And if variety be of absolute necessity in every one of them, according to the etymology of the word, yet it may arise naturally from one sub-ject[4] as it is diversely treated in the several subordinate branches of it, all relating to the chief. It may be illustrated accordingly with variety of examples in the subdivisions of it, and with as many pre-cepts as there are members of it; which, altogether, may complete that *olla* or hotchpotch which is properly a satire.

Under this unity of theme or subject is comprehended another rule for perfecting the design of true satire. The poet is bound, and that *ex officio*,[5] to give his reader some one precept of moral virtue, and to caution him against some one particular vice or folly. Other virtues subordinate to the first may be recommended under that chief head, and other vices or follies may be scourged besides that which he principally intends. But he is chiefly to inculcate one virtue and insist on that. . . .

Of the best and finest manner of satire, I have said enough in the comparison betwixt Juvenal and Horace: 'tis that sharp, well-man-nered way of laughing a folly out of countenance, of which your Lordship is the best master of this age. I will proceed to the versifi-cation which is most proper for it, and add somewhat to what I have said already on that subject. The sort of verse which is called

---

[3] Published 1660–66. *L'Art poétique* appeared in 1674 and nine Horatian epistles 1669–77.

[4] Dryden's governing standard of "propriety." *Cf.* Preface to *Albion and Albanius* (1685): "Propriety of thought is that fancy which arises naturally from the subject or which the poet adapts to it."

[5] being privileged in one office by dint of holding another office. The satirist is committed to unity and moral instruction because all poets are.

burlesque, consisting of eight syllables or four feet, is that which our excellent Hudibras has chosen. I ought to have mentioned him[6] before, when I spoke of Donne, but by a slip of an old man's memory he was forgotten. The worth of his poem is too well known to need my commendation, and he is above my censure. His satire is of the Varronian kind, though unmixed with prose. The choice of his numbers is suitable enough to his design, as he has managed it, but in any other hand, the shortness of his verse, and the quick returns of rhyme, had debased the dignity of style. And besides, the double rhyme (a necessary companion of burlesque writing) is not so proper for manly satire, for it turns earnest too much to jest, and gives us a boyish kind of pleasure. It tickles awkwardly with a kind of pain, to the best sort of readers: we are pleased ungratefully, and, if I may say so, against our liking. We thank him not for giving us that unseasonable delight, when we know he could have given us a better and more solid. He might have left that task to others who, not being able to put in thought, can only make us grin with the excrescence of a word of two or three syllables in the close. 'Tis indeed below so great a master to make use of such a little instrument. But his good sense is perpetually shining through all he writes; it affords us not the time of finding faults. We pass through the levity of his rhyme, and are immediately carried into some admirable, useful thought. After all, he has chosen this kind of verse, and has written the best in it; and had he taken another, he would always have excelled; as we say of a court favorite, that whatsoever his office be, he still makes it uppermost and most beneficial to himself.

The quickness of your imagination, my Lord, has already prevented[7] me, and you know beforehand that I would prefer the verse of ten syllables, which we call the English heroic, to that of eight. This is truly my opinion. For this sort of number is more roomy; the thought can turn itself with greater ease in a larger compass. When the rhyme comes too thick upon us, it straitens the expression; we are thinking of the close when we should be employed in adorning the thought. It makes a poet giddy with turning in a space too narrow for his imagination; he loses many beauties without gaining one advantage. For a burlesque rhyme I have already concluded to be none, or, if it were, 'tis more easily purchased in ten syllables than in eight. In both occasions 'tis as in a tennis court when the strokes of greater force are given when we strike

---

[6] Samuel Butler.
[7] anticipated.

out and play at length. Tassoni[8] and Boileau have left us the best examples of this way in the *Secchia Rapita* and the *Lutrin,*[9] and next them Merlin Coccaius[1] in his *Baldus.* I will speak only of the two former, because the last is written in Latin verse. The *Secchia Rapita* is an Italian poem, a satire of the Varronian kind. 'Tis written in the stanza of eight,[2] which is their measure for heroic verse. The words are stately, the numbers smooth, the turn both of thoughts and words is happy. The first six lines of the stanza seems majestical and severe, but the two last turn them all into a pleasant ridicule. Boileau, if I am not much deceived, has modeled from hence his famous *Lutrin.* He had read the burlesque poetry of Scarron[3] with some kind of indignation, as witty as it was, and found nothing in France that was worthy of his imitation; but he copied the Italian so well that his own may pass for an original. He writes it in the French heroic verse and calls it a heroic poem; his subject is trivial but his verse is noble. I doubt not but he had Virgil in his eye, for we find many admirable imitations of him and some parodies. . . . This, I think, my Lord, to be the most beautiful and most noble kind of satire. Here is the majesty of the heroic finely mixed with the venom of the other, and raising the delight, which otherwise would be flat and vulgar, by the sublimity of the expression. I could say somewhat more of the delicacy of this and some others of his satires, but it might turn to his prejudice if 'twere carried back to France.

I have given your Lordship but this bare hint in what verse and in what manner this sort of satire may be best managed. Had I time, I could enlarge on the beautiful turns[4] of words and thought which are as requisite in this as in heroic poetry itself, of which the satire is undoubtedly a species.

---

[8] Alessandro Tassoni (1565–1635) claimed that his *La Secchia Rapita* (1622), "the stolen bucket," was the first modern mock-heroic.

[9] *Le Lutrin* means "the reading desk"; a mock-epic, it was published in four cantos in 1674; two other cantos were added in 1683.

[1] The pen name of Teofilo Folengo (1491–1554), an Italian Benedictine famous for his macaronics. *Baldus* (1517) is a mock-romance in Latin hexameters, whose fabulous adventures suggest Rabelais.

[2] *ottava rima.*

[3] Paul Scarron (1610–60), French *abbé* whose most famous burlesque was *Virgile Travesti* (1648–53), imitated in English by Charles Cotton as *Scarronides* (1664). Scarron's greatest work, however, was his *Le Roman comique* (1651–57), an anti-romance and prototype of the realistic novel influential on Le Sage, Fielding, and Smollett.

[4] A "turn" is a graceful repetition or variation which Dryden believed to be characteristic of Virgil, Ovid, Tasso, "that immortal poem called the *Fairy Queen,*" and contemporary French poets, as also Waller and Denham.

* * * *

FROM

Fables, Ancient and Modern [1700]

—◦⟡⟡◦—

from Preface

I proceed to Ovid and Chaucer, considering the former only in relation to the latter. With Ovid ended the Golden Age of the Roman tongue; from Chaucer the purity of the English tongue began. The manners of the poets were not unlike. Both of them were well-bred, well-natured, amorous, and libertine, at least in their writings: it may also be in their lives. Their studies were the same, philosophy and philology.[1] Both of them were knowing in astronomy, of which Ovid's books of the *Roman Feasts* and Chaucer's *Treatise of the Astrolabe* are sufficient witnesses. But Chaucer was likewise an astrologer, as were Virgil, Horace, Persius, and Manilius. Both writ with wonderful facility and clearness; neither were great inventors, for Ovid only copied the Grecian fables, and most of Chaucer's stories were taken from his Italian contemporaries or their predecessors. Boccace his *Decameron* was first published, and from thence our Englishman has borrowed many of his *Canterbury Tales;*[2] yet that of Palamon and Arcite[3] was written, in all probability, by some Italian wit in a former age, as I shall prove hereafter. The tale of Griselda was the invention of Petrarch, by him sent to Boccace, from whom it came to Chaucer.[4] *Troilus and Criseyde* was also written by a Lombard author,[5] but much amplified by our English translator as well as beautified: the genius of our countrymen, in general, rather being to improve an invention than to invent themselves, as is evident not only in our poetry but

---

[1] the study of literature in general, polite learning.

[2] Modern scholarship disagrees. Chaucer knew other works of Boccaccio, however.

[3] "The Knight's Tale," Dryden's favorite—a "noble poem. . . . of the epic kind and perhaps not much inferior to the *Iliad* or the *Aeneid*."

[4] Modern scholarship shows the reverse: Petrarch borrowed the tale from the last novella of the *Decameron*. Chaucer used Petrarch's Latin version or perhaps a French translation of it.

[5] In *Troilus and Criseyde* Chaucer "improves" and "beautifies" Boccaccio's *Il Filostrato*, saying that he follows "myn auctor called Lollius." The latter has never been identified.

in many of our manufactures. I find I have anticipated already and taken up from Boccace before I come to him; but there is so much less behind; and I am of the temper of most kings, who love to be in debt, are all for present money, no matter how they pay it afterwards; besides, the nature of a preface is rambling, never wholly out of the way nor in it. This I have learned from the practice of honest Montaigne, and return at my pleasure to Ovid and Chaucer, of whom I have little more to say.

Both of them built on the inventions of other men; yet since Chaucer had something of his own, as *The Wife of Bath's Tale*, *The Cock and the Fox*,[6] which I have translated, and some others, I may justly give our countryman the precedence in that part, since I can remember nothing of Ovid which was wholly his. Both of them understood the manners,[7] under which name I comprehend the passions, and, in a larger sense the descriptions of persons, and their very habits. For an example, I see Baucis and Philemon as perfectly before me as if some ancient painter had drawn them; and all the pilgrims in the *Canterbury Tales*, their humors, their features, and the very dress, as distinctly as if I had supped with them at the Tabard in Southwark. Yet even there, too, the figures of Chaucer are much more lively, and set in a better light; which though I have not time to prove, yet I appeal to the reader, and am sure he will clear me from partiality. The thoughts and words remain to be considered [8] in the comparison of the two poets; and I have saved myself one half of that labor by owning that Ovid lived when the Roman tongue was in its meridian, Chaucer in the dawning of our language; therefore that part of the comparison stands not on an equal foot, any more than the diction of Ennius and Ovid, or of Chaucer and our present English. The words are given up, as a post not to be defended in our poet, because he wanted the modern art of fortifying. The thoughts remain to be considered; and they

---

[6] "The Nun's Priest's Tale."

[7] A key term in eighteenth-century criticism, to which Dryden devotes ten pages of discussion in the Preface to *Troilus and Cressida* (1679). In substance, "the manners in a poem are understood to be those inclinations, whether natural or acquired, which move and carry us to actions, good, bad, or indifferent. . . . The manners arise from many causes, and are either distinguished by complexion, as choleric and phlegmatic, or by the differences of age or sex, of climates, or quality of the persons, or their present condition. . . . From the manners, the characters of persons are derived, for indeed the characters are no other than the inclinations as they appear in the several persons of the poem; a character being thus defined—that which distinguishes one man from another."

[8] Dryden loosely follows the conventional scheme of analysis—fable, characters, sentiments (thoughts), and language.

are to be measured only by their propriety, that is, as they flow more or less naturally from the persons described on such and such occasions. The vulgar judges, which are nine parts in ten of all nations, who call conceits and jingles *wit*, who see Ovid full of them and Chaucer altogether without them, will think me little less than mad for preferring the Englishman to the Roman. Yet, with their leave, I must presume to say that the things they admire are only glittering trifles, and so far from being witty that in a serious poem they are nauseous, because they are unnatural. Would any man who is ready to die for love describe his passion like Narcissus? Would he think of *inopem me copia fecit*[9] and a dozen more of such expressions, poured on the neck of one another and signifying all the same thing? If this were wit, was this a time to be witty, when the poor wretch was in the agony of death? This is just John Littlewit, in *Bartholomew-Fair*, who had a conceit (as he tells you) left him in his misery, a miserable conceit.[1] On these occasions the poet should endeavor to raise pity, but instead of this, Ovid is tickling you to laugh. Virgil never made use of such machines when he was moving you to commiserate the death of Dido:[2] he would not destroy what he was building. Chaucer makes Arcite violent in his love and unjust in the pursuit of it; yet when he came to die, he made him think more reasonably: he repents not of his love, for that had altered his character, but acknowledges the injustice of his proceedings, and resigns Emilia to Palamon. What would Ovid have done on this occasion? He would certainly have made Arcite witty on his death-bed: he had complained he was further off from possession by being so near, and a thousand such boyisms which Chaucer rejected as below the dignity of the subject. They who think otherwise would, by the same reason, prefer Lucan and Ovid to Homer and Virgil, and Martial to all four of them. As for the turn of words, in which Ovid particularly excels all poets, they are sometimes a fault and sometimes a beauty, as they are used properly or improperly; but in strong passions always to be shunned, because passions are serious and will admit no playing. The French have a high value for them; and I confess, they are often what they call delicate, when they are introduced with judgment; but Chaucer writ with more simplicity, and followed nature more closely than to use them. I have thus far, to the best

---

[9] Ovid, *Metamorphoses*, III, 466: "my abundance has made me poor."
[1] Inaccurately quoted from a passage near the beginning of the play by Ben Jonson.
[2] *Aeneid*, IV.

of my knowledge, been an upright judge betwixt the parties in competition, not meddling with the design nor the disposition of it, because the design was not their own, and in the disposing of it they were equal. It remains that I say somewhat of Chaucer in particular.

In the first place, as he is the father of English poetry, so I hold him in the same degree of veneration as the Grecians held Homer or the Romans Virgil. He is a perpetual fountain of good sense, learned in all sciences, and therefore speaks properly on all subjects. As he knew what to say, so he knows also when to leave off—a continence which is practiced by few writers and scarcely by any of the ancients excepting Virgil and Horace. One of our late great poets[3] is sunk in his reputation because he could never forgive any conceit which came in his way, but swept, like a dragnet, great and small. There was plenty enough, but the dishes were ill-sorted: whole pyramids of sweet-meats for boys and women, but little of solid meat for men. All this proceeded not from any want of knowledge, but of judgment. Neither did he want that in discerning the beauties and faults of other poets, but only indulged himself in the luxury of writing; and perhaps knew it was a fault, but hoped the reader would not find it. For this reason, though he must always be thought a great poet, he is no longer esteemed a good writer; and for ten impressions which his works have had in so many successive years, yet at present a hundred books are scarcely purchased once a twelve-month; for as my last Lord Rochester said, though somewhat profanely, "Not being of God, he could not stand."

Chaucer followed Nature everywhere, but was never so bold to go beyond her; and there is a great difference of being *poeta* and *nimis poeta*,[4] if we may believe Catullus, as much as betwixt a modest behavior and affectation. The verse of Chaucer, I confess, is not harmonious to us, but 'tis like the eloquence of one whom Tacitus commends: it was *auribus istius temporis accommodata:*[5] they who lived with him, and some time after him, thought it musical; and it continues so, even in our judgment, if compared with the numbers of Lydgate and Gower, his contemporaries: there is the rude sweetness of a Scotch tune in it, which is natural and pleasing, though not perfect. 'Tis true, I cannot go so far as he who

---

[3] Abraham Cowley.

[4] a "poet" and "too much a poet." *Nimis poeta* is from Martial, *Epigrams*, III, 44, not Catullus.

[5] "adapted to the ears of that time." Altered from Tacitus, *Dialogus de Oratoribus*, ch. 21. The historically conscious phrase "of that time" is Dryden's addition.

published the last edition of him,[6] for he would make us believe the fault is in our ears, and that there were really ten syllables in a verse where we find but nine; but this opinion is not worth confuting; 'tis so gross and obvious an error, that common sense (which is a rule in everything but matters of faith and revelation) must convince the reader that equality of numbers, in every verse which we call heroic, was either not known or not always practiced in Chaucer's age. It were an easy matter to produce some thousands of his verses which are lame for want of half a foot, and sometimes a whole one, and which no pronunciation can make otherwise. We can only say that he lived in the infancy of our poetry, and that nothing is brought to perfection at the first. We must be children before we grow men. There was an Ennius, and in process of time a Lucilius and a Lucretius, before Virgil and Horace; even after Chaucer there was a Spenser, a Harington,[7] a Fairfax,[8] before Waller and Denham were in being; and our numbers were in their nonage till these last appeared. I need say little of his parentage, life, and fortunes; they are to be found at large in all the editions of his works. He was employed abroad and favored by Edward the Third, Richard the Second, and Henry the Fourth, and was poet, as I suppose, to all three of them. In Richard's time, I doubt, he was a little dipped in the rebellion of the Commons: and being brother-in-law to John of Gaunt, it was no wonder if he followed the fortunes of that family and was well with Henry the Fourth when he had deposed his predecessor. Neither is it to be admired[9] that

---

[6] Thomas Speght's standard edition of Chaucer (1597) was reprinted in 1687. Though he drops many of the final "e's" in Chaucer's verse, Speght argues that it once was regular, and blames irregularities on Chaucer's scrivener Adam. The true pronunciation was not understood until the edition in 1775 by Thomas Tyrwhitt.

[7] Sir John Harington (1561–1612) translated Ariosto's *Orlando Furioso in English Heroical Verse* (1591).

[8] Edward Fairfax (c. 1580–1635) translated Tasso's *Jerusalemme Liberata* under the title *Godfrey of Bulloigne* (1600). Dryden had previously said: "Spenser and Fairfax both flourished in the reign of Queen Elizabeth, great masters in our language and who saw much farther into the beauties of our numbers than those who immediately followed them. Milton was the poetical son of Spenser, and Mr. Waller of Fairfax, for we have our lineal descents and clans as well as other families. Spenser more than once insinuates that the soul of Chaucer was transfused into his body and that he was begotten by him two hundred years after his decease. Milton has acknowledged to me that Spenser was his original; and many besides myself have heard our famous Waller own that he derived the harmony of his numbers from *Godfrey of Bulloigne*, which was turned into English by Mr. Fairfax."

[9] wondered at.

Henry, who was a wise as well as a valiant prince, who claimed by succession, and was sensible that his title was not sound but was rightfully in Mortimer, who had married the heir of York—it was not to be admired, I say, if that great politician should be pleased to have the greatest wit of those times in his interests and to be the trumpet of his praises. Augustus had given him the example, by the advice of Maecenas, who recommended Virgil and Horace to him; whose praises helped to make him popular while he was alive and after his death have made him precious to posterity. As for the religion of our poet, he seems to have some little bias towards the opinions of Wycliffe,[1] after John of Gaunt his patron; somewhat of which appears in the tale of Piers Plowman;[2] yet I cannot blame him for inveighing so sharply against the vices of the clergy in his age; their pride, their ambition, their pomp, their avarice, their worldly interest, deserved the lashes which he gave them, both in that and in most of his *Canterbury Tales*. Neither has his contemporary Boccace spared them; yet both those poets lived in much esteem with good and holy men in orders, for the scandal which is given by particular priests reflects not on the sacred function. Chaucer's Monk, his Canon, and his Friar, took not from the character of his Good Parson. A satirical poet is the check of the laymen on bad priests. We are only to take care that we involve not the innocent with the guilty in the same condemnation. The good cannot be too much honored, nor the bad too coarsely used, for the corruption of the best becomes the worst. When a clergyman is whipped, his gown is first taken off, by which the dignity of his order is secured. If he be wrongfully accused, he has his action of slander; and 'tis at the poet's peril if he transgress the law. But they will tell us that all kind of satire, though never so well deserved by particular priests, yet brings the whole order into contempt. Is then the peerage of England anything dishonored when a peer suffers for his treason? If he be libeled or any way defamed, he has his *scandalum magnatum*[3] to punish the offender. They who use this kind of argument seem to be conscious to themselves of somewhat which has deserved the poet's lash, and are less concerned for their public capacity than for their private: at least there is pride at the bottom of their reasoning. If the faults of men in orders are only to be

---

[1] John Wycliffe (c. 1320–84), early reformer and first translator of the Bible into English.

[2] *The Plowman's Tale*, once thought to be by Chaucer and printed at the end of the *Canterbury Tales*.

[3] A legal term for slandering those in high positions of power.

judged among themselves, they are all in some sort parties; for, since they say the honor of their order is concerned in every member of it, how can we be sure that they will be impartial judges? How far I may be allowed to speak my opinion in this case I know not, but I am sure a dispute of this nature caused mischief in abundance betwixt a King of England and an Archbishop of Canterbury,[4] one standing up for the laws of his land and the other for the honor (as he called it) of God's Church; which ended in the murder of the prelate and in the whipping of his Majesty from post to pillar for his penance. The learned and ingenious Dr. Drake[5] has saved me the labor of inquiring into the esteem and reverence which the priests have had of old, and I would rather extend than diminish any part of it; yet I must needs say that when a priest provokes me without occasion given him, I have no reason, unless it be the charity of a Christian, to forgive him: *prior laesit*[6] is justification sufficient in the civil law. If I answer him in his own language, self-defense I am sure must be allowed me; and if I carry it further, even to a sharp recrimination, somewhat may be indulged to human frailty. Yet my resentment has not wrought so far but that I have followed Chaucer in his character of a holy man, and have enlarged on that subject with some pleasure, reserving to myself the right, if I shall think fit hereafter, to describe another sort of priests, such as are more easily to be found than the Good Parson, such as have given the last blow to Christianity in this age by a practice so contrary to their doctrine. But this will keep cold till another time. In the meanwhile, I take up Chaucer where I left him.

He must have been a man of a most wonderful comprehensive nature, because, as it has been truly observed of him, he has taken into the compass of his *Canterbury Tales* the various manners and humors (as we now call them) of the whole English nation in his age. Not a single character has escaped him. All his pilgrims are severally distinguished from each other, and not only in their inclinations but in their very physiognomies and persons. Baptista Porta[7] could not have described their natures better than by the marks which the poet gives them. The matter and manner of their tales, and of their telling, are so suited to their different educations,

[4] Henry II and Thomas à Becket.

[5] James Drake replied to Jeremy Collier's attack on the stage (and on Dryden) in *The Ancient and Modern Stages Reviewed: or Mr. Collier's View of the Immorality and Profaneness of the Stage set in a True Light* (1699).

[6] Terence, *Eunuchus*, prologue, 6: "he hit me first."

[7] Giambattista della Porta (1538–1615) wrote a famous Latin treatise on physiognomy, as also several comedies.

humors, and callings, that each of them would be improper in any other mouth. Even the grave and serious characters are distinguished by their several sorts of gravity: their discourses are such as belong to their age, their calling, and their breeding; such as are becoming of them, and of them only. Some of his persons are vicious and some virtuous; some are unlearned or, as Chaucer calls them, *lewd*, and some are learned. Even the ribaldry of the low characters is different: the Reeve, the Miller, and the Cook, are several [8] men, and distinguished from each other as much as the mincing Lady-Prioress and the broad-speaking, gap-toothed Wife of Bath. But enough of this; there is such a variety of game springing up before me that I am distracted in my choice and know not which to follow. 'Tis sufficient to say, according to the proverb, that *here is God's plenty.* We have our forefathers and great-grand-dames all before us, as they were in Chaucer's days: their general characters are still remaining in mankind, and even in England, though they are called by other names than those of monks, and friars, and canons, and lady-abbesses, and nuns; for mankind is ever the same, and nothing lost out of Nature, though everything is altered. . . .

---

[8] different.

---❧❦❧---

Thomas Rymer

1643?–1713

---❧❦❧---

THE LIBERAL and many-sided greatness of Dryden is best measured alongside the pharisaism of Thomas Rymer who, until the 1690's, was the second-best critic in Dryden's England.

Not altogether justly, Rymer's name has hardened into a byword for critical pedant—"the worst critic that ever lived," Macaulay has said. Such a transformation, from man to legend, began in his own lifetime. Recent scholarship, however, has put his ideas into a more accurate and humane perspective. Rymer had the misfortune to adopt French rationalistic criticism at just the moment in England when a current was setting against it; he attacked Shakespeare just as Shakespeare was being rediscovered and consecrated to national pride; he showed off his learning in a seventeenth-century scribal manner already antiquated by Augustan fashions; and he was, by temperament, a fault-finder. His arguments will still appear, on the whole, wrong-headed. His style of invective, though vivid and often charming, still seems old-fashioned, rather brutal, and, after a time, annoying. Yet he is by no means the ogre of dullness which he is made out by satire and tradition, and once his premises are understood, he is not irrelevant to an understanding of the eighteenth century.

He was a Whig lawyer, antiquarian, and poet *manqué*, the son of a Roundhead justice of the peace who, four years after the Restoration, was hanged for rebellion. In 1681 Rymer wrote a tract defending the rights of Parliament, and in 1692, after the bloodless Whig Revolution, he was appointed royal historiographer, succeeding Thomas Shadwell. He spent the last twenty years of his life on *Foedera* (1704–13), a gigantic feat of editing which rescued from must all the treaties in English history, plus other state documents. His other works include a bad rhymed tragedy *Edgar* (1677), scattered verses, translations (including the brilliant "Life of Nicias" in Dryden's Plutarch[1]), and prefaces including one to Rochester's collected poems (1691). But his reputation as a critic rests on three works from which the following excerpts are taken—the preface to his translation of Rapin's *Réflexions sur la poétique d'Aristote* (1674), *Tragedies of the Last Age* (1677), and the ambitious *Short View of Tragedy* (1692) which includes, in its sweeping glance at tragedy through the ages, the crude outline of a history of English literature. The full titles are worth study: they hint almost all the salient premises of his criticism.

"Action," Rymer says, the element of story, "finds the blind side of human kind a hundred ways"; spectacle "prepossesses the head strangely"; and so "most people" acquiesce in ornaments and accidents "without ever troubling their noddle farther." His purpose as critic was to force people to think, to examine the inner reason or unreason of plays and poems, and to find out the "universal rules" by which each kind of poetry pleases, or ought to please, by its nature. He was convinced that English language and genius, dating from Chaucer, had the potentiality of greatness beyond that of all other nations, but with few exceptions, such as *Gorboduc* and more recently the verses of Waller, it was lacking in correctness and critical knowledge. Spenser, for example, had "a genius for heroic poetry perhaps above any that ever writ since Virgil," but he lacked "a true *idea*" and so lost himself in the improbabilities of a medieval fairyland. Rymer accepted a role of critical gadfly for his age and cultivated a style deliberately vexing.

English comedy (he mentions *The Rehearsal*) seemed to him already the best in modern times, but English tragedy, as created by Shakespeare, Jonson, Beaumont and Fletcher, had a "brutish" soul. Apparently he disapproved of Milton also, for he promised, what was never written, reflections on "that *Paradise Lost* of Milton's which some are pleased to call a poem." Rymer intended to "assert rhyme against the slender sophistry wherewith he attacks it."

Like Dryden, his operative premises were decorum (or propriety)

---

[1] Still to be read, with Clough's revisions, in the Modern Library edition.

and common sense. But unlike Dryden, instead of staying open to live and various experience—instead of enlarging criticism to include new practice—Rymer tried to strait-jacket practice by the laws of Aristotle as sifted through the Cartesian rationalism of France. He was not a partisan of French literature, although he ranked Corneille at the top of tragedy, alongside Sophocles: French language and manners lacked "sinews for great and heroic subjects." But he admired the spirit of the French Academy and the formalism of French Aristotelian critics, from whom he borrowed most of his ideas—particularly, as Professor Zimansky has shown, La Mesnardière, Abbé d'Aubignac, Rapin, André Dacier, and Le Bossu. Rymer insisted upon strict probability in plot, meaning at least two things: truth to familiar life as, by common sense, we all know it is, and truth to the moral order which reason and Christianity tell us ought to be. (He coined the phrase "poetical justice.") In the same way, decorum of characterization includes lifelikeness and conformity to type, but also moral comeuppance: "the fire must roar in the conscience of the criminal." He exacted similar strictness in other elements of machinery, thought, and diction. For example, he came to believe that the chorus is "the root and original" and "certainly always the most necessary part of tragedy."

Unlike Dryden, he had no poet's gift for appreciation; his knack was exposure of "deformity." He was expert as a lawyer in finding "blind sides" while ignoring unassimilable and unwelcome facts. At his best, he made a case which had to be answered. The most notorious instance is his *examen* of *Othello*—the first full-scale analysis of a Shakespearean play—which occupies almost half of his *Short View.* As Dryden remarked in a letter, "Almost all the faults he has discovered are truly there; yet who will read Mr. Rymer or not read Shakespeare?" Given his premises, and allowing for playful sarcasms, Rymer was perhaps unanswerable, and yet his conclusions, despite their claim to "common sense," contradicted common feelings of equal authority; he had chosen *Othello* for his attack just because, he said, in his time it was the most admired tragedy of the "last age." With single-minded logic he ripped into a central problem of English criticism in his generation, and for some time to come: the gulf existing between authoritative theory and actual English tastes, perceptions, and facts of practice. He could only be answered, as Dryden quickly recognized, by refashioning the premises of theory itself.

Dryden filled the blank leaves of his copy of *Tragedies of the Last*

Age with copious notes for an answer,[2] in which he acknowledged in passing that "all writers ought to study this critique, as the best account I have ever seen of the ancients; that the model of tragedy he has here given is excellent and extreme correct." But "'tis not enough," he continued, "that Aristotle has said so, for Aristotle drew his models of tragedy from Sophocles and Euripides, and if he had seen ours, might have changed his mind." His intended reply is the Preface to *Troilus and Cressida*, which, however, is among his most conservative performances: even Dryden is unable to shake the fundamentals of Rymer's position.

Rymer's clearest disciple was the reforming churchman Jeremy Collier whose *Short View of the Immorality and Profaneness of the English Stage* (1698) is Rymerian in title, substance, and style, though ironically it is aimed against English comedy, the one part of English literature which Rymer had claimed to admire. His spirit, however, and many of his ideas are to be found in Sir Richard Blackmore (see p. 188), and in a lesser but still significant extent, in Dennis and Shaftesbury, all three of them Whigs and would-be reformers. Voltaire adopted Rymerian invective and *reductio* in his numerous attacks on Shakespeare, and as late as 1765, Dr. Johnson still felt it necessary to answer Rymer's objections.[3] Perhaps the most instructive contrast is with Morgann (see pp. 570 ff.) who, in 1777, takes the trouble to ridicule Rymer and to deny the argument from rational decorum: the kind of incongruities which Rymer detects, and rightly detects, in Shakespeare's characters become, in Morgann, the sure sign of truth to nature, the higher propriety which only feeling can grasp. Thus, Rymer's insights are vindicated, though his tastes are denied.

---

[2] Reprinted by Dr. Johnson; see "Dryden," *Lives of the Poets*, ed. Hill, I, 471–79.

[3] See pp. 445–48 and *cf.* p. 497.

* * * *

FROM Preface to
Reflections on Aristotle's Treatise of Poesy,
Containing the Necessary, Rational, and Universal
Rules for Epic, Dramatic, and the Other Sorts
of Poetry, with Reflections on the Works of
the Ancient and Modern Poets, and Their Faults Noted
by R. Rapin [1674]

from Preface of the Translator

The artist would not take pains to polish a diamond if none besides himself were quick-sighted enough to discern the flaw; and poets would grow negligent if the critics had not a strict eye over their miscarriages. Yet it often happens that this eye is so distorted by envy or ill nature that it sees nothing aright. Some critics are like wasps, that rather annoy the bees than terrify the drones.

For this sort of learning, our neighbor nations have got far the start of us; in the last century, Italy swarmed with critics, where, amongst many of less note, Castelvetro[1] opposed all comers, and the famous Academy [del]la Crusca[2] was always impeaching some or other of the best authors. Spain in those days bred great wits but, I think, was never so crowded that they needed to fall out and quarrel amongst themselves. But from Italy, France took the cudgels, and though some light strokes passed in the days of Marot, Baif,[3] etc., yet they fell not to it in earnest, nor was any noble contest amongst them, till the Royal Academy was founded [4] and Cardinal Richelieu encouraged and rallied all the scattered wits under his banner. Then Malherbe[5] reformed their ancient licentious poetry,

---

[1] See p. 94, n. 6.
[2] The prototype of academies to watch over the purity of language and standard of literature, founded 1572.
[3] Clement Marot (1496–1544) and Jean Antoine dè Baïf (1532–89), French poets, members of the Pléiade.
[4] In 1629.
[5] Francois de Malherbe (1555–1628), French poet, who rebeled against the manner of Ronsard and promoted a verse of sharp, rational clarity.

and Corneille's *Cid* raised many factions amongst them. At this time with us, many great wits flourished, but Ben Jonson, I think, had all the critical learning to himself; and till of late years, England was as free from critics as it is from wolves, that a harmless, well-meaning book might pass without any danger. But now this privilege, whatever extraordinary talent it requires, is usurped by the most ignorant, and they who are least acquainted with the game are aptest to bark at everything that comes in their way. Our fortune is [that] Aristotle, on whom our author makes these *Reflections*, came to this great work better accomplished . . . and him antiquity first honored with the name of *critic*.

It is indeed suspected that he dealt not always fairly with the philosophers, misreciting sometimes and misinterpreting their opinions. But I find him not taxed of that injustice to the poets, in whose favor he is so ingenious that, to the disadvantage of his own profession, he declares that "tragedy more conduces to the instruction of mankind than even philosophy itself." [6] And however cried down in the schools and vilified by some Modern philosophers—since men have had a taste for *good sense* and could discern the beauties of correct writing, he is preferred in the *politest* courts of Europe, and by the poets held in great veneration. Not that these can servilely yield to his authority, who, of all men living, affect liberty. The truth is, what Aristotle writes on this subject are not the dictates of his own magisterial will or dry deductions of his metaphysics, but the poets were his masters, and what was their practice he reduced to principles. Nor would the Modern poets blindly resign to this practice of the Ancients were not the reasons convincing and clear as any demonstration in mathematics. 'Tis only needful that we understand them for our consent to the truth of them.

---

[6] Not in Aristotle; *cf. Poetics*, IX, 3.

* * * *

FROM

The Tragedies of the Last Age Considered and Examined by the Practice of the Ancients, and by the Common Sense of All Ages, in a Letter to Fleetwood Shepherd, Esq.[1] [1677]

from Preface

Having several mornings, and early, traveled to St. James's[2] with the only design of being with you, and missing you as often, I became so mortified with the misfortune that I resolved to come into the Town no more till assured of your return from Copt Hall.[3] But because I meant not altogether to kill myself, for my entertainment I provided me some of those "masterpieces" of wit so renowned everywhere and so edifying to the stage: I mean the choicest and most applauded English tragedies of this last age as *Rollo, A King and No King,* [and] *The Maid's Tragedy* by Beaumont and Fletcher, *Othello* and *Julius Caesar* by Shakespeare, and *Cataline* by Worthy Ben.

These I perused with some attention, and some reflections I made, in which how far I mistake your sense, that is, how far I am mistaken, I desire to be informed.

I had heard that the theatre was wont to be called the "school of virtue" [4] and tragedy a "poem for kings"; that they who first brought tragedy to perfection were made viceroys and governors of islands, were honored everywhere with statues of marble and statues of brass, were styled the "wise Sophocles," "wise Euripides" by God and man, by oracles and philosophers; that for teaching morality, Crantor and Chrysippus[5] were nobody to 'em (this latter transcribed the whole *Medea* of Eurpides into his works); that so refined a people and so frugal a commonwealth as Athens did tax and assess

---

[1] Courtly wit (1634–98), member of the Earl of Dorset circle, later the patron of Prior.
[2] St. James park, whose Mall was a fashionable resort.
[3] Earl of Dorset's country home.
[4] Rapin, *Reflections*, II, IV.
[5] *Cf.* Horace, *Epistles*, I, ii, 3–4.

themselves and laid out more of their public exchequer upon the representation of these plays than all their wars stood them in, though sometimes both seas and land were covered with pagan enemies that invaded them. And not Athens only but (who hated Athens) so austere and glum a generation as those of Sparta, by the care of Lycurgus, agreed the same honor to these Athenian poets.

These things coming into my mind, surely (thought I) men's brains lie not in the same place as formerly, or else poetry is not now the same thing it was in those days of yore.

I therefore made inquiry what difference might be in our philosophy and manners; I found that our philosophers agreed well enough with theirs, in the main; however, that our poets have forced another way to the wood, a byroad that runs directly cross to that of Nature, Manners, and Philosophy, which gained the Ancients so great veneration.

I would not examine the proportions, the unities and outward regularities, the *mechanical part* of tragedies: there is no talking of beauties when there wants essentials; 'tis not necessary for a man to have a nose on his face nor to have two legs: he may be a true man, though awkward and unsightly as the monster in *The Tempest*.

Nor have I much troubled their phrase and expression; I have not vexed their language with the "doubts," and "remarks," and eternal triflings of the French grammaticasters. Much less have I cast about for jests and gone a quibble-catching.

I have chiefly considered the *fable* or *plot*, which all conclude to be the soul of a tragedy—which with the Ancients is always found to be a reasonable soul, but with us, for the most part, a brutish, and often worse than brutish.

And certainly there is not required much learning, or that a man must be some Aristotle and doctor of subtleties, to form a right judgment in this particular; common sense suffices; and rarely have I known the women-judges mistake in these points when they have the patience to think and (left to their own heads) they decide with their own sense. But if people are prepossessed, if they will judge of *Rollo* by *Othello*, and one crooked line by another, we can never have a certainty.

Amongst those who will be objecting against the doctrine I lay down may peradventure appear a sort of men who have remembered so and so, and value themselves upon their "experience." I may write by the book (say they) what I have a mind, but they know what will "please." These are a kind of stage-quacks and empirics in poetry who have got a receipt to "please," and no collegiate like 'em for purging the passions.

These say, for instance, A *King and No King* pleases. I say the *comical* part pleases.

I say that Mr. Hart[6] "pleases"; most of the business falls to his share, and what he delivers, everyone takes upon content; their eyes are prepossessed and charmed by his action before aught of the poets can approach their ears; and to the most wretched of characters, he gives a lustre and *brillant*[7] which dazzles the sight, that the deformities in the poetry cannot be perceived.

Therefore a distinction is to be made between what *pleases naturally* in itself and what "pleases" upon the account of machines, actors, dances, and circumstances which are merely accidental to the tragedy.

Aristotle observes that, in his time, some who (wanting the talent to write that might please) made it their care that the actors should help out where the Muses failed.[8]

These objectors urge that there is also another great accident, which is that Athens and London have not the same meridian.

Certain it is that Nature is the same and Man is the same: he loves, grieves, hates, envies, has the same affections and passions in both places, and the same springs that give them motion. What moved pity there will here also produce the same effect.

This must be confessed unless they will, in effect, say that we have not that "delicate taste" of things; we are not so refined nor so virtuous; that Athens was more civilized by their philosophers than we with both our philosophers and Twelve Apostles.

But were it to be supposed that Nature with us is a corrupt and depraved nature, that we are barbarians, and humanity dwells not amongst us, shall our poet therefore pamper this corrupt nature and indulge our barbarity? Shall he not rather purge away the corruption and reform our manners? Shall he not with Orpheus rather choose to draw the brutes after him than be himself a follower of the herd? Was it thus that the Ancient poets, by the best philosophers, became styled the "fathers of knowledge" and "interpreters of the gods?"

Lastly, though tragedy is a poem chiefly for men of *sense*, yet I cannot be persuaded that the people are so very mad of acorns[9] but

---

[6] Charles Hart (d. 1693), a famous Restoration actor.
[7] Fr. "brilliancy."
[8] *Poetics*, XIV, 2.
[9] like hogs.

that they could be well content to eat the bread of civil [1] persons.

Say others: "Poetry and reason, how come these to be cater cousins? Poetry is the child of *fancy*, and is never to be schooled and disciplined by reason; poetry," say they, "is *blind* inspiration, is pure *enthusiasm*, is *rapture* and *rage* all over."

But fancy, I think, in poetry, is like faith in religion; it makes far discoveries and soars above reason, but never clashes or runs against it. Fancy leaps and frisks and away she's gone; whilst reason rattles the chains and follows after. Reason must consent and ratify whatever by fancy is attempted in its absence, or else 'tis all null and void in law. However, in the contrivance and economy of a play, reason is always principally to be consulted. Those who object against reason are the *fanatics* in poetry and are never to be saved by their good works.

Others imagine that these rules and restraints on the plot and argument of tragedy would hinder much good intrigue, would clog invention, and make all plays alike and uniform.

But certainly Nature affords plenty and variety enough of beauties, that no man need complain if the deformed are cloistered up and shut from him. Such a painter has been who could draw nothing but a rose; yet other painters can design one and the same good face in a thousand several figures.[2] It may be remembered that there are but five vowels, or be considered, from seven planets and their several positions, how many fates and fortunes the astrologer distributes to the people. And has not a poet more virtues and vices within his circle? cannot he observe them and their influences in their several *situations*, in their *oppositions* and *conjunctions*, in their *altitudes* and *depressions*? And he shall sooner find his ink than the stores of Nature exhausted.[3]

Other objections may be answered as they fall in the way. I would only have you beforehand advertised that you will find me tied to no certain style, nor laying my reasons together in form and method. You will find me sometimes reasoning, sometimes declaiming, sometimes citing authority for common sense; sometimes uttering as my own what may be had at any bookshop in the nation; sometimes doubting when I might be positive, and sometimes confident out of season; sometimes turning tragedy into what is light and comical, and sporting when I should be serious. This variety made the travel more easy. And you know I am not cut out for writing a

---

[1] civilized.
[2] variations, angles of vision.
Cf. Johnson, p. 410.

treatise, nor have a genius to pen anything exactly; so long as I am true to the *main sense* before me, you will pardon me in the rest. Nor will it, I hope, give offense that I handle these tragedies with the same liberty that I formerly had taken[4] in examining the epic poems of Spenser, Cowley, and such names as will ever be sacred to me. Rapin tells us, for his own countrymen, that none of them had writ a good tragedy nor was ever like to write one. And an eminent Italian[5] confesses that the best of theirs exceeded not a mediocrity; and yet their divine Tasso had then writ a tragedy and *Torrismondo* strutted it in buskins.

But I have elsewhere declared my opinion that the English want neither genius nor language for so great a work. And certainly, had our authors begun with tragedy as Sophocles and Euripides left it, had they either built on the same foundation or after their model, we might ere this day have seen poetry in greater perfection and boasted such monuments of wit as Greece or Rome never knew in all their glory.

* * * *

FROM

A Short View of Tragedy,
Its Original, Excellency, and Corruption,
with Some Reflections on Shakespeare
and Other Practitioners
for the Stage [1692]

FROM CHAPTER VII

THE FABLE

Othello, a blackamoor captain, by talking of his prowess and feats of war, makes Desdemona, a Senator's daughter, to be in love with him and to be married to him without her parents' knowledge; and having preferred [1] Cassio to be his lieutenant (a place which his ensign Iago sued for), Iago in revenge works the Moor into a jealousy that Cassio cuckolds him, which he effects by

---

[4] In the preface to Rapin.
[5] Alessandro Tassoni, *De Pensieri diversi* (1665); see p. 110, n. 8.
[1] promoted.

stealing and conveying a certain handkerchief which had, at the wedding, been by the Moor presented to his bride. Hereupon, Othello and Iago plot the deaths of Desdemona and Cassio; Othello murders her, and soon after is convinced of her innocence. And as he is about to be carried to prison in order to be punished for the murder, he kills himself.

Whatever rubs or difficulty may stick on the bark, the moral, sure, of this fable is very instructive:

First, this may be a caution to all maidens of quality how, without their parents' consent, they run away with blackamoors. *Di non si accompagnare con huomo, cui la natura e il cielo e il modo della vita disgiunge da noi*—Cinthio.[2]

Secondly, this may be a warning to all good wives that they look well to their linen.

Thirdly, this may be a lesson to husbands that before their jealousy be tragical, the proofs may be mathematical. . . .

What poet would give a villainous blackamoor this ascendant? What tramontane[3] could fancy the Venetians so low, so despicable, or so patient? This outrage to an injured lady, the "divine Desdemona," might in a colder climate have provoked somebody to be her champion; but the Italians may well conclude we have a strange genius for poetry. In the next scene[4] Othello is examining the supposed bawd; then follows another storm of horror and outrage against the poor chicken, his wife. Some drayman or drunken tinker might possibly treat his drab at this sort of rate and mean no harm by it, but for his excellency, "a my lord General," to serenade a Senator's daughter with such a volly of scoundrel, filthy language is sure the most absurd maggot that ever bred from any poet's addle brain.

And she is in the right who tells us:

> *Emil.*   A beggar in his drink
> Could not have laid such terms upon his callet.[5]

This is not to describe passion. Seneca had another notion in the case:

---

[2] Giraldi Cinthio whose *Hecatommithi* was believed to be Shakespeare's source: "not to take up with a man whom Nature, Heaven, and the manner of his life sets apart from us."

[3] one living beyond the mountains, as seen from Italy; hence, a barbarian.

[4] IV, ii.

[5] IV, ii, 121–22.

Parvae loquuntur curae, ingentes stupent.[6]

And so had the painter who drew Agamemnon with his face covered. Yet to make all worse, her murder and the manner of it had before been resolved upon and concerted. But nothing is to provoke a Venetian: she takes all in good part; had the scene lain in Russia, what could we have expected more? With us a tinker's trull would be nettled, would repartee with more spirit, and not appear so void of spleen.

> *Desd.*   O good Iago,
> What shall I do to win my Lord again? [7]

No woman bred out of a pig sty could talk so meanly. After this, she is called to supper with Othello, Lodovico, etc.; after that comes a filthy sort of pastoral scene, where the "wedding sheets" and song of "willow" and her mother's maid "poor Barbara" are not the least moving things in this entertainment. But that we may not be kept too long in the dumps, nor the melancholy scenes lie too heavy, undigested on our stomach, this act gives us for a farewell the *salsa O picante*,[8] some quibbles and smart touches, as Ovid had prophesied:

> *Est et in obscenos deflexa tragoedia risus.*[9] . . .

But for our comfort, however felonious is the heart, hear with what soft language he does approach her, with a candle in his hand:

> *Oth.*   Put out the light and then put out the light;
> If I quench thee, thou flaming minister,
> I can again thy former light restore—[1]

Who would call him a barbarian, monster, savage? Is this a blackamoor?

> *Soles occidere et redire possunt*—[2]

The very soul and quintessence of Sir George Etherege.[3]

---

[6] *Hippolytus,* 607 (misquoted): "trivia express anxiety, but vast things astonish."

[7] IV, ii, 149–50.

[8] Sp. "Oh, piquant sauce!"

[9] *Tristia,* II, 409: "and tragedy digresses into filthy laughter."

[1] V, ii, 7–9.

[2] Catullus, V, 4: "Suns may set and rise again."

[3] The Restoration playwright (1635?–92). That is, Othello now speaks like a refined and witty gentleman.

One might think the General should not glory much in this action but make a hasty work on't, and have turned his eyes away from so unsoldierly an execution. Yet is he all pause and deliberation, handles her as calmly and is as careful of her soul's health as it had been her father confessor: "Have you prayed tonight, Desdemona?" But the suspense is necessary that he might have a convenient while so to roll his eyes and so to gnaw his nether lip to the spectators. Besides the greater cruelty—*sub tam lentis maxillis.*[4]

But hark! a most tragical thing laid to her charge:

> *Oth.* That handkerchief that I so loved and gave thee,
> Thou gavest to Cassio.
> *Desd.* No by my life and soul;
> Send for the man and ask him.
> *Oth.* By Heaven, I saw my handkerchief in his hand—
> I saw the handkerchief.[5]

So much ado, so much stress, so much passion and repetition about a handkerchief! What can be more absurd than, as Quintilian expresses it, *in parvis litibus has tragoedias movere?* [6] We have heard of Fortunatus his purse[7] and of the invisible cloak, long ago worn threadbare and stowed up in the wardrobe of obsolete romances: one might think that were a fitter place for this handkerchief than that it—at this time of day—be worn on the stage to raise everywhere all this clutter and turmoil. Had it been Desdemona's garter, the sagacious Moor might have smelled a rat, but the handkerchief is so remote a trifle, no booby on this side Mauritania could make any consequence from it. . . .

Then for the *unraveling* of the plot, as they call it, never was old deputy recorder in a country town with his spectacles, in summoning up the evidence, at such a puzzle, so blundered and bedoltified, as is our poet, to have a good riddance and get the catastrophe off his hands.

What can remain with the audience to carry home with them from this sort of poetry for their use and edification? How can it work unless (instead of settling the mind and purging our passions) to delude our senses, disorder our thoughts, addle our brain, pervert our affections, hair[8] our imaginations, corrupt our appetite, and fill

---

[4] Suetonius, *Tiberius*, XXI, 2: "within such lingering jaws."
[5] *Cf.* V, ii, 48–49, 62, 66–67.
[6] *Institutes*, VI, i, 36: "to excite these tragic events by such trivial disputes."
[7] As in Dekker's *Old Fortunatus* (1599), based on the folk tale of the miraculous purse.
[8] harry (?)

our head with vanity, confusion, *tintamarre*,⁹ and jingle-jangle beyond what all the parish clerks of London, with their Old Testament farces and interludes in Richard the Second's time, could
ever pretend to? Our only hopes, for the good of their souls, can be
that these people go to the playhouse as they do to church, to sit
still, look on one another, make no reflection, nor mind the play
more than they would a sermon.

There is in this play some burlesque, some humor and ramble of
comical wit, some show, and some mimicry to divert the spectators,
but the tragical part is plainly none other than a bloody farce, without salt or savor.

---

⁹ Fr. "hubbub."

John Dennis

1657–1734

In the 1690's Dennis moved in the best coffeehouse circles with aging Dryden, Wycherly, and productive Congreve, wrote bad though respected Pindarics and plays, and began unfolding a varied, independent, often pioneering criticism which still repays study, both for itself and for what it reveals of Augustan culture. His leadership in replying to Jeremy Collier's *Short View* (1698), a moralistic assault on the stage, seems to have crystallized his thinking. As so often in the history of English (and American) criticism, defense against excessive moralism forced a liberal and sensitive man to think through fundamentals. Throughout his career, however, Dennis was always rebutting something or somebody; most of what he had to say was said by 1704 when Swift coupled him with Rymer, as a modernist, in *A Tale of a Tub*. He sometimes wrote in a Rymerian style of insolent sarcasm and literal-minded "common sense." He neither understood nor liked the age he grew old in, the age of Swift, Pope, and Gay. A critic, he believed, "who writes to the knowing few at present writes to the race of mankind in all succeeding ages." But convinced of his worth, he resented neglect. Cantankerous, vain, high-serious, and astute, he figured in the eyes of Scriblerians (and later of Fielding when he wrote *Tom Thumb*) as a type of the ill-natured, ill-mannered, uncreating critic, unwilling to discern "beauties." Off and on for twenty years after Dennis inveighed against the *Essay on Criticism* (1711), Pope baited the old man into displays of self-condemning fury, although in fact the *Essay* may owe something to Dennis, whose eclectic and restorative classicism (though Whig and anti-Catholic) often suggests Pope's. As early as 1702, in *A Large Account of the Taste in Poetry, and the Causes of the Degeneracy of It*, he was idealizing the England of his young manhood, Charles II's brilliant "reign of poetry and pleasure," whose homogeneous, cultivated audience, at leisure to be foolish and to observe their folly, helped explain, he believed, its excellence in comedy—an early instance of sociological criticism. He further analyzed the theory of Restoration comedy in *A Defence of Sir Fopling Flutter* and other essays in the 1720's. As vehemently as the Scriblerians, he jeremiahed a new "reign of politics and of business" which seemed to him superficial, conformist, and philistine. Anxiety of war, business, and taxes had made everybody dully alike. He left cogent appreciations of *Hudibras* and *The Plain Dealer*, and an *Essay on the Genius and Writings of Shakespeare*. He wrote an illuminating attack on the vogue of Italian operas, exposed the pseudo-classicism of Addison's popular *Cato*, and, with much prescience, objected to outcroppings of sentimentalism in the comedy of Cibber and Steele. His high-minded conception of the critic as guardian of public taste was earnestly, if unavailingly, performed for the stage.

In seeking (against Collier) a moral justification for the stage, Dennis came to realize that poetry itself, indeed "all those arts which respect humanity," were at issue. Like Shaftesbury after him, he carefully thought through the functions of criticism in general, in a day when it was suspect, and evolved a consistent ethics to underpin his own. Besides Aristotle, Longinus, and the French formalists like Rapin and Le Bossu, his English mentors were Bacon, Milton, Dryden, and Hobbes. *The Grounds of Criticism in Poetry* (1704),[1] from which the present selection is taken, incorporates or touches on most of his premises, but an earnest student will not neglect *The Advancement and Reformation of Modern Poetry* (1701), Dennis's brilliant and massive mediation of the Ancients-Moderns controversy.

In his ethics, he managed in his way, as Pope in another, to compromise a theological notion of fallen man and a classical idea of regular nature with a hedonistic psychology of self-love. At the Fall, human passion and the senses, in which is included all our Hobbesian appetite and capacity for pleasure, revolted from human

---

[1] The title suggests Dryden's *Preface* [to *Troilus and Cressida*] *containing the Grounds of Criticism in Tragedy* (1679).

reason and the bliss of God; they corruptly affected the world. As the goal of every genuine religion is to redeem human happiness, so the function of all liberal arts, throughout human history, has been, in their way and measure, to redeem man from his misery and lethargy—"to delight and reform mankind by exciting the passions in such a manner as to reconcile them to reason and restore the harmony of the human faculties." Poetry is the noblest and completest art since it provides for "the satisfaction of the whole man together." Without its aesthetic excitement, religion will not have its due force on the minds of men; poetry is the natural language of religion—witness the Ancients, *Job*, "Solomon's song," the Old Testament prophets, and the parables of Christ. Conversely, religious ideas are the source of the greatest poetry. *Paradise Lost* Dennis considered "the greatest poem that ever was written by man," and he wrote tasteful, intelligent appreciations of it, the first of importance, almost a decade before Addison's famous but less excited *Spectator* papers. Dennis was seized by the glorious hope of reforming poetry in his time as much as a critic could, and reaching back to older ideas of the poet as *vates* and divine restorer, he passed them on, transformed, to later critics in the century such as Trapp, Bishop Lowth, and Young. Prophesying the demise of rhyme by mid-century, he defended blank verse on the psychological ground that rhyming falsifies, that the particular "sentiment" and "spirit" of the poet's intention have only one "harmony" and "expression" that "of right" belong to them. "True poetical genius is a great and sacred thing." Like Wordsworth, who seems to have learned from him, Dennis believed that poetry, in origin and effect, is harmony of "passion," which he divided into "enthusiastic" passion and "vulgar" (ordinary) passion.[2] Poetry of enthusiasm is rare, intense, and subtle: it arouses in the qualified soul a state of contemplative emotion that imagines the uncommon or mysterious, and like religion, as it "speaks to the senses, brings the wonders of another world more home to us." Dennis associated enthusiasm with Longinus's description of transport—a joyful amazement and pride (pleased vanity) proceeding from the soul's consciousness of its own power to conceive. His discovery that "terror . . . chiefly to be derived from religious ideas"—including enchantments and witchcraft—is the source of sublimity signaled the weather of much to come in

---

[2] "Vulgar" is not pejorative. The vulgar passions belong to dramatic action, the enthusiastic to parts of epic and ode "where the poet speaks himself, or the eldest of the Muses for him." Vulgar passions are excited in epic, but are more characteristic of tragedy.

later eighteenth-century criticism and poetry, and furthered the growing interest among English critics in the psychology of poetic creation and response. He effected the first advance by an Englishman in defining the sublime as an emotionalistic category, and was accordingly ridiculed by Pope and Gay, in their farce *Three Hours After Marriage*, as "Sir Tremendous Longinus." [3] Besides sublimity and passion, many other, perhaps most of the critical issues of the next several decades are touched on somewhere in his criticism— for example, taste,[4] genius, originality, the rules, wit and humor— often with surprising point. He surely ranks as one of the most independent and prescient critics in the early eighteenth century, whom poets as divers as Wordsworth, Coleridge, Landor, and Swinburne have condescended to praise.

* * * *

FROM

The Grounds of Criticism in Poetry [1704]

---◦•◦[◦|◦]◦•◦---

Specimen[1]

The next poet of whom we shall treat is Milton, one of the greatest and most daring geniuses that has appeared in the world, and who has made his country a glorious present of the most lofty, but most irregular poem that has been produced by the mind of man. That

---

[3] "Tremendous" and "furious" (he was also ridiculed as Rinaldo Furioso) seem to have been favorite exclamations of his. *Cf. Essay on Criticism*, III, 26–27.

[4] "Want of taste is want of sense. . . . they who pretend to like nothing will at the playhouses be pleased with everything, and they who would be thought to approve of everything like nothing long; for nothing but Truth can be long esteemed."

[1] sample of what is to come. Part of Dennis's advertisement. As Hooker notes, the *Grounds* "was the first work of English criticism to be published by subscription," though with little success. What survives is a fragment of the *magnum opus* in folio which Dennis projected. Among other things it was to explain poetry in general, the rules of each genre, the beauties and defects of Milton, Spenser, Cowley, and other "English poets who have written any thing that comes near to heroic poetry," Longinus and sublimity, satire and comedy (the first criticism "of any moment that will be extant upon it in any language"), and the decline of modern tragedy; it was to include a translation of *Oedipus Rex* and parts of Homer, Tasso, and the Bible; and for "the greater variety, the lives of the several English poets will be added in their proper places."

great man had a desire to give the world something like an epic poem; but he resolved at the same time to break through the rules of Aristotle. Not that he was ignorant of them or condemned them. On the contrary, no man knew them better or esteemed them more, because no man had an understanding that was more able to comprehend the necessity of them; and therefore when he mentioned them in the little treatise which he wrote to Mr. Hartlib,[2] he calls the art which treats of them a "sublime art." But at the same time he had discernment enough to see that if he wrote a poem which was within the compass of them, he should be subjected to the same fate which has attended all who have written epic poems ever since the time of Homer, and that is, to be a copyist instead of an original. 'Tis true, the epic poets who have lived since Homer have, most of them, been originals in their fables,[3] which are the very souls of their poems, but in their manner of treating those fables, they have too frequently been copyists. They have copied the spirit and the images of Homer; even the great Virgil himself is not to be excepted.[4] Milton was the first who in the space of almost 4000 years resolved, for his country's honor and his own, to present the world with an original poem, that is to say, a poem that should have his own thoughts, his own images, and his own spirit. In order to do this, he was resolved to write a poem that, by virtue of its extraordinary subject, cannot so properly be said to be against the rules as it may be affirmed to be above them all. He had observed that Aristotle had drawn his rules which he has given us for epic poetry from the reflections which he had made upon Homer. Now, he knew very well that in Homer the action lay chiefly between man and man, for Achilles and Hector are properly the principals and the gods are but seconds. He was resolved, therefore, that his principals should be the Devil on one side and Man on the other; and the Devil is properly his hero[5] because he gets the better. All the persons in his poem, excepting two, are either divine or infernal. So that most of the persons and particularly one of the principals, being so very different from what Homer or Aristotle ever thought of,

---

[2] "Treatise of Education" (1664).

[3] Stories or plots, but also the "moral" which each plot carries within it.

[4] Dennis is not condemning imitation of authors, however. He proposed, in his grand project, to show "what Virgil has done; because that great poet is so exact that he may be said to have written a *criticism* upon epic poetry by examples, and because he is now, by Mr. Dryden's translation, to be reckoned among our own poets, and so comes within the compass of my design."

[5] This famous opinion, echoed later by Blake and Shelley among others, was originated by Dryden in *Dedication of the Aeneis* (1697).

could not possibly be subject to their rules, either for the characters or the incidents. We shall now show for what reasons the choice of Milton's subject, as it set him free from the obligation which he lay under to the poetical laws, so it necessarily threw him upon new thoughts, new images, and an original spirit. In the next place, we shall show that besides their newness they have vastly the advantage of those of Homer and Virgil. And we shall make this appear from several things, but principally from the description of Hell, which has been described by those three great poets with all their force and with all their art. After that, we shall come to mark his defects with so much the more exactness, because some of them ought to be avoided with the utmost caution, as being so great that they would be insupportable in any one who had not his extraordinary distinguishing qualities.

CHAPTER I

The design of the following treatise is the re-establishment of poetry

The design of the ensuing treatise, whether we consider the importance or the extent of it, is perhaps the greatest in this kind of writing that has been conceived by the Moderns, for 'tis no less than an attempt to restore and re-establish the noblest art in every branch of it—an art that by the barbarity of the times is fallen and sunk in them all and has been driven and banished from every country excepting England alone, and is even here so miserably fallen, for the most part by the extravagance of its professors[6] and by the unskillfulness of its admirers, that we have reason to apprehend it to be departing from hence, too.

That poetry is the noblest of all arts, and by consequence the most instructive and most beneficial to mankind, may be proved by the concording testimony of the greatest men who have lived in every age: the greatest philosophers, the greatest heroes, and the greatest statesmen, who have, as it were, unanimously cherished, esteemed, admired it; and never has it been disesteemed or neglected by any but some pretenders to wisdom and by some contemptible politicasters, persons who have got into the management of affairs only by the weakness of those who have employed them, and who have utterly wanted capacity to know what a glorious use may be made of it for the benefit of civil society. But in the sequel

---

[6] practitioners.

of this discourse, by discovering the nature of poetry in general (which seems to me to have been hitherto but little understood), I shall clearly show its excellence and the importance of this undertaking. And by laying down either the general rules of it, or by tracing out that "sublime art" which, to make use of Milton's expression, teaches "what the laws are of a true epic poem, what of a dramatic, what of a lyric, what decorum is, what[7] is the grand masterpiece to observe," I shall not only lay a good foundation for the judging of the performance of the several poets whose works I have undertaken to examine, but shall, as Milton says in his *Treatise of Education* to Mr. Hartlib, soon make the world perceive "what despicable creatures our common rhymers and playwrights are, and show them what religious, what glorious and magnificent use may[8] be made of poetry, both in divine and in human things."

CHAPTER II

That poetry is to be established by laying down the rules

That an art so divine in its institution is sunk and profaned and miserably debased is a thing that is confessed by all. But since poetry is fallen from the excellence which it once attained to, it must be fallen either by the want of parts,[9] or want of industry, or by the errors of its professors. But that it cannot be for want of parts we have shown clearly in *The Advancement of Modern Poetry*;[1] nor can it be supposed to be for want of industry, since so many of its professors have no other dependence. It remains then that it must have fallen by their errors, and for want of being guided right.

---

[7] Milton says "which."

[8] Milton says "might."

[9] gifts, talents.

[1] Two opposed lines of thought converged in the same conclusion, that modern poetry was fallen. A Christian belief in the Fall of Man sometimes carried a pessimistic corollary of decaying nature: history is running down and human nature along with it: Moderns, much diminished, live in the old age of the world. The notion appeared in Donne (*First Anniversary*), Browne, Walton, and many others. It seems implied in the allegorical sections of *A Tale of a Tub*, and in parts of Pope's *An Essay on Criticism*. This view Dennis rejected, believing in a moral fall, not a historistic one: Moderns are not wanting in "parts." The other, more optimistic belief, e.g., in Rymer and Blackmore, was that in epic and tragedy, the Moderns were fallen (though not in comedy) but that poetry can and should be reformed by the rules and/or by liberty of experiment. Dennis further imbibed the spirit of Milton and Cowley who sought reform by cultivating Christian poetry in the grand manner.

Since, therefore, it is for want of knowing by what rules they ought to proceed that poetry is fallen so low, it follows then that it is the laying down of those rules alone that can re-establish it. In short, poetry is either an art, or whimsy and fanaticism. If it is an art, it follows that it must propose an end to itself, and afterwards lay down proper means for the attaining that end; for this is undeniable, that there are proper means for the attaining of every end, and those proper means in poetry we call the rules. Again, if the end of poetry be to instruct and reform the world, that is, to bring mankind from irregularity, extravagance, and confusion, to rule and order, how this should be done by a thing that is in itself irregular and extravagant is difficult to be conceived. Besides, the work of every reasonable creature must derive its beauty from regularity, for reason is rule and order, and nothing can be irregular either in our conceptions or our actions any further than it swerves from rule, that is, from reason. As man is the more perfect the more he resembles his Creator, the works of man must needs be more perfect the more they resemble his Maker's. Now the works of God, though infinitely various, are extremely regular.

The universe is regular in all its parts, and it is to that exact regularity that it owes its admirable beauty. The microcosm owes the beauty and health, both of its body and soul, to order, and the deformity and distempers of both to nothing but the want of order. Man was created, like the rest of the creatures, regular, and as long as he remained so, he continued happy; but as soon as he fell from his primitive state by transgressing order, weakness and misery was the immediate consequence of that universal disorder that immediately followed in his conceptions, in his passions and actions.

The great design of arts is to restore the decays that happened to human nature by the Fall, by restoring order.[2] The design of logic is to bring back order and rule and method to our conceptions, the want of which causes most of our ignorance and all our errors. The design of moral philosophy is to cure the disorder that is found in our passions, from which proceeds all our unhappiness and all our vice, as from the due order that is seen in them comes all our virtue and all our pleasure. But how should these arts re-establish order unless they themselves were regular? Those arts that make the senses instrumental to the pleasure of the mind, as painting and music, do it by a great deal of rule and order. Since, therefore, poetry

---

[2] *Cf.* another remark of Milton in his letter to Hartlib: "The end of learning is to repair the ruins of our first parents by regaining to know God aright."

comprehends the force of all these arts of logic, of ethics, of eloquence, of painting, of music, can anything be more ridiculous than
to imagine that poetry itself should be without rule and order?

FROM CHAPTER III

What poetry is, and that it attains its end
by exciting of passion

We have said above that as poetry is an art, it must have a certain
end, and that there must be means that are proper for the attaining
that end, which means are otherwise called the rules. But that we
may make this appear the more plainly, let us declare what poetry
is. Poetry, then, is an art by which a poet excites passion (and for
that very cause entertains sense)[3] in order to satisfy and improve,
to delight and reform, the mind, and so to make mankind happier
and better; from which it appears that poetry has two ends, a subordinate and a final one: the subordinate one is pleasure, and the
final one is instruction.

First, the subordinate end of poetry is to please, for that pleasure
is the business and design of poetry is evident, because poetry, unless it pleases, nay and pleases to a height, is the most contemptible
thing in the world. Other things may be borne with if they are
indifferent, but poetry, unless it is transporting, is abominable—nay,
it has only the name of poetry, so inseparable is pleasure from the
very nature of the thing.

But, secondly, the final end of poetry is to reform the manners.
As poetry is an art, instruction must be its final end; but either that
instruction must consist in reforming the manners, or it cannot instruct at all, and consequently be an art; for poetry pretends to no
other instruction as its final end. But since the final end of poetry
is to reform the manners, nothing can be according to the true art
of it which is against religion, or which runs counter to moral virtue,
or to the true politics and to the liberty of mankind; and everything
which is against the last tends to the corruption and destruction of
mankind; and consequently everything against the last must be
utterly inconsistent with the true art of poetry.

Now the proper means for poetry to attain both its subordinate
and final end is by exciting passion. . . .

1. The greater poetry is an art by which a poet justly and reason-

---

[3] Because in empirical psychology, the passions are mechanically linked to
the physical senses.

ably excites great passion that he may please and instruct, and comprehends epic, tragic, and the greater lyric poetry.

2. The less poetry is an art by which a poet excites less passion for the forementioned ends, and includes in it comedy and satire, and the little ode, and elegiac and pastoral poems. But first we shall treat of the former.

What the greater poetry is; what enthusiasm is

The greater poetry, then, is an art by which a poet justly and reasonably excites great passion in order to please and instruct and make mankind better and happier; so that the first and grand rule in the greater poetry is that a poet must everywhere excite great passion. But in some branches of the greater poetry, it is impossible for the poet everywhere to excite in a very great degree that which we vulgarly call passion—as in the ode, for example, and in the narration of the epic poem. It follows, then, that there must be two sorts of passion: first, that which we call vulgar passion; and secondly, enthusiasm.

First, vulgar passion, or that which we commonly call passion, is that which is moved by the objects themselves, or by the ideas of them in the ordinary course of life—I mean, that common society which we find in the world. As for example, anger is moved by an affront that is offered us in our presence, or by the relation of one; pity, by the sight of a mournful object or the relation of one; admiration or wonder (the common passion, I mean, for there is an enthusiastic admiration, as we shall find anon) by the sight of a strange object or the relation of one. But,

Secondly, enthusiastic passion, or enthusiasm, is a passion which is moved by the ideas in contemplation, or the meditation of things that belong not to common life. Most of our thoughts in meditation are naturally attended with some sort and some degree of passion; and this passion, if it is strong, I call enthusiasm. Now the enthusiastic passions are chiefly six—admiration, terror, horror, joy, sadness, desire[4]—caused by ideas occurring to us in meditation, and producing the same passions that the objects of those ideas would raise in us if they were set before us in the same light that those ideas give us of them. And here I desire the reader to observe that ideas

---

[4] Dennis discusses only admiration and terror, though he had planned to discuss all six passions.

in meditation are often very different from what ideas of the same objects are in the course of common conversation. As, for example, the sun mentioned in ordinary conversation gives the idea of a round, flat, shining body of about two foot diameter. But the sun occurring to us in meditation gives the idea of a vast and glorious body, and the top of all the visible creation, and the brightest material image of the Divinity. I leave the reader therefore to judge if this idea must not necessarily be attended with admiration; and that admiration I call enthusiasm. So thunder mentioned in common conversation gives an idea of a black cloud and a great noise, which makes no great impression upon us. But the idea of it occurring in meditation sets before us the most forcible, most resistless, and consequently the most dreadful phenomenon in Nature; so that this idea must move a great deal of terror in us, and 'tis this sort of terror that I call enthusiasm. And 'tis this sort of terror, or admiration, or horror, and so of the rest, which expressed in poetry make that spirit, that passion, and that fire which so wonderfully please. . . .

First, ideas producing terror contribute extremely to the sublime. All the examples that Longinus brings of the loftiness of the thought consist of terrible ideas. And they are principally such ideas that work the effects which he takes notice of in the beginning of his treatise, viz., that ravish and transport the reader and produce a certain admiration mingled with astonishment and with surprise. For the ideas which produce terror are necessarily accompanied with admiration (because everything that is terrible is great to him to whom it is terrible), and with surprise (without which terror cannot subsist), and with astonishment (because everything which is very terrible is wonderful and astonishing); and as terror is perhaps the violentest of all the passions, it consequently makes an impression which we cannot resist, and which is hardly to be defaced; and no passion is attended with greater joy than enthusiastic terror, which proceeds from our reflecting that we are out of danger at the very time that we see it before us. And as terror is one of the violentest of all passions, if it is very great, and the hardest to be resisted, nothing gives more force nor more vehemence to a discourse.

But, secondly, it is plain from the same Longinus that this enthusiastic terror is chiefly to be derived from religious ideas. For all the examples which he has brought of the sublime, in his chapter of the sublimity of the thoughts, consist of most terrible and most religious ideas; and at the same time every man's reason will inform him that everything that is terrible in religion is the most terrible thing in the world.

But that we may set this in a clearer light, let us lay before the reader the several ideas which are capable of producing this enthusiastic terror, which seem to me to be those which follow: *viz.*, gods, demons, hell, spirits and souls of men, miracles, prodigies, enchantments, witchcrafts, thunder, tempests, raging seas, inundations, torrents, earthquakes, volcanoes, monsters, serpents, lions, tigers, fire, war, pestilence, famine, etc.

Now of all these ideas none are so terrible as those which show the wrath and vengeance of an angry God, for nothing is so wonderful in its effects; and consequently the images or ideas of those effects[5] must carry a great deal of terror with them, which we may see was Longinus's opinion by the examples which he brings in his chapter of the sublimity of the thoughts. Now of things which are terrible, those are the most terrible which are the most wonderful, because that seeing them both threatening and powerful, and not being able to fathom the greatness and extent of their power, we know not how far and how soon they may hurt us. . . . But here it will be convenient to answer an objection: For how come some of the forementioned ideas, which seem to have but little to do with religion, to be terrible to great and to wise men? as it is plain that such, when they read the descriptions of them in Homer and Virgil, *are* terrified.

To which we answer that the care, which Nature has inrooted in all, of their own preservation is the cause that men are unavoidably terrified with anything that threatens approaching evil. 'Tis now our business to show how the ideas of serpents, lions, tigers, etc., were made by the art of those great poets to be terrible to their readers, at the same time that we are secure from their objects.[6]

'Tis very plain that it is the apprehension of danger which causes that emotion in us which we call terror, and it signifies nothing at all to the purpose whether the danger is real or imaginary; and 'tis as plain, too, that the soul never takes the alarm from anything so soon as it does from the senses, especially those two noble ones of the eye and the ear, by reason of the strict affinity which they have with the imagination; and the evil always seems to be very

---

[5] Dennis's exposition is sometimes tortured because he is struggling to explain complex spiritual and aesthetic experience in a materialistic language of Hobbesian psychology.

[6] I.e., from real serpents, lions, and tigers.

near when those two senses give notice of it; and the nearer the evil is, the greater still is the terror. But now let us see how those two poets did, by virtue of their ideas, bring even absent terrible objects within the reach of those two noble senses. First then, to bring an absent terrible object before our sight, they drew an image or picture of it; but to draw an image or picture of a terrible object so as to surprise and astonish the soul by the eye, they never failed to draw it in violent action or motion; and in order to that, they made choice of words and numbers which might best express the violence of that action or motion.[7] For an absent object can never be set before the eye in a true light unless it be shown in violent action or motion, because unless it is shown so, the soul has leisure to reflect upon the deceit. But violent motion can never be conceived without a violent agitation of spirit, and that sudden agitation surprises the soul and gives it less time to reflect, and at the same time causes the impressions that the objects make to be so deep, and their traces to be so profound, that it makes them in a manner as present to us, as if they were really before us. For the spirits being set in a violent emotion, and the imagination being fired by that agitation, and the brain[8] being deeply penetrated by those impressions, the very objects themselves are set as it were before us, and consequently we are sensible of the same passion that we should feel from the things themselves. For the warmer the imagination is, the less able we are to reflect, and consequently the things are the more present to us of which we draw the images; and therefore when the imagination is so inflamed as to render the soul utterly incapable of reflecting, there is no difference between the images and the things themselves, as we may see, for example, by men in raging fevers. But those two great poets were not satisfied with setting absent objects before our eyes by showing them in violent motion, but if their motion occasioned any extraordinary sounds that were terrifying, they so contrived their numbers and expressions as that they might be sure to ring those sounds in the very ears of their readers.[9] . . .

---

[7] Elledge compares Aristotle's *Rhetoric* (III, xi) in which, praising Homer, Aristotle says, "Things are set before the eyes by words that signify actuality . . . and actuality is movement."

[8] The language is materialistic, with the result that Dennis is carried logically to compare aesthetic experience with a physical fever.

[9] to make the sound an echo to the sense. *Cf.* Pope's *Essay on Criticism*, II, 137–82.

Recapitulation; and that religion is the basis and foundation of the greater poetry

But now let us recapitulate. We have shown in the foregoing part of this discourse that passion is the characteristical mark of poetry and that all poetry is pathetic; and then we divided it into two kinds, the greater and the less, and showed that the greater poetry comprehends epic, tragic, and the greater lyric, and that our design was in the first place to treat of it. Then we proceeded to show that as passion is the characteristical mark of poetry, great passion must be the characteristical mark of the greater poetry, and consequently that this last must have everywhere great passion; but since what we commonly call passion cannot be everywhere, there must be something distinct from ordinary passion, and that must be enthusiasm. Then we endeavored to discover what enthusiasm is, and how many several sorts there are of it; and that admiration and terror make the principal greatness of poetry, and are the chief of the enthusiastic passions; that those two passions are to bear proportion with the ideas from which they are derived, and that consequently the greatest must flow from religious ideas. We shall show too in the sequel of this discourse that not only the remaining enthusiastic passions, horror, sadness, joy, and desire, but that even the ordinary passions which contribute most to the greatness of poetry, as admiration, terror, and pity, are chiefly to be derived from religion; but that the passions of both sorts must, for the most part, flow greater from revelation than from natural religion, because all revealed religion, whether true or pretended, speaks to the senses, brings the wonders of another world more home to us, and so makes the passions which it raises the greater.

The fundamental rule then that we pretend to lay down for the succeeding or excelling in the greater poetry is that the constitution of the poem be religious, that it may be throughout pathetic.

And we pretend to prove undeniably that not only the gentlemen whose works we design to examine have succeeded and excelled no further than their poems have been so constituted, but that never any poets of any nation or any age ever did or can excel without it. I have already proved in *The Advancement of Modern Poetry*, beyond all manner of doubt, to those who have capacity enough to comprehend the arguments, that the Ancient poets excelled the Moderns in the greatness of poetry for no other reason but because their subjects were religious in their constitution. And therefore, all that I shall say of it here is that poetry is the natural language of religion, and that religion at first produced it as a cause produces its effect. In the first ages of writing, among the Grecians, there was nothing writ but verse, because they wrote of nothing but religion, which was necessary for the cementing the societies which in those times were but just united; and Nature had taught them that poetry was the only language in which they could worthily treat of the most important parts of religion, or worthily perform its most important duties. But as soon as religion was sufficiently imprinted in the minds of men, and they had leisure to treat of human things in their writings, they invented prose, and invented it in imitation of verse, as Strabo tells us in the First Book of his *Geography*;[1] but after that prose was invented by them, never any of them treated of their gods or their religious matters in prose before the age of Socrates, because they found that that way of writing was by no means proper for it. For the wonders of religion naturally threw them upon harmony and figurative language, as they must of necessity do any poet, as long as he continues master of them.[2] Which is known by experience to all who are poets; for never anyone, while he was rapt with enthusiasm or with ordinary passion, wanted either words or harmony, and therefore poetry is more harmonious than prose because it is more pathetic. Even in prose, your orators and all who pretend to move the passions have more harmonious periods than they who barely speak to the reason. And in poetry, they who write with a great deal of passion are generally very harmonious, whereas those who write with but little are not so musical. Horace is an illustrious example of this: no man who has read his *Odes* can doubt of the fineness and the delicacy of his ear; and therefore his *Satires* are often harsh and rugged because the spirit in them is mean and little. No man can believe that Juvenal had a finer ear than Horace, but yet his satires are more musical, because they have a greater spirit in them. At the same time, 'tis a little odd to consider that passion, which disturbs the soul, should occasion it to produce harmony, which seems to imply the order and composure of it. Whether this proceeds from the secret effort that the soul makes to compose itself, or whatever the cause is, the effect is certain. . . . But we shall have occasion to treat of harmony more at large when we come to the particular sorts of poems; in the

---

[1] I, ii, 6.
[2] *Cf.* Dryden, p. 96, on figurative language in passion.

meantime let us return to the business from which we may seem to have digressed.

As we have formerly undeniably proved in *The Advancement of Modern Poetry* that the Ancient poets derived that advantage which they have over the Moderns to the constituting their subjects after a religious manner, so I shall make it appear in the sequel of this discourse that it was owing to the same thing that the Ancient poets very often excelled themselves.

And I have reason to believe that one of the principal reasons that has made the Modern poetry so contemptible is that, by divesting itself of religion, it is fallen from its dignity and its original nature and excellence, and from the greatest production of the mind of man is dwindled to an extravagant and a vain amusement. For the Modern poetry, being for the most part profane, has either very little spirit, or if it has a great one, that spirit is out of Nature,[3] because it bears no manner of proportion to the ideas from which it is forcibly derived, nor the ideas very often to the objects from which they are taken, for as Mr. Waller says:

> *In boundless verse the fancy soars too high*
> *For any object but the Deity,*
> *What mortal can with heaven pretend to share*
> *In the superlatives of wise and fair?*
> *A meaner subject when with these we grace,*
> *A giant's habit on a dwarf we place.*[4]

But that the Modern poetry, as miserably as it is fallen from the dignity of its original nature, might gloriously arise and lift up its head, surpassing even that of the Ancients, if the poets would but constitute their subjects religious, I have formerly clearly shown, in the second part of *The Advancement of Modern Poetry*, by showing that the design of the Christian religion is the very same with that of poetry, which can be said of no other religion: that the business of both is to delight and reform mankind by exciting the passions in such a manner as to reconcile them to reason and restore the harmony of the human faculties. . . .

For this is certain, that there are not wanting great geniuses to every age; but they do not equally appear[5] in every age, sometimes for want of knowing themselves, and sometimes for want of en-

---

[3] unnatural.
[4] From "Upon the Earl of Roscommon's Translation of Horace, *De Arte Poetica*; and of the Use of Poetry."
[5] become known. *Cf.* Young, pp. 361–66.

couragement and leisure to exert themselves. The business of the treatise intended is to show them how they may try, and know, and form themselves, which is all that I am capable of attempting towards the restoring so useful and so noble an art. If I were in a condition to give them encouragement[e] too, they should not be long without it. If they who so much exceed me in power did but equal me in will, we should soon see poetry raise up its dejected head, and our own might come to emulate the happiest of Grecian and Roman Ages.

And thus much may suffice to show the nature of poetry, but chiefly of the greater poetry, and the importance of this design. For since poetry has been thought not only by heathens, but by the writers of the Old Testament, and consequently by God himself, who inspired them, to be the fittest method for the enforcing religion upon the minds of men; and since religion is the only solid foundation of all civil society; it follows that whoever endeavors to re-establish poetry makes a generous attempt to restore an art that may be highly advantageous to the public and beneficial to mankind.

---

[e] patronage.

ON

WIT and HUMOR

THE RESURGENCE of *wit* in early twentieth-century criticism and of witty poetry and fiction had its prototype during the Restoration and early eighteenth century. Critical terms are likely to be vaguest, and indispensable, when they are near the vital center of creativity. Almost every critic, great or small, tried to define wit; one could easily list fifty or more essays or chapters or commentaries on it between 1650 and 1800. Nor was such anxiety of definition merely faddish. At stake was the whole question of what qualities in literature and the literary life are valuable, and sometimes whether they are valuable; for wit was a historic English term for creativity in language. Other terms could be synonymous with it—*invention, imagination, fancy, eloquence, genius, taste, judgment*; sometimes it translated the Latin *ingenium* or French *l'esprit*. But the native term wit gathered to itself historic, special meanings—free, erudite, or quick intellect, intensity and indirection, power of form, ingenuity of rhetoric, and an urbane understanding, often comic but not necessarily so, of relativities, alternatives, and incongruities in the facts of experience. Furthermore, it focused historic controversies of faith, ethics, tradition, class, and the value of language itself. The position which one took on wit mattered, and still may matter. As T. S. Eliot has remarked:

> We are baffled in the attempt to translate the quality indicated by the dim and antiquated term wit into the equally unsatisfactory nomenclature of our time. . . . It is confused

with erudition because it belongs to an educated mind, rich in generations of experience; and it is confused with cynicism because it implies a constant inspection and criticism of experience. It involves, probably, a recognition, implicit in the expression of every experience, of other kinds of experience which are possible.[1]

Three interpenetrative classes of meaning—intellectual, artistic, and social (or moral)—had their roots in the English Renaissance. Wit (AS. *witan*, "to know, learn, be aware of") early accumulated meanings as varied as whatever can be learned, the faculty of mind which learns it, or the condition of a mind which has learned. It meant wisdom, especially spiritual wisdom, but also the worldly intellect (*cf.* "motherwit" or "sharp-witted Aristotle") and occasionally the senses. The Five Wits, that is, the five senses, troop on stage near the end of *Everyman*, and the meaning of wit as an organ of sensation can be found sporadically in Sir Thomas Elyot's *The Book Named the Governor* (1531). As Renaissance humanists identified the moral and intellectual faculties, however, the equation of wit to wise or spiritual understanding was normal throughout the sixteenth century, often tinged with Christian Platonism. As humanists were educators, wit often meant the innate (or God-given) capacity of intellect—always endangered by "will" or "carnal affections"—which must be trained to the wisdom proper in statesmen and gentlemen, training which included a selection of great books. And so it appears, for example, in Lyly's *Euphues: The Anatomy of Wit* (1578).

The meaning of wit as trained, gentlemanly intelligence, morally upright (if possible) and knowing in both tradition and public affairs, persisted throughout the seventeenth century, though gradually wit and the humanists' wisdom, which itself was sometimes prudishly restrictive, became dissociated and even opposed to each other. Looking back from 1779, Dr. Johnson observed that about a century before, "*wit*, which had till then been used for intellection, in contradistinction to *will*, took the meaning, whatever it is, which it now bears." [2] In the opening paragraph of his essay "Of Poetry" (1692), Sir William Temple recommends a "happy mixture" of both "faculties of the mind" in poetry, but distinguishes *wisdom*, which pertains to "inventions or productions of things generally esteemed the most necessary, useful, or profitable to human life,"

---

[1] "Andrew Marvell," *Selected Essays, 1917–32*, p. 262.
[2] See p. 480.

from *wit*, which pertains to things merely "pleasing or entertaining." An illuminating exercise is to follow the terms in Swift's youthful (and curiously Platonistic) odes and epistles in which wit figures as "a mighty light" but a "lost language." Angry and self-divided, he blames the civil war for corruptions in English religious and literary culture; instead of questing for "wisdom," people nowadays are intimidated by those who are called "wits," especially atheists, Cartesians, Epicurean or Hobbesian materialists, pedants, enthusiasts, and madmen; whereas true wit is philosophy, learning, and language unfallen and rightly used. As "wit is the noblest and most useful gift of human nature," Swift wrote in the "Apology" to *A Tale of a Tub*, "so humor is the most agreeable, and where these two enter far into the composition of any work, they will render it always acceptable to the world." He "wrote only to the men of wit and taste," though in the preface to *The Battle of the Books* one is reminded that "wit without knowledge" is "a sort of cream, which gathers in a night to the top and by a skillful hand may be soon whipt into froth; but once scummed away, what appears underneath will be fit for nothing but to be thrown to the hogs." The threatened dissociation of wit from wisdom (that is, from knowledge of truth and nature) reflected profound changes of philosophy, culture, and general sense of reality between, say, Spenser and Dryden, Elyot and Hobbes. The spider and the bee in *The Battle of the Books* merrily symbolize opposite notions of wit—the one modernist, solipsistic, mathematical, proudly narrow, "conceited," and satyrical; the other, like a classically trained, tradition-conscious mind, "ranging through every corner of nature" to fill its hive "with honey and wax, thus furnishing mankind with the two noblest of things, which are sweetness and light"—that is, truly wise humor and wit.

A bye-meaning during the Renaissance had restricted wit to that part of the mind which inquires or ranges through experience. Sir Thomas Elyot speaks of "that power the property whereof is to espy, seek for, ensearch, and find out, which virtue is referred to wit, which is, as it were, the instrument of understanding." [3] Some such notion of wit as inquiry or discovery became central in its definition, as in Davenant's definition of wit (see p. 167) as "rounding the world like the sun, with unimaginable motion, and bringing swiftly home to the memory universal surveys," in search of "truth operative," as also Temple's "sprightly imagination or fancy, fertile in a thousand productions, ranging over infinite ground, piercing into

---

[3] *The Book Named the Governor*, III, xxiii.

every corner, and, by the light of that true poetical fire, discovering a thousand little bodies or images in the world, and similitudes among them, unseen to common eyes." Frequently, after Hobbes and Locke, it might be called *sagacity* (L. *sagax*, "keen-scented"): hence Hobbes's comparison of "invention" to a spaniel snuffling through the field of memory (see p. 19 and *cf*. p. 24 on *fancy*), which Dryden copied and renamed wit (see p. 169), Sagacity reappears as late as 1786 in Reynolds (see p. 539), though by this time the term *wit* is obsolescent, to name the process of wise intuition by which an artist, as his hand creates, draws on his habitual and only partly conscious reservoir of experience. Wit as inquiry implied an encounter with things new or unpredictable and therefore with surprise or luck or mystery of discovery.

A further specialized meaning of wit as "that which cunningly contrives," appears as early as Chaucer's Wife of Bath who

> *broughte it so aboute by me wit*
> *That they moste yive it up as for the beste.*

The very title *Merry Jests and Witty Shifts of Scoggin* (1566) suggests, already, a Falstaffian meaning. A nobler and more formal contrivance is meant, however, by the "witty" devices in Thomas Wilson's *The Art of Rhetoric* (1553); or when Surrey speaks in 1557 of the glory of Chaucer's wit, or "E. K." in his commentary on *The Shepherd's Calendar* (1579) of Spenser's "wittiness in devising" and of poetry as "poured into the wit by a certain ἐνθυσιασμός," or Nashe in 1589 of "divine Master Spenser, the miracle of wit." The generic meaning is succinctly, if insipidly, expressed in the prologue to Alexander Barclay's *Certain Eclogues* (1570):

> *The famous poets with the muses nine,*
> *With wit inspired, fresh, pregnant, and divine,*
> *Say, "Boldly indite in style substantial!"*
> *Some in poems high and heroical,*
> *Some them delight in heavy tragedies,*
> *And some in wanton or merry comedies;*
> *Some in satires against vices dare carp,*
> *Some in sweet songs accordant with the harp;*
> *And each of these all had laud and excellence*
> *After their reason and style of eloquence.*

The passage, with its hierarchy of genres, matches the belief, a century later, of Temple and of Dryden (see p. 169) that "the composition of all poems is, or ought to be, of wit," each genre having its own laws and proprieties; and of Cowley whose "Ode on Wit" (1668) reaffirms its inspired genius and its grasp of enduring truth.

As a generic term for the creative process, whether inspired or rhetorical, wit took on the dye of changing artistic fashions from the sixteenth through the eighteenth century, but any restrictive application to "metaphysical" wit was late, gradual, and never complete. During the lifetime of Dryden, however, the search for an idiom in poetry both new and natural—one more proper, perspicuous, and public—encouraged distinctions between true and false wit. Cowley's ode initiated the fashion, defining true wit as a constructive or harmonizing power of mind which, somewhat mysteriously, assimilates each element of a poem to every other, as distinct from mere jest or "laughter at a feast," "florid talk," gaudy ornament, puns, anagrams, acrostics, or metaphorical bombast. As epic was the norm of poetic theory in neoclassicism, so epic wit like that of Homer or Virgil controlled the term's noblest meaning. To Dryden, wit was propriety of thought and language to the subject (see p. 98, n. 9), but "heroical" wit in particular he early defined (see p. 169) as a lively, comprehensive, accurate imaging which "sets before your eyes the absent object, as perfectly, and more delightfully than nature." Especially after Boileau's translation of Longinus in 1674, and the critical dialogues of Bouhours, a beautiful, Homeric simplicity of thought and style which vividly images (makes "obvious") the nature of things human seemed to major Augustans, from Pope to Johnson, the highest reach of poetry, and therefore presumably of wit. It grandly fills the mind with true lifelikeness, as distinct from the ingenuity of wordplay, the extravagance or contortion of image permissible in lesser genres like satire and epigram.

> *True Wit is Nature to advantage dressed,*
> *What oft was thought, but ne'er so well expressed:*
> *Something, whose truth convinced at sight we find,*
> *That gives us back the image of our mind.*[4]

The "glaring chaos and wild heap of wit" in Donne, Herbert, Crashaw, Cleveland, and Cowley himself sank in reputation, as also of course the puns and quibbles in Shakespeare; but the wit of conceits bequeathed by them, and perhaps more importantly, the kind of unheroic, densely allusive and topical ridicule in which Augustans excelled, whatever their theory, gradually specialized the term wit and undermined its use for the higher genres. By the middle of the

---

[4] Pope, *Essay on Criticism*, II, 97–100.

eighteenth century, wit as the source and quality of the highest
achievement in poetry was displaced by new concepts of *imagination*, as in the selection from Joseph Warton (see p. 203). Even
Dryden, who embraced all complications, could "safely say it of
this present age that if we are not so great wits as Donne, yet certainly we are better poets." He also was first to distinguish between
imagination and *fancy* (see p. 169). Pope vacillated notoriously in
his usage: *wit* is a key term in his *Essay on Criticism* (1711), but
is displaced in the Preface to the *Iliad* (1715) by *invention, genius,
imagination*, and *fire*. In *The Dunciad* of 1744, however, *wit* is
a key term for understanding Pope's critical position, and when wit
"expires" (IV, 634), it carries with it all art, science, philosophy, and
religion. In his six *Spectator* papers on wit (nos. 58–63), Addison
reaffirmed that "the basis of all wit is truth" and distinguished the
true wit of congruous ideas and beautiful thought, which delights
and surprises, from the false wit of external and literal ornament,
including puns, and the "mixed wit" of Cowley, Italian romantic
epics, Greek epigrammatists, Ovid, and Martial. But wit for Addison
could not include "the similitudes of heroic poets, who endeavor
rather to fill the mind with great conceptions than to divert it with
such as are new and surprising."

Dr. Johnson reflected on wit more profoundly than anyone else
during the late eighteenth century and endeavored to save the term
(see p. 478), but even as he wrote, he was reaching back, as in so
much else, to elucidate and bring into currency values from a dying
past. Before Johnson was born, the issue had become whether or
how wit is cognitive—that is, whether wisdom, strength and complication of intellect, is intrinsic to poetry, or whether poetry is only
an escapist or technical pastime.

Two other seventeenth-century developments, one social, the other
philosophic, worked to undermine the generic dignity of the term as
well as greatly to enlarge its range of applications.

If wit might be the badge of a Renaissance gentleman, and little
wit a sign of commonness, changing ideals of gentlemanliness between, say, Sidney and Rochester, altered the meaning of the term
in practice. It was taken over by Cavaliers and courtly gentlemen-
poets to describe their refined conversation (*repartee* entered the
language c. 1645, *raillery* c. 1653) or else the kind of neatly finished,
gaily paradoxical, or plaintive epigrams, songs, and epistles which
they were writing during the civil war. The very titles of fashionable
miscellanies are significant: *Wit's Recreations* (1640, repr. 1641,
1645, 1650, 1654, 1663, 1667), *Wit's Interpreter* (1655), *Sportive*

Wit (1656), *Wit and Drollery* (1656), *Wit a-Sporting* (1657), *Wit Restored* (1658). They included attacks, usually impudent, against Commonwealthmen; and the term wit became a self-conscious class distinction, even more triumphantly self-conscious after the Restoration, as the names of many characters in Restoration comedy suggest—Truewit, Witwoud, Witless. A courtly sophistication, coolly ironic if not libertine, tinged the popular (or unpopular) meaning of wit.

At one extreme, a wit might signify a freethinking young rake or epicurean who sinned gloriously and fleered at cits or parsons. As Johnson was once to remark, "One may say of him as was said of a French wit, *Il n'a de l'esprit que contre Dieu.* . . . his trade is wit. It would be as wild in him to come into company without merriment as for a highwayman to take the road without his pistols." Wit in many minds would suggest scandalous levity or obscenity, irresponsible jokes, pretty turns, and in general, ridicule. The vernacular of Augustans was rich in "witty" terms once relatively precise: to *bite* (tell a lie with a straight face so as to arouse an emotion like anger or pity which, because it has no basis, makes the victim look foolish),[5] *smoke out, bubble, set by the ears* (cause two people to quarrel who had not planned to), *flam, bamboozle, fall foul on, wipe, gibe, flirt* (make contemptuous or ill-mannered remarks), *chouse* (swindle), *fob off* (shift by an artifice, dismiss by a trick), *cully* (make a fool of). Swift complained in *Tatler* 230, not without irony of his own, about "all modern terms of art—*sham, banter, mob,*[6] *bubble, bully,*[7] *cutting, shuffling, and palming.*" More formally, wit might also imply mastery of rhetorical tropes and figures, still part of a gentleman's education, especially those tropes, in Barrow's phrase, "wherein the lepid way doth consist"—"biting sarcasms, sly ironics, strong metaphors, lofty hyperboles, paranomasias, oxymorons, and the like." But in general, classical rhetoric of verbal intensity and formal design would split during the eighteenth century under the combined weight of theories of practical communication on the one hand, and theories of genius and emotion on the other. At the other social extreme, a wit might possess dignified ease and correctness, a noble refinement and purity of language or deportment. In *An Essay on the Dramatic Poetry of the Last Age* (1672) Dryden mentioned two orders of wit: "wit in a larger signification," the generic act of imitation, repre-

---

[5] See p. 196.
[6] to wrap in a cowl or veil, to conceal the face; hence to be ironic.
[7] to overbear with invective.

sentation, imaging; "wit in the stricter sense, that is, sharpness of conceit"; and, what amounts virtually to a third order, the well-bred refinement of Augustans. The wit of Shakespeare, Jonson, even Fletcher, great as it was, "was not that of gentlemen; there was ever somewhat that was ill-bred and clownish in it, and which confessed the conversation[8] of the authors." Similarly, Dennis praised the wit of Samuel Butler because there is "much of a gentleman" in it, good sense, purity and vivacity of language "that could proceed from nothing but a generous education and from a happy nature."

Wit had come to imply a certain liberty of thought and especially, in Hutcheson's phrase, a "liberty of laughing." The sermon from Barrow, written sometime during the late 1660's or early 1670's, brilliantly catalogues qualities of rhetoric and satire which flowered from laughing wit, especially at court, and expresses the worried attitude of latitudinarian churchmen, as also of gentlemen like Temple, who looked back on Sir Philip Sidney as the noblest genius of modern Europe and what a wise wit ought to be. Invoking Scripture and Socrates, Barrow wished not to repress the "facetious wit" of the age but to redirect it toward rational, good-natured ends—to reconcile liberty of laughing with the wisdom of faith. A flurry of extreme revulsion, however, came at the turn of the century from high churchmen like Jeremy Collier, and generally from a growingly powerful, moralistic and businesslike middle class, for whom vivacious liberty of wit might seem, as indeed by common standards it often was, obscene or snobbish or both. Their antagonist watchword became not *wisdom*, but, more narrowly, *sense* (*good sense, common sense*); and so one encounters a further confusion that *wit* and *sense* may be confederate if not identical (as in Dryden's *Mac Flecknoe* or Pope's *Essay on Criticism*) or bitter opposites, depending on the critic. The selection from Blackmore's "Essay on Wit" (see p. 188) represents, for its time, the recurring philistinism in English society, which persists through Utilitarians and Positivists in the nineteenth century to the present day. Despite his enthusiasm for Longinus and religious poetry, Blackmore reduced the profession of wit to the lowest in society and opposed it to the "useful" occupation held by men of plain understanding and good sense. Wit itself he defined as ornamentality of fancy and prettiness of sentiment, and he totally excluded it from serious subjects. The dilemma which such contradictory notions of wit posed for Swift and Pope helps account for a defiantly surreal non-"sense" in their

---

[8] revealed the level of society in which they usually moved.

art as well as for complexity of tone in their moral war on dullness
and dunces. The public-spirited plan of Addison (*Spectator* No.
10) "to enliven morality with wit and to temper wit with morality," and thereby to heal what he called the "dreadful spirit of division" in society, reverted to a gentler latitudinarianism like that of
Barrow, without ceasing, at its best, to be current and exact in satire. But it edged also toward a feminizing of wit and reduction to
mere levity. It cramped the freedom of comic and satiric intellect
by social taboos, turned victims of satire into objects of compassion,
and shut out certain realities such as class or ideological conflict,
"hard" learning, "obscenity," and moral ambiguity. By mid-century
the reputation of complex, laughing wits like Swift and Pope was
falling rapidly; wit itself was increasingly identified with satire, and
satire with malignant laughter and self-centered intellect. Defend-
ers of wit like Fielding (with whom Barrow was a favorite) and
Sterne found themselves caught in a dilemma of heart and head,
which both just barely and not always solved.

The most original theory of laughing wit was probably that of
Francis Hutcheson (see p. 192), a Presbyterian minister as well as
aesthetician, who published three essays signed Philomeides (that
is, "laughter-loving") in *The Dublin Journal* (1725), posthumously
reprinted in Scotland as *Reflections upon Laughter* (1750). He rejected Hobbes's theory of egoistic or self-loving laughter (see p.
27) since it "overlooked everything which is generous and kind"
in men—"the old notions of natural affections and kind instincts,
the *sensus communis*, the *decorum*, the *honestum*." [9] Furthermore,
Addison had accepted Hobbes's theory and given it wide currency
in *Spectator* No. 47. To refute both, Hutcheson borrowed from *Spectator* No. 62 the distinction of "serious" or "grave wit" which pleases
us with its detection of unsuspected but true resemblances—fusing
the natural and the new—from the different wit of laughter. This
he coalesced with a theory of association of ideas derived from
Locke, and a theory of "inner senses" of beauty, regularity, harmony, and their opposites, derived from Shaftesbury. In that "great
fund of pleasantry, the parody and burlesque allusion," Hutcheson
argued, laughter "often arises without any imagined superiority of
ourselves," for we may have "the highest veneration for the writing
alluded to"—for example, Homer and Virgil—and "also admire
the wit of the person who makes the allusion." Conversely, if imagined superiority of well-being were the only source of laughter, an

---

[9] See Shaftesbury, p. 216.

"infirmary or lazar-house" would be hilarious. Laughter in general, he argued, must be distinguished from ridicule: laughing *because* or *with*, in which our moral sympathies are intact, must be distinguished from laughing *at* somebody. The efficient cause of laughter, in any culture, is not self-love, as Hobbes had argued, but impropriety, incongruity—the joining of "ideas" which are in fact contradictory, the juxtaposition of "ideas" which by custom are associated with the dignified, beautiful, perfect, or sacred, with contrasting "ideas" associated with the mean, ugly, deformed, or indecent. After a temporary eclipse, Hutcheson's distinction between laughter, whose "final cause" is fellowship, and ridicule, which exposes false grandeur, was revived by Scottish critics at mid-century, and, with subtleties of variation, dominated comic theory.[1]

His theory of incongruity was new at the time, objective and causal, and in the abstract is still a theory of laughter to be reckoned with. An additional appeal of his essay is its being *engagé* with many facts of Augustan writing. Hutcheson was theorizing in a literary climate when the creative resources of parodic, burlesque, and allusive wit were exploited by major writers more deliberately than at any time before Eliot, Pound, and Joyce in the twentieth century. From Rymer, Temple, Dennis, and Addison to Joseph Warton[2] and Goldsmith, it was common opinion, not altogether flattering, that in comic wit and humor the Moderns excelled the Ancients. Variously in various critics, the Moderns might include Erasmus, More, Rabelais, Cervantes, Shakespeare and Jonson, Molière, Le Sage, Etherege, Wycherley, and Congreve, Butler, *The Rehearsal*, Swift, Pope, later Fielding and Sterne. Hutcheson draws examples from Butler and Swift, but his remarks illuminate the practices of a hundred others. By separating "laughter" from "truth" however—that is, by separating incongruities in literature from intellectual grasp—he missed his chance for greatness. And in the long run, his theory encouraged a certain mindlessness of laughter. He perpetuated, in a new version, a Lockian depression of wit to pleasantry.

---

[1] The term incongruity was first used in Gerard's *Essay on Taste* (1759), which, borrowing from Hutcheson, numbers "ridicule" among the seven internal senses of the mind; see p. 275. Kames in 1762 distinguished between "ridicule" (implying contempt for that which pains us emotionally) and the "risible," the "true emotion" of sympathetic laughter. Beattie in his essay "On Laughter and Ludicrous Composition" (1776) further distinguished "animal" from "sentimental" (that is, humane) laughter. All were associationists for whom *wit* was increasingly restricted to ridicule.

[2] See *The Adventurer*, nos. 127 and 133 (1754).

Fielding's distinction in the Preface to *Joseph Andrews*—between burlesque, whose incongruities rouse a healthy but mindless, neurological laughter, and refined comic irony that "discovers" the human truth but causes little or no laughter—suggests the limits of Hutcheson's theory and the artistic dilemma concealed within it. Wit was divided against itself.

Finally, at work within all this, were other efforts to define wit "philosophically," that is, to abstract it with some scientific finality as a principle.[3] As in the twentieth century, there were generally two approaches—theoretical and inductive. Like Freud (*Wit and Its Relation to the Unconscious,* 1905) one could arrive at a notion of wit incidentally, as a by-product of a larger account of the mind, or like T. S. Eliot, one could saturate oneself in the literary facts and cautiously reflect in their presence. Hobbes (see p. 168) and Locke (see p. 184) represent the first; poet-critics like Dryden and Johnson, having absorbed empirical philosophy, lean toward the second, though fineness of distinction would be arbitrary, especially in professed philosophic inquirers like Burke (see p. 336) or Kames (see p. 309). The new epistemology, defining mind as a succession and storage of unit "ideas" imprinted from external objects, necessarily restricted activity of the mind to relation of ideas—combining, comparing, enlarging or diminishing, or "abstracting" one from the mass. Fancy or imagination, licentious and unpredictable, is a pleasure principle which finds new similitudes (resemblances, affinities, congruities) among things which in reality are different, and therefore is the origin of fiction and metaphor. But as it inures one to trivial or false relationships, fancy nears or is madness.

> As all is dullness, when the Fancy's bad,
> So without Judgment, Fancy is but mad.[4]

Judgment, the reality principle, is a dissociating power, the source of true knowledge, which discerns things as they are, puts them in right order, refusing to be abused by false resemblances. Those who followed Locke in depressing wit to fancy—and they were legion— were haunted by an antithesis of wit and judgment whose implications were hostile to imaginative literature generally. Historians may have made too much of this "Magna Charta of stupidity," as Tristram Shandy called it. No major critic from Dryden to Johnson, including Hobbes himself, denied that both fancy (wit, extravagance) and judgment (reason, sense), indeed all faculties of the mind,

---

[3] *Cf.* Johnson on metaphysical wit, p. 478.
[4] John Sheffield, Duke of Buckingham, *An Essay on Poetry* (1682), II, 35–36.

must cooperate in the creative act. Poetry, Dennis said, provides for "the satisfaction of the whole man together." But the anxious care to reconcile them testifies to a felt problem. Generally, the distinction encouraged constraint and timidity. It undermined confidence in the "truth" of fiction and the resources of language: words, narrowly, should deliver so many things as they are, as in science.[5]

Few discussions of *wit* failed sooner or later to drop alongside the complementary term *humor*. Humor defined something congeneric but somehow distinct. Generally, humor is nature; wit is art. Wit is intellectual, impersonal, and learned, and causes surprise; humor is of unforced growth, has something warm, individual, and odd about it, and causes delight. Both cooperate in the comic act. Augustans had a knack for coupling opposite terms, then struggling to reconcile them: superimposition of nature-art upon humor-wit became as commonplace as the distinction of Shakespeare's "original" genius from Jonson's "imitative" learning. An increasingly common corollary was the superiority of humor to wit (as of Shakespeare to Jonson), explicitly stated by Dennis, Addison, Corbyn Morris, Young, Sterne, Goldsmith, and Sheridan. Humor, like wit, opens up the literary values and practices of an era, though unlike wit, values of humor thrust vigorously into the nineteenth century, partly because of their immanence in the novel. Between, say, Ben Jonson and Dickens, the term *humor* enjoyed an appreciation or ennoblement—precisely the reverse fortune of *wit*, whose association with obscenity, impiety, or misanthropy helped redefine and elevate the term most often coupled with it.

From the start, humor (a term derived from medieval and Renaissance psycho-medical theory) was connected with character, and therefore later with characterization. As Elyot explains, for example, in *The Castle of Health* (1541), the four elements from which all physical things derive, each with its special qualities, produce four "humors" or fluids in the body: earth (cold and dry) "hath dominion" over the humor melancholy or black bile, water (cold and moist) over phlegm, air (hot and moist) over blood, and fire (hot and dry) over choler or yellow bile. In a healthy man or woman, the humors continue in a right proportion of nature, but if one humor breaks out and overspreads the personality, the result is sickness, distemper: the man becomes passionately melancholic, phlegmatic, sanguine, or choleric. Well before the comedy of humors

---

[5] See A. C. Howell, "*Res et Verba*: Words and Things," *ELH*, XIII (1946), 131–42.

created by Jonson, Chapman, Marston, and others in the late 1590's and early 1600's, the term humor had escaped the tidiness of medical theory and accumulated complex literary associations—for example, with type-characters in Roman comedy (as in the prologue to *Ralph Roister Doister*, c. 1553) and with allegorical figures of the morality play (as in Nashe's prose satiric-fantasy *Pierre Penniless*, 1592). It came generically to mean diseased or unbalanced egotism of some sort—comic vainglory or a monstrous, possibly evil compulsion, real or affected. Secondarily, it might mean an eccentricity, a socially unacceptable quirk, whim, tic, or mannerism in individuals or types, especially in the Theophrastan prose "characters" revived in the early 1600's by Bishop Hall and Sir Thomas Overbury and popular throughout the seventeenth century. In *Every Man out of his Humor* (1599) Jonson carefully distinguished the two meanings, defining true humor as an ethically diseased monomania that individuates, is "peculiar" to a man; but despite his authority, the term humor mellowed toward the socially typical and harmlessly eccentric. The definition of a man of humor in Butler's *Characters* (1677–80, pub. 1759) is transitional: "a peculiar fantastic, that has a wonderful natural affection to some particular kind of folly, to which he applies himself and in time becomes eminent. 'Tis commonly some outlying whimsy of Bedlam that, being tame and unhurtful, is suffered to go at liberty." A more genial and fond twentieth-century slang-meaning, as in "He's a character," is present in Corbyn Morris's discussion of humor in 1748.

Dryden's usage, as one might expect, is compromising and contextual (see p. 88). It ranges from a generically noble or neutral sense ("the soul of poesy . . . is imitation of humor and passions") to an equation of humor with whatever quality of character deserves ridicule. Generally, "by humor is meant some extravagant habit, passion, or affection, particular (as I said before) to some one person, by the oddness of which he is immediately distinguished from the rest of men." It usually provokes laughter, "as all things which are deviations from common customs," but not necessarily: "laughter is only accidental, as the person represented is fantastic or bizarre, but pleasure is essential to it as the imitation of what is natural." Humor has the generality of ἦθος in Greek New Comedy; but the Moderns excel the Ancients in variety and subtlety of individuation, especially the English, and among the English, especially Jonson and Chaucer.[6] Dryden's argument was continued and refined by Sir

---

[6] Sir William Temple believed that "Shakespeare was the first that opened this vein upon our stage."

William Temple (*Of Poetry,* 1692) who grounds the superiority of English humor in a stubborn originality and individualism within the national character and therefore in the honest variety of English life, in the liberty of England's government, and in the variability of its climate. Humor is "a picture of particular life, as comedy is of general." Temple was followed, in turn, by Dennis and, finally, by Congreve (see p. 174) for whom humor is a just imitation of the particular and extravagant diversities really to be found among men, especially Englishmen. Humor "shows us as we are." In humor, an individual is drawn after the life, in all his particularity, yet at the same time, human nature is realized as a type within the particular. Such humor is not easily discriminated, ever: it would be "the work of a long life to make one comedy true in all its parts and give every character in it a true and distinct humor." Yet it is found more in English comic writers because of "the greater freedom, privilege, and liberty which the common people of England enjoy. Any man that has a humor is under no restraint or fear of giving it vent." [7] In a society in which people are free to be eccentrically themselves, nature's diversities spring into actual view, ready for copying.

Nature, delightful oddity or grotesqueness (usually harmless but sometimes, as in Swift and Hogarth, sharply satirized), individuality, the variety of eccentric or irrational life springing wild from the liberty diffused through common English society—humor throughout the eighteenth century in England exploits such notions in a climate of growing benevolism. In *Intelligencer* 3 (1728), his defense of "low" humor in Gay's *The Beggar's Opera,* Swift protested chauvinistic definitions, and citing Cervantes, Rabelais, and the *commedia dell'arte,* argued that each nation, not England alone, cultivates its own manner of humor: humor is nature. But that humor-characters, at their best, were somehow natively English continued a commonplace. For example, Boswell's biographical image of Johnson—Mr. Oddity, a true-born Englishman—owes much to the tradition.

Corbyn Morris, Boswell's friend, seems first to have articulated the distinction between a "humorist" or humor-character and his creator "the man of humor." During the century humor was gradually generalized to include the artist's state of mind or character, or even genius itself: Tristram Shandy, for example, apostrophizes not the Muse, but the spirit of "native humor." Later in the century humor coalesced, as in Morgann's essay on Falstaff (see p. 572), with an idea of "natural," Shakespearean characterization as

---

[7] *Cf.* Shaftesbury, pp. 213–15.

a three-dimensional grasp of latent, irrational, organic peculiarities in an individual.

By a humorist, Morris specifically had in mind a splenetic, proud English type, contemptuous of a mad or drunken world in which he affects to be the only man sober, though in fact, if carried to excess, his humor would be madness. He nevertheless is a lover of reason and liberty with the honest courage to cry out against abuses and to be himself. A kind of inverted benevolist, rough-mannered and hypersensitive, he lives in terror of defeat and contempt from others, for "it sets him upon suspecting himself." The type suggests Matthew Bramble in Smollett's *The Expedition of Humphrey Clinker* or the Man in Black in Goldsmith's *The Citizen of the World*. Morris's own examples, however—Addison's Sir Roger de Coverley, Falstaff, Don Quixote—lean toward a slightly different type, the "amiable humorist," [8] whose foibles are "not mischievous or sneaking, but free, jocund, and liberal, and such as result from a generous flow of spirits and a warm universal benevolence." Morris's theory anticipates the good-natured and lovable (if ironically contemplated and often battered) eccentrics who stride through the eighteenth-century comic novel—Parson Adams, Commodore Trunnion, Uncle Toby and all the Shandys, Geoffrey Wildgoose, Dr. Primrose—usually older men as sexless as a child, often crusty and blunt, but despite their manias, inwardly gentle, charitable, good-hearted. The type is still vital in Austen, Thackeray, and Dickens, who all three, incidentally, like Fielding before and Twain afterward, began their careers by writing burlesque and parody. Hutcheson's theory of laughter was taken over by mid-century critics partly because it justified the pitiably affectionate, sympathetic, and later "picturesque" mirth, the healthy vent of kindly emotion, which "highest" humor was thought to elicit. As Meredith would later say of the humor-character (*An Essay on Comedy*, 1877):

> If you laugh all round him, tumble him, roll him about, deal
> him a smack, and drop a tear on him, own his likeness to you,
> and yours to your neighbor, spare him as little as you shun,
> pity him as much as you expose, it is a spirit of Humor that
> is moving you.

To get inside the term *wit*, in all its befuddling multiplicity, is to near the heart of Renaissance literary intelligence in England and

---

[8] See the comprehensive study by Stuart M. Tave, *The Amiable Humorist: A Study in the Comic Theory and Criticism of the Eighteenth and Early Nineteenth Centuries* (Chicago, 1960).

Augustan redactions of it. *Humor,* however, a standard of judgment in comedy inverted to a standard of sympathy, thrusts beyond the eighteenth century.

* * * *

SIR WILLIAM DAVENANT (1606–1668)[1]

FROM

Gondibert, a Heroic Poem:
the Author's Preface to his Much Honored Friend, Mr. Hobbes [1650]

But first give me leave (remembering with what difficulty the world can show any heroic poem, that in a perfect glass[2] of Nature gives us a familiar and easy view of ourselves) to take notice of those quarrels which the living have with the dead. And I will (according as all times have applied their reverence) begin with Homer, who though he seems to me standing upon the poets' famous hill, like the eminent sea-mark by which they have in former ages steered; and though he ought not to be removed from that eminence, lest posterity should presumptuously mistake their course; yet some (sharply observing how his successors have proceeded no farther than a perfection of imitating him) say that as sea-marks are chiefly useful to coasters, and serve not those who have the ambition of discoverers, that love to sail in untried seas, so he hath proved a guide for those whose satisfied Wit will not venture beyond the track of others, than to them who affect a new and remote way of thinking, who esteem it a deficiency and meanness of mind to stay and depend upon the authority of example. . . .

Having described the outward frame [of the poem *Gondibert*], the large rooms within, the lesser conveyances, and now the furniture, it were orderly to let you examine the matter of which that furniture is made. But though every owner who hath the vanity to

---

[1] Poet laureate to Charles I, driven to Parisian exile during much of the civil war. His opera *The Siege of Rhodes* (1656) helped revive drama in England, especially heroic plays: he became poet laureate to Charles II after the Restoration. His epic poem *Gondibert* was composed in Paris; its preface, together with Hobbes's *Answer,* forecast the new aesthetic in England.

[2] mirror.

show his ornaments or hangings must endure the curiosity and censure of him that beholds them, yet I shall not give you the trouble of inquiring what is, but tell you what I designed their substance, which is, Wit. And Wit is the laborious and lucky resultances of thought, having towards its excellence (as we say of the strokes of painting) as well a happiness as care.

Wit is not only the luck and labor, but also the dexterity of thought, rounding the world like the sun, with unimaginable motion, and bringing swiftly home to the memory universal surveys. It is the soul's powder[3] which when suppressed (as forbidden from flying upward) blows up the restraint and loseth all force in a farther ascension towards Heaven, and yet by nature is much less able to make any inquisition downward towards Hell, but breaks through all about it (as far as the utmost it can reach), removes, uncovers, makes way for light where darkness was inclosed, till great bodies are more examinable by being scattered into parcels,[4] and till all that find its strength (but most of mankind are strangers to Wit, as Indians are to powder) worship it for the effects, as derived from the Deity. It is in divines, humility, exemplariness, and moderation; in statesmen, gravity, vigilance, benign complacency,[5] secrecy, patience, and dispatch; in leaders of armies, valor, painfulness,[6] temperance, bounty, dexterity in punishing and rewarding, and a sacred certitude of promise. It is in poets a full comprehension of all recited in all these, and an ability to bring those comprehensions into action, when they shall so far forget the true measure of what is of greatest consequence to humanity (which are things righteous, pleasant, and useful) as to think the delights of greatness equal to that of poesy, or the chiefs of any profession more necessary to the world than excellent poets. Lastly, though Wit be not the envy of ignorant men, 'tis often of evil statesmen and of all such imperfect great spirits as have it in a less degree than poets; for though no man envies the excellence of that which in no proportion he ever tasted (as men cannot be said to envy the condition of angels) yet we may say the Devil envies the supremacy of God because he was in some degree partaker of His Glory. . . .

But I will proceed no farther . . . in recording mistakes, lest finding so many more than there be verities, we might believe we walk in as great obscurity as the Egyptians when darkness was their

---

[3] gunpowder.
[4] parts, pieces.
[5] disposition to please, civility.
[6] laborious exertion.

plague.[7] Nor will I presume to call the matter of which the ornaments or substantial parts of this poem are composed, Wit; but only tell you my endeavor was, in bringing Truth, too often absent, home to men's bosoms, to lead her through unfrequented and new ways and from the most remote shades, by representing Nature, though not in an affected, yet in an unusual dress.

* * * *

THOMAS HOBBES (1588–1679)
FROM
Treatise of Human Nature [1650]

FROM CHAPTER X, SECTION 3

The contrary [to dullness] . . . is that quick ranging of mind described chapter iv, section 3, which is joined with curiosity of comparing the things that come into the mind, one with another; in which comparison a man delighteth himself either with finding unexpected similitude of things otherwise much unlike, in which men place the excellence of *fancy* and from whence proceed those grateful [1] similes, metaphors, and other tropes by which both poets and orators have it in their power to make things please or displease, and show well or ill to others, as they like themselves; or else in discerning suddenly dissimilitude in things that otherwise appear the same. And this virtue of the mind is that by which men attain to exact and perfect knowledge; and the pleasure thereof consisteth in continual instruction, and in distinction of places, persons, and seasons, and is commonly termed by the name of *judgment*. For to judge is nothing else but to distinguish or discern; and both *fancy* and *judgment* are commonly comprehended under the name of *wit*, which seemeth to be a tenuity[2] and agility of spirits contrary to that restiness[3] of the spirits supposed in those that are dull.

---

[7] Exodus, 10:21–23.
[1] pleasing.
[2] rare fineness.
[3] sluggishness.

* * * *

JOHN DRYDEN (1631–1700)
FROM
Annus Mirabilis [1667]

—◦◦§◦◦—

from Preface

The composition of all poems is, or ought to be, of wit; and wit in the poet, or *wit writing* (if you will give me leave to use a school-distinction) is no other than the faculty of imagination in the writer, which, like a nimble spaniel, beats over and ranges through the field of memory, till it springs the quarry it hunted after; or, without metaphor, which searches over all the memory for the spe cies or ideas of those things which it designs to represent. *Wit written* is that which is well defined, the happy result of thought, or product of imagination. But to proceed from wit, in the general notion of it, to the proper wit of a heroic or historical poem, I judge it chiefly to consist in the delightful imaging of persons, actions, passions, or things. 'Tis not the jerk or sting of an epigram, nor the seeming contradiction of a poor antithesis (the delight of an ill-judging audience in a play of rhyme), nor the jingle of a more poor *paronomasia;*[1] neither is it so much the morality of a grave sentence, affected by Lucan, but more sparingly used by Virgil; but it is some lively and apt description, dressed in such colors of speech that it sets before your eyes the absent object, as perfectly, and more delightfully than nature.[2] So then, the first happiness of the poet's imagination is properly invention, or finding of the thought; the second is fancy, or the variation, deriving, or molding, of that thought, as the judgment represents it proper to the subject; the third is elocution, or the art of clothing and adorning that thought, so found and varied, in apt, significant, and sounding words: the quickness of the imagination is seen in the invention, the fertility in the fancy, and the accuracy in the expression. For the two first of these, Ovid is famous among the poets; for the latter, Virgil.

---

[1] pun.
[2] The rhetorical concept of *enargeia* or pictorial vividness. See Hagstrum, *The Sister Arts,* p. 179, and in general pp. 10–13, 134–40.

Ovid images more often the movements and affections of the mind, either combating between two contrary passions, or extremely discomposed by one. His words therefore are the least part of his care; for he pictures nature in disorder, with which the study and choice of words is inconsistent. This is the proper wit of dialogue or discourse, and consequently of the drama, where all that is said is supposed to be the effect of sudden thought; which, though it excludes not the quickness of wit in repartees, yet admits not a too curious election of words, too frequent allusions, or use of tropes, or, in fine, anything that shows remoteness of thought or labor in the writer.

* * * *

ISAAC BARROW (1630–1677)[1]

FROM

Sermon against Foolish Talking and Jesting [1669?]

But first it may be demanded what the thing we speak of is, or what this *facetiousness* doth import?[2] To which question I might reply as Democritus did to him that asked the definition of a man: " 'Tis that which we all see and know": anyone better apprehends what it is by acquaintance than I can inform him by description. It is indeed a thing so versatile and multiform, appearing in so many shapes, so many postures, so many garbs, so variously apprehended by several eyes and judgments, that it seemeth no less hard to settle a clear and certain notion thereof than to make a portrait of Proteus or to define the figure of the fleeting air. Sometimes it lieth in pat

---

[1] One of the most learned, and endearing, men of his age, one-time professor of Greek, Master of Trinity College and founder of its library, expert also in medicine and Arabic. In 1669 he resigned a professorial chair in mathematics to Sir Isaac Newton, to devote himself to theology and sermons, for which he became famous as a "latitudinarian" and a long speaker. Because of his royalist sympathies, he had traveled during the civil war, as far as Turkey; "his wit," Tillotson said, "was pure and peaceable," who adds that he was "intemperate in the love of fruit" and "free too in the use of tobacco, believing it did help to regulate his thinking." Barrow's sermon on wit was quoted, or borrowed from, by Swift, Addison, Hutcheson, Corbyn Morris, Boswell, later Coleridge, Hazlitt, and Leigh Hunt; he was a favorite of Fielding.

[2] Previously Barrow has said that in "this pleasant and jocular age" which is "so infinitely addicted to this sort of speaking," all reputation appears "to veil and stoop to that of being a wit: to be learned, to be wise, to be good, are nothing in comparison thereto."

allusion to a known story, or in seasonable application of a trivial saying, or in forging an apposite tale; sometimes it playeth in words and phrases, taking advantage from the ambiguity of their sense or the affinity of their sound; sometimes it is wrapped in a dress of humorous expression; sometimes it lurketh under an odd similitude; sometimes it is lodged in a sly question, in a smart answer, in a quirkish reason, in a shrewd imitation, in cunningly diverting or cleverly retorting an objection; sometimes it is couched in a bold scheme of speech, in a tart irony, in a lusty hyperbole, in a startling metaphor, in a plausible reconciling of contradictions, or in acute nonsense; sometimes a scenical representation of persons or things, a counterfeit speech, a mimical look or gesture passeth for it; sometimes an affected simplicity, sometimes a presumptuous bluntness giveth it being; sometimes it riseth only from a lucky hitting upon what is strange, sometimes from a crafty wresting obvious matter to the purpose; often it consisteth in one knows not what and springeth up one can hardly tell how. Its ways are unaccountable and inexplicable, being answerable to the numberless rovings of fancy and windings of language. It is, in short, a manner of speaking, out of the simple and plain way (such as reason teacheth and proveth things by), which, by a pretty surprising uncouthness in conceit or expression, doth affect and amuse the fancy, stirring in it some wonder and breeding some delight thereto. It raiseth admiration, as signifying a nimble sagacity of apprehension, a special felicity of invention, a vivacity of spirit, and reach of wit more than vulgar, it seeming to argue a rare quickness of parts that one can fetch in remote conceits applicable, a notable skill that he can dexterously accommodate them to the purpose before him, together with a lively briskness of humor not apt to damp those sportful flashes of imagination. (Whence in Aristotle[3] such persons are termed ἐπιδέξιοι, "dexterous men," and εὔτροποι, men of facile or versatile manners who can "easily turn" themselves to all things or turn all things to themselves.) It also procureth delight by gratifying curiosity with its rareness or semblance of difficulty (as monsters not for their beauty but their rarity, as juggling tricks not for their use but their abstruseness, are beheld with pleasure); by diverting the mind from its road by serious thoughts; by instilling gaiety and airiness of spirit; by provoking to such dispositions of spirit in way of emulation or complaisance; and by seasoning matters, otherwise distasteful or insipid, with an unusual, and thence grateful tang. . . .

Facetiousness is allowable when it is the most proper instrument

---

[3] *Nichomachean Ethics*, IV, viii, 3.

of exposing things apparently base and vile to due contempt. It is many times expedient that things really ridiculous should appear such, that they may be sufficiently loathed and shunned, and to render them such is the part of a facetious wit, and usually can only be compassed thereby. When to impugn them with downright reason or to check them by serious discourse would signify nothing, then representing them in a shape strangely ugly to the fancy, and thereby raising derision at them, may effectually discountenance them. Thus did the prophet Elias expose the wicked superstition of those who worshipped Baal: "Elias (sayeth the text) mocked them, and said, 'Cry aloud, for he is a god; either he is talking, or he is pursuing, or he is in a journey, or peradventure he sleeps, and must be awaked.'" [4] By which one pregnant instance, it appeareth that reasoning, pleasantly abusive, in some cases may be useful. The Holy Scripture doth not indeed use it frequently (it not suiting the divine simplicity and stately gravity thereof to do so); yet its condescension thereto at any time sufficiently doth authorize a cautious use thereof. When sarcastical twitches are needful to pierce the thick skins of men, to correct their lethargic stupidity, to rouse them out of their drowsy negligence, then may they well be applied; when plain declarations will not enlighten people to discern the truth and weight of things, and blunt arguments will not penetrate to convince or persuade them to their duty, then doth reason freely resign its place to wit, allowing it to undertake its work of instruction and reproof. . . .

If it be lawful (as by the best authorities it plainly doth appear to be) in using rhetorical schemes, poetical strains, involutions of sense in allegories, fables, parables and riddles, to discoast[5] from the plain and simple way of speech, why may not facetiousness, issuing from the same principles, directed to the same ends, serving to like purposes, be likewise used blamelessly? If those exorbitancies of speech may be accommodated to instill good doctrine into the head, to excite good passions in the heart, to illustrate and adorn the truth in a delightful and taking way, and facetious discourse be sometime notoriously conducible to the same ends, why, they being retained, should it be rejected? especially considering how difficult often it may be to distinguish those forms of discourse from this, or exactly to define the limits which sever rhetoric and raillery. Some elegant figures and tropes of rhetoric (biting sarcasms, sly ironies,

---

[4] I Kings 18:27.
[5] depart.

strong metaphors, lofty hyperboles, paronomasias, oxymorons, and the like, frequently used by the best speakers and not seldom even by sacred writers) do lie very near upon the confines of jocularity, and are not easily differenced from those sallies of wit wherein the lepid [6] way doth consist; so that were this wholly culpable, it would be matter of scruple[7] whether one hath committed a fault or no when he meant only to play the orator or the poet, and hard surely it would be to find a judge who could precisely set out the difference between a jest and a flourish.

I shall only add that, of old, even the sagest and gravest persons (persons of most rigid and severe virtue) did much affect this kind of discourse and did apply it to noble purposes. The great introducer of moral wisdom among the pagans[8] did practice it so much (by it, repressing the windy pride and fallacious vanity of sophisters in his time) that he thereby got the name of ὁ εἴρων, "the droll"; and the rest of those who pursued his design do by numberless stories and apophthegms recorded of them appear well skilled and much delighted in this way. Many great princes (as Augustus Caesar for one, many of whose jests are extant in Macrobius), many grave statesmen (as Cicero particularly, who composed several books of jests), many famous captains (as Fabius M. Cato the censor, Scipio Africanus, Epaminondas, Themistocles, Phocion, and many others whose witty sayings, together with their martial exploits, are reported by historians) have pleased themselves herein and made it a condiment of their weighty businesses. So that practicing thus (within certain rule and compass), we cannot err without great patterns and mighty patrons.[9] . . .

To conclude, as we need not be demure, so must we not be impudent; as we should not be sour, so ought we not to be fond: as we may be free, so we should not be vain; as we may well stoop to friendly complaisance, so we should take heed of falling into contemptible levity. If without wronging others or derogating from ourselves, we can be facetious; if we can use our wits in jesting innocently and conveniently,[1] we may sometimes do it; but let us, in

---

[6] jocose.
[7] hard to decide.
[8] Socrates.
[9] The two greatest men and gravest divines of their time (St. Gregory Nazianzus and St. Basil) could entertain one another with facetious epistles. (Barrow's note.)
[1] with propriety.

compliance with St. Paul's direction, beware of "foolish talking and jesting, which are not convenient." [2]

* * * *

WILLIAM CONGREVE (1670–1729) [1]
Letter to Mr. Dennis,
Concerning Humor in Comedy [July 10, 1695][2]

—◦◦❧❧◦◦—

DEAR SIR:

You write to me that you have entertained yourself two or three days with reading several comedies of several authors, and your observation is that there is more of humor in our English writers than in any of the other comic poets, ancient or modern. You desire to know my opinion and, at the same time, my thought of that which is generally called humor in a comedy.

I agree with you in an impartial preference of our English writers in that particular. But if I tell you my thoughts of humor, I must at the same time confess that what I take for true humor has not been so often written, even by them, as is generally believed, and some who have valued themselves, and have been esteemed by others, for that kind of writing have seldom touched upon it. To make this appear to the world would require a long and labored discourse, and such as I neither am able nor willing to undertake. But such little remarks as may be contained within the compass of a letter, and such unpremeditated thoughts as may be communicated between friend and friend, without incurring the censure of the world or setting up for a dictator, you shall have from me since you have enjoined it.

To define humor perhaps were as difficult as to define wit, for like that, it is of infinite variety. To enumerate the several humors of men were a work as endless as to sum up their several opinions.

---

² Ephesians 5:4, the text of the sermon.

¹ The famous playwright, born and educated in Ireland.

² In the 1690's Dennis addressed letters to Congreve, Dryden, Wycherley, and Walter Moyle which, together with answers, were published as *Letters Upon Several Occasions* (1696), with a preface by Dennis on the art of letter-writing.

And in my mind, the *quot homines, tot sententiae*[3] might have been more properly interpreted of humor, since there are many men of the same opinion in many things who are yet quite different in humors. But though we cannot certainly tell what wit is or what humor is, yet we may go near to show something which is not wit or not humor and yet often mistaken for both. And since I have mentioned wit and humor together, let me make the first distinction between them and observe to you that *wit is often mistaken for humor.*

I have observed that when a few things have been wittily and pleasantly spoken by any character in a comedy, it has been very usual for those who make their remarks on a play while it is acting to say, "Such a thing is very humorously spoken. There is a great deal of humor in that part." Thus the character of the person speaking, [as it] may be surprisingly and pleasantly, is mistaken for a character of humor, which indeed is a character of wit. But there is a great difference between a comedy wherein there are many things humorously (as they call it, which is [to say] pleasantly) spoken, and one where there are several characters of humor, distinguished by the particular and different humors appropriated [4] to the several persons represented, and which naturally arise from the different constitutions, complexions, and dispositions of men. The saying of humorous things does not distinguish characters, for every person in a comedy may be allowed to speak them. From a witty man they are expected, and even a fool may be permitted to stumble on 'em by chance. Though I make a difference betwixt wit and humor, yet I do not think that humorous characters exclude wit. No, but the manner of wit should be adapted to the humor. As, for instance, a character of a splenetic and peevish humor should have a satyrical wit. A jolly and sanguine humor should have a facetious wit. The former should speak positively,[5] the latter carelessly. For the former observes and shows things as they are; the latter rather overlooks Nature and speaks things as he would have them, and his wit and humor have both of them a less alloy of judgment than the other's.

As wit, so its opposite *folly is sometimes mistaken for humor.*

When a poet brings a character on the stage committing a thousand absurdities and talking impertinencies, roaring aloud and

---

[3] "as many opinions as there are men."

[4] made or shown to be proper.

[5] in a dogmatic or peremptory manner.

laughing immoderately on every or rather upon no occasion—this is a character of humor.[6]

Is anything more common than to have a pretended comedy stuffed with such grotesque figures and farce fools? things that either are not in Nature or, if they are, are monsters and births of mischance, and consequently as such should be stifled and huddled out of the way, like sooterkins,[7] that mankind may not be shocked with an appearing possibility of the degeneration of a Godlike species. For my part, I am as willing to laugh as anybody, and as easily diverted with an object truly ridiculous, but at the same time I can never care for seeing things that force me to entertain low thoughts of my nature. I don't know how it is with others, but I confess freely to you I could never look long upon a monkey without very mortifying reflections, though I never heard anything to the contrary why that creature is not originally of a distinct species. As I don't think humor exclusive of wit, neither do I think it inconsistent with folly, but I think the follies should be only such as men's humors may incline 'em to, and not follies entirely abstracted from both humor and Nature.

Sometimes *personal defects are misrepresented for humor.*

I mean, sometimes characters are barbarously exposed on the stage, ridiculing natural deformities, casual defects in the senses, and infirmities of age. Sure the poet must both be very ill-natured himself, and think his audience so, when he proposes by showing a man deformed, or deaf, or blind, to give them an agreeable entertainment, and hopes to raise their mirth by what is truly an object of compassion. But much need not be said upon this head to anybody, especially to you who in one of your letters to me,[8] concerning Mr. Jonson's *Fox*,[9] have justly excepted against this immoral part of ridicule in Corbaccio's character; and there I must agree with you to blame him, whom otherwise I cannot enough admire for his great mastery of true humor in comedy.

External habit of body is often mistaken for humor.

By external habit I do not mean the ridiculous dress or clothing of a character, though that goes a good way in some received characters. (But undoubtedly a man's humor may incline him to dress

---

[6] The tone is ironical.

[7] It was a fabulous joke that Dutch women, who, to keep warm, sat with a stove under their petticoats, secretly gave birth to mouselike creatures called "sooterkins." See Pope's *Dunciad*, I, 126.

[8] Reprinted in E. N. Hooker, *Critical Works of Dennis*, II, 384–85.

[9] *Volpone.*

differently from other people.) But I mean a singularity of manners, speech, and behavior peculiar to all or most of the same country, trade, profession, or education. I cannot think that a humor which is only a habit, or disposition contracted by use or custom; for by a disuse or compliance with other customs, it may be worn off or diversified.

Affectation is generally mistaken for humor.

These are indeed so much alike that, at a distance, they may be mistaken one for the other. For what is humor in one may be affectation in another, and nothing is more common than for some to affect particular ways of saying and doing things peculiar to others whom they admire and would imitate. Humor is the life, affectation the picture. He that draws a character of affectation shows humor at the second hand; he at best but publishes a translation, and his pictures are but copies.

But as these two last distinctions are the nicest,[1] so it may be most proper to explain them by particular instances from some author of reputation. Humor I take either to be born with us, and so of a natural growth, or else to be grafted into us by some accidental change in the constitution or revolution of the internal habit of body, by which it becomes, if I may so call it, naturalized.

Humor is from Nature, habit from custom, and affectation from industry.

Humor shows us as we *are*.

Habit shows us as we appear under a forcible impression.[2]

Affectation shows what we would be[3] under a voluntary disguise.

Though here I would observe, by the way, that a continued affectation may in time become a habit.

The character of Morose in *The Silent Woman* I take to be a character of humor. And I choose to instance this character to you from many others of the same author because I know it has been condemned by many as unnatural and farce. And you have yourself hinted some dislike of it for the same reason, in a letter to me concerning some of Jonson's plays.

Let us suppose Morose to be a man naturally splenetic and melancholy; is there anything more offensive to one of such a disposition than noise and clamor? Let any man that has the spleen (and there are enough in England) be judge. We see common examples of this humor, in little, every day. 'Tis ten to one, but three parts in

---

[1] most subtle.
[2] compulsion (from *impress*, "to compel one to enter the army or navy").
[3] wish to be.

four of the company that you dine with are discomposed and startled at the cutting of a cork, or scratching a plate with a knife. It is a proportion of the same humor that makes such or any other noise offensive to the person that hears it, for there are others who will not be disturbed at all by it. Well, but Morose, you will say, is so extravagant he cannot bear any discourse or conversation above a whisper. Why, it is his excess of this humor that makes him become ridiculous, and qualifies his character for comedy. If the poet had given him but a moderate proportion of that humor, 'tis odds but half the audience would have sided with the character, and have condemned the author, for exposing a humor which was neither remarkable nor ridiculous. Besides, the distance of the stage requires the figure represented to be something larger than the life, and sure a picture may have features larger in proportion and yet be very like the original. If this exactness of quantity were to be observed in wit, as some would have it in humor, what would become of those characters that are designed for men of wit? I believe if a poet should steal a dialogue of any length from the *extempore* discourse of the two wittiest men upon earth, he would find the scene but coldly received by the town. But to the purpose.

The character of Sir John Daw in the same play is a character of affectation. He everywhere discovers an affectation of learning, when he is not only conscious to himself, but the audience also plainly perceives that he is ignorant. Of this kind are the characters of Thraso in the *Eunuch* of Terence, and Pyrgopolinices in the *Miles Gloriosus* of Plautus. They affect to be thought valiant when both themselves and the audience know they are not. Now, such a boasting of valor in men who were really valiant would undoubtedly be a humor, for a fiery disposition might naturally throw a man into the same extravagance which is only affected in the characters I have mentioned.

The character of Cob in *Every Man in his Humour* and most of the under characters in *Bartholomew Fair* discover only a singularity of manners appropriated to the several educations and professions of the persons represented. They are not humors but habits contracted by custom. Under this head may be ranged all country clowns, sailors, tradesmen, jockeys, gamesters, and such like, who make use of cants or peculiar dialects in their several arts and vocations. One may almost give a receipt[4] for the composition of such

---

[4] recipe, formula.

a character. For the poet has nothing to do but to collect a few proper phrases and terms of art, and to make the person apply them by ridiculous metaphors in his conversation with characters of different natures. Some late characters of this kind have been very successful, but in my mind they may be painted without much art or labor, since they require little more than a good memory and superficial observation. But true humor cannot be shown without a dissection of Nature and a narrow search to discover the first seeds from whence it has its root and growth.

If I were to write to the world, I should be obliged to dwell longer upon each of these distinctions and examples, for I know that they would not be plain enough to all readers. But a bare hint is sufficient to inform you of the notions which I have on this subject. And I hope by this time you are of my opinion, that humor is neither wit, nor folly, nor personal defect, nor affectation, nor habit, and yet that each and all of these have been both written and received for humor.

I should be unwilling to venture even on a bare description of humor, much more to make a definition of it, but now my hand is in, I'll tell you what serves me instead of either. I take it to be *a singular and unavoidable manner of doing or saying anything, peculiar and natural to one man only, by which his speech and actions are distinguished from those of other men.*

Our humor has relation to us and to what proceeds from us as the accidents have to a substance; it is a color, taste, and smell diffused through all; though our actions are never so many and different in form, they are all splinters of the same wood and have naturally one complexion, which, though it may be disguised by art, yet cannot be wholly changed. We may paint it with other colors, but we cannot change the grain. So the natural sound of an instrument will be distinguished, though the notes expressed by it are never so various and the divisions never so many. Dissimulation may by degrees become more easy to our practice, but it can never absolutely transubstantiate us into what we would seem: it will always be, in some proportion, a violence upon Nature.

A man may change his opinion, but I believe he will find it a difficulty to part with his humor, and there is nothing more provoking than the being made sensible of that difficulty. Sometimes one shall meet with those who, perhaps innocently enough but at the same time impertinently, will ask the question: "Why are you not merry? Why are you not gay, pleasant, and cheerful?" Then, instead of answering, could I ask such a one: "Why are you not handsome? Why have you not black eyes and a better complexion?" Nature abhors to be forced.

The two famous philosophers of Ephesus and Abdera[5] have their different sects at this day. Some weep and others laugh at one and the same thing.

I don't doubt but you have observed several men laugh when they are angry, others who are silent, some that are loud; yet I cannot suppose that it is the passion of anger which is in itself different, or more or less in one than t'other, but that it is the humor of the man that is predominant, and urges him to express it in that manner. Demonstrations of pleasure are as various: one man has a humor of retiring from all company when anything has happened to please him beyond expectation; he hugs himself alone and thinks it an addition to the pleasure to keep it secret. Another is upon thorns till he has made proclamation of it, and must make other people sensible of his happiness before he can be so himself. So it is in grief and other passions. Demonstrations of love and the effects of that passion upon several humors are infinitely different; but here the ladies who abound in servants are the best judges. Talking of the ladies, methinks something should be observed of the humor of the fair sex, since they are sometimes so kind as to furnish out a character for comedy. But I must confess I have never made any observation of what I apprehend to be true humor in women. Perhaps passions are too powerful in that sex to let humor have its course, or maybe, by reason of their natural coldness, humor cannot exert itself to that extravagant degree which it often does in the male sex. For if ever anything does appear comical or ridiculous in a woman, I think it is little more than an acquired folly or an affectation. We may call them the weaker sex, but I think the true reason is because our follies are stronger and our faults are more prevailing.

One might think that the diversity of humor, which must be allowed to be diffused throughout mankind, might afford endless matter for the support of comedies. But when we come closely to consider that point, and nicely to distinguish the difference of humors, I believe we shall find the contrary. For though we allow every man something of his own and a peculiar humor, yet every

[5] Heraclitus of Ephesus (fl. 500 B.C.), known as "the weeping philosopher" because of his gloomy view of the human condition, and Democritus of Abdera (fl. 5th cent. B.C.), known as "the laughing philosopher" because of his scornful view of human follies.

man has it not in quantity to become remarkable by it; or, if many do become remarkable by their humors, yet all those humors may not be diverting. Nor is it only requisite to distinguish what humor will be diverting, but also how much of it, what part of it to show in light and what to cast in shades, how to set it off by preparatory scenes and by opposing other humors to it in the same scene. Through a wrong judgment, sometimes men's humors may be opposed when there is really no specific difference between them, only a greater proportion of the same in one than t'other, occasioned by his having more phlegm or choler or whatever the constitution is from whence their humors derive their source.

There is infinitely more to be said on this subject, though perhaps I have already said too much; but I have said it to a friend who I am sure will not expose it if he does not approve of it. I believe the subject is entirely new and was never touched upon before, and if I would have anyone to see this private essay, it should be someone who might be provoked by my errors in it to publish a more judicious treatise on the subject. Indeed I wish it were done, that the world, being a little acquainted with the scarcity of true humor and the difficulty of finding and showing it, might look a little more favorably on the labors of them who endeavor to search into Nature for it, and lay it open to the public view.

I don't say but that very entertaining and useful characters, and proper for comedy, may be drawn from affectations and those other qualities which I have endeavored to distinguish from humor, but I would not have such imposed on the world for humor, nor esteemed of equal value with it. It were perhaps the work of a long life to make one comedy true in all its parts and to give every character in it a true and distinct humor. Therefore, every poet must be beholding to other helps to make out his number of ridiculous characters. But I think such a one deserves to be broke[6] who makes all false musters, who does not show one true humor in a comedy, but entertains his audience to the end of the play with everything out of Nature.

I will make but one observation to you more, and have done; and that is grounded upon an observation of your own, and which I mentioned at the beginning of my letter, viz., that there is more of humor in our English comic writers than in any others. I do not at all wonder at it, for I look upon humor to be almost of English growth; at least, it does not seem to have found such increase on

---

[6] broken in rank.

any other soil. And what appears to me to be the reason of it is the greater freedom, privilege, and liberty which the common people of England enjoy. Any man that has a humor is under no restraint or fear of giving it vent; they have a proverb among them which, may be, will show the bent and genius of the people as well as a longer discourse: "He that will have a Maypole shall have a Maypole." This is a maxim with them, and their practice is agreeable to it. I believe something considerable too may be ascribed to their feeding so much on flesh, and the grossness of their diet in general. But I have done; let the physicians agree [on] that. Thus you have my thoughts of humor, to my power of expressing them in so little time and compass. You will be kind to show me wherein I have erred, and as you are very capable of giving me instruction, so I think I have a very just title to demand it from you, being without reserve,

Your real friend and humble servant,
W. CONGREVE.

* * * *

JOSEPH ADDISON (1672–1719)
FROM *Spectator No.* 61

—◦🙤🙦◦—

Thursday, May 10, 1711

Aristotle, in the eleventh chapter of his book of *Rhetoric*, describes two or three kinds of puns, which he calls "paragrams," among the beauties of good writing, and produces instances of them out of some of the greatest authors in the Greek tongue. Cicero has sprinkled several of his works with puns, and in his book where he lays down the rules of oratory, quotes abundance of sayings as pieces of wit, which also upon examination prove arrant puns. But the age in which the pun chiefly flourished was the reign of King James the First. That learned monarch was himself a tolerable punster, and made very few bishops or privy-counsellors that had not some time or other signalized themselves by a clinch or a conundrum. It was therefore in this age that the pun appeared with pomp and dignity. It had before been admitted into merry speeches and ludicrous compositions, but was now delivered with great gravity from the pulpit, or pronounced in the most solemn manner at the council table. The greatest authors in their most serious works made frequent use of puns. The sermons of Bishop Andrews[1] and the tragedies of Shakespeare are full of them. The sinner was punned into repentance by the former, as in the latter nothing is more usual than to see a hero weeping and quibbling for a dozen lines together.

I must add to these great authorities, which seem to have given a kind of sanction to this piece of false wit, that all the writers of rhetoric have treated of punning with very great respect, and divided the several kinds of it into hard names that are reckoned among the figures of speech and recommended as ornaments of discourse. . . .

To account for this, we must consider that the first race of authors, who were the great heroes in writing, were destitute of all rules and arts of criticism; and for that reason, though they excel later writers in greatness of genius, they fall short of them in accuracy and correctness. The Moderns cannot reach their beauties but can avoid their imperfections. When the world was furnished with these authors of the first eminence, there grew up another set of writers who gained themselves a reputation by the remarks which they made on the works of those who preceded them. It was one of the employments of these secondary authors to distinguish the several kinds of wit by terms of art[2] and to consider them as more or less perfect according as they were founded in truth. It is no wonder therefore that even such authors as Isocrates, Plato, and Cicero should have such little blemishes as are not to be met with in authors of a much inferior character who have written since those several blemishes were discovered.

I do not find that there was a proper separation made between puns and true wit by any of the Ancient authors except Quintillian and Longinus. But when this distinction was once settled, it was very natural for all men of sense to agree in it. As for the revival of this false wit, it happened about the time of the Revival of Letters,[3] but as soon as it was once detected, it immediately vanished and disappeared. At the same time there is no question but as it has sunk in one age and rose in another, it will again recover itself in some distant period of time, as pedantry and ignorance shall prevail upon wit and sense. . . .

But to return to punning. Having pursued the history of a pun

---

[1] Lancelot Andrews (1555–1626), theologian and prose stylist, one of the group appointed by James I to translate the Bible.
[2] rhetoric.
[3] the Renaissance.

from its original to its downfall, I shall here define it to be a conceit arising from the use of two words that agree in the sound but differ in the sense. The only way therefore to try a piece of wit is to translate it into a different language. If it bears the test, you may pronounce it true; but if it vanishes in the experiment, you may conclude it to have been a pun.

* * * *

FROM *Spectator No. 62*

Friday, May 11, 1711

Scribendi recte sapere est et principium et fons.[4]

Mr. Locke has an admirable reflection upon the difference of wit and judgment, whereby he endeavors to show the reason why they are not always the talents of the same person. His words are as follows: "And hence, perhaps, may be given some reason of that common observation that men who have a great deal of wit and prompt memories have not always the clearest judgment or deepest reason. For wit lying most in the assemblage of ideas, and putting those together with quickness and variety wherein can be found any resemblance or congruity, thereby to make up pleasant pictures and agreeable visions in the fancy; judgment, on the contrary, lies quite on the other side, in separating carefully, one from another, ideas wherein can be found the least difference, thereby to avoid being misled by similitude and by affinity to take one thing for another. This is a way of proceeding quite contrary to metaphor and allusion, wherein, for the most part, lies that entertainment and pleasantry of wit which strikes so lively on the fancy, and is therefore so acceptable to all people." [5]

This is, I think, the best and most philosophical account that I have ever met with of wit, which generally, though not always, consists in such a resemblance and congruity of ideas as this author mentions. I shall only add to it, by way of explanation, that every resemblance of ideas is not that which we call wit unless it be such

---

[4] Horace, *Ars Poetica*, 309: "Wisdom is the origin and underlying principle of good writing."
[5] *An Essay Concerning Human Understanding*, II, xi, 2.

an one that gives *delight* and *surprise* to the reader. These two properties seem essential to wit, more particularly the last of them. In order therefore that the resemblance in the ideas be wit, it is necessary that the ideas should not lie too near one another in the nature of things, for where the likeness is obvious, it gives no surprise. To compare one man's singing to that of another, or to represent the whiteness of any object by that of milk and snow, or the variety of its colors by those of the rainbow, cannot be called wit, unless besides this obvious resemblance there be some further congruity discovered in the two ideas, that is capable of giving the reader some surprise. Thus, when a poet tells us the bosom of his mistress is as white as snow, there is no wit in the comparison, but when he adds, with a sigh, that it is as cold too, it then grows into wit. Every reader's memory may supply him with innumerable instances of the same nature. For this reason, the similitudes in heroic poets, who endeavor rather to fill the mind with great conceptions than to divert it with such as are new and surprising, have seldom anything in them that can be called wit. Mr. Locke's account of wit, with this short explanation, comprehends most of the species of wit, as metaphors, similitudes, allegories, enigmas, mottos, parables, fables, dreams, visions, dramatic writings, burlesque, and all the methods of allusion: as there are many other pieces of wit (how remote soever they may appear at first sight from the foregoing description) which, upon examination, will be found to agree with it.

As *true wit* generally consists in this resemblance and congruity of ideas, *false wit* chiefly consists in the resemblance and congruity sometimes of single letters, as in anagrams, chronograms, lipograms, and acrostics; sometimes of syllables, as in echoes and doggerel rhymes; sometimes of words, as in puns and quibbles; and sometimes of whole sentences or poems cast into the figures of eggs, axes, or altars. Nay, some carry the notion of wit so far as to ascribe it even to external mimicry, and to look upon a man as an ingenious person that can resemble the tone, posture, or face of another.

As *true wit* consists in the resemblance of ideas, and *false wit* in the resemblance of words, according to the foregoing instances, there is another kind of wit which consists partly in the resemblance of ideas and partly in the resemblance of words, which for distinction sake I shall call *mixed wit*. This kind of wit is that which abounds in Cowley more than in any author that ever wrote. Mr. Waller has likewise a great deal of it. Mr. Dryden is very sparing in it. Milton had a genius much above it. Spenser is in the same class with Milton. The Italians, even in their epic poetry, are full of it. Monsieur Boileau, who formed himself upon the Ancient poets, has everywhere rejected it with scorn. If we look after mixed wit among the Greek writers, we shall find it nowhere but in the epigrammatists. There are indeed some strokes of it in the little poem ascribed to Musaeus, which by that, as well as many other marks, betrays itself to be a Modern composition. If we look into the Latin writers, we find none of this mixed wit in Virgil, Lucretius, or Catullus, very little in Horace, but a great deal of it in Ovid, and scarce anything else in Martial.

Out of the innumerable branches of mixed wit, I shall choose one instance which may be met with in all the writers of this class. The passion of love, in its nature, has been thought to resemble fire, for which reason the words *fire* and *flame* are made to signify love. The witty poets therefore have taken an advantage from the doubtful meaning of the word *fire* to make an infinite number of witticisms. Cowley, observing the cold regard of his mistress's eyes and at the same time their power of producing love in him, considers them as burning-glasses made of ice; and finding himself able to live in the greatest extremities of love, concludes the torrid zone to be habitable. When his mistress has read his letter, written in juice of lemon, by holding it to the fire, he desires her to read it over a second time by love's flames. When she weeps, he wishes it were inward heat that distilled those drops from the limbeck. When she is absent, he is beyond eighty, that is, thirty degrees nearer the pole than when she is with him. His ambitious love is a fire that naturally mounts upwards; his happy love is the beams of Heaven, and his unhappy love flames of Hell. When it does not let him sleep, it is a flame that sends up no smoke; when it is opposed by counsel and advice, it is a fire that rages the more by the wind's blowing upon it. Upon the dying of a tree in which he had cut his loves, he observes that his written flames had burnt up and withered the tree. When he resolves to give over his passion, he tells us that one burnt like him forever dreads the fire. His heart is an Aetna that, instead of Vulcan's shop, encloses Cupid's forge in it. His endeavoring to drown his love in wine is throwing oil upon the fire. He would insinuate to his mistress that the fire of love, like that of the sun (which produces so many living creatures) should not only warm but beget. Love, in another place, cooks pleasure at his fire. Sometimes the poet's heart is frozen in every breast, and sometimes scorched in every eye. Sometimes he is drowned in tears, and burnt in love, like a ship set on fire in the middle of the sea.

The reader may observe in every one of these instances that the poet mixes the qualities of fire with those of love; and in the same sentence, speaking of it both as a passion and as real fire, surprises the reader with those seeming resemblances or contradictions that make up all the wit in this kind of writing. Mixed wit therefore is a composition of pun and true wit, and is more or less perfect as the resemblance lies in the ideas or in the words. Its foundations are laid partly in falsehood and partly in truth. Reason puts in her claim for one half of it, and extravagance for the other. The only province therefore for this kind of wit is epigram, or those little occasional poems that in their own nature are nothing else but a tissue of epigrams. I cannot conclude this head of *mixed wit* without owning that the admirable poet out of whom I have taken the examples of it had as much true wit as any author that ever writ, and indeed all other talents of an extraordinary genius.

It may be expected, since I am upon this subject, that I should take notice of Mr. Dryden's definition of wit, which, with all the deference that is due to the judgment of so great a man, is not so properly a definition of wit as of good writing in general. Wit, as he defines it, is "a propriety of words and thoughts adapted to the subject." [6] If this be a true definition of wit, I am apt to think that Euclid was the greatest wit that ever set pen to paper. It is certain that never was a greater propriety of words and thoughts adapted to the subject than what that author has made use of in his *Elements*. I shall only appeal to my reader if this definition agrees with any notion he has of wit. If it be a true one, I am sure Mr. Dryden was not only a better poet but a greater wit than Mr. Cowley, and Virgil a much more facetious man than either Ovid or Martial.

Bouhours,[7] whom I look upon to be the most penetrating of all the French critics, has taken pains to show that it is impossible for any thought to be beautiful which is not just, and has not its foundation in the nature of things; that the basis of all wit is truth; and that no thought can be valuable of which good sense is not the groundwork. Boileau has endeavored to inculcate the same notion in several parts of his writings, both in prose and verse. This is that natural way of writing, that beautiful simplicity, which we so much admire in the compositions of the Ancients, and which nobody de-

---

[6] See p. 98.

[7] Dominique Bouhours (1628–1702), French priest. His *Entretiens d'Artiste et d'Eugène* (1671) and *La Manière de bien penser dans les ouvrages d'esprit* (1687) popularized a *je ne sais quoi* taste for classic simplicity, beauty, and truth.

viates from but those who want strength of genius to make a thought shine in its own natural beauties. Poets who want this strength of genius to give that majestic simplicity to Nature, which we so much admire in the works of the Ancients, are forced to hunt after foreign ornaments, and not to let any piece of wit of what kind soever escape them. I look upon these writers as *Goths* in poetry, who, like those in architecture, not being able to come up to the beautiful simplicity of the old Greeks and Romans, have endeavored to supply its place with all the extravagances of an irregular fancy. . . .

I must not dismiss this subject without observing that as Mr. Locke, in the passage above-mentioned, has discovered the most fruitful source of wit, so there is another of a quite contrary nature to it, which does likewise branch itself out into several kinds. For not only the *resemblance* but the *opposition* of ideas does very often produce wit, as I could show in several little points, turns, and antitheses, that I may possibly enlarge upon in some future speculation.

* * * *

SIR RICHARD BLACKMORE (c. 1650–1729)[1]

FROM

Essays upon Several Subjects [1716]

from An Essay upon Wit

Though perhaps the talent which we call wit, like that of humor, is as clearly understood by its simple term as by the most labored description—an argument of which is this, that many ingenious persons, by their unsuccessful essays[2] to explain it, have rather obscured than illustrated its idea—I will notwithstanding adventure to give the definition of it, which, though it may fall short of perfection, yet I imagine will come nearer to it than any that has yet appeared. *Wit is a qualification of the mind that raises and enlivens*

---

[1] Physician, author of heroic poems—*Prince Arthur* (1695), *King Arthur* (1697), *Eliza* (1705), *Alfred* (1723)—and Longinian "sublime," reflective poems such as *The Nature of Man* (1711) in three books, *Creation, a Philosophical Poem* (1712) in seven books, *Redemption, a Divine Poem* (1722) in six books. In *Peri Bathous* Pope satirized him as the Homer of bathos.

[2] attempts.

*cold sentiments and plain propositions by giving them an elegant
and surprising turn.*

It is evident that wit cannot essentially consist in the justness
and propriety of the thoughts, that is, the conformity of our conceptions to the objects we conceive, for this is the definition of
Truth. . . . The addition of wit to proper subjects is like the
artful improvement of the cook who by his exquisite sauce gives to
a plain dish a pleasant and unusual relish. A man of this character
works on simple propositions a rich embroidery of flowers and
figures, and imitates the curious artist[3] who studs and inlays his prepared steel with devices of gold and silver. But wit is not only the
improvement of a plain piece by intellectual enameling; besides
this, it animates and warms a cold sentiment, and makes it glow
with life and vigor; and this it effects, as is expressed in the last part
of the definition, by giving it an elegant and surprising turn. It always conveys the thought of the speaker or writer clothed in a
pleasing but foreign dress, in which it never appeared to the hearer
before, who, however, had been long acquainted with it; and this
appearance in the habit[4] of a stranger must be admirable, since surprise naturally arises from novelty, as delight and wonder result
from surprise. . . .

Wit is employed in its own province when the possessor of it
exercises his genius on the ordinary customs and manners of life,
either in conversation or comic writing. It has therefore no place
in the works where severe knowledge and judgment are chiefly
exercised; those superior productions of the understanding must be
expressed in a clear and strong manner, without intervening strains
of wit or facetious fancies, which, were they admitted, would appear incongruous and impertinent, and diminish the merit of the
writing. Hence wit has no place in history, philology,[5] philosophy,
or in the greater lyric or epic poem, the two last of which containing either the praises of deities or demigods, or treating of lofty
and illustrious subjects, such as the foundation, rise, and revolution
of kingdoms, commotions of state, battles, triumphs, solemn em-
bassies, and various other important actions of princes and heroes,
are exalted above the sphere of wit and humor. The strength and
dignity of the sublime style is debased and adulterated by the foreign and improper mixture of light sentiments and pretty fancies. . . .

---

[3] careful craftsman.
[4] dress, attire.
[5] scholarship and criticism, any study of literature as such.

Hence the labors of the meanest persons that conduce to the welfare and benefit of the public are more valuable, because more useful, than the employments of those who apply themselves only or principally to divert and entertain the fancy; and therefore must be as much preferable to the occupation or profession of a wit as the improvement and happiness of men is to be regarded above their mirth and recreation. I allow that the talents of these ingenious men are very much to be esteemed in their proper place, that is, as they unbend the mind, relieve the satiety of contemplation and labor, and by the delight which they give, refresh the spirits, and fit them for the returns of study and employment. But then, it must be granted that, as I have said, this is the meanest, as being the least beneficial province in which our intellectual faculties can be engaged. . . .

The truth of what I have asserted will farther appear if we reflect that generally men of a plain understanding and good sense, but of great industry and capacity for business, are in all governments advanced to posts of trust and great employments in the state, while mere wits are regarded as men of the lowest merit, and accordingly are promoted to the meaner and less profitable places, being looked on, by reason of their inapplication and volatile temper, as unfit for a higher station.

Another pernicious abuse of wit is that which appears in the writings of some ingenious men who are so hardy as to expose from the press the most venerable subjects, and treat virtue and sobriety of manners with raillery and ridicule. Several in their books have many sarcastical and spiteful strokes at religion in general, while others make themselves pleasant with[6] the principles of the Christian. Of the last kind, this age has seen a most audacious example in the book entitled A Tale of a Tub. Had this writing been published in a pagan or Popish nation, who are justly impatient of all indignity offered to the established religion of their country, no doubt but the author would have received the punishment he deserved. But the fate of this impious buffoon is very different, for in a Protestant kingdom, zealous of their civil and religious immunities, he has not only escaped affronts and the effects of public resentment, but has been caressed and patronized by persons of great figure and of all denominations.

But the most extensive abuse of parts and ingenuity appears in the loose productions of our writers to the stage. It was the complaint of the celebrated wit of Spain, Michael de Cervantes, before-

---

[6] banter or jest at; a Gallicism.

cited, that the comedies in his time were not only extravagant and monstrous in their contrivance, but likewise the exemplars of vice, and representations of lewdness. But had the plays in Spain at that time been as immoral and unchaste as the daily entertainments of the British theatre, which have a manifest tendency to vitiate the taste of the people, fill their imaginations with obscene ideas, and their lives with levity, idleness, and luxury—I say, if that great man, whose judgment was equal to his admirable genius, had seen religion and virtue so derided, and modesty, reservedness, and decency so insulted and exposed, his zeal for the honor of his country and his love of mankind would have animated him to have attacked the comic poets, with the same spirit with which he assaulted the prevailing folly of his age, the romantic achievements of knights-errant; his wit and good sense would have made those merry authors as odious for poisoning the people with their loose and immoral writings as he made the others ridiculous for their extravagant and idle tales. . . .

It would prove an effectual remedy for this evil if the ladies would discountenance these loose comedies, by expressing their dislike and refusing to be present when they are acted. And this no doubt they would do, were they informed that the comedies which they encourage by their appearance at the theatre are full of wanton sentiments, obscene allusions, and immodest ideas contained in expressions of a double meaning; for it cannot be imagined they would bear with unconcernedness, much less with pleasure, discourses in public which they detest as unsufferable in private conversation, if they knew them to be unchaste. . . .

The clergy lie under such manifest obligations to attack public immorality, wherever it is found, and by whatsoever patrons of power, dignity, and interest it is sheltered and supported, that, as I have suggested, it is not easy to imagine whence their lenity and tenderness for the theatre can proceed. But if the true reason of it, whatever it is, and which is so hard to be accounted for, were removed, and our divines would interest themselves with zeal in the cause of virtue in respect to our dramatic entertainments, as they espouse and defend it in all other instances, I cannot believe that the stage, without a regulation,[7] would be able to stand, when battered with vigor from the pulpit. The poets and players would soon find themselves obliged to restrain their licentious conduct, reform the theatre, and present to the town, if not instructive, at least inoffensive and unshocking diversions. And it is very desirable

---

[7] without censorship.

that this expedient were set on foot, that the honor of the English theatre may be retrieved; that while we justly boast of our priority in wit and humor to our neighbors, we may not be obliged to acknowledge the great inferiority of our comedies in respect of cleanness and moral beauty; that we may not be reproached that while we profess a reformed and pure religion, we encourage an immodest and unreformed theatre, and that we are very defective in the practice of virtue and regularity of manners, while these abominations are indulged, and these unhallowed groves and high places of immorality are frequented without disturbance.

* * * *

FRANCIS HUTCHESON (1694–1746) [1]

FROM

The Dublin Journal No. 11

Saturday, June 12, 1725

*Humano capiti cervicem pictor equinam
Iungere si velit, et varias inducere plumas,
Undique collatis membris, ut turpiter atrum
Desinat in piscem mulier formosa superne,
Spectatum admissi risum teneatis, amici?* [2]

---

[1] Irish-born, Presbyterian minister who, after attending the University of Glasgow, became professor of moral philosophy in 1729, where he was enormously influential on mid-century Scottish critics. In his best-known critical work, *An Inquiry into the Original of Our Ideas of Beauty and Virtue* (1725), Hutcheson announced a defense of "the principles of the late Earl of Shaftesbury" against Mandeville, "the author of the *Fable of the Bees,*" and argued the reality of instinctual "inner senses" of beauty and virtue. He distinguished the principle of "absolute" beauty, which consists always and everywhere of uniformity observed in variety (the more variety brought into form, the more intense the beauty), from "relative" beauty, which consists of the conformity of an imitation to an original. Fanciful variations in taste, from individual to individual, or from culture to culture, derive from customary association of ideas, as explained by Locke.

[2] Horace, *Ars Poetica*, 1–5: "If a painter decided to join a human head to the neck of a horse, and to stick varicolored feathers on limbs gathered here and there, so that a beautiful woman at the top should end below in a foul black fish, could you keep from laughing, my friends, when admitted to the spectacle?"

SIR,

In my former letter I attempted to show that Mr. Hobbes's account of laughter[3] was not just. I shall now endeavour to discover some other ground of that sensation, action, passion, or affection, I know not which of them a philosopher would call it.

The ingenious Mr. Addison, in his treatise of *The Pleasures of the Imagination*, has justly observed many sublimer sensations than those commonly mentioned among philosophers. He observes particularly that we receive sensations of pleasure from those objects which are great, new, or beautiful; and on the contrary, that objects which are more narrow and confined, or deformed and irregular, give us disagreeable ideas.[4] It is unquestionable that we have a great number of perceptions which one can scarcely reduce to any of the five senses as they are commonly explained, such as either the ideas of grandeur, dignity, decency, beauty, harmony; or on the other hand, of meanness, baseness, indecency, deformity; and that we apply these ideas not only to material objects, but to characters, abilities, actions.

It may be farther observed that by some strange association of ideas, made in our infancy, we have frequently some of these ideas recurring along with a great many objects with which they have no other connection than what custom and education, or frequent allusions, give them, or at most, some very distant resemblance. The very affections of our minds are ascribed to inanimate objects; and some animals, perfect enough in their own kind, are made constant emblems of some vices or meanness, whereas other kinds are made emblems of the contrary qualities. For instances of these associations, partly from nature, partly from custom, we may take the following ones: *sanctity* in our churches; *magnificence* in public buildings; *affection* between the oak and ivy, the elm and vine; *hospitality* in a shade; a pleasant sensation of *grandeur* in the sky, the sea, and mountains, distinct from a bare apprehension or image of their extension; *solemnity* and *horror* in shady woods. An ass is the common emblem of *stupidity* and *sloth*; a swine of *selfish luxury*; an eagle of a *great genius*; a lion of *intrepidity*; an ant or bee of *low industry* and *prudent economy*. Some inanimate objects have in like manner some accessory ideas of meanness, either for some natural reason or oftener by mere chance and custom.

Now, the same ingenious author observes, in the *Spectator*, Vol.

---

[3] See p. 27, n. 2.
[4] See p. 242 ff.

I, No. 62, that what we call a *great genius*, such as becomes a heroic poet, gives us pleasure by filling the mind with great conceptions; and therefore they bring most of their similitudes and metaphors from objects of dignity and grandeur, where the resemblance is generally very obvious. This is not usually called *wit*, but something nobler. What we call grave *wit* consists in bringing such resembling ideas together as one could scarce have imagined had so exact a relation to each other, or when the resemblance is carried on through many more particulars than we could have at first expected; and this therefore gives the pleasure of surprise. In this serious wit, though we are not solicitous about the grandeur of the images, we must still beware of bringing in ideas of baseness or deformity, unless we are studying to represent an object as base and deformed. Now this sort of wit is seldom apt to move laughter, more than heroic poetry.

That, then, which seems generally the cause of laughter is the bringing together of images which have contrary additional ideas as well as some resemblance in the principal idea. This contrast between the ideas of grandeur, dignity, sanctity, perfection, and ideas of meanness, baseness, profanity, seems to be the very spirit of burlesque, and the greatest part of our raillery and jest is founded upon it.

We also find ourselves moved to laughter by an overstraining of wit, by bringing resemblances from subjects of a quite different kind from the subject to which they are compared. When we see, instead of the easiness and natural resemblance which constitutes true wit, a forced straining of a likeness, our laughter is apt to arise; as also when the only resemblance is not in the idea, but in the sound of the words. And this is the matter of laughter in the pun.

Let us see if this thought may not be confirmed in many instances. If any writing has obtained a high character for grandeur, sanctity, inspiration, or sublimity of thoughts and boldness of images, the application of any known sentence of such writings to low, vulgar, or base subjects never fails to divert the audience and set them a laughing. This fund of laughter the Ancients had by allusions to Homer: of this, the lives of some of the philosophers in Diogenes Laertius[5] supply abundance of instances. Our late burlesque writers derive a great part of their pleasantry from their introducing on the most trifling occasions allusions to some of the bold schemes or figures or sentences of the great poets upon the most solemn subjects. *Hudibras* and *Don Quixote* will supply one with instances of

---

[5] (Fl. 2nd cent. A.D.), author of *Lives of the Greek Philosophers* in ten books.

this in almost every page. It were to be wished that the boldness of our age had never carried their ludicrous allusions to yet more venerable writings We know that allusions to the phrases of Holy Writ have obtained to some gentlemen a character of wit, and often furnished laughter to their hearers, when their imaginations have been too barren to give any other entertainment. But I appeal to the religious themselves if these allusions are not apt to move laughter, unless a more strong affection of the mind, a religious horror at the profanity of such allusions, prevents their allowing themselves the liberty of laughing at them. Now, in this affair, I fancy anyone will acknowledge that an opinion of superiority is not at all the occasion of the laughter.

Again, any little accident to which we have joined the idea of meanness, befalling a person of great gravity, ability, dignity, is a matter of laughter for the very same reason; thus the strange contortions of the body in a fall, the dirtying of a decent dress, the natural functions which we study to conceal from sight, are matter of laughter when they occur to observation in persons of whom we have high ideas: nay, the very human form has the ideas of dignity so generally joined with it that even in ordinary persons such mean accidents are matter of jest; but still the jest is increased by the dignity, gravity, or modesty of the person; which shows that it is this contrast or opposition of ideas of dignity and meanness which is the occasion of laughter.

We generally imagine in mankind some degree of wisdom above other animals and have high ideas of them on this account. If then, along with our notion of wisdom in our fellows, there occurs any instance of gross inadvertence or great mistake, this is a great cause of laughter. Our countrymen[6] are very subject to little trips of this kind, and furnish often some diversion to their neighbors, not only by mistakes in their speech but in actions. Yet even this kind of laughter cannot well be said to arise from our sense of superiority. This alone may give a sedate joy, but not be a matter of laughter, since we shall find the same kind of laughter arising in us where this opinion of superiority does not attend it. For if the most ingenious person in the world, whom the whole company esteems, should, through inadvertent hearing or any other mistake, answer quite from the purpose, the whole audience may laugh heartily without the least abatement of their good opinion. Thus we know some very ingenious men have not in the least suffered in their characters by an extempory pun, which raises the laugh very

---

[6] the Irish.

readily, whereas a premeditated pun, which diminishes our opinion of a writer, will seldom raise any laughter.

Again, the more violent passions, as fear, anger, sorrow, compassion, are generally looked upon as something great and solemn; the beholding of these passions in another strikes a man with gravity. Now if these passions are artfully or accidentally raised upon a small or a fictitious occasion, they move the laughter of those who imagine the occasions to be small and contemptible or who are conscious of the fraud. This is the occasion of the laugh in *biting*, as they call such deceptions.

According to this scheme, there must necessarily arise a great diversity in men's sentiments of the ridiculous in actions or characters according as their ideas of dignity and wisdom are various. A truly wise man, who places the dignity of human nature in good affections and suitable actions, may be apt to laugh at those who employ their most solemn and strong affections about what, to the wise man, appears perhaps very useless or mean. The same solemnity of behavior and keenness of passion about a place or ceremony, which ordinary people only employ about the absolute necessaries of life, may make them laugh at their betters. When a gentleman of pleasure, who thinks that good fellowship and gallantry are the only valuable enjoyments of life, observes men with great solemnity and earnestness heaping up money without using it, or encumbering themselves with purchases and mortgages, which the gay gentleman, with his paternal revenues, thinks very silly affairs, he may make himself very merry upon them. And the frugal man, in his turn, makes the same jest of the man of pleasure. The successful gamester, whom no disaster forces to lay aside the trifling ideas of an amusement in his play, may laugh to see the serious looks and passions of the gravest business arising in the loser, amidst the ideas of a recreation. There is indeed in these last cases an opinion of superiority in the laughter, but this is not the proper occasion of his laughter; otherwise I see not how we should ever meet with a composed countenance anywhere. Men have their different relishes of life; most people prefer their own taste to that of others; but this moves no laughter unless, in representing the pursuits of others, they do join together some whimsical image of opposite ideas.

In the more polite nations there are certain modes of dress, behavior, ceremony, generally received by all the *better sort*, as they are commonly called. To these modes, ideas of decency, grandeur, and dignity are generally joined; hence men are fond of imitating the mode. And if in any polite assembly, a contrary dress, behavior, or ceremony appear, to which we have joined in our country the contrary ideas of meanness, rusticity, sullenness, a laugh does ordinarily arise, or a disposition to it, in those who have not the thorough good breeding, or reflection, to restrain themselves or break through these customary associations.

And hence we may see that what is counted ridiculous in one age or nation may not be so in another. We are apt to laugh at Homer when he compares Ajax unwillingly retreating to an ass driven out of a corn field,[7] or when he compares him to a boar, or Ulysses tossing all night without sleep through anxiety to a pudding frying on the coals.[8] Those three similes have got low mean ideas joined to them with us, which it is very probable they had not in Greece in Homer's days. Nay, as to one of them, the boar, it is well known that in some countries of Europe where they have wild boars for hunting, even in our times, they have not these low sordid ideas joined to that animal, which we have in these kingdoms who never see them but in their dirty sties or on dunghills. This may teach us how impertinent a great many jests are which are made upon the style of some other ancient writings in ages when manners were very different from ours, though perhaps fully as rational and every way as human and just.

* * * *

CORBYN MORRIS (1710–1779)[1]

FROM

An Essay towards Fixing the True Standards of Wit, Humor, Raillery, Satire, and Ridicule, to Which is Added an Analysis of the Characters of a Humorist, Sir John Falstaff, Sir Roger de Coverley, and Don Quixote [1744]

Wit is the *lustre* resulting from the *quick elucidation* of one subject by a *just* and *unexpected arrangement* of it with another subject. . . .

---

[7] *Iliad*, XI, 670 ff.
[8] *Odyssey*, V, 626 ff.
[1] Walpolian Whig, writer of pamphlets on economics and the song birds of England, customs officer and statistician, friend of Hume and Boswell, and

But metaphor goes further, and not content with arranging the two subjects together and exhibiting from thence their agreement or contrast, it actually snatches the properties of the auxiliary one and fits them at once upon the original subject.

It is evident from hence that there may be Wit without any metaphor, but in every just metaphor there is Wit. . . .

Upon the Restoration, Mr. Waller presented a congratulatory copy of verses to King Charles. His Majesty, after reading them, said: "Mr. Waller, these are very good but not so fine as you made upon the Protector." To which Mr. Waller replied: "Your Majesty will please to recollect that we poets always write best upon fictions." . . . He unexpectedly exhibits his more excellent verses to Cromwell as a plain elucidation of the fictitious glory of the Protector, and intimates at the same time that the inferiority of his present performance was a natural illustration of his Majesty's real glory. . . .

An instance of Wit in the opposition [of subjects] I remember to have read somewhere in the *Spectator*, where Sir Roger de Coverley, intimating the splendor which the perverse Widow should have appeared in if she had commenced Lady Coverley, says that "he would have given her a coal pit to have kept her in clean linen" and that "her finger should have sparkled with one hundred of his richest acres."

The joint introduction of these opposite subjects, as a coal pit with clean linen, and dirty acres with the lustre of a jewel, is *just*[2] in this instance as they really produce each other in their consequences.[3] The natural opposition between them, which is strongly *elucidated* by their *arrangement* together, and at the same time their *unexpected connection* in their consequences, strike us with a *surprise* which exhibits the brilliancy and sparkling of Wit. . . .

[Wit] is also sometimes obtained by transitions from one subject to another by the help of an equivocal word, which, like a bridge with two roads meeting at the end of it, leads to two different places. Transitions thus made from the right course have indeed the pretense of being natural, but they ought . . . not to end only at a ridiculous pun, void of all spirit and poignancy.[4]

---

after 1757 fellow of the Royal Society. Morris ventured into criticism only once, amateurishly, at thirty-three. His introduction quotes definitions of wit or humor from Cowley, Barrow, Dryden, Locke, Congreve, and Addison.

[2] true to reality.

[3] That is, the income from such property would enable the Widow to dress fashionably.

[4] significant point.

The Wit in such instances results, as in all others, from the quick arrangement together of two subjects; but that which was first intended for the original one is dropped, and a new original subject is started, through the double meaning of a word, and suddenly enlightened.

To give a trite instance of this kind of Wit.

A peer coming out of the House of Lords and wanting his servant called out, "Where's my fellow?" To which another peer, who stood by him, returned: "Faith, my Lord, not in England." . . .

It is also proper to add that there may be Wit in a picture, landscape, or in any prospect[5] where a gay unexpected assemblage of similar or opposite objects is presented. . . .

Humor is any *whimsical oddity* or *foible* appearing in the temper or conduct of a *person* in *real life*. . . . I call such a person in the book of mankind a "character." So that the chief subjects of Humor are persons in real life who are "characters."

It is easy to be perceived that Humor and Wit are extremely different. . . .

Humor is the whimsical oddity or foible which fairly appears in its subject of itself; whereas Wit is the lustre which is thrown upon one subject by the sudden introduction of another subject. . . .

A Man of Wit is he who is happy in elucidating any subject by a just and unexpected arrangement and comparison of it with another subject.

It may also be proper to describe a Man of Humor and a Humorist, which are very different persons.

A Man of Humor is one who can happily exhibit a weak and ridiculous "character" in real life, either by assuming it himself or representing another in it so naturally that the whimsical oddities and foibles of that character shall be palpably exposed.

Whereas a Humorist is a person in real life, obstinately attached to sensible[6] peculiar oddities of his own genuine growth, which appear in his temper and conduct. . . . He flourishes only in a land of freedom, and when that ceases, he dies too, the last and noblest weed of the soil of liberty. . . . In writing to Englishmen, who are generally tinged, deeply or slightly, with the dye of the Humorist, it seemed not improper to insist the longer upon this character.[7]

---

[5] something seen, a view. Wit is not necessarily verbal.

[6] perceptible, obvious.

[7] In a portion omitted, Morris made a lengthy, seven-page type-portrait of the Humorist. See discussion, p. 165.

However, let none be too fond of it, for though a Humorist with his roughness is greatly to be preferred to a smooth insipid, yet the extremes of both are equally wretched, idiots being only the lowest scale of insipids as madmen are no other than Humorists in excess. . . .

It has from hence been observed that there is more Humor in the English comedies than in others, as we have more various odd "characters" in real life than any other nation, or perhaps than all other nations together. . . .

Humor is more interesting than Wit, in general, as the oddities and foibles of persons in real life are more apt to affect our passions than any oppositions or relations between inanimate objects.

Humor is nature, or what really appears in the subject, without any embellishments; Wit [is] only a stroke of art. . . .

Humor generally appears in such foibles as each of the company thinks himself superior to. Whereas Wit shows the quickness and abilities of the person who discovers it, and places him superior to the rest of the company.

Humor . . . frequently exhibits very generous, benevolent sentiments of heart, and these, though exerted in a particular odd manner, justly command our fondness and love. Whereas in the allusions of Wit, severity, bitterness, and satire are frequently exhibited; and where these are avoided, not worthy amiable sentiments of the heart, but quick unexpected efforts of the fancy are presented. . . .

However, the most agreeable representations or compositions of all others appear not where they separately exist, but where they are united together in the same fabric: where Humor is the groundwork and chief substance, and Wit, happily spread, quickens the whole with embellishments.

This is the excellency of the character of Sir John Falstaff. The groundwork is Humor, or the representation and detecting of a bragging and vaunting coward in real life. . . . But here the inimitable Wit of Sir John comes in to his support and gives a new rise and lustre to his character. For the sake of his Wit, you forgive his cowardice, or rather, are fond of his cowardice for the occasions it gives to his Wit. . . .

At the first entrance of the knight, your good humor and tendency to mirth are irresistibly excited by his jolly appearance and corpulency; you feel and acknowledge him to be the fittest subject imaginable for yielding diversion and merriment; but when you see him immediately set up for enterprise and activity, with his evident weight and unwieldiness, your attention is all called forth, and you are eager to watch him to the end of his adventures, your imagination pointing out with a full scope his future embarrassments. All the while, as you accompany him forwards, he heightens your relish for his future disasters by his happy opinion of his own sufficiency and the gay vaunts which he makes of his talents and accomplishments, so that at last when he falls into a scrape, your expectation is exquisitely gratified and you have the full pleasure of seeing all his trumpeted honor laid in the dust. When in the midst of his misfortunes, instead of being utterly demolished and sunk, he rises again by the superior force of his Wit, and begins a new course with fresh spirit and alacrity, this excites you the more. . . .

It may also deserve to be remarked of Falstaff that the figure of his person is admirably suited to the turn of his mind, so that there arises before you a perpetual allusion from one to the other, which forms an incessant series of Wit,[8] whether they are in contrast or agreement together. When he pretends to activity, there is Wit in the contrast between his mind and person, and Wit in their agreement when he triumphs in jollity.

To complete the whole, you have in this character of Falstaff not only a free course of Humor, supported and embellished with admirable Wit; but this Humor is of a species the most jovial and gay in all Nature. Sir John Falstaff possesses generosity, cheerfulness, alacrity, invention, frolic, and fancy superior to all other men. The figure of his person is the picture of jollity, mirth, and good nature, and banishes at once all other ideas from your breast. He is happy himself and makes you happy. If you examine him further, he has no fierceness, reserve, malice, or peevishness lurking in his heart. His intentions are all pointed at innocent riot and merriment, nor has the knight any inveterate design except against sack, and that too he loves.[9] . . .

Ben Jonson has Humor in his characters, drawn with the most masterly skill and judgment. In accuracy, depth, propriety, and truth, he has no superior or equal among ancients or moderns; but the characters he exhibits are of a satirical and deceitful or of a

---

[8] The Wit, or enlightening arrangement, in this instance is Shakespeare the artist's, not Falstaff's.

[9] In his introduction, Morris explains away Falstaff's villainy, punishment, and death as Shakespeare's compliance with "the austerity of the times . . . in order to avoid the imputation of encouraging idleness and mirthful riot by too amiable and happy an example." Johnson mentions that "the reign of Elizabeth is commonly supposed to have been a time of stateliness, formality and reserve."

peevish or despicable species, as Volpone, Subtle, Morose, and Abel Drugger. . . . Whereas Shakespeare, besides the peculiar gaiety in the humor of Falstaff, has guarded him from disgusting you with his forward advances by giving him rank and quality; from being despicable, by his real good sense and excellent abilities; from being odious, by his harmless plots and designs; and from being tiresome, by his inimitable Wit and his new and incessant sallies of highest fancy and frolic.

This discovers the secret of carrying comedy to the highest pitch of delight, which lies in drawing the persons exhibited with such cheerful and amiable oddities and foibles as you would choose in your own companions in real life. Otherwise, though you may be diverted at first with the novelty of a character and with a proper detection and ridicule of it, yet its peevishness, meanness, or immorality will begin to disgust you . . . it being certain that whoever cannot be endured as an accidental companion in real life will never become, for the very same reasons, a favorite comic character in the theatre. . . .

It may be added that Humor is the most exquisite and delightful when the oddities and foibles introduced are not mischievous or sneaking, but free, jocund, and liberal, and such as result from a generous flow of spirits and a warm universal benevolence.

It is obviously from hence that the character of Sir Roger de Coverley in the *Spectator* is so extremely agreeable. His foibles are all derived from some amiable cause. If he believes that one Englishman can conquer two Frenchmen, you laugh at his foible and are fond of a weakness in the knight which proceeds from his high esteem of his own countrymen. If he chooses you should employ a waterman or porter with one leg, you readily excuse the inconvenience he puts you to, for his worthy regard to the suffering of a brave soldier. In short, though he is guilty of continual absurdities and has little understanding or real abilities, you cannot but love and esteem him for his honor, hospitality, and universal benevolence.

It is indeed true that his dignity, age, and rank in his country are of constant service in upholding his character. These are a perpetual guard to the knight and preserve him from contempt upon many occasions. All which corresponds entirely with the foregoing remark. For you would be fond of Sir Roger's acquaintance and company in real life, as he is a gentleman of quality and virtue. You love and admire him in the *Spectator* for the same reasons, and for these also he would become, if he was rightly exhibited, a favorite character in the theatre.

* * * *

JOSEPH WARTON (1722–1800) [1]
FROM
An Essay on the Writings and Genius of Pope [1756] [2]

We do not, it should seem, sufficiently attend to the difference there is betwixt a man of wit, a man of sense, and a true poet. Donne and Swift were undoubtedly men of wit and men of sense, but what traces have they left of *pure poetry?* It is remarkable that Dryden says of Donne, "He was the greatest wit, though not the greatest poet, of this nation." Fontenelle[3] and La Motte[4] are entitled to the former character, but what can they urge to gain the latter? Which of these characters is the most valuable and useful is entirely out of the question. All I plead for is to have their several provinces kept distinct from each other and to impress on the reader that a clear head and acute understanding are not sufficient alone to make a poet; that the most solid observations on human life expressed with the utmost elegance and brevity are *morality,* and not *poetry;* that the *Epistles* of Boileau in rhyme are not more poetical than the *Characters* of La Bruyère in prose; and that it is a creative and glowing IMAGINATION, *acer spiritus ac vis,*[5] and that alone, that can stamp a writer with this exalted and very uncommon character which so few possess and of which so few can properly judge.

For one person who can adequately relish and enjoy a work of imagination, twenty are to be found who can taste and judge of

---

[1] Rector, headmaster of Winchester College, friend of Johnson, brother of Thomas Warton, the poet, critic, and Oxford professor of poetry. His *Odes on Various Subjects* (1746), reacting against Pope, tried to "bring back poetry into its right channel" of imagination. A critic of extraordinary learning and catholic taste, and a good writer, he edited and translated part of Virgil in 1753, and contributed twenty-four essays to The Adventurer at Johnson's behest, most notably essays on the *Odyssey,* Milton, *The Tempest,* and *King Lear,* which carry on the "particular" exposition of beauties begun by Addison in his essays on *Paradise Lost.* He also edited Pope and Dryden.
[2] Dedicated to Edward Young; see p. 358, n. 6.
[3] Bernard de Bovier de Fontenelle (1657–1757), French satirist and critic who sided with Moderns in the controversy with the Ancients.
[4] Antoine Houdar de la Motte (1672–1731), French playwright and critic.
[5] Horace, *Satires,* I, iv, 46: "a spirit of fire and force."

observations on familiar life and the manners of the age. The satires of Ariosto are more read than the *Orlando Furioso*, or even Dante. Are there so many cordial admirers of Spenser and Milton as of *Hudibras*, if we strike out of the number of these supposed admirers those who appear such out of fashion and not of feeling? Swift's "Rhapsody on Poetry" is far more popular than Akenside's noble "Ode to Lord Huntingdon." The epistles on the characters of men and women and your sprightly satires, my good friend,[6] are more frequently perused and quoted than "L'Allegro" and "Il Penseroso" of Milton. Had you written only these satires, you would, indeed, have gained the title of a man of wit and a man of sense, but, I am confident, would not insist on being denominated a *poet, merely* on their account. . . .

The sublime and the pathetic are the two chief nerves of all genuine poesy. What is there transcendently sublime or pathetic in Pope? In his works there is, indeed, *nihil inane, nihil arcessitum: puro tamen fonti quam magno flumini proprior*, as the excellent Quintilian remarks of Lysias.[7] And because I am, perhaps, unwilling to speak out in plain English, I will adopt the following passage of Voltaire, which in my opinion as exactly characterizes Pope as it does his model Boileau, for whom it was originally designed:

> *Incapable peut-être du sublime qui élève l'âme, et du senti-*
> *ment qui l'attendrit, mais fait pour éclairer ceux à qui la*
> *nature accorda l'un et l'autre, laborieux, sévère, précis, pur,*
> *harmonieux, il devint, enfin, le poète de la Raison.*[8]

Our English poets may, I think, be disposed in four different classes and degrees. In the first class I would place our only three sublime and pathetic poets: Spenser, Shakespeare, Milton. In the second class should be ranked such as possessed the true poetical genius in a more moderate degree, but who had noble talents for moral, ethical, and panegyrical poesy. At the head of these are Dryden, Prior, Addison, Cowley, Waller, Garth, Fenton, Gay, Denham, Parnell. In the third class may be placed men of wit, of elegant

---

[6] Young's *Love of Fame* (1725).

[7] *Institutes*, X, i, 78: "nothing pointless, nothing far-fetched—nevertheless more like a pure spring than a mighty river." Lysias was a Greek orator (fl. 5th cent. B.C.).

[8] *Discours à sa réception à l'Académie française* (1746): "incapable perhaps of the sublime which lifts the heart or of the feeling which softens it, but made to clarify them for those to whom Nature has given one or the other; hard-working, strict, precise, pure, harmonious, he has become, in short, the poet of Reason."

taste, and lively fancy in describing familiar life, though not the higher scenes of poetry. Here may be numbered Butler, Swift, Rochester, Donne, Dorset, Oldham. In the fourth class the mere versifiers, however smooth and mellifluous some of them may be thought, should be disposed. Such as Pitt, Sandys, Fairfax, Broome, Buckingham, Lansdowne. This enumeration is not intended as a complete catalogue but only to mark out briefly the different species of our celebrated authors. In which of these classes Pope deserves to be placed, the following work is intended to determine.[9]

> *I am, Dear Sir,*
> *Your affectionate*
> *And faithful servant.*

---

[9] A place next to Milton and just above Dryden.

Anthony Ashley Cooper,

Third Earl

of Shaftesbury 1671–1713

A MERE catalogue of Shaftesbury's premises may look like the most frigid neoclassic orthodoxy. Fixed standards of Nature and Reason, formalistic imitation, aristocratic taste, simplicity of style, self-knowledge and impersonality in the artist, symmetry and proportion, the rules, the kinds, refinement of society, superiority of Ancients to Moderns, disdain of puns, of Gothicism and "Moorish fancy"—it is all there, irritatingly bland, confident, and explicit. An idealizing Hellenist, he ruled against tragicomedy and regretted the archaic rudeness of Shakespeare and Milton (if measured against Corneille and Boileau); he praised Le Bossu's formalistic *Traité du poème épique* (1675) as the greatest piece of criticism in modern Europe, and, in passing, admired the common sense of Rymer.[1] Blind to its irony, he detested the extravagance of Swift's great *A Tale of a Tub*. Yet his philosophic intelligence liberalized the orthodox with fresh if miscellaneous suggestion. Before his early death, "Europe's amiable Plato" had opened new possibilities of thought for many of the best philosophical and critical minds of the eighteenth century—Voltaire, Montesquieu, Diderot,

---

[1] Like Rymer, he believed that English literature is profounder, freer, more energetic than that of France but in need of refinement. Regrettably, "the *limae labor* is the greatest grievance with our countrymen. An English author would be all genius." Yet he praised Shakespeare and Milton as "the first of Europeans" to throw off Gothic rhyme; they "asserted ancient poetic liberty." *Hamlet* is the play "which appears to have most affected English hearts."

Rousseau, Herder, Winckelmann, Goethe, Kant. In Scotland, he directly inspired Francis Hutcheson and Thomas Blackwell, and through them later Scottish critics (see Alison, p. 581), and he laid much of the groundwork for the new English poetry of sublime landscape and aesthetic idealism. Though he preferred the title "moralist," he may qualify as the first aesthetician in modern English, despite his lack of system. He analyzed the disinterestedness of aesthetic pleasure and developed a theory of beauty and creative form. If his judgment of non-Hellenic literature was hyperopic and over-civilized, his statement of principle was enthusiastically broad, lordly, astute, and liberating.

Like Matthew Arnold in the nineteenth century, he had two self-appointed enemies—philistinism in English society, and the world-view of the "new philosophy" of empiricism, which was sweeping English thought.

With Puritans in mind, he grounded a plea for intellectual tolerance on a defense of "ridicule" (the witty, satiric, or comic arts)—one of the most original and closely reasoned of several such defenses during the century. He assumed, however, what his contemporary Swift surely doubted, the accessible goodness of Nature and the therapy of natural emotion freely expressed. A Whig patriot by birth and breeding, he believed that the highest genres of art, such as tragedy, can be brought to greatness only in a "free nation"—that is, an intellectual climate in which rational Nature, by "trial and experience of what is best," can search freely for perfection, and therefore a society in which toleration, intelligent taste, and good humor are progressively diffused among a general public led by sophisticated gentlemen. Bad taste, folly, morbid emotion, and perversities too subtle or personal for the law should be corrected by satire, not censorship. "There are certain humors in mankind which of necessity must have vent." Yet "in healthy bodies Nature dictates remedies of her own"—namely, ridicule and laughter, not repression. "If men are forbid to speak their minds seriously on certain subjects, they will do it ironically." Ironic ridicule, though not the highest art, is a weapon of civilized reform and progress toward freedom. In England, he argued, it had emerged in response to repressive Puritanism, in Italy and France to Roman Catholicism: " 'Tis the persecuting spirit has raised the bantering one." He praised *The Rehearsal* and *Hudibras* and suggested that "our home wits" might well "refine upon this pattern"—that is, satire and serious-minded parody—for the most effective English criticism in his time, both literary and social, must border most, he

predicted, on "the manner of earliest Greek comedy." [2] Shaftesbury assumed the dependence of literature, and therefore of criticism, upon a given stage in the growth of a society. He never
claimed, as later controvertists accused him, that ridicule, usurping
the role of reason, can be "the test of truth." It only prepares the
way for truth by testing "gravity"—the seriousness or sincerity behind appearances. It dissipates impostures in society and brings to
light morbid fancies and self-deceptions, "idol-notions . . . which
are kept thus choicely in some dark corner of our minds." Many
contemporary wits, for example Pope and Bishop Berkeley, mistook
him for a deist in disguise, licensing attacks upon revelation and
the establishment; twentieth-century evidence makes him out a
practicing, if very cheerfully, broad-minded Anglican.

His avowed masters in metaphysics were seventeenth-century
liberal theologians, the so-called Cambridge Platonists or "latitude
men," especially Benjamin Whichcote (whose sermons he edited),
Henry More, and Ralph Cudworth. Like them he believed that Nature in the new mechanico-corpuscular philosophy, so far from
being the art of God, as in older humanism, was emptied of values;
that the spirit of man, autonomous in knowing, was being narrowed
to an environmentally determined self.

> Hence Hobbes, Locke, etc. Still the same man, same genus
> at the bottom.—"Beauty is nothing."—"Virtue is noth-
> ing."—So "perspective nothing—Music nothing."—but these
> are the greatest realities of things, especially the beauty and
> order of affections. These philosophers together with the anti-
> virtuosi may be called by one common name, viz., barbar
> [ians].[3]

He wished to reclothe "dead matter" with sacred purpose and
beauty, to lead moderns out of their relativistic, sensual, and selfish
cave into the daylight of universals and of urbane *beaux-arts*. Like
Addison, who belonged to the same generation, he was anxious
to bring philosophy out of colleges and cells into common life—
the philosophy of Plato, Xenophon, and Marcus Aurelius, however,
not of Newton and Locke. Locke was, in fact, Shaftesbury's child-

---

[2] In classical Greece, ridicule emerged in ancient parodies and in Aristophanes, inevitably and naturally, as a corrective to the false sublimity of tragedy
and oratory. The remedy in time became a disease and was in turn improved
into the New Comedy of Menander. Such is the Shaftesburian way, of polite
refinement in a free, intelligent society.

[3] *Second Characters, or the Language of Forms*, p. 178.

hood tutor, but what he owed his master he sublimated in a mystique of Nature. Sooner or later, everything in Shaftesbury's criticism reverts to his idea of Nature, which, eclectic in its sources, is further blurred by his fervid and digressive, if always gracious, style and his liking for genteel playfulness.

In his theory of beauty and form, he was virtually alone in turn-of-the-century England. The quasi–Neo-Platonic view that the artist creates in his poem an autonomous second Nature, second world, or second being, often echoed in later criticism of Shakespeare, was not uncommon in seventeenth-century English theory between Puttenham and Pope, but on metaphysical grounds, Shaftesbury made a unique exposition of it. From Cudworth he borrowed (and reinterpreted) a concept of "plastic Nature"—the forming principle of organic life which, infinitely varied and diffused through every imperfect particular, transcends mechanism and chance because it expresses Nature's *mind*.[4] Beauty belongs only to mind— "the beautifying, not the beautified, is the really beautiful"—but is objectively characterized by the striving of parts toward harmony, just proportion and symmetry, "interior numbers." "What is beautiful is harmonious and proportionable; what is harmonious and proportionable is true; and what is at once both beautiful and true is, of consequence, agreeable[5] and good." Even rude, asymmetrical landscape that evokes melancholy, "the horrid graces of the wilderness itself," invites contemplation of its "natural" beauty, though one should not mistake outward shadows apprehended by the senses for the higher beauty which is inward and rational. Since art imitates Nature, "poetical truth" is literally that—a transposition into art of plastic Nature. The artist, "a second *maker*, a just Prometheus under Jove," imitates plastic Nature by forming a beautiful "whole, coherent and proportioned in itself, with due subjection and subordinacy of constituent parts," in which, as in a mirror, men discover the inward truth of themselves and of their times.

---

[4] A problem of mechanistic theory was that having resolved everything into particles or "atoms" of matter in motion, it was hard pressed to explain how they come back together to constitute values and wholes, and how anything valuable and whole can be made. Association-theory attempted one answer (see p. 14). The term *plastic* had a quiet, uneven history as an alternative before emerging, transformed, in the "esemplastic" imagination of Coleridge. It might be invoked—for example, by Pope and by Burke—whenever one had to account for vital (non-mechanical) organization of any kind, in nature, art, or society. See Meyer Abrams, *The Mirror and the Lamp*, pp. 156–67, and J. W. Beach, *The Concept of Nature in Nineteenth-Century English Poetry*, pp. 54–78.
[5] fitted to the ends of life; therefore, useful, healthful.

The artist may select his materials from empirical reality—"men, manners, opinions, times"—but he imitates only by virtue of his form. As Nature makes every particular man unlike any other, so the artist makes (he does not copy) individually distinct characters, which, however, are related to universals and, as it were, measured, by his form. Like Homer or Plato, the artist is thoroughly impersonal, "scarce discoverable in his poem." Despite his own miscellanarian manner, Shaftesbury claimed to despise the "coquetry" of a modern author, "talking eternally of himself, dressing and sprucing up himself . . . so many affected graces, designed to draw the attention from the subject towards himself." Form expresses the artist's vision, his "moral taste," within his selected materials, but his form will be truth-revealing and beautiful only as he has cultivated a taste for perfection by philosophy.

"'Tis we ourselves create and form our taste." His *Advice to an Author* (1710) recommended Socratic self-inspection to both artist and audience, for in no other way can taste, an immediacy of right understanding of values, be developed from its latency. Taste, philosophically considered, is a kind of knowledge which all men have, in some degree, by nature. A dynamic, affective urge to know the beautiful and the good, an "enthusiasm" for it, expresses itself throughout human life; in dress, manners, sports, play, as well as in art and philosophy. But if it is not to be corruptly limited by the senses, as in the English taste for brutality, it must be instructed. Right taste grows from a disinterested cultivation of an "inward model" of perfection. In one respect, it is indistinguishable from the "moral sense." The latter phrase, which Hutcheson would popularize, named an inborn (natural) power to discriminate values—"the honestum, the pulchrum, τὸ καλόν"—as inevitably as the five senses discriminate the physical world. Of course, it too must be trained. Thus, the gentleman, the virtuoso,[6] the artist, the

---

[6] See "Miscellaneous Reflections" in *Characteristics* II, 252–53: "the sort of ridicule or raillery which is apt to fall upon philosophers is of the same kind with that which falls commonly on the virtuosi or refined wits of the age. In this latter general denomination we include the real fine gentlemen, the lovers of art and ingenuity, such as have seen the world and informed themselves of the manners and customs of the several nations of Europe; searched into their antiquities and records; considered police, laws, and constitutions; observed the situation, strength, and ornaments of their cities, their architecture, sculpture, painting, music, and their taste in poetry, learning, language, and conversation.

"Hitherto there can lie no ridicule, nor the least scope for satiric wit or raillery. But when we push this virtuoso character a little further and lead our polished gentleman into . . . contemplation of the insect life, the conveniences, habitations, and economy of a race of shell-fish . . . he then indeed

virtuous man, and the philosopher, all of them "moralists," students of the highest happiness, differ only by degree. Indeed, "to philosophize, in a just signification, is but to carry good breeding a step higher." By a spread of intelligent taste throughout England, the freest nation of Europe, Shaftesbury hoped for a renaissance in English culture excelling that in classical Greece. And indeed, when all is said, his criticism is governed by its liberal thrust toward reform and the future. "Let but the search go freely on."

* * * *

FROM

Characteristics of Men, Manners, Opinions, Times [1711]

A Letter Concerning Enthusiasm to My Lord [Somers] [1708]

FROM SECTION II

If the knowing well how to expose any infirmity or vice were a sufficient security for the virtue which is contrary, how excellent an age might we be presumed to live in! Never was there in our nation a time known when folly and extravagance of every kind were more sharply inspected, or more wittily ridiculed. And one might hope, at least from this good symptom, that our age was in no declining state, since whatever our distempers are, we stand so well affected to our remedies. To bear the being told of faults is in private persons the best token of amendment. 'Tis seldom that a public is thus disposed. For where jealousy of state, or the ill lives of the great people, or any other cause is powerful enough to restrain the freedom of censure in any part, it in effect destroys the benefit of it in the whole. There can be no impartial and free censure of manners where any peculiar custom or national opinion is set apart, and not only exempted from criticism but even flattered with the highest art. 'Tis only in a free nation, such as ours, that imposture has no privilege, and that neither the credit of a court, the power of a nobility, nor the awfulness of a church can

---

becomes the subject of sufficient raillery, and is made the jest of common conversations."

give her protection or hinder her from being arraigned in every shape and appearance. 'Tis true, this liberty may seem to run too far. We may perhaps be said to make ill use of it. So every one will say when he himself is touched, and his opinion freely examined. But who shall be judge of what may be freely examined and what may not, where liberty may be used and where it may not? What remedy shall we prescribe to this in general? Can there be a better than from that liberty itself which is complained of? If men are vicious, petulant, or abusive, the magistrate may correct them, but if they reason ill, 'tis reason still must teach them to do better. Justness of thought and style, refinement in manners, good breeding, and politeness of every kind can come only from the trial and experience of what is best. Let but the search go freely on, and the right measure of everything will soon be found. Whatever humor has got the start, if it be unnatural, it cannot hold; and the ridicule, if ill-placed at first, will certainly fall at last where it deserves.

I have often wondered to see men of sense so mightily alarmed at the approach of anything like ridicule on certain subjects, as if they mistrusted their own judgment. For what ridicule can lie against reason? or how can any one of the least justness of thought endure a ridicule wrongly placed? Nothing is more ridiculous than this itself. The vulgar, indeed, may swallow any sordid jest, any mere drollery or buffoonery, but it must be a finer and truer wit which takes with the men of sense and breeding. How comes it to pass, then, that we appear such cowards in reasoning, and are so afraid to stand the test of ridicule? O! say we, the subjects are too grave. Perhaps so, but let us see first whether they are really grave or no; for in the manner we may conceive them, they may, peradventure, be very grave and weighty in our imagination but very ridiculous and impertinent in their own nature. *Gravity* is of the very essence of imposture. It does not only make us mistake other things, but is apt perpetually almost to mistake itself. For even in common behavior, how hard is it for the grave character to keep long out of the limits of the formal [1] one? We can never be too grave if we can be assured we are really what we suppose. And we can never too much honor or revere anything for grave if we are assured the thing is grave, as we apprehend it. The main point is to know always true gravity from the false; and this can only be by carrying the rule constantly with us, and freely applying it, not only to the things about us but to ourselves; for if unhappily we lose the meas-

---

[1] form-ridden, falsely punctilious (with a glance at Puritans and pedants).

ure in ourselves, we shall soon lose it in everything besides. Now what rule or measure is there in the world except in the considering of the real temper of things, to find which are truly serious and which ridiculous? And how can this be done, unless by applying the ridicule to see whether it will bear? But if we fear to apply this rule in anything, what security can we have against the imposture of formality in all things? . . .

It was heretofore the wisdom of some wise nations to let people be fools as much as they pleased, and never to punish seriously what deserved only to be laughed at, and was, after all, best cured by that innocent remedy. There are certain humors[2] in mankind which of necessity must have vent. The human mind and body are both of them naturally subject to commotions; and as there are strange ferments in the blood, which in many bodies occasion an extraordinary discharge, so in reason, too, there are heterogeneous particles which must be thrown off by fermentation. Should physicians endeavor absolutely to allay those ferments of the body, and strike in the humors which discover themselves in such eruptions, they might, instead of making a cure, bid fair perhaps to raise a plague and turn a spring-ague or an autumn-surfeit into an epidemical malignant fever. They are certainly as ill physicians in the body-politic who would needs be tampering with these mental eruptions. . . .

Not only the visionaries and enthusiasts[3] of all kinds were tolerated, your lordship knows, by the Ancients, but, on the other side, philosophy had as free a course and was permitted as a balance against superstition. And whilst some sects, such as the Pythagorean and latter Platonic, joined in with the superstition and enthusiasm of the times, the Epicurean, the Academic, and others were allowed to use all the force of wit and raillery against it. And thus matters were happily balanced; reason had fair play; learning and science flourished. Wonderful was the harmony and temper which arose from all these contrarieties. Thus superstition and enthusiasm were mildly treated; and being let alone, they never raged to that degree as to occasion bloodshed, wars, persecutions, and devastation in the world. . . . I am sure the only way to save men's sense, or preserve wit at all in the world, is to give liberty to wit. Now wit

---

[2] bodily fluids.

[3] irrational fanatics, pretenders to inspiration. The purport of Shaftesbury's letter, however, is to warn against imprecision in the term which confuses vulgar delusion with "a real feeling of the Divine Presence" and with the "noble enthusiasm" animating "heroes, statesmen, poets, orators, musicians, and even philosophers themselves."

214 ANTHONY ASHLEY COOPER

can never have its liberty where the freedom of raillery is taken away, for against serious extravagances and splenetic humors there is no other remedy than this.

Sensus Communis: an Essay on the Freedom of Wit and Humor in a Letter to a Friend [1709]

FROM PART I, SECTIONS I, II, IV

We may be charged perhaps with willful ignorance and blind idolatry for having taken opinions upon trust, and consecrated in ourselves certain idol-notions, which we will never suffer to be unveiled or seen in open light. They may perhaps be monsters, and no divinities or sacred truths, which are kept thus choicely in some dark corner of our minds. The spectres may impose on us whilst we refuse to turn them every way and view their shape and complexions in every light. For that which can be shown only in a certain light is questionable. Truth, 'tis supposed, may bear all lights; and one of those principal lights, or natural mediums, by which things are to be viewed in order to a thorough recognition, is ridicule itself, or that manner of proof by which we discern whatever is liable to just raillery in any subject. . . .

The only danger is the laying an embargo. The same thing happens here as in the case of trade. Impositions and restrictions reduce it to a low ebb. Nothing is so advantageous to it as a free port.

We have seen in our own time the decline and ruin of a false sort of wit, which so much delighted our ancestors that their poems and plays, as well as sermons, were full of it. All humor had something of the quibble. The very language of the court was punning.[4] But 'tis now banished the town and all good company; there are only some few footsteps of it in the country; and it seems at last confined to the nurseries of youth, as the chief entertainment of pedants and their pupils. And thus in other respects, wit will mend upon our hands, and humor will refine itself, if we take care not to tamper with it and bring it under constraint by severe usage and rigorous prescriptions. All politeness is owing to liberty. We polish one another and rub off our corners and rough sides by a sort of amicable collision. To restrain this is inevitably to bring a rust upon men's understandings. 'Tis a destroying of civility, good breeding, and even charity itself under pretense of maintaining it. . . .

The same thing therefore happens here as in strong and healthy bodies which are debarred their natural exercise and confined in a

---

[4] Cf. Addison, Spectator No. 62.

narrow space. They are forced to use odd gestures and contortions. They have a sort of action and move still, though with the worst grace imaginable. For the animal spirits in such sound and active limbs cannot lie dead or without employment. And thus the natural free spirits of ingenious men, if imprisoned and controlled, will find out other ways of motion to relieve themselves in their constraint; and whether it be in burlesque, mimicry, or buffoonery, they will be glad at any rate[5] to vent themselves and be revenged on their constrainers.

If men are forbid to speak their minds seriously on certain subjects, they will do it ironically. If they are forbid to speak at all upon such subjects, or if they find it really dangerous to do so, they will then redouble their disguise, involve themselves in mysteriousness, and talk so as hardly to be understood, or at least not plainly interpreted, by those who are disposed to do them a mischief. And thus raillery is brought more in fashion and runs into an extreme. 'Tis the persecuting spirit has raised the bantering one, and want of liberty may account for want of a true politeness and for the corruption or wrong use of pleasantry and humor.

If in this respect we strain the just measure of what we call urbanity, and are apt sometimes to take a buffooning rustic air, we may thank the ridiculous solemnity and sour humor of our pedagogues; or rather, they may thank themselves if they in particular meet with the heaviest of this kind of treatment. For it will naturally fall heaviest where the constraint has been the severest. The greater the weight is, the bitterer will be the satire. The higher the slavery, the more exquisite the buffoonery.

That this is really so may appear by looking on those countries where the spiritual tyranny is highest. For the greatest of buffoons are the Italians; and in their writings, in their freer sort of conversations, on their theaters, and in their streets, buffoonery and burlesque are in the highest vogue. 'Tis the only manner in which the poor cramped wretches can discharge a free thought.[6]

FROM PART IV, SECTIONS II, III

The admirers of beauty in the fair sex would laugh, perhaps, to hear of a moral part in their amours. Yet what a stir is made about

---

[5] at any cost.

[6] Defending all ridicule in principle, Shaftesbury argues the superiority of clear, sweet-tempered raillery, like his own. Intense irony, ambiguity, and burlesque are not in the highest taste, but inevitable outgrowths of a society in which artistic and intellectual freedom are repressed. They express psychological constraint and rebellion against it.

a heart! . . . Why else is the very air of foolishness enough to cloy a lover at first sight? Why does an idiot-look and manner destroy the effect of all those outward charms and rob the fair one of her power, though regularly armed in all the exactness of features and complexion? We may imagine what we please of a substantial solid part of beauty; but were the subject to be well criticized, we should find, perhaps, that what we most admired, even in the turn of outward features, was only a mysterious expression and a kind of shadow of something inward in the temper; and that when we were struck with a majestic air, a sprightly look, an Amazon bold grace or a contrary soft and gentle one, 'twas chiefly the fancy of these characters or qualities which wrought on us, our imagination being busied in forming beauteous shapes and images of this rational kind, which entertained the mind and held it in admiration whilst other passions of a lower species were employed another way. . . .

Nor can the men of cooler passions and more deliberate pursuits withstand the force of beauty in other subjects. Every one is a virtuoso of a higher or lower degree. Every one pursues a Grace and courts a Venus of one kind or another. The *venustum*, the *honestum*, the *decorum* of things[7] will force its way. They who refuse to give it scope in the nobler subjects of a rational and moral kind will find its prevalency elsewhere in an inferior order of things. . . . The models of houses, buildings, and their accompanying ornaments; the plans of gardens and their compartments; the ordering of walks, plantations, avenues; and a thousand other symmetries will succeed in the room of[8] that happier and higher symmetry and order of a mind. The species[9] of fair, noble, and handsome will discover itself on a thousand occasions and in a thousand subjects. The spectre still will haunt us in some shape or other. . . .

And thus, after all, the most natural beauty in the world is honesty and moral truth. For all beauty is truth. True features make the beauty of a face and true proportions the beauty of architecture, as true measures that of harmony and music. In poetry, which is all fable, truth still is the perfection. And whoever is scholar enough to read the Ancient philosopher or his Modern copyists[1] upon the nature of a dramatic and epic poem will easily understand this account of truth.

---

[7] "loveliness," "moral nobility," and "fitness," each considered as an aspect of the one beauty.
[8] take the place of.
[9] idea.
[1] The French translator, no doubt, has justly hit our author's thought by

A painter, if he has any genius, understands the truth and unity of design, and knows he is even then unnatural when he follows Nature too close and strictly copies life. For his art allows him not to bring all Nature into his piece, but a part only. However, his piece, if it be beautiful and carries truth, must be a whole by itself, complete, independent, and withal as great and comprehensive as he can make it. So that particulars, on this occasion, must yield to the general design, and all things be subservient to that which is principal, in order to form a certain easiness of sight, a simple, clear, and united view,[2] which would be broken and disturbed by the expression of anything peculiar or distinct.

Now the variety of Nature is such as to distinguish everything she forms by a peculiar original character which, if strictly observed, will make the subject appear unlike to anything extant in the world besides. But this effect the good poet and painter seek industriously to prevent. They hate minuteness and are afraid of singularity, which would make their images or characters appear capricious and fantastical. The mere face-painter indeed has little in common with the poet, but like the mere historian, copies what he sees and minutely traces every feature and odd mark. 'Tis otherwise with the men of invention and design. 'Tis from the many objects of Nature, and not from a particular one, that those geniuses form the idea of their work. Thus the best artists are said to have been indefatigable in studying the best statues, as esteeming them a better rule than the perfectest human bodies could afford. And thus some considerable wits have recommended the best poems as preferable to the best of histories, and better teaching the truth of characters and nature of mankind.

Nor can this criticism be thought high-strained. Though few confine themselves to these rules, few are insensible of them. Whatever quarter we may give to our vicious poets or other composers of irregular and short-lived works, we know very well that the standing pieces of good artists must be formed after a more uniform way.

---

naming in his margin the excellent Bossu *Du poème épique*, who in that admirable comment and explanation of Aristotle has perhaps not only shown himself the greatest of the French critics, but presented the world with a view of Ancient literature and just writing beyond any other Modern of whatever nation. (Shaftesbury's note.)

[2] The τὸ εὐσύνοπτον, as the great master of arts calls it in his *Poetics* . . . where he shows "that the τὸ καλόν, the beautiful or the sublime in these abovementioned arts, is from the expression of greatness with order. . . . The dramatic kind is confined within the convenient and proper time of a spectacle. The epic is left more at large. Each work, however, must aim at vastness. . . ." (Shaftesbury's note and translation.)

Every just work of theirs comes under those natural rules of proportion and truth. The creature of their brain must be like one of Nature's formation. It must have a body and parts proportionable, or the very vulgar will not fail to criticize the work when it has neither head nor tail. For so common sense (according to just philosophy) judges of those works which want the justness of a whole, and show their author, however curious and exact in particulars, to be in the main a very bungler—

> *Infelix operis summa, quia ponere totum*
> *Nesciet.*[3]

Such is poetical and such (if I may so call it) graphical or plastic truth.[4]

The Moralists, a Philosophical Rhapsody [1709] [5]
FROM PART III, SECTION I

"O glorious Nature! supremely fair and sovereignly good! all-loving and all-lovely, all-divine! whose looks are so becoming and of such infinite grace, whose study brings such wisdom and whose contemplation such delight, whose every single work affords an ampler scene and is a nobler spectacle than all which ever art presented! O mighty Nature! wise substitute of Providence! impowered creatress! Or thou impowering Deity, supreme creator! Thee I invoke and thee alone adore. To thee this solitude, this place, these rural meditations are sacred; whilst thus inspired with harmony of thought, though unconfined by words, and in loose numbers, I sing of Nature's order in created beings and celebrate the beauties which resolve in thee, the source and principle of all beauty and perfection.

"Thy being is boundless, unsearchable, impenetrable. In thy im-

---

[3] Horace, *Ars Poetica*, 34–35: "He is unsuccessful in his effects because he cannot represent a whole."

[4] The preceding passage is typical. It resumes neoclassic commonplaces but with a very special interpretation of them. Aristotle, Horace, Le Bossu, the unities, rules, common sense, imitation of authors, the inferior truth of history and particulars, all are fused with plastic Nature, sublime vastness, genius, inward beauty, Platonic eros, and selective idealization.

[5] An imitation of a Platonic dialogue, lengthy and beautifully controlled, which Shaftesbury considered his "principal performance" where he appeared "a poet, in due form." It is narrated by Philocles, a sensitive skeptic, to Palemon, a gentleman of fashion. The Socratic hero of the piece is named Theocles, who, in the course of discussion, converts Philocles to Shaftesbury's philosophy of Nature.

mensity all thought is lost; fancy gives over its flight; and wearied imagination spends itself in vain, finding no coast nor limit of this ocean, nor, in the widest tract through which it soars, one point yet nearer the circumference than the first center whence it parted. Thus having oft essayed, thus sallied forth into the wide expanse, when I return again within myself, struck with the sense of this so narrow being and of the fullness of that immense one, I dare no more behold the amazing depths nor sound the abyss of Deity." . . .

Here he[6] stopped short, and starting as out of a dream: "Now, Philocles," said he, "inform me, how have I appeared to you in my fit? Seemed it a sensible kind of madness, like those transports which are permitted to our poets? or was it downright raving?"

FROM PART III, SECTION II

" 'Tis true," said I, "Theocles, I own it. Your genius, the genius of the place, and the Great Genius have at last prevailed. I shall no longer resist the passion growing in me for things of a natural kind, where neither art nor the conceit or caprice of man has spoiled their genuine order by breaking in upon that primitive state. Even the rude rocks, the mossy caverns, the irregular unwrought grottoes and broken falls of waters, with all the horrid graces of the wilderness itself, as representing Nature more, will be the more engaging, and appear with a magnificence beyond the formal mockery of princely gardens. But tell me, I entreat you, how comes it that, excepting a few philosophers of your sort, the only people who are enamored in this way, and seek the woods, the rivers, or seashores, are your poor vulgar lovers?"

"Say not this," replied he, "of lovers only. For is it not the same with poets, and all those other students in Nature and the arts which copy after her? In short, is not this the real case of all who are lovers either of the Muses or the Graces?"

"However," said I, "all those who are deep in this romantic way are looked upon, you know, as a people either plainly out of their wits or overrun with melancholy and enthusiasm." . . .

"No wonder," replied he, "if we are at a loss when we pursue the shadow for the substance. For if we may trust to what our reasoning has taught us, whatever in Nature is beautiful or charming is only the faint shadow of that first beauty. So that every real love depending on the mind, and being only the contemplation of beauty either as it really is in itself or as it appears imperfectly in

---

[6] Theocles.

the objects which strike the sense, how can the rational mind rest here or be satisfied with the absurd enjoyment which reaches the sense alone? . . . If you are already," replied he, "such a proficient in this new love that you are sure never to admire the representative beauty except for the sake of the original, nor aim at other enjoyment than of the rational kind, you may then be confident." . . .

"O Theocles!" said I, "well do I remember now the terms in which you engaged me that morning when you bespoke my love of this mysterious beauty. You have indeed made good your part of the condition and may now claim me for a proselyte. If there be any seeming extravagance in the case, I must comfort myself the best I can and consider that all sound love and admiration is enthusiasm: 'The transports of poets, the sublime of orators, the rapture of musicians, the high strains of the virtuosi—all mere enthusiasm! Even learning itself, the love of arts and curiosities, the spirit of travelers and adventurers, gallantry, war, heroism—all, all enthusiasm!' 'Tis enough; I am content to be this new enthusiast in a way unknown to me before."

"And I," replied Theocles, "am content you should call this love of ours enthusiasm, allowing it the privilege of its fellow passions. For is there a fair and plausible enthusiasm, a reasonable ecstasy and transport allowed to other subjects, such as architecture, painting, music; and shall it be exploded here? Are there senses by which all those other graces and perfections are perceived, and none by which this higher perfection and grace is comprehended? . . .

"Thus then," said he, smiling, "whatever passion you may have for other beauties, I know, good Philocles, you are no such admirer of wealth in any kind as to allow much beauty to it, especially in a rude heap or mass. But in medals, coins, embossed work, statues, and well-fabricated pieces of whatever sort, you can discover beauty and admire the kind."

"True," said I, "but not for the metal's sake."

"'Tis not then the metal or matter which is beautiful with you?"

"No."

"But the art?"

"Certainly."

"The art then is the beauty."

"Right."

"And the art is that which beautifies?"

"The same."

"So that the beautifying, not the beautified, is the really beautiful?"

"It seems so."

"For that which is beautified, is beautiful only by the accession of something beautifying, and by the recess or withdrawing of the same, it ceases to be beautiful?"

"Be it."

"In respect of bodies therefore, beauty comes and goes?"

"So we see."

"Nor is the body itself any cause either of its coming or staying?"

"None."

"So that there is no principle of beauty in body?"

"None at all."

"For body can no way be the cause of beauty to itself?"

"No way."

"Nor govern nor regulate itself?"

"Nor yet this."

"Nor mean nor intend itself?"

"Nor this neither."

"Must not that, therefore, which means and intends for it, regulates and orders it, be the principle of beauty to it? "

"Of necessity."

"And what must that be?"

"Mind, I suppose, for what can it be else?"

"Here then," said he, "is all I would have explained to you before. 'That the beautiful, the fair, the comely, were never in the matter but in the art and design, never in body itself but in the form or forming power.' Does not the beautiful form confess this, and speak the beauty of the design whenever it strikes you? What is it but the design which strikes? What is it you admire but mind or the effect of mind? 'Tis mind alone which forms. All which is void of mind is horrid, and matter formless is deformity itself."

"Of all forms then," said I, "those according to your scheme are the most amiable, and in the first order of beauty, which have a power of making other forms themselves. From whence methinks they may be styled the forming forms. So far I can easily concur with you and gladly give the advantage to the human form above those other beauties of man's formation. The palaces, equipages, and estates shall never in my account be brought in competition with the original living forms of flesh and blood. And for the other, the dead forms of Nature, the metals and stones, however precious

222 ~ ANTHONY ASHLEY COOPER

and dazzling, I am resolved to resist their splendor and make abject things of them, even in their highest pride, when they pretend to set off human beauty and are officiously brought in aid of the fair."

"Do you not see then," replied Theocles, "that you have established three degrees or orders of beauty?"

"As how?"

"Why first, the dead forms, as you properly have called them, which bear a fashion, and are formed, whether by man or Nature, but have no forming power, no action or intelligence."

"Right."

"Next, and as the second kind, the forms which form, that is, which have intelligence, action, and operation."

"Right still."

"Here therefore is double beauty. For here is both the form (the effect of mind) and mind itself. The first kind low and despicable in respect of this other, from whence the dead form receives its luster and force of beauty. For what is a mere body, though a human one, and ever so exactly fashioned, if inward form be wanting, and the mind be monstrous or imperfect, as in an idiot or savage?"

"This too I can apprehend," said I, "but where is the third order?"

"Have patience," replied he, "and see first whether you have discovered the whole force of this second beauty. How else should you understand the force of love or have the power of enjoyment? Tell me, I beseech you, when first you named these the forming forms, did you think of no other productions of theirs besides the dead kinds, such as the palaces, the coins, the brazen or the marble figures of men? Or did you think of something nearer life?"

"I could easily," said I, "have added that these forms of ours had a virtue of producing other living forms like themselves. But this virtue of theirs, I thought, was from another form above them, and could not properly be called their virtue or art, if in reality there was a superior art, or something artist-like, which guided their hand and made tools of them in this specious[7] work."

"Happily thought," said he. "You have prevented a censure which I hardly imagined you could escape. And here you have unawares discovered that third order of beauty, which forms not only such as we call mere forms, but even the forms which form. For we ourselves are notable architects in matter, and can show lifeless bodies brought into form and fashioned by our own hands, but that which fashions even minds themselves, contains in itself all

---

[7] beautiful or right, but not entirely what it seems.

the beauties fashioned by those minds, and is consequently the principle, source, and fountain of all beauty."

Soliloquy, or Advice to an Author [1710]
FROM PART I, SECTION III

Scribendi recte sapere est et principium et fons;
Rem tibi Socraticae poterunt ostendere chartae.[8] . . .

The horse alone can never make the horseman, nor limbs the wrestler or the dancer. No more can a genius alone make a poet, or good parts a writer in any considerable kind. The skill and grace of writing is founded, as our wise poet tells us, in knowledge and good sense, and not barely in that knowledge which is to be learnt from common authors or the general conversation of the world, but from those particular rules of art which philosophy alone exhibits.

The philosophical writings to which our poet in his *Art of Poetry* refers were in themselves a kind of poetry. . . . They were either real dialogues, or recitals of such personated discourses, where the persons themselves had their characters preserved throughout, their manners, humors, and distinct turns of temper and understanding maintained, according to the most exact poetical truth. 'Twas not enough that these pieces treated fundamentally of morals and in consequence pointed out real characters and manners: they exhibited them alive, and set the countenances and complexions of men plainly in view. And by this means they not only taught us to know others but, what was principal and of highest virtue in them, they taught us to know ourselves.

The philosophical hero of these poems,[9] whose name they carried both in their body and front, and whose genius and manner they were made to represent, was in himself a perfect character, yet in some respects so veiled, and in a cloud, that to the unattentive surveyor he seemed often to be very different from what he really was, and this chiefly by reason of a certain exquisite and refined raillery which belonged to his manner, and by virtue of which he could treat the highest subjects and those of the commonest capacity both together, and render them explanatory of each other. So that in this genius of writing there appeared both the heroic and

---

[8] Horace, *Ars Poetica*, 309–10: "Wisdom is the origin and underlying principle of good writing. The Socratic dialogues can provide you with material."
[9] Socrates.

the simple, the tragic and the comic vein. However, it was so ordered that, notwithstanding the oddness or mysteriousness of the principal character, the underparts or second characters showed human nature more distinctly and to the life. We might here, therefore, as in a looking-glass, discover ourselves, and see our minutest features nicely delineated, and suited to our own apprehension and cognizance. No one who was ever so little a while an inspector, could fail of becoming acquainted with his own heart. And, what was of singular note in these magical glasses, it would happen that, by constant and long inspection, the parties accustomed to the practice would acquire a peculiar speculative habit, so as virtually to carry about with them a sort of pocket mirror, always ready and in use. In this, there were two faces which would naturally present themselves to our view: one of them like the commanding genius, the leader and chief above-mentioned; the other like that rude, undisciplined, and headstrong creature whom we ourselves in our natural capacity most exactly resembled. Whatever we were employed in, whatever we set about, if once we had acquired the habit of this mirror we should, by virtue of the double reflection, distinguish ourselves into two different parties. And in this dramatic method, the work of self-inspection would proceed with admirable success. . . .

For poetry itself was defined an imitation chiefly of men and manners, and was that in an exalted and noble degree which in a low one we call mimicry. 'Tis in this that the great mimographer, the father and prince of poets,[1] excels so highly, his characters being wrought to a likeness beyond what any succeeding masters were ever able to describe. Nor are his works, which are so full of action, any other than an artful series or chain of dialogues which turn upon one remarkable catastrophe or event. He describes no qualities or virtues, censures no manners, makes no encomiums, nor gives characters himself, but brings his actors still in view. 'Tis they who show themselves. 'Tis they who speak in such a manner as distinguishes them in all things from all others and makes them ever like themselves. Their different compositions and alloys so justly made, and equally carried on through every particle of the action, give more instruction than all the comments or glosses in the world. The poet, instead of giving himself to those dictating and masterly airs of wisdom, makes hardly any figure at all, and is scarce discoverable in his poem. This is being truly a master. He paints so as to need no inscription over his figures to tell us what

---

[1] Homer.

they are or what he intends by them. A few words let fall on any slight occasion, from any of the parties he introduces, are sufficient to denote their manners and distinct character. From a finger or a toe he can represent to our thoughts the frame and fashion of a whole body. He wants no other help of art to personate his heroes and make them living. There was no more left for tragedy to do after him than to erect a stage and draw his dialogues and characters into scenes, turning in the same manner upon one principal action or event, with that regard to place and time which was suitable to a real spectacle.[2] Even comedy itself was adjudged to this great master, it being derived from those parodies or mock humors of which he had given the specimen[3] in a concealed sort of raillery intermixed with the sublime. A dangerous stroke of art! and which required a masterly hand, like that of the philosophical hero whose character was represented in the dialogue writings above mentioned.

From hence possibly we may form a notion of that resemblance which on so many occasions was heretofore remarked between the prince of poets and the divine philosopher[4] who was said to rival him and who, together with his contemporaries of the same school, writ wholly in that manner of dialogue above described. . . .

I have formerly wondered indeed why a manner which was familiarly used in treatises upon most subjects with so much success among the Ancients should be so insipid and of little esteem with us Moderns.[5] But I afterwards perceived that, besides the difficulty of the manner itself, and that mirror faculty which we have observed it to carry in respect to ourselves, it proves also of necessity a kind of mirror or looking-glass to the age. If so, it should of consequence (you will say) be the more agreeable and entertaining.

True, if the real view of ourselves be not perhaps displeasing to us. But why more displeasing to us than to the Ancients? Because perhaps they could with just reason bear to see their natural countenances represented. And why not we the same? What should discourage us? For are we not as handsome, at least in our

---

[2] The preceding passage on Homer neatly capsules Aristotelian doctrines of imitation, unity of action, impersonality, consistency and reality of characterization. Shaftesbury is discreetly ambiguous regarding the pseudo-Aristotelian unities of time and place.

[3] Not only in his *Margites*, but even in his *Iliad* and *Odyssey*. (Shaftesbury's note.)

[4] Plato.

[5] Dialogues, popular throughout the Renaissance, became increasingly a fashion of criticism: Dryden and Dennis preceded Shaftesbury himself, and later they were cultivated by Berkeley, Hurd, Hume, Franklin and others.

own eyes? Perhaps not, as we shall see when we have considered a little further what the force is of this mirror-writing and how it differs from that more complacent modish way in which an author, instead of presenting us with other natural characters, sets off his own with the utmost art, and purchases his reader's favor by all imaginable compliances and condescensions.

An author who writes in his own person has the advantage of being who or what he pleases. He is no certain man, nor has any certain or genuine character, but suits himself on every occasion to the fancy of his reader whom, as the fashion is nowadays, he constantly caresses and cajoles. All turns upon their two persons. And, as in an amour or commerce of love letters, so here the author has the privilege of talking eternally of himself, dressing and sprucing himself up, whilst he is making diligent court and working upon the humor of the party to whom he addresses. This is the coquetry of a Modern author, whose epistles dedicatory, prefaces, and addresses to the reader are so many affected graces, designed to draw the attention from the subject towards himself, and make it generally observed, not so much what he says as what he appears, or is, and what figure he already makes or hopes to make in the fashionable world. . . . The whole writing of this age is become indeed a sort of memoir-writing. Though in the real memoirs of the Ancients, even when they writ at any time concerning themselves, there was neither the *I* nor *thou* throughout the whole work. So that all this pretty amour and intercourse of caresses between the author and reader was thus entirely taken away.

Much more is this the case in dialogue. For here the author is annihilated, and the reader, being no way applied to, stands for nobody. The self-interesting parties both vanish at once. The scene presents itself as by chance and undesigned. You are not only left to judge coolly and with indifference of the sense delivered, but of the character, genius, elocution, and manner of the persons who deliver it. . . . It must be seen from what bottom they speak, from what principle, what stock or fund of knowledge they draw, and what kind or species of understanding they possess. For the understanding here must have its mark, its characteristic note, by which it may be distinguished. It must be such and such an understanding, as when we say, for instance, such or such a face, since Nature has characterized tempers and minds as peculiarly as faces. And for an artist who draws naturally, 'tis not enough to show us merely faces which may be called men's: every face must be a certain man's.

Now as a painter who draws battles or other actions of Christians, Turks, Indians, or any distinct and peculiar people, must of necessity draw the several figures of his piece in their proper and real proportions, gestures, habits, arms, or at least with as fair a resemblance as possible, so in the same manner that writer, whoever he be among us Moderns, who shall venture to bring his fellow Moderns into dialogue, must introduce them in their proper manners, genius, behavior and humor. And this is the mirror or looking-glass above described.

For instance, a dialogue, we will suppose, is framed after the manner of our Ancient authors. In it a poor philosopher, of a mean figure, accosts one of the powerfullest, wittiest, handsomest, and richest noblemen of the time as he is walking leisurely towards the temple. "You are going then," says he (calling him by his plain name), "to pay your devotions yonder at the temple?" . . . I see a thousand ridicules arising from the manner, the circumstances and action itself, compared with Modern breeding and civility.[6] Let us therefore mend the matter if possible, and introduce the same philosopher addressing himself in a more obsequious manner to *his Grace, his Excellency,* or *his Honor,* without failing in the least tittle of the ceremonial. . . . Let his garb and action be of the more modish sort in order to introduce him better and gain him audience. And with these advantages and precautions, imagine still in what manner he must accost this pageant of state, if at any time he finds him at leisure, walking in the fields alone and without his equipage. Consider how many bows and simpering faces! how many preludes, excuses, compliments! Now put compliments, put ceremony into a dialogue, and see what will be the effect!

This is the plain dilemma against that Ancient manner of writing which we can neither well imitate nor translate, whatever pleasure or profit we may find in reading those originals. . . . If we avoid ceremony, we are unnatural; if we use it and appear as we naturally are, as we salute, and meet, and treat one another, we hate the sight. What's this but hating our own faces? Is it the painter's fault? Should he paint falsely or affectedly, mix Modern with Ancient, join shapes preposterously, and betray his art? If not, what medium is there? What remains for him but to throw away the pencil? No more designing after the life; no more mirror-writing or personal representation of any kind whatever.

Thus dialogue is at an end. The Ancients could see their own faces, but we cannot. And why this? Why, but because we have less

---

[6] *Cf.* Blackwell, p. 282.

beauty, for so our looking-glass can inform us. . . . Our commerce and manner of conversation, which we think the politest imaginable, is such, it seems, as we ourselves cannot endure to see represented to the life. 'Tis here as in our real portraitures, particularly those at full length, where the poor pencil-man is put to a thousand shifts whilst he strives to dress us in affected habits such as we never wore, because should he paint us in those we really wear, they would of necessity make the piece to be so much more ridiculous as it was more natural and resembling.

Thus much for antiquity and those rules of art, those philosophical sea-cards, by which the adventurous genuises of the times were wont to steer their courses and govern their impetuous muse. These were the *chartae*[7] of our Roman masterpoet, and these the pieces of art, the mirrors, the exemplars he bids us place before our eyes—

vos exemplaria Graeca
Nocturna versate manu, versate diurna.[8] . . .

I must confess there is hardly anywhere to be found a more insipid race of mortals than those whom we Moderns are contented to call poets for having attained the chiming faculty of a language with an injudicious random use of wit and fancy. But for the man who truly and in a just sense deserves the name of poet, and who as a real master, or architect in the kind, can describe both men and manners, and give to an action its just body and proportions, he will be found, if I mistake not, a very different creature. Such a poet is indeed a second *maker*, a just Prometheus under Jove. Like that sovereign artist or universal plastic Nature, he forms a whole, coherent and proportioned in itself, with due subjection and subordinacy of constituent parts. He notes the boundaries of the passions and knows their exact tones and measures, by which he justly represents them, marks the sublime of sentiments and action, and distinguishes the beautiful from the deformed, the amiable from the odious. The moral artist who can thus imitate the Creator, and is thus knowing in the inward form and structure of his fellow creature, will hardly, I presume, be found unknowing in himself, or at a loss in those numbers which make the harmony of a mind. For knavery is mere dissonance and disproportion. And though villains may have strong tones and natural capacities of action, 'tis

---

[7] See the quotation from Horace, p. 223.
[8] Horace, *Ars Poetica*, 268–69: "For your part, handle the Greek models night and day."

impossible that true judgment and ingenuity should reside where harmony and honesty have no being.

However difficult or desperate it may appear in any artist to endeavor to bring perfection into his work, if he has not at least the idea of perfection to give him aim, he will be found very defective and mean in his performance. Though his intention be to please the world, he must nevertheless be, in a manner, above it, and fix his eye upon that consummate grace, that beauty of Nature, and that perfection of numbers which the rest of mankind, feeling only by the effect whilst ignorant of the cause, term the *je ne sais quoi*, the unintelligible or the I know not what, and suppose to be a kind of charm or enchantment of which the artist himself can give no account. . . .

Could we once convince ourselves of what is in itself so evident, "That in the very nature of things there must of necessity be the foundation of a right and wrong taste, as well in respect of inward characters and features as of outward person, behavior, and action," we should be far more ashamed of ignorance and wrong judgment in the former than in the latter of these subjects. Even in the arts, which are mere imitations of that outward grace and beauty, we not only confess a taste, but make it a part of refined breeding to discover amidst the many false manners and ill styles the true and natural one, which represents the real beauty and Venus of the kind. 'Tis the like moral grace and Venus which, discovering itself in the turns of character and the variety of human affection, is copied by the writing artist. If he knows not this Venus, these graces, nor was ever struck with the beauty, the decorum of this inward kind, he can neither paint advantageously after the life nor in a feigned subject where he has full scope. . . .

And thus the sense of inward numbers, the knowledge and practice of the social virtues, and the familiarity and favor of the moral graces are essential to the character of a deserving artist and just favorite of the Muses. Thus are the arts and virtues mutually friends; and thus the science of virtuosi and that of virtue itself become, in a manner, one and the same.

One who aspires to the character of a man of breeding and politeness is careful to form his judgment of arts and sciences upon right models of perfection. If he travels to Rome, he inquires which are the truest pieces of architecture, the best remains of statues, the best paintings of a Raphael or a Carracci.[9] However antiquated, rough, or dismal they may appear to him at first sight, he resolves to view them over and over till he has brought himself to relish them, and finds their hidden graces and perfections. He takes particular care to turn his eye from everything which is gaudy, luscious, and of a false taste. Nor is he less careful to turn his ear from every sort of music besides that which is of the best manner and truest harmony.

'Twere to be wished we had the same regard to a right taste in life and manners. What mortal being, once convinced of a difference in inward character, and of a preference due to one kind above another, would not be concerned to make his own the best? If civility and humanity be a taste, if brutality, insolence, riot, be in the same manner a taste, who, if he could reflect, would not choose to form himself on the amiable and agreeable rather than the odious and perverse model? Who would not endeavor to force Nature as well in this respect as in what relates to a taste or judgment in other arts and sciences? For in each place the force on Nature is used only for its redress. If a natural good taste be not already formed in us, why should not we endeavor to form it, and cultivate it till it become natural?

"I like! I fancy! I admire! How? By accident, or as I please? No. But I learn to fancy, to admire, to please, as the subjects themselves are deserving and can bear me out. Otherwise, I like at this hour but dislike the next. I shall be weary of my pursuit, and upon experience find little pleasure in the main, if my choice and judgment in it be from no other rule than that single one, because I please. Grotesque and monstrous figures often please. Cruel spectacles and barbarities are also found to please and, in some tempers, to please beyond all other subjects. But is this pleasure right? And shall I follow it if it presents? not strive with it or endeavor to prevent its growth or prevalency in my temper? . . . How stands the case in a more soft and flattering kind of pleasure? . . . Effeminacy pleases me. The Indian figures, the Japan work, the enamel strikes my eye. The luscious colors and glossy paint gain upon my fancy.[1] A French

***

[9] Raffaello Sanzio (1483–1520) was generally considered by neoclassicists as the greatest of modern painters, until the later eighteenth century when he was dethroned in favor of the more "sublime" Michelangelo. The Carracci family—Annibale (1540–1609), Ludovico (1555–1619), Agostino (1557–1602)—also had a favored place in the neoclassic pantheon. See Hagstrum, *The Sister Arts*, pp. 162–70 *et passim*.

[1] Shaftesbury alludes to the growing fashion for Oriental decoration and

or Flemish style is highly liked by me at first sight, and I pursue my liking.[2] But what ensues? . . . Do I not for ever forfeit my good relish? How is it possible I should thus come to taste the beauties of an Italian master, or of a hand happily formed on Nature and the Ancients? 'Tis not by wantonness and humor that I shall attain my end and arrive at the enjoyment I propose. The art itself is severe, the rules rigid. And if I expect the knowledge should come to me by accident, or in play, I shall be grossly deluded and prove myself, at best, a mock virtuoso or mere pedant of the kind."

Miscellaneous Reflections
on the Preceding Treatises [1711]
FROM MISCELLANY III, CHAPTER II

'Tis impossible we can advance the least in any relish or taste of outward symmetry and order without acknowledging that the proportionate and regular state is the truly prosperous and natural in every subject. The same features which make deformity create incommodiousness and disease. And the same shapes and proportions which make beauty afford advantage by adapting to activity and use. Even in the imitative or designing arts (to which our author[3] so often refers), the truth or beauty of every figure or statue is measured from the perfection of Nature in her just adapting of every limb and proportion to the activity, strength, dexterity, life and vigor of the particular species or animal designed.

Thus beauty and truth are plainly joined with the notion of utility and convenience, even in the apprehension of every ingenious artist, the architect, the statuary, or the painter. 'Tis the same in the physician's way. Natural health is the just proportion, truth, and regular course of things in a constitution. 'Tis the inward beauty of the body. And when the harmony and just measures of the rising pulses, the circulating humors, and the moving airs or spirits are disturbed or lost, deformity enters, and with it, calamity and ruin.

Should not this (one would imagine) be still the same case and

---

chinoiserie in furniture and movables, building, gardening, and the like. Its unclassical asymmetry and gaudiness seem to him bad taste.

[2] Flemish (and Dutch) painters are disvalued because of their particularity or minuteness of copying, unlike the "Roman and Bolognian schools" who idealize nature and "address themselves to our best and noblest faculties" (Reynolds, *Discourse* VII).

[3] Here Shaftesbury writes of himself in the third person, an act of "self-inspection."

hold equally as to the mind? Is there nothing there which tends to disturbance and dissolution? Is there no natural tenor, tone, or order of the passions or affections? No beauty or deformity in this moral kind? Or allowing that there really is, must it not, of consequence, in the same manner imply health or sickliness, prosperity or disaster? Will it not be found in this respect, above all, "that what is beautiful is harmonious and proportionable; what is harmonious and proportionable is true; and what is at once both beautiful and true is, of consequence, agreeable and good?"

Where then is this beauty or harmony to be found? How is this symmetry to be discovered and applied? Is it any other art than that of philosophy or the study of inward numbers and proportions which can exhibit this in life? If no other, who then can possibly have a taste of this kind without being beholden to philosophy? Who can admire the outward beauties and not recur instantly to the inward, which are the most real and essential, the most naturally affecting, and of the highest pleasure as well as profit and advantage?

In so short a compass does that learning and knowledge lie on which manners and life depend. 'Tis we ourselves create and form our taste. If we resolve to have it just, 'tis in our power. We may esteem and resolve, approve and disapprove, as we would wish. For who would not rejoice to be always equal and consonant to himself and have constantly that opinion of things which is natural and proportionable? But who dares search opinion to the bottom or call in question his early and prepossessing taste? Who is so just to himself as to recall his fancy from the power of fashion and education to that of reason?

Joseph Addison

1672–1719

EVEN IN the eighteenth century, Addison weathered charges of superficiality, which Dr. Johnson answered (see p. 501). Before judging his criticism, one should remember its historical and biographical context.

Addison resided twelve years at Oxford, as student, tutor, and fellow; earned his M.A. in classics, and the notice of Dryden. In 1699, at age twenty-seven, he accepted a government grant, to prepare for a diplomatic career, and for the next four years, traveled in France, Italy, Switzerland, Austria, Germany, and Holland. He became, after his return, Undersecretary of State (1706–8); Secretary for the Irish Government in Dublin (1708–10, 1714); Member of Parliament (1710); and later still, Secretary to the Regency (1714) after the death of Queen Anne; Commissioner of Trade (1715); and finally, the highest office of his life, Secretary of State (1717–18). Along the route he performed as Whig publicist. He completed his best criticism, the *Spectator* essays, during the brief period 1711–14 when he was out of office. He died relatively young, at forty-seven, after a series of illnesses aggravated by overwork. Most if not all that he had to say took shape during his freer, less hurried university days before he was thirty, and though it was refined by his years on the continent, it changed very little. The same was true for his poems and plays: the most valuable were written or planned by 1706 as he began his administrative career. Even

Cato (1714) was rough-drafted at Oxford, in time for Dryden to see it, and was carried along by Addison on his travels.

His adult ambition was partially letters but increasingly social reform and public service. Of the almost three hundred papers which he contributed to the *Spectator* from 1711 to 1714, about fifty qualify as criticism: those on tragedy (39, 40, 42, 44), wit (58, 59, 60, 61, 62, 63), comedy (65, 446), ballads (70, 74, 85), genius (160), laughter and ridicule (249), Pope's *Essay on Criticism* (253) and the idea of a true critic (291, 592), *Paradise Lost* (eighteen weekly papers from 267 to 369), taste (409), the pleasures of imagination (411 to 421 consecutively), and mythology in poetry (523). To these may be added a scattering of papers contributed to the *Tatler* (e.g., 158 on Tom Folio the pedant, 163 on Ned Softly the easy poet, 165 on criticism) and to the *Guardian* (e.g., 115 and 119 on criticism).

If Addison helped create the periodical essay, its limits no less helped create the "superficial" pitch of his criticism. It forbade the rambling, personal freedom which Dryden enjoyed in his prefaces, the slow massive building of concepts in the treatises of Shaftesbury and Dennis. It exacted wise surface with now and then a risk—a short flight or series of flights on a single, limited topic, in a politic style leveled to the busy, miscellaneous, socially divided public of 1711, who must somehow be won to the next installment. It allowed no probing at the abstruse edges of fact and argument, which Addison certainly knew were there, and it exacted speed. Addison wrote his *Spectator* essays under the pressure of deadlines, and of course dredged up what he could from all that he had ever thought; e.g., the essays on wit, Milton, and the pleasures of imagination were among those resurrected from earlier notes and drafts.

Finally, one should remember his Whig idealism, not only to reach a mixed, general public, but to improve them with up-to-date learning, to bring "philosophy" out of libraries, schools, and colleges, to dwell in clubs and assemblies, at tea tables and coffee houses (no. 10). Even if one denied the undeniable—Addison's uncommon charm of style and satire, his bold precise grasp of live manners and live thought, his enormous influence throughout England, Scotland, America, Europe, and into the next century—he would still be a significant critic by example: he succeeded, in a way for which the twentieth century well may be wistful, in bridging the gulf between advanced learning and common life, between the literary, scientific, and popular cultures of his day.

In short, Addison's criticism is sometimes "superficial" because he intended it to be, and sometimes seems more superficial than it really is. He is so easily underestimated that, once discovered, he is likely to be overvalued.

As Dr Johnson said, "What he attempted he performed." For almost a decade after the Collier controversy and the death of Dryden, there was an interim pause in which criticism in England lacked direction and a spokesman, despite the efforts of Dennis. "That general knowledge," Johnson noticed, "which now circulates in common talk was in his time rarely to be found. Men not professing learning were not ashamed of ignorance." Addison set himself to awaken *inquiry*, which, reaching a general audience, spread after him down the eighteenth century. Later critics cited or borrowed from him almost to a man; his judgments were liberating as well as facile. If his irony was light, condescending, and tentative, it was also subversive. A masterful journalist, he seemed to know just how far his audience could be made to go. As Boswell later would remark: "His readers fancy that a wise and accomplished companion is talking to them, so that he insinuates his sentiments and tastes into their minds by an imperceptible influence."

Addison kept alive one side of the neoclassicism of Dryden, though he wrote with an eye more to society and the good life, in which poetry may be part, than to a life of good poetry. In his first influential work, *An Essay on Virgil's "Georgics"* (1697), published under Dryden's auspices, he defined the rules for an eighteenth-century poetry of practical and didactic statement. Repeatedly thereafter, he referred to classical poets for a standard of truth to human nature and majestic simplicity of manner and thought (e.g., *Spectator* 249, 253, 523). He chided would-be critics who, shabbily or not at all disciplined in classical language, could not really understand what was at issue (no. 291). In 1711 he still argued that Moderns "fall short at present of the Ancients in poetry, painting, oratory, history, architecture, and all the noble arts and sciences which depend more upon genius than experience." He excepted only "doggerel, humor, burlesque, and all the trivial arts of ridicule" (no. 249). The very missionary impulse which underlay the *Spectator*, to refine the age and banish bad taste, proceeded from a neoclassical standard of reconciling the natural and the familiar. Aside from Dryden, the critics which meant most to him were, seemingly, Boileau, whom he met on his first trip to Paris, and among the ancients, Longinus; occasionally he made use of Aristotle, Bouhours, Rapin, or Le Bossu. All in all, however, little in Addison's criticism is not implicit somewhere in the rich common-sense medley of Dryden, including his popular touch, versatility, and tolerance. As an example of the latter: Addison claimed to prefer *King Lear* as Shakespeare had written it, not in the prettified and poetically "just" adaptation by Nahum Tate which held the eighteenth-century stage (no. 40). And in no. 592 he declared: "Our inimitable Shakespeare is a stumbling-block to the whole tribe of these rigid critics. Who would not rather read one of his plays, where there is not a single rule of the stage observed, than any production of a modern critic where there is not one of them violated?"

The new appreciative criticism, luxuriant but random in Dryden, was trimmed by Addison into an official plain method which anybody could understand and aspire to use. It had at least three dimensions which Addison brought self-consciously together: examination of a poem by its genre, as in Aristotle or, more recently, in Hobbes; detection of Longinian "beauties" and "defects," as in Dennis; and the unraveling of structural "particulars" as in the polemics of Rymer. In the latter especially, Addison took a forward step in his papers on *Paradise Lost*. After a "general survey" of "beauties" in the fable, characters, sentiments, and language, general remarks on the duty of a critic to emphasize "beauties," and a general survey of "defects," Addison then bestowed a paper upon each book—"to particularize those innumerable kinds of beauty which it would be tedious to recapitulate but which are essential to poetry and which may be met with in the works of this great author." If the *kinds* of beauty *essential* to poetry are *innumerable,* then the Aristotelian scheme of analysis is no more than a useful way of classifying evidence, among other ways which might be just as useful. Criticism by rules and form was splintering into appreciation of particulars in a single aesthetic effect created by a particular poet at a particular time in history. As Dryden had remarked, if Aristotle had seen later poetry he might have changed his mind; so Addison hoped that his particularizing of beauties would "not only serve as a comment upon Milton but upon Aristotle." The same subversion of formalism is latent in his essays on "Chevy Chase"— ostensibly a sniping at false wit, but actually reaching further—for if both the *Aeneid* and an old English song have the same "kinds of beauty," then genres would seem expendable.

On balance, despite his sometime conservatism and his adoration of classics, Addison perhaps did more to loosen up neoclassicism, and ultimately to undermine it, than any other English critic in the first half of the century, especially by his series of eleven consecutive papers *On the Pleasures of the Imagination.* They are "superficial" in the Addisonian way—that is, pitched at a modest public level, unexplored at the edges, pregnant with contradictions, subversive without forewarning—but they crystallize something for the first time, a set of problems, a set of distinctions, whose implications required the rest of the century to work out. If not the first aesthetician in English, he was among the first.

Unlike Shaftesbury, who sought an alternative to it, Addison assimilated to criticism the world-view of "new philosophy." At twenty-one, as an Oxford tutor, he had delivered a Latin oration *Nova philosophia veteri praeferenda est,* and steeped himself in miscellaneous "philosophic" studies including Bacon, Descartes, Malebranche (whom he met in Paris), Hobbes, Newton, and Locke. The "great modern discovery" in optics, that light and color "are only ideas in the mind and not qualities that have any existence in matter," led him to a rigid distinction between nature as apprehended in common life by the senses and imagination, and nature as it is revealed really to be by the scientist—matter in motion, in Whitehead's language, "a dull affair, soundless, scentless, colorless; merely the hurrying of material, endlessly, meaninglessly." Later aesthetic theorists such as Hutcheson and Burke would explore its mechanism, in which Addison seems uninterested. Opposite nature stood, in Locke's psychology, the perceiving mind (or soul), born into a body no less material, and dependent on its organs for the development of all vital experience and knowledge. The Lockian model of the mind is vividly evident in Addison's metaphors—*awaken, open, enlarge, fill, enlighten,* implying that the mind before "experience" is a sleeping, closed, narrow, empty, and dark affair, in fact, a mere "power" or "capacity," like a prenatal embryo; and after experience, is still, outside science, a denizen of unsubstantial if pleasing images, like "a man in a dungeon" who entertains himself with visions (no. 411), like "the enchanted hero of a romance" who is " lost and bewildered in a pleasing delusion" · (no. 413).

The controlling premises of his argument are stated in the first three papers (nos. 411–413). In the first, Addison locates *imagination* between *understanding* and *sensation,* limits it to the visual, and distinguishes between two kinds of imaginative pleasures: *primary* (seeing physical objects with the physical eye) and *secondary* (seeing with the mind's eye, memory and imaging). Pleasures of imagination, necessary to mental health, are immediate, and require no act of reason: they strike at once (cf. Johnson,

p. 481). Thereafter, Addison ascends rhetorically through the whole scale of being, stage by stage, from nature seen by the eye to the most rarefied limits of spiritual vision. From "primary pleasures," such as looking at huge heaps of rocks or an expanse of ocean, he moves to a border region (nos. 414, 415) where art conspires with "matter," as in cultivated landscape, gardens, the camera obscura, and architecture. Nos. 416 to 419 pass over to "secondary pleasures" of imagination, and within this category Addison ascends from statuary, which "is likest nature," to painting, which still has "a real resemblance to its original," to the arts of verbal description, and finally to the most immaterial and unvisual of all arts, music. In nos. 417 to 419 Addison focuses upon description and continues his ascent from mere representation (memory or photographic imaging) to poetic "mending" or reshuffling of matter (no. 418) to poetic invention beyond the possibilities of matter, as in fairies and ghosts (no. 419). In the last two essays (nos. 420, 421) he passes over into realms of understanding where imagination, still valuable, bumps nevertheless against the outer limits of its powers—historians and scientists who "describe objects of a real existence," matters of fact; and secondly, moralists, critics, and others who deal with truth "abstracted from matter." In the last three paragraphs of no. 421, Addison passes beyond human normality—throughout he has assumed the normal mind—to glance at madness, and finally at the power of God Himself to regulate human happiness or misery by imagination. For the first time, the whole range of aesthetic and affective experience has been outlined, however roughly, and set apart for investigation.

By his rigid fencing-off of imagination, Addison opened new doors in English imagination-theory and encouraged a poetry of pictorial and irrational effects. He undermined the authority of rules of criticism and invited "philosophic" inquiry into nature instead of poetic tradition, and into "poetic truth" (cf. Hurd, p. 384) or such "ideas as are most apt to affect the imagination" (cf. Reynolds, p. 539). By anchoring imagination in memory of objects, he invited inquiry into the historical objects which particular poets had seen—pictures, medals, tapestries, customs, artifacts (cf. Hurd, p. 374; Whiter, p. 590). Indeed, his implications were revolutionary, and no one later critic exploited them all at once.

In his second essay, Addison stated his second major premise, the three modalities of all imaginative response: the great, the uncommon (novel or strange), and the beautiful. The great, corresponding to the later "sublime," may be either sensual bulk (mountain, ocean, towering cathedral or pyramid) or, more fundamentally, any wholeness or grandeur of view which "fills" or "enlarges" the imagination; its identifying pleasure is astonishment or admiration. The *uncommon* results from sensual motion or from experience of variety, and produces pleasurable surprise or horror. The *beautiful*, originating in sexuality or in response to color, symmetry, and proportion, produces "inward joy" or "complacency." Addison's categories shift criticism away from genres to psychological effects. His discussions of novelty and strangeness are especially transvaluing: novelty opens up *all* experience for poetic use, not just subjects great or beautiful in themselves; strangeness, which underlies "the fairy way of writing," leads directly to the use of subjects which never really existed, to Gothic superstitions, for example, and the possibility of poetry itself as magic.

Addison's third premise, in no. 413, is that a critic can investigate "final" but not "efficient" causes. Though not strictly a literary idea, its influence on later criticism and poetry was enormous (*cf.* Hutcheson, p. 160; Burke, p. 329; Alison, p. 556). It not only posed a problem for aesthetics, but, as Professor Tuveson has shown, issued in an eighteenth-century mystique which underlies the poetry of Thomson, Young, Akenside, and others for whom imagination was a "means of grace."

Finally, the contributions of Addison to the psychology of imagination itself are substantial, especially in no. 417. He defines "secondary imagination" as an activity of comparison which gives more pleasure than the sight of the objects themselves, for it "awakens numberless ideas that before slept in the imagination": it evokes an associational response which "has something in it like creation." Though Addison limits imagination to picture-making, his associational theory leads directly to theories more complicated (*cf.* Alison, p. 555). Here too, as in so much else, Addison drew upon his youthful speculations at Oxford. In his essay on the *Georgics*, in 1697, he observed that Virgil loved "to suggest a truth indirectly, and without giving us a full and open view of it, to let us see just so much as will naturally lead the imagination into all the parts that lie concealed. . . . For here the mind, which is always delighted with its own discoveries, only takes the hint from the poet, and seems to work out the rest by the strength of her own faculties."

Such "superficiality" is rare.

* * * *

FROM

On the Pleasures of the Imagination, Spectators Nos. 411–421

—◦◦❖||❖◦◦—

from No. 411, Saturday, June 21, 1712

*Avia Pieridum peragro loca nullius ante
trita solo; juvat integros accedere fonteis
atque haurire.*
—LUCR.[1]

Our sight is the most perfect and most delightful of all our senses. It fills the mind with the largest variety of ideas, converses with its objects at the greatest distance, and continues the longest in action without being tired or satiated with its proper enjoyments. The sense of feeling can indeed give us a notion of extension, shape, and all other ideas that enter at the eye, except colors; but at the same time it is very much straitened and confined in its operations, to the number, bulk, and distance of its particular objects. Our sight seems designed to supply all these defects, and may be considered as a more delicate and diffusive kind of touch, that spreads itself over an infinite multitude of bodies, comprehends the largest figures, and brings into our reach some of the most remote parts of the universe.

It is this sense which furnishes the imagination with its ideas, so that by the pleasures of the imagination or fancy (which I shall use promiscuously) I here mean such as arise from visible objects, either when we have them actually in our view, or when we call up their ideas into our minds by paintings, statues, descriptions, or any the like occasion. We cannot indeed have a single image in the fancy that did not make its first entrance through the sight; but we have the power of retaining, altering, and compounding those images which we have once received into all the varieties of picture and vision that are most agreeable to the imagination; for by this faculty a man in a dungeon is capable of entertaining himself with scenes

---

[1] *De rerum natura*, I, 926–28: "I wander in the solitary places of the Pierides, never yet trodden by any foot; it is a joy to approach those virgin springs and to drink."

and landscapes more beautiful than any that can be found in the whole compass of nature.

There are few words in the English language which are employed in a more loose and uncircumscribed sense than those of the *fancy* and the *imagination*. I therefore thought it necessary to fix and determine the notion of these two words as I intend to make use of them in the thread of my following speculations, that the reader may conceive rightly what is the subject which I proceed upon. I must therefore desire him to remember that by the pleasures of the imagination, I mean only such pleasures as arise originally from sight, and that I divide these pleasures into two kinds: my design being first of all to discourse of those primary pleasures of the imagination which entirely proceed from such objects as are before our eyes; and in the next place, to speak of those secondary pleasures of the imagination which flow from the ideas of visible objects when the objects are not actually before the eye, but are called up into our memories, or formed into agreeable visions of things that are either absent or fictitious.[2]

The pleasures of the imagination, taken in their full extent, are not so gross as those of sense, nor so refined as those of the understanding. The last are indeed more preferable, because they are founded on some new knowledge or improvement in the mind of man; yet it must be confessed that those of the imagination are as great and as transporting as the other. A beautiful prospect[3] delights the soul as much as a demonstration,[4] and a description in Homer has charmed more readers than a chapter in Aristotle. Besides, the pleasures of the imagination have this advantage above those of the understanding, that they are more obvious and more easy to be acquired. It is but opening the eye, and the scene enters. The colors paint themselves on the fancy, with very little attention of thought or application of mind in the beholder. We are struck, we know not how, with the symmetry of anything we see, and immediately assent to the beauty of an object, without inquiring into the particular causes and occasions of it.

A man of a polite imagination is let into a great many pleasures that the vulgar are not capable of receiving. He can converse with a picture and find an agreeable companion in a statue. He meets with a secret refreshment in a description, and often feels a greater satisfaction in the prospect of fields and meadows than another

---

[2] *Cf.* Dennis, p. 143, on "vulgar" and "enthusiastic" passion.
[3] view of scenery.
[4] logical proof.

does in the possession. It gives him, indeed, a kind of property in everything he sees, and makes the most rude uncultivated parts of nature administer to his pleasures, so that he looks upon the world, as it were, in another light, and discovers in it a multitude of charms that conceal themselves from the generality of mankind. . . .

We might here add that the pleasures of the fancy are more conducive to health than those of the understanding, which are worked out by dint of thinking and attended with too violent a labor of the brain. Delightful scenes, whether in nature, painting, or poetry, have a kindly influence on the body as well as the mind, and not only serve to clear and brighten the imagination, but are able to disperse grief and melancholy, and to set the animal spirits in pleasing and agreeable motions. For this reason Sir Francis Bacon, in his essay "Upon Health," has not thought it improper to prescribe to his reader a poem or a prospect, where he particularly dissuades him from knotty and subtle disquisitions, and advises him to pursue studies that fill the mind with splendid and illustrious objects, as histories, fables, and contemplations of nature.

*

from No. 412, Monday, June 23, 1712

Divisum sic breve fiet opus.
—MART.[5]

I shall first consider those pleasures of the imagination which arise from the actual view and survey of outward objects. And these, I think, all proceed from the sight of what is *great, uncommon,* or *beautiful.*[6] There may indeed be something so terrible or offensive that the horror or loathsomeness of an object may overbear the pleasure which results from its greatness, novelty, or beauty; but still there will be such a mixture of delight in the very disgust it gives us as any of these three qualifications are most conspicuous and prevailing.

By *greatness* I do not only mean the bulk of any single object, but the largeness of a whole view, considered as one entire piece. Such are the prospects of an open champaign country, a vast uncultivated desert, of huge heaps of mountains, high rocks and precipices, or a wide expanse of waters, where we are not struck with the novelty or beauty of the sight, but with that rude kind of

---

[5] *Epigrams*, IV, lxxxii, 8: "Divided, the work will thus become brief."

[6] *Cf.* Longinus, XXXV, 3, who, however, says "striking" instead of "new or uncommon" or, as Addison later says, "strange." *Cf.* Hutcheson, p. 193.

magnificence which appears in many of these stupendous works of nature. Our imagination loves to be filled with an object, or to grasp at anything that is too big for its capacity. We are flung into a pleasing astonishment at such unbounded views, and feel a delightful stillness and amazement in the soul at the apprehension of them. The mind of man naturally hates everything that looks like a restraint upon it, and is apt to fancy itself under a sort of confinement when the sight is pent up in a narrow compass, and shortened on every side by the neighborhood of walls or mountains. On the contrary, a spacious horizon is an image of liberty, where the eye has room to range abroad, to expatiate at large on the immensity of its views, and to lose itself amidst the variety of objects that offer themselves to its observation. Such wide and undetermined prospects are as pleasing to the fancy as the speculations of eternity or infinitude are to the understanding. But if there be a beauty or uncommonness joined with this grandeur, as in a troubled ocean, a heaven adorned with stars and meteors, or a spacious landscape cut out into rivers, woods, rocks, and meadows, the pleasure still grows upon us, as it arises from more than a single principle.

Everything that is *new* or *uncommon* raises a pleasure in the imagination, because it fills the soul with an agreeable surprise, gratifies its curiosity, and gives it an idea of which it was not before possessed. We are indeed so often conversant with one set of objects, and tired out with so many repeated shows of the same things, that whatever is new or uncommon contributes a little to vary human life, and to divert our minds for a while with the strangeness of its appearance. It serves us for a kind of refreshment, and takes off from that satiety we are apt to complain of in our usual and ordinary entertainments. It is this that bestows charms on a monster, and makes even the imperfections of nature please us. It is this that recommends variety, where the mind is every instant called off to something new, and the attention not suffered to dwell too long and waste itself on any particular object. It is this, likewise, that improves what is great or beautiful, and makes it afford the mind a double entertainment. Groves, fields, and meadows are at any season of the year pleasant to look upon, but never so much as in the opening of the spring, when they are all new and fresh with their first gloss upon them, and not yet too much accustomed and familiar to the eye. For this reason there is nothing that more enlivens a prospect than rivers, jetteaus, or falls of water, where the scene is perpetually shifting and entertaining the sight every moment with something that is new. We are quickly tired with looking upon hills and

244 ~ JOSEPH ADDISON

valleys, where everything continues fixed and settled in the same place and posture, but find our thoughts a little agitated and relieved at the sight of such objects as are ever in motion,[7] and sliding away from beneath the eye of the beholder.

But there is nothing that makes its way more directly to the soul than *beauty*, which immediately diffuses a secret satisfaction and complacency through the imagination, and gives a finishing to anything that is great or uncommon. The very first discovery of it strikes the mind with an inward joy, and spreads a cheerfulness and delight through all its faculties. There is not perhaps any real beauty or deformity more in one piece of matter than another, because we might have been so made that whatsoever now appears loathsome to us, might have shown itself agreeable; but we find by experience that there are several modifications of matter which the mind, without any previous consideration, pronounces at first sight beautiful or deformed. Thus we see that every different species of sensible creatures has its different notions of beauty, and that each of them is most affected with the beauties of its own kind. This is nowhere more remarkable than in birds of the same shape and proportion, where we often see the male determined in his courtship by the single grain or tincture of a feather, and never discovering any charms but in the color of its species. . . .

There is a second kind of beauty that we find in the several products of art and nature, which does not work in the imagination with that warmth and violence as the beauty that appears in our proper[8] species, but is apt, however, to raise in us a secret delight and a kind of fondness for the places or objects in which we discover it. This consists either in the gaiety or variety of colors, in the symmetry and proportion of parts, in the arrangement and disposition of bodies, or in a just mixture and concurrence of all together. Among these several kinds of beauty, the eye takes most delight in colors. We nowhere meet with a more glorious or pleasing show in nature than what appears in the heavens at the rising and setting of the sun, which is wholly made up of those different stains of light that show themselves in clouds of a different situation. For this reason we find the poets, who are always addressing themselves to the imagination, borrowing more of their epithets from colors than from any other topic.

As the fancy delights in everything that is great, strange, or beautiful, and is still more pleased the more it finds of these per-

---

[7] *Cf.* Dennis, p. 146.
[8] own.

On the Pleasures of the Imagination ⌐ 245

fections in the same object, so it is capable of receiving a new satisfaction by the assistance of another sense. Thus any continued sound, as the music of birds, or a fall of water, awakens every moment the mind of the beholder, and makes him more attentive to the several beauties of the place that lie before him. Thus if there arises a fragrancy of smells or perfumes, they heighten the pleasures of the imagination, and make even the colors and verdure of the landscape appear more agreeable; for the ideas of both senses recommend each other, and are pleasanter together than when they enter the mind separately—as the different colors of a picture, when they are well disposed, set off one another, and receive an additional beauty from the advantage of their situation.

*

No. 413, Tuesday, June 24, 1712

Causa latet, vis est notissima.
—OVID[9]

Though in yesterday's paper we considered how everything that is great, new, or beautiful is apt to affect the imagination with pleasure, we must own that it is impossible for us to assign the necessary cause of this pleasure, because we know neither the nature of an idea nor the substance of a human soul, which might help us to discover the conformity or disagreeableness of the one to the other; and therefore, for want of such a light, all that we can do in speculations of this kind is to reflect on those operations of the soul that are most agreeable, and to range under their proper heads what is pleasing or displeasing to the mind, without being able to trace out the several necessary and efficient causes from whence the pleasure or displeasure arises.

Final causes lie more bare and open to our observation, as there are often a great variety that belong to the same effect; and these, though they are not altogether so satisfactory, are generally more useful than the other, as they give us greater occasion of admiring the goodness and wisdom of the First Contriver.

One of the final causes of our delight in anything that is *great* may be this: the Supreme Author of our being has so formed the soul of man that nothing but Himself can be its last, adequate, and proper happiness. Because, therefore, a great part of our happiness must arise from the contemplation of His Being, that He might

---

[9] *Metamorphoses*, IV, 287: "The cause is secret, but th' effect is known" (Addison's translation seven years earlier).

give our souls a just relish of such a contemplation, He has made them naturally delight in the apprehension of what is great or unlimited. Our admiration, which is a very pleasing motion of the mind, immediately arises at the consideration of any object that takes up a great deal of room in the fancy, and by consequence, will improve into the highest pitch of astonishment and devotion when we contemplate His nature, that is neither circumscribed by time nor place, nor to be comprehended by the largest capacity of a created being.

He has annexed a secret pleasure to the idea of anything that is *new* or *uncommon* that He might encourage us in the pursuit after knowledge, and engage us to search into the wonders of His creation; for every new idea brings such a pleasure along with it as rewards any pains we have taken in its acquisition, and consequently serves as a motive to put us upon fresh discoveries.

He has made everything that is *beautiful* in our own species pleasant that all creatures might be tempted to multiply their kind and fill the world with inhabitants; for it is very remarkable that wherever nature is crossed in the production of a monster (the result of any unnatural mixture), the breed is incapable of propagating its likeness and of founding a new order of creatures; so that unless all animals were allured by the beauty of their own species, generation would be at an end, and the earth unpeopled.

In the last place, He has made everything that is beautiful in all other objects pleasant, or rather has made so many objects appear beautiful, that He might render the whole creation more gay and delightful. He has given almost everything about us the power of raising an agreeable idea in the imagination, so that it is impossible for us to behold His works with coldness or indifference, and to survey so many beauties without a secret satisfaction and complacency. Things would make but a poor appearance to the eye if we saw them only in their proper figures and motions. And what reason can we assign for this exciting in us many of those ideas, which are different from anything that exists in the objects themselves (for such are light and colors), were it not to add supernumerary ornaments to the universe and make it more agreeable to the imagination? We are everywhere entertained with pleasing shows and apparitions: we discover imaginary glories in the heavens and in the earth, and see some of this visionary beauty poured out upon the whole creation; but what a rough, unsightly sketch of nature should we be entertained with, did all her coloring disappear and the several distinctions of light and shade vanish? In short, our souls are at present delightfully lost and bewildered in a pleasing delusion; and we walk about like the enchanted hero of a romance, who sees beautiful castles, woods, and meadows, and at the same time hears the warbling of birds and the purling of streams; but upon the finishing of some secret spell, the fantastic scene breaks up, and the disconsolate knight finds himself on a barren heath or in a solitary desert. It is not improbable that something like this may be the state of the soul after its first separation[1] in respect of the images it will receive from matter, though indeed the ideas of colors are so pleasing and beautiful in the imagination that it is possible the soul will not be deprived of them, but perhaps find them excited by some other occasional cause, as they are at present by the different impressions of the subtle matter on the organ of sight.

I have here supposed that my reader is acquainted with that great modern discovery which is at present universally acknowledged by all the inquirers into natural philosophy—namely, that light and colors as apprehended by the imagination are only ideas in the mind, and not qualities that have any existence in matter. As this is a truth which has been proved incontestably by many modern philosophers,[2] and is indeed one of the finest speculations in that science, if the English reader would see the notion explained at large, he may find it in the eighth chapter of the second book of Mr. Locke's *Essay on Human Understanding*.

*

from No. 414, Wednesday, June 25, 1712

Alterius sic
altera poscit opem res, et conjurat amice.
—Hor.[3]

If we consider the works of nature and art as they are qualified to entertain the imagination, we shall find the last very defective in comparison of the former, for though they [works of art] may sometimes appear as beautiful or strange, they can have nothing in them of that vastness and immensity which afford so great an entertainment to the mind of the beholder. The one may be as polite and delicate as the other, but can never show herself so august and magnificent in the design. There is something more bold and masterly in the rough, careless strokes of nature than in the nice

---

[1] That is, after death.

[2] For example, Newton and Berkeley.

[3] *Ars Poetica*, 410–11: "So much does each [nature, art] require the other's help, and mutually conspire."

touches and embellishments of art. The beauties of the most stately garden or palace lie in a narrow compass: the imagination immediately runs them over, and requires something else to gratify her; but in the wide fields of nature, the sight wanders up and down without confinement, and is fed with an infinite variety of images, without any certain stint or number. For this reason we always find the poet in love with a country life, where nature appears in the greatest perfection, and furnishes out all those scenes that are most apt to delight the imagination. . . .

But though there are several of these wild scenes that are more delightful than any artificial shows, yet we find the works of nature still more pleasant the more they resemble those of art. For in this case, our pleasure rises from a double principle—from the agreeableness of the objects to the eye, and from their similitude to other objects. We are pleased as well with comparing their beauties as with surveying them, and can represent them to our minds either as copies or originals. Hence it is that we take delight in a prospect which is well laid out, and diversified with fields and meadows, woods and rivers; in those accidental landscapes of trees, clouds, and cities that are sometimes found in the veins of marble; in the curious fretwork of rocks and grottoes; and, in a word, in anything that hath such a variety or regularity as may seem the effect of design in what we call the works of chance.

If the products of nature rise in value according as they more or less resemble those of art, we may be sure that artificial works receive a greater advantage from their resemblance of such as are natural, because here the similitude is not only pleasant but the pattern more perfect. The prettiest landscape I ever saw was one drawn on the walls of a dark room,[4] which stood opposite on one side to a navigable river and on the other to a park. The experiment is very common in optics. Here you might discover the waves and fluctuations of the water in strong and proper colors, with the picture of a ship entering at one end and sailing by degrees through the whole piece. On another there appeared the green shadows of trees, waving to and fro with the wind, and herds of deer among them in miniature, leaping about upon the wall. I must confess, the novelty of such a sight may be one occasion of its pleasantness to the imagination, but certainly the chief reason is its near resemblance to nature, as it does not only, like other pictures, give the color and figure, but the motion of the things it represents.

We have before observed that there is generally in nature some-

---

[4] Addison refers to a camera obscura.

thing more grand and august than what we meet with in the curiosities of art. When, therefore, we see this imitated in any measure, it gives us a nobler and more exalted kind of pleasure than what we receive from the nicer and more accurate productions of art. On this account, our English gardens are not so entertaining to the fancy as those in France and Italy, where we see a large extent of ground covered over with an agreeable mixture of garden and forest, which represent everywhere an artificial rudeness much more charming than that neatness and elegancy which we meet with in those of our own country. It might, indeed, be of ill consequence to the public, as well as unprofitable to private persons, to alienate so much ground from pasturage and the plow, in many parts of a country that is so well peopled and cultivated to a far greater advantage. But why may not a whole estate be thrown into a kind of garden by frequent plantations, that may turn as much to the profit as the pleasure of the owner? A marsh overgrown with willows or a mountain shaded with oaks are not only more beautiful but more beneficial than when they lay bare and unadorned. Fields of corn make a pleasant prospect, and if the walks were a little taken care of that lie between them, if the natural embroidery of the meadows were helped and improved by some small additions of art, and the several rows of hedges set off by trees and flowers that the soil was capable of receiving, a man might make a pretty landscape of his own possessions.

Writers[5] who have given us an account of China tell us the inhabitants of that country laugh at the plantations of our Europeans, which are laid by the rule and line, because, they say, anyone may place trees in equal rows and uniform figures. They choose rather to show a genius in works of this nature, and therefore always conceal the art by which they direct themselves. They have a word, it seems, in their language by which they express the particular beauty of a plantation that thus strikes the imagination at first sight without discovering what it is that has so agreeable an effect. Our British gardeners, on the contrary, instead of humoring nature, love to deviate from it as much as possible. Our trees rise in cones, globes, and pyramids. We see the marks of the scissors upon every plant and bush. I do not know whether I am singular in my opinion, but for my own part, I would rather look upon a tree in all its luxuriancy and diffusion of boughs and branches than when it is thus cut and trimmed into a mathematical figure, and cannot but

---

[5] Addison borrows directly from Sir William Temple's essay "Upon the Gardens of Epicurus."

fancy that an orchard in flower looks infinitely more delightful than all the little labyrinths of the most finished parterre.

*

from No. 416, Friday, June 27, 1712

Quatenus hoc simile est oculis, quod mente videmus.

—LUCR.[6]

I at first divided the pleasures of the imagination into such as arise from objects that are actually before our eyes, or that once entered in at our eyes and are afterwards called up into the mind, either barely by its own operations, or an occasion of something without us, as statues or descriptions. We have already considered the first division,[7] and shall therefore enter on the other, which, for distinction's sake, I have called the secondary pleasures of the imagination. When I say the ideas we receive from statues, descriptions, or such like occasions are the same that were once actually in our view, it must not be understood that we had once seen the very place, action, or person which are carved or described. It is sufficient that we have seen places, persons, or actions in general, which bear a resemblance or at least some remote analogy with what we find represented—since it is in the power of the imagination, when it is once stocked with particular ideas, to enlarge, compound, and vary them at her own pleasure.

Among the different kinds of representation, *statuary* is the most natural, and shows us something *likest* the object that is represented. To make use of a common instance, let one who is born blind take an image in his hands and trace out with his fingers the different furrows and impressions of the chisel, and he will easily conceive how the shape of a man or beast may be represented by it; but should he draw his hand over a *picture*, where all is smooth and uniform, he would never be able to imagine how the several prominences and depressions of a human body could be shown on a plain piece of canvas, that has in it no unevenness or irregularity. *Description* runs yet further from the things it represents than painting, for a picture bears a real resemblance to its original, which letters and syllables are wholly void of. Colors speak all languages, but words

---

[6] *De rerum natura*, IV, 750: "Since what we see in the mind is like what we see with the eyes."

[7] In *Spectator* No. 415, Addison considered architecture—"that particular art which has a more immediate tendency than any other to produce those primary pleasures of the imagination."

are understood only by such a people or nation. For this reason, though men's necessities quickly put them on finding out speech, writing is probably of a later invention than painting; particularly we are told that in America, when the Spaniards first arrived there, expresses[8] were sent to the Emperor of Mexico in paint, and the news of his country delineated by the strokes of a pencil—which was a more natural way than that of writing, though at the same time much more imperfect, because it is impossible to draw the little connections of speech or to give the picture of a conjunction or an adverb. It would be yet more strange to represent visible objects by sounds that have no ideas annexed to them, and to make something like description in *music*. Yet it is certain there may be confused, imperfect notions of this nature raised in the imagination by an artificial composition of notes, and we find that great masters in the art are able sometimes to set their hearers in the heat and hurry of a battle, to overcast their minds with melancholy scenes and apprehensions of deaths and funerals, or to lull them into pleasing dreams of groves and Elysiums.

In all these instances, this secondary pleasure of the imagination proceeds from that action of the mind which compares the ideas arising from the original objects with the ideas we receive from the statue, picture, description, or sound that represents them. It is impossible for us to give the necessary reason[9] why this operation of the mind is attended with so much pleasure, as I have before observed on the same occasion; but we find a great variety of entertainments derived from this single principle, for it is this that not only gives us a relish of statuary, painting, and description, but makes us delight in all the actions and arts of mimicry. It is this that makes the several kinds of wit pleasant, which consists, as I have formerly shown, in the affinity of ideas. . . . The *final cause*, probably, of annexing pleasure to this operation of the mind, was to quicken and encourage us in our searches after truth, since the distinguishing one thing from another, and the right discerning betwixt our ideas, depends wholly upon our comparing them together and observing the congruity or disagreement that appears among the several works of nature.

But I shall here confine myself to those pleasures of the imagination which proceed from ideas raised by *words*, because most of the observations that agree with descriptions are equally applicable to painting and statuary.

---

[8] messages.
[9] That is, the "efficient cause."

Words, when well chosen, have so great a force in them that a description often gives us more lively ideas than the sight of things themselves. The reader finds a scene drawn in stronger colors and painted more to the life in his imagination, by the help of words, than by an actual survey of the scene which they describe. In this case the poet seems to get the better of nature; he takes, indeed, the landscape after her, but gives it more vigorous touches, heightens its beauty, and so enlivens the whole piece that the images which flow from the objects themselves appear weak and faint in comparison of those that come from the expressions. The reason, probably, may be because in the survey of any object, we have only so much of it painted on the imagination as comes in at the eye; but in its description, the poet gives us as free a view of it as he pleases, and discovers to us several parts that either we did not attend to or that lay out of our sight when we first beheld it. As we look on any object, our idea of it is perhaps made up of two or three simple ideas, but when the poet represents it, he may either give us a more complex idea of it, or only raise in us such ideas as are most apt to affect the imagination.

*

from No. 417, Saturday, June 28, 1712

Quem tu Melpomene semel
nascentem placido lumine videris,
   non illum labor Isthmius
clarabit pugilem, non equus impiger. . . .
Sed quae Tibur aquae fertile praefluunt,
   et spissae nemorum comae
fingent Aeolio carmine nobilem.
                                          —Hor.[1]

We may observe that any single circumstance of what we have formerly seen often raises up a whole scene of imagery, and awakens numberless ideas that before slept in the imagination; such a particular smell or color is able to fill the mind on a sudden with the picture of the fields or gardens where we first met with it, and to bring up into view all the variety of images that once attended it.

---

[1] *Odes*, IV, iii, 1–4, 10–12: "Him, Melpomene, whom once, at his birth, thou hast noticed with calm eye, no Isthmian struggle shall distinguish as a boxer, or impetuous horse [as a victor] . . . but the waters that flow past fertile Tiber and thick leaves from the groves shall make him renowned for Aeolian song."

Our imagination takes the hint, and leads us unexpectedly into cities or theatres, plains or meadows. We may further observe, when the fancy thus reflects on the scenes that have passed in it formerly, those which were at first pleasant to behold appear more so upon reflection, and that the memory heightens the delightfulness of the original. A Cartesian[2] would account for both these instances in the following manner:

The set of ideas, which we received from such a prospect or garden, having entered the mind at the same time, have a set of traces belonging to them in the brain, bordering very near upon one another; when, therefore, any one of these ideas arises in the imagination, and consequently dispatches a flow of animal spirits[3] to its proper trace,[4] these spirits, in the violence of their motion, run not only into the trace to which they were more particularly directed, but into several of those that lie about it. By this means, they awaken other ideas of the same set, which immediately determine a new dispatch of spirits that, in the same manner, open other neighboring traces, till at last the whole set of them is blown up, and the whole prospect or garden flourishes in the imagination. But because the pleasure we received from these places far surmounted and overcame the little disagreeableness we found in them, for this reason there was at first a wider passage worn in the pleasure traces, and on the contrary, so narrow a one in those which belonged to the disagreeable ideas that they were quickly stopped up and rendered incapable of receiving any animal spirits, and, consequently, of exciting any unpleasant ideas in the memory.

It would be in vain to inquire whether the power of imagining things strongly proceeds from any greater perfection in the soul or from any nicer texture in the brain of one man than of another. But this is certain, that a noble writer should be born with this faculty in its full strength and vigor, so as to be able to receive lively ideas from outward objects, to retain them long, and to range them together, upon occasion, in such figures and representations as are most likely to hit the fancy of the reader. A poet should take as much pains in forming his imagination as a philosopher in cultivating his understanding. He must gain a due relish of the works of nature, and be thoroughly conversant in the various scenery of a country life.

---

[2] a follower of Descartes.
[3] In old physiology, a muscular fluid which transmitted nerve impulses. See Locke, p. 31.
[4] track.

When he is stored with country images, if he would go beyond pastoral and the lower kinds of poetry, he ought to acquaint himself with the pomp and magnificence of courts. He should be very well versed in everything that is noble and stately in the productions of art, whether it appear in painting or statuary, in the great works of architecture which are in their present glory, or in the ruins of those which flourished in former ages.

Such advantages as these help to open a man's thoughts and to enlarge his imagination, and will therefore have their influence on all kinds of writing if the author knows how to make right use of them. And among those of the learned languages who excel in this talent, the most perfect in their several kinds are perhaps Homer, Virgil, and Ovid. The first strikes the imagination wonderfully with what is great, the second with what is beautiful, and the last with what is strange. Reading the *Iliad* is like traveling through a country uninhabited, where the fancy is entertained with a thousand savage prospects of vast deserts, wide uncultivated marshes, huge forests, misshapen rocks and precipices. On the contrary, the *Aeneid* is like a well-ordered garden, where it is impossible to find out any part unadorned or to cast our eyes upon a single spot that does not produce some beautiful plant or flower. But when we are in the *Metamorphoses*, we are walking on enchanted ground, and see nothing but scenes of magic lying round us. . . .

If I were to name a poet that is a perfect master in all these arts of working on the imagination, I think Milton may pass for one. And if his *Paradise Lost* falls short of the *Aeneid* or *Iliad* in this respect, it proceeds rather from the fault of the language in which it is written than from any defect of genius in the author. So divine a poem in English is like a stately palace built of brick, where one may see architecture in as great a perfection as in one of marble, though the materials are of a coarser nature. But to consider it only as it regards our present subject: what can be conceived greater than the battle of angels, the majesty of Messiah, the stature and behavior of Satan and his peers? what more beautiful than Pandemonium, Paradise, Heaven, Angels, Adam and Eve? what more strange than the creation of the world, the several metamorphoses of the fallen angels, and the surprising adventures their leader meets with in his search after Paradise? No other subject could have furnished a poet with scenes so proper to strike the imagination, as no other poet could have painted those scenes in more strong and lively colors.

*

from No. 418, Monday, June 30, 1712

Ferat et rubus asper amonum.
—VIRG.[5]

The pleasures of these secondary views of the imagination arc of a wider and more universal nature than those it has when joined with sight; for not only what is great, strange, or beautiful, but anything that is disagreeable when looked upon pleases us in an apt description. Here, therefore, we must inquire after a new principle of pleasure, which is nothing else but the action of the mind which *compares* the ideas that arise from words with the ideas that arise from the objects themselves; and why this operation of the mind is attended with so much pleasure, we have before considered. For this reason therefore, the description of a dunghill is pleasing to the imagination if the image be represented to our minds by suitable expressions, though perhaps this may be more properly called the pleasure of the understanding than of the fancy, because we are not so much delighted with the image that is contained in the description as with the aptness of the description to excite the image.

But if the description of what is little, common, or deformed be acceptable to the imagination, the description of what is great, surprising, or beautiful is much more so, because here we are not only delighted with *comparing* the representation with the original, but are highly pleased with the original itself. Most readers, I believe, are more charmed with Milton's description of Paradise than of Hell; they are both, perhaps, equally perfect in their kind, but in the one the brimstone and sulphur are not so refreshing to the imagination as the beds of flowers and the wilderness of sweets in the other.

There is yet another circumstance which recommends a description more than all the rest, and that is if it represents to us such objects as are apt to raise a secret ferment in the mind of the reader and to work, with violence, upon his passions. For in this case, we are at once warmed and enlightened, so that the pleasure becomes more universal and is several ways qualified to entertain us. Thus, in painting it is pleasant to look on the picture of any face where the resemblance is hit, but the pleasure increases if it be the picture of a face that is beautiful, and is still greater if the beauty be softened with an air of melancholy or sorrow. The two

---

[5] *Eclogues*, III, 89: "And may the rough bramble bear spice."

leading passions which the more serious parts of poetry endeavor to stir up in us are terror and pity. And here, by the way, one would wonder how it comes to pass that such passions as are very unpleasant at all other times are very agreeable when excited by proper descriptions. It is not strange that we should take delight in such passages as are apt to produce hope, joy, admiration, love, or the like emotions in us, because they never rise in the mind without an inward pleasure which attends them. But how comes it to pass that we should take delight in being terrified or dejected by a description, when we find so much uneasiness in the fear or grief which we receive from any other occasion?

If we consider, therefore, the nature of this pleasure, we shall find that it does not arise so properly from the description of what is terrible as from the reflection we make on ourselves at the time of reading it. When we look on such hideous objects, we are not a little pleased to think we are in no danger of them. We consider them, at the same time, as dreadful and harmless, so that the more frightful appearance they make, the greater is the pleasure we receive from the sense of our own safety. . . .

In the like manner, when we read of torments, wounds, deaths, and the like dismal accidents, our pleasure does not flow so properly from the grief which such melancholy descriptions give us as from the secret comparison which we make between ourselves and the person who suffers. Such representations teach us to set a just value upon our own condition, and make us prize our good fortune, which exempts us from the like calamities. This is, however, such a kind of pleasure as we are not capable of receiving when we see a person actually lying under the tortures that we meet with in a description, because in this case the object presses too close upon our senses and bears so hard upon us that it does not give us time or leisure to reflect on ourselves. Our thoughts are so intent upon the miseries of the sufferer that we cannot turn them upon our own happiness; whereas, on the contrary, we consider the misfortunes we read in history or poetry either as past or as fictitious, so that the reflection upon ourselves rises in us insensibly and overbears the sorrow we conceive for the sufferings of the afflicted.

But because the mind of man requires something more perfect in matter than what it finds there, and can never meet with any sight in nature which sufficiently answers its highest ideas of pleasantness—or in other words, because the imagination can fancy to itself things more great, strange, or beautiful than the eye ever saw, and is still sensible of some defect in what it has seen—on this account, it is the part of a poet to humor the imagination in its own notions by mending and perfecting nature where he describes a reality, and by adding greater beauties than are put together in nature where he describes a fiction.

He is not obliged to attend her in the slow advances which she makes from one season to another, or to observe her conduct in the successive production of plants and flowers. He may draw into his description all the beauties of the spring and autumn, and make the whole year contribute something to render it the more agreeable. His rose trees, woodbines, and jessamines may flower together, and his beds be covered at the same time with lilies, violets, and amaranths. His soil is not restrained to any particular set of plants, but is proper either for oaks or myrtles, and adapts itself to the products of every climate. Oranges may grow wild in it; myrrh may be met with in every hedge; and if he thinks it proper to have a grove of spices, he can quickly command sun enough to raise it. If all this will not furnish out an agreeable scene, he can make several new species of flowers, with richer scents and higher colors than any that grow in the gardens of nature. His consorts of birds may be as full and harmonious, and his woods as thick and gloomy as he pleases. He is at no more expense in a long vista than a short one, and can as easily throw his cascades from a precipice of half a mile high as from one of twenty yards. He has his choice of the winds, and can turn the course of his rivers in all the variety of *meanders* that are most delightful to the reader's imagination. In a word, he has the modeling of nature in his own hands, and may give her what charms he pleases, provided he does not reform her too much and run into absurdities by endeavoring to excel.

*

from No. 419, Tuesday, July 1, 1712

Mentis gratissimus error.
—Hor.[6]

There is a kind of writing wherein the poet quite loses sight of nature, and entertains his reader's imagination with the characters and actions of such persons as have many of them no existence but what he bestows on them. Such are fairies, witches, magicians, demons, and departed spirits. This Mr. Dryden calls *the fairy way*

---

[6] *Epistles*, II, ii, 140: "The most charming extravagance of the mind."

of writing, which is indeed more difficult than any other that depends on the poet's fancy, because he has no pattern to follow in it, and must work altogether out of his own invention.

There is a very odd turn of thought required for this sort of writing, and it is impossible for a poet to succeed in it who has not a particular cast of fancy, and an imagination naturally fruitful and superstitious. Besides this, he ought to be very well versed in legends and fables, antiquated romances, and the traditions of nurses and old women, that he may fall in with our natural prejudices, and humor those notions which we have imbibed in our infancy. For, otherwise, he will be apt to make his fairies talk like people of his own species, and not like other sets of beings who converse with different objects and think in a different manner from that of mankind. . . .

These descriptions raise a pleasing kind of horror in the mind of the reader, and amuse his imagination with the strangeness and novelty of the persons who are represented in them. They bring up into our memory the stories we have heard in our childhood, and favor those secret terrors and apprehensions to which the mind of man is naturally subject. We are pleased with surveying the different habits and behaviors of foreign countries; how much more must we be delighted and surprised when we are led, as it were, into a new creation, and see the persons and manners of another species? Men of cold fancies and philosophical dispositions object to this kind of poetry that it has not probability enough to affect the imagination. But to this it may be answered that we are sure, in general, there are many intellectual beings in the world besides ourselves, and several species of spirits who are subject to different laws and economies from those of mankind; when we see, therefore, any of these represented naturally, we cannot look upon the representation as altogether impossible; nay, many are prepossessed with such false opinions as dispose them to believe these particular delusions; at least, we have all heard so many pleasing relations in favor of them that we do not care for seeing through the falsehood, and willingly give ourselves up to so agreeable an imposture.

The ancients have not much of this poetry among them, for indeed almost the whole substance of it owes its original to the darkness and superstition of later ages, when pious frauds were made use of to amuse mankind and frighten them into a sense of their duty. Our forefathers looked upon nature with more reverence and horror before the world was enlightened by learning and philosophy, and loved to astonish themselves with the apprehensions of witchcraft, prodigies, charms, and enchantments. There was not a village in England that had not a ghost in it; the churchyards were all haunted; every large common had a circle of fairies belonging to it; and there was scarce a shepherd to be met with who had not seen a spirit.

Among all the poets of this kind, our English are much the best by what I have yet seen, whether it be that we abound with more stories of this nature, or that the genius of our country is fitter for this sort of poetry. For the English are naturally fanciful, and very often disposed, by that gloominess and melancholy of temper which is so frequent in our nation, to many wild notions and visions to which others are not so liable.

Among the English, Shakespeare has incomparably excelled all others. That noble extravagance of fancy which he had in so great perfection thoroughly qualified him to touch this weak superstitious part of his reader's imagination, and made him capable of succeeding where he had nothing to support him besides the strength of his own genius. There is something so wild and yet so solemn in the speeches of his ghosts, fairies, witches, and the like imaginary persons, that we cannot forbear thinking them natural, though we have no rule by which to judge of them, and must confess, if there are such beings in the world, it looks highly probable they should talk and act as he has represented them.

There is another sort of imaginary beings that we sometimes meet with among the poets, when the author represents any passion, appetite, virtue, or vice under a visible shape, and makes it a person or an actor in his poem. Of this nature are the descriptions of Hunger and Envy in Ovid, of Fame in Virgil, and of Sin and Death in Milton. We find a whole creation of the like shadowy persons in Spenser, who had an admirable talent in representations of this kind. I have discoursed of these emblematical persons in former papers,[7] and shall therefore only mention them in this place. Thus we see how many ways poetry addresses itself to the imagination, as it has not only the whole circle of nature for its province, but makes new worlds of its own, shows us persons who are not to be found in being, and represents even the faculties of the soul, with her several virtues and vices, in a sensible shape and character.

I shall, in my two following papers, consider in general how other kinds of writing are qualified to please the imagination, with which I intend to conclude this essay.

---

[7] *Cf. Spectator* No. 273, on allegory in Milton.

*

No. 420, Wednesday, July 2, 1712

Quocunque volent animum auditoris agunto.
—Hor.[8]

As the writers in poetry and fiction borrow their several materials from outward objects and join them together at their own pleasure, there are others who are obliged to follow nature more closely and to take entire scenes out of her. Such are historians, natural philosophers, travelers, geographers, and in a word, all who describe visible objects of a real existence.

It is the most agreeable talent of a historian to be able to draw up his armies and fight his battles in proper expressions, to set before our eyes the divisions, cabals, and jealousies of great men, and to lead us step by step into the several actions and events of his history. We love to see the subject unfolding itself by just degrees and breaking upon us insensibly, that so we may be kept in a pleasing suspense, and have time given us to raise our expectations and to side with one of the parties concerned in the relation. I confess this shows more the art than the veracity of the historian, but I am only to speak of him as he is qualified to please the imagination. And in this respect, Livy has perhaps excelled all who went before him or have written since his time. He describes everything in so lively a manner that his whole history is an admirable picture, and touches on such proper circumstances in every story that his reader becomes a kind of spectator, and feels in himself all the variety of passions which are correspondent to the several parts of the relation.

But among this set of writers, there are none who more gratify and enlarge the imagination than the authors of the new philosophy, whether we consider their theories of the earth or heavens, the discoveries they have made by glasses,[9] or any other of their contemplations on nature. We are not a little pleased to find every green leaf swarm with millions of animals, that at their largest growth are not visible to the naked eye. There is something very engaging to the fancy, as well as to our reason, in the treatises of metals, minerals, plants, and meteors. But when we survey the whole earth at once, and the several planets that lie within its neighborhood, we are filled with a pleasing astonishment to see so many worlds

---

[8] *Ars Poetica*, 100: "They must lead the imagination of a hearer wherever they choose."
[9] microscope and telescope.

hanging one above another, and sliding round their axles in such an amazing pomp and solemnity. If, after this, we contemplate those wide fields of *ether* that reach in height as far as from Saturn to the fixed stars, and run abroad almost to an infinitude, our imagination finds its capacity filled with so immense a prospect, and puts itself upon the stretch to comprehend it. But if we yet rise higher, and consider the fixed stars as so many vast oceans of flame, that are each of them attended with a different set of planets, and still discover new firmaments and new lights that are sunk farther in those unfathomable depths of *ether*, so as not to be seen by the strongest of our telescopes, we are lost in such a labyrinth of suns and worlds, and confounded with the immensity and magnificence of nature.

Nothing is more pleasant to the fancy than to enlarge itself, by degrees, in its contemplation of the various proportions which its several objects bear to each other, when it compares the body of man to the bulk of the whole earth, the earth to the circle it describes around the sun, that circle to the sphere of the fixed stars, the sphere of the fixed stars to the circuit of the whole creation, the whole creation itself to the infinite space that is everywhere diffused about it; or when the imagination works downward, and considers the bulk of a human body in respect of an animal a hundred times less than a mite, the particular limbs of such an animal, the different springs which actuate the limbs, the spirits which set these springs a going, and the proportionable minuteness of these several parts before they have arrived at their full growth and perfection. But if, after all this, we take the least particle of these animal spirits, and consider its capacity of being wrought into a world that shall contain within these narrow dimensions a heaven and earth, stars and planets, and every different species of living creatures, in the same analogy and proportion they bear to each other in our own universe—such a speculation, by reason of its nicety, appears ridiculous to those who have not turned their thoughts that way, though at the same time it is founded on no less than the evidence of a demonstration. Nay, we might yet carry it farther, and discover in the smallest particle of this little world a new and inexhausted fund of matter, capable of being spun out into another universe.

I have dwelt the longer on this subject because I think it may show us the proper limits as well as the defectiveness of our imagination, how it is confined to a very small quantity of space and immediately stopped in its operations when it endeavors to take in anything that is very great or very little. Let a man try to conceive the different bulk of an animal which is twenty, from another which is a hundred times less than a mite, or to compare in his thoughts a length of a thousand diameters of the earth with that of a million, and he will quickly find that he has no different measures in his mind adjusted to such extraordinary degrees of grandeur or minuteness. The understanding, indeed, opens an infinite space on every side of us, but the imagination, after a few faint efforts, is immediately at a stand, and finds herself swallowed up in the immensity of the void that surrounds it. Our reason can pursue a particle of matter through an infinite variety of divisions, but the fancy soon loses sight of it, and feels in itself a kind of chasm that wants to be filled with matter of a more sensible bulk. We can neither widen nor contract the faculty to the dimensions of either extreme. The object is too big for our capacity when we would comprehend the circumference of a world, and dwindles into nothing when we endeavor after the idea of an atom.

It is possible this defect of imagination may not be in the soul itself but as it acts in conjunction with the body. Perhaps there may not be room in the brain for such a variety of impressions, or the animal spirits may be incapable of figuring them in such a manner as is necessary to excite so very large or very minute ideas. However it be, we may well suppose that beings of a higher nature very much excel us in this respect, as it is probable the soul of man will be infinitely more perfect hereafter in this faculty, as well as in all the rest; insomuch that perhaps the imagination will be able to keep pace with the understanding, and to form in itself distinct ideas of all the different modes and quantities of space.

*

from No. 421, Thursday, July 3, 1712

Ignotis errare locis, ignota videre
flumina gaudebat, studio minuente laborem.
—OVID[1]

The pleasures of the imagination are not wholly confined to such particular authors as are conversant in material objects, but are often to be met with among the polite masters of morality, criticism, and other speculations abstracted from matter, who, though they do not directly treat of the visible parts of nature, often draw from them their similitudes, metaphors, and allegories. By these allusions,

---

[1] *Metamorphoses*, IV, 294–95: "He delighted to stray in unfrequented places, to see unknown streams, his labor lessened by his eagerness."

a truth in the understanding is, as it were, reflected by the imagination: we are able to see something like color and shape in a notion and to discover a scheme of thought traced out upon matter. And here the mind receives a great deal of satisfaction, and has two of its faculties gratified at the same time, while the fancy is busy in copying after the understanding and transcribing ideas out of the intellectual world into the material.

The great art of a writer shows itself in the choice of pleasing allusions, which are generally to be taken from the great or beautiful works of art or nature; for though whatever is new or uncommon is apt to delight the imagination, the chief design of an allusion being to illustrate and explain the passages of an author, it should be always borrowed from what is more known and common than the passages which are to be explained.

Allegories, when well chosen, are like so many tracks of light in a discourse, that make everything about them clear and beautiful. A noble metaphor, when it is placed to an advantage, casts a kind of glory round it and darts a lustre through a whole sentence. These different kinds of allusion are but so many different manners of similitude, and that they may please the imagination, the likeness ought to be very exact or very agreeable, as we love to see a picture where the resemblance is just or the posture and air graceful. But we often find eminent writers very faulty in this respect; great scholars are apt to fetch their comparisons and allusions from the sciences in which they are most conversant, so that a man may see the compass of their learning in a treatise on the most indifferent subject. I have read a discourse upon love which none but a profound chemist could understand and have heard many a sermon that should only have been preached before a congregation of Cartesians. On the contrary, your men of business usually have recourse to such instances as are too mean and familiar. They are for drawing the reader into a game of chess or tennis, or for leading him from shop to shop in the cant of particular trades and employments. It is certain there may be found an infinite variety of very agreeable allusions in both these kinds; but for the generality, the most entertaining ones lie in the works of nature, which are obvious to all capacities and more delightful than what is to be found in arts and sciences.

It is this talent of affecting the imagination that gives an embellishment to good sense and makes one man's compositions more agreeable than another's. It sets off all writings in general, but is the very life and highest perfection of poetry. Where it shines in an eminent degree, it has preserved several poems for many ages, that have nothing else to recommend them; and where all the other beauties are present, the work appears dry and insipid if this single one be wanting. It has something in it like creation; it bestows a kind of existence and draws up to the reader's view several objects which are not to be found in being. It makes additions to nature and gives a greater variety to God's works. In a word, it is able to beautify and adorn the most illustrious scenes in the universe or to fill the mind with more glorious shows and apparitions than can be found in any part of it.

We have now discovered the several originals of those pleasures that gratify the fancy; and here perhaps it would not be very difficult to cast under their proper heads those contrary objects which are apt to fill it with distaste and terror, for the imagination is as liable to pain as pleasure. When the brain is hurt by any accident, or the mind disordered by dreams or sickness, the fancy is overrun with wild, dismal ideas and terrified with a thousand hideous monsters of its own framing. . . .

There is not a sight in nature so mortifying as that of a distracted person when his imagination is troubled and his whole soul disordered and confused. Babylon in ruins is not so melancholy a spectacle. But to quit so disagreeable a subject, I shall only consider, by way of conclusion, what an infinite advantage this faculty gives an Almighty Being over the soul of man, and how great a measure of happiness or misery we are capable of receiving from the imagination only.

We have already seen the influence that one man has over the fancy of another, and with what ease he conveys into it a variety of imagery; how great a power then may we suppose lodged in Him who knows all the ways of affecting the imagination, who can infuse what ideas He pleases and fill those ideas with terror and delight to what degree He thinks fit? He can excite images in the mind without the help of words, and make scenes rise up before us and seem present to the eye without the assistance of bodies or exterior objects. He can transport the imagination with such beautiful and glorious visions as cannot possibly enter into our present conceptions, or haunt it with such ghastly spectres and apparitions as would make us hope for annihilation and think existence no better than a curse. In short, He can so exquisitely ravish or torture the soul through this single faculty as might suffice to make up the whole heaven or hell of any finite being.

THE ANGLO-SCOTS
INQUIRY:
Academics and Aestheticians

--◦◦◦◦◦--

THE AWAKENING of criticism in Scotland, largely after mid-century, centered in the university towns of Edinburgh, Aberdeen, and Glasgow. The patriotic note was sometimes sounded, especially in the controversy over Ossian, in appraisals of Anglo-Scots writers and works such as Dr. Arbuthnot (whom Lord Kames considered a greater humorist than Swift), Thomson's *The Seasons*, John Home's *Douglas*, Thomas Willkie's *Epigoniad*, and in early appreciation of Burns. Yet, its unity, such as it had, derived less from patriotism than from other facts of Scottish life and intellectual history: ancient ties with France; Calvinism (or reaction against it) with its peculiar blend of argumentative bookishness, distrust of tradition, concern for practical society, and worry about inner states of emotion; the university system; and the long-standing divorce of Scottish intellect from Scottish language.

Since Reformation days, business or controversy had been conducted in Latin or English; talent emigrated to England or France; and hence, the intelligentsia was partially uprooted from local culture. The spoken language had a rich, if underground and half-forgotten poetry, dating from the fifteenth century, but had never evolved a learned prose. Hence, no matter how patriotic, Scots were never practicing poet-critics like Dryden, Addison, Pope, Gray or Johnson. They carefully purged themselves of Scotticisms; they wrote in what Saintsbury calls "the full-dress plain style" of one, part of whose vital idiom is split off from learned occasions. Their tone was fastidious, rationalizing, and teacherly; they were likely to be drily dialectic, shrewd and independent in their apprehension of arguments and in "improving" on them, but narrow or genteel in particular tastes. Many, especially university professors, had a discursive and classifying mentality, a flair for defining elegant problems—e.g., Is Music an Imitative Art?—then covering the ground inductively by examples drawn from very broad, up-to-date, and eclectic reading. At worst, again to quote Saintsbury, they had "a tendency to substitute for actual reasoning long chains of only plausibly connected propositions."

Yet they imported into eighteenth-century English criticism a special angle of vision. Because they aspired to be systematically comprehensive and because they argued points to an end, they left a copious record, and in some cases the most subtle record we have, of transitions in eighteenth-century critical consciousness. In particular, they forwarded inquiry into problems of:

1) taste, imagination, emotion, moral sentiment, sympathy—all those problems which, in the phrase of Lord Kames, concern "the culture of the heart";
2) association-theory and aesthetics, the new discovery of rules in human nature and psychology;
3) the relation of literature to a historically determined society;
4) poetic genius and the metaphorical origins of language, especially in a "primitive" society;
5) philosophic definition of concepts and terms.

Scottish universities had long excelled in mathematics and medicine. By the end of the eighteenth century, they were eminent throughout Europe, and sometimes front-running, in natural sciences, "philosophy," and what may be called professionalism—the application of new philosophy to traditional disciplines and to public affairs. They assimilated the scientific spirit faster than Oxford or Cambridge, and they continued a Scottish heritage of "practical" training and willingness to meet social needs. Dr. Johnson noticed the "diffusion of learning . . . widely and thinly spread" which made a Scottish merchant as learned as a clergyman. "Their learning is like bread in a besieged town: every man gets a little, but no man gets a full meal."

In the traditional system of lectures, modeled after that on the continent, a Scottish professor had to be method-conscious, consecutive, and broadly interdisciplinary. He would instruct in the principles of logic, as a propaedeutic, then advance through the various branches of knowledge, taking the logic with him. During the eighteenth century, Latin lectures yielded gradually to English, and the system became more specialized; but habits of mind lingered. A "moral philosopher" like Adam Smith ranged over all which would now be called the social sciences, with excursions into ethics and aesthetics. Hutcheson lectured on natural religion, ethics, law, government, Greek and Latin moralists, and on Sunday evenings, "the evidences of Christianity." Reid lectured on the latest applied science and mathematics as well as metaphysics. Instead of traditional logic, however, a mid-century professor was more likely to proceed from "experimental method" and association-psychology, the "science of mind." He inherited a sense of the encyclopaedic unity of all disciplines in philosophy, and a desire at all points to insinuate philosophy in common life. A typical Scottish inquiry—e.g., Hutcheson, Kames, Gerard, Alison—opens with chapters defining first principles or explaining how the mind works, as a propaedeutic to criticism or aesthetic theory. Almost all Scottish critics think of themselves as investigating a "branch" of what belongs to a much larger, communal investigation of Man in Nature and Society, and most of them write books on one or more subjects besides literature.

For the history of literary criticism and theory, the most notable writers and titles are:

Francis Hutcheson, *An Inquiry into the Original of Our Ideas of Beauty and Virtue* (1725), *Reflections on Laughter* (1750, first published 1725)

Thomas Blackwell, *An Inquiry into the Life and Writings of Homer* (1735)

David Hume, philosophical and literary essays between 1739 and 1776

Alexander Gerard, *An Essay on Taste* (1759), *An Essay on Genius* (1774)

Adam Smith, *The Theory of Moral Sentiments* (1759)

Henry Home, Lord Kames, *Elements of Criticism* (1762)

Hugh Blair, *A Critical Dissertation on the Poems of Ossian* (1763), *Lectures on Rhetoric and Belles-Lettres* (1783)

William Duff, *An Essay on Original Genius* (1767), *Critical Observations on the Writings of the Most Celebrated Original Geniuses in Poetry* (1770)

James Beattie, *Essays on Poetry and Music as They Affect the Mind* (1776), *Dissertations, Moral and Critical* (1783)

George Campbell, *The Philosophy of Rhetoric* (1776)

Henry MacKenzie, *Spectator*-like essays in *The Mirror* (1779–80) and *The Lounger* (1785–87)

Archibald Alison, *Essays on the Nature and Principles of Taste* (1790)

More than half are university professors: Hutcheson (Moral Philosophy), Blackwell (Greek), Gerard (Philosophy, Divinity), Smith (Moral Philosophy), Blair (Rhetoric and Belles-Lettres), Beattie (Moral Philosophy), Campbell (Principal of Marischal College). Hume aspired to professorships at both Edinburgh and Glasgow, but was rejected by city authorities for his presumed "atheism" and "skepticism." Kames was a judge, MacKenzie a lawyer better known for his sentimental novels such as *The Man of Feeling* (1771); Hume also had legal training. Duff and Alison were clergymen as, incidentally, were Hutcheson, Gerard, Blair, and Campbell, who all published sermons or theological works; all were Presbyterian except Alison. Together with luminaries like the "common sense" philosopher (and minister) Thomas Reid, the historian (and minister) William Robertson, and the philosopher-historian Alan Ferguson, one of the founders of modern sociology—all of them professors—they belonged to an Anglo-Scots intelligentsia which seemed to Hume in 1757, and to many other Scotsmen, "the most distinguished for literature in Europe."

The Scots knew one another intimately—Edinburgh at mid-century had only about 35,000 people, perhaps twice as many by 1800—and they often belonged to the same clubs or service-organizations such as The Philosophical Society, the Select Society, the Highlands Society, the Society of Antiquaries of Scotland. And they linked through generations. When Hutcheson died, his chair at Glasgow was filled by his student Adam Smith; when Smith moved to Edinburgh, the chair was filled by Reid, who moved from Aberdeen. When Ferguson died in 1785, his chair at Edinburgh was filled by Dugald Stewart, a disciple of Reid, who in turn numbered among his students many luminaries of the next generation: Sir Walter Scott, James Mill, and the founders of the later *Edinburgh Review* (Francis Jeffrey, Henry Brougham, Sydney Smith, and Francis Horner.)

Despite complicated comings and goings, the Scots are perhaps best classified by university circles. Clustered in Edinburgh, the literary capital, were Hume, Smith, Kames, Blair, and MacKenzie, and, one may add, Lord Monboddo the learned and eccentric judge,

whose *Origin and Progress of Language* (1773–92) in six volumes
has a mixed claim to be considered criticism or anthropology.

Though in twentieth-century eyes Hume towers over all the
Scots in philosophic importance, Thomas Reid enjoyed a like reputation through much of the nineteenth century as one who, like
Kant, had "answered" Hume's skepticism. What may be called
the Aberdeen professors—Gerard, Beattie, and Campbell—belonged
to a Philosophical Society (or "Wise Club") founded by Reid, in
1758, more or less in friendly opposition to Hume. For fifteen
years, it met fortnightly at the Red Lion Inn in Aberdeen and
presented papers, some of them literary, such as Gerard's on genius,
Beattie's on laughter, and Campbell's on eloquence. Also at Marischal College, Aberdeen, though of an older generation, was Thomas
Blackwell, who had founded an earlier club enlisting Gerard, Beattie,
and Campbell, all of them former students. Blackwell was apparently a great teacher, and among other students whom he interested both in Greek and in his theories of cultural history and
language were Lord Monboddo, William Duff, and James Macpherson of Ossian fame.

Though no literary circle clustered in Glasgow, it has some claim
to originating the Scottish inquiry: the aesthetic moralism of
Francis Hutcheson (see p. 192), professor from 1729 to 1746, pervades Scottish thought incalculably.

In the following selections from Blackwell, Hume, Kames, and
Gerard, many of the more interesting preoccupations of the Scots
emerge. For Alison, see p. 555.

Thomas Blackwell (1701–57). Blackwell asks why Homer, "a
blind strolling bard," should still be unequaled after 2700 years. In
his answer, probably for the first time in criticism, poetry and the
poet are *causally* submerged in social history. A "concourse of
natural causes" in Homer's environment—we should say "factors"
—"conspired to produce" great poetry and to "cultivate" Homer's
genius, a concourse of causes so rare that it is unlikely to be repeated more than once every 3000 years or so:

1) a geographical climate of temperate variety, beauty, and
   fertility;
2) a "primitive" society, neither barbarous nor wholly civilized,
   progressing out of "dark ages" but not yet so disciplined or
   refined as to have lost a "natural" simplicity and passionate
   openness; "as he grew up" Homer could be "a spectator of

all the various situations of the human race" from the extreme of barbarous war and piracy to the cultivated peace and growth of cities;

3) a language that, becoming refined, had not lost its "original" metaphorical character and racy quaintness;

4) a fund of humanly expressive myth, close to "natural" religion, and an audience eager to hear its marvels.

When "the united influence" of these, Blackwell says, "were applied to so rich a subject as the war between Greece and Troy, they produced the *Iliad* and the *Odyssey*." The historical approach, which in Dryden, Pope, and Addison was a minor aid to understanding poetry, becomes for the first time a sociological theory of its origin and value, self-contained and backed by scholarship.

To be sure, in one light Blackwell merely transsumes Augustan commonplaces: Homer, the father of poetry, and Nature are the same; "Know well each ancient's proper character;/His fable, subject, scope in every page;/Religion, country, genius of his age";[1] a great poet must have a great subject; the language of the poet's society, considered as an impersonal fact, conditions the possibilities of his poetry; many ancient and especially Oriental geniuses, Homer or Job, are more passionately metaphorical than later, more correct poets. Moderns excel in arts of ridicule but have lost ancient simplicity. The poet imitates nature but *istius temporis,* in a given society at a given time, and therefore he imitates "manners," including prevalent religious beliefs. (*Cf.* Dryden, p. 114: Chaucer "followed Nature everywhere"; that is, he painted "the various manners and humors, as we now call them, of the whole English nation in his age.") The implied theory of imitation—catching the manners living as they rise, in a contemporary environment— underlies Restoration comedy, Scriblerian satire, and mid-century apologias for the novel.[2] Wherever it appears, it threatens to displace form by content, or to make form a separate, overlaying act of imitation, as in mock-forms.

But what transmutes commonplaces into a revolutionary work is Blackwell's submerging poetry and the poet so completely in environment. The manners in vogue in one's generation and country "make us what we are." [3] To adopt alien manners is artistically

---

[1] Pope, *Essay on Criticism*, I, 119–21.

[2] *Cf.* Johnson, *Rambler* No. 4, p. 406; Fielding, Preface and interchapters to *Joseph Andrews* and interchapters to *Tom Jones*.

[3] *Cf.* Congreve, p. 177: humor "shows us as we are," whether "born with us" or "grafted into us by some accidental change."

sterile; a poet writes from himself, and must confine his poetry, if
it is to be successful, to manners that he knows from practice or
observes around him. Hence the excellence of Congreve's *The Way
of the World* and Pope's *The Rape of the Lock*. Unfortunately, the
artificialities of eighteenth-century civilization, though they produce
good order, are at the same time repressive, prosaic, hostile to the
highest poetry, as Shaftesbury had noted.[4]

Blackwell hedges few implications, and later critics worked out
still others. If poetry is "produced" by social history, then of course
we must study customs and manners of the past in order to understand its poetry; but more, part of the value of poetry, and sometimes perhaps all of its value, may be to document social history,
to "picture life." The forms of poetry, such as epic or comedy, grow
from and express the inner life of the poet in a society, and are not
equally possible at all times. If the poet is "produced" by history,
one should collect as much biographical and social information as
possible in order to explain him. If the greatest poetry known was
produced by "primitive" Greece, other "primitive" societies may
have produced heroic poetry as great or greater; hence the credibility of Ossian, and the serious study of Scandinavian Edda,
Arabian or Indian poetry, Anglo-Saxon or Welsh bardic poetry,
medieval ballads and medieval romances. If the greatest poet was
produced by primitive society, perhaps all natural and original poetic
genius has something primitive about it. If contemporary manners
are hypercivilized, the poet is still free to be bardic in landscape
descriptions; hence Blackwell's praise of *The Seasons* by his Scottish
countryman James Thomson.

David Hume (1711–76). To isolate Hume's criticism of literature
from his philosophy as a whole and its world importance is almost
inevitably to distort, but cannot be helped in short compass. He
had one of the best analytical minds, and one of the seminal minds,
of the century, and those who learned from him, if only by re-
pugnance, learned as one learns now, miscellaneously from the consistent whole.

His criticism, as criticism, is scattered through a lifetime of es-
says, most notably "Of the Delicacy of Taste and Passion," "Of
Eloquence," "Of the Rise and Progress of the Arts and Sciences,"
"Of Simplicity and Refinement in Writing," "Of Tragedy," "Of
Essay Writing." But his letters, like Pope's, are full of revealing

---

[4] *Cf.* pp. 227–28.

asides; other essays, such as "Of Civil Liberty," often digress into literary judgment—e.g., "the first polite prose" in English, he believed, was written by Swift; his *History of England* (1754–61) pronounces, with Gallo-Scots partiality, on English writers from Spenser to Dryden; it is characteristic that explaining the doctrine of association in *An Enquiry Concerning Human Understanding* (1748), Hume should illustrate, in a footnote, from Milton. A "passion for literature," a "love of literary fame," he described as the ruling passion of his life. He insisted that philosophic analysis be subservient to the "easy and humane," that is, the literate, common-sense, social world, and that the easy and humane criticize and feed back into the "accurate and abstract." Indeed, from such sly, difficult, and surprising juxtapositions, Hume gets his irony, which is also the trajectory of forward thought.

His tastes are best summarized as neoclassical-conservative. Virgil and Racine seem to him "nearest the center" and therefore nearest the top of the literary hierarchy, along with Cicero and Terence. French drama, he said, "excelled even the Greeks, who far excelled the English." In English literature, his tastes ran to Queen Anne writers of his youth—Swift, Addison, Pope, and Parnell who "after the fiftieth reading is as fresh as at the first." Unlike Blackwell, he concluded that the more refined and civilized the society, the better for poetry, including epic; and he regretted that Milton, who in his best moments is "the most wonderfully sublime of any poet in any language," had not "lived in a later age and learned to polish some rudeness in his verses."

A traveled man of the world, Hume worshiped cosmopolitan politeness with a self-conscious fervor almost provincial. He polished his English prose style into glistening, classic simplicity— deceptive simplicity; and he labored, with other Scots, to make Edinburgh a capital of civilized intellect. Civilization, progress of refined experience in society, any society, is close to his heart. "Though a philosopher may live remote from business," he remarked, "the genius of philosophy, if carefully cultivated by several, must gradually diffuse itself throughout the whole society and bestow a similar correctness on every art and calling."

To be socially useful, he applied his civilized surgery to almost every subject, from miracles and taxes to polygamy and suicide; a kind of cerebral Scottish Addison, he loosened up the intellectual life of his time in ways almost too subtle to prove. In criticism, as in philosophy, he is most important for his demolition of common-sense certitudes—that each man knows who he is, and who others are, in a world of rationally understood values, causes and effects. If "common sense," self, reason, and knowledge are all a glide of imagination along sealed, accustomed grooves, if in the outer world anything can happen so far as one really knows, if belief or experience is truly all that can be known of reality—then the implications are tremendous, but not quickly worked out. For example, one implication may be that reality is history or process, in which are latent irrationalities.

The conviction of mid-century critics like Burke and Kames that rules cannot be drawn from dogmatic tradition owes much to Hume's example. At the age of eighteen, he underwent a nine-months dark night of the soul, a kind of skeptical epiphany, which convinced him that he must "derive every truth in criticism as well as morality" from "experience of human nature," that philosophy and criticism contain "little more than endless disputes, even in the most fundamental articles." [5] The subtitle of his trial run, the *Treatise of Human Nature* (1739–40), announces "an attempt to introduce the experimental [Newtonian] method of reasoning into moral subjects." In his doctrine of total association, Hume hoped that he had discovered "a kind of *attraction*" in the mental world corresponding to the Newtonian law of gravity in the physical world. Having subverted rationalism as a moral guide, he introduced a neutral instinct of "sympathy," based on association by resemblance, from which moral values could evolve.

His essay "Of the Standard of Taste" typifies the kind of dilemma in which he landed and the pragmatic brilliance of analysis by which he extricated himself. Throughout, he struggles to align neoclassical tastes and values with a skeptical-empirical doctrine which threatens at every turn to dissolve them in relativism. To establish a standard, he must counterpoint two contrary realities— general nature, truth, and beauty, of whose existence there is sufficient evidence, if only one could know them, and the welter of subjective impressions which constitute experience in a particular man. Particular men can be physiologically insensitive, unpracticed, deficient in comparisons, prejudiced (personally, historically, nationally, or religiously), or lacking in sufficient intellect to grasp relationships of part to whole. A standard of taste can be apprehended, then, in men of good taste, civilized men of "strong sense, united to delicate sentiment, improved by practice, perfected by comparison, and cleared of all prejudice," wherever and when-

[5] Letter to George Cheyne (?), 1734.

ever they are to be found. Hume assumes that the consensus of such men, or at least the consensus of their qualities, will prevail in a progressively civilized society.

Henry Home, Lord Kames (1696–1782). Kames represents an eighteenth-century gentleman-aristocrat at his best, erudite, affluent, independent in a charmingly gruff manner, liberal-minded, devoted to "culture." A relative of Hume's, prominent in the Edinburgh circle, he was also Lord Justice of the Supreme Criminal Court, president of The Philosophical Society, and in his old age, one of the most influential and famous Scotsmen of his day. Boswell considered writing his biography. The titles of a few of his eighteen books may suggest his miscellaneous reach, and in their tentativeness, something of his aristocratic-scholarly air: *Decisions of the Court of Sessions . . . in the form of a dictionary* (1741), *Essays upon Several Subjects Concerning British Antiquities* (1747), *Essays on the Principles of Morality and Natural Religion* (1751), *Introduction to the Art of Thinking* (1761) written for his children, *Sketches of the History of Man* (1774), *The Gentleman Farmer; being an attempt to improve agriculture by subjecting it to the test of rational principles* (1776), *Loose Hints on Education, or the Culture of the Heart* (1781). They may not so clearly suggest Kames's practical, public-spirited temper and interest in experimental science, which vaguely reminds one of his American friend Ben Franklin.

In the *Elements of Criticism* (1762), his best-known work today, Kames attempts a Newtonian induction, in the manner of Burke. Beginning with an associationist account of "Perceptions and Ideas in a Train," followed by a lengthy discussion of "Emotions and Passions," he tries to keep his terminology precise and appends a glossary, at the very end, which defines his terms. What sets him apart from all other critics in the century is his attempt, in one treatise, to survey exhaustively the whole ground of criticism in all the fine arts, to isolate criticism itself as a science, to "improve" criticism as he would try to improve agriculture, "by subjecting it to the test of rational principles." What other critics entertain piecemeal or in ambition, Kames attempts in fact. To make his induction credible, he must illustrate his principles from an enormously wide range of particulars, from both criticism and literature. If his taste is often narrowly-expressed, understandably so given his sweeping plan, Kames, a hard-minded judge of sixty-six, is also independent and freshly observant. His organized wilderness of a book touches on most of the topics of mid-century thought, often with clarifying precision and shrewdness. His illustrations of human nature by Shakespeare, and of Shakespeare by human nature, are almost always interesting.

In the selected passages, one can observe, once more, the coexistence of neoclassical tastes with an empiricism which complicates or threatens them. Though Kames believes in genres, he sees that they run into one another like colors. Though he believes in a standard of taste, he is driven back, like Hume, upon historical evidence and a kind of floating faith in the permanent common sense not just of mankind, but of civilized man, indeed of the non-laboring classes. In exploding the unities of place and time, he is driven, on psychological grounds, to re-establish them in separate acts. Imagination is so like memory that he must struggle to distinguish them, in Hume's language, by their different "vivacity." His doctrine of "ideal presence," which he believed an original contribution to criticism, defines aesthetic experience as a "waking dream" which is sustained by a memory-like flow of associated emotions, images, and ideas. Yet it is placed in the service of neoclassic tastes for probability and realism: only a true imitation of nature will arouse "sympathy."

Alexander Gerard (1728–95). Gerard, of the Aberdeen circle, is better known for his *Essay on Taste* (1759), a scholastic, three-part treatise with sub-sections, perhaps the most thorough digest of mid-century speculation on the subject. Following Hutcheson, he thought of taste as planted in human nature by Providence for human happiness—a distinct faculty of the mind, built up associatively in the course of experience by the interworking of passions with innate "senses" of novelty, grandeur and sublimity, beauty, imitation, harmony, ridicule, and virtue. Gerard explained how such sensibility of taste might be educated or "refined" to higher intensity within individual limits, its interrelations with imagination and genius, and the constructive role of knowledge and judgment. An *Essay on Genius* was begun, and much of it written, about the same time, though it was not published until 1774. It is an equally exhaustive, professorial treatise in three parts. Gerard was not an innovative thinker, though he was individualistic, well read, and analytic, and for that reason he is often valuable as a record of what was often thought but unexpressed. His exposition of association-psychology and its implications for the literary culture is especially full and illuminating. Unlike Hume and Kames, however, he argued that a standard of taste is to be found in objective principles within works of art themselves, not in the consensus of aristocratic critics.

In the following passages, Gerard attributes to imagination many of the qualities once stated of wit, but in a context of association-psychology. He restates traditional antinomies of nature and art, imagination and judgment, rules and genius; he exemplifies from Homer and Newton. But his associationism is clearly dissolving old boundaries. Imagination which in a genius is always creating spontaneous, new linkages of association, is also seen as a constructive power in both poetry and science. The form of a poem, though vaguely purposed, actually is brought into being under the influence of passion, by a kind of imaginative magic; it emerges from the associative reservoir of an individual genius, who himself is less a designing artist than a natural force that converts experience as a vegetable converts moisture from surrounding soil. The implication is to make the form of a poem relative and particular, and to submerge rules in a creative process essentially irrational.[6]

The section quoted from Part II, as Professor Elledge has been first to observe, shows Gerard at his best. He distinguishes more clearly than Kames, who stated the same distinction, between description and representation in Shakespeare—between associations which belong merely to the poet, and associations which, by an act of sympathetic imagination, belong to the passion felt by a character. Gerard is helping to forge, from association theory, a new tool for Shakespearean analysis.

* * * *

THOMAS BLACKWELL (1701–1757)

FROM

*An Inquiry into the Life
and Writings of Homer* [1735]

FROM SECTION I

It is Homer, my Lord, and a question concerning him which has been looked upon as hitherto unresolved—by what fate or disposi-

---

[6] In Section IV immediately following, however, Gerard explores the necessary role of "judgment" in governing genius.

tion of things it has happened that none have equalled him in epic poetry for two thousand seven hundred years, the time since he wrote, nor any that we know ever surpassed him before. For this is the man whose works for many ages were the delight of princes and the support of priests, as well as the wonder of the learned, which they still continue to be.

How unsafe soever it might have been to have said so of old at Smyrna, where Homer was deified, or at Chios[1] among his posterity, I believe it would be difficult to persuade your Lordship that there was a miracle in the case. That, indeed, would quickly put an end to the question. For were we really of the same opinion as the ancients, that Homer was inspired from heaven, that he sang and wrote as the "prophet and interpreter of the gods,"[2] we should hardly be apt to wonder. Nor would it surprise us much to find a book of a heavenly origin without an equal among human compositions; to find the subject of it equally useful and great, the style just and yet sublime, the order both simple and exquisite; to find the sentiments natural without lowness, the manners real and withal so extensive as to include even the *varieties* of the chief characters of mankind. We should expect no less, considering whence it came. And that I take to have been the reason why none of the ancients have attempted to account for this prodigy. They acquiesced, it is probable, in the pretensions which the poet constantly makes to celestial instruction, and seem to have been of Tacitus' opinion "that it is more pious and respectful to believe than to inquire into the works of the gods."[3]

But the happy change that has been since wrought upon the face of religious affairs leaves us at liberty to be of contrary opinion. Though in ancient times it might have gone near to banish us from Smyrna or Colophon, yet at present it is become perfectly harmless, and we may anywhere assert that Homer's poems are of *human composition*, inspired by no other power than his own natural faculties, assisted by the chances of his education; in a word, that a *concourse* of *natural* causes conspired to produce and cultivate that mighty genius, and gave him the noblest field to exercise it in that ever fell to the share of a poet.

Here, my Lord, there seems to be occasion for a little philosophy,

---

[1] Two of many cities which claimed to be Homer's birthplace; see below, Colophon.

[2] "Plato, *Alcibiades*, ii." (Blackwell's note. Most of his heavy annotation in Greek, Latin, Italian, and Spanish has been omitted.)

[3] *Germania*, 34.

to put us, if possible, upon the track of this singular phenomenon. It has shone for upwards of two thousand years in the poetic world, and so dazzled men's eyes that they have hitherto been more employed in gazing at it than in inquiring "What formed it?" or "How it came there?" And very fortunately, the author of all antiquity who seems to have made the happiest union of the courtier and the scholar[4] has determined a point that might have given us some trouble. He has laid it down as a principle that the greatest genius cannot excel without culture, nor the finest education produce anything noble without natural endowments.[5] Taking this for granted, we may assure ourselves that Homer hath been happy in them both, and must now follow the dark hints afforded us by antiquity to find out how a blind strolling bard could come by them.

I do not choose to entertain your Lordship with the accidents about his birth, though some naturalists would look upon them as the beginnings of his good fortune. I incline rather to observe that he is generally reputed to have been a native of Asia the Less, a tract of ground that for the temperature of the climate and qualities of the soil may vie with any in Europe. It is not so fat and fruitful as the plains of Babylon or banks of the Nile, to effeminate the inhabitants, and beget laziness and inactivity. But the purity and benignity of the air, the varieties of the fruits and fields, the beauty and number of the rivers, and the constant gales from the happy isles of the western sea—*all conspire* to bring its productions of every kind to the highest perfection. They inspire that mildness of temper and flow of fancy which favor the most extensive views, and give the finest conceptions of *nature* and *truth*.

In the division commonly made of climates, the rough and cold are observed to produce the strongest bodies and most martial spirits; the hotter, lazy bodies with cunning and obstinate passions; but the temperate regions, lying under the benign influences of a genial sky, have the best chance for a fine perception and a proportioned eloquence. Good sense is indeed said to be the product of every country, and I believe it is; but the richest growth and fairest shoots of it spring, like other plants, from the happiest exposition[6] and most friendly soil.[7] . . .

If Homer, then, came into the world in such a country and under so propitious an aspect of nature, we must next inquire what recep-

---

[4] Horace.
[5] *Cf.* Horace, Ars Poetica, 409–10.
[6] exposure.
[7] In support, Blackwell cites Hippocrates, Plato, Quintus Curtius, and Galen.

tion he met with upon his arrival, in what condition he found things, and what dispositions they must produce in an exalted genius and comprehensive mind. This is a difficult speculation, and I should be under some apprehensions how to get through if I did not know that men moving, like your Lordship, in the higher spheres of life are well acquainted with the effects of *culture* and *education*. They know the changes they are able to produce, and are not surprised to find them, as it were, new-molding human creatures and transforming them more than Urganda or Circe. The influence of example and discipline is, in effect, so extensive that some very acute writers have mistaken it for the only source of our morals, though their root lies deeper and is more interwoven with our original frame. However, as we have at present only to do with Homer in his poetical capacity, we need give ourselves no further trouble in considering the tenor of his life than as it served to raise him to be the prince of his profession.

In this search, we must remember that young minds are apt to receive such strong impressions from the circumstances of the country where they are born and bred that they contract a mutual kind of *likeness* to those circumstances, and bear the marks of the course of life through which they have passed. A man who has had great misfortunes is easily distinguished from one who has lived all his days in high prosperity, and a person bred to business has a very different appearance from another brought up in sloth and pleasure. Both our understanding and behavior receive a stamp from our station and adventures; and as a liberal education forms a gentleman, and the contrary a clown, in the same manner, if we take things a little deeper, are our minds and manners influenced by the strain of our lives. In this view, the circumstances that may reasonably be thought to have the greatest effect upon us may perhaps be reduced to these following:

First, the state of the country where a person is born and bred, in which I include the common manners of the inhabitants, their constitution, civil and religious, with its causes and consequences. Their manners are seen in the ordinary way of living as it happens to be polite or barbarous, luxurious or simple.

Next, the manners of the times or the prevalent humors and professions in vogue. These two are public, and have a common effect on the whole generation. Of a more confined nature is, first, private education, and, after that, the particular way of life we choose and pursue, with our fortunes in it.

From these accidents, men in every country may be justly said to draw their character and derive their manners. They make us *what we are*, in so far as they reach our sentiments and give us a peculiar turn and appearance. A change in any one of *them* makes an alteration upon *us*; and taken together, we must consider them as the molds that form us into those habits and dispositions which sway our conduct and distinguish our actions.

FROM SECTION II

There are some things, my Lord, which though they happen in all ages, are yet very hard to describe. Few people are capable of observing them; and therefore terms have not been contrived to express perceptions which are taken from the widest views of human affairs. Of this kind is a circumstance which attends the fate of every nation. It may be called a *progression of manners,* and depends for the most part upon our fortunes: as they flourish or decline, so we live and are affected; and the greatest revolutions in them produce the most conspicuous alterations in the other. For the manners of a people seldom stand still, but are either polishing or spoiling. In nations where for many years no considerable changes of fortune happen, the various rises and falls in their moral character are the less observed. But when by an invasion and conquest the face of things is wholly changed, or when the original planters of a country, from a state of ignorance and barbarity, advance by policy and order to wealth and power, it is then that the steps of the progression become observable: we can see everything on the growing hand, and the very soul and genius of the people rising to higher attempts and a more liberal manner.

From the accounts left us of the state of ancient Greece by the most accurate of their historians,[8] we may perceive three periods in their affairs: the first, from the dark ages, of which they had little or no knowledge, to the time of the Trojan War; the second, from the taking of Troy to the Persian invasion under Xerxes; the third, from that time to the loss of their liberty, first by the Macedonians and then by the Romans. Greece was peopled in the first; she grew, and the constitution was settled, in the second; she enjoyed it in the third, and was in all her glory. From the two first periods, Homer drew his *imagery* and *manners,* learned his *language,* and took his *subject,* which makes it necessary for us to review them. . . .

Thus, for some ages after the taking of Troy, Greece was indeed increasing in wealth and numbers of inhabitants, but was continu-

---

[8] "Thucydides, i." (Blackwell's note.)

ally engaged in wars; taking of towns, battles of tribes, piracy, and incursions were common adventures.

In the second or third age of this period was Homer born; that is, at a time when he might, as he grew up, be a spectator of all the various situations of the human race, might observe them in great calamities and in high felicity; but more generally they were increasing in wealth and discipline. For I cannot help observing that from these hard beginnings and jarring interests, the Greeks became early masters of the military art, and, by degrees, of all others that tend to enrich or adorn a city and raise a commonwealth. Shipping and commerce, domestic order, and foreign influence, with every subservient art of policy and government, were invented or improved, and some of them brought to a very great degree of perfection.

And truly, it could not be otherwise while each city was independent, rivaling its neighbor, and trying its genius in peace and its strength in war. Upon good or bad success, the citizens, all concerned in the administration, made a careful inquiry into the cause of it: What fault in their conduct had procured the one, or what excellency in their constitution the other? This liberty produced hardiness and discipline, which at length arose to that height that ten thousand Greeks were an overmatch for the Persian monarch with all the power of the Asiatic plains.

This indeed happened long after, but the struggle was fresh in Homer's days. Arms were in repute, and force decided possession. He saw towns taken and plundered, the men put to the sword, and the women made slaves; he beheld their despairing faces and suppliant postures, heard their moanings over their murdered husbands, and prayers for their infants to the victor.

On the other hand, he might view cities blessed with peace, spirited by liberty, flourishing in trade, and increasing in wealth. He was not engaged in affairs himself, to draw off his attention; but he wandered through the various scenes and observed them at leisure. Nor was it the least instructive sight to see a colony led out, a city founded, the foundations of order and policy laid, with all the provisions for the security of the people. Such scenes afford extended views, and natural ones too, as they are the immediate effect of the great parent of invention, necessity, in its young and untaught essays.

The importance of this good fortune will best appear if we reflect on the pleasure which arises from a representation of *natural* and *simple* manners. It is irresistible and enchanting; they best show human wants and feelings; they give us back the emotions of an artless mind, and the plain methods we fall upon to indulge them. Goodness and honesty have their share in the delight; for we begin to love the men, and would rather have to do with them than with more refined but *double* characters. Thus, the various works neces- sary for building a house or a ship, for planting a field, or forging a weapon, if described with an eye to the sentiments and attention of the man so employed, give us great pleasure *because we feel the same.* Innocence, we say, is beautiful, and the sketches of it, wher- ever they are truly hit off, never fail to charm. Witness the few strokes of that nature in Mr. Dryden's *Conquest of Mexico* and the *Enchanted Island.*[9]

Accordingly, we find Homer describing very minutely the houses, tables, and way of living of the ancients; and we read these descrip- tions with pleasure. But on the contrary, when we consider our own customs, we find that our first business when we sit down to poetize in the higher strains is to *unlearn* our daily way of life, to forget our manner of sleeping, eating, and diversions. We are obliged to adopt a set of *more natural* manners, which, however, are foreign to us, and must be like plants raised up in hotbeds or greenhouses, in com- parison of those which grow in soils fitted by nature for such pro- ductions. Nay, so far are we from enriching poetry with *new* images drawn from nature that we find it difficult to understand the old. We live within doors, covered, as it were, from nature's face, and passing our days supinely ignorant of her beauties. We are apt to think the similes taken from her "low," and the ancient manners "mean" or absurd. But let us be ingenuous, my Lord, and confess that while the moderns admire nothing but pomp, and can think nothing *great* or *beautiful* [1] but what is the produce of wealth, they exclude themselves from the pleasantest and most natural images that adorned the old poetry. State and form disguise man; and wealth and luxury disguise nature. Their effects in writing are an- swerable. A Lord Mayor's show or grand procession of any kind [2] is not very delicious reading if described minutely and at length, and great ceremony is at least equally tiresome in a poem as in ordinary conversation.

It has been an old complaint that we love to disguise everything, and most of all *ourselves.* All our titles and distinctions have been represented as coverings, and additions of grandeur to what nature

---

[9] *The Indian Emperor* and *The Tempest.*
[1] See Addison, p. 242.
[2] Apparently an allusion to Pope's *The Dunciad.*

gave us[3]—happy indeed for the best of ends (I mean the public tranquillity and good order), but incapable of giving delight in fiction or poetry.

By this time, your Lordship sees I am in the case of a noble historian who, having related the constant superiority his Greeks had over the inhabitants of the Assyrian vales, concludes "that it has not been given by the gods, to one and the same country, to produce rich crops and warlike men." [4] Neither indeed does it seem to be given to one and the same kingdom to be thoroughly civilized and afford proper subjects for poetry.

The *marvelous* and *wonderful* is the nerve of the epic strain. But what marvelous things happen in a well-ordered state? We can hardly be surprised; we know the springs and method of acting; everything happens in order and according to custom or law. But in a wide uncultivated country, not under a regular government or split into many, whose inhabitants live scattered and ignorant of laws and discipline—in such a country the manners are simple, and accidents will happen every day: exposition and loss of infants, encounters, escapes, rescues, and every other thing that can inflame the human passions while acting, or awake them when described and recalled by imitation.

These are not to be found in a well-governed state, except it be during the time of a civil war, when it ceases to be so; and yet, with all the disorder and misery that attends that last of ills, the period while it rages is a fitter subject for an epic poem than the most glorious campaign that ever was made in Flanders. Even the things that give the greatest luster in a regular government, the greatest honors and highest trusts, will scarcely bear poetry. The Muse refuses to bestow her embellishments on a duke's patent or a general's commission. They can neither raise our wonder nor gain our heart. For peace, harmony, and good order, which make the happiness of a people, are the bane of a poem that subsists by wonder and surprise. . . .

It is thus that a people's felicity clips the wings of their verse. It affords few materials for admiration or pity; and though the pleasure arising from the sublimer kinds of writing may make us regret the silence of the Muses, yet I am persuaded your Lordship will join in the wish *that we may never be a proper subject* of a heroic poem.

But now that I have ventured so far, I begin to apprehend that I shall be deserted. The habit of reconciling extremes when a public

---

[3] Blackwell quotes from Guarini's pastoral play *Il Pastor Fido* (1585).
[4] "Herodotus." (Blackwell's note.)

concern calls for attention is become so natural to your Lordship that it must incline you to wish our epic affairs not so desperate; and your knowledge of the poetical privilege will immediately suggest "that our private manners, it is possible, admit not such representation; nor will our mercenary wars and state intrigues receive the stamp of simplicity and heroism. But why may not a poet *feign?* Can't he counterfeit manners and contrive accidents as he sees good? Is he not entitled to shift scenes and introduce persons and characters at pleasure? Let him but exercise his prerogative, and all will be well. Our manners need be no impediment; he may give his new-raised generation what turn and cast he pleases."

Though this seems to promise fair, yet in the end, I am afraid, it will not hold good. Your Lordship will judge whether my fears are just when, relying on that penetration which attends your opinions, I venture to affirm that a poet describes nothing so happily as what he has seen, nor talks masterly but in his native language and proper idiom, nor mimics truly other manners than those whose originals he has practiced and known.[5]

This maxim will, no doubt, appear severe, and yet, I believe upon inquiry it will hold true in fact. If we cast an eye backward upon antiquity, it will be found that none of the great *original* writers have excelled but where they spoke of the things they were most conversant with, and in the language and dialect they constantly used.[6] The satyrical buffoonish temper of Archilochus[7] is well known, nor is it a secret that he indulged his passions, which were neither weak nor few. The sententious writings of Euripides, and Menander's polite pictures of life, represented their daily conversation. Plato's admired dialogues are but corrected transcripts of what passed in the Academy. And Lucilius,[8] preferred by some Romans to all that ever wrote, wrote himself just as he spoke. Herodotus' history shows the traveler, Thucydides' the politician, Dionysius' [9] the scholar, Xenophon's the captain and the philosopher, as truly as

---

[5] Plato, *Republic*, iii: "the human genius is, if I may use the expression, clipped or coined into a still smaller compass than what I have mentioned, so as neither to be able to imitate many different things perfectly nor to act the things themselves of which these imitations are copies or resemblances." (Blackwell's note.)

[6] As for the poets in particular, says Cervantes, "all the ancient poets wrote in the language which they sucked in with their milk, and did not seek foreign tongues in order to express their sublime conceptions." *Don Quixote*, II, 5, 16. (Blackwell's note.)

[7] See p. 101, n. 1.

[8] See p. 100, n. 6.

[9] Dionysius of Halicarnassus (fl. 1st cent. B.C.), literary critic and historian whose *Archaeologia* recounts the history of Rome to 264 B.C.

they acted those characters in their lives. Nor could those heroes have excelled, each in his different way, had they done otherwise.

But the truth of this maxim will best appear if we observe its influence in conversation and behavior. He who affects no other than his natural manners has a better chance to excel than if he should attempt to copy another man's way, though perhaps preferable both in language and gesture to his own. It is a small circle of acquaintance which does not afford some diverting proofs of this common mistake. And if it was not a disagreeable occupation to blame and find fault, it were easy to produce many instances of the same miscarriage in writing. I will only put your Lordship in mind of two great men who, with everything besides to recommend them, have split upon this single rock; and for that reason, as well as their being dead near two hundred years ago, they may be mentioned with less reluctancy. The persons I mean are both Italians who had the happiness to see the golden age of learning in that country, the pontificate[1] of Leo X.

Pietro Bembo was of a noble family in Venice; his early merit recommended him to Leo, who loved to fill his court with learned men, and had a true judgment in such things himself. Bembo was made secretary for the apostolic briefs, and after two successions to the pontificate, was raised to the dignity of the purple, chiefly for his reputation in literature. And indeed his learning and abilities are unquestionable. But at the same time, this great man, admiring only the Roman eloquence and manners, wrote a history of his own country[2] so much upon the model of a Latin annal, that not only the general turn and cast of the work is servilely copied, but the peculiarities of their style, their computation of miles and time, and the forms of their religion and government are with infinite labor wrought into a Venetian story. The effect of it is to enervate and deaden his work, which a writer of half his knowledge and accomplishments would have told better without his affectation.

A little younger than the Cardinal was Giovanni Giorgio Trissino, a native of Vicenza. He was looked upon as one of the greatest masters of ancient learning, both Greek and Roman, of his age; and, which rarely happens, was blessed at the same time with a flow of Tuscan eloquence. A man so qualified easily saw the faults of his contemporary writers, and thought it not impossible, with his talents and judgment, "to produce such a poem in Italian as Homer had done in Greek."

---

[1] 1513–21.
[2] *Rerum Veneticarum, Libri XII* (1551).

He set about it, and placed this great model before his eyes. He abandoned the use of rhyme, followed the natural run of speech in his verse, and endeavored to adapt his inventions to the state and temper of his age and nation. He took Italy for the subject of his poem, as Homer had taken Greece. He has champions of the same country, as Homer has Grecian heroes. He uses angels for his divinities, and supplies[3] the ancient Furies with modern devils. In his geography, as Homer described Greece and chiefly Thessaly, Trissino describes Italy and dwells on Lombardy. He has even attempted fable, and interwoven allegorical stories of life and morals with the body of the narration. But after all, the *native Italian* manners are lost, and the high spirit and secret force which bewitches a reader and dazzles his eyes, [so] that he can see no faults in Dante and Ariosto, is here crushed by imitation. Its fate has been answerable: the *Italia Liberata* (for so he called his poem) being no more read or known than Chapelain's *Pucelle*[4] would be without Boileau, or Sir R***'s A***d without the D***.[5] Trissino owes his fame to his *Sophonisba*, a tragedy, and to his *Miscellanies*; and the Cardinal is preserved from oblivion by his letters and love verses; and there, too, the same inclination to copy has made him check his natural fire, that he might attain Cicero's elegance in the one, and Petrarch's purity and softness in the other.

To say the truth, my Lord, we are born but with narrow capacities. Our minds are not able to master two sets of manners, or comprehend with facility different ways of life. Our company, education, and circumstances make deep impressions, and form us into a *character* of which we can hardly divest ourselves afterwards. The manners not only of the age and nation in which we live, but of our city and family, stick closely to us, and betray us at every turn when we try to dissemble and would pass for foreigners. These we understand, and can paint to perfection; and there is no one so undiscerning as not to see how happy we have been in describing those parts of *modern* life we have undertaken. Was there ever a more natural picture than the *Way of the World*? Or can anything in its kind surpass the *Rape of the Lock*? The authors, doubtless, perfectly knew the life and manners they were painting, and have succeeded accordingly.

---

[3] replaces.
[4] A twenty-four book epic by the French poet and critic Jean Chapelain (1595–1674), mocked by Boileau.
[5] Sir Richard Blackmore's *Arthuriad* without Pope's *Dunciad*.

Here then was Homer's first happiness: he took his plain natural images from *life*. He saw warriors and shepherds and peasants, such as he drew, and was daily conversant among such people as he intended to represent. The manners used in the Trojan times were not disused in his own. The same way of living in private, and the same pursuits in public, were still prevalent, and gave him a model for his design, which would not allow him to exceed the truth in his draught. By frequently and freely looking it over, he could discern what parts of it were fit to be represented and what to be passed over.

For so unaffected and simple were the manners of those times that the folds and windings of the human breast lay open to the eye. People were not as yet taught to be ashamed of themselves and their natural appetites, nor consequently to dissemble them. They made no scruple of owning the inclinations of their heart, and openly indulged their passions, which were entirely void of art and design.[6] This was Homer's happiness, with respect to mankind and the living part of his poetry. As for the other parts, and what a painter would call "still life," he could have little advantage over the moderns. For we are not to imagine that he could discover the entertaining prospects or rare productions of a country better than we can. That is a subject still remaining to us, if we will quit our towns and look upon it. We find it, accordingly, nobly executed by many of the moderns, and the most illustrious instance of it within these few years doing honor to the British poetry.[7]

In short, it may be said of Homer, and of every poet who has wrote well, that what he felt and saw, that he described; and that Homer had the good fortune to see and learn the Grecian manners at their true pitch and happiest temper for verse. Had he been born much sooner, he could have seen nothing but nakedness and barbarity. Had he come much later, he had fallen either in times of peace, when a wide and settled policy prevailed over Greece, or in general wars, regularly carried on by civilized states, when private passions are buried in the common order and established discipline.

---

[6] *Bold Homer durst not so great virtue feign*
In his best pattern. Of Patroclus slain,
With such amazement as weak mothers use,
And frantic gesture, he receives the news. —WALLER (Blackwell's note.)
[7] *The Seasons,* by Mr. Thomson. (Blackwell's note.)

* * * *

DAVID HUME (1711–1776)
Of the Standard of Taste [1757]

The great variety of taste, as well as of opinion, which prevails in the world is too obvious not to have fallen under everyone's observation. Men of the most confined knowledge are able to remark a difference of taste in the narrow circle of their acquaintance, even where the persons have been educated under the same government, and have early imbibed the same prejudices. But those who can enlarge their view to contemplate distant nations and remote ages are still more surprised at the great inconsistence and contrariety. We are apt to call *barbarous* whatever departs widely from our own taste and apprehension, but soon find the epithet of reproach retorted on us. And the highest arrogance and self-conceit is at last startled on observing an equal assurance on all sides, and scruples amidst such a contest of sentiment to pronounce positively in its own favor.

As this variety of taste is obvious to the most careless inquirer, so will it be found, on examination, to be still greater in reality than in appearance. The sentiments of men often differ with regard to beauty and deformity of all kinds, even while their general discourse is the same. There are certain terms in every language which import blame and others praise, and all men who use the same tongue must agree in their application of them. Every voice is united in applauding *elegance, propriety, simplicity, spirit* in writing, and in blaming *fustian, affectation, coldness*, and a *false brilliancy*. But when critics come to particulars, this seeming unanimity vanishes, and it is found that they had affixed a very different meaning to their expressions. In all matters of opinion and science,[1] the case is opposite: the difference among men is there oftener found to lie in generals than in particulars and to be less in reality than in appearance. An explanation of the terms commonly ends the controversy, and the disputants are surprised to find that they had been quarreling while at bottom they agreed in their judgment.

Those who found morality on sentiment more than on reason are inclined to comprehend ethics under the former observation, and

---

[1] knowledge.

to maintain that in all questions which regard conduct and manners, the difference among men is really greater than at first sight it appears. It is indeed obvious that writers of all nations and all ages concur in applauding justice, humanity, magnanimity, prudence, veracity, and in blaming the opposite qualities. Even poets and other authors whose compositions are chiefly calculated to please the imagination are yet found, from Homer down to Fénelon,[2] to inculcate the same moral precepts and to bestow their applause and blame on the same virtues and vices. This great unanimity is usually ascribed to the influence of plain reason, which, in all these cases, maintains similar sentiments in all men, and prevents those controversies to which the abstract sciences are so much exposed. So far as the unanimity is real, this account may be admitted as satisfactory. But we must also allow that some part of the seeming harmony in morals may be accounted for from the very nature of language. The word *virtue*, with its equivalent in every tongue, implies praise, as that of *vice* does blame; and no one, without the most obvious and grossest impropriety, could affix reproach to a term which in general acceptation is understood in a good sense, or bestow applause where the idiom requires disapprobation. Homer's general precepts, where he delivers any such, will never be controverted; but it is obvious that when he draws particular pictures of manners, and represents heroism in Achilles and prudence in Ulysses, he intermixes a much greater degree of ferocity in the former, and of cunning and fraud in the latter, than Fénelon would admit of. The sage Ulysses, in the Greek poet, seems to delight in lies and fictions, and often employs them without any necessity or even advantage. But his more scrupulous son, in the French epic writer, exposes himself to the most imminent perils rather than depart from the most exact line of truth and veracity.

The admirers and followers of the Alcoran[3] insist on the excellent moral precepts interspersed throughout that wild and absurd performance. But it is to be supposed that the Arabic words which correspond to the English *equity, justice, temperance, meekness, charity*, were such as, from the most constant use of that tongue, must always be taken in a good sense, and it would have argued the greatest ignorance, not of morals but of language, to have mentioned them with any epithets besides those of applause and approbation. But would we know whether the pretended prophet had really attained a just sentiment of morals? Let us attend to his nar-

---

[2] See p. 393, n. 3.
[3] the Koran.

ration, and we shall soon find that he bestows praise on such instances of treachery, inhumanity, cruelty, revenge, bigotry, as are utterly incompatible with civilized society. No steady rule of right seems there to be attended to, and every action is blamed or praised so far only as it is beneficial or hurtful to the true believers.

The merit of delivering true general precepts in ethics is indeed very small. Whoever recommends any moral virtues really does no more than is implied in the terms themselves. That people who invented the word *charity* and used it in a good sense, inculcated more clearly and much more efficaciously the precept "Be charitable" than any pretended legislator or prophet who should insert such a *maxim* in his writings. Of all expressions, those which together with their other meaning imply a degree either of blame or approbation are the least liable to be perverted or mistaken.

It is natural for us to seek a "standard of taste," a rule by which the various sentiments of men may be reconciled, at least a decision afforded confirming one sentiment and condemning another.

There is a species of philosophy[4] which cuts off all hopes of success in such an attempt, and represents the impossibility of ever attaining any standard of taste. The difference, it is said, is very wide between judgment and sentiment. All sentiment is right, because sentiment has a reference to nothing beyond itself, and is always real wherever a man is conscious of it. But all determinations of the understanding are not right, because they have a reference to something beyond themselves, to wit, real matter of fact, and are not always conformable to that standard. Among a thousand different opinions which different men may entertain of the same subject, there is one, and but one, that is just and true, and the only difficulty is to fix and ascertain it. On the contrary, a thousand different sentiments excited by the same object are all right, because no sentiment represents what is really in the object. It only marks a certain conformity or relation between the object and the organs or faculties of the mind; and if that conformity did not really exist, the sentiment could never possibly have being. Beauty is no quality in things themselves: it exists merely in the mind which contemplates them, and each mind perceives a different beauty. One person may even perceive deformity where another is sensible of beauty, and every individual ought to acquiesce in his own sentiment without pretending to regulate those of others. To seek the real beauty or real deformity is as fruitless an inquiry as to pretend to ascertain

---

[4] Hume's usual strategy of argument is to state a skeptical position, then bring it into conflict with common sense.

the real sweet or real bitter. According to the disposition of the organs, the same object may be both sweet and bitter, and the proverb[5] has justly determined it to be fruitless to dispute concerning tastes. It is very natural, and even quite necessary, to extend this axiom to mental as well as bodily taste; and thus common sense, which is so often at variance with philosophy, especially with the skeptical kind, is found, in one instance at least, to agree in pronouncing the same decision.

But though this axiom by passing into a proverb seems to have attained the sanction of common sense, there is certainly a species of common sense which opposes it, at least serves to modify and restrain it. Whoever would assert an equality of genius and elegance between Ogilby[6] and Milton, or Bunyan[7] and Addison, would be thought to defend no less an extravagance than if he had maintained a molehill to be as high as Teneriffe,[8] or a pond as extensive as the ocean. Though there may be found persons who give the preference to the former authors, no one pays attention to such a taste, and we pronounce without scruple the sentiment of these pretended critics to be absurd and ridiculous. The principle of the natural equality of tastes is then totally forgot, and while we admit it on some occasions where the objects seem near an equality, it appears an extravagant paradox, or rather a palpable absurdity, where objects so disproportioned are compared together.

It is evident that none of the rules of composition are fixed by reasonings *a priori*, or can be esteemed abstract conclusions of the understanding, from comparing those habitudes and relations of ideas which are eternal and immutable. Their foundation is the same with that of all the practical sciences, experience; nor are they anything but general observations concerning what has been universally found to please in all countries and in all ages. Many of the beauties of poetry and even of eloquence are founded on falsehood and fiction, on hyperboles, metaphors, and an abuse or perversion of terms from their natural meaning. To check the sallies of the imagination and to reduce every expression to geometrical truth and exactness would be the most contrary to the laws of criticism because it would produce a work which, by universal experience, has

---

[5] *De gustibus non disputandum.*

[6] John Ogilby (1600–76), Scottish printer and map-maker, whose translations of Homer and Virgil had been ridiculed by Dryden and Pope.

[7] Bunyan is considered a lower-class religious writer; according to one account in the 1740's, *Pilgrim's Progress* could be found in almost every cottage in Scotland.

[8] mountain peak in the Canary Islands, proverbial for height.

been found the most insipid and disagreeable. But though poetry can never submit to exact truth, it must be confined by rules of art, discovered to the author either by genius or observation. If some negligent or irregular writers have pleased, they have not pleased by their transgressions of rule or order, but in spite of these transgressions: they have possessed other beauties which were conformable to just criticism, and the force of these beauties has been able to overpower censure, and give the mind a satisfaction superior to the disgust arising from the blemishes. Ariosto pleases, but not by his monstrous and improbable fictions, by his bizarre mixture of the serious and comic styles, by the want of coherence in his stories, or by the continual interruptions of his narration. He charms by the force and clearness of his expression, by the readiness and variety of his inventions, and by his natural pictures of the passions, especially those of the gay and amorous kind; and however his faults may diminish our satisfaction, they are not able entirely to destroy it. Did our pleasure really arise from those parts of his poem which we denominate faults, this would be no objection to criticism in general; it would only be an objection to those particular rules of criticism which would establish such circumstances to be faults, and would represent them as universally blamable. If they are found to please, they cannot be faults, let the pleasure which they produce be ever so unexpected and unaccountable.

But though all the general rules of art are founded only on experience and on the observation of the common sentiments of human nature, we must not imagine that on every occasion the feelings of men will be conformable to these rules. Those finer emotions of the mind are of a very tender and delicate nature, and require the concurrence of many favorable circumstances to make them play with facility and exactness, according to their general and established principles. The least exterior hindrance to such small springs, or the least internal disorder, disturbs their motion and confounds the operation of the whole machine. When we would make an experiment of this nature and would try the force of any beauty or deformity, we must choose with care a proper time and place, and bring the fancy to a suitable situation and disposition. A perfect serenity of mind, a recollection of thought, a due attention to the object—if any of these circumstances be wanting, our experiment will be fallacious, and we shall be unable to judge of the catholic and universal beauty. The relation which nature has placed between the form and the sentiment will at least be more obscure, and it will require accuracy to trace and discern it. We shall be able to ascertain its influence, not so much from the operation of each particular beauty, as from the durable admiration which attends those works that have survived all the caprices of mode and fashion, all the mistakes of ignorance and envy.

The same Homer who pleased at Athens and Rome two thousand years ago is still admired at Paris and at London. All the changes of climate, government, religion, and language[9] have not been able to obscure his glory. Authority or prejudice may give a temporary vogue to a bad poet or orator, but his reputation will never be durable or general. When his compositions are examined by posterity or by foreigners, the enchantment is dissipated, and his faults appear in their true colors. On the contrary, a real genius, the longer his works endure, and the more wide they are spread, the more sincere is the admiration which he meets with. Envy and jealousy have too much place in a narrow circle, and even familiar acquaintance with his person may diminish the applause due to his performances; but when these obstructions are removed, the beauties which are naturally fitted to excite agreeable sentiments immediately display their energy; and while the world endures, they maintain their authority over the minds of men.

It appears, then, that amidst all the variety and caprice of taste, there are certain general principles of approbation or blame whose influence a careful eye may trace in all operations of the mind. Some particular forms or qualities, from the original structure of the internal fabric, are calculated to please, and others to displease, and if they fail of their effect in any particular instance, it is from some apparent defect or imperfection in the organ. A man in a fever would not insist on his palate as able to decide concerning flavors, nor would one affected with the jaundice pretend to give a verdict with regard to colors. In each creature there is a sound and a defective state, and the former alone can be supposed to afford us a true standard of taste and sentiment. If in the sound state of the organ there be an entire or a considerable uniformity of sentiment among men, we may thence derive an idea of the perfect beauty, in like manner as the appearance of objects in daylight to the eye of a man in health is denominated their true and real color, even while color is allowed to be merely a phantasm of the senses.

Many and frequent are the defects in the internal organs which

---

[9] See Blackwell, p. 269. In an essay "Of Eloquence," Hume said, seemingly against Blackwell: "a man who should inquire why such a particular poet, as Homer for instance, existed at such a place, in such a time, would throw himself headlong into chimera." Knowledge is general, not particular.

prevent or weaken the influence of those general principles on which depends our sentiment of beauty or deformity. Though some objects, by the structure of the mind, be naturally calculated to give pleasure, it is not to be expected that in every individual the pleasure will be equally felt. Particular incidents and situations occur which either throw a false light on the objects, or hinder the true from conveying to the imagination the proper sentiment and perception.

One obvious cause why many feel not the proper sentiment of beauty is the want of that *delicacy* of imagination which is requisite to convey a sensibility of those finer emotions.[1] This delicacy everyone pretends to; everyone talks of it, and would reduce every kind of taste or sentiment to its standard. But as our intention in this essay is to mingle some light of the understanding with the feelings of sentiment, it will be proper to give a more accurate definition of delicacy than has hitherto been attempted. And not to draw our philosophy from too profound a source, we shall have recourse to a noted story in *Don Quixote*.[2]

It is with good reason, says Sancho to the squire with the great nose, that I pretend to have a judgment in wine: this is a quality hereditary in our family. Two of my kinsmen were once called to give their opinion of a hogshead which was supposed to be excellent, being old and of a good vintage. One of them tastes it, considers it, and, after mature reflection, pronounces the wine to be good, were it not for a small taste of leather which he perceived in it. The other, after using the same precautions, gives also his verdict in favor of the wine, but with the reserve of a taste of iron, which he could easily distinguish. You cannot imagine how much they were both ridiculed for their judgment. But who laughed in the end? On emptying the hogshead, there was found at the bottom an old key with a leather thong tied to it.

The great resemblance between mental and bodily taste will easily teach us to apply this story. Though it be certain that beauty and deformity, no more than sweet and bitter, are not qualities in objects, but belong entirely to the sentiment, internal or external, it must be allowed that there are certain qualities in objects which are fitted by nature to produce those particular feelings. Now, as these qualities may be found in a small degree or may be mixed and confounded with each other, it often happens that the taste is not affected with such minute qualities, or is not able to distinguish all

---

[1] See Hume's essay "Of the Delicacy of Taste and Passion."
[2] Pt. II, ch. 13.

the particular flavors amidst the disorder in which they are presented. Where the organs are so fine as to allow nothing to escape them, and at the same time so exact as to perceive every ingredient in the composition, this we call *delicacy of taste*, whether we employ these terms in the literal or metaphorical sense. Here then the general rules of beauty are of use, being drawn from established models and from the observation of what pleases or displeases when presented singly and in a high degree; and if the same qualities, in a continued composition and in a smaller degree, affect not the organs with a sensible delight or uneasiness, we exclude the person from all pretensions to this delicacy. To produce these general rules or avowed patterns of compositions is like finding the key with the leather thong, which justified the verdict of Sancho's kinsmen, and confounded those pretended judges who had condemned them. Though the hogshead had never been emptied, the taste of the one was still equally delicate, and that of the other equally dull and languid, but it would have been more difficult to have proved the superiority of the former, to the conviction of every bystander. In like manner, though the beauties of writing had never been methodized or reduced to general principles, though no excellent models had ever been acknowledged, the different degrees of taste would still have subsisted, and the judgment of one man been preferable to that of another; but it would not have been so easy to silence the bad critic, who might always insist upon his particular sentiment and refuse to submit to his antagonist. But when we show him an avowed principle of art; when we illustrate this principle by examples, whose operation, from his own particular taste, he acknowledges to be conformable to the principle; when we prove that the same principle may be applied to the present case, where he did not perceive or feel its influence; he must conclude, upon the whole, that the fault lies in himself, and that he wants the delicacy which is requisite to make him sensible of every beauty and every blemish in any composition or discourse.

It is acknowledged to be the perfection of every sense or faculty to perceive with exactness its most minute objects, and allow nothing to escape its notice and observation. The smaller the objects are which become sensible to the eye, the finer is that organ, and the more elaborate its make and composition. A good palate is not tried by strong flavors, but by a mixture of small ingredients, where we are still sensible of each part, notwithstanding its minuteness and its confusion with the rest. In like manner, a quick and acute perception of beauty and deformity must be the perfection of our mental taste, nor can a man be satisfied with himself while he suspects that any excellence or blemish in a discourse has passed him unobserved. In this case, the perfection of the man and the perfection of the sense or feeling are found to be united. A very delicate palate, on many occasions, may be a great inconvenience both to a man himself and to his friends; but a delicate taste of wit or beauty must always be a desirable quality, because it is the source of all the finest and most innocent enjoyments of which human nature is susceptible. In this decision the sentiments of all mankind are agreed. Wherever you can ascertain a delicacy of taste, it is sure to meet with approbation, and the best way of ascertaining it is to appeal to those models and principles which have been established by the uniform consent and experience of nations and ages.

But though there be naturally a wide difference in point of delicacy between one person and another, nothing tends further to increase and improve this talent than *practice* in a particular art, and the frequent survey or contemplation of a particular species of beauty. When objects of any kind are first presented to the eye or imagination, the sentiment which attends them is obscure and confused, and the mind is, in a great measure, incapable of pronouncing concerning their merits or defects. The taste cannot perceive the several excellencies of the performance, much less distinguish the particular character of each excellency, and ascertain its quality and degree. If it pronounce the whole in general to be beautiful or deformed, it is the utmost that can be expected; and even this judgment, a person so unpracticed will be apt to deliver with great hesitation and reserve. But allow him to acquire experience in those objects, his feeling becomes more exact and nice: He not only perceives the beauties and defects of each part, but marks the distinguishing species of each quality, and assigns it suitable praise or blame. A clear and distinct sentiment attends him through the whole survey of the objects; and he discerns that very degree and kind of approbation or displeasure which each part is naturally fitted to produce. The mist dissipates which seemed formerly to hang over the object; the organ acquires greater perfection in its operations, and can pronounce, without danger of mistake, concerning the merits of every performance. In a word, the same address and dexterity which practice gives to the execution of any work is also acquired by the same means in the judging of it.

So advantageous is practice to the discernment of beauty that before we can give judgment on any work of importance, it will even be requisite that that very individual performance be more than

once perused by us, and be surveyed in different lights with attention and deliberation. There is a flutter or hurry of thought which
attends the first perusal of any piece, and which confounds the genuine sentiment of beauty. The relation of the parts is not discerned;
the true characters of style are little distinguished; the several perfections and defects seem wrapped up in a species of confusion,
and present themselves indistinctly to the imagination. Not to mention that there is a species of beauty which, as it is florid and superficial, pleases at first, but being found incompatible with a just expression either of reason or passion, soon palls upon the taste, and
is then rejected with disdain, at least rated at a much lower value.

It is impossible to continue in the practice of contemplating any
order of beauty without being frequently obliged to form *compari-*
sons between the several species and degrees of excellence, and estimating their proportion to each other. A man who has had no opportunity of comparing the different kinds of beauty is indeed totally
unqualified to pronounce an opinion with regard to any object presented to him. By comparison alone we fix the epithets of praise or
blame, and learn how to assign the due degree of each. The coarsest
daubing contains a certain lustre of colors and exactness of imitation, which are so far beauties, and would affect the mind of a
peasant or Indian with the highest admiration. The most vulgar
ballads are not entirely destitute of harmony or nature, and none
but a person familiarized to superior beauties would pronounce
their numbers harsh, or narration uninteresting. A great inferiority
of beauty gives pain to a person conversant in the highest excellence
of the kind, and is for that reason pronounced a deformity, as the
most finished object with which we are acquainted is naturally supposed to have reached the pinnacle of perfection, and to be entitled
to the highest applause. One accustomed to see, and examine, and
weigh the several performances admired in different ages and nations, can alone rate the merits of a work exhibited to his view, and
assign its proper rank among the productions of genius.

But to enable a critic the more fully to execute this undertaking,
he must preserve his mind free from all *prejudice*, and allow nothing
to enter into his consideration but the very object which is submitted
to his examination. We may observe that every work of art, in order
to produce its due effect on the mind, must be surveyed in a certain
point of view, and cannot be fully relished by persons whose situation, real or imaginary, is not conformable to that which is required
by the performance. An orator addresses himself to a particular
audience, and must have a regard to their particular genius, interests,

opinions, passions, and prejudices; otherwise he hopes in vain to govern their resolutions and inflame their affections. Should they even have entertained some prepossessions against him, however unreasonable, he must not overlook this disadvantage, but before he enters upon the subject, must endeavor to conciliate their affection and acquire their good graces. A critic of a different age or nation who should peruse this discourse must have all these circumstances in his eye, and must place himself in the same situation as the audience in order to form a true judgment of the oration. In like manner, when any work is addressed to the public, though I should have a friendship or enmity with the author, I must depart from this situation, and considering myself as a man in general, forget, if possible, my individual being and my peculiar circumstances. A person influenced by prejudice complies not with this condition, but obstinately maintains his natural position, without placing himself in that point of view which the performance supposes. If the work be addressed to persons of a different age or nation, he makes no allowance for their peculiar views and prejudices, but full of the manners of his own age and country, rashly condemns what seemed admirable in the eyes of those for whom alone the discourse was calculated. If the work be executed for the public, he never sufficiently enlarges his comprehension, or forgets his interest as a friend or enemy, as a rival or commentator. By this means his sentiments are perverted; nor have the same beauties and blemishes the same influence upon him as if he had imposed a proper violence on his imagination and had forgotten himself for a moment. So far his taste evidently departs from the true standard, and of consequence loses all credit and authority.

It is well known that in all questions submitted to the understanding, prejudice is destructive of sound judgment, and perverts all operations of the intellectual faculties. It is no less contrary to good taste, nor has it less influence to corrupt our sentiment of beauty. It belongs to *good sense* to check its influence in both cases; and in this respect, as well as in many others, reason, if not an essential part of taste, is at least requisite to the operations of this latter faculty. In all the nobler productions of genius, there is a mutual relation and correspondence of parts, nor can either the beauties or blemishes be perceived by him whose thought is not capacious enough to comprehend all those parts and compare them with each other, in order to perceive the consistence and uniformity of the whole. Every work of art has also a certain end or purpose for which it is calculated, and is to be deemed more or less perfect as it is more or less fitted to attain this end. The object of eloquence is to persuade, of history to instruct, of poetry to please by means of the passions and the imagination. These ends we must carry constantly in our view when we peruse any performance, and we must be able to judge how far the means employed are adapted to their respective purposes. Besides, every kind of composition, even the most poetical, is nothing but a chain of propositions and reasonings, not always, indeed, the justest and most exact, but still plausible and specious, however disguised by the coloring of the imagination. The persons introduced in tragedy and epic poetry must be represented as reasoning, and thinking, and concluding, and acting suitably to their characters and circumstances; and without judgment, as well as taste and invention, a poet can never hope to succeed in so delicate an undertaking. Not to mention that the same excellence of faculties which contributes to the improvement of reason, the same clearness of conception, the same exactness of distinction, the same vivacity of apprehension, are essential to the operations of true taste, and are its infallible concomitants. It seldom or never happens that a man of sense who has experience in any art cannot judge of its beauty; and it is no less rare to meet with a man who has a just taste without a sound understanding.

Thus, though the principles of taste be universal, and nearly if not entirely the same in all men, yet few are qualified to give judgment on any work of art, or establish their own sentiment as the standard of beauty. The organs of internal sensation are seldom so perfect as to allow the general principles their full play, and produce a feeling correspondent to those principles. They either labor under some defect, or are vitiated by some disorder, and by that means excite a sentiment which may be pronounced erroneous. When the critic has no delicacy, he judges without any distinction, and is only affected by the grosser and more palpable qualities of the object; the finer touches pass unnoticed and disregarded. Where he is not aided by practice, his verdict is attended with confusion and hesitation. Where no comparison has been employed, the most frivolous beauties, such as rather merit the name of defects, are the object of his admiration. Where he lies under the influence of prejudice, all his natural sentiments are perverted. Where good sense is wanting, he is not qualified to discern the beauties of design and reasoning, which are the highest and most excellent. Under some or other of these imperfections, the generality of men labor, and hence a true judge in the finer arts is observed, even during the most polished ages, to be so rare a character. Strong sense, united to delicate sentiment, improved by practice, perfected by comparison, and cleared of all prejudice, can alone entitle critics to this valuable character; and the joint verdict of such, wherever they are to be found, is the true standard of taste and beauty.

But where are such critics to be found? By what marks are they to be known? How distinguish them from pretenders? These questions are embarrassing, and seem to throw us back into the same uncertainty from which during the course of this essay we have endeavored to extricate ourselves.

But if we consider the matter aright, these are questions of fact, not of sentiment. Whether any particular person be endowed with good sense and a delicate imagination, free from prejudice, may often be the subject of dispute, and be liable to great discussion and inquiry. But that such a character is valuable and estimable will be agreed in by all mankind. Where these doubts occur, men can do no more than in other disputable questions which are submitted to the understanding: they must produce the best arguments that their invention suggests to them; they must acknowledge a true and decisive standard to exist somewhere, to wit, real existence and matter of fact; and they must have indulgence to such as differ from them in their appeals to this standard. It is sufficient for our present purpose if we have proved that the taste of all individuals is not upon an equal footing, and that some men in general, however difficult to be particularly pitched upon, will be acknowledged by universal sentiment to have a preference above others.

But in reality the difficulty of finding, even in particulars, the standard of taste, is not so great as it is represented. Though in speculation we may readily avow a certain criterion in science and deny it in sentiment, the matter is found in practice to be much more hard to ascertain in the former case than in the latter. Theories of abstract philosophy, systems of profound theology, have prevailed during one age; in a successive period these have been universally exploded; their absurdity has been detected; other theories and systems have supplied their place, which again gave place to their successors; and nothing has been experienced more liable to the revolutions of chance and fashion than these pretended decisions of science. The case is not the same with the beauties of eloquence and poetry. Just expressions of passion and nature are sure, after a little time, to gain public applause, which they maintain forever. Aristotle and Plato and Epicurus and Descartes may successively yield to each other, but Terence and Virgil maintain a universal, undisputed empire over the minds of men. The abstract philosophy of Cicero has lost its credit; the vehemence of his oratory is still the object of our admiration.

Though men of delicate taste be rare, they are easily to be distinguished in society by the soundness of their understanding and the superiority of their faculties above the rest of mankind. The ascendant which they acquire gives a prevalence to that lively approbation with which they receive any productions of genius, and renders it generally predominant. Many men when left to themselves have but a faint and dubious perception of beauty, who yet are capable of relishing any fine stroke which is pointed out to them. Every convert to the admiration of the real poet or orator is the cause of some new conversion. And though prejudices may prevail for a time, they never unite in celebrating any rival to the true genius, but yield at last to the force of nature and just sentiment. Thus, though a civilized nation may easily be mistaken in the choice of their admired philosopher, they never have been found long to err in their affection for a favorite epic or tragic author.

But notwithstanding all our endeavors to fix a standard of taste, and reconcile the discordant apprehensions of men, there still remain two sources of variation, which are not sufficient indeed to confound all the boundaries of beauty and deformity, but will often serve to produce a difference in the degrees of our approbation or blame. The one is the different humors of particular men; the other, the particular manners and opinions of our age and country. The general principles of taste are uniform in human nature; where men vary in their judgments, some defect or perversion in the faculties may commonly be remarked, proceeding either from prejudice, from want of practice, or want of delicacy; and there is just reason for approving one taste and condemning another. But where there is such a diversity in the internal frame or external situation as is entirely blameless on both sides, and leaves no room to give one the preference above the other, in that case a certain degree of diversity in judgment is unavoidable, and we seek in vain for a standard by which we can reconcile the contrary sentiments.

A young man, whose passions are warm, will be more sensibly touched with amorous and tender images than a man more advanced in years, who takes pleasure in wise, philosophical reflections concerning the conduct of life and moderation of the passions. At twenty, Ovid may be the favorite author, Horace at forty, and perhaps Tacitus at fifty. Vainly would we, in such cases, endeavor to enter into the sentiments of others and divest ourselves of those propensities which are natural to us. We choose our favorite author

302 ~ DAVID HUME

as we do our friend, from a conformity of humor and disposition. Mirth or passion, sentiment or reflection, whichever of these most predominates in our temper, it gives us a peculiar sympathy with the writer who resembles us.

One person is more pleased with the sublime, another with the tender, a third with raillery. One has a strong sensibility to blemishes, and is extremely studious of correctness; another has a more lively feeling of beauties, and pardons twenty absurdities and detects for one elevated or pathetic stroke. The ear of this man is entirely turned towards conciseness and energy; that man is delighted with a copious, rich, and harmonious expression. Simplicity is affected by one; ornament by another. Comedy, tragedy, satire, odes have each its partisans who prefer that particular species of writing to all others. It is plainly an error in a critic to confine his approbation to one species or style of writing, and condemn all the rest. But it is almost impossible not to feel a predilection for that which suits our particular turn and disposition. Such preferences are innocent and unavoidable, and can never reasonably be the object of dispute, because there is no standard by which they can be decided.

For a like reason, we are more pleased in the course of our reading with pictures and characters that resemble objects which are found in our own age or country than with those which describe a different set of customs. It is not without some effort that we reconcile ourselves to the simplicity of ancient manners, and behold princesses carrying water from the spring, and kings and heroes dressing their own victuals. We may allow in general that the representation of such manners is no fault in the author, nor deformity in the piece; but we are not so sensibly touched with them. For this reason, comedy is not easily transferred from one age or nation to another. A Frenchman or Englishman is not pleased with the *Andria* of Terence, or *Clitia* of Machiavelli: where the fine lady upon whom all the play turns never once appears to the spectators, but is always kept behind the scenes, suitably to the reserved humor of the ancient Greeks and modern Italians. A man of learning and reflection can make allowance for these peculiarities of manners, but a common audience can never divest themselves so far of their usual ideas and sentiments as to relish pictures which nowise resemble them.

But here there occurs a reflection which may, perhaps, be useful in examining the celebrated controversy concerning ancient and modern learning, where we often find the one side excusing any seeming absurdity in the ancients from the manners of the age, and

the other refusing to admit this excuse, or at least admitting it only
as an apology for the author, not for the performance. In my opinion, the proper boundaries in this subject have seldom been fixed
between the contending parties. Where any innocent peculiarities
of manners are represented, such as those above mentioned, they
ought certainly to be admitted, and a man who is shocked with them
gives an evident proof of false delicacy and refinement. The poet's
"monument more durable than brass"[3] must fall to the ground like
common brick or clay, were men to make no allowance for the continual revolutions of manners and customs, and would admit of
nothing but what was suitable to the prevailing fashion. Must we
throw aside the pictures of our ancestors because of their ruffs and
farthingales? But where the ideas of morality and decency alter
from one age to another, and where vicious manners are described
without being marked with the proper characters of blame and disapprobation, this must be allowed to disfigure the poem, and to be a
real deformity. I cannot, nor is it proper I should, enter into such
sentiments; and however I may excuse the poet on account of the
manners of his age, I never can relish the composition. The want of
humanity and of decency so conspicuous in the characters drawn
by several of the ancient poets, even sometimes by Homer and the
Greek tragedians, diminishes considerably the merit of their noble
performances and gives modern authors an advantage over them.
We are not interested in the fortunes and sentiments of such rough
heroes; we are displeased to find the limits of vice and virtue so
much confounded; and whatever indulgence we may give to the
writer on account of his prejudices, we cannot prevail on ourselves
to enter into his sentiments, or bear an affection to characters which
we plainly discover to be blamable.

The case is not the same with moral principles as with speculative
opinions of any kind. These are in continual flux and revolution.
The son embraces a different system from the father. Nay, there
scarcely is any man who can boast of great constancy and uniformity
in this particular. Whatever speculative errors may be found in the
polite writings of any age or country, they detract but little from
the value of those compositions. There needs but a certain turn of
thought or imagination to make us enter into all the opinions
which then prevailed, and relish the sentiments or conclusions derived from them. But a very violent effort is requisite to change our
judgment of manners, and excite sentiments of approbation or
blame, love or hatred, different from those to which the mind,

[3] Horace, *Odes*, III, xxx, l.

from long custom, has been familiarized. And where a man is confident of the rectitude of that moral standard by which he judges, he is justly jealous of it, and will not pervert the sentiments of his heart for a moment, in complaisance to any writer whatsoever.

Of all speculative errors, those which regard religion are the most excusable in compositions of genius, nor is it ever permitted to judge of the civility or wisdom of any people, or even of single persons, by the grossness or refinement of their theological principles. The same good sense that directs men in the ordinary occurrences of life is not hearkened to in religious matters, which are supposed to be placed altogether above the cognizance of human reason. On this account, all the absurdities of the pagan system of theology must be overlooked by every critic who would pretend to form a just notion of ancient poetry; and our posterity, in their turn, must have the same indulgence to their forefathers. No religious principles can ever be imputed as a fault to any poet while they remain merely principles, and take not such strong possession of his heart as to lay him under the imputation of *bigotry* or *superstition*. Where that happens, they confound the sentiments of morality and alter the natural boundaries of vice and virtue. They are therefore eternal blemishes, according to the principle above mentioned; nor are the prejudices and false opinions of the age sufficient to justify them.

It is essential to the Roman Catholic religion to inspire a violent hatred of every other worship, and to represent all pagans, Mohammedans, and heretics as the objects of divine wrath and vengeance. Such sentiments, though they are in reality very blamable, are considered as virtues by the zealots of that communion, and are represented in their tragedies and epic poems as a kind of divine heroism. This bigotry has disfigured two very fine tragedies of the French theatre, *Polyeucte*[4] and *Athalie*,[5] where an intemperate zeal for particular modes of worship is set off with all the pomp imaginable, and forms the predominant character of the heroes. "What is this," says the sublime Joad[6] to Josabet, finding her in discourse with Mathan, the priest of Baal, "Does the daughter of David speak to this traitor? Are you not afraid lest the earth should open, and pour forth flames to devour you both? Or lest these holy walls should fall and crush you together? What is his purpose? Why comes that enemy of God hither to poison the air which we breathe, with his horrid presence?" Such sentiments are received with great

---

[4] By Corneille.
[5] By Racine.
[6] Jewish high-priest in *Athalie*.

applause on the theatre of Paris, but at London the spectators would be full as much pleased to hear Achilles tell Agamemnon that he was a dog in his forehead and a deer in his heart, or Jupiter threaten Juno with a sound drubbing if she will not be quiet.[7]

Religious principles are also a blemish in any polite composition when they rise up to superstition, and intrude themselves into every sentiment, however remote from any connection with religion. It is no excuse for the poet that the customs of his country had burthened life with so many religious ceremonies and observances that no part of it was exempt from that yoke. It must for ever be ridiculous in Petrarch to compare his mistress, Laura, to Jesus Christ. Nor is it less ridiculous in that agreeable libertine, Boccaccio, very seriously to give thanks to God Almighty and the ladies, for their assistance in defending him against his enemies.

* * * *

HENRY HOME, LORD KAMES (1696–1782)
FROM
Elements of Criticism [1762]

from Introduction

We stand therefore engaged in honor as well as interest to second the purposes of nature by cultivating the pleasures of the eye and ear, those especially that require extraordinary culture, such as arise from poetry, painting, sculpture, music, gardening, and architecture. This especially is the duty of the opulent, who have leisure to improve their minds and their feelings. The fine arts are contrived to give pleasure to the eye and the ear, disregarding the inferior senses. A taste for these arts is a plant that grows naturally in many soils, but, without culture, scarce to perfection in any soil: it is susceptible of much refinement, and is by proper care greatly improved. In this respect, a taste in the fine arts goes hand in hand with the moral sense, to which indeed it is nearly allied: both of them discover what is right and what is wrong; fashion, temper, and education have an influence to vitiate both, or to preserve them pure and un-

---

[7] *Iliad*, I, 225, 560–67.

tainted; neither of them are arbitrary nor local, being rooted in human nature and governed by principles common to all men. The design of the present undertaking, which aspires not to morality, is to examine the sensitive branch of human nature, to trace the objects that are naturally agreeable as well as those that are naturally disagreeable, and by these means to discover, if we can, what are the genuine principles of the fine arts. . . . Hence a foundation for reasoning upon the taste of any individual and for passing sentence upon it: where it is comfortable to principles, we can pronounce with certainty that it is correct; otherwise, that it is incorrect and perhaps whimsical. Thus, the fine arts, like morals, become a rational science, and like morals, may be cultivated to a high degree of refinement. . . .

With respect to the present undertaking, it is not the author's intention to compose a regular treatise upon each of the fine arts, but only, in general, to exhibit their fundamental principles drawn from human nature, the true source of criticism. . . . His plan is to ascend gradually to principles from facts and experiments,[1] instead of beginning with the former, handled abstractedly, and descending to the latter. But though criticism is thus his only declared aim, he will not disown that all along it has been his view to explain the Nature of Man. . . . He is, however, too sensible of its extent and difficulty to undertake it professedly or to avow it as the chief purpose of the present work. . . .

Neither pretends he to justify his taste in every particular: that point must be extremely clear which admits not variety of opinion, and in some matters susceptible of great refinement, time is perhaps the only infallible touchstone of taste; to that he appeals, and to that he cheerfully submits.

FROM CHAPTER 1

Perceptions and Ideas in a Train

A man, while awake, is conscious of a continued train of perceptions and ideas passing in his mind. It requires no activity on his part to carry on the train, nor can he at will add any idea to the train.[2] At the same time, we learn from daily experience that the

---

[1] So in the first, epistemological half of the book; in the second half, treating more specific topics of criticism and rhetoric, Kames loosely follows the reverse procedure of submitting principles to the test of facts. So doing, he is self-consciously applying the Newtonian method of "analysis" and "synthesis."

[2] For how should this be done? What idea is it that we are to add? If we can specify the idea, that idea is already in the mind, and there is no occasion for

train of our thoughts is not regulated by chance, and if it depend not upon will, nor upon chance, by what law is it governed? The question is of importance in the science of human nature, and I promise beforehand that it will be found of great importance in the fine arts.

It appears that the relations by which things are linked together have a great influence in directing the train of thought. Taking a view of external objects, their inherent properties are not more remarkable than the various relations that connect them together: cause and effect, contiguity in time or in place, high and low, prior and posterior, resemblance, contrast, and a thousand other relations connect things together without end. Not a single thing appears solitary and altogether devoid of connection; the only difference is that some are intimately connected, some more slightly; some near, some at a distance.

Experience will satisfy us of what reason makes probable, that the train of our thoughts is in a great measure regulated by the foregoing relations: an external object is no sooner presented to us in idea than it suggests to the mind other objects to which it is related, and in that manner is a train of thoughts composed. Such is the law of succession, which must be natural because it governs all human beings. The law, however, seems not to be inviolable: it sometimes happens that an idea arises in the mind without any perceived connection, as, for example, after a profound sleep.

But though we cannot add to the train an unconnected idea, yet in a measure we can attend to some ideas and dismiss others. There are few things but what are connected with many others, and when a thing thus connected becomes a subject of thought, it commonly suggests many of its connections; among these a choice is afforded; we can insist upon one, rejecting others; and sometimes we insist on what is commonly held the slighter connection. . . .

Will is not the only cause that prevents a train of thought from being continued through the strictest connections: much depends on the present tone of mind, for a subject that accords with that tone is always welcome. Thus, in good spirits a cheerful subject will be introduced by the slightest connection, and one that is melan-

---

any act of the will. If we cannot specify any idea, I next demand how can a person will, or to what purpose, if there be nothing in view? We cannot form a conception of such a thing. If this argument need confirmation, I urge experience: whoever makes a trial will find that ideas are linked together in the mind, forming a connected chain, and that we have not the command of any idea independent of the chain. (Kames's note.)

choly no less readily in low spirits. An interesting subject is recalled, from time to time, by any connection indifferently strong or weak—which is finely touched by Shakespeare, with relation to a rich cargo at sea:

> My wind cooling my broth
> Would blow me to an ague, when I thought
> What harm a wind too great at sea might do.
> I should not see the sandy hour-glass run,
> But I should think of shallows and of flats,
> And see my wealthy Andrew dock'd in sand,
> Vailing her high top lower than her ribs
> To kiss her burial. Should I go to church
> And see the holy edifice of stone,
> And not bethink me straight of dangerous rocks? [3] . . .

Another cause clearly distinguishable from that now mentioned hath also a considerable influence to vary the natural train of ideas, which is that, in the minds of some persons, thoughts and circumstances crowd upon each other by the slightest connections. I ascribe this to a bluntness in the discerning faculty, for a person who cannot accurately distinguish between a slight connection and one that is more intimate is equally affected by each; such a person must necessarily have a great flow of ideas. . . . This doctrine is, in a lively manner, illustrated by Shakespeare:

> *Falstaff.* What is the gross sum that I owe thee?
> *Hostess.* Marry, if thou wert an honest man, thyself and the money too. Thou didst swear to me upon a parcel-gilt goblet, sitting in my Dolphin-chamber, at the round table, by a sea-coal fire, on Wednesday in Whitsun-week, when the Prince broke thy head for liking his father to a singing-man of Windsor, thou didst swear to me then, as I was washing thy wound, to marry me, and make me my lady thy wife. Canst thou deny it? Did not Goodwife Keech, the butcher's wife, come in then and call me Gossip Quickly? coming in to borrow a mess of vinegar; telling us she had a good dish of prawns; whereby thou didst desire to eat some; whereby I told thee they were ill for a green wound? And didst thou not, when she was gone down stairs, desire me to be no more so familiarity with such poor

---

[3] *The Merchant of Venice,* I, i, 23–31.

people; saying that ere long they should call me
madam? And didst thou not kiss me and bid me fetch
thee thirty shillings? I put thee now to thy book-oath;
deny it, if thou canst?[4]

On the other hand, a man of accurate judgment cannot have a
great flow of ideas, because the slighter relations, making no figure
in his mind, have no power to introduce ideas. . . . Wit, upon
that account, is in a good measure incompatible with solid judgment, which, neglecting trivial relations, adheres to what are substantial and permanent. . . .

Every work of art that is conformable to the moral course of our
ideas is so far agreeable; and every work of art that reverses that
course is so far disagreeable. Hence it is required in every such work
that, like an organic system, its parts be orderly arranged and mutually connected, bearing each of them a relation to the whole, some
more intimate, some less, according to their destination; when due
regard is had to these particulars, we have a sense of just composition, and so far are pleased with the performance. Homer is defective in order and connection, and Pindar more remarkably.
Regularity, order, and connection are painful restraints on a bold
and fertile imagination, and are not patiently submitted to but after
much culture and discipline.

FROM CHAPTER 2, PART 1, SECTION 7
Emotions caused by Fiction

By the power of memory, a thing formerly seen may be recalled
to the mind with different degrees of accuracy. We commonly are
satisfied with a slight recollection of the capital circumstances; and
in such recollection, the thing is not figured as in our view, nor any
image formed; we retain the consciousness of our present situation
and barely remember that formerly we saw that thing. But with respect to an interesting object or event that made a strong impression, I am not satisfied with a cursory review, but must dwell upon
every circumstance. I am imperceptibly converted into a spectator,
and perceive every particular passing in my presence, as when I was
in reality a spectator. For example, I saw yesterday a beautiful
woman in tears for the loss of an only child, and was greatly moved
with her distress; not satisfied with a slight recollection or bare remembrance, I ponder upon the melancholy scene; conceiving my-

---

[4] *2 Henry IV*, II, i, 91–112.

self to be in the place where I was an eye-witness, every circumstance appears to me as at first; I think I see the woman in tears and hear her moans. Hence it may be justly said that, in a complete idea of memory, there is no past nor future: a thing recalled to the mind, with the accuracy I have been describing, is perceived as in our view, and consequently as existing at present. Past time makes part of an incomplete idea only. . . .

As many rules of criticism depend on ideal presence, the reader, it is hoped, will take some pains to form an exact notion of it, as distinguished on the one hand from real presence, and on the other from superficial or reflective remembrance. In contradistinction to real presence, ideal presence may be properly termed *a waking dream*, because, like a dream, it vanisheth the moment we reflect upon our situation. Real presence, on the contrary, vouched by eyesight, commands our belief, not only during the direct perception but in reflecting afterward on the object. . . .

Though ideal presence is thus distinguished from real presence on the one side, and from reflective remembrance on the other, it is however variable, without any precise limits, rising sometimes toward the former, and often sinking toward the latter. . . .

Hitherto I have spoken of an idea of memory. I proceed to consider the idea of a thing I never saw, raised in me by speech, by writing, or by painting. That idea, with respect to the present subject, is of the same nature with an idea of memory, being either complete or incomplete. A lively and accurate description of an important event raises in me ideas no less distinct than if I had been originally an eye-witness: I am insensibly transformed into a spectator, and have an impression that every incident is passing in my presence. On the other hand, a slight or superficial narrative produces but a faint and incomplete idea, of which ideal presence makes no part. Past time is a circumstance that enters into this idea, as it does into an incomplete idea of memory. I believe that Scipio existed about 2000 years ago, and that he overcame Hannibal in the famous battle of Zama. When I reflect so slightly upon that memorable event, I consider it as long past. But let it be spread out in a lively and beautiful description, I am insensibly transformed into a spectator: I perceive these two heroes in act to engage; I perceive them brandishing their swords, and cheering their troops; and in that manner I attend them through the battle, every incident of which appears to be passing in my sight. . . .

The power of language to raise emotions depends entirely on the raising such lively and distinct images as are here described; the reader's passions are never sensibly moved till he be thrown into a kind of reverie, in which state, forgetting that he is reading, he conceives every incident as passing in his presence, precisely as if he were an eye-witness. . . .

To support the foregoing theory, I add what I reckon a decisive argument, which is that even genuine history has no command over our passions but by ideal presence only, and consequently that, in this respect, it stands upon the same footing with fable. To me it appears clear that in neither can our sympathy hold firm against reflection, for if the reflection that a story is a pure fiction prevent our sympathy, so will equally the reflection that the persons described are no longer existing. What effect, for example, can the belief of the rape of Lucretia have to raise our sympathy, when she died above 2000 years ago, and hath at present no painful feeling of the injury done her? The effect of history, in point of instruction, depends in some measure upon its veracity. But history cannot reach the heart while we indulge any reflection upon the facts; such reflection, if it engage our belief, never fails at the same time to poison our pleasure by convincing us that our sympathy for those who are dead and gone is absurd. And if reflection be laid aside, history stands upon the same footing with fable: what effect either may have to raise our sympathy depends on the vivacity of the ideas they raise, and with respect to that circumstance, fable is generally more successful than history.

Of all the means for making an impression of ideal presence, theatrical representation is the most powerful. That words, independent of action, have the same power in a less degree, every one of sensibility must have felt; a good tragedy will extort tears in private, though not so forcibly as upon the stage. That power belongs also to painting: a good historical picture makes a deeper impression than words can, though not equal to that of theatrical action. Painting seems to possess a middle place between reading and acting: in making an impression of ideal presence, it is not less superior to the former than inferior to the latter.

It must not, however, be thought that our passions can be raised by painting to such a height as by words. A picture is confined to a single instant of time, and cannot take in a succession of incidents. Its impression indeed is the deepest that can be made instantaneously, but seldom is a passion raised to any height in an instant or by a single impression. It was observed above that our passions, those especially of the sympathetic kind, require a succession of impressions, and for that reason, reading and acting have greatly the advantage by reiterating impressions without end. . . .

The foregoing theory must have fatigued the reader with much dry reasoning; but his labor will not be fruitless, because from that theory are derived many useful rules in criticism, which shall be mentioned in their proper places. One specimen shall be our present entertainment. Events that surprise by being unexpected, and yet are natural, enliven greatly an epic poem; but in such a poem, if it pretend to copy human manners and actions, no improbable incident ought to be admitted; that is, no incident contrary to the order and course of nature. A chain of imagined incidents linked together according to the order of nature finds easy admittance into the mind; and a lively narrative of such incidents occasions complete images, or, in other words, ideal presence. But our judgment revolts against an improbable incident; and if we once begin to doubt of its reality, farewell relish and concern—an unhappy effect; for it will require more than ordinary effort to restore the waking dream, to make the reader conceive even the more probable incidents as passing in his presence.

I never was an admirer of machinery in an epic poem, and I now find my taste justified by reason; the foregoing argument concluding still more strongly against imaginary beings than against improbable facts. Fictions of that nature may amuse by their novelty and singularity, but they never move the sympathetic passions, because they cannot impose on the mind any perception of reality. I appeal to the discerning reader whether that observation be not applicable to the machinery of Tasso and of Voltaire; such machinery is not only in itself cold and uninteresting, but gives an air of fiction to the whole composition. A burlesque poem, such as the *Lutrin*[5] or the *Dispensary*,[6] may employ machinery with success, for these poems, though they assume the air of history, give entertainment chiefly by their pleasant and ludicrous pictures, to which machinery contributes: it is not the aim of such a poem to raise our sympathy, and for that reason, a strict imitation of nature is not required.

---

[5] See p. 110, n. 9.
[6] Mock-epic (1699) by Dr. Samuel Garth (1661–1719), a friend of Pope.

FROM CHAPTER 21
Narration and Description

Abstract or general terms have no good effect in any composition for amusement, because it is only of particular objects that images can be formed. Shakespeare's style in that respect is excellent: every article in his description is particular, as in nature; and if accidentally a vague expression slip in, the blemish is discernible by the bluntness of its impression. Take the following example: Falstaff, excusing himself for running away at a robbery, says:

> By the Lord, I knew ye, as well as he that made ye. Why, hear ye, my masters; was it for me to kill the heir-apparent? should I turn upon the true prince? Why, thou knowest, I am as valiant as Hercules; but beware instinct, the lion will not touch the true prince: *instinct is a great matter.* I was a coward on instinct: I shall think the better of myself and thee, during my life; I for a violent lion, and thou for a true prince. But, by the Lord, lads, I am glad you have the money. Hostess, clap to the doors, watch tonight, pray tomorrow. Gallants, lads, boys, heart of gold, all the titles of good fellowship come to you! What! Shall we be merry? shall we have a play extempore? [7]

The sentence I object to is, *instinct is a great matter,* which makes but a poor figure compared with the liveliness of the rest of the speech. It was one of Homer's advantages that he wrote before general terms were multiplied. The superior genius of Shakespeare displays itself in avoiding them after they were multiplied. Addison describes the family of Sir Roger de Coverley in the following words:

> You would take his valet de chambre for his brother, his butler is gray-headed, his groom is one of the gravest men that I have ever seen, and his coachman has the looks of a privy counsellor. [8]

The description of the groom is less lively than of the others; plainly because the expression, being vague and general, tends not to form any image. *Dives opum variarum* [9] is an expression still more vague.

---

[7] *1 Henry IV*, II, iv, 272–87.
[8] *Spectator* No. 106.
[9] Virgil, *Georgics*, II, 468: "rich in varied wealth."

Epic and Dramatic Compositions

It is not a little diverting to see so many profound critics hunting for what is not; they take for granted, without the least foundation, that there must be some precise criterion to distinguish epic poetry from every other species of writing. Literary compositions run into each other precisely like colors: in their strong tints they are easily distinguished, but are susceptible of so much variety, and of so many different forms, that we never can say where one species ends and another begins. As to the general taste, there is little reason to doubt that a work where heroic actions are related in elevated style will, without further requisite, be deemed an epic poem.

The Three Unities

Thus the Grecian drama is a continued representation without interruption—a circumstance that merits attention. A continued representation without a pause affords not opportunity to vary the place of action, nor to prolong the time of the action beyond that of the representation. . . . Hence it is that the unities of place and of time were, or ought to have been, strictly observed in the Greek tragedies; which is made necessary by the very constitution of their drama,[1] for it is absurd to compose a tragedy that cannot be justly represented.

Modern critics who, for our drama, pretend to establish rules founded on the practice of the Greeks are guilty of an egregious blunder. The unities of place and of time were in Greece, as we see, a matter of necessity, not of choice; and I am now ready to show that if we submit to such fetters, it must be from choice, not necessity. . . . By dropping the chorus, opportunity is afforded to divide the representation by intervals of time, during which the stage is evacuated and the spectacle suspended. This qualifies our drama for subjects spread through a wide space both of time and of place. . . . This doctrine may be illustrated by comparing a modern play to a set of historical pictures; let us suppose them five in number, and the resemblance will be complete. Each of the pictures resembles an act in one of our plays; there must necessarily be the strictest unity of place and of time in each picture; and the same necessity requires these two unities during each act of a play, be-

---

[1] That is, of their stage and its conventions.

cause during an act there is no interruption of the spectacle. Now, when we view in succession a number of such historical pictures— let it be, for example, the history of Alexander by Le Brun[2]—we have no difficulty to conceive that months or years have passed between the events exhibited in two different pictures, though the interruption is imperceptible in passing our eye from the one to the other; and we have as little difficulty to conceive a change of place, however great. In which view, there is truly no difference between five acts of a modern play and five such pictures. Where the representation is suspended, we can with the greatest facility suppose any length of time or any change of place. The spectator, it is true, may be conscious that the real time and place are not the same with what are employed in the representation, but this is a work of reflection; and by the same reflection he may also be conscious that Garrick is not King Lear, that the playhouse is not Dover cliffs, nor the noise he hears thunder and lightning. In a word, after an interruption of the representation, it is no more difficult for a spectator to imagine a new place or a different time than, at the commencement of the play, to imagine himself at Rome or in a period of time two thousand years back. And indeed, it is abundantly ridiculous that a critic who is willing to hold candlelight for sunshine, and some painted canvasses for a palace or a prison, should be so scrupulous about admitting any latitude of place or of time in the fable beyond what is necessary in the representation. . . .[3]

The unities of place and time ought to be strictly observed during each act, for during the representation, there is no opportunity for the smallest deviation from either. Hence it is an essential requisite that during an act the stage be always occupied, for even a momentary vacuity makes an interval or interruption. Another rule is no less essential: it would be a gross breach of the unity of action to exhibit upon the stage two separate actions at the same time; and therefore, to preserve that unity, it is necessary that each personage introduced during an act be linked to those in possession of the stage, so as to join all in one action.[4] These things follow from the very conception of an act, which admits not the slightest interruption: the moment the representation is intermitted, there is an end of that act; and we have no notion of a new act but where, after a pause or interval, the representation is again put in motion.[5]

---

[2] Charles Le Brun (1619–90), history painter of enormous influence in his time, picked by Louis XIV to decorate Versailles.

[3] *Cf.* Johnson, p. 454.

[4] *Liaison des scènes.*

[5] Kames is deducing the logical consequences of his psychology. To interrupt

French writers, generally speaking, are correct in this particular. The English, on the contrary, are so irregular as scarce to deserve a criticism. . . . From the foregoing censure must be excepted the *Mourning Bride* of Congreve, where regularity concurs with the beauty of sentiment and of language to make it one of the most complete pieces England has to boast of. . . . In *The Way of the World* of the same author, unity of place is preserved during every act, and a stricter unity of time during the whole play than is necessary.

FROM CHAPTER 25
Standard of Taste

History informs us that nothing is more variable than taste in the fine arts; judging by numbers, the Gothic taste of architecture must be preferred before that of Greece, and the Chinese taste probably before either. It would be endless to recount the various tastes that have prevailed in different ages with respect to gardening, and still prevail in different countries. Despising the modest coloring of nature, women of fashion in France daub their cheeks with a red powder; nay, an unnatural swelling in the neck peculiar to the inhabitants of the Alps is relished by that people. But we ought not to be discouraged by such untoward instances when we find as great variety in moral opinions: was it not among some nations held lawful for a man to sell his children for slaves, to expose them in their infancy to wild beasts, and to punish them for the crimes of their parents? Was anything more common than to murder an enemy in cold blood? Nay more, did not law once authorize the abominable practice of human sacrifices, no less impious than immoral? Such aberrations from the rules of morality prove only that men, originally savage and brutal, acquire not rationality nor delicacy of taste till they be long disciplined in society. To ascertain the rules of morality, we appeal not to the common sense of savages, but of men in their more perfect state, and we make the same appeal in forming the rules that ought to govern the fine arts; in neither can we safely rely on a local or transitory taste, but on what is the most general and the most lasting among polite nations.

In this very manner, a standard for morals has been ascertained with a good deal of accuracy and is daily applied by able judges

---

the representation is to destroy the "ideal presence," which in turn depends upon an ordered continuity of associated ideas by which our emotions of sympathy are gradually aroused.

with general satisfaction. . . . True it is indeed that in gathering
the common sense of mankind, more circumspection is requisite
with respect to the fine arts than with respect to morals: upon the
latter any person may be consulted, but in the former a wary choice
is necessary, for to collect votes indifferently would certainly mislead us. Those who depend for food on bodily labor are totally
void of taste, of such a taste, at least, as can be of use in the fine
arts. This consideration bars the greater part of mankind, and of
the remaining part, many by a corrupted taste are unqualified for
voting. The common sense of mankind must then be confined to
the few that fall not under these exceptions. . . .

The exclusion of classes so many and numerous reduces within
a narrow compass those who are qualified to be judges in the fine
arts. Many circumstances are necessary to form such a judge: there
must be a good natural taste, that is, a taste approaching, at least
in some degree, to the delicacy of taste above described [Chapter
2, Part 2]; that taste must be improved by education, reflection,
and experience;[6] it must be preserved in vigor by living regularly,
by using the goods of fortune with moderation, and by following
the dictates of improved nature, which give welcome to every
rational pleasure without indulging any excess. This is the tenor
of life which of all contributes the most to refinement of taste,
and the same tenor of life contributes the most to happiness in
general.

* * * *

ALEXANDER GERARD (1728–1795)
FROM
An Essay on Genius [1774]

FROM PART I, SECTION III
How Genius Arises from the Imagination

When memory presents ideas, it annexes to them a conviction
that the ideas themselves, or the objects from which they are

---

[6] The very populace in Athens were critics in language, in pronunciation,
and even in eloquence, harangues being their daily entertainment. In Rome at
present, the most illiterate shopkeeper is a better judge of statues and of pictures
than persons of refined education in London. . . . convincing evidence that a
discerning taste depends still more on experience than on nature. (Kames's
note.)

copied, were formerly perceived; and it exhibits the ideas in the same form and order in which the things themselves appeared. In time remembrance fails, ideas are perceived without being referred to any prior sensations of their originals, the order of the parts is forgotten. But even then, ideas do not lie in the mind without any connection or dependence. Imagination can connect them by new relations. It knits them together by other ties than what connected the real things from which they are derived, and often bestows a union upon ideas whose archetypes had no relation. In this operation, it is far from being capricious or irregular, but for the most part observes general and established rules. There are certain qualities which either really belong, or at least are supposed to belong, to all the ideas that are associated by the imagination. These qualities must be considered as, by the constitution of our nature, rendering ideas fit to be associated. It is impossible to give a reason why these qualities unite ideas: it is not necessary at present to explain particularly what they are. Experience informs us that the influence of association is very great. By means of it, multitudes of ideas originally distinct and unconnected rise always in company, so that one of them cannot make its appearance without introducing all the rest. On this account, human thought is perfectly restless. It requires no labor to run from one idea to others. We have so great a propensity to do it that no resolution has force enough to restrain us from it, nor will the strongest efforts be able to confine us long to the contemplation of a single idea. We are incessantly looking round to every side without intending it; we employ ourselves about many objects almost at the same instant.[1] Nay, association is often so strong that it bestows a sort of cohesion on several separate ideas, and makes them start up in numberless combinations, many of them different from every form which the senses have perceived; and thus produces a new creation. In this operation of the imagination, its associating power, we shall, on a careful examination, discover the origin of genius.

Association being an operation of fancy common to all men, some of its effects are universal. In every individual it displays itself in many instances. Not to mention such cases as are totally unconnected with our present subject, scarce any person is so stupid as not to have sometime in his life produced a bright flash

---

[1] Gerard's Latin note quotes Quintilian, *Institutes*, I, xii: "The nature of the human mind [*ingenium*] is so agile and quick, it so looks in every direction, if I may say so, that it cannot care for just one thing, but spends its strength on several, not only in the same day but at the same moment."

of imagination, though surrounded, it may be, with a wide extent of darkness. But such transient blazes do not necessarily imply real genius. It is something more permanent and uniform. It requires a peculiar vigor of association. In order to produce it, the imagination must be comprehensive, regular, and active.

Genius implies such *comprehensiveness* of imagination as enables a man, on every occasion, to call in the conceptions that are necessary for executing the designs or completing the works in which he engages. . . . When the associating principles are vigorous, imagination, conscious as it were of its own strength, sallies forth, without needing support or asking assistance, into regions hitherto unexplored, and penetrates into their remotest corners, unfatigued with the length of the way. In a man of genius, the power of association is so great that when any idea is present to his mind, it immediately leads him to the conception of those that are connected with it. No sooner almost is a design formed, or the hint of a subject started, than all the ideas which are requisite for completing it rush into his view, as if they were conjured up by the force of magic. His daring imagination traverses all nature, and collects materials fit for his purpose from all the most distant corners of the universe, and presents them at the very instant when they become useful or necessary. In consequence of this, he takes in a comprehensive view of every subject to which his genius is adapted.

Thus, when the associating principles are strong and have an extensive influence, they naturally form, in proportion to the degree of their strength, that boundless fertility, that inexhaustible copiousness of invention, which is not only one necessary ingredient in true genius, but the first and most essential constituent of it. . . . There is no particular, perhaps, in the works of Homer that has been more universally remarked and admired than the prodigious compass of imagination which they show. His penetration has gained him access to all the magazines of ideas, and enabled him to draw materials from every part of nature, and from the whole circle of human arts. . . . A comprehensive imagination gave Newton so great command over the natural and the intellectual world that, in his philosophical inquiries, he misses no experiment which is necessary for promoting his investigation, and in his mathematical researches, discovers every idea which can be a proper medium for inferring his conclusion, and includes in his problems almost every case that can occur. . . .

Genius implies *regularity* as well as comprehensiveness of imagination. Regularity arises in a great measure from such a turn of imagination as enables the associating principles, not only to introduce proper ideas, but also to connect the design of the whole with every idea that is introduced. When the design is steadily kept in view, and the mind so formed as to be strongly affected by that associating quality by which the design is related to the means of executing it, the imagination can scarce fail of being regular and correct. Any conception that is present will introduce most readily those ideas which are related to the main design, as well as to itself, though there should be a thousand others bearing the same relation to itself, but unconnected with the general subject. These latter have only one tie, but the former have a double relation, and will therefore rush into the thoughts with double violence. They will occur and be observed while the rest never come into view, or if they make their appearance, are rejected so quickly that we instantly forget our ever having thought of them. No sooner does the imagination, in a moment of wandering, suggest any idea not conducive to the design, than the conception of this design breaks in of its own accord, and, like an antagonist muscle, counteracting the other association, draws us off to the view of a more proper idea.

In this manner, an attachment to the design naturally produces that regularity of imagination, that capacity of avoiding foreign, useless, and superfluous conceptions, at the same time that none necessary or proper are passed by, which is always most perfect in the greatest geniuses, and constitutes no inconsiderable part of their excellence. As acuteness of smell carries a dog along the path of the game for which he searches, and secures him against the danger of quitting it upon another scent; so this happy structure of imagination leads the man of genius into those tracks where the proper ideas lurk, and not only enables him to discover them, but, by a kind of instinctive infallibility, prevents him from turning aside to wander in improper roads, or to spend his time in the contemplation of unapposite ideas. As the bee extracts from such flowers as can supply them the juices which are proper to be converted into honey, without losing its labor in sipping those juices which would be pernicious, or in examining those vegetables which are useless, so true genius discovers at once the ideas which are conducive to its purpose, without at all thinking of such as are unnecessary or would obstruct it. The extent of Homer's imagination is not more remarkable than its regularity. . . . His correct imagination admits no detail inconsistent with the unity of the fable,[2] no shining episode that can be deemed unconnected with the subject, nor a single image unsuitable to the nature of the work. . . .

Genius implies likewise *activity* of imagination. Whenever a fine imagination possesses healthful vigor, it will be continually starting hints, and pouring in conceptions upon the mind. As soon as any of them appears, fancy, with the utmost alertness, places them in every light and enables us to pursue them through all their consequences, that we may be able to determine whether they will promote the design which we have in eye. This activity of imagination, by which it darts with the quickness of lightning through all possible views of the ideas which are presented, arises from the same perfection of the associating principles which produces the other qualities of genius. . . .

This faculty bears a greater resemblance to *nature* in its operations than to the less perfect energies of *art*. When a vegetable draws in moisture from the earth, nature, by the same action by which it draws it in, and at the same time, converts it to the nourishment of the plant; it at once circulates through its vessels, and is assimilated to its several parts. In like manner, genius arranges its ideas by the same operation, and almost at the same time that it collects them. The same force of association which makes us perceive the connection of all the ideas with the subject, leads us soon to perceive also the various degrees of that connection. By means of it, these ideas, like a well-disciplined army, fall of their own accord into rank and order, and divide themselves into different classes according to their different relations. The most strongly related unite, of course, in the same member, and all the members are set in that position which association leads us to assign to them as the most natural. If the principles of association should not at first lead readily to any disposition, or should lead to one which is disapproved on examination, they continue to exert themselves, labor in searching for some other method, project new ones, throw out the unapposite ideas which perplex the mind and impede its operations, and thus by their continued efforts and unremitted activity, conduct us at length to a regular form, in which reason can find scarce any idea that is misplaced.

Thus imagination is no unskillful architect; it collects and chooses the materials; and though they may at first lie in a rude and undigested chaos, it in a great measure, by its own force, by

---

[2] Gerard's note quotes Aristotle's *Poetics*, VIII, 3, and XXIII, 3.

means of its associating power, after repeated attempts and transpositions, designs a regular and well-proportioned edifice.

Of the Influence of the Passions on Association

It will be proper, however, to attempt a fuller explication of the manner in which the passions influence the association of ideas. To understand this is of great importance in a theory of the varieties of genius, for to give a just representation of the passions is one of the greatest efforts of genius, and it can be accomplished only following those paths into which the passions naturally direct the thoughts. But the influence of the passions on the succession of our ideas, though thus important, relates only to one species of genius, genius for the *arts*. It would therefore be improper to enter on a full discussion of it at present when we are tracing out the *general* sources of the varieties of genius. In the observations which we are now to make on this subject, some examples will be necessary both for illustrating and for confirming our principles. It may perhaps be thought most proper to draw these from our own experience in real life. But to be able to select examples from real life, and to set them in a striking light, would require no small degree of one of the highest and rarest kinds of poetical genius. It will therefore be both the safest and the best way to take our examples from such representations of the passions in poetry as are confessedly natural, and will approve themselves natural to the taste of the reader. Such examples have as great authority as instances which a person himself observes in ordinary life. Shakespeare alone will almost supply us with as many as are necessary. . . .

When Alonzo's companions are endeavoring to alleviate his grief for the supposed loss of his son, by diverting his thoughts to his daughter's marriage with the King of Tunis, in their return from which they now suffered shipwreck, he answers them:

> *You cram these words into mine ears against*
> *The stomach of my sense. Would I had never*
> *Married my daughter there! for coming thence*
> *My son is lost; and, in my rate, she too,*
> *Who is so far from Italy remov'd,*
> *I ne'er again shall see her: O thou mine heir*

Of Naples and of Milan, what strange fish
Hath made his meal on thee? ³

This example illustrates and confirms almost every observation we have had occasion to make concerning the influence of the passions upon association. His grief keeps his attention fixed on the loss of his son, an object immediately connected with it ⁴ as being its cause, and that in spite of every thought by which his companions endeavored to divert it. This object suggests an idea related to it by causation,⁵ his daughter's marriage at Tunis, the event which occasioned that loss. This event carries his thoughts back again to the death of his son; which, when thus again presented to his imagination, suggests a second time his daughter's marriage, by means of its resemblance to it in one particular, that her distance deprived him of all intercourse with her, as much as if she too had been dead. But sorrow for his son allows him not to rest long upon this thought, suitable as it is to his passion, or to pursue any others which this might have introduced; it makes his imagination instantly to recur to the loss of his son, to view it in every light, to conceive many circumstances relating⁶ to him— his being his heir, his being entitled to large dominions, his being devoured by fishes. This example is thus a new illustration of the principles formerly explained, that a passion tends to fix the view on objects intimately connected with it, or to make it often recur to them, not only on the slightest hint, but even without any occasion, and that these objects suggest ideas related to them. It is likewise a direct illustration of the principle now under consideration, and for the sake of which we have cited it. It is a striking instance of the power of a passion to enable a perception connected with it to introduce, not indiscriminately any ideas related to itself, but only such as are at the same time suitable to the nature of the passion. No ideas are conceived but such as are perfectly suitable to Alonzo's sorrow. Claribel's marriage was in itself fully as fit for suggesting ideas of the mirth or pomp which

---

³ *The Tempest*, II, i, 106–13.
⁴ That is, his grief.
⁵ In the *Treatise of Human Nature* (1739–40), Hume classifies associations by *resemblance* (or *contrariety*), *contiguity* in time or place, and *cause-effect*. Sometimes one encounters *analogy*, a special kind of resemblance. Alison added *coexistence* to the list to account for associations more vital than mere contiguity (which he calls *vicinity*). On the whole question, see Bate, *From Classic to Romantic*, ch. iv.
⁶ Relations of coexistence.

attended it, or of the circumstances which rendered it desirable and moved Alonzo to urge it, as for suggesting ideas of its disagreeable circumstances and consequences. It had actually suggested ideas of the former kind to the rest of the company; but Alonzo's sorrow hinders them from occurring to him, and forces into his view such thoughts as are unpleasant and excite regret.

Further, a passion has an influence on the *number* as well as on the nature of the ideas introduced. . . . Alonzo's grief made the loss of his son to suggest the distance of his daughter and the consequence of that distance, the improbability of his ever seeing her; but without allowing him to pursue that thought, hurries him back to the loss of his son and sets him a thinking on new circumstances connected with it. The marriage of his daughter, the loss of his son, the loss of his daughter, her distance, the little chance for his seeing her again, the loss of his son, his being heir to extensive territories, his being devoured by fishes—all succeed one another in his thoughts with great abruptness and rapidity.

There is a fault very common in dramatic poetry: persons are made to express their passions, not as if they were really actuated by them, but as if they were spectators of them in others; the poet gives, not a natural *representation* of the passion, but a labored *description* of it. The observations just now made lead us to a discovery of the source of this fault. An object which is in a particular instance strictly connected with a passion, and forced into the mind by it, may be considered, not only in this particular point of view but also simply in itself, as a present perception. Its influence on association is very different according as it stands in one of these situations or the other. When it is in the mind simply as a present perception, it tends to suggest any ideas whatever that are connected with it by any of the associating qualities, and to cause the mind [to] run from one of these through a long train of ideas, successively introducing one another. But when it is brought into the mind by a passion to which it is intimately related, it receives a tincture from that passion; it is wholly under the direction of that passion; it exerts its power of association only in such ways and so far as the passion permits; it introduces such ideas alone as are suitable to the passion; and it introduces no long trains of ideas, but suffers the mind to return quickly to the conception of itself, or of some other object as intimately related to the passion. . . . Now, an indifferent poet, having conceived some of the objects strictly connected with a passion, considers that object only in general and abstractly, as a present perception; he therefore allows himself to run into such a train of thought as that object present to the mind would dictate if it were unconnected with any passion; he goes on coolly imagining such ideas as it suggests by means of any of the principles of association; and he makes the person possessed by the passion to express all these ideas. He feels not the passion; he has not force of genius or sensibility of heart sufficient for conceiving how it would affect a person who felt it, or for entering into the sentiments which it would produce in him. The sentiments which he makes him utter might all be very proper in a description, a discourse, or a meditation occasioned by the view of such an object, but they are not natural to a person in whom that object produces a suitable passion. In order to conceive sentiments natural to him, the poet ought. . . . to indulge only such a train of thought as it would lead to in these circumstances, or such a train as the passion with which it is presently connected would introduce into the mind of a person under the power of that passion.

This is indeed so difficult that the best poets cannot always perfectly attain it. Shakespeare makes the Duchess of Gloucester, in parting with John of Gaunt, to express her grief in this manner:

> *Yet one word more; grief boundeth where it falls,*
> *Not with the empty hollowness, but weight:*
> *I take my leave before I have begun,*
> *For sorrow ends not when it seemeth done.*
> *Commend me to thy brother, Edmund York;*
> *Lo, this is all—nay yet depart not so;*
> *Though this be all, do not so quickly go:*
> *I shall remember more. Bid him—oh what?*
> *With all good speed at Plashy visit me.*
> *Alack, and what shall good old York see there,*
> *But empty lodgings, and unfurnish'd walls,*
> *Unpeopled offices, untrodden stones?*
> *And what hear there for welcome, but my groans?*
> *Therefore commend me—let him not come there*
> *To seek out sorrow that dwells every where!*
> *All desolate will I from hence, and die;*
> *The last leave of thee takes my weeping eye.*[7]

The latter part of the speech is a natural expression of grief, and of violent grief; the first four lines are a description, not an ex-

---

[7] *Richard II*, I, ii, 58–74.

pression of it, and therefore unsuitable to the duchess's state of mind; the reflection which they contain is just, but too cool for the temper of the speaker. . . .

Coexistence and the relation of *cause and effect* are the principles of association which the passions employ most frequently, and which suggest the longest trains of ideas. These give ideas the most perfect relation to a passion, and almost every idea introduced by means of these principles really influences the passion. Co-existence suggests the qualities, the circumstances, the accessories, and the concomitants of those objects which are closely connected with the passion; and the more of these we have in our view, the stronger and livelier is our conception of those objects. All the objects almost which the relation of cause and effect can suggest, contribute either more immediately or more remotely to the pro-duction of the passion itself, and therefore are strongly connected with it. Accordingly, in most of the examples which have been produced, the ideas suggested by objects strictly connected with the passions are such as are suggested by means of these two principles of association.

FROM PART II, SECTION IV

Reflections on the Principles of Association.
Ideas suggested either by Sensations, or by other Ideas

From the account which has been already given of the principles of association, it is easy to collect that there is a broad foundation laid in the nature of the human imagination for great extent and variety of genius. There are many relations of ideas which fit them for being associated; almost every perception bears some of these relations to many different ideas; habit and the passions multiply and vary the instruments of association: by these means there are innumerable handles by which the imagination may seize such ideas as it has occasion for. Genius has, in some men, great force and compass, but a vigorous construction of the associating prin-ciples is sufficient to account for it, however great it be; for if they be vigorous, any one perception may introduce a great multitude of others, and that by means of many different relations. The principles of association likewise being so various, cannot but admit many distinct combinations and modifications, by which genius will be molded into a great diversity of forms.

Edmund Burke

1729–1797

THE GREATEST political thinker in eighteenth-century England and one of the great English prose stylists made his youthful reputation by A *Philosophical Inquiry into the Origin of Our Ideas of the Sublime and Beautiful* (1757). It was "rolling in his thoughts" from the age of nineteen, when he was still an undergraduate in Trinity College, Dublin. Burke published it at age twenty-eight, after he had settled in London as a free-lance literary gentleman out-at-elbows, almost a decade before he entered the House of Commons. The elder statesman—"haughtier-headed Burke that proved the State a tree" [1]—would be embarrassed later by mechanistic naïvetés in the *Inquiry*, or so the report goes. Its radical empiricism has a somehow boyish gusto for self-study and for knocking down fashionable opinions. But in it Burke first revealed his genius for large-scale, lucid, and logical argument, at once practical and investigative. Seen in its eighteenth-century context, it is a bold book whose many-sided importance eludes easy or quick summary—"an example of true criticism," Dr. Johnson said. Discriminations from it made their way into the thinking of Diderot, Lessing, and Kant, of Scottish critics such as Kames and Alison, of Johnson, Reynolds, and numerous minor writers such as the "picturesque" theorists of the 1790's, and, in time, into the art of Wordsworth and even, as Pro-

---

[1] W. B. Yeats, "Blood and the Moon," l. 22.

fessor Boulton has shown recently, into the art of Thomas Hardy's novels.

Its title, inviting comparison with Francis Hutcheson's *Inquiry into the Original of Our Ideas of Beauty and Virtue* (1725), fixes its lineage in the family of aesthetic philosophies begotten of Addison, Longinus, empirical psychology, and Shaftesburian idealism. By mid-century, perhaps most critics were convinced that, in one way or another, true criticism must be "philosophical," and that a standard of taste must be discovered not in neoclassic tradition—in particular poems or the "rules" deduced from them—but in the "principles" of nature and the human mind. Poets since antiquity, Burke says, have been "confined in so narrow a circle" because they have been "rather imitators of one another than of nature"; at the same time, critics "have generally sought the rule of the arts in the wrong place; they sought it among poems, pictures, engravings, statues, and buildings. But art can never give the rules that make an art." Significantly, he glances at tragedy (Part I, Section XV) not to analyze it as a neoclassic genre, but to discuss a psychological question popularized by Addison—on what principle the mind can be pleased by painful events. Burke is not studying artistic tradition, which he can afford to take for granted, but mental mechanics, the principles by which any aesthetic effect is enjoyed "antecedent to any reasoning," not just in arts but in nature and life. By mid-century, one consequence of such speculation was confusion of art with life and one art with another, the absence of rational justification for classical good taste, and a threatened collapse of all taste in subjectivity. The *Inquiry* is one of several efforts by mid-century critics—e.g., Hume, Gerard, Kames, Hurd—to re-establish a standard.

Burke protested against two trends in aesthetics which seemed to him sophistical, although he learned from both. Moralizing and mathematicizing followers of Shaftesbury and Addison, such as Hutcheson and the poet Akenside, committed the "sophism" of imposing human wishes upon nature instead of "extending our ideas to take in all that nature comprehends, according to her manner of combining." Thus they "left us no standard or rule to judge by that was not even more uncertain and fallacious than our own fancies." They spoke of taste or "inner sense" as if it were a means of knowing nature, and thus they separated good taste from trained, rational judgment. At the other extreme, and more formidable, was the psychology of Hume, which doubted the possibility of knowing anything, and reduced even reason to a stream of customary associations. In answer to both trends, Burke reverted to the more realistic and practical psychology of Locke, which attributes knowledge, limited as it must be, to rational judgment, and distinguishes, in a normal mind, between natural and customary associations. At the same time, Burke based his *Inquiry* on "physical causes," including the human body, whose mechanical laws could be known, as he tried to know them, by Newtonian induction.

The *Inquiry* is one of the first interdisciplinary attempts in the history of criticism, perhaps the first in its rigor, to base aesthetics upon physics and physiology. As many have remarked, a historic side-effect of science in the eighteenth century, unlike that in the twentieth, was to encourage a layman to try his hand at it. A popular belief grew up—epitomized by the story of Newton's discovery of gravitation while he watched a falling apple—that though the great mechanism of nature is subtle, nevertheless it operates in the ordinary world and in ordinary experience, and applying the right key, any man has a chance to make discoveries. Or in Burke's words: "The true standard of the arts is in every man's power; and an easy observation of the most common, sometimes of the meanest things in nature, will give the truest lights." Both Addison and Hutcheson had felt the certitude of mechanism in matter, but turning away from investigation of it, had softened its implications by optimistic theories of imagination and moral sense, and by admitting "final causes." Burke had moments of Addisonian piety, in which he remarked Providential design in the "great chain of causes . . . linking one to another even to the throne of God himself," and he admitted a principle of "sympathy" in the mind. But he also assumed that if "we go but one step beyond the immediate sensible qualities of things, we go out of our depth." Final causes may exist, but they are not to be known. Short of revelation, a man must inhabit his ignorant, practical isthmus, as Locke had said; with patient investigation, he may know "efficient causes" in nature, the how of many things, but not the why.

After Dennis, critics tended increasingly to discuss the Sublime not as a property of language and rhetoric, the grand style, but as a state of awe-struck, even redemptive, emotion, the most intense which is humanly possible. It might be excited, in real life or in poetry, by various "objects" of thought such as God, the starry universe, or turbulent scenery. The Sublime and the Beautiful were often blurred together, but sometimes beauty was traced to abstract principles such as Hutcheson's "uniformity in variety" or the curving spiral proposed by Hogarth in *The Analysis of Beauty*

(1752). Burke firmly separated the two aesthetic categories, and reduced both to particular states of bodily sensation and feeling, excited, in life or poetry, according to fixed mechanical laws, by the natural properties of objects. Unlike Addison, he admitted all five senses, which are only "different sorts of feelings," into aesthetic response. The "delight" or pleasurable pain of sublimity—"a sort of tranquility tinged with terror"—is to feel in safety that which otherwise would threaten pain, sickness, or death, arouse the animal instinct for self-preservation with its muscular contraction and tension of the nerves. *Terror, obscurity, power, privation* (i.e., *vacuity, darkness, silence, solitude*), *vastness* and *infinity, difficulty, magnificence,* the *artificial infinite*—a glance at his table of contents is instructive. As Professor Monk observes, the concept of the Sublime gathered to itself all those emotionalist and irrational elements which the Beautiful of neoclassic art tended not to have. Its history is entangled with the poetry (and painting) of graveyards, storms, ruins, and primitive or preternatural terror, from Thomson to Gray to Cowper, as well as with changing views of Shakespeare and Milton, with Ossian and the Gothic novel. The "pleasure" of Beauty, whose origin is either sexual or social, is to experience, in life or poetry, that which "as effectually causes some degree of love in us as the application of ice or fire produces the ideas of heat or cold." Qualities of finitude (often diminutive), smoothness, gradual variation, delicacy, clarity, bright but not glaring color, relax the nerves and evoke secure, amiable feelings of tenderness. Later theories of the Picturesque, by establishing a third category, tried to take care of experiences which Burke had overlooked.

Burke understood, of course, that "in the infinite variety of natural combinations, we must expect to find the qualities of things the most remote imaginable from each other united in the same object. We must expect also to find combinations of the same kind in works of art." But having established two bed-rock categories of aesthetic response, prior to any reasoning, he had therefore proved that the most irrational elements in taste—or "sensibility," as Hume had called them—obey the same laws in all normal men. Unless a man is born with a dull sensibility or his sensibility is dulled by life, he can be brought to agree on all matters of taste, by close study and the habit of reasoning. Accordingly, to a second edition of the *Inquiry* in 1759, he added a discourse "On Taste," in which he concluded, *quod erat demonstrandum,* that "a standard both of reason and taste is the same in all human creatures."

Finally, in the last section of the *Inquiry,* turning to words and poetry, Burke attacked two traditional beliefs: that poetry is imitation of nature, and that poetry is like painting (*ut pictura poesis*). By mid-century, *imitation* had disintegrated meanings: copying or borrowing from other poets (Pope's "stealing wisely"), a representation of sense-impressions (painting to the imagination, as in Thomson) or comparison of such impressions with the real world that one knows, fiction in general, the likeness of a stage-play to real life, and still other meanings. Many troubled critics struggled to define it—e.g., Hurd, Young, Kames, Reynolds. Cutting through such confusion, Burke concluded that only drama is strictly imitative (it has physical characters who can be watched as they act and speak in a physical setting); poetry, purely verbal, presupposes a speaker at some remove but has no *necessary* relation to a physical, verifiable world. It may or may not evoke pictures; if it does, they had best be grandly obscure, crowded, and confused. "A clear idea is . . . another name for a little idea." Poetry is more like music than painting. Words are mere sounds associated by custom, by just living along, with feelings and ideas. Poetry, "a union of affecting words," excites such associated feelings and ideas into new combinations, whose value or truth must be judged tastefully. The business of poetry, then, and of rhetoric, is "to affect rather by sympathy than imitation, to display rather the effect of things on the mind of the speaker, or of others, than to present a clear idea of the things themselves." Burke is groping toward the concept of "sympathetic imagination" more elaborately developed by later aestheticians, as well as toward the art of his later great speeches; but more importantly perhaps, destroying the basis for poetry of mere painterly description, he lays a new and clear basis for a modern poetry of sensibility.

* * * *

FROM

A *Philosophical Inquiry into the Origin of Our Ideas of the Sublime and Beautiful* [1757]

from the Preface

The characters of nature are legible, it is true; but they are not plain enough to enable those who run to read them. We must make use of a cautious, I had almost said a timorous method of proceeding. We must not attempt to fly when we can scarcely pretend to creep. In considering any complex matter, we ought to examine every distinct ingredient in the composition, one by one, and reduce everything to the utmost simplicity, since the condition of our nature binds us to a strict law and very narrow limits. We ought afterwards to re-examine the principles by the effect of the composition as well as the composition by that of the principles. We ought to compare our subject with things of a similar nature and even with things of a contrary nature, for discoveries may be and often are made by the contrast, which would escape us on the single view. The greater number of the comparisons we make, the more general and the more certain our knowledge is like to prove, as built upon a more extensive and perfect induction. . . .

I could wish that in examining this theory, the same method were pursued which I endeavored to observe in forming it. The objections, in my opinion, ought to be proposed either to the several principles as they are distinctly considered, or to the justness of the conclusion which is drawn from them. But it is common to pass over both the premises and conclusion in silence, and to produce as an objection some poetical passage which does not seem easily accounted for upon the principles I endeavor to establish. This manner of proceeding I should think very improper. The task would be infinite if we could establish no principle until we had previously unravelled the complex texture of every image or description to be found in poets and orators. And though we should never be able to reconcile the effect of such images to our principles, this can never overturn the theory itself whilst it is founded on certain and indisputable facts. A theory founded on experiment, and not assumed, is always good for so much as it explains. Our inability to push it indefinitely is no argument at all against it. This inability may be owing to our ignorance of some necessary mediums, to a want of proper application, to many other causes besides a defect in the principles we employ. In reality, the subject requires a much closer attention than we dare claim from our manner of treating it.

If it should not appear on the face of the work, I must caution the reader against imagining that I intended a full dissertation on the Sublime and Beautiful. My inquiry went no farther than to the origin of these ideas. If the qualities which I have ranged under the head of the Sublime be all found consistent with each other, and all different from those which I place under the head of beauty, and if those which compose the class of the Beautiful have the same consistency with themselves and the same opposition to those which are classed under the denomination of Sublime, I am in little pain whether anybody chooses to follow the name I give them or not, provided he allows that what I dispose under different heads are in reality different things in nature. The use I make of the words may be blamed, as too confined or too extended; my meaning cannot well be misunderstood.

To conclude: whatever progress may be made towards the discovery of truth in this matter, I do not repent the pains I have taken in it. The use of such inquiries may be very considerable. Whatever turns the soul inward on itself tends to concenter its forces, and to fit it for greater and stronger flights of science. By looking into physical causes, our minds are opened and enlarged; and in this pursuit, whether we take or whether we lose our game, the chase is certainly of service. Cicero, true as he was to the Academic philosophy, and consequently led to reject the certainty of physical as of every other kind of knowledge, yet freely confesses its great importance to the human understanding: *Est animorum ingeniorumque nostrorum naturale quoddam quasi pabulum consideratio contemplatioque naturae.*[1] If we can direct the lights we derive from such exalted speculations upon the humbler field of the imagination, whilst we investigate the springs and trace the courses of our passions, we may not only communicate to the taste a sort of philosophical solidity, but we may reflect back on the severer sciences some of the graces and elegancies of taste, without which the great-

---

[1] *Academica*, II, 127: "Scrutiny and contemplation of nature is, so to speak, a kind of natural food for our minds and characters."

est proficiency in those sciences will always have the appearance of
something illiberal.

*

from Introduction on Taste [1759]

On a superficial view we may seem to differ very widely from each
other in our reasonings, and no less in our pleasures. But notwithstanding this difference, which I think to be rather apparent than
real, it is probable that the standard both of reason and taste is the
same in all human creatures. For if there were not some principles
of judgment as well as of sentiment common to all mankind, no
hold could possibly be taken, either on their reason or their passions,
sufficient to maintain the ordinary correspondence of life. . . .
And indeed, it is very necessary at the entrance into such an inquiry as our present, to make this point as clear as possible; for if
taste has no fixed principles, if the imagination is not affected
according to some invariable and certain laws, our labor is likely to
be employed to very little purpose, as it must be judged a useless, if
not an absurd undertaking to lay down rules for caprice, and to set
up for a legislator of whims and fancies. . . .

But to cut off all pretense for cavilling, I mean by the word *taste*
no more than that faculty, or those faculties of the mind which are
affected with, or which form a judgment of the works of imagination and the elegant arts. That is, I think, the most general idea of
the word, and what is the least connected with any particular
theory. And my point in this inquiry is to find whether there are
any principles on which the imagination is affected, so common to
all, so grounded and certain, as to supply the means of reasoning
satisfactorily about them. And such principles of taste I fancy there
are, however paradoxical it may seem to those who, on a superficial
view, imagine that there is so great a diversity of tastes, both in kind
and degree, that nothing can be more indeterminate.

All the natural powers in man which I know, that are conversant
about external objects, are the senses, the imagination, and the judgment. And first with regard to the senses. We do and we must suppose that as the conformation of their organs are nearly or altogether the same in all men, so the manner of perceiving external
objects is in all men the same, or with little difference. We are satisfied that what appears to be light to one eye appears light to another, that what seems sweet to one palate is sweet to another, that
what is dark and bitter to this man is likewise dark and bitter to

that; and we conclude in the same manner of great and little, hard and soft, hot and cold, rough and smooth, and indeed of all the natural qualities and affections of bodies. If we suffer ourselves to imagine that their senses present to different men different images of things, this sceptical proceeding will make every sort of reasoning on every subject vain and frivolous, even that sceptical reasoning itself which had persuaded us to entertain a doubt concerning the agreement of our perceptions. . . . It is confessed that custom and some other causes[2] have made many deviations from the natural pleasures or pains which belong to these several tastes, but then the power of distinguishing between the natural and the acquired relish remains to the very last. A man frequently comes to prefer the taste of tobacco to that of sugar, and the flavor of vinegar to that of milk, but this makes no confusion in tastes whilst he is sensible that the tobacco and vinegar are not sweet, and whilst he knows that habit alone has reconciled his palate to these alien pleasures. Even with such a person we may speak, and with sufficient precision, concerning tastes. But should any man be found who declares that to him tobacco has a taste like sugar, and that he cannot distinguish between milk and vinegar, or that tobacco and vinegar are sweet, milk bitter, and sugar sour, we immediately conclude that the organs of this man are out of order, and that his palate is utterly vitiated. We are as far from conferring with such a person upon tastes as from reasoning concerning the relations of quantity with one who should deny that all the parts together were equal to the whole. We do not call a man of this kind wrong in his notions but absolutely mad. Exceptions of this sort, in either way, do not at all impeach our general rule, nor make us conclude that men have various principles concerning the relations of quantity or the taste of things. So that when it is said "taste cannot be disputed," it can only mean that no one can strictly answer what pleasure or pain some particular man may find from the taste of some particular thing. This indeed cannot be disputed; but we may dispute, and with sufficient clearness too, concerning the things which are naturally pleasing or disagreeable to the sense. But when we talk of any peculiar or acquired relish, then we must know the habits, the prejudices, or the distempers of this particular man, and we must draw our conclusion from those. . . .

Besides the ideas, with their annexed pains and pleasures, which are presented by the sense, the mind of man possesses a sort of creative power of its own, either in representing at pleasure the

---

[2] "unnatural" associations.

images of things, in the order and manner in which they were received by the senses, or in combining those images in a new manner and according to a different order. This power is called imagination, and to this belongs whatever is called wit, fancy, invention, and the like. But it must be observed that this power of the imagination is incapable of producing anything absolutely new; it can only vary the disposition of those ideas which it has received from the senses. Now, the imagination is the most extensive province of pleasure and pain, as it is the region of our fears and our hopes and of all our passions that are connected with them; and whatever is calculated to affect the imagination with these commanding ideas, by force of any original natural impression, must have the same power pretty equally over all men. For since the imagination is only the representation of the senses, it can only be pleased or displeased with the images from the same principle on which the sense is pleased or displeased with the realities, and consequently there must be just as close an agreement in the imaginations as in the senses of men. A little attention will convince us that this must of necessity be the case.

But in the imagination, besides the pain or pleasure arising from the properties of the natural object, a pleasure is perceived from the resemblance which the imitation has to the original. The imagination, I conceive, can have no pleasure but what results from one or other of these causes. And these causes operate pretty uniformly upon all men, because they operate by principles in nature, and which are not derived from any particular habits or advantages. Mr. Locke very justly and finely observes of wit that it is chiefly conversant in tracing resemblances; he remarks, at the same time, that the business of judgment is rather in finding differences. It may perhaps appear, on this supposition, that there is no material distinction between the wit and the judgment as they both seem to result from different operations of the same faculty of *comparing*. But in reality, whether they are or are not dependent on the same power of the mind, they differ so very materially in many respects that a perfect union of wit and judgment is one of the rarest things in the world. When two distinct objects are unlike to each other, it is only what we expect; things are in their common way; and therefore they make no impression on the imagination. But when two distinct objects have a resemblance, we are struck, we attend to them, and we are pleased. The mind of man has naturally a far greater alacrity and satisfaction in tracing resemblances than in searching for differences, because by making resem-

blances we produce *new images;* we unite, we create, we enlarge
our stock; but in making distinctions we offer no food at all to the
imagination; the task itself is more severe and irksome, and what
pleasure we derive from it is something of a negative and indirect
nature. A piece of news is told me in the morning; this, merely as
a piece of news, as a fact added to my stock, gives me some pleasure.
In the evening I find there was nothing in it. What do I gain by
this but the dissatisfaction to find that I had been imposed upon?
Hence it is that men are much more naturally inclined to belief
than to incredulity. And it is upon this principle that the most
ignorant and barbarous nations have frequently excelled in similitudes, comparisons, metaphors, and allegories, who have been weak
and backward in distinguishing and sorting their ideas. And it is
for a reason of this kind that Homer and the Oriental writers,
though very fond of similitudes, and though they often strike out
such as are truly admirable, seldom take care to have them exact;
that is, they are taken with the general resemblance, they paint it
strongly, and they take no notice of the difference which may be
found between the things compared. . . .

So far then as taste belongs to the imagination, its principle is
the same in all men; there is no difference in the manner of their
being affected, nor in the causes of the affection; but in the *degree*
there is a difference, which arises from two causes principally:
either from a greater degree of natural sensibility, or from a closer
and longer attention to the object. To illustrate this by the procedure of the senses, in which the same difference is found, let us
suppose a very smooth marble table to be set before two men; they
both perceive it to be smooth, and they are both pleased with it
because of this quality. So far they agree. But suppose another,
and after that another table, the latter still smoother than the
former, to be set before them. It is now very probable that these
men, who are so agreed upon what is smooth, and in the pleasure
from thence, will disagree when they come to settle which table
has the advantage in point of polish. Here is indeed the great difference between tastes, when men come to compare the excess or
diminution of things which are judged by degree and not by measure. Nor is it easy, when such a difference arises, to settle the point
if the excess or diminution be not glaring. If we differ in opinion
about two quantities, we can have recourse to a common measure
which may decide the question with the utmost exactness; and this,
I take it, is what gives mathematical knowledge a greater certainty
than any other. But in things whose excess is not judged by greater

or smaller, as smoothness and roughness, hardness and softness, darkness and light, the shades of color, all these are very easily distinguished when the difference is any way considerable, but not when it is minute, for want of some common measures, which perhaps may never come to be discovered. In these nice cases, supposing the acuteness of the sense equal, the greater attention and habit in such things will have the advantage. In the question about the tables, the marble-polisher will unquestionably determine the most accurately. But notwithstanding this want of a common measure for settling many disputes relative to the senses, and their representative the imagination, we find that the principles are the same in all, and that there is no disagreement until we come to examine into the pre-eminence or difference of things, which brings us within the province of the judgment.

So long as we are conversant with the sensible qualities of things, hardly any more than the imagination seems concerned; little more also than the imagination seems concerned when the passions are represented, because by the force of natural sympathy they are felt in all men without any recourse to reasoning, and their justness recognized in every breast. Love, grief, fear, anger, joy, all these passions have, in their turns, affected every mind; and they do not affect it in an arbitrary or casual manner, but upon certain, natural, and uniform principles. But as many of the works of imagination are not confined to the representation of sensible objects, nor to efforts upon the passions, but extend themselves to the manners, the characters, the actions, and designs of men, their relations, their virtues and vices, they come within the province of the judgment, which is improved by attention and by the habit of reasoning. All these make a very considerable part of what are considered as the objects of taste, and Horace sends us to the schools of philosophy and the world for our instruction in them.[3] Whatever certainty is to be acquired in morality and the science of life, just the same degree of certainty have we in what relates to them in works of imitation. Indeed it is for the most part in our skill in manners, and in the observances of time and place, and of decency in general, which is only to be learned in those schools to which Horace recommends us, that what is called taste, by way of distinction, consists, and which is in reality no other than a more refined judgment. On the whole, it appears to me that what is called taste, in its most general acceptation, is not a simple idea, but is partly made up of a perception of the primary pleasures of sense, of the secondary pleasures of

---

[3] *Ars Poetica*, 309 ff.

the imagination, and of the conclusions of the reasoning faculty concerning the various relations of these, and concerning the human passions, manners, and actions. All this is requisite to form taste, and the groundwork of all these is the same in the human mind; for as the senses are the great originals of all our ideas and consequently of all our pleasures, if they are not uncertain and arbitrary, the whole groundwork of taste is common to all, and therefore there is a sufficient foundation for a conclusive reasoning on these matters.

Whilst we consider taste merely according to its nature and species, we shall find its principles entirely uniform; but the degree in which these principles prevail, in the several individuals of mankind, is altogether as different as the principles themselves are similar. For sensibility and judgment, which are the qualities that compose what we commonly call a *taste*, vary exceedingly in various people. From a defect in the former of these qualities arises a want of taste; a weakness in the latter constitutes a wrong or a bad one. . . .

The cause of a wrong taste is a defect of judgment. And this may arise from a natural weakness of understanding (in whatever the strength of that faculty may consist), or, which is much more commonly the case, it may arise from a want of a proper and well-directed exercise, which alone can make it strong and ready. Besides that, ignorance, inattention, prejudice, rashness, levity, obstinacy, in short, all those passions, and all those vices, which pervert the judgment in other matters, prejudice it no less in this its more refined and elegant province. These causes produce different opinions upon everything which is an object of the understanding, without inducing us to suppose that there are no settled principles of reason. And indeed, on the whole, one may observe that there is rather less difference upon matters of taste among mankind than upon most of those which depend upon the naked reason, and that men are far better agreed on the excellence of a description in Virgil than on the truth or falsehood of a theory of Aristotle.

A rectitude of judgment in the arts, which may be called a good taste, does in a great measure depend upon sensibility, because if the mind has no bent to the pleasures of the imagination, it will never apply itself sufficiently to works of that species to acquire a competent knowledge of them. But though a degree of sensibility is requisite to form a good judgment, yet a good judgment does not necessarily arise from a quick sensibility to pleasure; it frequently happens that a very poor judge, merely by force of a greater complexional sensibility, is more affected by a very poor piece than the best judge by the most perfect; for as everything new, extraordinary, grand, or passionate, is well calculated to affect such a person, and that the faults do not affect him, his pleasure is more pure and unmixed; and as it is merely a pleasure of the imagination, it is much higher than any which is derived from a rectitude of judgment; the judgment is for the greater part employed in throwing stumbling-blocks in the way of the imagination, in dissipating the scenes of its enchantment, and in tying us down to the disagreeable yoke of our reason. For almost the only pleasure that men have in judging better than others consists in a sort of conscious pride and superiority, which arises from thinking rightly, but then this is an indirect pleasure, a pleasure which does not immediately result from the object which is under contemplation. In the morning of our days, when the senses are unworn and tender, when the whole man is awake in every part and the gloss of novelty fresh upon all the objects that surround us, how lively at that time are our sensations, but how false and inaccurate the judgments we form of things! I despair of ever receiving the same degree of pleasure from the most excellent performances of genius, which I felt at that age from pieces which my present judgment regards as trifling and contemptible. Every trivial cause of pleasure is apt to affect the man of too sanguine a complexion; his appetite is too keen to suffer his taste to be delicate, and he is in all respects what Ovid says of himself in love:

> Molle meum levibus cor est violabile telis,
> Et semper causa est, cur ego semper amem.[4]

One of this character can never be a refined judge, never what the comic poet calls *elegans formarum spectator*.[5] The excellence and force of a composition must always be imperfectly estimated from its effect on the minds of any except we know the temper and character of those minds. The most powerful effects of poetry and music have been displayed, and perhaps are still displayed, where these arts are but in a very low and imperfect state. The rude hearer is affected by the principles which operate in these arts even in their rudest condition, and he is not skilful enough to perceive the defects. But as the arts advance toward their perfection, the science of criticism advances with equal pace, and the pleasure of

---

[4] *Heroides*, XV, 79–80 (misquoted): "my heart is tender, easily pierced by light arrows, and there is always a reason why I should always be in love."
[5] Terence, *Eunuchus*, 566: "a tasteful observer of beautiful things."

judges is frequently interrupted by the faults which are discovered in the most finished compositions.

Before I leave this subject, I cannot help taking notice of an opinion which many persons entertain, as if the taste were a separate faculty of the mind and distinct from the judgment and imagination—a species of instinct, by which we are struck naturally, and at first glance, without any previous reasoning, with the excellencies or the defects of a composition. So far as the imagination and the passions are concerned, I believe it true that the reason is little consulted; but where disposition, where decorum, where congruity are concerned, in short, wherever the best taste differs from the worst, I am convinced that the understanding operates and nothing else; and its operation is in reality far from being always sudden, or, when it is sudden, it is often far from being right. Men of the best taste by consideration come frequently to change these early and precipitate judgments which the mind, from its aversion to neutrality and doubt, loves to form on the spot. It is known that the taste (whatever it is) is improved exactly as we improve our judgment, by extending our knowledge, by a steady attention to our object, and by frequent exercise. They who have not taken these methods, if their taste decides quickly, it is always uncertainly, and their quickness is owing to their presumption and rashness, and not to any sudden irradiation that in a moment dispels all darkness from their minds. But they who have cultivated that species of knowledge which makes the object of taste, by degrees and habitually attain not only a soundness, but a readiness of judgment, as men do by the same methods on all other occasions. At first they are obliged to spell, but at last they read with ease and with celerity; but this celerity of its operation is no proof that the taste is a distinct faculty. Nobody, I believe, has attended the course of a discussion which turned upon matters within the sphere of mere naked reason but must have observed the extreme readiness with which the whole process of the argument is carried on, the grounds discovered, the objections raised and answered, and the conclusions drawn from premises, with a quickness altogether as great as the taste can be supposed to work with; and yet where nothing but plain reason either is or can be suspected to operate. To multiply principles for every different appearance is useless, and unphilosophical too in a high degree.

This matter might be pursued much farther; but it is not the extent of the subject which must prescribe our bounds, for what subject does not branch out to infinity? It is the nature of our particular scheme, and the single point of view in which we consider it, which ought to put a stop to our researches.

Of the passions which belong to self-preservation

Most of the ideas which are capable of making a powerful impression on the mind, whether simply of pain or pleasure, or of the modifications of those, may be reduced very nearly to these two heads, *self-preservation* and *society*; to the ends of one or the other of which all our passions are calculated to answer. The passions which concern self-preservation turn mostly on pain or danger. The ideas of *pain, sickness,* and *death* fill the mind with strong emotions of horror; but *life* and *health,* though they put us in a capacity of being affected with pleasure, they make no such impression by the simple enjoyment. The passions therefore which are conversant about the preservation of the individual turn chiefly on *pain* and *danger,* and they are the most powerful of all the passions.

Of the Sublime

Whatever is fitted in any sort to excite the ideas of pain and danger, that is to say, whatever is any sort terrible, or is conversant about terrible objects, or operates in a manner analogous to terror, is a source of the *sublime;* that is, it is productive of the strongest emotion which the mind is capable of feeling. I say the strongest emotion, because I am satisfied the ideas of pain are much more powerful than those which enter on the part of pleasure. Without all doubt, the torments which we may be made to suffer are much greater in their effect on the body and mind than any pleasures the most learned voluptuary could suggest, or than the liveliest imagination and the most sound and exquisitely sensible body could enjoy. Nay, I am in great doubt whether any man could be found who would earn a life of the most perfect satisfaction at the price of ending it in the torments which justice inflicted in a few hours on the late unfortunate regicide in France. But as pain is stronger in its operation than pleasure, so death is in general a much more affecting idea than pain, because there are very few pains, however exquisite, which are not preferred to death. Nay, what generally makes pain itself, if I may say so, more painful is that it is considered as an emissary of this king of terrors. When danger or pain press too nearly, they are incapable of giving any delight and are simply terrible; but at certain distances, and with certain modifications, they are delightful, as we every day experience. The cause of this I shall endeavor to investigate hereafter.

FROM PART I, SECTION X
Of Beauty

The passion which belongs to generation, merely as such, is lust only. This is evident in brutes, whose passions are more unmixed, and which pursue their purposes more directly than ours. The only distinction they observe with regard to their mates is that of sex. It is true that they stick severally to their own species in preference to all others. But this preference, I imagine, does not arise from any sense of beauty which they find in their species, as Mr. Addison supposes, but from a law of some other kind to which they are subject; and this we may fairly conclude from their apparent want of choice amongst those objects to which the barriers of their species have confined them. But man, who is a creature adapted to a greater variety and intricacy of relation, connects with the general passion the idea of some *social* qualities, which direct and heighten the appetite which he has in common with all other animals; and as he is not designed like them to live at large, it is fit that he should have something to create a preference and fix his choice; and this in general should be some sensible quality, as no other can so quickly, so powerfully, or so surely produce its effect. The object therefore of this mixed passion which we call love is the *beauty* of the *sex*. Men are carried to the sex in general, as it is the sex, and by the common law of nature, but they are attached to particulars by personal *beauty*. I call beauty a social quality; for where women and men, and not only they, but when other animals give us a sense of joy and pleasure in beholding them (and there are many that do so), they inspire us with sentiments of tenderness and affection towards their persons; we like to have them near us.

FROM PART I, SECTION XIII
Sympathy

It is by [sympathy] . . . that we enter into the concerns of others, that we are moved as they are moved and are never suffered to be indifferent spectators of almost anything which men can do or suffer. For sympathy must be considered as a sort of substitution, by which we are put into the place of another man and affected in many respects as he is affected. So that this passion may either partake of the nature of those which regard self-preservation, and turning upon pain may be a source of the sublime; or it may turn upon ideas of pleasure; and then whatever has been said of the social affections, whether they regard society in general or only some particular mode of it, may be applicable here. It is by this principle chiefly that poetry, painting, and other affecting arts transfuse their passions from one breast to another, and are often capable of grafting a delight on wretchedness, misery, and death itself. It is a common observation that objects which in the reality would shock are in tragical, and such like representations, the source of a very high species of pleasure. This, taken as a fact, has been the cause of much reasoning. The satisfaction has been commonly attributed, first, to the comfort we receive in considering that so melancholy a story is no more than a fiction; and next, to the contemplation of our own freedom from the evils which we see represented. I am afraid it is a practice much too common in inquiries of this nature to attribute the cause of feelings which merely arise from the mechanical structure of our bodies, or from the natural frame and constitution of our minds, to certain conclusions of the reasoning faculty on the objects presented to us; for I should imagine that the influence of reason in producing our passions is nothing near so extensive as it is commonly believed.

FROM PART I, SECTION XIV

The effects of sympathy in the distresses of others

To examine this point concerning the effect of tragedy in a proper manner, we must previously consider how we are affected by the feelings of our fellow-creatures in circumstances of real distress. I am convinced that we have a degree of delight, and that no small one, in the real misfortunes and pains of others. . . . Terror is a passion which always produces delight when it does not press too closely; and pity is a passion accompanied with pleasure, because it arises from love and social affection. Whenever we are formed by nature to any active purpose, the passion which animates us to it is attended with delight or a pleasure of some kind, let the subject-matter be what it will; and as our Creator has designed that we should be united by the bond of sympathy, he has strengthened that bond by a proportionable delight; and there most where our sympathy is most wanted—in the distresses of others. If this passion was simply painful, we would shun with the greatest care all persons and places that could excite such a passion, as some, who are so far gone in indolence as not to endure any strong impression, actually do. But the case is widely different with the greater part of mankind; there is no spectacle we so eagerly pursue as that of some uncommon and grievous calamity; so that whether the misfortune is before our eyes, or whether they are turned back to it in history, it always touches with delight. This is not an unmixed delight, but blended with no small uneasiness. The delight we have in such things hinders us from shunning scenes of misery; and the pain we feel prompts us to relieve ourselves in relieving those who suffer; and all this antecedent to any reasoning, by an instinct that works us to its own purposes without our concurrence.

FROM PART I, SECTION XV

Of the effects of tragedy

It is thus in real calamities. In imitated distresses the only difference is the pleasure resulting from the effects of imitation; for it is never so perfect but we can perceive it is imitation, and on that principle are somewhat pleased with it. And indeed, in some cases, we derive as much or more pleasure from that source than from the thing itself. But then I imagine we shall be much mistaken if we attribute any considerable part of our satisfaction in tragedy to the consideration that tragedy is a deceit, and its representations no realities. The nearer it approaches the reality, and the further it removes us from all idea of fiction, the more perfect is its power. But be its power of what kind it will, it never approaches to what it represents. Choose a day on which to represent the most sublime and affecting tragedy we have; appoint the most favorite actors; spare no cost upon the scenes and decorations; unite the greatest efforts of poetry, painting, and music; and when you have collected your audience, just at the moment when their minds are erect with expectation, let it be reported that a state criminal of high rank is on the point of being executed in the adjoining square; in a moment the emptiness of the theatre would demonstrate the comparative weakness of the imitative arts, and proclaim the triumph of the real sympathy. . . . Nor is it, either in real or fictitious distresses, our immunity from them which produces our delight; in my own mind I can discover nothing like it. I apprehend that this mistake is owing to a sort of sophism by which we are frequently imposed upon; it arises from our not distinguishing between what is indeed a necessary condition to our doing or suffering anything in general, and what is the cause of some particular act. If a man kills me with a sword, it is a necessary condition to this that we should have been both of us alive before the fact; and yet it would be absurd to say that our being both living creatures was the cause of his crime and my death. So it is certain that it is absolutely necessary my life should be out of any imminent hazard before I can take a delight in the sufferings of others, real or imaginary, or indeed in anything else from any cause whatsoever. But then it is a sophism to argue from thence that this immunity is the cause of my delight either on these or on any occasions.

FROM PART I, SECTION XIX

The conclusion

A consideration of the rationale of our passions seems to me very necessary for all who would affect them upon solid and sure principles. It is not enough to know them in general. To affect them after a delicate manner, or to judge properly of any work designed to affect them, we should know the exact boundaries of their several jurisdictions; we should pursue them through all their variety of operations, and pierce into the inmost and what might appear inaccessible parts of our nature:

Quod latet arcana non enarrabile fibra.[6]

Without all this it is possible for a man, after a confused manner, sometimes to satisfy his own mind of the truth of his work, but he can never have a certain determinate rule to go by, nor can he ever make his propositions sufficiently clear to others. Poets and orators and painters and those who cultivate other branches of the liberal arts have, without this critical knowledge, succeeded well in their several provinces, and will succeed, as among artificers there are many machines made and even invented without any exact knowledge of the principles they are governed by. It is, I own, not uncommon to be wrong in theory and right in practice, and we are happy that it is so. Men often act right from their feelings who afterwards reason but ill on them from principle; but as it is impossible to avoid an attempt at such reasoning, and equally impossible to prevent its having some influence on our practice, surely it is worth taking some pains to have it just, and founded on the basis of sure experience. We might expect that the artists them-

---

[6] Persius, *Satires*, V, 29: "what lies in the deep and inexpressible interior."

selves would have been our surest guides, but the artists have been too much occupied in the practice. The philosophers have done little, and what they have done was mostly with a view to their own schemes and systems. And as for those called critics, they have generally sought the rule of the arts in the wrong place; they sought it among poems, pictures, engravings, statues, and buildings. But art can never give the rules that make an art. This is, I believe, the reason why artists in general, and poets principally, have been confined in so narrow a circle; they have been rather imitators of one another than of nature, and this with so faithful a uniformity and to so remote an antiquity that it is hard to say who gave the first model. Critics follow them, and therefore can do little as guides. I can judge but poorly of anything whilst I measure it by no other standard than itself. The true standard of the arts is in every man's power; and an easy observation of the most common, sometimes of the meanest things in nature will give the truest lights, where the greatest sagacity and industry that slights such observation must leave us in the dark, or what is worse, amuse and mislead us by false lights.

FROM PART II, SECTION III
Obscurity

To make anything very terrible, obscurity seems in general to be necessary. When we know the full extent of any danger, when we can accustom our eyes to it, a great deal of the apprehension vanishes. Everyone will be sensible of this who considers how greatly night adds to our dread in all cases of danger, and how much the notions of ghosts and goblins, of which none can form clear ideas, affect minds which give credit to the popular tales concerning such sorts of beings. Those despotic governments, which are founded on the passions of men and principally upon the passion of fear, keep their chief as much as may be from the public eye. The policy has been the same in many cases of religion. Almost all the heathen temples were dark. Even in the barbarous temples of the Americans at this day, they keep their idol in a dark part of the hut, which is consecrated to his worship. For this purpose too the druids performed all their ceremonies in the bosom of the darkest woods and in the shade of the oldest and most spreading oaks. No person seems better to have understood the secret of heightening, or of setting terrible things, if I may use the expression, in their strongest light, by the force of a judicious obscurity, than Milton.

The same subject continued:
Of the difference between clearness and obscurity
with regard to the passions

We do not anywhere meet a more sublime description than this justly celebrated one of Milton, wherein he gives the portrait of Satan with a dignity so suitable to the subject:

> He above the rest
> *In shape and gesture proudly eminent*
> *Stood like a tower; his form had yet not lost*
> *All her original brightness, nor appeared*
> *Less than Archangel ruined, and the excess*
> *Of glory obscured: as when the sun new-risen*
> *Looks through the horizontal misty air*
> *Shorn of his beams, or from behind the moon*
> *In dim eclipse disastrous twilight sheds*
> *On half the nations, and with fear of change*
> *Perplexes monarchs.*[7]

Here is a very noble picture; and in what does this poetical picture consist? in images of a tower, an archangel, the sun rising through mists, or in an eclipse, the ruin of monarchs, and the revolutions of kingdoms. The mind is hurried out of itself by a crowd of great and confused images, which affect because they are crowded and confused. For separate them, and you lose much of the greatness; and join them, and you infallibly lose the clearness. The images raised by poetry are always of this obscure kind, though in general the effects of poetry are by no means to be attributed to the images it raises; which point we shall examine more at large hereafter. But painting, when we have allowed for the pleasure of imitation, can only affect simply by the images it presents; and even in painting, a judicious obscurity in some things contributes to the effect of the picture; because the images in painting are exactly similar to those in nature; and in nature, dark, confused, uncertain images have a greater power on the fancy to form the grander passions than those have which are more clear and determinate. But where and when this observation may be applied to practice, and how far it shall be extended, will be better deduced from the nature of the subject and from the occasion than from any rules that can be given.

---

[7] *Paradise Lost*, I, 589–99.

I am sensible that this idea has met with opposition, and is likely to be rejected by several. But let it be considered that hardly anything can strike the mind with its greatness which does not make some sort of approach towards infinity, which nothing can do whilst we are able to perceive its bounds; but to see an object distinctly and perceive its bounds is one and the same thing. A clear idea is therefore another name for a little idea.

PART III, SECTION XXVII

The Sublime and Beautiful compared

On closing this general view of beauty, it naturally occurs that we should compare it with the sublime, and in this comparison there appears a remarkable contrast. For sublime objects are vast in their dimensions, beautiful ones comparatively small. Beauty should be smooth and polished; the great, rugged and negligent. Beauty should shun the right line, yet deviate from it insensibly; the great in many cases loves the right line, and when it deviates, it often makes a strong deviation. Beauty should not be obscure; the great ought to be dark and gloomy. Beauty should be light and delicate; and great ought to be solid and even massive. They are indeed ideas of a very different nature, one being founded on pain, the other on pleasure; and however they may vary afterwards from the direct nature of their causes, yet these causes keep up an eternal distinction between them, a distinction never to be forgotten by any whose business it is to affect the passions. In the infinite variety of natural combinations, we must expect to find the qualities of things the most remote imaginable from each other united in the same object. We must expect also to find combinations of the same kind in the works of art. But when we consider the power of an object upon our passions, we must know that when anything is intended to affect the mind by the force of some predominant property, the affection produced is like to be the more uniform and perfect if all the other properties or qualities of the object be of the same nature and tending to the same design as the principal.

> *If black and white blend, soften, and unite*
> *A thousand ways, are there no black and white?* [8]

If the qualities of the sublime and beautiful are sometimes found united, does this prove that they are the same; does it prove that they are any way allied; does it prove even that they are not oppo-

---

[8] Pope, *Essay on Man*, II, 213–14.

site and contradictory? Black and white may soften, may blend, but they are not therefore the same. Nor, when they are so softened and blended with each other, or with different colors, is the power of black as black, or of white as white, so strong as when each stands uniform and distinguished.

FROM PART V, SECTION V
Examples that words may affect
without raising images

The truth is, if poetry gives us a noble assemblage of words, corresponding to many noble ideas, which are connected by circumstances of time or place, or related to each other as cause and effect, or associated in any natural way, they may be molded together in any form, and perfectly answer their end. The picturesque connection is not demanded, because no real picture is formed, nor is the effect of the description at all the less upon this account. What is said of Helen by Priam and the old men of his council is generally thought to give us the highest possible idea of that fatal beauty:

> οὐ νέμεσις, Τρῶας καὶ ἐϋκνήμιδας ᾿Αχαιοὺς
> τοιῇδ᾿ ἀμφὶ γυναικὶ πολὺν χρόνον ἄλγεα πάσχειν
> αἰνῶς ἀθανάτῃσι θεῇς εἰς ὦπα ἔοικεν.[9]

> *They cried: no wonder such celestial charms*
> *For nine long years have set the world in arms;*
> *What winning graces! what majestic mien!*
> *She moves a goddess, and she looks a queen.*[1]

Here is not one word said of the particulars of her beauty, nothing which can in the least help us to any precise idea of her person; but yet we are much more touched by this manner of mentioning her than by those long and labored descriptions of Helen, whether handed down by tradition or formed by fancy, which are to be met with in some authors. I am sure it affects me much more than the minute description which Spenser has given of Belphoebe,[2] though I own that there are parts in that description, as there are in all the descriptions of that excellent writer, extremely fine and poetical.

---

[9] *Iliad*, III, 156–58.
[1] Pope's *Iliad*, III, 205–8.
[2] *Faerie Queene*, II, iii, 21–31.

The terrible picture which Lucretius has drawn of religion, in order to display the magnanimity of his philosophical hero in opposing her, is thought to be designed with great boldness and spirit:

> *Humana ante oculos foede cum vita jaceret,*
> *In terris, oppressa gravi sub religione,*
> *Quae caput e caeli regionibus ostendebat*
> *Horribili desuper visu mortalibus instans;*
> *Primus Graius homo mortales tollere contra*
> *Est oculos ausus.*[3]

What idea do you derive from so excellent a picture? None at all most certainly; neither has the poet said a single word which might in the least serve to mark a single limb or feature of the phantom, which he intended to represent in all the horrors imagination can conceive. In reality, poetry and rhetoric do not succeed in exact description so well as painting does; their business is to affect rather by sympathy than imitation, to display rather the effect of things on the mind of the speaker, or of others, than to present a clear idea of the things themselves. This is their most extensive province, and that in which they succeed the best.

PART V, SECTION VI

Poetry not strictly an imitative art

Hence we may observe that poetry, taken in its most general sense, cannot with strict propriety be called an art of imitation. It is indeed an imitation so far as it describes the manners and passions of men which their words can express, where *animi motus effert interprete lingua*.[4] There it is strictly imitation, and all merely *dramatic* poetry is of this sort. But *descriptive* poetry operates chiefly by *substitution*, by the means of sounds, which by custom have the effect of realities. Nothing is an imitation further than as it resembles some other thing, and words undoubtedly have no sort of resemblance to the ideas for which they stand.

---

[3] *De Rerum Natura*, I, 62–67 (misquoted): "When human life lay visibly and foully sick upon the earth, crushed under harsh religion, whose head showed against the heavens with dreadful appearance as it pressed from above on mortal men, a Greek was the first man who dared lift up his mortal eyes against it."

[4] Horace, *Ars Poetica*, 111: "with the tongue as interpreter, it expresses motions of the heart."

How words influence the passions

Now, as words affect not by any original power but by representation, it might be supposed that their influence over the passions
should be but light; yet it is quite otherwise, for we find by experience that eloquence and poetry are as capable, nay indeed much
more capable of making deep and lively impressions than any other
arts, and even than nature itself in very many cases. And this arises
chiefly from these three causes. First, that we take an extraordinary
part in the passions of others, and that we are easily affected and
brought into sympathy by any tokens which are shown of them;
and there are no tokens which can express all the circumstances of
most passions so fully as words; so that if a person speaks upon any
subject, he can not only convey the subject to you, but likewise the
manner in which he is himself affected by it. Certain it is that the
influence of most things on our passions is not so much from the
things themselves as from our opinions concerning them; and these
again depend very much on the opinions of other men, conveyable
for the most part by words only. Secondly, there are many things
of a very affecting nature which can seldom occur in the reality,
but the words which represent them often do; and thus they have
an opportunity of making a deep impression and taking root in the
mind, whilst the idea of the reality was transient and to some perhaps never really occurred in any shape, to whom it is notwithstanding very affecting, as war, death, famine, &c. Besides, many
ideas have never been at all presented to the senses of any men
but by words, as God, angels, devils, heaven and hell, all of which
have however a great influence over the passions. Thirdly, by words
we have it in our power to make such *combinations* as we cannot
possibly do otherwise. By this power of combining we are able, by
the addition of well-chosen circumstances, to give a new life and
force to the simple object. In painting we may represent any fine
figure we please, but we never can give it those enlivening touches
which it may receive from words. To represent an angel in a picture,
you can only draw a beautiful young man winged; but what painting can furnish out any thing so grand as the addition of one word,
"the angel of the *Lord?*" It is true, I have here no clear idea, but
these words affect the mind more than the sensible image did;
which is all I contend for. A picture of Priam dragged to the altar's
foot, and there murdered, if it were well executed, would undoubt-

edly be very moving, but there are very aggravating circumstances which it could never represent.

> *Sanguine foedantem* quos ipse sacraverat *ignes*[5]

As a further instance, let us consider those lines of Milton, where he describes the travels of the fallen angels through their dismal habitation:

> *O'er many a dark and dreary vale*
> *They pass'd, and many a region dolorous;*
> *O'er many a frozen, many a fiery Alp;*
> *Rock, caves, lakes, fens, bogs, dens and shades of death,*
> *A universe of death.*[6]

Here is displayed the force of union in

> *Rocks, caves, lakes, fens, bogs, dens and shades*

which yet would lose the greatest part of their effect if they were not the

> *Rocks, caves, lakes, dens, bogs, fens and shades———*
> *———of death.*

This idea of this affection caused by a word, which nothing but a word could annex to the others, raises a very great degree of the sublime, and this sublime is raised yet higher by what follows, a "universe of death." Here are again two ideas not presentable but by language, and a union of them great and amazing beyond conception, if they may properly be called ideas which present no distinct image to the mind. But still, it will be difficult to conceive how words can move the passions which belong to real objects, without representing these objects clearly. This is difficult to us because we do not sufficiently distinguish, in our observations upon language, between a clear expression and a strong expression. These are frequently confounded with each other, though they are in reality extremely different. The former regards the understanding; the latter belongs to the passions. The one describes a thing as it is; the other describes it as it is felt. Now, as there is a moving tone of voice, an impassioned countenance, an agitated gesture, which affect independently of the things about which they are exerted, so there are words, and certain dispositions of words, which being

---

[5] *Aeneid*, II, 502: "polluting with his blood the altar fires *which he himself had consecrated.*"

[6] *Paradise Lost*, II, 618–22.

peculiarly devoted to passionate subjects, and always used by those who are under the influence of any passion, they touch and move us more than those which far more clearly and distinctly express the subject matter. We yield to sympathy, what we refuse to description. The truth is, all verbal description, merely as naked description, though never so exact, conveys so poor and insufficient an idea of the thing described that it could scarcely have the smallest effect if the speaker did not call in to his aid those modes of speech that mark a strong and lively feeling in himself.

Edward Young

1683–1765

YOUNG BELONGED to the generation of Pope. Yet he lived long enough to see a decline in Pope's reputation and to articulate, however vaguely, some of the values of a new-developing era. Until middle age, he lived at Oxford, studying law and theology, where it is reported—perhaps apocryphally—he wrote in artificially darkened seclusion, in a room lit only by a candle stuck in the eye of a skull. In frequent trips to London and court, he passed as an Augustan man of the town, morally urbane, libertarian, ambitious, a member of Addison's "Little Senate" until the latter's death. He wrote odd pseudo-Elizabethan suicide-tragedies in the early 1720's, followed by *The Love of Fame* (1725–28), heroic-couplet moral essays on worldly vanity, which made his reputation second only to Pope's and preceded Pope in this form of satire. In 1730 he became a country rector, and remained such for the rest of his life. A somber, perhaps neurasthenic ennui and obsession with death was latent in his poetry from the start. In his early sixties, after a life of increasing personal sorrow and disappointed ambition, he wrote *The Complaint; or, Night Thoughts on Life, Death, and Immortality* (1742–46), nine blank-verse outpourings of subjective reflection, world-sorrow, and Christian apologetics, which spread throughout Europe his fame as an original poet. *Conjectures on Original Composition* was written, with "unsteady pen," at the lively old age of seventy-six, partly at the instigation of

Samuel Richardson, the novelist, who was Young's friend and the publisher of *Night Thoughts*. Richardson, also a Protestant apologist, actually wrote some of the paragraphs and encouraged in others a tone of moral squeamishness (apparent in the criticism of Swift) and polemic against tradition (apparent in the criticism of Pope).

The novel, a truly "original" form, as its name suggests, had ambiguous critical status at mid-century, despite Fielding's brave attempt to reconcile it with the neoclassic system, as a comic epic in prose.[1] Aristocratic neoclassicists could doubt its legitimacy or despise its popularity.[2] Both Defoe and Richardson were in turn anti-classical for reasons more religious and sociological than artistic. Young, who greatly admired Richardson's *Clarissa*—"his last amour"—embraced the new form as merely another historic "species of composition." The old man knew nothing from the inside about the art of the novel; he was interested in semi-ethical principles by which to encourage writers of every kind. He praised "original, unindebted energy" wherever he found it, even in medieval schoolmen, Aquinas and Scotus. But if one keeps in mind the outlook of a mid-century novelist like Richardson, the *Conjectures* takes on an extra dimension.

Three other forces in mid-century England converged on Young to enlarge and partially to revolutionize his taste: science, Protestant Christianity, and middle-class democratic feeling. All three strengthened his faith in progress and his belief that human subjectivity, in the race and in the individual, has unimagined bounds and dimensions.

"The arts mechanic are in perpetual progress," he observed, because scientists are "ever endeavoring to go beyond their predecessors." Liberal arts, however, tend unnaturally to stagnate in tradition and timidity. The issue reached back to the quarrel of Ancients and Moderns during the Restoration, and beyond that to Bacon, and of course continues unresolved into the twentieth century. Unlike their counterparts in France, who were more arty and academic, Englishmen since Bacon had quarreled largely on the grounds of science and philosophy vs. older humanistic culture; and among partisans of "new philosophy" pleas for originality, liberty, openness to Nature, had accompanied attacks upon ancient

---

[1] In the preface to *Joseph Andrews*. For critical discussion by Richardson, see in addition to scattered remarks in his correspondence, the prefaces to his novels and the postscript to *Clarissa*.

[2] *Cf.* Hurd, p. 393.

authority and the rules. Dr. Johnson, however, was "surprised to find Young receive as novelties what he thought very common maxims." The antithesis of great-souled invention (originating or discovering the new) to imitation of authors had certainly been a commonplace of criticism since Davenant's Preface to *Gondibert* and the rediscovery of Longinus.[3] And though the terms *original* and *genius* would become "Romantic" shibboleths during the late eighteenth century, both were in common usage much earlier, even during the Restoration.[4]

As a Protestant moralist, Young loved and feared a living God who works an inscrutable, perhaps millennial change in history; and since on Christians is poured "a marvellous light, unenjoyed of old," he speculated that "heaven's latest editions of the human mind may be the most correct and fair; that the day may come when the moderns may proudly look back on the comparative darkness of former ages, on the children of antiquity." Neoclassicism like that of Dryden, Swift, and Pope (two of them Papists after all) figured in his aging eyes as idolatry of tradition, canonization of literary saints. He believed, or came to believe, in radical individuality and the openness of life. Nature "brings us into the world all originals; no two faces, no two minds, are just alike. . . . Born *originals*, how comes it to pass that we die *copies*?" Men during any civilized epoch are, by the justice of Providence, the equals of men during any other, but intimidated by past authority, lacking in full self-knowledge, they neglect their "dormant, unsuspected abilities." Thus genius, more abundant than most people suppose, is lost or undeveloped: it is only a special case, divine in origin, of the individuality given to all, at all times.

"Who hath fathomed the mind of man? Its bounds are as unknown as those of the creation." A further corollary of Young's subjectivism is the irrationality of the creative process. Great poetry, like that of Shakespeare or Pindar, is a kind of "magic"; it originates in passive, spontaneous, and mysterious eruptions of the psyche; it is discovered in the depths of selfhood. An original work "may be said to be of a *vegetable* nature; it rises spontaneously[5]

---

[3] Among predecessors who stated the antithesis in favor of invention or originality could be named Davenant, Hobbes, Cowley, Dryden, Temple, Blackmore, Dennis, Shaftesbury, Addison, and Pope. *Cf.* Addison's *Spectator* No. 160.

[4] *Cf.* Dryden, pp. 93, 105; Dennis, p. 138.

[5] In the preface to *Night Thoughts*, Young describes his poetry, which is full of conceits, hyperboles, and paradoxes, as "what spontaneously rose in the author's mind."

from the vital root of genius; it *grows*, it is not *made*. Imitations
are often a sort of *manufacture,* wrought up by those *mechanics,
art* and *labor,* out of pre-existent materials not their own." The
biological metaphor is significant. To be sure, one should beware
of claiming too much for a metaphor in an essay glittering with
them. Young's ornamental comparison of literature to a pleasure-
garden full of "flowers" is as old as Vida, and had been exploited
to define natural genius by Addison and Pope, among others.
Yet, in its subjectivistic context, it signifies a profound shift of
thought, gradually developing in the eighteenth century, from
mechanistic to organic and vitalistic standards—especially in Germany, where the *Conjectures* was immediately acclaimed.

Young by no means abandoned neoclassicism. Regretting the
imagined loss of what Dryden, Swift, and Pope might have become
if less "imitative" and tradition-conscious, he took for granted
their limited excellence. The *Conjectures* culminates in a panegyric
to Addison,[6] which praises the heroic Christian mildness of his
death, his "intellectual power," and "his sweet, elegant, Virgilian
prose . . . in the taste of the ancients." Addison had written to
posterity, Young believed, "on truly *classic ground.*" Exalting
unfettered genius—blank verse is "verse unfallen, uncurst, verse
reclaimed"—he cautioned nevertheless against failures of literacy
and moral self-discipline in those "automaths, those self-taught
philosophers of our age, who set up genius, and often mere
fancied genius, not only above human learning but divine truth."
He still had, if shakily, a neoclassic habit of letting extremes
criticize one another—genius and learning, art and nature, vegetable and mechanic, ancient and modern, invention (or originality) and imitation. Imitation, he assumed, "must be the lot (and
often an honorable lot it is) of most writers." But even imitative
writers, struggling to keep past standards alive, should seek the
"noble contagion" urged by Longinus, which inspires one to write
"with the spirit and in the taste of the ancients, but not with
their materials." To imitate the *Iliad* is not to imitate Homer.
"He that admires not ancient authors . . . tells the world that he
does not understand them. Let us be as far from neglecting, as
from copying, their admirable compositions. . . . Let our understanding feed on theirs; they afford the noblest nourishment; but
let them nourish, not annihilate our own."

---

[6] Cut from the following selection. His judgment of Pope should be compared with Joseph Warton's (see p. 203). Warton dedicated to Young his
historic *Essay on the Genius and Writings of Pope* (1756), but felt that Young
had gone too far in the *Conjectures.*

All in all, Young had little if anything unprecedented to say. But he spoke from himself. "There is a mine in man, which must be deeply dug ere we can conjecture its contents." Young mined his vein with personal urgency that makes his *Conjectures* a spirited piece of exhortatory criticism, perhaps the most spirited in English before Emerson. He restated freshly, brought up to date, ideas scattered and tentative during the hundred years before.

* * * *

FROM

Conjectures on Original Composition, in a Letter to the Author of Sir Charles Grandison [1759]

I begin with *original* composition,[1] and the more willingly as it seems an original subject to me, who have seen nothing hitherto written on it. But first, a few thoughts on composition in general. Some are of opinion that its growth at present is too luxuriant, and that the press is overcharged.[2] Overcharged, I think, it could never be if none were admitted but such as brought their imprimatur from *sound understanding* and the *public good*. Wit, indeed, however brilliant, should not be permitted to gaze self-enamored on its useless charms in that fountain of fame (if so I may call the press), if beauty is all that it has to boast; but, like the first Brutus,[3] it should sacrifice its most darling offspring to the sacred interests of virtue and real service of mankind.

This restriction allowed, the more composition the better. To men of letters and leisure, it is not only a noble amusement but a sweet refuge; it improves their parts, and promotes their peace. It opens a back door out of the bustle of this busy and idle world into a delicious garden of moral and intellectual fruits and flowers, the key of which is denied to the rest of mankind. When stung

---

[1] Young planned a second letter on "*moral* composition," which was never published. Its substance was probably incorporated in the last half of the *Conjectures.*

[2] overcrowded.

[3] Lucius Junius Brutus (fl. 500 B.C.), founder of the Roman Republic. He condemned to death his two sons when they plotted to restore the monarchy.

with idle anxieties, or teased with fruitless impertinence, or yawning over insipid diversions, then we perceive the blessing of a lettered recess. With what a gust[4] do we retire to our disinterested and immortal friends in our closet, and find our minds, when applied to some favorite theme, as naturally and as easily quieted and refreshed as a peevish child (and peevish children are we all till we fall asleep) when laid to the breast? Our happiness no longer lives on charity, nor bids fair for a fall by leaning on that most precarious and thorny pillow, another's pleasure, for our repose. How independent of the world is he who can daily find new acquaintance that at once entertain and improve him, in the little world, the minute but fruitful creation of his own mind? . . .

The mind of a man of genius is a fertile and pleasant field, pleasant as Elysium and fertile as Tempe; it enjoys a perpetual spring. Of that spring, *originals* are the fairest flowers: *imitations* are of quicker growth but fainter bloom. Imitations are of two kinds, one of nature, one of authors. The first we call *originals*, and confine the term *imitation* to the second. I shall not enter into the curious inquiry of what is or is not, strictly speaking, original, content with what all must allow, that some compositions are more so than others; and the more they are so, I say, the better. Originals are, and ought to be, great favorites, for they are great benefactors; they extend the republic of letters and add a new province to its dominion. Imitators only give us a sort of duplicates of what we had, possibly much better before, increasing the mere drug of books, while all that makes them valuable, *knowledge* and *genius*, are at a stand. The pen of an original writer, like Armida's wand,[5] out of a barren waste calls a blooming spring. Out of that blooming spring an imitator is a transplanter of laurels, which sometimes die on removal, always languish in a foreign soil. . . .

Still farther: an imitator shares his crown, if he has one, with the chosen object of his imitation; an original enjoys an undivided applause. An original may be said to be of a *vegetable* nature; it rises spontaneously from the vital root of genius; it *grows*, it is not *made*. Imitations are often a sort of *manufacture*, wrought up by those *mechanics*, *art* and *labor*, out of pre-existent materials not their own.

Again: we read imitation with somewhat of his languor who

---

[4] gusto.

[5] Armida: a Circean enchantress in Tasso's *Jerusalemme Liberata*, whose garden in cantos xv–xvi is the model for Spenser's bower of Acrasia in *The Faerie Queene*, Book II.

listens to a twice-told tale. Our spirits rouse at an original; that is a perfect stranger, and all throng to learn what news from a foreign land. And though it comes like an Indian prince, adorned with feathers only, having little of weight, yet of our attention it will rob the more solid, if not equally new. Thus every telescope is lifted at a new-discovered star; it makes a hundred astronomers in a moment, and denies equal notice to the sun. But if an original, by being as excellent as new, adds admiration to surprise, then are we at the writer's mercy; on the strong wing of his imagination we are snatched from Britain to Italy, from climate to climate, from pleasure to pleasure; we have no home, no thought, of our own till the magician drops his pen. And then, falling down into ourselves, we awake to flat realities, lamenting the change, like the beggar who dreamt himself a prince.

It is with thoughts as it is with words, and with both as with men: they may grow old and die. Words tarnished by passing through the mouths of the vulgar are laid aside as inelegant and obsolete. So thoughts, when become too common, should lose their currency, and we should send new metal to the mint, that is, new meaning to the press. . . .

But why are originals so few? Not because the writer's harvest is over, the great reapers of antiquity having left nothing to be gleaned after them; nor because the human mind's teeming time is past, or because it is incapable of putting forth unprecedented births; but because illustrious examples *engross*, *prejudice*, and *intimidate*. They *engross* our attention, and so prevent a due inspection of ourselves; they *prejudice* our judgment in favor of their abilities, and so lessen the sense of our own; and they *intimidate* us with the splendor of their renown, and thus under diffidence bury our strength. Nature's impossibilities and those of diffidence lie wide asunder.

Let it not be suspected that I would weakly insinuate anything in favor of the moderns as compared with ancient authors; no, I am lamenting their great inferiority. But I think it is no necessary inferiority, that it is not from divine destination, but from some cause far beneath the moon.[6] I think that human souls, through all periods, are equal. . . .

After all, the first ancients had no merit in being originals. They could *not* be imitators. Modern writers have a *choice* to make, and therefore have a merit in their power. They may soar in the regions of *liberty* or move in the soft fetters of easy *imitation*; and

---

[6] *Cf.* Blackwell, p. 277.

imitation has as many plausible reasons to urge as Pleasure had to offer to Hercules. Hercules made the choice of a hero, and *so* became immortal.[7]

Yet let not assertors of classic excellence imagine that I deny the tribute it so well deserves. He that admires not ancient authors betrays a secret he would conceal, and tells the world that he does not understand them. Let us be as far from neglecting as from copying their admirable compositions. Sacred be their rights, and inviolable their fame. Let our understanding feed on theirs; they afford the noblest nourishment. But let them nourish, not annihilate, our own. When we read, let our imagination kindle at their charms; when we write, let our judgment shut them out of our thoughts; treat even Homer himself as his royal admirer was treated by the cynic:[8] bid him stand aside, nor shade our composition from the beams of our own genius; for nothing original can rise, nothing immortal can ripen, in any other sun.

Must we then, you say, not imitate ancient authors? Imitate them, by all means, but imitate aright. He that imitates the divine *Iliad* does not imitate Homer, but he who takes the same method which Homer took for arriving at a capacity of accomplishing a work so great. Tread in his steps to the sole fountain of immortality; drink where he drank, at the true Helicon, that is, at the breast of nature. Imitate, but imitate not the *composition*, but the *man*. For may not this paradox pass into a maxim? viz. "The less we copy the renowned ancients, we shall resemble them the more."

But possibly you may reply, that you must either imitate Homer or depart from nature. Not so. For suppose you was to change place in time with Homer; then, if you write naturally, you might as well charge Homer with an imitation of you. Can you be said to imitate Homer for writing *so*, as you would have written if Homer had never been? As far as a regard to nature and sound sense will permit a departure from your predecessors, so far, ambitiously, depart from them; the farther from them in *similitude*, the nearer are you to them in *excellence*; you rise by it into an original, become a noble collateral, not a humble descendant from them. Let us build our compositions with the spirit and in the taste of the

---

[7] The allegory of Hercules's choice between Virtue and Pleasure derives from Xenophon, *Memorabilia*, II, i, 21. It was a favorite of Shaftesbury, was retold by Addison, and painted by Reynolds.

[8] Alexander the Great visited Diogenes the Cynic, who was reading, and asked what he could do for him. Diogenes replied: "You can stand out of the sunshine"—that is, "You can get out of my light."

ancients, but not with their materials. Thus will they resemble the structures of Pericles at Athens, which Plutarch commends[9] for having had an air of antiquity as soon as they were built. All eminence and distinction lies out of the beaten road; excursion and deviation are necessary to find it; and the more remote your path from the highway, the more reputable, if like poor Gulliver (of whom anon) you fall not into a ditch[1] in your way to glory.

What glory to come near, what glory to reach, what glory (presumptuous thought) to surpass, our predecessors? And is that then, in nature, absolutely impossible? Or is it not, rather, contrary to nature to fail in it? Nature herself sets the ladder; all wanting is our ambition to climb. For by the bounty of nature we are as strong as our predecessors, and by the favor of time (which is but another round in nature's scale), we stand on higher ground. As to the first, were *they* more than men? or are *we* less? Are not our minds cast in the same mold with those before the Flood? The Flood affected matter; mind escaped. As to the second, though we are moderns, the world is an ancient, more ancient far than when they whom we most admire filled it with their fame. . . . It is by a sort of noble contagion, a general familiarity with their writings, and not by any particular sordid theft, that we can be the better for those who went before us. . . .

A *genius* differs from a *good understanding* as a magician from a good architect; that raises his structure by means invisible; this by the skillful use of common tools. Hence genius has ever been supposed to partake of something divine. *Nemo unquam vir magnus fuit, sine aliquo afflatu divino.*[2]

Learning, destitute of this superior aid, is fond and proud of what has cost it much pains, is a great lover of rules, and boaster of famed examples. As beauties less perfect who owe half their charms to cautious art, learning inveighs against natural unstudied graces and small harmless inaccuracies, and sets rigid bounds to that liberty to which genius owes its supreme glory, but the no-genius its frequent ruin. For unprescribed beauties and unexampled excellence, which are characteristics of *genius*, lie without the pale of *learning's* authorities and laws; which pale, genius must leap to come at them. But by that leap, if genius is wanting, we break our necks; we lose that little credit which possibly we might have enjoyed before. For

---

[9] In the *Life of Pericles*.

[1] The "ditch" of misanthropy and obscenity.

[2] Cicero, *De Natura Deorum*, II, lvi, 167: "No one was ever a great man without some divine inspiration."

rules, like crutches, are a needful aid to the lame, though an impediment to the strong. A Homer casts them away, and like his Achilles,

Jura negat sibi nata, nihil non arrogat,[3]

by native force of mind. There is something in poetry beyond prose-reason; there are mysteries in it not to be explained, but admired, which render mere prose-men infidels to their divinity. . . .

Of genius there are two species, an earlier and a later, or call them *infantine* and *adult*. An adult genius comes out of nature's hand, as Pallas out of Jove's head, at full growth and mature: Shakespeare's genius was of this kind. On the contrary, Swift stumbled at the threshold and set out for distinction on feeble knees. His was an infantine genius, a genius which, like other infants, must be nursed and educated, or it will come to nought. Learning is its nurse and tutor; but this nurse may overlay with an indigested load, which smothers common sense; and this tutor may mislead with pedantic prejudice, which vitiates the best understanding. As too great admirers of the fathers of the church have sometimes set up their authority against the true sense of Scripture; so too great admirers of the classical fathers have sometimes set up their authority or example against reason. . . . I know but one book that can justify our implicit acquiescence in it.[4] And by the way, on that book a noble disdain of undue deference to prior opinion has lately cast, and is still casting, a new and inestimable light. . . .

"But, you say, since originals can arise from genius only, and since genius is so very rare, it is scarce worthwhile to labor a point so much from which we can reasonably expect so little." To show that genius is not so very rare as you imagine, I shall point out strong instances of it in a far distant quarter from that mentioned above. The minds of the schoolmen were almost as much cloistered as their bodies; they had but little learning and few books; yet may the most learned be struck with some astonishment at their so singular natural sagacity and most exquisite edge of thought. Who would expect to find Pindar and Scotus, Shakespeare and Aquinas of the same party? Both equally show an original, unindebted energy: the *vigor igneus* and *caelestis origo*[5] burns in both, and leaves us in doubt whether genius is more evident in the sublime flights

---

[3] Horace, *Ars Poetica*, 122: "denies that laws were made for him; nothing he does not arrogate to himself."

[4] The Bible.

[5] "fiery energy" and "heavenly source."

and beauteous flowers of poetry or in the profound penetrations and marvelously keen and minute distinctions called the thorns of the schools. There might have been more able consuls called from the plow than ever arrived at that honor,[6] Many a genius, probably, there has been which could neither write nor read. So that genius, that supreme lustre of literature, is less rare than you conceive. . . .

But here a caution is necessary against the most fatal of errors in those automaths, those self-taught philosophers of our age, who set up genius, and often mere *fancied* genius, not only above human learning but divine truth. I have called genius wisdom, but let it be remembered that in the most renowned ages of the most refined heathen wisdom (and theirs is not Christian) "the world by wisdom knew not God, and it pleased God by the foolishness of preaching to save those that believed." [7] In the fairyland of fancy, genius may wander wild; there it has a creative power, and may reign arbitrarily over its own empire of chimeras. The wide field of nature also lies open before it, where it may range unconfined, make what discoveries it can, and sport with its infinite objects uncontrolled, as far as visible nature extends, painting them as wantonly as it will. But what painter of the most unbounded and exalted genius can give us the true portrait of a seraph? He can give us only what by his own or others' eyes has been seen, though that indeed infinitely compounded, raised, burlesqued, dishonored, or adorned. In like manner, who can give us divine truth unrevealed? Much less should any presume to set aside divine truth when revealed as incongruous to their own sagacities.—Is this too serious for my subject? I shall be more so before I close. . . .

But farther still: a spirit of imitation hath many ill effects. I shall confine myself to three. First, it deprives the liberal and politer arts of an advantage which the mechanic enjoy. In these, men are ever endeavoring to go beyond their predecessors; in the former, to follow them. And since copies surpass not their originals, as streams rise not higher than their spring, rarely so high, hence while arts mechanic are in perpetual progress and increase, the liberal are in retrogradation and decay. *These* resemble pyramids, are broad at bottom but lessen exceedingly as they rise. *Those* resemble rivers which, from a small fountainhead, are spreading ever wider and wider as they run. Hence it is evident that different portions of

---

[6] Alluding to Lucius Quintius Cincinnatus (c. 519–438 B.C.) who was plowing on his farm when notified of his election to the consulship.
[7] I Corinthians 1:21.

understanding are not (as some imagine) allotted to different periods of time, for we see, in the same period, understanding rising in one set of artists and declining in another. Therefore, nature stands absolved, and our inferiority in composition must be charged on ourselves.

Nay, so far are we from complying with a necessity which nature lays us under, that, secondly, by a spirit of imitation we counteract nature and thwart her design. She brings us into the world all originals. No two faces, no two minds, are just alike, but all bear nature's evident mark of separation on them. Born *originals*, how comes it to pass that we die *copies?* That meddling ape imitation, as soon as we come to years of indiscretion (so let me speak), snatches the pen and blots out nature's mark of separation, cancels her kind intention, destroys all mental individuality; the lettered world no longer consists of singulars: it is a medley, a mass, and a hundred books at bottom are but one. . . .

The third fault to be found with a spirit of imitation is that, with great incongruity, it makes us poor and proud: makes us think little and write much; gives us huge folios which are little better than more reputable cushions to promote our repose. . . .

But notwithstanding these disadvantages of imitation, imitation must be the lot (and often an honorable lot it is) of most writers. If there is a famine of *invention* in the land, like Joseph's brethren we must travel far for food;[8] we must visit the remote and rich ancients; but an inventive genius may safely stay at home; that, like the widow's cruse,[9] is divinely replenished from within, and affords us a miraculous delight. Whether our own genius be such or not, we diligently should inquire, that we may not go a begging with gold in our purse. For there is a mine in man which must be deeply dug ere we can conjecture its contents. Another often sees that in us which we see not ourselves; and may there not be that in us which is unseen by both? . . .

Quite clear of the dispute concerning *ancient and modern learning,* we speak not of performance, but powers. The modern powers are equal to those before them; modern performance in general is deplorably short. . . . Reasons there are why talents may not *appear,* none why they may not *exist,* as much in one period as another. An evocation of vegetable fruits depends on rain, air, and sun; an evocation of the fruits of genius no less depends on externals. What a marvellous crop bore it in Greece and Rome? And

---

[8] See Genesis 42:1.
[9] See I Kings 17.

what a marvellous sunshine did it there enjoy? What encouragement from the nature of their governments and the spirit of their
people? Virgil and Horace owed their divine talents to Heaven,
their immortal works to men; thank Maecenas and Augustus[1] for
them. Had it not been for these, the genius of those poets had lain
buried in their ashes. . . . And has there arisen but one Tully, one
Demosthenes, in so long a course of years? The powerful eloquence
of them both in one stream should never bear me down into the
melancholy persuasion that several have not been born, though they
have not emerged. The sun as much exists in a cloudy day as in a
clear; it is outward, accidental circumstances that with regard to
genius, either in nation or age,

Collectas fugat nubes, solemque reducit.[2]

As great, perhaps greater, than those mentioned (presumptuous
as it may sound) may possibly arise, for who hath fathomed the
mind of man? Its bounds are as unknown as those of the creation,
since the birth of which, perhaps, not one has so far exerted as not
to leave his possibilities beyond his attainments, his powers beyond
his exploits. Forming our judgments altogether by what *has* been
done, without knowing or at all inquiring what possibly *might* have
been done, we naturally enough fall into too mean an opinion of
the human mind. If a sketch of the divine *Iliad*, before Homer
wrote, had been given to mankind by some superior being or otherwise, its execution would probably have appeared beyond the power
of man. Now to surpass it, we think impossible. As the first of these
opinions would evidently have been a mistake, why may not the
second be so too? Both are founded on the same bottom, on our
ignorance of the possible dimensions of the mind of man. . . .
  But here,

Cynthius aurem
  Vellit,[3]

and demands justice for his favorite, and ours.[4] Great things he has
done, but he might have done greater. What a fall is it from Homer's numbers, free as air, lofty and harmonious as the spheres, into
childish shackles and tinkling sounds! But in his fall, he is still great,

---

[1] Their patrons.
[2] Virgil, *Aeneid*, I, 143: "drives away gathered clouds, and brings back the
sun."
[3] Virgil, *Eclogues*, VI, 3–4: "Apollo plucks my ear."
[4] Alexander Pope, who translated the *Iliad*.

> *Nor appears*
> *Less than archangel ruin'd, and the excess*
> *Of glory obscur'd.*[5]

Had Milton never wrote, Pope had been less to blame. But when in Milton's genius, Homer, as it were, personally rose to forbid Britons doing him that ignoble wrong, it is less pardonable, by that *effeminate* decoration, to put Achilles in petticoats a second time. How much nobler had it been if his numbers had rolled on in full flow through the various modulations of *masculine* melody into those grandeurs of solemn sound which are indispensably demanded by the native dignity of heroic song? How much nobler if he had resisted the temptation of that Gothic daemon,[6] which modern poesy tasting became mortal? . . . Harmony as well as eloquence is essential to poesy, and a murder of his music is putting half Homer to death. *Blank* is a term of diminution; what we mean by blank verse is verse unfallen, uncurst, verse reclaimed, reinthroned in the true *language of the gods*, who never thundered nor suffered their Homer to thunder in rhyme. . . .

But supposing Pope's *Iliad* to have been perfect in its kind, yet it is a *translation* still, which differs as much from an original as the moon from the sun.

> *Phoeben alieno jusserat igne*
> *Impleri, solemque suo.*[7]

But as nothing is more easy than to write originally wrong, originals are not here recommended but under the strong guard of my first rule—*Know thyself.* Lucian, who was an original, neglected not this rule if we may judge by his reply to one who took some freedom with him. He was at first an apprentice to a statuary, and when he was reflected on[8] as such by being called Prometheus, he replied: "I am indeed the inventor of new work, the model of which I owe to none, and if I do not execute it well, I deserve to be torn by twelve vultures instead of one."

If so, O Gulliver! dost thou not shudder at thy brother Lucian's vultures hovering o'er thee? Shudder on! They cannot shock thee more than decency has been shocked by thee. How have thy Hou-

---

[5] *Paradise Lost*, I, 592–94.

[6] That is, rhyme.

[7] Claudian, *In Rufinum*, I, 9–10 (misquoted): "He had ordered Phoebe to shine with borrowed fire, the sun with its own."

[8] derided.

yhnhnms thrown thy judgment from its seat and laid thy imagination in the mire? In what ordure hast thou dipt thy pencil? What a monster hast thou made of the

Human face divine? [9]

This writer has so satirized human nature as to give a demonstration in himself that it deserves to be satirized. But, say his wholesale admirers, few could *so* have written; true, and fewer *would*. If it required great abilities to commit the fault, greater still would have saved him from it. . . . He has given us some beauties which deserve all our praise, and our comfort is that his faults will not become common, for none can be guilty of them but who have wit as well as reputation to spare. His wit had been less wild if his temper had not jostled his judgment. If his favorite Houyhnhnms could write, and Swift had been one of them, every horse with him would have been an ass, and he would have written a panegyric on mankind, saddling with much reproach the present heroes of his pen. On the contrary, being born amongst men, and, of consequence, piqued by many and peevish at more, he had blasphemed a nature little lower than that of angels, and assumed [1] by far higher than they. But surely the contempt of the world is not a greater virtue than the contempt of mankind is a vice. Therefore I wonder that, though forborne by others, the laughter-loving Swift was not reproved by the venerable Dean, who could sometimes be very grave.

For I remember, as I and others were taking with him an evening's walk, about a mile out of Dublin he stopped short; we passed on; but perceiving that he did not follow us, I went back, and found him fixed as a statue, and earnestly gazing upward at a noble elm, which in its uppermost branches was much withered and decayed. Pointing at it, he said: "I shall be like that tree, I shall die at top." As in this he seemed to prophesy like the Sybils: if, like one of them, he had burnt part of his works, especially *this* blasted branch of a noble genius, like her too he might have risen in his demand for the rest.

Would not his friend Pope have succeeded better in an *original* attempt? Talents untried are talents unknown. All that I know is that, contrary to these sentiments, he was not only an avowed professor of imitation, but a zealous recommender of it also. . . . His

---

[9] *Paradise Lost*, III, 44. But *cf.* Swift's ironic "A Panegyric on Dean Swift" (1730), 1. 176: "The horse's countenance divine."
[1] acted as if he were.

taste partook the error of his religion; it denied not worship to saints and angels, that is, to writers who, canonized for ages, have received their apotheosis from established and universal fame. True poesy, like true religion, abhors idolatry, and though it honors the memory of the exemplary, and takes them willingly (yet cautiously) as guides in the way to glory, real, though unexampled, excellence is its only aim; nor looks it for any inspiration less than divine.

Though Pope's noble muse may boast her illustrious descent from Homer, Virgil, Horace, yet is an original author more nobly born. As Tacitus says[2] of Curtius Rufus, an original author is born of himself, is his own progenitor, and will probably propagate a numerous offspring of imitators to eternize his glory, while mule-like imitators die without issue. Therefore, though we stand much obliged for his giving us Homer, yet had he doubled our obligation by giving us—a *Pope*. Had he a strong imagination and the true sublime? . . .

Bacon, under the shadow of whose great name I would shelter my present attempt in favor of originals, says: "Men seek not to know their own stock and abilities, but fancy their possessions to be greater, and their abilities less, than they really are." [3] Which is, in effect, saying "that we ought to exert more than we do, and that, on exertion, our probability of success is greater than we conceive." . . .

And why not? For consider, *since* an impartial Providence scatters talents indifferently, as through all orders of persons, so through all periods of time; *since* a marvellous light, unenjoyed of old, is poured on us by revelation, with larger prospects extending our understanding, with brighter objects enriching our imagination, with an inestimable prize setting our passions on fire, thus strengthening every power that enables composition to shine; *since* there has been no fall in man on this side Adam, who left no works, and the works of all other ancients are our auxiliars against themselves, as being perpetual spurs to our ambition, and shining lamps in our path to fame; *since* this world is a school, as well for intellectual as moral advance, and the longer human nature is at school, the better scholar it should be; *since* as the moral world expects its glorious millennium, the world intellectual may hope, by the rules of analogy, for some superior degrees of excellence to crown her later scenes; nor may it only hope, but must enjoy them too, for Tully, Quintilian,

---

[2] *Annals*, XI, xxi, 10–11.
[3] Preface to *The Advancement of Learning*.

and all true critics allow that virtue assists genius, and that the writer will be more able when better is the man—all these particulars, I say, considered, why should it seem altogether impossible that heaven's latest editions of the human mind may be the most correct and fair, that the day may come when the moderns may proudly look back on the comparative darkness of former ages, on the children of antiquity, reputing Homer and Demosthenes as the dawn of divine genius, and Athens as the cradle of infant fame; what a glorious revolution would this make in the rolls of renown?

What a rant, say you, is here? I partly grant it. Yet consider, my friend! knowledge physical, mathematical, moral, and divine increases; all arts and sciences are making considerable advance, with them all the accommodations, ornaments, delights, and glories of human life; and these are new food to the genius of a polite writer; these are as the root, and composition as the flower; and as the root spreads and thrives, shall the flower fail? As well may a flower flourish when the root is dead. It is prudence to read, genius to relish, glory to surpass ancient authors, and wisdom to try our strength in an attempt in which it would be no great dishonor to fail.

Why condemned Maro his admirable epic to the flames? [4] Was it not because his discerning eye saw some length of perfection beyond it? And what he saw, may not others reach? And who bid fairer than our countrymen for that glory? Something new may be expected from *Britons* particularly, who seem not to be more severed from the rest of mankind by the surrounding sea than by the current in their veins, and of whom little more appears to be required in order to give us originals than a consistency of character, and making their compositions of a piece with their lives. May our genius shine and proclaim us in that nobler view!

> . . . *minima contentos nocte Britannos.*[5]

And so it does, for in polite composition, in natural and mathematical knowledge, we have great originals already: Bacon, Boyle, Newton, Shakespeare, Milton, have showed us that all the winds cannot blow the British flag farther than an original spirit can convey the British fame; their names go round the world; and what foreign genius strikes not as they pass? Why should not their posterity embark in the same bold bottom of new enterprise and hope the same

---

[4] According to one story, the dying Virgil desired to burn his *Aeneid* because he had not finished polishing it. At the persuasion of friends, he relented, on condition that it never be published.

[5] Juvenal, *Satires*, II, 161: "Britons content with the shortest possible night."

success? Hope it they may, or you must assert either that those originals which we already enjoy were written by angels or deny that
we are men. As Simonides said to Pausanias, reason should say to
the writer: "Remember thou art a man." And for man not to grasp
at all which is laudable within his reach is a dishonor to human nature, and a disobedience to the divine; for as heaven does nothing
in vain, its gift of talents implies an injunction of their use.

A friend of mine[6] has obeyed that injunction; he has relied on
himself, and with a genius as well *moral* as *original* (to speak in
bold terms) has cast out evil spirits, has made a convert to virtue
of a species of composition[7] once most its foe; as the first Christian
emperors expelled daemons, and dedicated their temples to the living God.

---

[6] Richardson himself.
[7] the novel.

Richard Hurd

1720–1808

THE ORNAMENTAL learning expected of churchmen, their relative leisure and access to libraries, their prominence as teachers, and in some cases their humility of spirit, enabled many to write good criticism.[1] Hurd entered Cambridge at the age of thirteen, and remained there, studying and teaching, more than twenty years. He was a friend of Thomas Gray. At mid-century he took orders, and began his long distinguished climb in the Anglican Church, as university preacher, then rector of Thurcaston, in 1774 Bishop of Lichfield and Coventry, then preceptor to the Prince of Wales, and after 1781 Bishop of Worcester. He declined the Archbishopric, but continued a royal intimate. Old, famous, and full of honors, he became known in end-of-the-century England as the "Beauty of Holiness." Most of his criticism was written before he became bishop.

While a fellow at Cambridge, he earned public attention by his editions, with commentary and notes, of Horace's *Ars Poetica* (1749) and *Epistola ad Augustum* (1751). To the latter he appended a discourse "On Poetical Imitation," in which he argued that since the same realities are "common stock" in human experi-

---

[1] Sprat, Burnet, King, Berkeley, Lowth, Warburton, Butler, Hurd, and Percy were all literary bishops, as Swift and Young aspired to be. Notable critics among rectors, vicars, or ministers were Isaac Watts, Young, Samuel Say, Hutcheson, Blair, Gerard, Campbell, Twining, Alison, Gilpin, among others. Many like Joseph Warton combined ecclesiastical with teaching careers. The same was true in France.

ence—only so much can ever be known—poets should not be accused of plagiarism, any more than scientists are, if they often resemble and "parallel" one another, or even if they borrow "materials of imitation" from one another. Poets of genius, however, will be original in their "manner" of imitation: they will see common reality from unexpected angles and will invent new styles; as common knowledge increases, they will find new uses for it. He had in mind educated poets like Milton, Pope, and Gray. To a second edition (1753) he added a dissertation "On the Provinces of Drama," in which he advocated the Greek chorus, as in *Samson Agonistes*; and for still a third edition (1776) he collected two other separately written pieces, "A Letter to Mr. Mason, on the Marks of Imitation" (1757) and "A Dissertation on the Idea of Universal Poety" (1766). Taken as a loose, growing unit, the four dissertations appended to Horace constitute another neoclassic inquiry into the nature and ends of poetry, academic in tone but no less personal, learnedly open, and compromising. Hurd also edited the *Select Works of Cowley* (1772) with preface and notes—perhaps the earliest anthology of its kind in English—the works of his friend Bishop Warburton (Pope's literary executor), and the works of Addison (published posthumously in 1811). He had a prim, dapper, sometimes insolent style, a liking for Pope and Scriblerian irony. But he was born to an interim generation, loosely including Gray (b. 1716), Joseph Warton (b. 1722) and Thomas Warton (b. 1728), Bishop Percy (b. 1729), even Gibbon (b. 1731); scholarly critics, whose neoclassic standards were half-dissolved in the acids of philosophic empiricism and historical sympathy.

His sense of history emerged [2] in "On the Golden Age of Queen Elizabeth," one of his *Moral and Political Dialogues* (1759). On a trip to the ruins of Kenilworth Castle, where Elizabeth had been feted, the Scriblerian Dr. Arbuthnot, Robert Digby, and Addison discuss Elizabethan manners and poetry. Arbuthnot, Hurd's persona, is made to argue a half-ironic case for nostalgia, against Addison's doubts. "We find in the phraseology and mode of thinking of that time, and of that time only, the essence of the truest and sublimest poetry." In the age of Elizabeth, Arbuthnot continues, masques, pageants, and festivals accustomed people "to animate and impersonate everything." Hence "the picturesque style" of Spenser and Shakespeare.[3] Taste and language flourished at the

---

[2] It was inchoate in his edition of *Ars Poetica:* Hurd argued that Horace's criticism was directed to the Roman stage of his own times.

[3] *Cf.* Whiter, p. 590.

unique moment in history when "the rude essays of uncorrected fancy"—the medieval heritage—coexisted with "the refinements of reason and science"—the modern dawning. Thus the spirit of the Elizabethan age was "romantic" but not barbarous, civilized but not repressed, golden for poetry.[4] In effect, Hurd transferred Blackwell's sociology of the fortunate moment[5] from Homeric Greece to Renaissance Europe. As with most erudite, half-hearted primitivists, even to the present day, to reconcile ancient, pre-logical habits of mind (fancy, imagination) with civilized reason (philosophy) was Hurd's chief critical problem. It pervaded his judgments of what the highest poetry is or should be, what the critic does, and, in this instance, what distinguishes an age congenial to great poetry. It is typical that, in later years, he could admire MacPherson's *Fingal* at the same time that, detecting its classical structure, he pronounced it a forgery.

To explain further, he wrote the famous *Letters on Chivalry and Romance* (1762). Building on hints in Addison's *Spectator* No. 419, he argued that "Gothic barbarism"—feudalism and chivalry of the Middle Ages, which gave birth to "romance"—was a repository of manners uniquely poetical. Its Christianized gallantry, charming faery, horrid fancies of superstition, were more "awakening to the imagination," more "sublime," than the classical barbarism and mythology which preceded Homer.[6] His purpose was not to eulogize the Middle Ages or its romances, which, unlike Thomas Warton and Bishop Percy,[7] he had not read. Nor did he recommend the medieval as a subject for contemporary poems; a point sometimes overlooked by those who have seen Hurd as a rebellious, "pre-Romantic" prophet. His purpose was to state a principle which Addison had not grasped, that manners in one age of history, properly imagined, may be as "natural" as those in any other, and to defend neomedievalism in the epic poetry of Ariosto, Tasso, and English poets under Renaissance Italian influence. To the old complaint against Spenser's irregularity, Hurd argued that the *Faerie Queene*

---

[4] In his *Essay on Dramatic Poetry of the Last Age* (1672) Dryden had alluded contemptuously to "those who call theirs 'the Golden Age of Poetry.' "

[5] See p. 269.

[6] Hurd assumed that the manners painted in Homer are "archetypes" of the barbarity which "actually subsists at this day." *Classic* meant to him that which perpetually tends to recur in nature.

[7] Percy's essay in *Reliques of English Poetry* (1765) first took the romances seriously. Trying to judge their worth by the rules of classical epic, Percy illustrates the aesthetic dilemma of his generation. *Cf.* Addison on "Chevy Chase," *Spectator* Nos. 70 and 74.

has unity if judged not by classical rules, but by its own: it is a "Gothic composition" deliberately, a mode of poetry which flowered from the "natural" manners and beliefs of the age of chivalry, gradually dying at the Renaissance but still in memory. Spenser "chose that the form of his work should be of a piece with his subject." Hurd's further concern, almost a century after Dryden had led the way,[8] was to discredit the doctrine of literal-minded verisimilitude stated by Hobbes. Like Dennis, he distinguished between drama, which is verisimilar, and "sublime" poetry which outstrips nature and justifiably "lies." His *bête noire* was Gallic rationalism "which looks like philosophy and is not," imported into England, he believed, by Davenant, Hobbes, and Rymer, and continued in Hume; even Shaftesbury and Addison had not escaped its "cant." He despised Voltaire, and in correspondence spoke appreciatively, even excitedly, of Rousseau's *Nouvelle Héloise*.

In Letter X he advanced to a defense of "poetical truth"—poetry as "magic," "miracle," and "fable" (myth)—where "experience has less to do than consistent imagination." Perhaps, one may think, Hurd reacted so strongly against "the trite maxim of *following Nature*" as virtually to divorce epic poetry from truth and to define its end as pleasurable escapism. The unexamined premise in Letter X was *imagination*, which continued in Hurd about as Addison, not Dryden, had left it.

Yet, such was his dilemma, the only true criticism, he believed, is the "philosophical" or "scientific." Traditional "rules" may be only classical superstitions; yet "principles" must be established by empirical investigation. Hurd cautiously envisioned a time when poetics might be based on cause-effect principles as systematic and verified as the laws of physical science. The true critic reasons from "sensible effects"—"impression," "sentiment," "feeling" of beauties and flaws in a work—to the "latent causes" which produce them, and thence, by progressively abstract classification, to "first principles" in the nature of poetry itself. Dr. Johnson described him, playfully, as "one of a set of men who account for everything systematically; for instance, it has been a fashion to wear scarlet breeches; these men would tell you that, according to causes and effects, no other wear could at that time have been chosen." Thomas Warton admired him for the same quality,[9] and Hurd referred to

---

[8] "Of Heroic Plays" (1673).

[9] To Hurd, Oct. 22, 1762, on the *Letters on Chivalry:* "I have the vanity to say that I was always of your opinion on this subject. But it was reserved for you to *display the system*, with that penetration, precision, and taste, which it requires, and which you, above all modern critics, so peculiarly possess."

himself as a "system-maker," with detached good humor. In practice, the good bishop-to-be was more deductive than empirical as
he struggled, elegantly, to keep his dilemmas in balance by "the
general dictates of common sense."

After such heady excursions, one may be surprised by the stubborn, if liberal, neoclassicism of "A Dissertation on the Idea of
Universal Poetry" (1766), Hurd's last venture into critical theory
and perhaps his most significant. Here as elsewhere, he had a knack
for pulling together fragmentary insights of many, adding his own,
and making graceful sense. His admiration for "true taste" does not
exclude "Gothic" poetry, though he is led by it to dislike tragicomedy, blank verse, and that popular new monster the novel. Aristotle
in his authority, but so is Bacon: Aristotle's rules apply only to
tragic drama, not to other kinds of poetry, and a new critical inquiry will be necessary for each kind before a complete "art of
poetry" exists. Hurd's main concern is to prepare for such inquiries
by defining poetry as such: "the name of poem will belong to every
composition whose primary end is to *please*, provided it be so constructed as to afford *all* the pleasure which its kind or 'sort' will
permit." The *sine qua non* of specifically poetic pleasure, in all
poems, past or to come, lies in three causes: novel rhythms and
figurative language, fiction, and meter. By disentangling poetic
structure from accessory questions of utility, instruction, or historical
subject-matter, Hurd recovered a more purely Aristotelian approach
than was common at mid-century. His psychologism, derived partly
from Bacon, partly from Longinus, emerges in his defense of fiction:
though fiction may outstrip "nature," it is justified because the aspiring mind of man naturally needs it: it answers a potentiality, it
fulfills the capacity, of mind.

*   *   *   *

FROM

Letters on Chivalry and Romance [1762]

from Letter I

The ages we call barbarous present us with many a subject of curious
speculation. What, for instance, is more remarkable than the Gothic

chivalry? or then the spirit of *romance,* which took its rise from that singular institution?

Nothing in human nature, my dear friend, is without its reasons. The modes and fashions of different times may appear, at first sight, fantastic and unaccountable. But they who look nearly into them discover some latent cause of their production.

> *Nature once known, no prodigies remain,*[1]

as sings our philosophical bard; but to come at this knowledge is the difficulty. Sometimes a close attention to the workings of the human mind is sufficient to lead us to it. Sometimes more than that, the diligent observation of what passes without us, is necessary.

This last I take to be the case here. The prodigies we are now contemplating had their origin in the barbarous ages. Why, then says the fastidious modern, look any farther for the reason? Why not resolve them at once into the usual caprice and absurdity of barbarians?

This, you see, is a short and commodious philosophy. Yet barbarians have their *own,* such as it is, if they are not enlightened by our reason. Shall we then condemn them unheard, or will it not be fair to let them have the telling of their own story?

Would we know from what causes the institution of chivalry was derived? The time of its birth, the situation of the barbarians, amongst whom it arose, must be considered. Their wants, designs, and policies must be explored. We must inquire when and where and how it came to pass that the western world became familiarized to this "prodigy," which we now start at.

Another thing is full as remarkable, and concerns us more nearly. The spirit of chivalry was a fire which soon spent itself; but that of romance, which was kindled at it, burnt long, and continued its light and heat even to the politer ages.

The greatest geniuses of our own and foreign countries, such as Ariosto and Tasso in Italy, and Spenser and Milton in England, were seduced by these barbarities of their forefathers, were even charmed by the Gothic romances. Was this caprice and absurdity in them? Or, may there not be something in the Gothic romance peculiarly suited to the views of a genius, and to the ends of poetry? And may not the philosophic moderns have gone too far, in their perpetual ridicule and contempt of it?

---

[1] Pope, *Moral Essays,* Epistle I, 208.

from Letter VI

Much has been said, and with great truth, of the felicity of Homer's age for poetical manners.[2] But as Homer was a citizen of the world, when he had seen in Greece, on the one hand, the manners he has described, could he, on the other hand, have seen in the west the manners of the feudal ages, I make no doubt but he would certainly have preferred the latter. And the grounds of this preference would, I suppose, have been the improved gallantry of the feudal times and the superior solemnity of their superstitions.

If any great poet, like Homer, had lived amongst, and sung of, the Gothic knights (for after all, Spenser and Tasso came too late, and it was impossible for them to paint truly and perfectly what was no longer seen or believed), this preference, I persuade myself, had been very sensible. But their fortune was not so happy.

> —*omnes illacrymabiles*
> *Urgentur, ignotique longa*
> *Nocte, carent quia vate sacro.*[3]

As it is, we may take a guess of what the subject was capable of affording to real genius from the rude sketches we have of it in the old romancers. And it is but looking into any of them to be convinced that the gallantry, which inspirited the feudal times, was of a nature to furnish the poet with finer scenes and subjects of description, in every view, than the simple and uncontrolled barbarity of the Grecian.

The principal entertainment arising from the delineation of these consists in the exercise of the boisterous passions, which are provoked and kept alive from one end of the *Iliad* to the other, by every imaginable scene of rage, revenge, and slaughter.[4] In the other, together with these, the gentler and more humane affections are awakened in us by the most interesting displays of love and friendship; of love, elevated to its noblest heights; and of friendship, operating on the purest motives. The mere variety of these paintings

---

[2] Hurd alludes to Blackwell's *Inquiry*.

[3] Horace, *Odes*, IV, ix, 26 ff: "All are overwhelmed with the long night of death, unwept and unknown because they lack a sacred bard."

[4] The shocking "spirit of cruelty" in the *Iliad* (remarked by Pope in a note to his translation of IV, 75) helped Christian apologists such as Defoe, Richardson, Hurd, and Young, to disengage their standards from pagan tradition and, on moral grounds, to look for superiority in post-Christian literature.

is a relief to the reader as well as writer. But their beauty, novelty, and pathos give them a vast advantage on the comparison. . . .

As to religious machinery, perhaps the popular system of each was equally remote from reason, yet the latter had something in it more amusing, as well as more awakening to the imagination.

The current popular tales of elves and fairies were even fitter to take the credulous mind, and charm it into a willing admiration of the specious miracles which wayward fancy delights in, than those of the old traditionary rabble of pagan divinities. And then, for the more solemn fancies of witchcraft and incantation, the horrors of the Gothic were above measure striking and terrible. The mummeries of the pagan priests were childish, but the Gothic enchanters shook and alarmed all nature.

We feel this difference very sensibly in reading the ancient and modern poets. You would not compare the Canidia of Horace with the Witches of *Macbeth*. And what are Virgil's myrtles dropping blood, to Tasso's enchanted forest? [5]

Ovid, indeed, who had a fancy turned to romance, makes Medea, in a rant, talk wildly. But was this the common language of their other writers? The enchantress in Virgil says coolly of the very chiefest prodigies of her charms and poisons,

> *His ego saepe lupum fieri, et se condere sylvis*
> *Moerin; saepe animas imis excire sepulchris,*
> *Atque satas alio vidi traducere messes.*[6]

The admirable poet has given an air of the marvellous to his subject by the magic of his expression. Else, what do we find here, but the ordinary effects of melancholy, the vulgar superstition of evoking spirits, and the supposed influence of fascination on the hopes of rural industry? . . .

Shakespeare, on the other hand, with a terrible sublime (which not so much the energy of his genius, as the nature of his subject drew from him) gives us another idea of the "rough magic," as he calls it, of fairy enchantment.

> *I have bedimm'd*
> *The noon-tide sun, call'd forth the mutinous winds,*
> *And 'twixt the green sea and the azure vault*

---

[5] *Aeneid*, III, 23 ff; *Jerusalemme Liberata*, XIII, st. 43 ff.

[6] *Eclogues*, VIII, 97–99: "Often I have seen Moeris become a wolf, and hide himself in the forest, and often I have seen him call forth souls from the depths of the tomb, and I have seen him remove crops from one place to another."

> *Set roaring war; to the dread rattling thunder*
> *Have I giv'n fire, and rifted Jove's stout oak*
> *With his own bolt; the strong-bas'd promontory*
> *Have I made shake, and by the spurs pluck'd up*
> *The pine and cedar, graves, at my command*
> *Have open'd, and let forth their sleepers.*[7]

The last circumstance, you will say, is but the *animas imis excire sepulchris* of the Latin poet. But a very significant word marks the difference. The pagan necromancers had a hundred little tricks by which they pretended to call up the ghosts, or shadows of the dead; but these, in the ideas of paganism, were quite another thing from Shakespeare's "sleepers."

This may serve for a cast of Shakespeare's magic. And I can't but think that when Milton wanted to paint the horrors of that night (one of the noblest parts in his *Paradise Regained*) which the Devil himself is feigned to conjure up in the wilderness, the Gothic language and ideas helped him to work up his tempest with such terror. You will judge from these lines:

> *Nor staid the terror there:*
> *Infernal ghosts and hellish furies round*
> *Environ'd thee; some howl'd, some yell'd, some shriek'd,*
> *Some bent at thee their fiery darts.*

But above all from the following:

> *Thus pass'd the night so foul, till morning fair*
> *Came forth with pilgrim steps in amice gray,*
> *Who with her* radiant finger *still'd the roar*
> *Of thunder, chas'd the clouds, and laid the winds*
> *And* grisly spectres.[8]

Where the "radiant finger" points at the potent wand of the Gothic magicians, which could reduce the calm of nature, upon occasion, as well as disturb it; and the "grisly spectres" laid by the approach of morn were apparently of their raising, as a sagacious critic[9] perceived when he took notice "how very injudicious it was to retail the popular superstition in this place." . . .

We are upon enchanted ground, my friend; and you are to think

---

[7] *The Tempest*, V, i, 41–49.
[8] *Paradise Regained*, IV, 421–30.
[9] Thomas Newton, who edited and annotated Milton's epics (1749). In the next omitted portion, Hurd quotes from Addison's *Spectator* No. 419. His debt to Addison is apparent.

yourself well used that I detain you no longer in this fearful circle. The glimpse you have had of it will help your imagination to conceive the rest. And without more words you will readily apprehend that the fancies of our modern bards are not only more gallant, but, on a change of the scene, more sublime, more terrible, more alarming than those of the classic fablers. In a word, you will find that the manners they paint, and the superstitions they adopt, are the more poetical for being Gothic.

from Letter VIII

When an architect examines a Gothic structure by Grecian rules, he finds nothing but deformity. But the Gothic architecture has its own rules, by which, when it comes to be examined, it is seen to have its merit as well as the Grecian. The question is not which of the two is conducted in the simplest or truest taste, but whether there be not sense and design in both, when scrutinized by the laws on which each is projected.

The same observation holds of the two sorts of poetry. Judge of the *Faerie Queene* by the classic models, and you are shocked with its disorder; consider it with an eye to its Gothic original, and you find it regular. The unity and simplicity of the former are more complete, but the latter has that sort of unity and simplicity which results from its nature.

The *Faerie Queene* then, as a Gothic poem, derives its *method*, as well as the other characters of its composition, from the established modes and ideas of chivalry.

It was usual, in the days of knight-errantry, at the holding of any great feast, for knights to appear before the prince who presided at it, and claim the privilege of being sent on any adventure, to which the solemnity might give occasion. For it was supposed that when such a "throng of knights and barons" [1] as Milton speaks of were got together, the distressed would flock in from all quarters, as to a place where they knew they might find and claim redress for all their grievances.

This was the real practice in the days of pure and ancient chivalry. And an image of this practice was afterwards kept in the castles of the great on any extraordinary festival or solemnity: of which, if you want an instance, I refer you to the description of a feast made at Lisle in 1453 in the court of Philip the Good, Duke of Burgundy, for a crusade against the Turks, as you may find it

---

[1] "L'Allegro," 119.

given at large in the memoirs of Matthieu de Conci, Olivier de la Marche, and Monstrelet.[2]

That feast was held for *twelve* days, and each day was distinguished by the claim and allowance of some adventure.

Now, laying down this practice as a foundation for the poet's design, you will see how properly the *Faerie Queene* is conducted.

"I devise," says the poet himself in his letter to Sir W. Raleigh,[3] "that the Faery Queen kept her annual feast xii days: upon which xii several days the occasions of the xii several adventures happened; which being undertaken by xii several knights, are in these xii books severally handled."

Here you have the poet delivering his own method, and the reason of it. It arose out of the order of his subject. And would you desire a better reason for his choice? . . .

So that if you will say anything against the poet's method, you must say that he should not have chosen this subject. But this objection arises from your classic ideas of unity, which have no place here, and are, in every view, foreign to the purpose if the poet has found means to give his work, though consisting of many parts, the advantage of unity. For in some reasonable sense or other, it is agreed, every work of art must be *one*, the very idea of a work requiring it.

If you ask then, what is this "unity" of Spenser's poem? I say, it consists in the relation of its several adventures to one common original, the appointment of the Faery Queen; and to one common end, the completion of the Faery Queen's injunctions. The knights issued forth on their adventures on the breaking up of this annual feast; and the next annual feast, we are to suppose, is to bring them together again from the achievement of their charges.

This, it is true, is not the classic unity, which consists in the representation of one entire action. But it is a unity of another sort, a unity resulting from the respect which a number of related actions have to one common purpose. In other words, it is a unity of *design*, and not of action.

from Letter X

The only criticism, indeed, that is worth regarding is the philosophical. But there is a sort which looks like philosophy, and is not. May not that be the case here?

---

[2] Fifteenth-century French chroniclers of their own times.
[3] January 23, 1589, appended to most editions of the *Faerie Queene*.

This criticism, whatever name it deserves, supposes that the poets, who are "liars by profession," [4] expect to have their lies believed. Surely they are not so unreasonable. They think it enough, if they can but bring you to *imagine* the possibility of them.

And how small a matter will serve for this? A legend, a tale, a tradition, a rumor, a superstition; in short, any thing is enough to be the basis of their air-formed visions. Does any capable reader trouble himself about the truth, or even the credibility, of their fancies? Alas, no; he is best pleased when he is made to conceive (he minds not by what magic) the existence of such things as his reason tells him did not, and were never likely to, exist. . . .

So little account does this wicked poetry make of philosophical or historical truth: all she allows us to look for is *poetical truth*; a very slender thing indeed, and which the poet's eye, when rolling in its finest frenzy, can just lay hold of. To speak in the philosophic language of Mr. Hobbes: it is something much "beyond the actual bounds, and only within the conceived possibility, of nature." [5]

But the source of bad criticism, as universally of bad philosophy, is the abuse of terms. A poet, they say, must "follow Nature";[6] and by Nature we are to suppose can only be meant the known and experienced course of affairs in this world. Whereas, the poet has a world of his own, where experience has less to do than consistent imagination.

He has, besides, a supernatural world to range in. He has gods, and fairies, and witches at his command: and,

> *O! who can tell*
> *The hidden pow'r of herbes, and might of magic spell?* [7]

Thus in the poet's world all is marvellous and extraordinary; yet not unnatural in one sense, as it agrees to the conceptions that are readily entertained of these magical and wonder-working Natures.

This trite maxim of "following Nature" is further mistaken in applying it indiscriminately to all sorts of poetry.

In those species which have men and manners professedly for their theme, a strict conformity with human nature is reasonably demanded.

---

[4] The phrase is Hume's, *Treatise of Human Nature*, I, iii, 10, who adds: "whatever emotion the poetical enthusiasm may give to the spirits, 'tis still the mere phantom of belief or persuasion."
[5] See *Answer to Davenant*, p. 26.
[6] Pope, *Essay on Criticism*, I, 68.
[7] Spenser, *Faerie Queene*, I, ii, 10.

Non hic Centauros, non Gorgonas, Harpyiasque Invenies:
hominem pagina nostra sapit:[8]

is a proper motto to a book of epigrams, but would make a poor
figure at the head of an epic poem.

Still further, in those species that address themselves to the heart,
and would obtain their end, not through the imagination, but
through the passions, there the liberty of transgressing Nature, I
mean the real powers and properties of human nature, is infinitely
restrained; and poetical truth is, under these circumstances, almost
as severe a thing as historical.

The reason is, we must first *believe*, before we can be affected.

But the case is different with the more sublime and creative
poetry. This species, addressing itself solely or principally to the
imagination (a young and credulous faculty, which loves to admire
and to be deceived) has no need to observe these cautious rules
of credibility so necessary to be followed by him who would touch
the affections and interest the heart.

This difference, you will say, is obvious enough. How came it
then to be overlooked? From another mistake: in extending a particular precept of the drama into a general maxim.

The *incredulus odi*[9] of Horace ran in the heads of these critics,
though his own words confine the observation singly to the stage.

Segnius irritant animos demissa per aurem
Quam quae sunt oculis subjecta fidelibus, et quae
Ipse sibi tradit Spectator.[1]

That which passes in representation and challenges, as it were,
the scrutiny of the eye, must be truth itself, or something very
nearly approaching to it. But what passes in narration, even on the
stage, is admitted without much difficulty:

multaque tolles
Ex oculis, quae mox narret facundia praesens.[2]

In the epic narration, which may be called *absens facundia*,[3] the

---

[8] Martial, *Epigrams*, X, iv, 9–10: "Not here will you find Centaurs, Gorgons
and Harpies: our page presents man."

[9] *Ars Poetica*, 188: "Unbelieving, I am disgusted [by whatever you show me
of this sort"].

[1] *Ibid.*, 180–83: "Things heard stir the mind more sluggishly than things
placed before the trusty eyes, things which the spectator sees for himself."

[2] A continuation of the passage above: "you will keep many things from
sight which in time an actor will narrate eloquently in our presence."

[3] A coinage from Horace's *facundia praesens* in the line just quoted; therefore, "eloquence by an absent narrator."

reason of the thing shows this indulgence to be still greater. It appeals neither to the eye nor the ear, but simply to the *imagination*, and so allows the poet a liberty of multiplying and enlarging his impostures at pleasure, in proportion to the easiness and comprehension of that faculty.

These general reflections hardly require an application to the present subject. The tales of faery are exploded as fantastic and incredible. They would merit this contempt if presented on the stage; I mean, if they were given as the proper subject of dramatic imitation, and the interest of the poet's plot were to be wrought out of the adventures of these marvellous persons. But the epic muse runs no risk in giving way to such fanciful exhibitions.

You may call them, as one does, "extraordinary dreams, such as excellent poets and painters, by being over studious, may have in the beginning of fevers." [4]

The epic poet would acknowledge the charge and even value himself upon it. He would say, "I leave to the sage dramatist the merit of being always broad awake, and always in his senses: the 'divine dream,' [5] and delirious fancy, are among the noblest of my prerogatives." . . .

Thus you see the apology of the Italian poets is easily made on every supposition. But I stick to my point and maintain that the fairy tales of Tasso do him more honor than what are called the more natural, that is, the classical parts of his poem. His imitations of the ancients have indeed their merit, for he was a genius in everything. But they are faint and cold and almost insipid when compared with his original fictions. We make a shift to run over the passages he has copied from Virgil. We are all on fire amidst the magical feats of Ismen and the enchantments of Armida.[6]

Magnanima mensogna, hor quando è il vero
Si bello, che si possa à te preporre? [7]

I speak at least for myself, and must freely own if it were not for these *lies* of Gothic invention, I should scarcely be disposed to give the *Jerusalemme Liberata* a second reading.

I readily agree to the lively observation, "That impenetrable armor, enchanted castles, invulnerable bodies, iron men, flying

---

[4] Davenant, Preface to *Gondibert*, speaking of Spenser's allegory. He had just finished attacking Tasso.

[5] "Θεῖος ὄνειρος. Homer." (Hurd's note.)

[6] Beautiful sorceress who enchants Rinaldo in *Jerusalemme Liberata*.

[7] "Noble lies, when is the truth so beautiful that it can be preferred to you?"

horses, and other such things, are easily feigned by them that dare." [8]
But, with the observer's leave, not so feigned as we find them in the
Italian poets, unless the writer have another quality besides that
of courage.

One thing is true, that the success of these fictions will not be
great when they have no longer any footing in the popular belief; [9]
and the reason is, that readers do not usually do, as they ought, put
themselves in the circumstances of the poet, or rather of those
of whom the poet writes. But this only shows that some ages are
not so fit to write epic poems in as others, not that they should be
otherwise written.

It is also true that writers do not succeed so well in painting
what they have heard as what they believe themselves, or at least
observe in others a facility of believing. [1] And on this account I
would advise no modern poet to revive these fairy tales in an epic
poem. But still, this is nothing to the case in hand, where we are
considering the merit of epic poems written under other circumstances.

The pagan gods and Gothic fairies were equally out of credit
when Milton wrote. He did well therefore to supply their room
with angels and devils. If these too should wear out of the popular
creed (and they seem in a hopeful way, from the liberty some late
critics have taken with them), I know not what other expedients
the epic poet might have recourse to; but this I know, the pomp
of verse, the energy of description, and even the finest moral paintings would stand him in no stead. Without admiration (which
cannot be effected but by the marvellous of celestial intervention—
I mean, the agency of superior natures really existing, or by the illu-
sion of the fancy taken to be so), no epic poem can be long-lived.

I am not afraid to instance in the *Henriade* [2] itself, which, notwithstanding the elegance of the composition, will in a short time
be no more read than the *Gondibert* of Sir W. Davenant, and for
the same reason.

Critics may talk what they will of "truth and nature," and abuse
the Italian poets, as they will, for transgressing both in their incredible fictions. But believe it, my friend, these fictions with which

---

[8] See *Answer to Davenant*, p. 25.

[9] Cf. Dryden, *Author's Apology*, p. 98.

[1] Hurd is adopting the position of Blackwell (see p. 286).

[2] Voltaire's heroic poem celebrating Henry IV and religious toleration. First
published as *La Ligue* (1723), it was banned in France. On his visit to England, Voltaire dedicated it to Queen Caroline with its new title *Henriade*.

they have studied to delude the world are of that kind of creditable deceits, of which a wise ancient pronounces with assurance, "That they who deceive are honester than they who do not deceive; and they who are deceived, wiser than they who are not deceived."

* * * *

FROM *Dissertation I.*
On the Idea of Universal Poetry [1766]

When we speak of poetry as an "art," we mean *such a way or method of treating a subject as is found most pleasing and delightful to us.* In all other kinds of literary composition, pleasure is subordinate to *use;* in poetry only, *pleasure* is the end, to which use itself (however it be, for certain reasons, always pretended) must submit.

This "idea" of the end of poetry is no novel one, but indeed the very same which our great philosopher entertained of it, who gives it as the essential note of this part of learning "that it submits the shows of things to the desires of the mind, whereas reason doth buckle and bow the mind unto the nature of things." [1] For to gratify the desires of the mind is to *please.* Pleasure, then, in the idea of Lord Bacon, is the ultimate and appropriate end of poetry, for the sake of which it accommodates itself to "the desires of the mind," and doth not (as other kinds of writing, which are under the control of reason) "buckle and bow the mind to the nature of things."

But they who like a principle the better for seeing it in Greek may take it in the words of an old philosopher, Eratosthenes,[2] who affirmed ποιητὴν πάντα στοχάζεσθαι ψυχαγωγίας ὃν διδασκαλίας,[3] of which words the definition given above is the translation.

This notion of the end of poetry, if kept steadily in view, will unfold to us all the mysteries of the poetic art. There needs but to

---

[1] Bacon, *Advancement of Learning,* II, iv, 2.

[2] Greek mathematician, philosopher, historian, poet, and critic (c. 275–195 B.C.). Famous for his encyclopedic learning, he became a librarian at Alexandria.

[3] Literally, "that the poet aims entirely at winning over men's souls (seducing them or calling them back from the dead by necromancy) not at instruction."

evolve the philosopher's idea, and to apply it, as occasion serves. The "art of poetry" will be universally *the art of pleasing*, and all its "rules" but so many *means* which experience finds most conducive to that end:

> Sic animis natum inventumque poema juvandis.[4]

Aristotle has delivered and explained these rules so far as they respect one species of poetry, the dramatic, or more properly speaking, the tragic. And when such a writer as he shall do as much by the other species, then, and not till then, a complete "art of poetry" will be formed.

I have not the presumption to think myself in any degree equal to this arduous task. But from the idea of this art, as given above, an ordinary writer may undertake to deduce some general conclusions concerning *universal poetry*, which seem preparatory to those nicer disquisitions concerning its *several sorts or species*.

I. It follows from that "idea" that it should neglect no advantage, that fairly offers itself, of appearing in such dress or mode of language as is most taking and agreeable to us. We may expect then, in the language or style of poetry, a choice of such words as are most sonorous and expressive, and such an arrangement of them as throws the discourse out of the ordinary and common phrase of conversation. Novelty and variety are certain sources of pleasure; a construction of words which is not vulgar is therefore more suited to the ends of poetry than one which we are everyday accustomed to in familiar discourse. Some manners of placing them are, also, more agreeable to the ear than others. Poetry, then, is studious of these, as it would by all means not manifestly absurd give pleasure. And hence a certain musical cadence, or what we call "rhythm," will be affected by the poet.

But of all the means of adorning and enlivening a discourse by words, which are infinite, and perpetually grow upon us, as our knowledge of the tongue in which we write and our skill in adapting it to the ends of poetry increases, there is none that pleases more than figurative expression.

By "figurative expression" I would be understood to mean here that which respects *the pictures or images of things*. And this sort of figurative expression is universally pleasing to us, because it tends to impress on the mind the most distinct and vivid conceptions; and truth of representation being of less account in this way of

---

[4] Horace, *Ars Poetica*, 377: "So a poem, which is born and created *to please the heart*."

composition than the liveliness of it, poetry, as such, will delight in tropes and figures, and those the most strongly and forcibly expressed. And though the application of figures will admit of great variety, according to the nature of the subject, and the management of them must be suited to the taste and apprehension of the people to whom they are addressed, yet, in some way or other, they will find a place in all works of poetry; and they who object to the use of them only show that they are not capable of being pleased by this sort of composition, or do, in effect, interdict the thing itself.

The ancients looked for so much of this force and spirit of expression in whatever they dignified with the name of *poem* that Horace tells us it was made a question by some whether comedy were rightly referred to this class, because it differed only in point of measure from mere prose.

> *Idcirco quidam comoedia necne poema*
> *Esset quaesivere, quod acer spiritus ac vis*
> *Nec verbis nec rebus inest, nisi quod pede certo*
> *Differt sermoni, sermo merus.*[5]

But they might have spared their doubt, or at least have resolved it, if they had considered that comedy adopts as much of this "force and spirit of words" [6] as is consistent with the *nature* and *degree* of that pleasure which it pretends to give. For the name of poem will belong to every composition whose primary end is to *please*, provided it be so constructed as to afford *all* the pleasure which its kind or "sort" will permit.

II. From the idea of the "end" of poetry, it follows that not only figurative and tropical terms will be employed in it, as these, by the images they convey, and by the air of novelty which such indirect ways of speaking carry with them, are found most delightful to us, but also that *fiction*, in the largest sense of the word, is essential to poetry. For its purpose is not to delineate truth simply, but to present it in the most taking forms; not to reflect the real face of things, but to illustrate and adorn it; not to represent the fairest objects only, but to represent them in the fairest lights, and to heighten all their beauties up to the possibility of their natures;

---

[5] *Satires*, I, iv, 45: "As a result, some have questioned whether comedy is poetry; for neither *in its language* nor in its subject matter is it inspired with fire and force, and except that it differs from prose in its regular measure, it is mere prose."

[6] *spiritus ac vis . . . verbis*; in the passage above.

nay, to outstrip nature, and to address itself to our wildest fancy, rather than to our judgment and cooler sense.

> Οὔτ' ἐπιδερκτὰ τά' ἀνράσιν, ὄυτ' ἐπακουστά
> Οὔτε νόῳ περίληπτα,

as sings one of the profession,[7] who seems to have understood his privileges very well.

For there is something in the mind of man, sublime and elevated, which prompts it to overlook all obvious and familiar appearances, and to feign to itself other and more extraordinary; such as correspond to the extent of its own powers, and fill out all the faculties and capacities of our souls. This restless and aspiring disposition, poetry, first and principally, would indulge and flatter, and thence take its name of *divine*, as if some power above human conspired to lift the mind to these exalted conceptions.

Hence it comes to pass that it deals in apostrophes and invocations; that it impersonates the virtues and vices; peoples all creation with new and living forms; calls up infernal spectres to terrify, or brings down celestial natures to astonish, the imagination; assembles, combines, or connects its ideas at pleasure; in short, prefers not only the agreeable and the graceful but, as occasion calls upon her, the vast, the incredible, I had almost said, the impossible, to the obvious truth and nature of things. For all this is but a feeble expression of that magic virtue of poetry which our Shakespeare has so forcibly described in those well-known lines:

> *The poet's eye, in a fine frenzy rolling,*
> *Doth glance from heaven to earth, from earth to heaven;*
> *And, as Imagination bodies forth*
> *The forms of things unknown, the poet's pen*
> *Turns them to shapes, and gives to airy nothing*
> *A local habitation and a name.*[8]

When the received system of manners or religion in any country happens to be so constituted as to suit itself in some degree to this extravagant turn of the human mind, we may expect that poetry will seize it with avidity, will dilate upon it with pleasure, and take a pride to erect its specious wonders on so proper and convenient a ground. Whence it cannot seem strange that, of all the forms in which poetry has appeared, that of pagan fable and Gothic romance

---

[7] "Empedocles. See Plutarch, Vol. I, p. 15, par. 1624." (Hurd's note.) "Things neither beheld nor listened to by men, nor comprehended by the prudent mind."

[8] *A Midsummer Night's Dream*, V, i, 12–17.

should, in their turns, be found the most alluring to the true poet. For, in defect of these advantages, he will ever adventure, in some sort, to supply their place with others of his own invention; that is, he will mold every system, and convert every subject, into the most amazing and miraculous form.[9] . . .

III. It follows from the same idea of the "end" which poetry would accomplish that not only rhythm but *numbers*, properly so called, is essential to it. . . .

Even the prose writer (when the art is enough advanced to produce prose), having been accustomed to have his ear consulted and gratified by the poet, catches insensibly the same harmonious affection, tunes his sentences and periods to some agreement with song, and transfers into his coolest narrative, or gravest instruction, something of that music with which his ear vibrates from poetic impressions.

In short, he leaves measured and determinate numbers, that is, *meter*, to the poet, who is to please up to the height of his faculties and the nature of his work; and only reserves to himself, whose purpose of giving pleasure is subordinate to another end, the looser musical measure, or what we call "rhythmical prose."

The reason appears from this deduction why *all* poetry aspires to please by melodious numbers. To *some* species it is thought more essential than to others because those species continue to be sung, that is, are more immediately addressed to the ear, and because they continue to be sung in concert with musical instruments, by which the ear is still more indulged. It happened in ancient Greece that even tragedy retained this accompaniment of musical instruments through all its stages, and even in its most improved state. Whence Aristotle includes *music*, properly so called, as well as rhythm and meter, in his idea of the tragic poem. He did this because he found the drama of his country *omnibus numeris absolutum*,[1] I mean in possession of all the advantages which could result from the union of rhythmical, metrical, and musical sounds. Modern tragedy has relinquished part of these; yet still, if it be true that this poem be more pleasing by the addition of the musical art, and there be nothing in the nature of the composition which forbids the use of it, I know not why Aristotle's idea should not be adopted, and his precept become a standing law of the tragic stage.[2] For this,

---

[9] Hurd seems to say that a poet may create his own myths.

[1] "perfected in all numbers."

[2] Hurd probably has the Greek chorus in mind, though the latitude of his expression could justify the use of music in any drama, Elizabethan tragedy or modern movie.

as every other poem, being calculated and designed properly and ultimately to *please*, whatever contributes to produce that end most perfectly, all circumstances taken into the account, must be thought of the nature or essence of the kind. . . .

These reflections will afford a proper solution of that question which has been agitated by the critics, whether a work of fiction and imagination (such as that of the Archbishop of Cambray,[3] for instance), conducted in other respects according to the rules of the epic poem, but written in prose, may deserve the name of *poem* or not. For though it be frivolous indeed to dispute about names, yet from what has been said, it appears that if meter be not incongruous to the nature of an epic composition, and it afford a pleasure which is not to be found in mere prose, meter is, for that reason, essential to this mode of writing; which is only saying in other words that an epic composition, to give all the pleasure which it is capable of giving, must be written in *verse*.

But secondly, this conclusion, I think, extends farther than to such works as aspire to the name of "epic." For instance, what are we to think of those "novels" or "romances," as they are called, that is, fables constructed on some private and familiar subject, which have been so current of late through all Europe? As they propose pleasure for their end, and prosecute it, besides, in the way of fiction, though without metrical numbers, and generally, indeed, in harsh and rugged prose, one easily sees what their pretensions are, and under what idea they are ambitious to be received. Yet, as they are wholly destitute of measured sounds (to say nothing of their other numberless defects), they can at most be considered but as hasty, imperfect, and abortive poems; whether spawned from the dramatic or narrative species, it may be hard to say.

> *Unfinished things, one knows not what to call,*
> *Their generation's so equivocal.*[4]

However, such as they are, these "novelties" have been generally well received: some for the real merit of their execution, others for their amusing subjects, *all* of them for the gratification they afford, or promise at least, to a vitiated, palled, and sickly imagination—that last disease of learned minds, and sure prognostic of expiring letters. But whatever may be the temporary success of

---

[3] François de Salignac de la Mothe Fénelon (1651–1715). His long allegory in narrative prose *Les Aventures de Télémaque* (1699) was defended by Fielding in the Preface to *Joseph Andrews* as "of the epic kind."

[4] Pope, *Essay on Criticism*, I, 42–43.

these things (for they vanish as fast as they are produced, and are produced as soon as they are conceived), good sense will acknowledge no work of art but such as is composed according to the laws of its kind. These "kinds," as arbitrary things as we account them (for I neither forget nor dispute what our best philosophy teaches concerning kinds and sorts), have yet so far their foundation in nature and the reason of things that it will not be allowed us to multiply or vary them at pleasure. We may, indeed, mix and confound them if we will (for there is a sort of literary luxury which would engross all pleasures at once, even such as are contradictory to each other), or, in our rage for incessant gratification, we may take up with half-formed pleasures, such as come first to hand and may be administered by anybody; but true taste requires chaste, severe, and simple pleasures, and true genius will only be concerned in administering such. . . .

In short, no method of gratifying the ear by *measured sound*, which experience has found pleasing, is to be neglected by the poet; and although from the different structure and genius of languages, these methods will be different, the studious application of such methods as each particular language allows becomes a necessary part of his office. He will only cultivate those methods most which tend to produce, in a given language, the most harmonious structure or measure of which it is capable.

Hence it comes to pass that the poetry of some modern languages cannot so much as subsist without rhyme; in others, it is only embellished by it. . . .

In the latter class of languages, whose poetry is only embellished by the use of rhyme, we may reckon the Italian and the English, which, being naturally more tuneful and harmonious than the French, may afford all the melody of sound which is expected in some sorts of poetry by its varied pause and quantity only; while in other sorts, which are more solicitous to please the ear, and where such solicitude, if taken notice of by the reader or hearer, is not resented, it may be proper, or rather it becomes a law of the English and Italian poetry, to adopt rhyme. Thus, our tragedies are usually composed in blank verse, but our epic and lyric compositions are found most pleasing when clothed in rhyme. Milton, I know it will be said, is an exception. But if we set aside some learned persons, who have suffered themselves to be too easily prejudiced by their admiration of the Greek and Latin languages, and still more perhaps by the prevailing notion of the monkish or Gothic original of rhymed verse, all other readers, if left to themselves, would, I dare say, be more delighted with this poet if, besides his various pause and measured quantity, he had enriched his numbers with rhyme. So that his love of liberty, the ruling passion of his heart, perhaps transported him too far when he chose to follow the example set him by one or two writers of "prime note" [5] (to use his own eulogium) rather than comply with the regular and prevailing practice of his favored Italy, which first and principally, as our best rhymist sings,

> *With pauses, cadence, and well-vowell'd words,*
> *And all the graces a good ear affords,*
> Made rhyme an art.[6]

Our comedy, indeed, is generally written in prose, but through the idleness or ill taste of our writers rather than from any other just cause. For though rhyme be not necessary, or rather would be improper in the comedy of our language, which can support itself in poetic numbers without the diligence of rhyme, yet some sort of meter is requisite in this humbler species of poem; otherwise it will not contribute all that is within its power and province to *please*. And the particular meter proper for this species is not far to seek. For it can plainly be no other than a careless and looser iambic, such as our language naturally runs into, even in conversation, and of which we are not without examples in our old and best writers for the comic stage. But it is not wonderful that those critics who take offense at English epic poems in rhyme, because the Greek and Latin only observed quantity, should require English comedies to be written in prose, though the Greek and Latin comedies were composed in verse. For the ill application of examples, and the neglect of them, may be well enough expected from the same men, since it does not appear that their judgment was employed, or the reason of the thing attended to, in either instance.

And thus much for the idea of universal poetry. It is the art of treating any subject in such a way as is found most delightful to us, that is, *in an ornamented and numerous style—in the way of fiction—and in verse*. Whatever deserves the name of *poem* must unite these three properties, only in different degrees of each, according to its nature. For the art of every "kind" of poetry is only this general art so modified as the *nature* of each, that is, its

---

[5] Preface to *Paradise Lost* (1668).
[6] Dryden, "To the Earl of Roscommon, on His Excellent Essay on Translated Verse," ll. 17–19.

more immediate and subordinate end, may respectively require.

We are now, then, at the wellhead of the poetic art; and they who drink deeply of this spring will be best qualified to perform the rest. But all heads are not equal to these copious draughts; and besides, I hear the sober reader admonishing me long since—

> Lusisti satis atque bibisti;
> Tempus abire tibi est, ne potum largius aequo
> Rideat et pulset lasciva decentius aetas.[7]

---

[7] Horace, *Epistles*, II, ii, 214: "You have played enough and *drunk* enough. It is time to leave, *having drunk so liberally*, lest *youth*, more gracefully wanton, should ridicule you and push you aside."

Samuel Johnson

1709–1784

THE SON of a poor small-town bookseller, Johnson attended Oxford briefly, then in 1737 came to London, where he survived by hack writing and odd jobs. The celebrated "Dr. Johnson" of Boswell's *Life* had acted and suffered fifty-four years before Boswell met him. From poverty of the bitterest sort, he rose to fame very slowly, against depressing odds. He learned realism from his own self-conquests and from the streets, and he always valued poets like Shakespeare who "caught his ideas from the living world," and like Samuel Butler who "had not suffered life to glide beside him unseen or unobserved." His critical genius is evident from the start, even in miscellaneous hired tracts, not to mention the great *Life of Savage* (1744). But it was after his success with *The Rambler* (1750–52), a periodical in the *Spectator* tradition, that his genius ripened. In subsequent works such as the *Dictionary* and its preface (1755), *The Idler* (1758–60), the philosophical romance *Rasselas* (1759), the edition of Shakespeare with its preface and notes (1765), the *Journey to the Western Isles of Scotland* (1775), and *Lives of the Poets* (1779–81), Johnson achieved the most vivid apology for neoclassic tradition since Dryden, perhaps the most vivid in English, and almost the last. Like Dryden, "the father of English criticism," he was practical and miscellaneous: his thought rose to generality in an experienced context, but deliberately resisted flight into system. He turned good-humored scorn on critics who "pry into worlds of conjecture" but are "totally blind to all that lies immediately before them." All that he thought is only to be gathered from all that he wrote, and from the massive records of his conversation preserved by Boswell, Mrs. Thrale, and other friends in his circle.

The most abstract premise in his criticism is a Neo-Platonist ideal nature—the realm of transcendent and timeless "ends" in which everything participates and toward which it moves when all its potentialities are being "perfected" as rationally and harmoniously as possible. Its opposite is particularity, irrational, fragmentary, and perishing. But as Johnson knew only too well, abstract perfection is impossible. Particulars are real, and nature cannot be realized apart from them. Hence, his practical or working premise is *general* nature—that which develops a particular (common reality, familiar life) as far as it can go in the direction of the ideal without ceasing to be itself. Art imitates nature by an act of "realizing imagination," or, if you wish, by "generalizing" particular realities. In either case (and there is a difference) nature is a standard not for escaping particulars, but for rising through them and by means of them to permanences. Unless the distinction is remembered, one may misunderstand Johnson's various strictures against *excessive* particularity in art: he disvalues the perishable and fragmentary, not the particular as such.

The "end" of literature is "to instruct by pleasing"; to energize knowledge of what is ideal and permanent by all the various means that artists can invent or imagine. But of course, particular works of art will be only more and less successful. The "end" of criticism is to explain the principles of relative success and failure, and to heighten consciousness of what is most nearly complete and enduring—"classic" in the large sense—as it is really to be found and enjoyed by particular readers in particular works produced by particular writers. Johnson is realistic. He does not say that nature will please all readers at all times, or that only nature will please: he knows that everyone, including himself, will take what pleasure he can wherever he can find it, because of "that hunger of imagination which preys incessantly upon life and must be always appeased by some employment." Particular readers in real life are more or less submerged at any given moment in custom, fashion, prejudice, opinion, caprice, vanity, or accident; and their human need for "pleasure"—for happiness or self-enhancement—drives them from one real or imagined novelty to the next, in literature as in all else. What he says, however, is that "nothing can *please many and please long* but just representations of general nature . . . the mind can only *repose* on the stability of truth."

The standard of nature, so understood, touches every dimension of his criticism. Ideally, he wrote in *Rasselas* chapter 10, the poet will "divest himself of the prejudices of his age and country . . . and rise to general and transcendental truths, which will always be the same. . . . He must write as the interpreter of nature and the legislator of mankind, and consider himself as presiding over the thoughts and manners of future generations." Shakespeare, "the poet of nature," probably comes closer than anyone else to realizing Johnson's ideal. His characters "are the genuine progeny of common humanity, such as the world will always supply and observation will always find. His persons act and speak by the influence of those general passions and principles by which all minds are agitated and the whole system of life is continued in motion." Homer, also, wrote "with very little dependence on local or contemporary customs." Yet, chapter 10 of *Rasselas* should be quoted alongside the opening paragraph of chapter 11, in which Johnson playfully undercuts his own noble idealism. In practice, he is willing to be pleased with much less: a catholic range of "thinking" and educated poets who exercise the wits and "bring realities to mind."

His ideal standard includes the *consensus gentium* or test of time, which implies an established tradition of classics. Works of literary art must be "estimated by their proportion to the general and collective ability of man, as it is discovered in a long succession of endeavors." They are proved "adequate to human faculties" by surviving changes of custom and fashion; their success in imitating nature is judged, in the final appeal, by the agreement of mankind in various nations and ages. Yet they are read, enjoyed or tossed aside, by particular *men*. "That book is good in vain which the reader throws away." Johnson perceived the test ongoing in familiar life, day by day, in "the common sense of readers uncorrupted with literary prejudices." The consensus continues to form itself "by the emulous diligence of contemporary students and the gradual discoveries of one age improving on another." Tradition is progressively open, because humanity's experience of nature is open. Works of literature appeal "wholly to observation and experience"; they are "tentative and experimental"; their excellence is "gradual and comparative." They belong to everybody, not just an elite. The good critic is only the common reader with greater sagacity, learning, and leisure, who tries to be useful by disentangling principles, not as ends in themselves but as means to insight:

> The eye of the intellect, like that of the body, is not equally perfect in all, nor equally adapted in any to all objects; the end of criticism is to supply its defects; rules are the instruments of mental vision.

Excellence, he once remarked, is that "with which the vulgar were pleased, and of which the learned could tell why it pleased."

In style he valued generality, a "simplicity of grandeur which fills the imagination" and has a "general power of gratifying every mind by recalling its conceptions." Yet he regretted a "perpetual tumor of phrase" in his own age—false generality—and he understood, as Addison had not, that "poetry cannot be translated." [1] The metaphysical poets, he observed, "were always analytic: they broke every image into fragments"; they "labored particularities" and never "attempted that comprehension and expanse of thought which at once fills the whole mind, and of which the first effect is sudden astonishment, and the second rational admiration." Yet, in the *Life of Cowley* he defined metaphysical wit almost for the first time and restored metaphysical poets to the English tradition. In his preface to the *Dictionary* he grasped the historical, assimilative, and changing character of English language—its rootedness in the particular; yet, at the same time, he perceived normative values within it: Shakespeare's comic dialogue fulfills the general nature of English. Spenserian stanza, sonnet, Pindaric ode, Gallicisms in Dryden, Latin pedantry in Milton, all deviate from naturalness.

A similar dual vision informs his discussion of individual artists and single works of art. Like other neoclassicists, Johnson maneuvers his way to judgments by observing the complex, relative balance of opposite qualities, such as knowledge and imagination —"imagination is useless without knowledge"—uniformity and variety, reason and emotion, the familiar and the wonderful, reality and fiction, learning and invention. The more nearly it approaches the ideal, the more a particular work will have developed through all such tensions into the fully realized harmony or "decorum" which belongs to it. Some tensions emerge from the duality of nature as both particular and ideal; others from the difference between art and the nature which it imitates. For example, one requisite of artistic pleasure is imaginative novelty. Hence John-

---

[1] Boswell's *Life*, ed. G. B. Hill (Oxford, 1934), III, 36.

son's definition of wit as that which "is at once natural and new; that which, though not obvious, is upon its first production acknowledged to be just. . . . that which he that never found it wonders how he missed." In Pope's *Rape of the Lock* "are exhibited in a very high degree the two most engaging powers of an author: new things are made familiar, and familiar things are made new." Shakespeare "approximates the remote and familiarizes the wonderful." A perceived disbalance between nature and novelty underlies much of his adverse criticism, when it is adverse, of Cowley, Butler, Milton, Gray, and Collins. In the *Life of Cowley*, Johnson's main objection to "metaphysical wit" is its failure, in many different ways, to resolve its implicit tensions and therefore to near the ideal completion of decorum.

His relation to neoclassic criticism, then, was complex, testing, and individualistic. "It ought to be the first endeavor of a writer to distinguish nature from custom, or that which is established because it is right from that which is right only because it is established." The task of criticism is "to establish principles," but "there is always an appeal open from criticism to nature." Again and again, he attacked "the cant of those who judge by principles rather than perception"—the most hilarious example being Dick Minim in *The Idler* nos. 60 and 61 who, perceiving nothing, masters all the neoclassical cliches and several new ones. There are three kinds of critics, Johnson once remarked, to Fanny Burney:

> The first are those who know no rules, but pronounce entirely from their natural taste and feelings; the second are those who know and judge by rules; and the third are those who know but are above the rules. These last are those you should wish to satisfy. Next to them rate the natural judges; but ever despise those opinions that are formed by the rules.[2]

In the Preface to Shakespeare he demolished the unities of time and place, defended tragicomedy, and attacked critics like Rymer and Voltaire who would enforce petty decorums, as in *Rambler* 156 he attacked "the arbitrary edicts of legislators, authorized only by themselves, who, out of various means by which the same end may be attained, selected such as happened to occur to their reflection, and then . . . prohibited new experiments of wit." In *Rambler* 4 he defended the new realistic novel and tried to work

---

[2] *Diary and Letters of Madame D'Arblay*, ed. Dobson (London, 1904), I, 183.

out a moral basis for it. Art and nature "have stores inexhaustible by human intellects," he argued in no. 121, because "imagination" is always pushing into "the boundless regions of possibility." Like Young, he repeatedly disdained "imitation" of authors, though he made common-sense allowances. "The highest praise of genius is original invention." Even *Paradise Lost*, which "with respect to design, may claim the first place . . . among the productions of the human mind," is not the greatest epic "because it is not the first." In *Rambler* 36 and 37 he blasted imitative conventionalities which had crept into pastoral, such as mythological allusion, rustic and archaic diction, setting in a golden age, ecclesiastical satire; and he argued that Virgil had understood the form more simply and realistically as "a poem in which any action or passion is represented by its effects upon a country life." The attack is typical in its trying to bypass "neoclassic" rules and recover more general and "classic" understanding, and in its urging modern poets to look at the real world freshly. "No man ever yet became great by imitation." In *Rambler* 125 he doubted the purity of any genre as such because "every genius produces some innovation which, once invented and approved, subverts the rules which the practice of foregoing authors had established." Shakespeare's plays, he would later argue, though "classic" in the large sense, are neither comedies nor tragedies, but "compositions of a distinct kind."

Johnson shared many preoccupations of the new mid-century criticism, though his relation to it, as to neoclassic tradition, was individualistic and complex. Like Hurd and Thomas Warton, he saw the relevance of historical learning to literary judgment; for example, with knowledge of seventeenth-century Puritanism, Butler's *Hudibras* becomes more valuable. As early as 1745 Johnson related the witches in *Macbeth* to sixteenth-century beliefs. His notes to the edition of Shakespeare draw on a wide range of learning. "Every man's performances, to be rightly estimated, must be compared with the state of the age in which he lived and with his own particular opportunities." Yet, historic particularity is a "perishable part" which only uncommon readers will bother to learn, and, once learned, it will be forgotten. He inquired into technicalities of the poetic process, in Pope's *Iliad*, in Milton's prosody (*Rambler* 86, 88, and 90). "When any work has been viewed and admired, the first question of intelligent curiosity is, how was it performed?" However, "it is not by comparing line with line that the merit of great works is to be estimated, but by their general effect and ultimate result." On the whole, like many other English critics at mid-century, he shifted the basis of criticism from authority to "philosophical" inquiry, from iteration of rules to study of the human mind and present experience. He perceived that, since the time of Hobbes, a developing fashion had been "to analyze the mind, to trace the passions to their sources, to unfold the seminal principles of vice and virtue, or sound the depths of the heart for the motives of actions"—in short, to psychologize, to attempt a "science of mind." Though he had misgivings about the fashion as such, as about criticism as such, he exploited its lights, without at all rejecting age-old alternatives. In 1769 he remarked of Lord Kames:

> the Scotchman has taken the right method in his *Elements of Criticism*. I do not mean that he has taught us anything, but he has told us old things in a new way. . . . We have an example of true criticism in Burke's *Essay on the Sublime and Beautiful*. . . . There is no great merit in telling how many plays have ghosts in them and how this ghost is better than that. You must show how terror is impressed on the human heart.[3]

Some of his borrowings from Burke are duly footnoted. Johnson had no scientific pretensions, however, and no interest in producing treatises like those of Kames and Burke. As a practical critic, he assumed the limits of individual intellect in a naked inquiry based on necessarily limited experience. As he forced neoclassic tradition to prove itself by experience, so he appealed beyond particular to general human experience as embodied in tradition. He conceived criticism as an ongoing, cooperative enterprise spanning centuries, "the collective labor of a thousand intellects." One of his many projected but unwritten books, according to Boswell,[4] was a "History of Criticism, as it relates to judging of authors, from Aristotle to the present age. An account of the rise and improvement of that art; of the different opinions of authors, ancient and modern"—a project put into print by no one, as Professor Bate points out, until late in the nineteenth century.

Nevertheless, the new psychologism, analyzing the mind and judging literature by its "effects" in real experience, undoubtedly freed his thought from rigidities and, in many various ways, en-

---

[3] Boswell's *Life*, II, 87–90.
[4] *Ibid.*, IV, 381.

larged his range of concern. It loosened up his restatement of neoclassicism. The brilliant impressionism in *Lives of the Poets* has a precedent in Dryden, but on so large a scale it is hardly conceivable apart from judgment by "effects"—a care for articulating the "feel" of things. The subtle relations of biography and art, as most brilliantly in the *Life of Pope*, depend, at least in part, on a psychological premise, that the value of a literary work may be increased by knowing psychic drives in its author and the circumstances of his life which called them forth. On the premise of general nature, Johnson evolved a new analytic biography, which probes the "real character" of a writer, his vital inwardness, with unprecedented depth. "The pathetic," the power of literature "in representing and moving the affections," is no less a traditional expectation of literature. It would never have occurred to Johnson, or perhaps any other English neoclassicist, that literature, or the judgment of it, could be divorced from the "heart"—imaginatively dominated emotion and feeling, response to beauty—any more than it could be divorced from reason or any other energy of the human mind. Failure to engage "sympathy" is part of his complaint against the metaphysical poets, *Lycidas*, and the burlesque mode of Butler. The decorum of a literary work requires that it harmonize all mental energies, in a proper order of subordination.

Finally, and most important of all, the new fashion of analyzing the mind helped Johnson to explore, more shrewdly than any other critic in modern times, the moral basis of neoclassicism. To discern where his literary criticism begins and his analysis of the human condition leaves off is almost impossible: each implicates the other. He approached literature as a worldly, practical human activity, a branch of "moral" learning, in which aesthetic or technical questions are implicit but secondary. By philosophical inquiry he meant largely "moral" inquiry, inquiry into the human as such and the ends of living. At their best, his judgments glow with freshly encountered and understood human experience; they energize and cleanse; and hence they are often less valuable for their documentation of eighteenth-century taste or belief than for their illumination of motives which still govern men in the living world—a still-existing human center, in literature, life, and the life of literature. Even at his worst, when he is aggressively moralistic, cranky, or dead wrong, when he is arguing for victory or merely teasing, he has such analytic power and such humanity that he instructs about *something*. And as a rule it is something worth keeping in mind: his remarks have had a way of waking up in later experience and in the later history of criticism, of slamming home with general wisdom.

* * * *

FROM

The Rambler [1750–1752]

--◦⊰⧉⊱◦--

No. 4, Saturday, March 31, 1750

Simul et jucunda et idonea dicere vitae.
—Hor. [*Ars. Poet.*, 334.]

And join both profit and delight in one.
—Creech.

The works of fiction with which the present generation seems more particularly delighted are such as exhibit life in its true state, diversified only by accidents that daily happen in the world, and influenced by passions and qualities which are really to be found in conversing with mankind.

This kind of writing may be termed not improperly the comedy of romance,[1] and is to be conducted nearly by the rules of comic poetry. Its province is to bring about natural events by easy means, and to keep up curiosity without the help of wonder. It is therefore precluded from the machines and expedients of the heroic romance, and can neither employ giants to snatch away a lady from the nuptial rites, nor knights to bring her back from captivity; it can neither bewilder its personages in deserts, nor lodge them in imaginary castles.

I remember a remark made by Scaliger[2] upon Pontanus, that all his writings are filled with the same images, and that if you take from him his lilies and his roses, his satyrs and his dryads, he will have nothing left that can be called poetry. In like manner almost all the fictions of the last age will vanish if you deprive them of a hermit and a wood, a battle and a shipwreck.

Why this wild strain of imagination found reception so long

---

[1] *Cf.* Fielding, Preface to *Joseph Andrews.*
[2] Probably *Poetics*, VI, 4.

in polite and learned ages, it is not easy to conceive; but we cannot wonder that while readers could be procured, the authors were willing to continue it; for when a man had by practice gained some fluency of language, he had no further care than to retire to his closet, let loose his invention, and heat his mind with incredibilities; a book was thus produced without fear of criticism, without the toil of study, without knowledge of nature or acquaintance with life.

The task of our present writers is very different; it requires, together with that learning which is to be gained from books, that experience which can never be attained by solitary diligence, but must arise from general converse and accurate observation of the living world. Their performances have, as Horace expresses it, *plus oneris quantum veniae minus*,[3] little indulgence, and therefore more difficulty. They are engaged in portraits of which every one knows the original, and can detect any deviation from exactness of resemblance. Other writings are safe except from the malice of learning, but these are in danger from every common reader; as the slipper ill executed was censured by a shoemaker who happened to stop in his way at the Venus of Apelles.[4]

But the fear of not being approved as just copiers of human manners is not the most important concern that an author of this sort ought to have before him. These books are written chiefly to the young, the ignorant, and the idle, to whom they serve as lectures of conduct and introductions into life. They are the entertainment of minds unfurnished with ideas, and therefore easily susceptible of impressions; not fixed by principles, and therefore easily following the current of fancy; not informed by experience, and consequently open to every false suggestion and partial account.

That the highest degree of reverence should be paid to youth, and that nothing indecent should be suffered to approach their eyes or ears, are precepts extorted by sense and virtue from an ancient writer[5] by no means eminent for chastity of thought. The same kind, though not the same degree, of caution is required in everything which is laid before them, to secure them from unjust prejudices, perverse opinions, and incongruous combinations of images.

In the romances formerly written, every transaction and senti-

[3] *Epistles*, II, 1, 170.
[4] Pliny, *Natural History*, XXXV, 36, 85.
[5] Juvenal, *Satires*, XIV.

ment was so remote from all that passes among men that the
reader was in very little danger of making any applications to
himself; the virtues and crimes were equally beyond his sphere
of activity; and he amused himself with heroes and with traitors,
deliverers and persecutors, as with beings of another species, whose
actions were regulated upon motives of their own, and who had
neither faults nor excellencies in common with himself.

But when an adventurer is leveled with the rest of the world,
and acts in such scenes of the universal drama as may be the lot
of any other man, young spectators fix their eyes upon him with
closer attention, and hope, by observing his behavior and success,
to regulate their own practices when they shall be engaged in the
like part.[6]

For this reason these familiar histories may perhaps be made of
greater use than the solemnities of professed morality, and convey
the knowledge of vice and virtue with more efficacy than axioms
and definitions. But if the power of example is so great as to take
possession of the memory by a kind of violence, and produce
effects almost without the intervention of the will, care ought to
be taken that, when the choice is unrestrained, the best examples
only should be exhibited; and that which is likely to operate so
strongly should not be mischievous or uncertain in its effects.

The chief advantage which these fictions have over real life is
that their authors are at liberty, though not to invent, yet to select
objects, and to cull from the mass of mankind those individuals
upon which the attention ought most to be employed; as a diamond, though it cannot be made, may be polished by art, and
placed in such a situation as to display that lustre which before
was buried among common stones.

It is justly considered as the greatest excellency of art to imitate
nature; but it is necessary to distinguish those parts of nature
which are most proper for imitation. Greater care is still required
in representing life, which is so often discolored by passion or
deformed by wickedness. If the world be promiscuously described,
I cannot see of what use it can be to read the account, or why it
may not be as safe to turn the eye immediately upon mankind,
as upon a mirror which shows all that presents itself without
discrimination.

It is therefore not a sufficient vindication of a character that it

---

[6] According to Arthur Murphy, throughout the essay Johnson intends a defense of the Richardsonian novel as against the newly popular *Roderick Random* (1748) and *Tom Jones* (1749).

is drawn as it appears, for many characters ought never to be drawn; nor of a narrative that the train of events is agreeable to observation and experience, for that observation which is called knowledge of the world will be found much more frequently to make men cunning than good. The purpose of these writings is surely not only to show mankind, but to provide that they may be seen hereafter with less hazard; to teach the means of avoiding the snares which are laid by Treachery for Innocence, without infusing any wish for that superiority with which the betrayer flatters his vanity; to give the power of counteracting fraud, without the temptation to practice it; to initiate youth by mock encounters in the art of necessary defense, and to increase prudence without impairing virtue.

Many writers, for the sake of following nature, so mingle good and bad qualities in their principal personages that they are both equally conspicuous; and as we accompany them through their adventures with delight, and are led by degrees to interest ourselves in their favor, we lose the abhorrence of their faults because they do not hinder our pleasure, or perhaps regard them with some kindness for being united with so much merit.

There have been men indeed splendidly wicked, whose endowments threw a brightness on their crimes, and whom scarce any villainy made perfectly detestable, because they never could be wholly divested of their excellencies; but such have been in all ages the great corrupters of the world, and their resemblance ought no more to be preserved than the art of murdering without pain.

Some have advanced, without due attention to the consequences of this notion, that certain virtues have their correspondent faults, and therefore that to exhibit either apart is to deviate from probability. Thus men are observed by Swift to be "grateful in the same degree as they are resentful." This principle, with others of the same kind, supposes man to act from a brute impulse, and pursue a certain degree of inclination without any choice of the object; for otherwise, though it should be allowed that gratitude and resentment arise from the same constitution of the passions, it follows not that they will be equally indulged when reason is consulted; yet unless that consequence be admitted, this sagacious maxim becomes an empty sound, without any relation to practice or to life.

Nor is it evident that even the first motions to these effects are always in the same proportion. For pride, which produces quickness of resentment, will obstruct gratitude by unwillingness to admit that inferiority which obligation implies; and it is very unlikely that he who cannot think he receives a favor will acknowledge or repay it.

It is of the utmost importance to mankind that positions of this tendency should be laid open and confuted; for while men consider good and evil as springing from the same root, they will spare the one for the sake of the other, and in judging, if not of others at least of themselves, will be apt to estimate their virtues by their vices. To this fatal error, all those will contribute who confound the colors of right and wrong, and instead of helping to settle their boundaries, mix them with so much art that no common mind is able to disunite them.

In narratives where historical veracity has no place, I cannot discover why there should not be exhibited the most perfect idea of virtue—of virtue not angelical nor above probability, for what we cannot credit[7] we shall never imitate, but the highest and purest that humanity can reach, which, exercised in such trials as the various revolutions of things shall bring upon it, may, by conquering some calamities and enduring others, teach us what we may hope and what we can perform. Vice, for vice is necessary to be shown, should always disgust; nor should the graces of gaiety or the dignity of courage be so united with it as to reconcile it to the mind. Wherever it appears, it should raise hatred by the malignity of its practices, and contempt by the meanness of its stratagems; for while it is supported by either parts or spirit,[8] it will be seldom heartily abhorred. The Roman tyrant was content to be hated if he was but feared,[9] and there are thousands of the readers of romances willing to be thought wicked if they may be allowed to be wits. It is therefore to be steadily inculcated that virtue is the highest proof of understanding and the only solid basis of greatness, and that vice is the natural consequence of narrow thoughts; that it begins in mistake and ends in ignominy.

---

[7] believe in.
[8] talents or vitality.
[9] See Suetonius, "Caligula," in *Lives*, XXX, 1.

*

from No. 36, Saturday, July 21, 1750

The range of pastoral is indeed narrow; for though nature itself, philosophically considered, be inexhaustible, yet its general effects on the eye and on the ear are uniform, and incapable of much variety of description. Poetry cannot dwell upon the minuter distinctions by which one species differs from another, without departing from that simplicity of grandeur which fills the imagination; nor dissect the latent qualities of things, without losing its general power of gratifying every mind by recalling its conceptions. However, as each age makes some discoveries and those discoveries are by degrees generally known, as new plants or modes of culture are introduced and by little and little become common, pastoral might receive from time to time small augmentations, and exhibit, once in a century, a scene somewhat varied.

But pastoral subjects have been often, like others, taken into the hands of those that were not qualified to adorn them, men to whom the face of nature was so little known that they have drawn it only after their own imagination, and changed or distorted her features, that their portraits might appear something more than servile copies from their predecessors.

*

from No. 92, Saturday, February 2, 1751

It has been long observed that the idea of beauty is vague and undefined, different in different minds, and diversified by time or place. It has been a term hitherto used to signify that which pleases us we know not why, and in our approbation of which we can justify ourselves only by the concurrence of numbers, without much power of enforcing our opinion upon others by any argument but example and authority. It is, indeed, so little subject to the examinations of reason that Pascal supposes it to end where demonstration begins, and maintains that without incongruity and absurdity we cannot speak of "geometrical beauty." [1]

To trace all the sources of that various pleasure which we ascribe to the agency of beauty, or to disentangle all the perceptions in-

---

[1] In the *Pensées*.

volved in its idea, would, perhaps, require a very great part of the life of an Aristotle or Plato. It is, however, in many cases, apparent that this quality is merely relative and comparative; that we pronounce things beautiful because they have something which we agree, for whatever reason, to call "beauty" in a greater degree than we have been accustomed to find it in other things of the same kind; and that we transfer the epithet as our knowledge increases, and appropriate it to higher excellence when higher excellence comes within our view.

Much of the beauty of writing is of this kind; and therefore Boileau justly remarks[2] that the books which have stood the test of time, and been admired through all the changes which the mind of man has suffered from the various revolutions of knowledge and the prevalence of contrary customs, have a better claim to our regard than any modern can boast, because the long continuance of their reputation proves that they are adequate to our faculties and agreeable to nature.

It is, however, the task of criticism to establish principles; to improve opinion into knowledge; and to distinguish those means of pleasing which depend upon known causes and rational deduction, from the nameless and inexplicable elegancies which appeal wholly to the fancy, from which we feel delight but know not how they produce it, and which may well be termed the enchantresses of the soul. Criticism reduces those regions of literature under the dominion of science which have hitherto known only the anarchy of ignorance, the caprices of fancy, and the tyranny of prescription.

*

No. 121, Tuesday, May 14, 1751

O imitatores, servum pecus!
HOR. [*Epist.* I, xix, 19.]

Away, ye imitators, servile herd!
ELPHINSTON.

I have been informed by a letter from one of the universities that, among the youth from whom the next swarm of reasoners is to learn philosophy, and the next flight of beauties to hear elegies and sonnets, there are many who, instead of endeavoring by books and meditation to form their own opinions, content themselves

---

[2] *Cf.* preface to *Works* (1701).

with the secondary knowledge which a convenient bench in a
coffee-house can supply; and without any examination or distinction, adopt the criticisms and remarks which happen to drop from
those who have risen, by merit or fortune, to reputation and
authority.

These humble retailers of knowledge my correspondent stigma-
tizes with the name of *Echoes,* and seems desirous that they should
be made ashamed of lazy submission, and animated to attempts
after new discoveries and original sentiments.

It is very natural for young men to be vehement, acrimonious,
and severe. For as they seldom comprehend at once all the consequences of a position, or perceive the difficulties by which cooler
and more experienced reasoners are restrained from confidence, they
form their conclusions with great precipitance. Seeing nothing that
can darken or embarrass the question, they expect to find their
own opinion universally prevalent, and are inclined to impute uncertainty and hesitation to want of honesty rather than of knowledge. I may perhaps, therefore, be reproached by my lively correspondent when it shall be found that I have no inclination to
persecute these collectors of fortuitous knowledge with the severity
required; yet, as I am now too old to be much pained by hasty
censure, I shall not be afraid of taking into protection those whom
I think condemned without a sufficient knowledge of their cause.

He that adopts the sentiments of another whom he has reason
to believe wiser than himself is only to be blamed when he claims
the honors which are not due but to the author, and endeavors
to deceive the world into praise and veneration; for to learn is the
proper business of youth; and whether we increase our knowledge
by books or by conversation, we are equally indebted to foreign
assistance.

The greater part of students are not born with abilities to con-
struct systems or advance knowledge, nor can have any hope beyond
that of becoming intelligent hearers in the schools of art, of being
able to comprehend what others discover and to remember what
others teach. Even those to whom Providence hath allotted greater
strength of understanding can expect only to improve a single science. In every other part of learning, they must be content to follow
opinions which they are not able to examine; and even in that
which they claim as peculiarly their own, can seldom add more
than some small particle of knowledge to the hereditary stock devolved to them from ancient times, the collective labor of a thousand intellects.

In science, which, being fixed and limited, admits of no other variety than such as arises from new methods of distribution or new arts of illustration, the necessity of following the traces of our predecessors is indisputably evident; but there appears no reason why imagination should be subject to the same restraint. It might be conceived that, of those who profess to forsake the narrow paths of truth, every one may deviate towards a different point, since, though rectitude is uniform and fixed, obliquity may be infinitely diversified. The roads of science are narrow, so that they who travel them must either follow or meet one another; but in the boundless regions of possibility which fiction claims for her dominion, there are surely a thousand recesses unexplored, a thousand flowers unplucked, a thousand fountains unexhausted, combinations of imagery yet unobserved, and races of ideal inhabitants not hitherto described.

Yet, whatever hope may persuade or reason evince, experience can boast of very few additions to ancient fable. The wars of Troy and the travels of Ulysses have furnished almost all succeeding poets with incidents, characters, and sentiments. The Romans are confessed to have attempted little more than to display in their own tongue the inventions of the Greeks. There is in all their writings such a perpetual recurrence of allusions to the tales of the fabulous age that they must be confessed often to want that power of giving pleasure which novelty supplies; nor can we wonder that they excelled so much in the graces of diction, when we consider how rarely they were employed in search of new thoughts.

The warmest admirers of the great Mantuan poet[3] can extol him for little more than the skill with which he has, by making his hero both a traveler and a warrior, united the beauties of the *Iliad* and the *Odyssey* in one composition. Yet his judgment was perhaps sometimes overborne by his avarice of the Homeric treasures; and for fear of suffering a sparkling ornament to be lost, he has inserted it where it cannot shine with its original splendor.

When Ulysses visited the infernal regions, he found among the heroes that perished at Troy his competitor, Ajax, who, when the arms of Achilles were adjudged to Ulysses, died by his own hand in the madness of disappointment. He still appeared to resent, as on earth, his loss and disgrace. Ulysses endeavored to pacify him with praises and submission, but Ajax walked away without reply.[4]

---

[3] Virgil.
[4] See *Odyssey*, XI, 563.

This passage has always been considered [5] as eminently beautiful, because Ajax, the haughty chief, the unlettered soldier of unshaken courage, of immovable constancy, but without the power of recommending his own virtues by eloquence, or enforcing his assertions by any other argument than the sword, had no way of making his anger known but by gloomy sullenness and dumb ferocity. His hatred of a man whom he conceived to have defeated him only by volubility of tongue was therefore naturally shown by silence, more contemptuous and piercing than any words that so rude an orator could have found, and by which he gave his enemy no opportunity of exerting the only power in which he was superior.

When Aeneas is sent by Virgil to the shades, he meets Dido the Queen of Carthage, whom his perfidy had hurried to the grave; he accosts her with tenderness and excuses; but the lady turns away like Ajax in mute disdain. [6] She turns away like Ajax, but she resembles him in none of those qualities which give either dignity or propriety to silence. She might, without any departure from the tenor of her conduct, have burst out like other injured women into clamor, reproach, and denunciation; but Virgil had his imagination full of Ajax, and therefore could not prevail on himself to teach Dido any other mode of resentment.

If Virgil could be thus seduced by imitation, there will be little hope that common wits should escape; and accordingly, we find that, besides the universal and acknowledged practice of copying the ancients, there has prevailed in every age a particular species of fiction. At one time all truth was conveyed in allegory; at another, nothing was seen but in a vision; at one period all the poets followed sheep, and every event produced a pastoral; at another, they busied themselves wholly in giving directions to a painter. [7]

It is indeed easy to conceive why any fashion should become popular by which idleness is favored and imbecility assisted, but surely no man of genius can much applaud himself for repeating a tale with which the audience is already tired, and which could bring no honor to any but its inventor.

There are, I think, two schemes of writing on which the laborious wits of the present time employ their faculties. One is the adaptation of sense to all the rhymes which our language can supply to some word that makes the burden of the stanza; but this, as it has

---

[5] E.g., by Longinus and by Addison (*Tatler* No. 133).

[6] See *Aeneid*, VI, 469.

[7] A late seventeenth-century poetic convention, as in Waller and Marvell.

been only used in a kind of amorous burlesque, can scarcely be censured with much acrimony. The other is the imitation of Spenser, which, by the influence of some men of learning and genius,[8] seems likely to gain upon the age, and therefore deserves to be more attentively considered.

To imitate the fictions and sentiments of Spenser can incur no reproach, for allegory is perhaps one of the most pleasing vehicles of instruction. But I am very far from extending the same respect to his diction or his stanza. His style was in his own time allowed to be vicious, so darkened with old words and peculiarities of phrase, and so remote from common use, that Jonson boldly pronounces him "to have written no language." [9] His stanza is at once difficult and unpleasing, tiresome to the ear by its uniformity, and to the attention by its length. It was at first formed in imitation of the Italian poets, without due regard to the genius of our language. The Italians have little variety of termination, and were forced to contrive such a stanza as might admit the greatest number of similar rhymes; but our words end with so much diversity that it is seldom convenient for us to bring more than two of the same sound together. If it be justly observed by Milton that rhyme obliges poets to express their thoughts in improper terms,[1] these improprieties must always be multiplied, as the difficulty of rhyme is increased by long concatenations.

The imitators of Spenser are indeed not very rigid censors of themselves, for they seem to conclude that when they have disfigured their lines with a few obsolete syllables, they have accomplished their design, without considering that they ought not only to admit old words, but to avoid new. The laws of imitation are broken by every word introduced since the time of Spenser, as the character of Hector is violated by quoting Aristotle in the play.[2] It would indeed be difficult to exclude from a long poem all modern phrases, though it is easy to sprinkle it with gleanings of antiquity. Perhaps, however, the style of Spenser might by long labor be justly copied; but life is surely given us for higher purposes than to gather what our ancestors have wisely thrown away, and to learn what is of no value but because it has been forgotten.

[8] See Johnson's lives of Gay and Collins.
[9] *Timber, or Discoveries*, ed. F. E. Schelling (1892), p. 57.
[1] Preface to *Paradise Lost*.
[2] *Troilus and Cressida*, II, ii, 166.

*

from No. 125, Tuesday, May 28, 1751

It is one of the maxims of the civil law that *definitions are hazardous*. Things modified by human understandings, subject to varieties of complication, and changeable as experience advances knowledge, or accident influences caprice, are scarcely to be included in any standing form of expression, because they are always suffering some alteration of their state. Definition is, indeed, not the province of man; everything is set above or below our faculties. The works and operations of nature are too great in their extent or too much diffused in their relations, and the performances of art too inconstant and uncertain, to be reduced to any determinate idea. It is impossible to impress upon our minds an adequate and just representation of an object so great that we can never take it into our view, or so mutable that it is always changing under our eye, and has already lost its form while we are laboring to conceive it.

Definitions have been no less difficult or uncertain in criticism than in law. Imagination, a licentious and vagrant faculty, unsusceptible of limitations and impatient of restraint, has always endeavored to baffle the logician, to perplex the confines of distinction, and burst the inclosures of regularity. There is therefore scarcely any species of writing of which we can tell what is its essence and what are its constituents; every new genius produces some innovation which, when invented and approved, subverts the rules which the practice of foregoing authors had established.

Comedy has been particularly unpropitious to definers; for though perhaps they might properly have contented themselves with declaring it to be *such a dramatic representation of human life, as may excite mirth*, they have embarrassed their definition with the means by which the comic writers attain their end, without considering that the various methods of exhilarating their audience, not being limited by nature, cannot be comprised in precept. Thus, some make comedy a representation of mean and others of bad men; some think that its essence consists in the unimportance, others in the fictitiousness of the transaction. But any man's reflections will inform him that every dramatic composition which raises mirth is comic; and that, to raise mirth, it is by no means universally necessary that the personages should be either mean or corrupt, nor always requisite that the action should be trivial, nor ever that it should be fictitious.

If the two kinds of dramatic poetry had been defined only by their effects upon the mind, some absurdities might have been prevented with which the compositions of our greatest poets are disgraced, who, for want of some settled ideas and accurate distinctions, have unhappily confounded tragic with comic sentiments. They seem to have thought that as the meanest of personages constituted comedy, their greatness was sufficient to form a tragedy, and that nothing was necessary but that they should crowd the scene with monarchs and generals and guards, and make them talk at certain intervals of the downfall of kingdoms and the rout of armies. They have not considered that thoughts or incidents, in themselves ridiculous, grow still more grotesque by the solemnity of such characters. . . .

*

No. 154, Saturday, September 7, 1751

Tibi res antiquae laudis et artis
Ingredior, sanctos ausus recludere fontes.
            —VIR. [*Georgics* II, 174.]

For thee my tuneful accents will I raise,
And treat of arts disclosed in ancient days;
Once more unlock for thee the sacred spring.
            —DRYDEN.

The direction of Aristotle to those that study politics is first to examine and understand what has been written by the ancients upon government, then to cast their eyes round upon the world and consider by what causes the prosperity of communities is visibly influenced, and why some are worse and others better administered.[3]

The same method must be pursued by him who hopes to become eminent in any other part of knowledge. The first task is to search books, the next to contemplate nature. He must first possess himself of the intellectual treasures which the diligence of former ages has accumulated, and then endeavor to increase them by his own collections.

The mental disease of the present generation is impatience of study, contempt of the great masters of ancient wisdom, and a disposition to rely wholly upon unassisted genius and natural sagacity. The wits of these happy days have discovered a way to fame which the dull caution of our laborious ancestors durst never attempt;

---

[3] *Politics*, II, 1.

they cut the knots of sophistry which it was formerly the business of years to untie, solve difficulties by sudden irradiations of intelligence, and comprehend long processes of argument by immediate intuition.

Men who have flattered themselves into this opinion of their own abilities look down on all who waste their lives over books as a race of inferior beings, condemned by nature to perpetual pupilage, and fruitlessly endeavoring to remedy their barrenness by incessant cultivation, or succor their feebleness by subsidiary strength. They presume that none would be more industrious than they, if they were not more sensible of deficiencies, and readily conclude that he who places no confidence in his own powers owes his modesty only to his weakness.

It is however certain that no estimate is more in danger of erroneous calculations than those by which a man computes the force of his own genius. It generally happens at our entrance into the world that, by the natural attraction of similitude, we associate with men like ourselves, young, sprightly, and ignorant, and rate our accomplishments by comparison with theirs; when we have once obtained an acknowledged superiority over our acquaintances, imagination and desire easily extend it over the rest of mankind; and if no accident forces us into new emulations, we grow old and die in admiration of ourselves.

Vanity, thus confirmed in her dominion, readily listens to the voice of idleness, and soothes the slumber of life with continual dreams of excellence and greatness. A man elated by confidence in his natural vigor of fancy and sagacity of conjecture, soon concludes that he already possesses whatever toil and inquiry can confer. He then listens with eagerness to the wild objections which folly has raised against the common means of improvement, talks of the dark chaos of indigested knowledge, describes the mischievous effects of heterogeneous sciences fermenting in the mind, relates the blunders of lettered ignorance, expatiates on the heroic merit of those who deviate from prescription or shake off authority, and gives vent to the inflations of his heart by declaring that he owes nothing to pedants and universities.

All these pretensions, however confident, are very often vain. The laurels which superficial acuteness gains in triumphs over ignorance unsupported by vivacity are observed by Locke[4] to be lost whenever real learning and rational diligence appear against her; the sallies of gaiety are soon repressed by calm confidence; and the artifices of

---

[4] *Of the Conduct of the Understanding*, par. 38.

subtlety are readily detected by those who, having carefully studied the question, are not easily confounded or surprised.

But though the contemner of books had neither been deceived by others nor himself, and was really born with a genius ourpassing the ordinary abilities of mankind, yet surely such gifts of Providence may be more properly urged as incitements to labor, than encouragements to negligence. He that neglects the culture of ground naturally fertile is more shamefully culpable than he whose field would scarcely recompense his husbandry.

Cicero remarks that not to know what has been transacted in former times is to continue always a child.[5] If no use is made of the labors of past ages, the world must remain always in the infancy of knowledge. The discoveries of every man must terminate in his own advantage, and the studies of every age be employed on questions which the past generation had discussed and determined. We may with as little reproach borrow science as manufactures from our ancestors; and it is as rational to live in caves, till our own hands have erected a palace, as to reject all knowledge of architecture which our understandings will not supply.

To the strongest and quickest mind it is far easier to learn than to invent. The principles of arithmetic and geometry may be comprehended by a close attention in a few days; yet who can flatter himself that the study of a long life would have enabled him to discover them, when he sees them yet unknown to so many nations whom he cannot suppose less liberally endowed with natural reason than the Grecians or Egyptians?

Every science was thus far advanced towards perfection by the emulous diligence of contemporary students and the gradual discoveries of one age improving on another. Sometimes unexpected flashes of instruction were struck out by the fortuitous collision of happy incidents, or an involuntary concurrence of ideas; in which the philosopher to whom they happened had no other merit than that of knowing their value, and transmitting unclouded to posterity that light which had been kindled by causes out of his power. The happiness of these casual illuminations, no man can promise to himself, because no endeavors can procure them; and therefore whatever be our abilities or application, we must submit to learn from others what perhaps would have lain hid forever from human penetration, had not some remote inquiry brought it to view, as treasures are thrown up by the plowman and the digger in the rude exercise of their common occupations.

---

[5] *Ad Marcam Brutum Orator,* XXXIV, 120.

The man whose genius qualifies him for great undertakings must at least be content to learn from books the present state of human knowledge, that he may not ascribe to himself the invention of arts generally known; weary his attention with experiments of which the event has been long registered; and waste, in attempts which have already succeeded or miscarried, that time which might have been spent with usefulness and honor upon new undertakings.

But though the study of books is necessary, it is not sufficient to constitute literary eminence. He that wishes to be counted among the benefactors of posterity must add by his own toil to the acquisitions of his ancestors, and secure his memory from neglect by some valuable improvement. This can only be effected by looking out upon the wastes of the intellectual world, and extending the power of learning over regions yet undisciplined and barbarous; or by surveying more exactly our ancient dominions, and driving ignorance from the fortresses and retreats where she skulks undetected and undisturbed. Every science has its difficulties which yet call for solution before we attempt new systems of knowledge; as every country has its forests and marshes, which it would be wise to cultivate and drain, before distant colonies are projected as a necessary discharge of the exuberance of inhabitants.

No man ever yet became great by imitation. Whatever hopes for the veneration of mankind must have invention in the design or the execution; either the effect must itself be new, or the means by which it is produced. Either truths hitherto unknown must be discovered, or those which are already known enforced by stronger evidence, facilitated by clearer method, or elucidated by brighter illustrations.

Fame cannot spread wide or endure long that is not rooted in nature and matured by art. That which hopes to resist the blast of malignity, and stand firm against the attacks of time, must contain in itself some original principle of growth. The reputation which arises from the detail or transposition of borrowed sentiments may spread for awhile, like ivy on the rind of antiquity, but will be torn away by accident or contempt, and suffered to rot unheeded on the ground.

*

from No. 156, Saturday, September 14, 1751

Every government, say the politicians, is perpetually degenerating towards corruption, from which it must be rescued at certain peri-

ods by the resuscitation of its first principles, and the re-establish-
ment of its original constitution. Every animal body, according to
the methodic physicians, is, by the predominance of some exuberant
quality, continually declining towards disease and death, which
must be obviated by a seasonable reduction of the peccant humor
to the just equipoise which health requires.

In the same manner the studies of mankind, all at least which,
not being subject to rigorous demonstration, admit the influence of
fancy and caprice, are perpetually tending to error and confusion.
Of the great principles of truth which the first speculatists discovered, the simplicity is embarrassed by ambitious additions, or the
evidence obscured by inaccurate argumentation; and as they descend from one succession of writers to another, like light transmitted from room to room, they lose their strength and splendor,
and fade at last in total evanescence.

The systems of learning therefore must be sometimes reviewed,
complications analyzed into principles, and knowledge disentangled
from opinion. It is not always possible, without a close inspection,
to separate the genuine shoots of consequential reasoning, which
grow out of some radical postulate, from the branches which art
has ingrafted on it. The accidental prescriptions of authority, when
time has procured them veneration, are often confounded with the
laws of nature; and those rules are supposed coëval with reason, of
which the first rise cannot be discovered.

Criticism has sometimes permitted fancy to dictate the laws by
which fancy ought to be restrained, and fallacy to perplex the principles by which fallacy is to be detected; her superintendence of
others has betrayed her to negligence of herself; and, like the ancient Scythians, by extending her conquests over distant regions, she
has left her throne vacant to her slaves.[6]

Among the laws of which the desire of extending authority or
ardor of promoting knowledge has prompted the prescription, all
which writers have received had not the same original right to our
regard. Some are to be considered as fundamental and indispensable, others only as useful and convenient; some as dictated by reason
and necessity, others as enacted by despotic antiquity; some as in-
vincibly supported by their conformity to the order of nature and
operations of the intellect; others as formed by accident, or instituted by example, and therefore always liable to dispute and alteration.

That many rules have been advanced without consulting nature

---

[6] See Herodotus, IV, 1–4.

or reason, we cannot but suspect when we find it peremptorily decreed by the ancient masters that *only three speaking personages should appear at once upon the stage*,[7] a law which, as the variety and intricacy of modern plays has made it impossible to be observed, we now violate without scruple and, as experience proves, without inconvenience. . . .

It ought to be the first endeavor of a writer to distinguish nature from custom, or that which is established because it is right from that which is right only because it is established; that he may neither violate essential principles by a desire of novelty, nor debar himself from the attainment of beauties within his view, by a needless fear of breaking rules which no literary dictator had authority to enact.

*

from No. 158, Saturday, September 21, 1751

Criticism, though dignified from the earliest ages by the labors of men eminent for knowledge and sagacity, and, since the revival of polite literature, the favorite study of European scholars, has not yet attained the certainty and stability of science. The rules hitherto received are seldom drawn from any settled principle or self-evident postulate, or adapted to the natural and invariable constitution of things; but will be found, upon examination, the arbitrary edicts of legislators, authorized only by themselves, who, out of various means by which the same end may be attained, selected such as happened to occur to their own reflection, and then, by a law which idleness and timidity were too willing to obey, prohibited new experiments of wit, restrained fancy from the indulgence of her innate inclination to hazard and adventure, and condemned all future flights of genius to pursue the path of the Meonian eagle.

This authority may be more justly opposed as it is apparently derived from them whom they endeavor to control; for we owe few of the rules of writing to the acuteness of critics, who have generally no other merit than that, having read the works of great authors with attention, they have observed the arrangement of their matter or the graces of their expression, and then expected honor and reverence for precepts which they never could have invented; so that practice has introduced rules, rather than rules have directed practice.

For this reason the laws of every species of writing have been

---

[7] Horace, *Ars Poetica*, 192; *cf.* Aristotle, *Poetics*, IV, 16.

settled by the ideas of him who first raised it to reputation, without inquiry whether his performances were not yet susceptible of improvement. The excellencies and faults of celebrated writers have been equally recommended to posterity, and so far has blind reverence prevailed, that even the number of their books has been thought worthy of imitation.

The imagination of the first authors of lyric poetry was vehement and rapid, and their knowledge various and extensive. Living in an age when science had been little cultivated, and when the minds of their auditors, not being accustomed to accurate inspection, were easily dazzled by glaring ideas, they applied themselves to instruct rather by short sentences and striking thoughts, than by regular argumentation; and finding attention more successfully excited by sudden sallies and unexpected exclamations, than by the more artful and placid beauties of methodical deduction, they loosed their genius to its own course, passed from one sentiment to another without expressing the intermediate ideas, and roved at large over the ideal world, with such lightness and agility that their footsteps are scarcely to be traced.

From this accidental peculiarity of the ancient writers, the critics deduce the rules of lyric poetry; which they have set free from all the laws by which other compositions are confined, and allow to neglect the niceties of transition, to start into remote digressions, and to wander without restraint from one scene of imagery to another.

A writer of later times has, by the vivacity of his essays, reconciled mankind to the same licentiousness in short dissertations; and he therefore who wants skill to form a plan, or diligence to pursue it, needs only entitle his performance an "essay" to acquire the right of heaping together the collections of half his life without order, coherence, or propriety.

In writing as in life, faults are endured without disgust when they are associated with transcendent merit, and may be sometimes recommended to weak judgments by the lustre which they obtain from their union with excellence; but it is the business of those who presume to superintend the taste or morals of mankind to separate delusive combinations, and distinguish that which may be praised from that which can only be excused. As vices never promote happiness, though when overpowered by more active and more numerous virtues they cannot totally destroy it, so confusion and irregularity produce no beauty, though they cannot always obstruct the brightness of genius and learning. To proceed from one truth to another, and connect distant propositions by regular consequences, is the great prerogative of man. Independent and unconnected sentiments flashing upon the mind in quick succession may, for a time, delight by their novelty, but they differ from systematical reasoning as single notes from harmony, as glances of lightning from the radiance of the sun.

When rules are thus drawn rather from precedents than reason, there is danger not only from the faults of an author, but from the errors of those who criticize his works, since they may often mislead their pupils by false representations, as the Ciceronians of the sixteenth century were betrayed into barbarisms by corrupt copies of their darling writer. . . .

*

from No. 176, Saturday, November 23, 1751

The eye of the intellect, like that of the body, is not equally perfect in all, nor equally adapted in any to all objects; the end of criticism is to supply its defects; rules are the instruments of mental vision, which may indeed assist our faculties when properly used, but produce confusion and obscurity by unskillful application.

Some seem always to read with the microscope of criticism, and employ their whole attention upon minute elegance, or faults scarcely visible to common observation. The dissonance of a syllable, the recurrence of the same sound, the repetition of a particle, the smallest deviation from propriety, the slightest defect in construction or arrangement, swell before their eyes into enormities. As they discern with great exactness, they comprehend but a narrow compass, and know nothing of the justness of the design, the general spirit of the performance, the artifice of connection, or the harmony of the parts; they never conceive how small a proportion that which they are busy in contemplating bears to the whole, or how the petty inaccuracies with which they are offended, are absorbed and lost in general excellence.

Others are furnished by criticism with a telescope. They see with great clearness whatever is too remote to be discovered by the rest of mankind, but are totally blind to all that lies immediately before them. They discover in every passage some secret meaning, some remote allusion, some artful allegory, or some occult imitation which no other reader ever suspected; but they have no perception of the cogency of arguments, the force of pathetic sentiments, the various colours of diction, or the flowery embellishments of fancy; of all that engages the attention of others, they are totally insensible, while they pry into worlds of conjecture, and amuse themselves with phantoms in the clouds.

In criticism, as in every other art, we fail sometimes by our weakness, but more frequently by our fault. We are sometimes bewildered by ignorance, and sometimes by prejudice, but we seldom deviate far from the right but when we deliver ourselves up to the direction of vanity.

* * * *

FROM

The Idler [1758–1760]

No. 60, Saturday, June 9, 1759

Criticism is a study by which men grow important and formidable at a very small expense. The power of invention has been conferred by nature upon few, and the labor of learning those sciences which may by mere labor be obtained is too great to be willingly endured; but every man can exert such judgment as he has upon the works of others; and he whom nature has made weak, and idleness keeps ignorant, may yet support his vanity by the name of a critic.

I hope it will give comfort to great numbers who are passing through the world in obscurity when I inform them how easily distinction may be obtained. All the other powers of literature are coy and haughty: they must be long courted, and at last are not always gained; but Criticism is a goddess easy of access and forward of advance, who will meet the slow and encourage the timorous; the want of meaning she supplies with words, and the want of spirit she recompenses with malignity.

This profession has one recommendation peculiar to itself, that it gives vent to malignity without real mischief. No genius was ever blasted by the breath of critics. The poison which, if confined, would have burst the heart, fumes away in empty hisses, and malice is set at ease with very little danger to merit. The critic is the only man whose triumph is without another's pain, and whose greatness does not rise upon another's ruin.

To a study at once so easy and so reputable, so malicious and so harmless, it cannot be necessary to invite my readers by a long or

426 - SAMUEL JOHNSON

labored exhortation; it is sufficient, since all would be critics if they could, to show by one eminent example that all can be critics if they will.

Dick Minim, after the common course of puerile studies, in which he was no great proficient, was put apprentice to a brewer, with whom he had lived two years when his uncle died in the city, and left him a large fortune in the stocks. Dick had for six months before used the company of the lower players, of whom he had learned to scorn a trade, and being now at liberty to follow his genius, he resolved to be a man of wit and humor. That he might be properly initiated in his new character, he frequented the coffee-houses near the theatres, where he listened very diligently, day after day, to those who talked of language and sentiments, and unities and catastrophes, till by slow degrees he began to think that he understood something of the stage, and hoped in time to talk himself.

But he did not trust so much to natural sagacity as wholly to neglect the help of books. When the theatres were shut, he retired to Richmond with a few select writers, whose opinions he impressed upon his memory by unwearied diligence; and when he returned with other wits to the town, was able to tell, in very proper phrases, that the chief business of art is to copy nature, that a perfect writer is not to be expected because genius decays as judgment increases, that the great art is the art of blotting,[1] and that, according to the rule of Horace, every piece should be kept nine years.[2]

Of the great authors, he now began to display the characters, laying down as an universal position that all had beauties and defects.[3] His opinion was that Shakespeare, committing himself wholly to the impulse of nature, wanted that correctness which learning would have given him, and that Jonson, trusting to learning, did not sufficiently cast his eyes on nature.[4] He blamed the stanzas of Spenser, and could not bear the hexameters of Sidney.[5] Denham and Waller he held the first reformers of English numbers,[6] and thought that if Waller could have obtained the strength of Denham, or Denham the sweetness of Waller, there had been nothing

---

[1] Cf. Pope's Essay on Criticism, 68, 253–54, 56–57, and Imitations of Horace, II, i, 281. The list of clichés in the next paragraph is amplified in G. B. Hill's edition of Select Essays of Dr. Johnson (1889).

[2] Ars Poetica, 388.

[3] Cf. Dryden, p. 41, or Addison, p. 236.

[4] Cf. Dryden, pp. 84–86; or Johnson himself in "Prologue at Opening of Drury-Lane Theatre."

[5] Pope, Imitations of Horace, II, i, 98; cf. Johnson himself, p. 415.

[6] Dryden, Preface to the Fables, par. 11.

wanting to complete a poet.[7] He often expressed his commiseration of Dryden's poverty, and his indignation at the age which suffered him to write for bread;[8] he repeated with rapture the first lines of *All for Love*, but wondered at the corruption of taste which could bear anything so unnatural as rhyming tragedies. In Otway he found uncommon powers of moving the passions, but was disgusted by his general negligence,[9] and blamed him for making a conspirator his hero;[1] and never concluded his disquisition, without remarking how happily the sound of the clock is made to alarm the audience. Southern would have been his favorite but that he mixes comic with tragic scenes, intercepts the natural course of the passions, and fills the mind with a wild confusion of mirth and melancholy. The versification of Rowe he thought too melodious for the stage and too little varied in different passions.[2] He made it the great fault of Congreve that all his persons were wits, and that he always wrote with more art than nature.[3] He considered *Cato* rather as a poem than a play,[4] and allowed Addison to be the complete master of allegory and grave humor, but paid no great deference to him as a critic.[5] He thought the chief merit of Prior was in his easy tales and lighter poems, though he allowed that his *Solomon* had many noble sentiments elegantly expressed. In Swift he discovered an inimitable vein of irony, and an easiness which all would hope and few would attain. Pope he was inclined to degrade from a poet to a versifier, and thought his numbers rather luscious than sweet. He often lamented the neglect of *Phaedra and Hippolytus*,[6] and wished to see the stage under better regulations.

These assertions passed commonly uncontradicted, and if now and then an opponent started up, he was quickly repressed by the suffrages of the company; and Minim went away from every dispute with elation of heart and increase of confidence.

He now grew conscious of his abilities, and began to talk of the present state of dramatic poetry, wondered what had become of the

---

[7] Pope, *Essay on Criticism*, 361.
[8] *Cf.* Pope, *Epistle to Arbuthnot*, 247.
[9] *Cf.* Pope, *Imitations of Horace*, II, i, 278.
[1] Addison, *Spectator* No. 39.
[2] Joseph Warton, *Essay on Writings and Genius of Pope* (1762), I, 271.
[3] Johnson's own opinion; *cf.* "Congreve" in *Lives*, pars. 16 and 33.
[4] Warton, *op. cit.*, I, 259.
[5] *Ibid.*, p. 269.
[6] By Edmund Smith, 1707. *Cf.* Addison's remark in *Spectator* No. 18, and Johnson's own discussion in "Smith," *Lives*, par. 49.

comic genius which supplied our ancestors with wit and pleasantry, and why no writer could be found that durst now venture beyond a farce.[7] He saw no reason for thinking that the vein of humor was exhausted, since we live in a country where liberty suffers every character to spread itself to its utmost bulk, and which, therefore, produces more originals than all the rest of the world together.[8] Of tragedy he concluded business[9] to be the soul, and yet often hinted that love predominates too much upon the modern stage.

He was now an acknowledged critic, and had his own seat in a coffee-house, and headed a party in the pit. Minim has more vanity than ill-nature, and seldom desires to do much mischief; he will, perhaps, murmur a little in the ear of him that sits next him, but endeavors to influence the audience to favor by clapping when an actor exclaims "Ye gods!" or laments the misery of his country.

By degrees he was admitted to rehearsals, and many of his friends are of opinion that our present poets are indebted to him for their happiest thoughts: by his contrivance the bell was rung twice in *Barbarossa*,[1] and by his persuasion the author of *Cleone*[2] concluded his play without a couplet; for what can be more absurd, said Minim, than that part of a play should be rhymed and part written in blank verse? and by what acquisition of faculties is the speaker, who never could find rhymes before, enabled to rhyme at the conclusion of an act?

He is the great investigator of hidden beauties, and is particularly delighted when he finds "the sound an echo to the sense."[3] He has read all our poets with particular attention to this delicacy of versification, and wonders at the supineness with which their works have been hitherto perused, so that no man has found the sound of a drum in this distich:

> *When pulpit, drum ecclesiastic,*
> *Was beat with fist instead of a stick;*[4]

and that the wonderful lines upon honor and a bubble have hitherto passed without notice:

---

[7] *Cf.* Johnson's Drury-Lane prologue, *op. cit.*
[8] See pp. 163–65.
[9] plot.
[1] By Dr. John Brown, 1754. Johnson once remarked that "the use of a bell is unknown to the Mohammedans."
[2] By Robert Dodsley, 1758.
[3] Pope, *Essay on Criticism*, 365. Johnson examines the doctrine in *Rambler* Nos. 92 and 94.
[4] *Hudibras*, I, i, 11–12 (misquoted).

Honor is like the glassy bubble,
Which costs philosophers such trouble;
Where, one part cracked, the whole does fly,
And wits are cracked to find out why.[5]

In these verses, says Minim, we have two striking accommodations of the sound to the sense. It is impossible to utter the first two lines emphatically without an act like that which they describe, *bubble* and *trouble* causing a momentary inflation of the cheeks by the retention of the breath, which is afterwards forcibly emitted, as in the practice of *blowing bubbles*. But the greatest excellence is in the third line, which is *cracked* in the middle to express a crack, and then shivers into monosyllables. Yet has this diamond lain neglected with common stones, and among the innumerable admirers of *Hudibras*, the observation of this superlative passage has been reserved for the sagacity of Minim.

*

No. 61, Saturday, June 16, 1759

Mr. Minim had now advanced himself to the zenith of critical reputation; when he was in the pit, every eye in the boxes was fixed upon him; when he entered his coffee-house, he was surrounded by circles of candidates, who passed their noviciate of literature under his tuition. His opinion was asked by all who had no opinion of their own, and yet loved to debate and decide; and no composition was supposed to pass in safety to posterity till it had been secured by Minim's approbation.

Minim professes great admiration of the wisdom and munificence by which the academies of the continent were raised, and often wishes for some standard of taste, for some tribunal, to which merit may appeal from caprice, prejudice, and malignity. He has formed a plan for an academy of criticism, where every work of imagination may be read before it is printed, and which shall authoritatively direct the theatres what pieces to receive or reject, to exclude or to revive.[6]

Such an institution would, in Dick's opinion, spread the fame of English literature over Europe and make London the metropolis of elegance and politeness,[7] the place to which the learned and ingen-

---

[5] *Ibid.*, II, ii, 385–88 (misquoted).

[6] Johnson disliked the notion of an English academy; see p. 435.

[7] In 1761 Johnson remarked that London is "now justly termed, the capital of literature."

ious of all countries would repair for instruction and improvement, and where nothing would any longer be applauded or endured that was not conformed to the nicest rules, and finished with the highest elegance.

Till some happy conjunction of the planets shall dispose our princes or ministers to make themselves immortal by such an academy, Minim contents himself to preside four nights in a week in a critical society selected by himself, where he is heard without contradiction, and whence his judgment is disseminated through the great vulgar and the small.

When[8] he is placed in the chair of Criticism, he declares loudly for the noble simplicity of our ancestors, in opposition to the petty refinements and ornamental luxuriance. Sometimes he is sunk in despair, and perceives false delicacy daily gaining ground, and sometimes brightens his countenance with a gleam of hope, and predicts the revival of the true sublime. He then fulminates his loudest censures against the monkish barbarity of rhyme; wonders how beings that pretend to reason can be pleased with one line always ending like another; tells how unjustly and unnaturally sense is sacrificed to sound, how often the best thoughts are mangled by the necessity of confining or extending them to the dimensions of a couplet; and rejoices that genius has, in our days, shaken off the shackles which had encumbered it so long. Yet he allows that rhyme may sometimes be borne, if the lines be often broken, and the pauses judiciously diversified.

From blank verse he makes an easy transition to Milton, whom he produces as an example of the slow advance of lasting reputation. Milton is the only writer in whose books Minim can read forever without weariness. What cause it is that exempts this pleasure from satiety, he has long and diligently inquired, and believes it to consist in the perpetual variation of the numbers by which the ear is gratified and the attention awakened. The lines that are commonly thought rugged and unmusical, he conceives to have been written to temper the melodious luxury of the rest, or to express things by a proper cadence. For he scarcely finds a verse that has not this favorite beauty; he declares that he could shiver in a hothouse when he reads that,

---

[8] The following paragraphs list still other clichés, which suggest the Longinian-Miltonic line of critics, e.g., Dennis.

> the ground
> *Burns frore, and cold performs th' effect of fire;*[9]

and that when Milton bewails his blindness, the verse

> *So thick a drop serene has quenched these orbs,*[1]

has, he knows not how, something that strikes him with an obscure sensation like that which he fancies would be felt from the sound of darkness.

Minim is not so confident of his rules of judgment as not very eagerly to catch new light from the name of the author. He is commonly so prudent as to spare those whom he cannot resist, unless, as will sometimes happen, he finds the public combined against them. But a fresh pretender to fame he is strongly inclined to censure, till his own honor requires that he commend him. Till he knows the success of a composition, he entrenches himself in general terms; there are some new thoughts and beautiful passages, but there is likewise much which he would have advised the author to expunge. He has several favorite epithets of which he has never settled the meaning, but which are very commodiously applied to books which he has not read or cannot understand. One is *manly*, another is *dry*, another *stiff*, and another *flimsy*; sometimes he discovers delicacy of style, and sometimes meets with *strange expressions*.

He is never so great or so happy as when a youth of promising parts is brought to receive his directions for the prosecution of his studies. He then puts on a very serious air; he advises the pupil to read none but the best authors; and when he finds one congenial to his own mind, to study his beauties but avoid his faults; and when he sits down to write, to consider how his favorite author would think at the present time on the present occasion.[2] He exhorts him to catch those moments when he finds his thoughts expanded and his genius exalted, but to take care lest imagination hurry him beyond the bounds of nature. He holds diligence the mother of success, yet enjoins him, with great earnestness, not to read more than he can digest, and not to confuse his mind by pursuing studies of contrary tendencies. He tells him that every man has his genius, and that Cicero could never be a poet. The boy retires illuminated, re-

---

[9] *Paradise Lost*, II, 594–95 (misquoted).
[1] *Ibid.*, III, 25 (misquoted).
[2] *Cf.* Longinus, XIV, 1.

solves to follow his genius, and to think how Milton would have thought; and Minim feasts upon his own beneficence till another day brings another pupil.

* * * *

FROM

Preface to

A *Dictionary of the English Language* [1755]

My purpose was to admit no testimony of living authors, that I might not be misled by partiality, and that none of my contemporaries might have reason to complain; nor have I departed from this resolution but when some performance of uncommon excellence excited my veneration, when my memory supplied me, from late books, with an example that was wanting, or when my heart, in the tenderness of friendship, solicited admission for a favorite name.

So far have I been from any care to grace my pages with modern decorations that I have studiously endeavored to collect examples and authorities from the writers before the Restoration, whose works I regard as "the wells of English undefiled," as the pure sources of genuine diction. Our language, for almost a century, has, by the concurrence of many causes, been gradually departing from its original Teutonic character and deviating towards a Gallic structure and phraseology, from which it ought to be our endeavor to recall it, by making our ancient volumes the groundwork of style, admitting among the additions of later times only such as may supply real deficiencies, such as are readily adopted by the genius of our tongue, and incorporate easily with our native idioms.

But as every language has a time of rudeness antecedent to perfection, as well as of false refinement and declension, I have been cautious lest my zeal for antiquity might drive me into times too remote, and crowd my book with words now no longer understood. I have fixed Sidney's works for the boundary, beyond which I make few excursions. From the authors which rose in the time of Elizabeth, a speech might be formed adequate to all the purposes of use and elegance. If the language of theology were extracted from Hooker and the translation of the Bible; the terms of natural knowledge from Bacon; the phrases of policy, war, and navigation from Raleigh; the dialect of poetry and fiction from Spenser and Sidney; and the diction of common life from Shakespeare, few ideas would be lost to mankind for want of English words in which they might be expressed. . . .

Those who have been persuaded to think well of my design will require that it should fix our language, and put a stop to those alterations which time and chance have hitherto been suffered to make in it without opposition. With this consequence I will confess that I flattered myself for a while; but now begin to fear that I have indulged expectation which neither reason nor experience can justify. When we see men grow old and die at a certain time, one after another, from century to century, we laugh at the elixir that promises to prolong life to a thousand years; and with equal justice may the lexicographer be derided who, being able to produce no example of a nation that has preserved their words and phrases from mutability, shall imagine that his dictionary can embalm his language, and secure it from corruption and decay, that it is in his power to change sublunary nature, and clear the world at once from folly, vanity, and affectation.

With this hope, however, academies have been instituted to guard the avenues of their languages, to retain fugitives and repulse intruders; but their vigilance and activity have hitherto been vain; sounds are too volatile and subtle for legal restraints; to enchain syllables and to lash the wind are equally the undertakings of pride, unwilling to measure its desires by its strength. The French language has visibly changed under the inspection of the Academy; the style of Amelot's translation of Father Paul [1] is observed by Le Courayer to be *un peu passé*; and no Italian will maintain that the diction of any modern writer is not perceptibly different from that of Boccaccio, Machiavelli, or Caro.[2]

Total and sudden transformations of a language seldom happen; conquests and migrations are now very rare. But there are other causes of change which, though slow in their operation, and invisible in their progress, are perhaps as much superior to human resistance as the revolutions of the sky or intumescence of the tide. Commerce, however necessary, however lucrative, as it depraves the manners, corrupts the language; they that have frequent intercourse with strangers, to whom they endeavor to accommodate themselves,

---

[1] Paolo Sarpi (1552–1623), Venetian professor of philosophy; *History of the Council of Trent* (1619), ed. Amelot (1683) and Courayer (1736).

[2] Annibale Caro (1507–66), Italian poet and prose writer.

must in time learn a mingled dialect, like the jargon which serves the traffickers[3] on the Mediterranean and Indian coasts. This will not always be confined to the exchange, the warehouse, or the port, but will be communicated by degrees to other ranks of the people, and be at last incorporated with the current speech.

There are likewise internal causes equally forcible. The language most likely to continue long without alteration would be that of a nation raised a little, and but a little, above barbarity, secluded from strangers, and totally employed in procuring the conveniences of life, either without books or, like some of the Mohammedan countries, with very few. Men thus busied and unlearned, having only such words as common use requires, would perhaps long continue to express the same notions by the same signs. But no such constancy can be expected in a people polished by arts and classed by subordination, where one part of the community is sustained and accommodated by the labor of the other. Those who have much leisure to think will always be enlarging the stock of ideas, and every increase of knowledge, whether real or fancied, will produce new words or combinations of words. When the mind is unchained from necessity, it will range after convenience; when it is left at large in the fields of speculation, it will shift opinions; as any custom is disused, the words that expressed it must perish with it; as any opinion grows popular, it will innovate speech in the same proportion as it alters practice.

As by the cultivation of various sciences, a language is amplified, it will be more furnished with words deflected from original sense; the geometrician will talk of a courtier's *zenith* or the *eccentric* virtue of a wild hero, and the physician of *sanguine* expectations and *phlegmatic* delays. Copiousness of speech will give opportunities to capricious choice, by which some words will be preferred and others degraded; vicissitudes of fashion will enforce the use of new, or extend the signification of known, terms. The tropes of poetry will make hourly encroachments, and the metaphorical will become the current sense; pronunciation will be varied by levity or ignorance, and the pen must at length comply with the tongue; illiterate writers will at one time or other, by public infatuation, rise into renown, who, not knowing the original import of words, will use them with colloquial licentiousness, confound distinction, and forget propriety. As politeness increases, some expressions will be considered as too gross and vulgar for the delicate, others as too formal and ceremoni-

---

[3] traders.

ous for the gay and airy; new phrases are therefore adopted which must, for the same reasons, be in time dismissed. Swift, in his petty treatise on the English language,[4] allows that new words must sometimes be introduced, but proposes that none should be suffered to become obsolete. But what makes a word obsolete, more than general agreement to forbear it? and how shall it be continued when it conveys an offensive idea, or recalled again into the mouths of mankind when it has once become unfamiliar by disuse and unpleasing by unfamiliarity?

There is another cause of alteration more prevalent than any other, which yet in the present state of the world cannot be obviated. A mixture of two languages will produce a third distinct from both, and they will always be mixed where the chief part of education, and the most conspicuous accomplishment, is skill in ancient or in foreign tongues. He that has long cultivated another language will find its words and combinations crowd upon his memory; and haste and negligence, refinement and affectation, will obtrude borrowed terms and exotic expressions.

The great pest[5] of speech is frequency of translation. No book was ever turned from one language into another without imparting something of its native idiom; this is the most mischievous and comprehensive innovation; single words may enter by thousands, and the fabric of the tongue continue the same; but new phraseology changes much at once: it alters not the single stones of the building, but the order of the columns. If an academy should be established for the cultivation of our style, which I, who can never wish to see dependence multiplied, hope the spirit of English liberty will hinder or destroy, let them, instead of compiling grammars and dictionaries, endeavor with all their influence to stop the license of translators, whose idleness and ignorance, if it be suffered to proceed, will reduce us to babble a dialect of France.

If the changes that we fear be thus irresistible, what remains but to acquiesce with silence, as in the other insurmountable distresses of humanity? It remains that we retard what we cannot repel, that we palliate what we cannot cure. Life may be lengthened by care, though death cannot be ultimately defeated: tongues, like governments, have a natural tendency to degeneration; we have long preserved our constitution, let us make some struggles for our language.

In hope of giving longevity to that which its own nature forbids

---

[4] A *Proposal for Correcting, Improving and Ascertaining the English Tongue* (1712).

[5] plague.

to be immortal, I have devoted this book, the labor of years, to the honor of my country, that we may no longer yield the palm of philology, without a contest, to the nations of the continent. The chief glory of every people arises from its authors. Whether I shall add anything by my own writings to the reputation of English literature must be left to time. Much of my life has been lost under the pressures of disease; much has been trifled away; and much has always been spent in provision for the day that was passing over me; but I shall not think my employment useless or ignoble if, by my assistance, foreign nations and distant ages gain access to the propagators of knowledge, and understand the teachers of truth; if my labors afford light to the repositories of science, and add celebrity to Bacon, to Hooker, to Milton, and to Boyle.

When I am animated by this wish, I look with pleasure on my book, however defective, and deliver it to the world with the spirit of a man that has endeavored well. That it will immediately become popular I have not promised to myself: a few wild blunders and risible absurdities, from which no work of such multiplicity was ever free, may for a time furnish folly with laughter, and harden ignorance in contempt; but useful diligence will at last prevail, and there never can be wanting some who distinguish desert; who will consider that no dictionary of a living tongue ever can be perfect, since while it is hastening to publication, some words are budding and some falling away; that a whole life cannot be spent upon syntax and etymology, and that even a whole life would not be sufficient; that he whose design includes whatever language can express must often speak of what he does not understand; that a writer will sometimes be hurried by eagerness to the end, and sometimes faint with weariness under a task which Scaliger compares to the labors of the anvil and the mine; that what is obvious is not always known, and what is known is not always present; that sudden fits of inadvertency will surprise vigilance, slight avocations will seduce attention, and casual eclipses of the mind will darken learning; and that the writer shall often in vain trace his memory, at the moment of need, for that which yesterday he knew with intuitive readiness, and which will come uncalled into his thoughts tomorrow.

In this work, when it shall be found that much is omitted, let it not be forgotten that much likewise is performed; and though no book was ever spared out of tenderness to the author, and the world is little solicitous to know whence proceeded the faults of that which it condemns, yet it may gratify curiosity to inform it that the *English Dictionary* was written with little assistance of the learned, and without any patronage of the great; not in the soft obscurities of retirement, or under the shelter of academic bowers, but amidst inconvenience and distraction, in sickness and in sorrow. It may repress the triumph of malignant criticism to observe that if our language is not here fully displayed, I have only failed in an attempt which no human powers have hitherto completed. If the lexicons of ancient tongues, now immutably fixed and comprised in a few volumes, be yet, after the toil of successive ages, inadequate and delusive; if the aggregated knowledge and cooperating diligence of the Italian academicians did not secure them from the censure of Beni; if the embodied critics of France, when fifty years had been spent upon their work, were obliged to change its economy and give their second edition another form, I may surely be contented without the praise of perfection, which, if I could obtain in this gloom of solitude, what would it avail me? I have protracted my work till most of those whom I wished to please have sunk into the grave, and success and miscarriage are empty sounds. I therefore dismiss it with frigid tranquillity, having little to fear or hope from censure or from praise.

*　*　*　*

FROM

The History of Rasselas, Prince of Abyssinia [1759]

—◦-⸙⧊⸙-◦—

CHAPTER 10

Imlac's History Continued. A Dissertation Upon Poetry

"Wherever I went, I found that poetry was considered as the highest learning, and regarded with a veneration somewhat approaching to that which man would pay to the Angelic Nature. And yet it fills me with wonder, that, in almost all countries, the most ancient poets are considered as the best: whether it be that every other kind of knowledge is an acquisition gradually attained, and poetry is a gift conferred at once; or that the first poetry of every nation surprised them as a novelty, and retained the credit by consent which it received by accident at first; or whether, as the province of poetry is to describe nature and passion, which are always the same, the first writers took possession of the most striking objects for description, and the most probable occurrences for fiction, and left nothing to those that followed them but transcription of the same events, and new combinations of the same images. Whatever be the reason, it is commonly observed that the early writers are in possession of nature, and their followers of art: that the first excel in strength and invention, and the latter in elegance and refinement.

"I was desirous to add my name to this illustrious fraternity. I read all the poets of Persia and Arabia, and was able to repeat by memory the volumes that are suspended in the mosque of Mecca. But I soon found that no man was ever great by imitation. My desire of excellence impelled me to transfer my attention to nature and to life. Nature was to be my subject, and men to be my auditors. I could never describe what I had not seen. I could not hope to move those with delight or terror, whose interests and opinions I did not understand.

"Being now resolved to be a poet, I saw everything with a new purpose; my sphere of attention was suddenly magnified: no kind of knowledge was to be overlooked. I ranged mountains and deserts for images and resemblances, and pictured upon my mind every tree of the forest and flower of the valley. I observed with equal care the crags of the rock and the pinnacles of the palace. Sometimes I wandered along the mazes of the rivulet, and sometimes watched the changes of the summer clouds. To a poet nothing can be useless. Whatever is beautiful and whatever is dreadful must be familiar to his imagination: he must be conversant with all that is awfully vast or elegantly little.[1] The plants of the garden, the animals of the wood, the minerals of the earth, and meteors of the sky, must all concur to store his mind with inexhaustible variety: for every idea is useful for the enforcement or decoration of moral or religious truth; and he who knows most will have most power of diversifying his scenes, and of gratifying his reader with remote allusions and unexpected instruction.

"All the appearances of nature I was therefore careful to study, and every country which I have surveyed has contributed something to my poetical powers."

"In so wide a survey," said the prince, "you must surely have left

---

[1] *Cf.* Burke, p. 349.

much unobserved. I have lived, till now, within the circuit of these mountains, and yet cannot walk abroad without the sight of something which I had never beheld before, or never heeded."

"The business of a poet," said Imlac, "is to examine not the individual but the species; to remark general properties and large appearances. He does not number the streaks of the tulip, or describe the different shades in the verdure of the forest. He is to exhibit in his portraits of nature such prominent and striking features as recall the original to every mind; and must neglect the minuter discriminations, which one may have remarked, and another have neglected, for those characteristics which are alike obvious to vigilance and carelessness.

"But the knowledge of nature is only half the task of a poet; he must be acquainted likewise with all the modes of life. His character requires that he estimate the happiness and misery of every condition; observe the power of all the passions in all their combinations, and trace the changes of the human mind, as they are modified by various institutions and accidental influences of climate or custom, from the sprightliness of infancy to the despondence of decrepitude. He must divest himself of the prejudices of his age or country; he must consider right and wrong in their abstracted and invariable state; he must disregard present laws and opinions, and rise to general and transcendental truths, which will always be the same: he must therefore content himself with the slow progress of his name; contemn the applause of his own time, and commit his claims to the justice of posterity. He must write as the interpreter of nature, and the legislator of mankind, and consider himself as presiding over the thoughts and manners of future generations, as a being superior to time and place.

"His labour is not yet at an end; he must know many languages and many sciences; and, that his style may be worthy of his thoughts, must by incessant practice familiarize to himself every delicacy of speech and grace of harmony."

FROM CHAPTER 11
Imlac's Narrative Continued

Imlac now felt the enthusiastic fit, and was proceeding to aggrandize his own profession, when the prince cried out, "Enough! thou has convinced me that no human being can ever be a poet." . . .

FROM CHAPTER 44
The Dangerous Prevalence of Imagination

"Disorders of intellect," answered Imlac, "happen much more often than superficial observers will easily believe. Perhaps, if we speak with rigorous exactness, no human mind is in its right state. There is no man whose imagination does not sometimes predominate over his reason, who can regulate his attention wholly by his will, and whose ideas will come and go at his command. No man will be found in whose mind airy notions do not sometimes tyrannize, and force him to hope or fear beyond the limits of sober probability. All power of fancy over reason is a degree of insanity; but while this power is such as we can control and repress, it is not visible to others, nor considered as any depravation of the mental faculties: it is not pronounced madness but when it comes ungovernable, and apparently[2] influences speech or action.

"To indulge the power of fiction, and send imagination out upon the wing, is often the sport of those who delight too much in silent speculation. When we are alone we are not always busy; the labor of excogitation is too violent to last long; the ardor of inquiry will sometimes give way to idleness or satiety. He who has nothing external that can divert him, must find pleasure in his own thoughts, and must conceive himself what he is not; for who is pleased with what he is? He then expatiates in boundless futurity, and culls from all imaginable conditions that which for the present moment he should most desire, amuses his desires with impossible enjoyments, and confers upon his pride unattainable dominion. The mind dances from scene to scene, unites all pleasures in all combinations, and riots in delights, which nature and fortune, with all their bounty, cannot bestow.

"In time, some particular train of ideas fixes the attention, all other intellectual gratifications are rejected, the mind, in weariness or leisure, recurs constantly to the favorite conception, and feasts on the luscious falsehood, whenever she is offended with the bitterness of truth. By degrees the reign of fancy is confirmed; she grows first imperious, and in time despotic. Then fictions begin to operate as realities, false opinions fasten upon the mind, and life passes in dreams of rapture or of anguish."

---

[2] obviously.

* * * *

FROM Preface to
The Plays of William Shakespeare [1765]

—◦◦⦃⦄◦◦—

That praises are without reason lavished on the dead, and that the honors due only to excellence are paid to antiquity, is a complaint likely to be always continued by those who, being able to add nothing to truth, hope for eminence from the heresies of paradox; or those who, being forced by disappointment upon consolatory expedients, are willing to hope from posterity what the present age refuses, and flatter themselves that the regard which is yet denied by envy will be at last bestowed by time.

Antiquity, like every other quality that attracts the notice of mankind, has undoubtedly votaries that reverence it not from reason, but from prejudice. Some seem to admire indiscriminately whatever has been long preserved, without considering that time has sometimes cooperated with chance; all perhaps are more willing to honor past than present excellence; and the mind contemplates genius through the shades of age, as the eye surveys the sun through artificial opacity. The great contention of criticism is to find the faults of the moderns and the beauties of the ancients. While an author is yet living, we estimate his powers by his worst performance, and when he is dead, we rate them by his best.

To works, however, of which the excellence is not absolute and definite, but gradual and comparative; to works not raised upon principles demonstrative and scientific, but appealing wholly to observation and experience, no other test can be applied than length of duration and continuance of esteem. What mankind have long possessed they have often examined and compared, and if they persist to value the possession, it is because frequent comparisons have confirmed opinion in its favor. As among the works of nature, no man can properly call a river deep or a mountain high without the knowledge of many mountains and many rivers, so in the productions of genius, nothing can be styled excellent till it has been compared with other works of the same kind. Demonstration immediately displays its power, and has nothing to hope or fear from the flux of years; but works tentative and experimental must be estimated by their proportion to the general and collective ability of man, as it is discovered in a long succession of endeavors. Of the first building that was raised, it might be with certainty determined that it was round or square, but whether it was spacious or lofty must have been referred to time. The Pythagorean scale of numbers was at once discovered to be perfect,[1] but the poems of Homer we yet know not to transcend the common limits of human intelligence, but by remarking that nation after nation and century after century has been able to do little more than transpose his incidents, new name his characters, and paraphrase his sentiments.

The reverence due to writings that have long subsisted arises therefore not from any credulous confidence in the superior wisdom of past ages, or gloomy persuasion of the degeneracy of mankind, but is the consequence of acknowledged and indubitable positions: that what has been longest known has been most considered, and what is most considered is best understood.

The poet of whose works I have undertaken the revision may now begin to assume the dignity of an ancient, and claim the privilege of established fame and prescriptive veneration. He has long outlived his century, the term commonly fixed as the test of literary merit.[2] Whatever advantages he might once derive from personal allusions, local customs, or temporary opinions have for many years been lost; and every topic of merriment or motive of sorrow, which the modes of artificial life afforded him, now only obscure the scenes which they once illuminated. The effects of favor and competition are at an end; the tradition of his friendships and his enmities has perished; his works support no opinion with arguments, nor supply any faction with invectives; they can neither indulge vanity nor gratify malignity, but are read without any other reason than the desire of pleasure, and are therefore praised only as pleasure is obtained; yet, thus unassisted by interest or passion, they have passed through variations of taste and changes of manners, and as they devolved from one generation to another, have received new honors at every transmission.

But because human judgment, though it be gradually gaining upon certainty, never becomes infallible; and approbation, though long continued, may yet be only the approbation of prejudice or fashion; it is proper to inquire by what peculiarities of excellence Shakespeare has gained and kept the favor of his countrymen.

Nothing can please many and please long but just representations of general nature. Particular manners can be known to few, and

---

[1] *Cf.* Aristotle, *Metaphysics*, I, 5.
[2] *Cf.* Horace, *Epistles*, II, i, 39; and Pope, *Imitations of Horace*, II, i, 55–56.

therefore few only can judge how nearly they are copied. The irregular combinations of fanciful invention may delight a while, by that novelty of which the common satiety of life sends us all in quest; but the pleasures of sudden wonder are soon exhausted, and the mind can only repose on the stability of truth.

Shakespeare is above all writers, at least above all modern writers, the poet of nature, the poet that holds up to his readers a faithful mirror of manners and of life. His characters are not modified by the customs of particular places, unpracticed by the rest of the world; by the peculiarities of studies or professions, which can operate but upon small numbers; or by the accidents of transient fashions or temporary opinions: they are the genuine progeny of common humanity, such as the world will always supply, and observation will always find. His persons act and speak by the influence of those general passions and principles by which all minds are agitated, and the whole system of life is continued in motion. In the writings of other poets a character is too often an individual; in those of Shakespeare it is commonly a species.[3]

It is from this wide extension of design that so much instruction is derived. It is this which fills the plays of Shakespeare with practical axioms and domestic wisdom. It was said of Euripides that every verse was a precept;[4] and it may be said of Shakespeare that from his works may be collected a system of civil and economical prudence. Yet his real power is not shown in the splendor of particular passages, but by the progress of his fable and the tenor of his dialogue; and he that tries to recommend him by select quotations will succeed like the pedant in Hierocles,[5] who, when he offered his house to sale, carried a brick in his pocket as a specimen.

It will not easily be imagined how much Shakespeare excels in accommodating his sentiments to real life but by comparing him with other authors. It was observed by the ancient schools of declamation that the more diligently they were frequented, the more was the student disqualified for the world, because he found nothing there which he should ever meet in any other place.[6] The same remark may be applied to every stage but that of Shakespeare. The theatre, when it is under any other direction, is peopled by such characters as were never seen, conversing in a language which was

---

[3] *Cf.* the paragraph with Fielding, *Joseph Andrews*, III, 1.

[4] Cicero, *Epistolae ad familiares*, XVI, 8.

[5] Neo-Platonist Alexandrian (fl. 5th cent. A.D.); see *Commentarius in Aurea Carmina*, ed. Needham (1709), p. 462.

[6] See Petronius, *Satyricon*, 1.

never heard, upon topics which will never arise in the commerce of mankind. But the dialogue of this author is often so evidently determined by the incident which produces it, and is pursued with so much ease and simplicity, that it seems scarcely to claim the merit of fiction, but to have been gleaned by diligent selection out of common conversation and common occurrences.

Upon every other stage the universal agent is love, by whose power all good and evil is distributed, and every action quickened or retarded. To bring a lover, a lady, and a rival into the fable; to entangle them in contradictory obligations, perplex them with oppositions of interest, and harass them with violence of desires inconsistent with each other; to make them meet in rapture and part in agony; to fill their mouths with hyperbolical joy and outrageous sorrow; to distress them as nothing human ever was distressed; to deliver them as nothing human ever was delivered, is the business of a modern dramatist. For this, probability is violated, life is misrepresented, and language is depraved. But love is only one of many passions, and as it has no great influence upon the sum of life, it has little operation in the dramas of a poet who caught his ideas from the living world, and exhibited only what he saw before him. He knew that any other passion, as it was regular or exorbitant, was a cause of happiness or calamity.

Characters thus ample and general were not easily discriminated and preserved; yet perhaps no poet ever kept his personages more distinct from each other. I will not say with Pope that every speech may be assigned to the proper speaker,[7] because many speeches there are which have nothing characteristical; but perhaps, though some may be equally adapted to every person, it will be difficult to find any that can be properly transferred from the present possessor to another claimant. The choice is right when there is reason for choice.

Other dramatists can only gain attention by hyperbolical or aggravated characters, by fabulous and unexampled excellence or depravity, as the writers of barbarous romances invigorated the reader by a giant and a dwarf; and he that should form his expectations of human affairs from the play, or from the tale, would be equally deceived. Shakespeare has no heroes; his scenes are occupied only by men, who act and speak as the reader thinks that he should himself have spoken or acted on the same occasion. Even where the agency is supernatural, the dialogue is level with life. Other writers

[7] Preface to Shakespeare (1725), par. 4.

disguise the most natural passions and most frequent incidents; so that he who contemplates them in the book will not know them in the world. Shakespeare approximates the remote, and familiarizes the wonderful; the event which he represents will not happen, but if it were possible, its effects would probably be such as he has assigned; and it may be said that he has not only shown human nature as it acts in real exigences, but as it would be found in trials to which it cannot be exposed.[8]

This therefore is the praise of Shakespeare, that his drama is the mirror of life; that he who has mazed his imagination, in following the phantoms which other writers raise up before him, may here be cured of his delirious ecstasies, by reading human sentiments in human language; by scenes from which a hermit may estimate the transactions of the world, and a confessor predict the progress of the passions.

His adherence to general nature has exposed him to the censure of critics who form their judgments upon narrower principles. Dennis[9] and Rymer[1] think his Romans not sufficiently Roman, and Voltaire censures his kings as not completely royal.[2] Dennis is offended that Menenius, a senator of Rome, should play the buffoon; and Voltaire perhaps thinks decency violated when the Danish usurper is represented as a drunkard. But Shakespeare always makes nature predominate over accident; and if he preserves the essential character, is not very careful of distinctions superinduced and adventitious. His story requires Romans or kings, but he thinks only on men. He knew that Rome, like every other city, had men of all dispositions; and wanting a buffoon, he went into the senate-house for that which the senate-house would certainly have afforded him. He was inclined to show a usurper and a murderer not only odious but despicable; he therefore added drunkenness to his other qualities, knowing that kings love wine like other men, and that wine exerts its natural power upon kings. These are the petty cavils of petty minds; a poet overlooks the casual distinction of country and condition, as a painter, satisfied with the figure, neglects the drapery.

---

[8] See Addison, p. 259.

[9] *An Essay on the Genius and Writings of Shakespeare* (1712), in *Works*, ed. Hooker, II, 5–6.

[1] *A Short View of Tragedy* (1692), in *Critical Works*, ed. Zimansky, pp. 164–69.

[2] See "L'Appel a toutes les nations de l'Europe" (1761), in *Oeuvres complètes*, ed. Moland, XXIV, 193 ff. Voltaire replied to Johnson's censure in "Du théâtre anglais," *Dictionnaire Philosophique*, and in 1776 renewed the attack on Shakespeare in "Lettre à l'Académie française," XXX, 349 ff.

The censure which he has incurred by mixing comic and tragic scenes, as it extends to all his works, deserves more consideration. Let the fact be first stated and then examined.

Shakespeare's plays are not in the rigorous and critical sense either tragedies or comedies, but compositions of a distinct kind; exhibiting the real state of sublunary nature, which partakes of good and evil, joy and sorrow, mingled with endless variety of proportion and innumerable modes of combination; and expressing the course of the world, in which the loss of one is the gain of another; in which, at the same time, the reveler is hasting to his wine, and the mourner burying his friend; in which the malignity of one is sometimes defeated by the frolic of another; and many mischiefs and many benefits are done and hindered without design.

Out of this chaos of mingled purposes and casualties the ancient poets, according to the laws which custom had prescribed, selected some the crimes of men, and some their absurdities; some the momentous vicissitudes of life, and some the lighter occurrences; some the terrors of distress, and some the gaieties of prosperity. Thus rose the two modes of imitation known by the names of *tragedy* and *comedy*,[3] compositions intended to promote different ends by contrary means, and considered as so little allied that I do not recollect among the Greeks or Romans a single writer who attempted both.

Shakespeare has united the powers of exciting laughter and sorrow not only in one mind, but in one composition. Almost all his plays are divided between serious and ludicrous characters, and, in the successive evolutions of the design, sometimes produce seriousness and sorrow, and sometimes levity and laughter.

That this is a practice contrary to the rules of criticism will be readily allowed; but there is always an appeal open from criticism to nature. The end of writing is to instruct; the end of poetry is to instruct by pleasing.[4] That the mingled drama may convey all the instruction of tragedy or comedy cannot be denied, because it includes both in its alternations of exhibition, and approaches nearer than either to the appearance of life, by showing how great machinations and slender designs may promote or obviate one another, and the high and the low cooperate in the general system by unavoidable concatenation.

It is objected [5] that by this change of scenes the passions are

---

[3] *Cf.* Aristotle, *Poetics*, IV, 7–10.
[4] *Cf.* Horace, *Ars Poetica*, 343.
[5] *Cf.* Kames, p. 315; and Hume, *Treatise of Human Nature*, ed. Selby-Bigge, p. 379.

interrupted in their progression, and that the principal event, being not advanced by a due gradation of preparatory incidents, wants at last the power to move, which constitutes the perfection of dramatic poetry. This reasoning is so specious that it is received as true even by those who in daily experience feel it to be false. The interchanges of mingled scenes seldom fail to produce the intended vicissitudes of passion. Fiction cannot move so much but that the attention may be easily transferred; and though it must be allowed that pleasing melancholy be sometimes interrupted by unwelcome levity, yet let it be considered likewise that melancholy is often not pleasing, and that the disturbance of one man may be the relief of another; that different auditors have different habitudes; and that, upon the whole, all pleasure consists in variety.[6]

The players, who in their edition[7] divided our author's works into comedies, histories, and tragedies, seem not to have distinguished the three kinds by any very exact or definite ideas.

An action which ended happily to the principal persons, however serious or distressful through its intermediate incidents, in their opinion constituted a comedy. This idea of a comedy continued long amongst us, and plays were written which, by changing the catastrophe, were tragedies today and comedies tomorrow.

Tragedy was not in those times a poem of more general dignity or elevation than comedy; it required only a calamitous conclusion, with which the common criticism of that age was satisfied, whatever lighter pleasure it afforded in its progress.

History was a series of actions with no other than chronological succession, independent of each other, and without any tendency to introduce or regulate the conclusion. It is not always very nicely distinguished from tragedy. There is not much nearer approach to unity of action in the tragedy of *Antony and Cleopatra* than in the history of *Richard the Second*. But a history might be continued through many plays; as it had no plan, it had no limits.

Through all these denominations of the drama, Shakespeare's mode of composition is the same: an interchange of seriousness and merriment, by which the mind is softened at one time and exhilarated at another. But whatever be his purpose, whether to gladden or depress, or to conduct the story, without vehemence or emotion, through tracts of easy and familiar dialogue, he never

---

[6] *Cf.* Dryden, p. 78.
[7] The First Folio, 1623, ed. by Heming and Condell.

fails to attain his purpose; as he commands us, we laugh or mourn, or sit silent with quiet expectation, in tranquillity without in- difference.

When Shakespeare's plan is understood, most of the criticisms of Rymer and Voltaire vanish away. The play of *Hamlet* is opened, without impropriety, by two sentinels; Iago bellows at Brabantio's window, without injury to the scheme of the play, though in terms which a modern audience would not easily endure; the character of Polonius is seasonable and useful; and the Grave-diggers them- selves may be heard with applause.

Shakespeare engaged in dramatic poetry with the world open before him; the rules of the ancients were yet known to few; the public judgment was unformed; he had no example of such fame as might force him upon imitation, nor critics of such authority as might restrain his extravagance. He therefore indulged his natural disposition, and his disposition, as Rymer has remarked, led him to comedy. In tragedy he often writes with great appearance of toil and study what is written at last with little felicity; but in his comic scenes he seems to produce without labor what no labor can improve. In tragedy he is always struggling after some occasion to be comic, but in comedy he seems to repose, or to luxuriate, as in a mode of thinking congenial to his nature. In his tragic scenes there is always something wanting, but his comedy often surpasses expectation or desire. His comedy pleases by the thoughts and the language, and his tragedy for the greater part by incident and action. His tragedy seems to be skill, his comedy to be instinct.

The force of his comic scenes has suffered little diminution from the changes made by a century and a half, in manners or in words. As his personages act upon principles arising from genuine passion, very little modified by particular forms, their pleasures and vexations are communicable to all times and to all places; they are natural and therefore durable; the adventitious peculiarities of personal habits are only superficial dyes, bright and pleasing for a little while, yet soon fading to a dim tinct, without any remains of former lustre; but the discriminations of true passion are the colors of nature; they pervade the whole mass, and can only perish with the body that exhibits them. The accidental compositions of heterogeneous modes are dissolved by the chance which combined them; but the uniform simplicity of primitive qualities neither admits increase, nor suffers decay. The sand heaped by one flood is scattered by another, but the rock always continues in its place. The stream of time, which is continually washing the dissoluble fabrics of other poets, passes without injury by the adamant of Shakespeare.

If there be, what I believe there is, in every nation, a style which never becomes obsolete, a certain mode of phraseology so consonant and congenial to the analogy and principles of its respective language as to remain settled and unaltered; this style is probably to be sought in the common intercourse of life, among those who speak only to be understood, without ambition of elegance. The polite are always catching modish innovations, and the learned depart from established forms of speech in hope of finding or making better; those who wish for distinction forsake the vulgar, when the vulgar is right; but there is a conversation above grossness and below refinement, where propriety resides, and where this poet seems to have gathered his comic dialogue. He is therefore more agreeable to the ears of the present age than any other author equally remote, and among his other excellencies deserves to be studied as one of the original masters of our language.

These observations are to be considered not as unexceptionably constant, but as containing general and predominant truth. Shakespeare's familiar dialogue is affirmed to be smooth and clear, yet not wholly without ruggedness or difficulty; as a country may be eminently fruitful, though it has spots unfit for cultivation. His characters are praised as natural, though their sentiments are sometimes forced, and their actions improbable; as the earth upon the whole is spherical, though its surface is varied with protuberances and cavities.

Shakespeare with his excellencies has likewise faults, and faults sufficient to obscure and overwhelm any other merit. I shall show them in the proportion in which they appear to me, without envious malignity or superstitious veneration. No question can be more innocently discussed than a dead poet's pretensions to renown; and little regard is due to that bigotry which sets candor higher than truth.

His first defect is that to which may be imputed most of the evil in books or in men. He sacrifices virtue to convenience, and is so much more careful to please than to instruct that he seems to write without any moral purpose. From his writings indeed a system of social duty may be selected, for he that thinks reasonably must think morally; but his precepts and axioms drop casually from him; he makes no just distribution of good or evil, nor is always careful to show in the virtuous a disapprobation of the wicked; he carries his persons indifferently through right and wrong, and at the close dismisses them without further care, and leaves their examples to operate by chance. This fault the barbarity of his age cannot extenuate; for it is always a writer's duty to make the world better, and justice is a virtue independent on time or place.

The plots are often so loosely formed that a very slight consideration may improve them, and so carelessly pursued that he seems not always fully to comprehend his own design. He omits opportunities of instructing or delighting which the train of his story seems to force upon him, and apparently rejects those exhibitions which would be more affecting, for the sake of those which are more easy.

It may be observed that in many of his plays the latter part is evidently neglected. When he found himself near the end of his work and in view of his reward, he shortened the labor to snatch the profit. He therefore remits his efforts where he should most vigorously exert them, and his catastrophe is improbably produced or imperfectly represented.

He had no regard to distinction of time or place, but gives to one age or nation, without scruple, the customs, institutions, and opinions of another, at the expense not only of likelihood, but of possibility. These faults Pope has endeavored, with more zeal than judgment, to transfer to his imagined interpolators.[8] We need not wonder to find Hector quoting Aristotle,[9] when we see the loves of Theseus and Hippolyta combined with the Gothic mythology of fairies. Shakespeare, indeed, was not the only violator of chronology, for in the same age Sidney, who wanted not the advantages of learning, has in his *Arcadia* confounded the pastoral with the feudal times, the days of innocence, quiet, and security, with those of turbulence, violence, and adventure.

In his comic scenes he is seldom very successful when he engages his characters in reciprocations of smartness and contests of sarcasm; their jests are commonly gross, and their pleasantry licentious; neither his gentlemen nor his ladies have much delicacy, nor are sufficiently distinguished from his clowns by any appearance of refined manners. Whether he represented the real conversation of his time is not easy to determine; the reign of Elizabeth is commonly supposed to have been a time of stateliness, formality, and reserve; yet perhaps the relaxations of that severity were not very elegant.

---

[8] Preface to Shakespeare (1725), par. 22 f.
[9] *Troilus and Cressida*, II, ii, 167.

There must, however, have been always some modes of gaiety preferable to others, and a writer ought to choose the best.

In tragedy his performance seems constantly to be worse as his labor is more. The effusions of passion which exigence forces out are for the most part striking and energetic, but whenever he solicits his invention or strains his faculties, the offspring of his throes is tumor, meanness, tediousness, and obscurity.

In narration he affects a disproportionate pomp of diction and a wearisome train of circumlocution, and tells the incident imperfectly in many words, which might have been more plainly delivered in few. Narration in dramatic poetry is naturally tedious, as it is unanimated and inactive, and obstructs the progress of the action; it should therefore always be rapid, and enlivened by frequent interruption. Shakespeare found it an encumbrance, and instead of lightening it by brevity, endeavored to recommend it by dignity and splendor.

His declamations or set speeches are commonly cold and weak, for his power was the power of nature; when he endeavored, like other tragic writers, to catch opportunities of amplification, and instead of inquiring what the occasion demanded, to show how much his stores of knowledge could supply, he seldom escapes without the pity or resentment of his reader.

It is incident to him to be now and then entangled with an unwieldy sentiment which he cannot well express, and will not reject; he struggles with it a while, and if it continues stubborn, comprises it in words such as occur, and leaves it to be disentangled and evolved by those who have more leisure to bestow upon it.

Not that always where the language is intricate the thought is subtle, or the image always great where the line is bulky; the equality of words to things is very often neglected, and trivial sentiments and vulgar ideas disappoint the attention, to which they are recommended by sonorous epithets and swelling figures.

But the admirers of this great poet have never less reason to indulge their hopes of supreme excellence, than when he seems fully resolved to sink them in dejection, and mollify them with tender emotions by the fall of greatness, the danger of innocence, or the crosses of love. He is not long soft and pathetic without some idle conceit or contemptible equivocation. He no sooner begins to move than he counteracts himself; and terror and pity, as they are rising in the mind, are checked and blasted by sudden frigidity.

A quibble is to Shakespeare what luminous vapors are to the

traveler: he follows it at all adventures; it is sure to lead him out of his way, and sure to engulf him in the mire. It has some malignant power over his mind, and its fascinations are irresistible. Whatever be the dignity or profundity of his disquisition, whether he be enlarging knowledge or exalting affection, whether he be amusing attention with incidents or enchaining it in suspense, let but a quibble spring up before him, and he leaves his work unfinished. A quibble is the golden apple for which he will always turn aside from his career, or stoop from his elevation. A quibble, poor and barren as it is, gave him such delight that he was content to purchase it by the sacrifice of reason, propriety, and truth. A quibble was to him the fatal Cleopatra for which he lost the world, and was content to lose it.

It will be thought strange that, in enumerating the defects of this writer, I have not yet mentioned his neglect of the unities, his violation of those laws which have been instituted and established by the joint authority of poets and of critics.

For his other deviations from the art of writing, I resign him to critical justice, without making any other demand in his favor than that which must be indulged to all human excellence, that his virtues be rated with his failings. But from the censure which this irregularity may bring upon him, I shall, with due reverence to that learning which I must oppose, adventure to try how I can defend him.

His histories, being neither tragedies nor comedies, are not subject to any of their laws; nothing more is necessary to all the praise which they expect than that the changes of action be so prepared as to be understood, that the incidents be various and affecting, and the characters consistent, natural, and distinct. No other unity is intended, and therefore none is to be sought.

In his other works he has well enough preserved the unity of action. He has not, indeed, an intrigue regularly perplexed and regularly unraveled; he does not endeavor to hide his design only to discover it, for this is seldom the order of real events, and Shakespeare is the poet of nature. But his plan has commonly what Aristotle requires, a beginning, a middle, and an end;[1] one event is concatenated with another, and the conclusion follows by easy consequence. There are perhaps some incidents that might be spared, as in other poets there is much talk that only fills up time upon the stage; but the general system makes gradual advances, and the end of the play is the end of expectation.

---

[1] *Poetics*, VII, 3.

To the unities of time and place he has shown no regard, and perhaps a nearer view of the principles on which they stand will diminish their value, and withdraw from them the veneration which, from the time of Corneille, they have very generally re ceived, by discovering that they have given more trouble to the poet than pleasure to the auditor.

The necessity of observing the unities of time and place arises from the supposed necessity of making the drama credible. The critics hold it impossible that an action of months or years can be possibly believed to pass in three hours, or that the spectator can suppose himself to sit in the theatre while ambassadors go and return between distant kings, while armies are levied and towns besieged, while an exile wanders and returns, or till he whom they saw courting his mistress shall lament the untimely fall of his son. The mind revolts from evident falsehood, and fiction loses its force when it departs from the resemblance of reality.

From the narrow limitation of time necessarily arises the con-traction of place. The spectator, who knows that he saw the first act at Alexandria, cannot suppose that he sees the next at Rome, at a distance to which not the dragons of Medea could in so short a time have transported him; he knows with certainty that he has not changed his place; and he knows that place cannot change itself: that what was a house cannot become a plain, that what was Thebes can never be Persepolis.

Such is the triumphant language with which a critic exults over the misery of an irregular poet, and exults commonly without resistance or reply. It is time therefore to tell him, by the authority of Shakespeare, that he assumes as an unquestionable principle a position which, while his breath is forming it into words, his un-derstanding pronounces to be false. It is false that any representa-tion is mistaken for reality; that any dramatic fable in its materi-ality was ever credible, or for a single moment was ever credited.

The objection arising from the impossibility of passing the first hour at Alexandria, and the next at Rome, supposes that when the play opens, the spectator really imagines himself at Alexandria, and believes that his walk to the theatre has been a voyage to Egypt, and that he lives in the days of Antony and Cleopatra. Surely he that imagines this may imagine more. He that can take the stage at one time for the palace of the Ptolemies, may take it in half an hour for the promontory of Actium. Delusion, if delu-sion be admitted, has no certain limitation; if the spectator can be once persuaded that his old acquaintance are Alexander and

Caesar, that a room illuminated with candles is the plain of Pharsalia or the bank of Granicus, he is in a state of elevation above the reach of reason or of truth, and from the heights of empyrean poetry may despise the circumscriptions of terrestrial nature. There is no reason why a mind thus wandering in ecstasy would count the clock, or why an hour should not be a century in that calenture of the brains that can make the stage a field.

The truth is that the spectators are always in their senses, and know, from the first act to the last, that the stage is only a stage, and that the players are only players. They come to hear a certain number of lines recited with just gesture and elegant modulation. The lines relate to some action, and an action must be in some place; but the different actions that complete a story may be in places very remote from each other; and where is the absurdity of allowing that space to represent first Athens, and then Sicily, which was always known to be neither Sicily nor Athens, but a modern theatre.

By supposition, as place is introduced, time may be extended; the time required by the fable elapses for the most part between the acts; for of so much of the action as is represented, the real and poetical duration is the same. If in the first act preparations for war against Mithridates are represented to be made in Rome, the event of the war may, without absurdity, be represented in the catastrophe as happening in Pontus; we know that there is neither war nor preparation for war; we know that we are neither in Rome nor Pontus, that neither Mithridates nor Lucullus are before us. The drama exhibits successive imitations of successive actions, and why may not the second imitation represent an action that happened years after the first, if it be so connected with it that nothing but time can be supposed to intervene? Time is, of all modes of existence, most obsequious to the imagination; a lapse of years is as easily conceived as a passage of hours. In contemplation we easily contract the time of real actions, and therefore willingly permit it to be contracted when we only see their imitation.

It will be asked how the drama moves if it is not credited. It is credited with all the credit due to a drama. It is credited, whenever it moves, as a just picture of a real original; as representing to the auditor what he would himself feel if he were to do or suffer what is there feigned to be suffered or to be done. The reflection that strikes the heart is not that the evils before us are real evils, but that they are evils to which we ourselves may be exposed. If there be any fallacy, it is not that we fancy the players, but that we fancy ourselves unhappy for a moment; but we rather lament the possibility than suppose the presence of misery, as a mother weeps over her babe when she remembers that death may take it from her. The delight of tragedy proceeds from our consciousness of fiction; if we thought murders and treasons real, they would please no more.

Imitations produce pain or pleasure, not because they are mistaken for realities, but because they bring realities to mind. When the imagination is recreated by a painted landscape, the trees are not supposed capable to give us shade, or the fountains coolness; but we consider how we should be pleased with such fountains playing beside us, and such woods waving over us. We are agitated in reading the history of *Henry the Fifth*; yet no man takes his book for the field of Agincourt. A dramatic exhibition is a book recited with concomitants that increase or diminish its effect. Familiar comedy is often more powerful on the theatre than in the page; imperial tragedy is always less. The humor of Petruchio may be heightened by grimace, but what voice or what gesture can hope to add dignity or force to the soliloquy of Cato? [2]

A play read affects the mind like a play acted. It is therefore evident that the action is not supposed to be real, and it follows that between the acts a longer or shorter time may be allowed to pass, and that no more account of space or duration is to be taken by the auditor of a drama than by the reader of a narrative, before whom may pass in an hour the life of a hero or the revolutions of an empire.

Whether Shakespeare knew the unities and rejected them by design, or deviated from them by happy ignorance, it is, I think, impossible to decide, and useless to inquire. We may reasonably suppose that when he rose to notice, he did not want the counsels and admonitions of scholars and critics, and that he at last deliberately persisted in a practice which he might have begun by chance. As nothing is essential to the fable but unity of action, and as the unities of time and place arise evidently from false assumptions, and, by circumscribing the extent of the drama, lessen its variety, I cannot think it much to be lamented that they were not known by him, or not observed. Nor if such another poet could arise, should I very vehemently reproach him that his first act passed at Venice and his next in Cyprus. Such violations of rules merely positive become the comprehensive genius of Shake-

[2] Addison's *Cato*, V, i.

speare, and such censures are suitable to the minute and slender criticism of Voltaire:

> *Non usque adeo permiscuit imis*
> *Longus summa dies, ut non, si voce Metelli*
> *Serventur leges, malint a Caesare tolli.*[3]

Yet when I speak thus slightly of dramatic rules, I cannot but recollect how much wit and learning may be produced against me; before such authorities I am afraid to stand, not that I think the present question one of those that are to be decided by mere authority, but because it is to be suspected that these precepts have not been so easily received but for better reasons than I have yet been able to find. The result of my inquiries, in which it would be ludicrous to boast of impartiality, is that the unities of time and place are not essential to a just drama; that though they may sometimes conduce to pleasure, they are always to be sacrificed to the nobler beauties of variety and instruction; and that a play written with nice observation of critical rules is to be contemplated as an elaborate curiosity, as the product of superfluous and ostentatious art, by which is shown rather what is possible than what is necessary.

He that, without diminution of any other excellence, shall preserve all the unities unbroken, deserves the like applause with the architect who shall display all the orders of architecture in a citadel, without any deduction from its strength; but the principal beauty of a citadel is to exclude the enemy; and the greatest graces of a play are to copy nature and instruct life.

Perhaps what I have here not dogmatically but deliberatively written may call the principles of the drama to a new examination. I am almost frighted at my own temerity; and when I estimate the fame and the strength of those that maintain the contrary opinion, am ready to sink down in reverential silence; as Aeneas withdrew from the defense of Troy when he saw Neptune shaking the wall, and Juno heading the besiegers.[4]

Those whom my arguments cannot persuade to give their approbation to the judgment of Shakespeare, will easily, if they consider the condition of his life, make some allowance for his ignorance.

---

[3] Lucan, *Pharsalia*, III, 138–40: "Time at long last has yet to work such depth of confusion that the laws would not prefer to be annulled by Caesar than saved by the voice of Metellus."

[4] *Aeneid*, II, 610–14.

Every man's performances, to be rightly estimated, must be compared with the state of the age in which he lived, and with his own particular opportunities; and though to the reader a book be not worse or better for the circumstances of the author, yet as there is always a silent reference of human works to human abilities, and as the inquiry how far man may extend his designs, or how high he may rate his native force, is of far greater dignity than in what rank we shall place any particular performance, curiosity is always busy to discover the instruments, as well as to survey the workmanship, to know how much is to be ascribed to original powers, and how much to casual and adventitious help. The palaces of Peru or Mexico were certainly mean and incommodious habitations, if compared to the houses of European monarchs; yet who could forbear to view them with astonishment who remembered that they were built without the use of iron?

The English nation in the time of Shakespeare was yet struggling to emerge from barbarity. The philology[5] of Italy had been transplanted hither in the reign of Henry the Eighth, and the learned languages had been successfully cultivated by Lily,[6] Linacre,[7] and More; by Pole, Cheke, and Gardiner;[8] and afterwards by Smith, Clerk, Haddon, and Ascham.[9] Greek was now taught to boys in the principal schools, and those who united elegance with learning read with great diligence the Italian and Spanish poets. But literature was yet confined to professed scholars, or to men and women of high rank. The public was gross and dark; and to be able to read and write was an accomplishment still valued for its rarity.

Nations, like individuals, have their infancy. A people newly awakened to literary curiosity, being yet unacquainted with the true state of things, knows not how to judge of that which is proposed as its resemblance. Whatever is remote from common

---

[5] literary learning.
[6] William Lily (1466–1522), grammarian.
[7] Thomas Linacre (1460–1524), Oxford professor who taught Greek to both Erasmus and Sir Thomas More.
[8] Cardinal Reginald Pole (1500–58), Bishop Stephen Gardiner (1483?–1555), both one-time chancellors of Cambridge, where Sir John Cheke (1514–57) was professor of Greek.
[9] Sir Thomas Smith (1514–77), statesman and Greek scholar at Cambridge; Bishop John Clerk (d. 1541); Walter Haddon (1516–72), vice-chancellor at Cambridge, later professor at Oxford; Roger Ascham (1516–72), Greek scholar at Cambridge, tutor to Queen Elizabeth, author of *The Schoolmaster*; see the short biography by Johnson.

appearances is always welcome to vulgar, as to childish credulity; and of a country unenlightened by learning, the whole people is the vulgar. The study of those who then aspired to plebeian learning was laid out upon adventures, giants, dragons, and enchantments. *The Death of Arthur* was the favorite volume.[1]

The mind which has feasted on the luxurious wonders of fiction has no taste of the insipidity of truth. A play which imitated only the common occurrences of the world would, upon the admirers of *Palmerin*[2] and *Guy of Warwick*,[3] have made little impression; he that wrote for such an audience was under the necessity of looking round for strange events and fabulous transactions, and that incredibility by which maturer knowledge is offended was the chief recommendation of writings to unskillful curiosity.

Our author's plots are generally borrowed from novels, and it is reasonable to suppose that he chose the most popular, such as were read by many and related by more; for his audience could not have followed him through the intricacies of the drama, had they not held the thread of the story in their hands.

The stories, which we now find only in remoter authors, were in his time accessible and familiar. The fable of *As You Like It*, which is supposed to be copied from Chaucer's *Gamelyn*,[4] was a little pamphlet of those times;[5] and old Mr. Cibber[6] remembered the tale of Hamlet in plain English prose, which the critics have now to seek in Saxo Grammaticus.[7]

His English histories he took from English chronicles and English ballads; and as the ancient writers were made known to his countrymen by versions, they supplied him with new subjects; he dilated some of Plutarch's lives into plays, when they had been translated by North.

His plots, whether historical or fabulous, are always crowded with incidents, by which the attention of a rude people was more easily caught than by sentiment or argumentation; and such is the power of the marvellous, even over those who despise it, that

---

[1] Malory's *Morte d'Arthur* (1485).

[2] Prose romance admired by Cervantes; Johnson read *Il Palmerino d'Inghilterra* "for the language" when he was planning a trip to Italy in 1776. Percy reported that as a boy Johnson was immoderately fond of reading romances.

[3] English metrical romance (c. 1300), published in the sixteenth century.

[4] *The Tale of Gamelyn*, not rejected from the Chaucer canon until Tyrwhitt's edition in 1775.

[5] Thomas Lodge's *Rosalynde* (1590).

[6] Colley Cibber (1671–1757), actor, playwright, hero of *The Dunciad*.

[7] In whose twelfth-century *Historia Danica* Hamlet first appears.

every man finds his mind more strongly seized by the tragedies of Shakespeare than of any other writer; others please us by particular speeches, but he always makes us anxious for the event, and has perhaps excelled all but Homer in securing the first purpose of a writer, by exciting restless and unquenchable curiosity, and compelling him that reads his work to read it through.

The shows and bustle with which his plays abound have the same original. As knowledge advances, pleasure passes from the eye to the ear, but returns, as it declines, from the ear to the eye. Those to whom our author's labors were exhibited had more skill in pomps or processions than in poetical language, and perhaps wanted some visible and discriminated events as comments on the dialogue. He knew how he should most please; and whether his practice is more agreeable to nature, or whether his example has prejudiced the nation, we still find that on our stage something must be done as well as said, and inactive declamation is very coldly heard, however musical or elegant, passionate or sublime.

Voltaire expresses his wonder that our author's extravagancies are endured by a nation which has seen the tragedy of *Cato*.[8] Let him be answered that Addison speaks the language of poets, and Shakespeare of men. We find in *Cato* innumerable beauties which enamor us of its author, but we see nothing that acquaints us with human sentiments or human actions; we place it with the fairest and the noblest progeny which judgment propagates by conjunction with learning, but *Othello* is the vigorous and vivacious offspring of observation impregnated by genius. *Cato* affords a splendid exhibition of artificial and fictitious manners, and delivers just and noble sentiments, in diction easy, elevated, and harmonious, but its hopes and fears communicate no vibration to the heart; the composition refers us only to the writer; we pronounce the name of *Cato*, but we think on Addison.

The work of a correct and regular writer is a garden accurately formed and diligently planted, varied with shades and scented with flowers; the composition of Shakespeare is a forest, in which oaks extend their branches, and pines tower in the air, interspersed sometimes with weeds and brambles, and sometimes giving shelter to myrtles and to roses; filling the eye with awful pomp, and gratifying the mind with endless diversity. Other poets display cabinets of precious rarities, minutely finished, wrought into shape, and polished unto brightness. Shakespeare opens a mine which

---

[8] *Lettres sur les Anglais* (1734), no. XVIII.

contains gold and diamonds in unexhaustible plenty, though clouded by incrustations, debased by impurities, and mingled with a mass of meaner minerals.

It has been much disputed whether Shakespeare owed his excellence to his own native force, or whether he had the common helps of scholastic education, the precepts of critical science, and the examples of ancient authors.

There has always prevailed a tradition that Shakespeare wanted learning, that he had no regular education, nor much skill in the dead languages. Jonson, his friend, affirms that "he had small Latin, and no Greek," [9] who, besides that he had no imaginable temptation to falsehood, wrote at a time when the character and acquisitions of Shakespeare were known to multitudes. His evidence ought therefore to decide the controversy, unless some testimony of equal force could be opposed.

Some have imagined that they have discovered deep learning in many imitations of old writers; but the examples which I have known urged were drawn from books translated in his time, or were such easy coincidences of thought as will happen to all who consider the same subjects, or such remarks on life or axioms of morality as float in conversation, and are transmitted through the world in proverbial sentences.

I have found it remarked [1] that in this important sentence, "Go before, I'll follow," [2] we read a translation of *i prae, sequar*.[3] I have been told that when Caliban, after a pleasing dream, says, "I cry'd to sleep again," [4] the author imitates Anacreon, who had, like every other man, the same wish on the same occasion.

There are a few passages which may pass for imitations, but so few that the exception only confirms the rule; he obtained them from accidental quotations or by oral communication, and as he used what he had, would have used more if he had obtained it.

The *Comedy of Errors* is confessedly taken from the *Menaechmi* of Plautus, from the only play of Plautus which was then in English. What can be more probable than that he who copied

---

[9] "To the Memory of Mr. William Shakespeare," written for the First Folio, l. 31. Jonson said "less" Greek.

[1] Zachary Grey, *Critical, historical, and explanatory notes on Shakespeare* (1754), II, 53.

[2] *Richard III*, I, i, 143.

[3] Terence, *Andria*, 171.

[4] *The Tempest*, III, ii, 155.

that would have copied more, but that those which were not translated were inaccessible?

Whether he knew the modern languages is uncertain. That his plays have some French scenes proves but little; he might easily procure them to be written, and probably, even though he had known the language in the common degree, he could not have written it without assistance. In the story of *Romeo and Juliet* he is observed to have followed the English translation where it deviates from the Italian; but this, on the other part, proves nothing against his knowledge of the original. He was to copy not what he knew himself, but what was known to his audience.

It is most likely that he had learned Latin sufficiently to make him acquainted with construction, but that he never advanced to an easy perusal of the Roman authors. Concerning his skill in modern languages I can find no sufficient ground of determination; but as no imitations of French or Italian authors have been discovered, though the Italian poetry was then high in esteem, I am inclined to believe that he read little more than English, and chose for his fables only such tales as he found translated.

That much knowledge is scattered over his works is very justly observed by Pope,[5] but it is often such knowledge as books did not supply. He that will understand Shakespeare must not be content to study him in the closet: he must look for his meaning sometimes among the sports of the field, and sometimes among the manufactures of the shop.

There is, however, proof enough that he was a very diligent reader, nor was our language then so indigent of books but that he might very liberally indulge his curiosity without excursion into foreign literature. Many of the Roman authors were translated, and some of the Greek; the Reformation had filled the kingdom with theological learning; most of the topics of human disquisition had found English writers; and poetry had been cultivated, not only with diligence, but success. This was a stock of knowledge sufficient for a mind so capable of appropriating and improving it.

But the greater part of his excellence was the product of his own genius. He found the English stage in a state of the utmost rudeness; no essays either in tragedy or comedy had appeared, from which it could be discovered to what degree of delight either one or other might be carried. Neither character nor dialogue were yet understood. Shakespeare may be truly said to have introduced

---

[5] Preface to Shakespeare, par. 15.

them both amongst us, and, in some of his happier scenes, to have carried them both to the utmost height.

By what gradations of improvement he proceeded is not easily known, for the chronology of his works is yet unsettled. Rowe is of opinion that "perhaps we are not to look for his beginning, like those of other writers, in his least perfect works; art had so little, and nature so large a share in what he did, that for aught I know," says he, "the performances of his youth, as they were the most vigorous, were the best." [6] But the power of nature is only the power of using to any certain purpose the materials which diligence procures, or opportunity supplies. Nature gives no man knowledge, and when images are collected by study and experience, can only assist in combining or applying them. Shakespeare, however favored by nature, could impart only what he had learned; and as he must increase his ideas, like other mortals, by gradual acquisition, he, like them, grew wiser as he grew older, could display life better as he knew it more, and instruct with more efficacy as he was himself more amply instructed.

There is a vigilance of observation and accuracy of distinction which books and precepts cannot confer; from this almost all original and native excellence proceeds. Shakespeare must have looked upon mankind with perspicacity, in the highest degree curious and attentive. Other writers borrow their characters from preceding writers, and diversify them only by the accidental appendages of present manners; the dress is a little varied, but the body is the same. Our author had both matter and form to provide; for except the characters of Chaucer, to whom I think he is not much indebted, there were no writers in English, and perhaps not many in other modern languages, which showed life in its native colors.

The contest about the original benevolence or malignity of man had not yet commenced.[7] Speculation had not yet attempted to analyze the mind, to trace the passions to their sources, to unfold the seminal principles of vice and virtue, or sound the depths of the heart for the motives of action. All those inquiries which from that time that human nature became the fashionable study, have been made sometimes with nice discernment, but often with idle subtlety, were yet unattempted. The tales, with which the infancy of learning was satisfied, exhibited only the

---

[6] Nicholas Rowe (1674–1718), poet and playwright. See "Some Account of the Life of William Shakespeare," preface to his edition (1709–10), par. 4.

[7] Elledge notes: "the contest initiated by Hobbes."

superficial appearances of action, related the events but omitted the causes, and were formed for such as delighted in wonders rather than in truth. Mankind was not then to be studied in the closet; he that would know the world was under the necessity of gleaning his own remarks by mingling as he could in its business and amusements.

Boyle congratulated himself upon his high birth, because it favored his curiosity by facilitating his access.[8] Shakespeare had no such advantage; he came to London a needy adventurer, and lived for a time by very mean employments. Many works of genius and learning have been performed in states of life that appear very little favorable to thought or to inquiry; so many, that he who considers them is inclined to think that he sees enterprise and perseverance predominating over all external agency, and bidding help and hindrance vanish before them. The genius of Shakespeare was not to be depressed by the weight of poverty, nor limited by the narrow conversation to which men in want are inevitably condemned; the incumbrances of his fortune were shaken from his mind "as dewdrops from a lion's mane." [9]

Though he had so many difficulties to encounter and so little assistance to surmount them, he has been able to obtain an exact knowledge of many modes of life and many casts of native dispositions; to vary them with great multiplicity; to mark them by nice distinctions; and to show them in full view by proper combinations. In this part of his performances he had none to imitate, but has himself been imitated by all succeeding writers; and it may be doubted whether from all his successors more maxims of theoretical knowledge or more rules of practical prudence can be collected, than he alone has given to his country.

Nor was his attention confined to the actions of men; he was an exact surveyor of the inanimate world; his descriptions have always some peculiarities, gathered by contemplating things as they really exist. It may be observed that the oldest poets of many nations preserve their reputation, and that the following generations of wit, after a short celebrity, sink into oblivion. The first, whoever they be, must take their sentiments and descriptions immediately from knowledge; the resemblance is therefore just, their descriptions are verified by every eye, and their sentiments acknowledged by every breast. Those whom their fame invites to

---

[8] See Thomas Birch, *Life of Robert Boyle* (1744), pp. 18–19. Robert Boyle (1627–91), famous English chemist.

[9] *Troilus and Cressida*, III, iii, 225.

the same studies, copy partly them and partly nature, till the books of one age gain such authority as to stand in the place of nature to another, and imitation, always deviating a little, becomes at last capricious and casual. Shakespeare, whether life or nature be his subject, shows plainly that he has seen with his own eyes; he gives the image which he receives, not weakened or distorted by the intervention of any other mind; the ignorant feel his representations to be just, and the learned see that they are complete.

Perhaps it would not be easy to find any author except Homer who invented so much as Shakespeare, who so much advanced the studies which he cultivated, or effused so much novelty upon his age or country. The form, the characters, the language, and the shows of the English drama are his. . . .

Yet it must be at last confessed that as we owe everything to him, he owes something to us; that if much of his praise is paid by perception and judgment, much is likewise given by custom and veneration. We fix our eyes upon his graces and turn them from his deformities, and endure in him what we should in another loathe or despise. If we endured without praising, respect for the father of our drama might excuse us; but I have seen in the book of some modern critic[1] a collection of anomalies which show that he has corrupted language by every mode of depravation, but which his admirer has accumulated as a monument of honor.

He has scenes of undoubted and perpetual excellence, but perhaps not one play which, if it were now exhibited as the work of a contemporary writer, would be heard to the conclusion. I am indeed far from thinking that his works were wrought to his own ideas of perfection; when they were such as would satisfy the audience, they satisfied the writer. It is seldom that authors, though more studious of fame than Shakespeare, rise much above the standard of their own age; to add a little to what is best will always be sufficient for present praise, and those who find themselves exalted into fame are willing to credit their encomiasts, and to spare the labor of contending with themselves.

It does not appear that Shakespeare thought his works worthy of posterity, that he levied any ideal tribute upon future times, or had any further prospect than of present popularity and present profit. When his plays had been acted, his hope was at an end; he solicited no addition of honor from the reader. He

---

[1] John Upton, *Critical Observations on Shakespeare* (1746).

therefore made no scruple to repeat the same jests in many dialogues, or to entangle different plots by the same knot of perplexity; which may be at least forgiven him by those who recollect that, of Congreve's four comedies, two are concluded by a marriage in a mask, by a deception which perhaps never happened, and which, whether likely or not, he did not invent.

So careless was this great poet of future fame that, though he retired to ease and plenty while he was yet little "declined into the vale of years," [2] before he could be disgusted with fatigue or disabled by infirmity, he made no collection of his works, nor desired to rescue those that had been already published from the depravations that obscured them, or secure to the rest a better destiny, by giving them to the world in their genuine state.

Of the plays which bear the name of Shakespeare in the late editions, the greater part were not published till about seven years after his death, and the few which appeared in his life are apparently thrust into the world without the care of the author, and therefore probably without his knowledge.

Of all the publishers, clandestine or professed, the negligence and unskillfulness has by the late revisers been sufficiently shown. The faults of all are indeed numerous and gross, and have not only corrupted many passages perhaps beyond recovery, but have brought others into suspicion, which are only obscured by obsolete phraseology, or by the writer's unskillfulness and affectation. To alter is more easy than to explain, and temerity is a more common quality than diligence. Those who saw that they must employ conjecture to a certain degree were willing to indulge it a little further. Had the author published his own works, we should have sat quietly down to disentangle his intricacies and clear his obscurities; but now we tear what we cannot loose, and eject what we happen not to understand.

The faults are more than could have happened without the concurrence of many causes. The style of Shakespeare was in itself ungrammatical, perplexed, and obscure; his works were transcribed for the players by those who may be supposed to have seldom understood them; they were transmitted by copiers equally unskillful, who still multiplied errors; they were perhaps sometimes mutilated by the actors for the sake of shortening the speeches; and were at last printed without correction of the press.

In this state they remained, not as Dr. Warburton supposes,

---

[2] *Othello*, III, iii, 265.

because they were unregarded,[3] but because the editor's art[4] was not yet applied to modern languages, and our ancestors were accustomed to so much negligence of English printers that they could very patiently endure it. . . .

Notes are often necessary, but they are necessary evils. Let him that is yet unacquainted with the powers of Shakespeare, and who desires to feel the highest pleasure that the drama can give, read every play from the first scene to the last, with utter negligence of all his commentators. When his fancy is once on the wing, let it not stoop at correction or explanation. When his attention is strongly engaged, let it disdain alike to turn aside to the name of Theobald and of Pope. Let him read on through brightness and obscurity, through integrity and corruption; let him preserve his comprehension of the dialogue and his interest in the fable. And when the pleasures of novelty have ceased, let him attempt exactness, and read the commentators.

Particular passages are cleared by notes, but the general effect of the work is weakened. The mind is refrigerated by interruption; the thoughts are diverted from the principal subject; the reader is weary, he suspects not why, and at last throws away the book which he has too diligently studied.

Parts are not to be examined till the whole has been surveyed; there is a kind of intellectual remoteness necessary for the comprehension of any great work in its full design and its true proportions; a close approach shows the smaller niceties, but the beauty of the whole is discerned no longer.

It is not very grateful to consider how little the succession of editors has added to this author's power of pleasing. He was read, admired, studied, and imitated, while he was yet deformed with all the improprieties which ignorance and neglect could accumulate upon him; while the reading was yet not rectified, nor his allusions understood; yet then did Dryden pronounce "that Shakespeare was the man who of all Modern, and perhaps Ancient poets, had the largest and most comprehensive soul. All the images of Nature were still present to him, and he drew them not laboriously but luckily; when he describes anything, you more than see it, you feel it too. Those who accuse him to have wanted learning, give

---

[3] Bishop William Warburton (1698–1779); see preface to his edition of Shakespeare (1747), par. 2.

[4] The remainder of Johnson's preface is an exposition of the art of editing and a surview of previous Shakespearean editors or commentators: Rowe, Pope, Theobald, Hammer, Upton, Warburton, Grey.

him the greater commendation: he was naturally learned; he needed not the spectacles of books to read Nature; he looked inwards and found her there. I cannot say he is everywhere alike; were he so, I should do him injury to compare him with the greatest of mankind. He is many times flat, insipid; his comic wit degenerating into clenches, his serious swelling into bombast. But he is always great when some great occasion is presented to him; no man can say he ever had a fit subject for his wit and did not then raise himself as high above the rest of poets,

> *Quantum lenta solent inter viburna cupressi*." [5]

It is to be lamented that such a writer should want a commentary; that his language should become obsolete, or his sentiments obscure. But it is vain to carry wishes beyond the condition of human things; that which must happen to all has happened to Shakespeare, by accident and time; and more than has been suffered by any other writer since the use of types[6] has been suffered by him, through his own negligence of fame, or perhaps by that superiority of mind which despised its own performances when it compared them with its powers, and judged those works unworthy to be preserved which the critics of following ages were to contend for the fame of restoring and explaining.

Among these candidates of inferior fame, I am now to stand the judgment of the public; and wish that I could confidently produce my commentary as equal to the encouragement which I have had the honor of receiving. Every work of this kind is by its nature deficient, and I should feel little solicitude about the sentence, were it to be pronounced only by the skillful and the learned.

---

[5] See p. 84.
[6] printing.

* * * *

Selected Notes on *The Plays*

1 Henry IV

Shakespeare has apparently designed a regular connection of these dramatic histories from *Richard the Second* to *Henry the Fifth*. King Henry, at the end of *Richard the Second*, declares his purpose to visit the Holy Land, which he resumes in this speech. The complaint made by King Henry in the last act of *Richard the Second*, of the wildness of his son, prepares the reader for the frolics which are here to be recounted, and the characters which are now to be exhibited.

I, ii, 218 ff: I know you all, and will a while uphold
        The unyok'd humor of your idleness, &c.

This speech is very artfully introduced to keep the Prince from appearing vile in the opinion of the audience; it prepares them for his future reformation, and, what is yet more valuable, exhibits a natural picture of a great mind offering excuses to itself, and palliating those follies which it can neither justify nor forsake.

I, iii, 201 ff: By heav'n, methinks it were an easy leap,
        To pluck bright honor from the pale-fac'd moon,
        Or dive into the bottom of the deep, &c.

"So that we see, though the expression be sublime and daring, yet the thought is the natural movement of a heroic mind. Euripides, at least, thought so, when he put the very same sentiment, in the same words, into the mouth of Eteocles: 'I will not, madam, disguise my thoughts; I could scale heaven, I could descend to the very entrails of the earth, if so be that by that price I could obtain a kingdom.'" [1]
—WARBURTON.

Though I am very far from condemning this speech, with Gildon and Theobald, as *absolute madness*, yet I cannot find in it that profundity of reflection and beauty of allegory which the learned

[1] *The Phoenician Women*, 11.

commentator has endeavored to display. This sally of Hotspur may be, I think, soberly and rationally vindicated as the violent eruption of a mind inflated with ambition and fired with resentment; as the boastful clamor of a man able to do much and eager to do more; as the hasty motion of turbulent desire; as the dark expression of indetermined thoughts. The passage from Euripides is surely not allegorical; yet it is produced, and properly, as parallel.

II, iv, 394–5:   You may buy land now as cheap as stinking mackerel.

In former times, the prosperity of the nation was known by the value of land as now by the price of stocks. Before Henry the Seventh made it safe to serve the king regnant, it was the practice at every revolution for the conqueror to confiscate the estates of those that opposed, and perhaps of those who did not assist him. Those, therefore, that foresaw a change of government, and thought their estates in danger, were desirous to sell them in haste for something that might be carried away.

IV, i, 97–9:   All furnisht, all in arms,
All plum'd like estridges, that with the wind
Baited like eagles.

I read:

All furnisht, all in arms,
All plum'd like estridges that *wing* the wind
Baited like eagles.

This gives a strong image. They were not only *plum'd like estridges*, but their plumes fluttered like those of an estridge on the wing, mounting against the wind. A more lively representation of young men ardent for enterprise perhaps no writer has ever given.

2 Henry IV

IV, v, 211:   To lead out many to the Holy Land.

This journey to the Holy Land, of which the king very frequently revives the mention, had two motives—religion and policy. He durst not wear the ill-gotten crown without expiation, but in the act of expiation he contrives to make his wickedness successful.

V, v, 67:   I banish thee, on pain of death.

Mr. Rowe observes that many readers lament to see Falstaff so hardly used by his old friend. But if it be considered that the fat knight has never uttered one sentiment of generosity, and with all his power of exciting mirth, has nothing in him that can be esteemed, no great pain will be suffered from the reflection that he is compelled to live honestly, and maintained by the king, with a promise of advancement when he shall deserve it.

I think the poet more blamable for Poins, who is always represented as joining some virtues with his vices, and is therefore treated by the prince with apparent distinction; yet he does nothing in the time of action, and though after the bustle is over he is again a favorite, at last vanishes without notice. Shakespeare certainly lost him by heedlessness, in the multiplicity of his characters, the variety of his action, and his eagerness to end the play.

V, v, 97:   Go, carry Sir John Falstaff to the Fleet.

I do not see why Falstaff is carried to the Fleet. We have never lost sight of him since his dismission from the king; he has committed no new fault, and therefore incurred no punishment; but the different agitations of fear, anger, and surprise in him and his company make a good scene to the eye; and our author, who wanted them no longer on the stage, was glad to find this method of sweeping them away.

I fancy every reader, when he ends this play, cries out with Desdemona, "O most lame and impotent conclusion!" [2] As this play was not, to our knowledge, divided into acts by the author, I could be content to conclude it with the death of Henry the Fourth.

In that Jerusalem shall Harry die.[3]

These scenes which now make the fifth act of *Henry the Fourth* might then be the first of *Henry the Fifth*; but the truth is that they do not unite very commodiously to either play. When these plays were represented, I believe they ended as they are now ended in the books; but Shakespeare seems to have designed that the whole series of action from the beginning of *Richard the Second* to the end of *Henry the Fifth* should be considered by the reader as one work, upon one plan, only broken into parts by the necessity of exhibition.[4]

---

[2] *Othello*, II, i, 162.
[3] Last line of Act IV.
[4] Johnson's discovery.

None of Shakespeare's plays are more read than the first and second parts of *Henry the Fourth*. Perhaps no author has ever in two plays afforded so much delight. The great events are interesting, for the fate of kingdoms depends upon them; the slighter occurrences are diverting, and, except one or two, sufficiently probable; the incidents are multiplied with wonderful fertility of invention, and the characters diversified with the utmost nicety of discernment, and the profoundest skill in the nature of man.

The prince, who is the hero both of the comic and tragic part, is a young man of great abilities and violent passions, whose sentiments are right, though his actions are wrong; whose virtues are obscured by negligence, and whose understanding is dissipated by levity. In his idle hours he is rather loose than wicked, and when the occasion forces out his latent qualities, he is great without effort, and brave without tumult. The trifler is roused into a hero, and the hero again reposes in the trifler. This character is great, original, and just.

Percy is a rugged soldier, choleric and quarrelsome, and has only the soldier's virtues, generosity and courage.

But Falstaff, unimitated, unimitable Falstaff, how shall I describe thee? Thou compound of sense and vice; of sense which may be admired but not esteemed, of vice which may be despised but hardly detested. Falstaff is a character loaded with faults, and with those faults which naturally produce contempt. He is a thief and a glutton, a coward and a boaster; always ready to cheat the weak and prey upon the poor, to terrify the timorous and insult the defenseless. At once obsequious and malignant, he satirizes in their absence those whom he lives by flattering. He is familiar with the prince only as an agent of vice, but of this familiarity he is so proud as not only to be supercilious and haughty with common men, but to think his interest of importance to the Duke of Lancaster. Yet the man thus corrupt, thus despicable, makes himself necessary to the prince that despises him, by the most pleasing of all qualities, perpetual gaiety; by an unfailing power of exciting laughter, which is the more freely indulged as his wit is not of the splendid or ambitious kind, but consists in easy escapes and sallies of levity, which make sport but raise no envy. It must be observed that he is stained with no enormous or sanguinary crimes, so that his licentiousness is not so offensive but that it may be borne for his mirth.

The moral to be drawn from this representation is that no man is more dangerous than he that with a will to corrupt hath the power to please; and that neither wit nor honesty ought to think themselves safe with such a companion when they see Henry seduced by Falstaff.

Henry V

I, i, 47–8:   When he speaks,
             The air, a charter'd libertine, is still.

This line is exquisitely beautiful.

II, iii, 25–6:   Cold as any stone.

Such is the end of Falstaff, from whom Shakespeare had promised us in his epilogue to *Henry IV* that we should receive more entertainment. It happened to Shakespeare as to other writers, to have his imagination crowded with a tumultuary confusion of images, which, while they were yet unsorted and unexamined, seemed sufficient to furnish a long train of incidents and a new variety of merriment, but which, when he was to produce them to view, shrunk suddenly from him, or could not be accommodated to his general design. That he once designed to have brought Falstaff on the scene again, we know from himself; but whether he could contrive no train of adventures suitable to his character, or could match him with no companions likely to quicken his humor, or could open no new vein of pleasantry, and was afraid to continue the same strain lest it should not find the same reception, he has here forever discarded him, and made haste to dispatch him, perhaps for the same reason for which Addison killed Sir Roger, that no other hand might attempt to exhibit him.

Let meaner authors learn from this example that it is dangerous to sell the bear which is yet not hunted, to promise to the public what they have not written.

This disappointment probably inclined Queen Elizabeth to command the poet to produce him once again, and to show him in love or courtship. This was indeed a new source of humor, and produced a new play from the former characters.

I forgot to note in the proper place, and therefore note here, that Falstaff's courtship, or *The Merry Wives of Windsor*, should be read between *Henry IV* and *Henry V*.

IV, vii, 50–1:   The fat knight with the great-belly doublet.

This is the last time that Falstaff can make sport. The poet was loath to part with him, and he continued his memory as long as he could.

V, i, 94: Exit Pistol.

The comic scenes of the history of *Henry the Fourth* and *Fifth* are now at an end, and all the comic personages are now dismissed. Falstaff and Mrs. Quickly are dead; Nym and Bardolph are hanged; Gadshill was lost immediately after the robbery; Poins and Peto have vanished since, one knows not how; and Pistol is now beaten into obscurity. I believe every reader regrets their departure.

V, ii, 125 ff: I' faith, Kate, . . . thou wouldst find me such a plain king, &c.

I know not why Shakespeare now gives the king nearly such a character as he made him formerly ridicule in Percy. This military grossness and unskillfulness in all the softer arts does not suit very well with the gaieties of his youth, with the general knowledge ascribed to him at his accession, or with the contemptuous message sent him by the Dauphin, who represents him as fitter for the ball-room than the field, and tells him that he is not *to revel into duchies* or win provinces *with a nimble galliard*.[5] The truth is that the poet's matter failed him in the fifth act, and he was glad to fill it up with whatever he could get; and not even Shakespeare can write well without a proper subject. It is a vain endeavor for the most skillful hand to cultivate barrenness or to paint upon vacuity.

King Lear

V, iii, 166: Let's exchange charity.

Our author by negligence gives his heathens the sentiments and practices of Christianity. In *Hamlet* there is the same solemn act of final reconciliation, but with exact propriety, for the personages are Christians.

Exchange forgiveness with me, noble Hamlet, &c.

The tragedy of *Lear* is deservedly celebrated among the dramas of Shakespeare. There is perhaps no play which keeps the attention so strongly fixed, which so much agitates our passions and interests our curiosity. The artful involutions of distinct interests, the strik-

[5] See I, ii, 252–53.

ing opposition of contrary characters, the sudden changes of fortune, and the quick succession of events, fill the mind with a perpetual tumult of indignation, pity, and hope. There is no scene which does not contribute to the aggravation of the distress or conduct of the action, and scarce a line which does not conduce to the progress of the scene. So powerful is the current of the poet's imagination that the mind, which once ventures within it, is hurried irresistibly along.

On the seeming improbability of Lear's conduct it may be observed that he is represented according to histories at that time, vulgarly received as true. And perhaps if we turn our thoughts upon the barbarity and ignorance of the age to which this story is referred, it will appear not so unlikely as while we estimate Lear's manners by our own. Such preference of one daughter to another, or resignation of dominion on such conditions, would be yet credible if told of a petty prince of Guinea or Madagascar. Shakespeare, indeed, by the mention of his Earls and Dukes, has given us the idea of times more civilized and of life regulated by softer manners; and the truth is that though he so nicely discriminates, and so minutely describes the characters of men, he commonly neglects and confounds the characters of ages, by mingling customs ancient and modern, English and foreign.

My learned friend Mr. Warton, who has in *The Adventurer* very minutely criticized this play,[6] remarks that the instances of cruelty are too savage and shocking, and that the intervention of Edmund destroys the simplicity of the story. These objections may, I think, be answered by repeating that the cruelty of the daughters is a historical fact, to which the poet has added little, having only drawn it into a series by dialogue and action. But I am not able to apologize with equal plausibility for the extrusion of Gloucester's eyes, which seems an act too horrid to be endured in dramatic exhibition, and such as must always compel the mind to relieve its distress by incredulity. Yet let it be remembered that our author well knew what would please the audience for which he wrote.

The injury done by Edmund to the simplicity of the action is abundantly recompensed by the addition of variety, by the art with which he is made to cooperate with the chief design, and the opportunity which he gives the poet of combining perfidy with perfidy, and connecting the wicked son with the wicked daughters, to impress this important moral: that villainy is never at a stop, that crimes lead to crimes, and at last terminate in ruin.

---

[6] Joseph Warton; see Nos. 113, 116, 122.

But though this moral be incidentally enforced, Shakespeare has suffered the virtue of Cordelia to perish in a just cause, contrary to the natural ideas of justice, to the hope of the reader, and, what is yet more strange, to the faith of chronicles. Yet this conduct is justified by the Spectator, who blames Tate[7] for giving Cordelia success and happiness in his alteration, and declares that, in his opinion, "the tragedy has lost half its beauty." [8] Dennis has remarked, whether justly or not, that to secure the favorable reception of *Cato*, "the town was poisoned with much false and abominable criticism," [9] and that endeavors had been used to discredit and decry poetical justice. A play in which the wicked prosper and the virtuous miscarry may doubtless be good, because it is a just representation of the common events of human life. But since all reasonable beings naturally love justice, I cannot easily be persuaded that the observation of justice makes a play worse; or that if other excellencies are equal, the audience will not always rise better pleased from the final triumph of persecuted virtue.

In the present case the public has decided. Cordelia, from the time of Tate, has always retired with victory and felicity. And if my sensations could add any thing to the general suffrage, I might relate that I was many years ago so shocked by Cordelia's death, that I know not whether I ever endured to read again the last scenes of the play till I undertook to revise them as an editor.

Othello

V, ii, 63–5: Oh perjur'd woman! thou dost stone my heart,
And mak'st me call what I intend to do
A murder, which I thought a sacrifice.

This line is difficult. "*Thou hast harden'd my heart, and mak'st me* kill *thee with the rage of a* murderer, *when I thought to have* sacrificed *thee to justice with the calmness of a priest striking a victim.*"

It must not be omitted that one of the elder quartos reads, *thou dost stone thy heart,* which I suspect to be genuine. The meaning

---

[7] Nahum Tate (1652–1715), Irish-born poet and playwright. In 1681 he adapted a happy ending to *Lear*, omitted the Fool, and constructed a love story between Cordelia and Edgar. His version held the stage throughout the eighteenth century.

[8] Addison in *Spectator* No. 40.

[9] *Remarks upon Cato, a Tragedy* (1713), in *Critical Works*, ed. Hooker, II, 43.

then will be: *"thou forcest me* to dismiss thee from the world in the state of the *murdered* without preparation for death, *when I intended* that thy punishment should have been *a sacrifice* atoning for thy crime."

I am glad that I have ended my revisal of this dreadful scene. It is not to be endured.

The beauties of this play impress themselves so strongly upon the attention of the reader that they can draw no aid from critical illustration. The fiery openness of Othello, magnanimous, artless, and credulous, boundless in his confidence, ardent in his affection, inflexible in his resolution, and obdurate in his revenge; the cool malignity of Iago, silent in his resentment, subtle in his designs, and studious at once of his interest and his vengeance; the soft simplicity of Desdemona, confident of merit, and conscious of innocence, her artless perseverance in her suit, and her slowness to suspect that she can be suspected, are such proofs of Shakespeare's skill in human nature as, I suppose, it is vain to seek in any modern writer. The gradual progress which Iago makes in the Moor's conviction, and the circumstances which he employs to inflame him, are so artfully natural that, though it will perhaps not be said of him as he says of himself, that he is a man "not easily jealous," yet we cannot but pity him when at last we find him "perplexed in the extreme." [1]

There is always danger lest wickedness conjoined with abilities should steal upon esteem, though it misses of approbation; but the character of Iago is so conducted that he is from the first scene to the last hated and despised.

Even the inferior characters of this play would be very conspicuous in any other piece, not only for their justness but their strength. Cassio is brave, benevolent, and honest, ruined only by his want of stubbornness to resist an insidious invitation. Roderigo's suspicious credulity, and impatient submission to the cheats which he sees practiced upon him, and which by persuasion he suffers to be repeated, exhibit a strong picture of a weak mind betrayed by unlawful desires to a false friend; and the virtue of Emilia is such as we often find, worn loosely but not cast off, easy to commit small crimes, but quickened and alarmed at atrocious villainies.

The scenes from the beginning to the end are busy, varied by happy interchanges, and regularly promoting the progression of the story; and the narrative in the end, though it tells but what is known already, yet is necessary to produce the death of Othello.

---

[1] V, ii, 345–46.

Had the scene opened in Cyprus, and the preceding incidents been occasionally related, there had been little wanting to a drama of the most exact and scrupulous regularity.

* * * *

FROM

Prefaces Biographical and Critical
to the Works of the Most Eminent English Poets
[Lives of the English Poets] [1779–1781]

—◦◦◦◦◦—

from Abraham Cowley

Cowley, like other poets who have written with narrow views, and instead of tracing intellectual pleasures in the mind of man, paid their court to temporary prejudices, has been at one time too much praised and too much neglected at another.

Wit, like all other things subject by their nature to the choice of man, has its changes and fashions, and at different times takes different forms. About the beginning of the seventeenth century appeared a race of writers that may be termed the metaphysical poets, of whom in a criticism on the works of Cowley it is not improper to give some account.

The metaphysical poets were men of learning, and to show their learning was their whole endeavor; but unluckily resolving to show it in rhyme, instead of writing poetry they only wrote verses, and very often such verses as stood the trial of the finger better than of the ear; for the modulation was so imperfect that they were only found to be verses by counting the syllables.

If the father of criticism has rightly denominated poetry τέχνη μιμητική "an imitative art," these writers will without great wrong lose their right to the name of poets, for they cannot be said to have imitated anything: they neither copied nature nor life, neither painted the forms of matter nor represented the operations of intellect.

Those however who deny them to be poets allow them to be wits. Dryden confesses of himself and his contemporaries that they fall below Donne in wit, but maintains that they surpass him in poetry.[1]

---

[1] See p. 107.

If Wit be well described by Pope as being that which has been often thought, but was never before so well expressed,[2] they certainly never attained nor ever sought it, for they endeavored to be singular in their thoughts, and were careless of their diction. But Pope's account of wit is undoubtedly erroneous; he depresses it below its natural dignity, and reduces it from strength of thought to happiness of language.

If by a more noble and more adequate conception that be considered as Wit which is at once natural and new;[3] that which, though not obvious, is upon its first production acknowledged to be just; if it be that which he that never found it, wonders how he missed; to wit of this kind the metaphysical poets have seldom risen. Their thoughts are often new but seldom natural; they are not obvious, but neither are they just; and the reader, far from wondering that he missed them, wonders more frequently by what perverseness of industry they were ever found.

But Wit, abstracted from its effects upon the hearer, may be more rigorously and philosophically considered as a kind of *discordia concors*: a combination of dissimilar images, or discovery of occult resemblances in things apparently unlike. Of wit, thus defined, they have more than enough. The most heterogeneous ideas are yoked by violence together; nature and art are ransacked for illustrations, comparisons, and allusions; their learning instructs, and their subtlety surprises; but the reader commonly thinks his improvement dearly bought, and though he sometimes admires, is seldom pleased.

From this account of their compositions it will be readily inferred that they were not successful in representing or moving the affections. As they were wholly employed on something unexpected and surprising, they had no regard to that uniformity of sentiment which enables us to conceive and to excite the pains and the pleasure of other minds; they never inquired what on any occasion they should have said or done, but wrote rather as beholders than partakers of human nature; as beings looking upon good and evil, impassive and at leisure; as Epicurean deities making remarks on the actions of men and the vicissitudes of life, without interest and without emotion. Their courtship was void of fondness and their lamentation of sorrow. Their wish was only to say what they hoped had been never said before.

---

[2] *Essay on Criticism*, II, 297–98.
[3] *Cf.* p. 519, on *The Rape of the Lock*.

Nor was the sublime more within their reach than the pathetic;[4] for they never attempted that comprehension and expanse of thought which at once fills the whole mind, and of which the first effect is sudden astonishment, and the second rational admiration. Sublimity is produced by aggregation, and littleness by dispersion.[5] Great thoughts are always general, and consist in positions not limited by exceptions, and in descriptions not descending to minuteness. It is with great propriety that *subtlety,* which in its original import means "exility of particles," is taken in its metaphorical meaning for "nicety of distinction." Those writers who lay on the watch for novelty could have little hope of greatness; for great things cannot have escaped former observation. Their attempts were always analytic: they broke every image into fragments, and could no more represent by their slender conceits and labored particularities the prospects of nature or the scenes of life, than he who dissects a sun-beam with a prism can exhibit the wide effulgence of a summer noon.

What they wanted however of the sublime, they endeavored to supply by hyperbole; their amplification had no limits: they left not only reason but fancy behind them, and produced combinations of confused magnificence that not only could not be credited, but could not be imagined.

Yet great labor directed by great abilities is never wholly lost: if they frequently threw away their wit upon false conceits, they likewise sometimes struck out unexpected truth; if their conceits were far-fetched, they were often worth the carriage. To write on their plan it was at least necessary to read and think. No man could be born a metaphysical poet, nor assume the dignity of a writer by descriptions copied from descriptions, by imitations borrowed from imitations, by traditional imagery and hereditary similes, by readiness of rhyme and volubility of syllables.

In perusing the works of this race of authors, the mind is exercised either by recollection or inquiry; either something already learned is to be retrieved, or something new is to be examined. If their greatness seldom elevates, their acuteness often surprises; if the imagination is not always gratified, at least the powers of reflection and comparison are employed; and in the mass of materials which ingenious absurdity has thrown together, genuine wit and use-

---

[4] *Cf.* Warton, p. 204.
[5] *Cf.* Burke, p. 349.

ful knowledge may be sometimes found, buried perhaps in grossness of expression, but useful to those who know their value, and such as, when they are expanded to perspicuity and polished to elegance, may give lustre to works which have more propriety though less copiousness of sentiment.

This kind of writing, which was, I believe, borrowed from Marino[6] and his followers, had been recommended by the example of Donne, a man of a very extensive and various knowledge, and by Jonson, whose manner resembled that of Donne more in the ruggedness of his lines than in the cast of his sentiments.

When their reputation was high, they had undoubtedly more imitators than time has left behind. . . . Denham and Waller sought another way to fame, by improving the harmony of our numbers. Milton tried the metaphysic style only in his lines upon Hobson the Carrier. Cowley adopted it and excelled his predecessors, having as much sentiment and more music. Suckling neither improved versification nor abounded in conceits. The fashionable style remained chiefly with Cowley; Suckling could not reach it, and Milton disdained it.

Critical remarks are not easily understood without examples; and I have therefore collected instances of the modes of writing by which this species of poets, for poets they were called, by themselves and their admirers, was eminently distinguished.[7] . . .

The ode "Of Wit" is almost without a rival. It was about the time of Cowley that *wit*, which had been till then used for intellection, in contradistinction to *will*, took the meaning, whatever it be, which it now bears. . . .

His diction was in his own time censured as negligent. He seems not to have known or not to have considered that words, being arbitrary, must owe their power to association, and have the influence, and that only, which custom has given them.

Truth indeed is always truth, and reason is always reason; they have an intrinsic and unalterable value, and constitute that intellectual gold which defies destruction. But gold may be so concealed in baser matter that only a chemist can recover it; sense may be so hidden in unrefined and plebeian words that none but philosophers can distinguish it; and both may be so buried in impurities as not to pay the cost of their extraction.

---

[6] Giambattista Marino (1569–1625), Italian poet best known for his long baroque poem *L'Adone* (1622); he initiated a Marinist school of conceits.

[7] Johnson quotes about forty-five illustrative passages from Cowley, Donne, and Cleveland.

The diction, being the vehicle of the thoughts, first presents itself to the intellectual eye, and if the first appearance offends, a further knowledge is not often sought. Whatever professes to benefit by pleasing must please at once. The pleasures of the mind imply something sudden and unexpected; that which elevates must always surprise. What is perceived by slow degrees may gratify us with consciousness of improvement, but will never strike with the sense of pleasure.

from John Milton

One of the poems on which much praise has been bestowed is *Lycidas*, of which the diction is harsh, the rhymes uncertain, and the numbers unpleasing. What beauty there is, we must therefore seek in the sentiments and images. It is not to be considered as the effusion of real passion, for passion runs not after remote allusions and obscure opinions. Passion plucks no berries from the myrtle and ivy, nor calls upon Arethuse and Mincius, nor tells of rough satyrs and fauns with cloven heel. Where there is leisure for fiction, there is little grief.

In this poem there is no nature, for there is no truth; there is no art, for there is nothing new. Its form is that of a pastoral, easy, vulgar, and therefore disgusting: whatever images it can supply are long ago exhausted; and its inherent improbability always forces dissatisfaction on the mind. When Cowley tells of Hervey that they studied together, it is easy to suppose how much he must miss the companion of his labors and the partner of his discoveries; but what image of tenderness can be excited by these lines!

> *We drove a field, and both together heard*
> *What time the grey fly winds her sultry horn,*
> *Battening our flocks with the fresh dews of night.*

We know that they never drove a field, and that they had no flocks to batten; and though it be allowed that the representation may be allegorical, the true meaning is so uncertain and remote that it is never sought because it cannot be known when it is found.

Among the flocks and copses and flowers appear the heathen deities, Jove and Phoebus, Neptune and Aeolus, with a long train of mythological imagery, such as a college easily supplies. Nothing can less display knowledge or less exercise invention than to tell how a shepherd has lost his companion and must now feed his flocks alone, without any judge of his skill in piping; and how one god asks another god what is become of Lycidas, and how neither god can tell. He who thus grieves will excite no sympathy; he who thus praises will confer no honor.

This poem has yet a grosser fault. With these trifling fictions are mingled the most awful and sacred truths, such as ought never to be polluted with such irreverent combinations. The shepherd likewise is now a feeder of sheep and afterwards an ecclesiastical pastor, a superintendent of a Christian flock. Such equivocations are always unskillful; but here they are indecent, and at least approach to impiety, of which, however, I believe the writer not to have been conscious.

Such is the power of reputation justly acquired that its blaze drives away the eye from nice examination. Surely no man could have fancied that he read *Lycidas* with pleasure had he not known its author. . . .

Those little pieces may be dispatched without much anxiety; a greater work calls for greater care. I am now to examine *Paradise Lost*, a poem which, considered with respect to design, may claim the first place, and with respect to performance the second, among the productions of the human mind.

By the general consent of critics, the first praise of genius is due to the writer of an epic poem, as it requires an assemblage of all the powers which are singly sufficient for other compositions. Poetry is the art of uniting pleasure with truth by calling imagination to the help of reason. Epic poetry undertakes to teach the most important truths by the most pleasing precepts, and therefore relates some great event in the most affecting manner. History must supply the writer with the rudiments of narration, which he must improve and exalt by a nobler art, must animate by dramatic energy, and diversify by retrospection and anticipation; morality must teach him the exact bounds and different shades of vice and virtue; from policy and the practice of life, he has to learn the discriminations of character and the tendency of the passions, either single or combined; and physiology must supply him with illustrations and images. To put these materials to poetical use is required an imagination capable of painting nature and realizing fiction. Nor is he yet a poet till he has attained the whole extension of his language, distinguished all the delicacies of phrase and all the colors of words, and learned to adjust their different sounds to all the varieties of metrical modulation. . . .

After the scheme and fabric of the poem must be considered its component parts, the sentiments and the diction.[8]

---

[8] In the omitted section of his analysis, Johnson formally but rather half-

The *sentiments*, as expressive of manners or appropriated to characters, are for the greater part unexceptionably just.

Splendid passages containing lessons of morality or precepts of prudence occur seldom. Such is the original formation of this poem that, as it admits no human manners till the Fall, it can give little assistance to human conduct. Its end is to raise the thoughts above sublunary cares or pleasures. Yet the praise of that fortitude, with which Abdiel maintained his singularity of virtue against the scorn of multitudes,[9] may be accommodated to all times; and Raphael's reproof of Adam's curiosity after the planetary motions, with the answer returned by Adam,[1] may be confidently opposed to any rule of life which any poet has delivered.

The thoughts which are occasionally called forth in the progress are such as could only be produced by an imagination in the highest degree fervid and active, to which materials were supplied by incessant study and unlimited curiosity. The heat of Milton's mind might be said to sublimate his learning, to throw off into his work the spirit of science, unmingled with its grosser parts.

He had considered creation in its whole extent, and his descriptions are therefore learned. He had accustomed his imagination to unrestrained indulgence, and his conceptions therefore were extensive. The characteristic quality of his poem is sublimity. He sometimes descends to the elegant, but his element is the great. He can occasionally invest himself with grace; but his natural port is gigantic loftiness. He can please when pleasure is required; but it is his peculiar power to astonish.

He seems to have been well acquainted with his own genius, and to know what it was that nature had bestowed upon him more bountifully than upon others—the power of displaying the vast, illuminating the splendid, enforcing the awful, darkening the gloomy, and aggravating the dreadful.[2] He therefore chose a subject on which too much could not be said, on which he might tire his fancy without the censure of extravagance.

The appearances of nature and the occurrences of life did not satiate his appetite of greatness. To paint things as they are requires a minute attention, and employs the memory rather than the fancy. Milton's delight was to sport in the wide regions of possibility; real-

---

heartedly follows the division, from Le Bossu and Addison, into fable and subject, characters, machinery and episodes, sentiments, and diction. After examining beauties, he turns to defects.

[9] V, 872.

[1] VIII, 66 ff.

[2] *Cf.* Burke on the Sublime.

ity was a scene too narrow for his mind. He sent his faculties out upon discovery, into worlds where only imagination can travel, and delighted to form new modes of existence, and furnish sentiment and action to superior beings, to trace the counsels of Hell, or accompany the choirs of Heaven.

But he could not be always in other worlds: he must sometimes revisit earth, and tell of things visible and known. When he cannot raise wonder by the sublimity of his mind, he gives delight by its fertility.

Whatever be his subject, he never fails to fill the imagination. But his images and descriptions of the scenes or operations of nature do not seem to be always copied from original form, nor to have the freshness, raciness, and energy of immediate observation. He saw nature, as Dryden expresses it, "through the spectacles of books," [3] and on most occasions calls learning to his assistance. The garden of Eden brings to his mind the vale of Enna, where Proserpine was gathering flowers.[4] Satan makes his way through fighting elements, like Argo between the Cyanean rocks, or Ulysses between the two Sicilian whirlpools, when he shunned Charybdis "on the larboard." [5] The mythological allusions have been justly censured,[6] as not being always used with notice of their vanity; but they contribute variety to the narration, and produce an alternate exercise of the memory and the fancy.

His similes are less numerous and more various than those of his predecessors. But he does not confine himself within the limits of rigorous comparison: his great excellence is amplitude, and he expands the adventitious image beyond the dimensions which the occasion required. Thus, comparing the shield of Satan to the orb of the Moon, he crowds the imagination with the discovery of the telescope and all the wonders which the telescope discovers.[7]

Of his moral sentiments it is hardly praise to affirm that they excel those of all other poets; for this superiority he was indebted to his acquaintance with the sacred writings. The ancient epic poets, wanting the light of Revelation, were very unskillful teachers of virtue: their principal characters may be great, but they are not amiable. The reader may rise from their works with a greater degree of active or passive fortitude, and sometimes of prudence, but he

[3] See p. 84.
[4] IV, 269.
[5] II, 1017–20.
[6] *Spectator* No. 297.
[7] I, 284–91.

will be able to carry away few precepts of justice and none of mercy. . . .

In Milton, every line breathes sanctity of thought and purity of manners, except when the train of the narration requires the introduction of the rebellious spirits; and even they are compelled to acknowledge their subjection to God in such a manner as excites reverence and confirms piety. . . .

As human passions did not enter the world before the Fall, there is in the *Paradise Lost* little opportunity for the pathetic; but what little there is has not been lost. That passion which is peculiar to rational nature, the anguish arising from the consciousness of transgression and the horrors attending the sense of the Divine displeasure, are very justly described and forcibly impressed. But the passions are moved only on one occasion; sublimity is the general and prevailing quality in this poem—sublimity variously modified, sometimes descriptive, sometimes argumentative.

The defects and faults of *Paradise Lost,* for faults and defects every work of man must have, it is the business of impartial criticism to discover. As in displaying the excellence of Milton I have not made long quotations, because of selecting beauties there had been no end, I shall in the same general manner mention that which seems to deserve censure; for what Englishman can take delight in transcribing passages which, if they lessen the reputation of Milton, diminish in some degree the honor of our country? . . .

The plan of *Paradise Lost* has this inconvenience, that it comprises neither human actions nor human manners. The man and woman who act and suffer are in a state which no other man or woman can ever know. The reader finds no transaction in which he can be engaged, beholds no condition in which he can by any effort of imagination place himself; he has, therefore, little natural curiosity or sympathy.

We all, indeed, feel the effects of Adam's disobedience; we all sin like Adam, and, like him, must all bewail our offences; we have restless and insidious enemies in the fallen angels, and in the blessed spirits we have guardians and friends; in the Redemption of mankind we hope to be included. In the description of Heaven and Hell we are surely interested, as we are all to reside hereafter either in the regions of horror or of bliss.

But these truths are too important to be new: they have been taught to our infancy; they have mingled with our solitary thoughts and familiar conversation, and are habitually interwoven with the whole texture of life. Being therefore not new, they raise no unaccustomed emotion in the mind: what we knew before we cannot learn; what is not unexpected cannot surprise.

Of the ideas suggested by these awful scenes, from some we recede with reverence, except when stated hours require their association; and from others we shrink with horror, or admit them only as salutary inflictions, as counterpoises to our interests and passions. Such images rather obstruct the career of fancy than incite it.

Pleasure and terror are indeed the genuine sources of poetry;[8] but poetical pleasure must be such as human imagination can at least conceive, and poetical terror such as human strength and fortitude may combat. The good and evil of Eternity are too ponderous for the wings of wit; the mind sinks under them in passive helplessness, content with calm belief and humble adoration.

Known truths, however, may take a different appearance, and be conveyed to the mind by a new train of intermediate images. This Milton has undertaken, and performed with pregnancy and vigor of mind peculiar to himself. Whoever considers the few radical positions which the Scriptures afforded him will wonder by what energetic operation he expanded them to such extent, and ramified them to so much variety, restrained as he was by religious reverence from licentiousness of fiction.

Here is a full display of the united force of study and genius, of a great accumulation of materials, with judgment to digest and fancy to combine them. Milton was able to select from nature or from story, from ancient fable or from modern science, whatever could illustrate or adorn his thoughts. An accumulation of knowledge impregnated his mind, fermented by study and exalted by imagination.

It has been therefore said without an indecent hyperbole, by one of his encomiasts, that in reading *Paradise Lost* we read a book of universal knowledge.

But original deficience cannot be supplied. The want of human interest is always felt. *Paradise Lost* is one of the books which the reader admires, and lays down, and forgets to take up again. None ever wished it longer than it is. Its perusal is a duty rather than a pleasure. We read Milton for instruction, retire harassed and overburdened, and look elsewhere for recreation; we desert our master and seek for companions. . . .

If *Paradise Regained* has been too much depreciated, *Samson Agonistes* has in requital been too much admired. It could only be by long prejudice and the bigotry of learning that Milton could

---

[8] *Cf.* Burke.

prefer the ancient tragedies, with their encumbrance of a chorus, to the exhibitions of the French and English stages; and it is only by a blind confidence in the reputation of Milton that a drama can be praised in which the intermediate parts have neither cause nor consequence, neither hasten or retard the catastrophe.[9]

In this tragedy are, however, many particular beauties, many just sentiments and striking lines; but it wants that power of attracting attention which a well-connected plan produces.

Milton would not have excelled in dramatic writing; he knew human nature only in the gross, and had never studied the shades of character, nor the combinations of concurring, or the perplexity of contending, passions. He had read much and knew what books could teach; but had mingled little in the world, and was deficient in the knowledge which experience must confer.

Through all his greater works there prevails a uniform peculiarity of *diction*, a mode and cast of expression which bears little resemblance to that of any former writer, and which is so far removed from common use that an unlearned reader, when he first opens his book, finds himself surprised by a new language.

This novelty has been, by those who can find nothing wrong in Milton, imputed to his laborious endeavors after words suitable to the grandeur of his ideas. "Our language," says Addison, "sunk under him." [1] But the truth is that, both in prose and verse, he had formed his style by a perverse and pedantic principle. He was desirous to use English words with a foreign idiom. This in all his prose is discovered and condemned; for there, judgment operates freely, neither softened by the beauty nor awed by the dignity of his thoughts; but such is the power of his poetry that his call is obeyed without resistance, the reader feels himself in captivity to a higher and nobler mind, and criticism sinks in admiration. . . .

Poetry may subsist without rhyme; but English poetry will not often please, nor can rhyme ever be safely spared, but where the subject is able to support itself. Blank verse makes some approach to that which is called the "lapidary style," has neither the easiness of prose nor the melody of numbers, and therefore tires by long continuance. Of the Italian writers without rhyme, whom Milton alleges as precedents, not one is popular; what reason could urge in its defense has been confuted by the ear.

But whatever be the advantage of rhyme, I cannot prevail on myself to wish that Milton had been a rhymer, for I cannot wish

---

[9] *Cf. Rambler* Nos. 139 and 140.
[1] *Spectator* No. 297.

his work to be other than it is; yet like other heroes he is to be admired rather than imitated. He that thinks himself capable of astonishing may write blank verse, but those that hope only to please must condescend to rhyme.

The highest praise of genius is original invention. Milton cannot be said to have contrived the structure of an epic poem, and therefore owes reverence to that vigor and amplitude of mind to which all generations must be indebted for the art of poetical narration, for the texture of the fable, the variation of incidents, the interposition of dialogue, and all the stratagems that surprise and enchain attention. But of all the borrowers from Homer, Milton is perhaps the least indebted. He was naturally a thinker for himself, confident of his own abilities and disdainful of help or hindrance; he did not refuse admission to the thoughts or images of his predecessors, but he did not seek them. From his contemporaries he neither courted nor received support; there is in his writings nothing by which the pride of other authors might be gratified or favor gained, no exchange of praise nor solicitation of support. His great works were performed under discountenance and in blindness, but difficulties vanished at his touch; he was born for whatever is arduous; and his work is not the greatest of heroic poems only because it is not the first.

from Samuel Butler

After his death were published three small volumes of his posthumous works, I know not by whom collected, or by what authority ascertained; and, lately two volumes more have been printed by Mr. Thyer[2] of Manchester, indubitably genuine. From none of these pieces can his life be traced or his character discovered. Some verses, in the last collection, show him to have been among those who ridiculed the institution of the Royal Society, of which the enemies were for some time very numerous and very acrimonious; for what reason it is hard to conceive, since the philosophers[3] professed not to advance doctrines but to produce facts; and the most zealous enemy of innovation must admit the gradual progress of experience, however he may oppose hypothetical temerity.

In this mist of obscurity passed the life of Butler, a man whose name can only perish with his language. The mode and place of

[2] Public librarian at Manchester who published Butler's characters and minor poems from manuscript, in 1759.
[3] I.e., scientists.

his education are unknown; the events of his life are variously related; and all that can be told with certainty is that he was poor.

The poem of *Hudibras* is one of those compositions of which a nation may justly boast, as the images which it exhibits are domestic, the sentiments unborrowed and unexpected, and the strain of diction original and peculiar. We must not, however, suffer the pride which we assume as the countrymen of Butler to make any encroachment upon justice, nor appropriate those honors which others have a right to share. The poem of *Hudibras* is not wholly English; the original idea is to be found in the history of *Don Quixote*, a book to which a mind of the greatest powers may be indebted without disgrace.[4]

Cervantes shows a man who, having by the incessant perusal of incredible tales subjected his understanding to his imagination, and familiarized his mind by pertinacious meditations to trains of incredible events and scenes of impossible existence, goes out in the pride of knighthood to redress wrongs and defend virgins, to rescue captive princesses, and tumble usurpers from their thrones; attended by a squire, whose cunning, too low for the suspicion of a generous mind, enables him often to cheat his master.

The hero of Butler is a Presbyterian justice, who, in the confidence of legal authority and the rage of zealous ignorance, ranges the country to repress superstition and correct abuses, accompanied by an Independent clerk, disputatious and obstinate, with whom he often debates, but never conquers him.

Cervantes had so much kindness for Don Quixote, that, however he embarrasses him with absurd distresses, he gives him so much sense and virtue as may preserve our esteem; wherever he is or whatever he does, he is made by matchless dexterity commonly ridiculous, but never contemptible.

But for poor Hudibras, his poet had no tenderness; he chooses not that any pity should be shown or respect paid him; he gives him up at once to laughter and contempt, without any quality that can dignify or protect him.

In forming the character of Hudibras and describing his person and habiliments, the author seems to labor with a tumultuous confusion of dissimilar ideas. He had read the history of the mock knights-errant; he knew the notions and manners of a Presbyterian magistrate, and tried to unite the absurdities of both, however dis-

---

[4] *Cf. Johnsonian Miscellanies*, I, 332: "Was there ever yet anything written by mere man that was wished longer by its readers excepting *Don Quixote, Robinson Crusoe*, and the *Pilgrim's Progress?*"

tant, in one personage. Thus he gives him that pedantic ostentation of knowledge which has no relation to chivalry, and loads him with martial encumbrances that can add nothing to his civil dignity. He sends him out "a colonelling," [5] and yet never brings him within sight of war.

If Hudibras be considered as the representative of the Presbyterians, it is not easy to say why his weapons should be represented as ridiculous or useless;[6] for, whatever judgment might be passed upon their knowledge or their arguments, experience had sufficiently shown that their swords were not to be despised.

The hero, thus compounded of swaggerer and pedant, of knight and justice, is led forth to action, with his squire Ralpho, an Independent enthusiast.

Of the contexture of events planned by the author, which is called the action of the poem, since it is left imperfect, no judgment can be made. It is probable that the hero was to be led through many luckless adventures, which would give occasion, like his attack upon the "bear and fiddle," [7] to expose the ridiculous rigor of the sectaries; like his encounter with Sidrophel and Whacum,[8] to make superstition and credulity contemptible; or like his recourse to the low retailer of the law, discover the fraudulent practices of different professions.[9] . . .

The discontinuity of the action might, however, have been easily forgiven if there had been action enough; but I believe every reader regrets the paucity of events, and complains that in the poem of *Hudibras*, as in the history of Thucydides, there is more said than done. The scenes are too seldom changed, and the attention is tired with long conversation.

It is, indeed, much more easy to form dialogues than to contrive adventures. Every position makes way for an argument, and every objection dictates an answer. When two disputants are engaged upon a complicated and extensive question, the difficulty is not to continue, but to end the controversy. But whether it be that we comprehend but few of the possibilities of life, or that life itself affords little variety, every man who has tried knows how much labor it will cost to form such a combination of circumstances, as shall

---

[5] I, i, 14.
[6] *Cf.* I, i, 351 ff.
[7] I, ii.
[8] II, iii.
[9] III, iii.

have at once the grace of novelty and credibility, and delight fancy without violence to reason.

Perhaps the dialogue of this poem is not perfect. Some power of engaging the attention might have been added to it by quicker reciprocation, by seasonable interruptions, by sudden questions, and by a nearer approach to dramatic sprightliness; without which fictitious speeches will always tire, however sparkling with sentences and however variegated with allusions.

The great source of pleasure is variety. Uniformity must tire at last, though it be uniformity of excellence. We love to expect, and when expectation is disappointed or gratified, we want to be again expecting. For this impatience of the present, whoever would please must make provision. The skillful writer *irritat, mulcet*,[1] makes a due distribution of the still and animated parts. It is for want of this artful intertexture and those necessary changes that the whole of a book may be tedious, though all the parts are praised.

If inexhaustible wit could give perpetual pleasure, no eye would ever leave half-read the work of Butler; for what poet has ever brought so many remote images so happily together? It is scarcely possible to peruse a page without finding some association of images that was never found before. By the first paragraph the reader is amused, by the next he is delighted, and by a few more strained to astonishment; but astonishment is a toilsome pleasure; he is soon weary of wondering, and longs to be diverted. . . .

Imagination is useless without knowledge: nature gives in vain the power of combination unless study and observation supply materials to be combined. Butler's treasures of knowledge appear proportioned to his expense: whatever topic employs his mind, he shows himself qualified to expand and illustrate it with all the accessories that books can furnish; he is found not only to have travelled the beaten road, but the bye-paths of literature; not only to have taken general surveys, but to have examined particulars with minute inspection.

If the French boast the learning of Rabelais, we need not be afraid of confronting them with Butler.

But the most valuable parts of his performance are those which retired study and native wit cannot supply. He that merely makes a book from books may be useful, but can scarcely be great. Butler had not suffered life to glide beside him unseen or unobserved. He had watched with great diligence the operations of human nature,

---

[1] Horace, *Epistles*, II, i, 212; "excites, then soothes."

and traced the effects of opinion, humor, interest, and passion. From such remarks proceeded that great number of sententious distichs which have passed into conversation, and are added as proverbial axioms to the general stock of practical knowledge.

When any work has been viewed and admired, the first question of intelligent curiosity is, how was it performed? *Hudibras* was not a hasty effusion; it was not produced by a sudden tumult of imagination or a short paroxysm of violent labor. To accumulate such a mass of sentiments at the call of accidental desire or of sudden necessity is beyond the reach and power of the most active and comprehensive mind. I am informed by Mr. Thyer of Manchester, the excellent editor of this author's reliques, that he could show something like *Hudibras* in prose. He has in his possession the commonplace book in which Butler reposited, not such events or precepts as are gathered by reading, but such remarks, similitudes, allusions, assemblages, or inferences, as occasion prompted or meditation produced—those thoughts that were generated in his own mind, and might be usefully applied to some future purpose. Such is the labor of those who write for immortality.

But human works are not easily found without a perishable part. Of the ancient poets every reader feels the mythology tedious and oppressive. Of *Hudibras*, the manners, being founded on opinions, are temporary and local, and therefore become every day less intelligible and less striking. What Cicero says of philosophy is true likewise of wit and humor, that "time effaces the fictions of opinion, and confirms the determinations of Nature." [2] Such manners as depend upon standing relations and general passions are co-extended with the race of man; but those modifications of life and peculiarities of practice which are the progeny of error and perverseness, or at best of some accidental influence or transient persuasion, must perish with their parents.

Much, therefore, of that humor which transported the last century with merriment is lost to us, who do not know the sour solemnity, the sullen superstition, the gloomy moroseness, and the stubborn scruples of the ancient Puritans; or, if we knew them, derive our information only from books or from tradition, have never had them before our eyes, and cannot, but by recollection and study, understand the lines in which they are satirized. Our grandfathers knew the picture from the life; we judge of the life by contemplating the picture.

It is scarcely possible, in the regularity and composure of the

---

[2] *De Natura Deorum*, II, ii, 5.

present time, to image the tumult of absurdity and clamor of contradiction which perplexed doctrine, disordered practice, and disturbed both public and private quiet in that age when subordination was broken, and awe was hissed away; when any unsettled innovator who could hatch a half-formed notion produced it to the public; when every man might become a preacher, and almost every preacher could collect a congregation.

The wisdom of the nation is very reasonably supposed to reside in the parliament. What can be concluded of the lower classes of the people when, in one of the parliaments summoned by Cromwell, it was seriously proposed that all the records in the Tower should be burnt, that all memory of things past should be effaced, and that the whole system of life should commence anew?

We have never been witnesses of animosities excited by the use of mince pies and plum porridge, nor seen with what abhorrence those who could eat them at all other times of the year would shrink from them in December. An old Puritan, who was alive in my childhood, being, at one of the feasts of the church, invited by a neighbor to partake his cheer, told him that if he would treat him at an alehouse with beer, brewed for all times and seasons, he should accept his kindness, but would have none of his superstitious meats and drinks.

One of the Puritanical tenets was the illegality of all games of chance; and he that reads Gataker upon Lots[3] may see how much learning and reason one of the first scholars of his age thought necessary, to prove that it was no crime to throw a die, or play at cards, or to hide a shilling for the reckoning.

Astrology, however, against which so much of the satire is directed, was not more the folly of the Puritans than of others. It had in that time a very extensive dominion. Its predictions raised hopes and fears in minds which ought to have rejected it with contempt. In hazardous undertakings, care was taken to begin under the influence of a propitious planet; and when the king was prisoner in Carisbrook Castle, an astrologer was consulted what hour would be found most favorable to an escape.

What effect this poem had upon the public, whether it shamed imposture or reclaimed credulity, is not easily determined. Cheats can seldom stand long against laughter. It is certain that the credit of planetary intelligence wore fast away; though some men of knowledge, and Dryden among them, continued to believe that

---

[3] Thomas Gataker (1574–1654), Puritan scholar; *Of The Nature and Use of Lots* (1616), a once controversial book.

conjunctions and oppositions had a great part in the distribution of good or evil, and in the government of sublunary things.

Poetical action ought to be probable upon certain suppositions, and such probability as burlesque requires is here violated only by one incident. Nothing can show more plainly the necessity of doing something, and the difficulty of finding something to do, than that Butler was reduced to transfer to his hero the flagellation of Sancho,[4] not the most agreeable fiction of Cervantes; very suitable indeed to the manners of that age and nation, which ascribed wonderful efficacy to voluntary penances, but so remote from the practice and opinions of the Hudibrastic time that judgment and imagination are alike offended.

The diction of this poem is grossly familiar, and the numbers purposely neglected, except in a few places where the thoughts, by their native excellence, secure themselves from violation, being such as mean language cannot express. The mode of versification has been blamed by Dryden,[5] who regrets that the heroic measure was not rather chosen. To the critical sentence of Dryden the highest reverence would be due were not his decisions often precipitate and his opinions immature. When he wished to change the measure, he probably would have been willing to change more. If he intended that when the numbers were heroic, the diction should still remain vulgar, he planned a very heterogeneous and unnatural composition. If he preferred a general stateliness both of sound and words, he can be only understood to wish Butler had undertaken a different work.

The measure is quick, sprightly, and colloquial, suitable to the vulgarity of the words and the levity of the sentiments. But such numbers and such diction can gain regard only when they are used by a writer whose vigor of fancy and copiousness of knowledge entitle him to contempt of ornaments, and who, in confidence of the novelty and justness of his conceptions, can afford to throw metaphors and epithets away. To another that conveys common thoughts in careless versification, it will only be said, *Pauper videri Cinna vult, et est pauper.*[6] The meaning and diction will be worthy of each other, and criticism may justly doom them to perish together.

Nor even though another Butler should arise would another

---

[4] II, iii.
[5] See p. 109.
[6] Martial, *Epigrams*, VIII, 19: "Cinna wishes to seem a pauper, and a pauper he is."

Hudibras obtain the same regard. Burlesque consists in a disproportion between the style and the sentiments, or between the adventitious sentiments and the fundamental subject. It therefore, like all bodies compounded of heterogeneous parts, contains in it a principle of corruption. All disproportion is unnatural; and from what is unnatural we can derive only the pleasure which novelty produces. We admire it awhile as a strange thing; but when it is no longer strange, we perceive its deformity. It is a kind of artifice which, by frequent repetition, detects itself; and the reader, learning in time what he is to expect, lays down his book, as the spectator turns away from a second exhibition of those tricks of which the only use is to show that they can be played.

from John Dryden

Dryden may be properly considered as the father of English criticism, as the writer who first taught us to determine upon principles the merit of composition. Of our former poets, the greatest dramatist [Shakespeare] wrote without rules, conducted through life and nature by a genius that rarely misled and rarely deserted him. Of the rest, those who knew the laws of propriety had neglected to teach them.

Two "arts of English poetry" were written in the days of Elizabeth by Webbe[7] and Puttenham,[8] from which something might be learned, and a few hints had been given by Jonson and Cowley; but Dryden's *Essay of Dramatic Poesy* was the first regular and valuable treatise on the art of writing.

He who, having formed his opinions in the present age of English literature, turns back to peruse this dialogue, will not perhaps find much increase of knowledge or much novelty of instruction; but he is to remember that critical principles were then in the hands of a few, who had gathered them partly from the ancients, and partly from the Italians and French. The structure of dramatic poems was not then generally understood. Audiences applauded by instinct, and poets perhaps often pleased by chance.

A writer who obtains his full purpose loses himself in his own lustre. Of an opinion which is no longer doubted, the evidence ceases to be examined. Of an art universally practised, the first teacher is forgotten. Learning once made popular is no longer

---

[7] William Webbe, *A Discourse of English Poetry* (1586).
[8] George Puttenham, *The Art of English Poesy* (1589).

learning: it has the appearance of something which we have bestowed upon ourselves, as the dew appears to rise from the field which it refreshes.

To judge rightly of an author we must transport ourselves to his time, and examine what were the wants of his contemporaries, and what were his means of supplying them. That which is easy at one time was difficult at another. Dryden at least imported his science, and gave his country what it wanted before; or rather, he imported only the materials, and manufactured them by his own skill.

The dialogue on the drama was one of his first essays of criticism, written when he was yet a timorous candidate for reputation, and therefore labored with that diligence which he might allow himself somewhat to remit when his name gave sanction to his positions, and his awe of the public was abated, partly by custom and partly by success. It will not be easy to find in all the opulence of our language a treatise so artfully variegated with successive representations of opposite probabilities, so enlivened with imagery, so brightened with illustrations. His portraits of the English dramatists are wrought with great spirit and diligence. The account of Shakespeare may stand as a perpetual model of encomiastic criticism; exact without minuteness, and lofty without exaggeration. The praise lavished by Longinus, on the attestation of the heroes of Marathon by Demosthenes, fades away before it.[9] In a few lines is exhibited a character so extensive in its comprehension, and so curious in its limitations, that nothing can be added, diminished, or reformed; nor can the editors and admirers of Shakespeare, in all their emulation of reverence, boast of much more than of having diffused and paraphrased this epitome of excellence, of having changed Dryden's gold for baser metal of lower value, though of greater bulk.

In this, and in all his other essays on the same subject, the criticism of Dryden is the criticism of a poet; not a dull collection of theorems, nor a rude detection of faults, which perhaps the censor was not able to have committed; but a gay and vigorous dissertation, where delight is mingled with instruction, and where the author proves his right of judgment by his power of performance.

The different manner and effect with which critical knowledge may be conveyed was perhaps never more clearly exemplified than in the performances of Rymer and Dryden. It was said of a dispute between two mathematicians, *malim cum Scaligero errare, quam cum Clavio recte sapere;* that "it was more eligible to go wrong with

---

[9] *On the Sublime,* XVI; Demosthenes, *On the Crown,* 263, II.

one than right with the other." A tendency of the same kind every mind must feel at the perusal of Dryden's prefaces and Rymer's discourses. With Dryden we are wandering in quest of Truth, whom we find, if we find her at all, dressed in the graces of elegance; and if we miss her, the labor of the pursuit rewards itself: we are led only through fragrance and flowers. Rymer, without taking a nearer, takes a rougher way; every step is to be made through thorns and brambles, and Truth, if we meet her, appears repulsive by her mien, and ungraceful by her habit. Dryden's criticism has the majesty of a queen; Rymer's has the ferocity of a tyrant.

As he had studied with great diligence the art of poetry, and enlarged or rectified his notions by experience perpetually increasing, he had his mind stored with principles and observations: he poured out his knowledge with little labor; for of labor, notwithstanding the multiplicity of his productions, there is sufficient reason to suspect that he was not a lover. To write *con amore*, with fondness for the employment, with perpetual touches and retouches, with unwillingness to take leave of his own idea, and an unwearied pursuit of unattainable perfection, was, I think, no part of his character.

His criticism may be considered as general or occasional. In his general precepts, which depend upon the nature of things and the structure of the human mind, he may doubtless be safely recommended to the confidence of the reader; but his occasional and particular positions were sometimes interested,[1] sometimes negligent, and sometimes capricious. It is not without reason that Trapp,[2] speaking of the praises which he bestows on *Palamon and Arcite*, says:

> *Novimus judicium Drydeni de poemate quodam Chauceri, pulchro sane illo, et admodum laudando, nimirum quod non modo vere epicum sit, sed* Iliada *etiam atque Æneida aequet, imo superet. Sed novimus eodem tempore viri illius maximi non semper accuratissimas esse censuras, nec ad*

---

[1] self-interested.

[2] Joseph Trapp (1679–1747), first Oxford professor of poetry, in Latin lectures published as *Praelectiones poeticae* (1711–19, trans. 1742). In 1748, in a preface to *The Preceptor*, Johnson asserted: "The art of poetry will best be learned from Bossu and Bouhours in French, together with Dryden's essays and prefaces, the critical papers of Addison, Spence on Pope's *Odyssey*, and Trapp's *Praelectiones poeticae*; but a more accurate and philosophical account is expected from a commentary upon Aristotle's *Art of Poetry*, with which the literature of this nation will be in a short time augmented."

*severissimam critices normam exactas: illo judice id plerum-
que optimum est, quod nunc prae manibus habet, et in quo
nunc occupatur.*[3]

He is therefore by no means constant to himself. His defense
and desertion of dramatic rhyme is generally known. Spence,[4] in
his remarks on Pope's *Odyssey*, produces what he thinks an uncon-
querable quotation from Dryden's preface to the *Aeneid* in favor
of translating an epic poem into blank verse; but he forgets that
when his author attempted the *Iliad* some years afterwards, he departed from his own decision and translated into rhyme.

When he has any objection to obviate or any license to defend,
he is not very scrupulous about what he asserts, nor very cautious,
if the present purpose be served, not to entangle himself in his own
sophistries. But when all arts are exhausted, like other hunted
animals, he sometimes stands at bay; when he cannot disown the
grossness of one of his plays, he declares that he knows not any
law that prescribes morality to a comic poet. . . .

What he wishes to say, he says at hazard; he cited *Gorbuduc*,
which he had never seen; gives a false account of Chapman's versification; and discovers in the preface to his *Fables* that he translated the first book of the *Iliad* without knowing what was in the
second.

It will be difficult to prove that Dryden ever made any great advances in literature.[5] As having distinguished himself at West-
minster under the tuition of Busby, who advanced his scholars to
a height of knowledge very rarely attained in grammar-schools, he
resided afterwards at Cambridge; it is not to be supposed that his

---

[3] *Lectures on Poetry*, trans. Clarke (1742), p. 348: "We know our countryman Mr. Dryden's judgment about a poem of Chaucer's, truly beautiful indeed
and worthy of praise; namely that it was not only equal, but even superior to
the *Iliad* and *Aeneid*. But we know likewise that his opinion was not always the
most accurate, nor formed upon the severest rules of criticism. What was in
hand was generally most in esteem; if it was uppermost in his thoughts it was
so in his judgment too."

[4] Joseph Spence (1699–1768), Oxford professor of poetry, friend of Pope,
best known for *Anecdotes*, a collection of table talk and miscellanea from Pope
and his circle. In 1727 he published an *Essay on Pope's "Odyssey": in which
Some Particular Beauties and Blemishes . . . are Consider'd*, in dialogue form;
and in 1747 *Polymetis*, a heavily illustrated dialogue in folio, illustrating Roman
poetry by Roman medals, bas-reliefs, and sculpture; it was much cited by pro-
ponents of *ut pictura poesis*, and toward the end of the century influenced the
Hellenistic revival in both England and Germany.

[5] literary learning.

skill in the ancient languages was deficient compared with that of common students; but his scholastic acquisitions seem not proportionate to his opportunities and abilities. He could not, like Milton or Cowley, have made his name illustrious merely by his learning. . . .

His literature, though not always free from ostentation, will be commonly found either obvious, and made his own by the art of dressing it; or superficial, which by what he gives, shows what he wanted; or erroneous, hastily collected, and negligently scattered.

Yet it cannot be said that his genius is ever unprovided of matter, or that his fancy languishes in penury of ideas. His works abound with knowledge, and sparkle with illustrations. There is scarcely any science or faculty that does not supply him with occasional images and lucky similitudes; every page discovers a mind very widely acquainted both with art and nature, and in full possession of great stores of intellectual wealth. Of him that knows much, it is natural to suppose that he has read with diligence; yet I rather believe that the knowledge of Dryden was gleaned from accidental intelligence and various conversation; by a quick apprehension, a judicious selection, and a happy memory, a keen appetite of knowledge, and a powerful digestion; by vigilance that permitted nothing to pass without notice, and a habit of reflection that suffered nothing useful to be lost. A mind like Dryden's, always curious, always active, to which every understanding was proud to be associated, and of which every one solicited the regard by an ambitious display of himself, had a more pleasant, perhaps a nearer way to knowledge than by the silent progress of solitary reading. I do not suppose that he despised books or intentionally neglected them; but that he was carried out by the impetuosity of his genius to more vivid and speedy instructors, and that his studies were rather desultory and fortuitous than constant and systematical. . . .

Of all this, however, if the proof be demanded, I will not undertake to give it; the atoms of probability, of which my opinion has been formed, lie scattered over all his works; and by him who thinks the question worth his notice, his works must be perused with very close attention.

Criticism, either didactic or defensive, occupies almost all his prose, except those pages which he has devoted to his patrons; but none of his prefaces were ever thought tedious. They have not the formality of a settled style, in which the first half of the sentence betrays the other. The clauses are never balanced, nor the periods modeled; every word seems to drop by chance, though it falls into its proper place. Nothing is cold or languid; the whole is airy, animated, and vigorous; what is little is gay; what is great is splendid. He may be thought to mention himself too frequently, but while he forces himself upon our esteem, we cannot refuse him to stand high in his own. Everything is excused by the play of images and the spriteliness of expression. Though all is easy, nothing is feeble; though all seems careless, there is nothing harsh; and though since his earlier works more than a century has passed, they have nothing yet uncouth or obsolete.

He who writes much will not easily escape a manner, such a recurrence of particular modes as may be easily noted. Dryden is "always another and the same";[6] he does not exhibit a second time the same elegances in the same form, nor appears to have any art other than that of expressing with clearness what he thinks with vigor. His style could not easily be imitated, either seriously or ludicrously, for being always equable and always varied, it has no prominent or discriminative characters. The beauty who is totally free from disproportion of parts and features cannot be ridiculed by an overcharged resemblance.

From his prose however Dryden derives only his accidental and secondary praise; the veneration with which his name is pronounced by every cultivator of English literature is paid to him as he refined the language, improved the sentiments, and tuned the numbers of English poetry. . . .

Of Dryden's works it was said by Pope that "he could select from them better specimens of every mode of poetry than any other English writer could supply." Perhaps no nation ever produced a writer that enriched his language with such variety of models. To him we owe the improvement, perhaps the completion of our meter, the refinement of our language, and much of the correctness of our sentiments. By him we were taught *sapere et fari*,[7] to think naturally and express forcibly. Though Davies has reasoned in rhyme before him, it may be perhaps maintained that he was the first who joined argument with poetry. He showed us the true bounds of a translator's liberty. What was said of Rome, adorned by Augustus, may be applied by an easy metaphor to English poetry embellished by Dryden, *lateritiam invenit, marmoream reliquit*,[8] he found it brick, and he left it marble.

---

[6] *Cf.* Pope's *Dunciad*, III, 40.
[7] Horace, *Epistles*, I, iv, 9.
[8] Suetonius, *Augustus*, XXVIII, 3.

from Joseph Addison

Addison is now to be considered as a critic, a name which the present generation is scarcely willing to allow him. His criticism is condemned as tentative or experimental rather than scientific, and he is considered as deciding by taste rather than by principles.

It is not uncommon for those who have grown wise by the labor of others to add a little of their own and overlook their masters. Addison is now despised by some who perhaps would never have seen his defects but by the lights which he afforded them. That he always wrote as he would think it necessary to write now cannot be affirmed; his instructions were such as the character of his readers made proper. That general knowledge which now circulates in common talk was in his time rarely to be found. Men not professing learning were not ashamed of ignorance, and in the female world any acquaintance with books was distinguished only to be censured. His purpose was to infuse literary curiosity by gentle and unsuspected conveyance into the gay, the idle, and the wealthy; he therefore presented knowledge in the most alluring form, not lofty and austere, but accessible and familiar. When he showed them their defects, he showed them likewise that they might be easily supplied. His attempt succeeded; inquiry was awakened, and comprehension expanded. An emulation of intellectual elegance was excited, and from his time to our own, life has been gradually exalted, and conversation purified and enlarged.

Dryden had not many years before scattered criticism over his *Prefaces* with very little parsimony; but though he sometimes condescended to be somewhat familiar, his manner was in general too scholastic for those who had yet their rudiments to learn, and found it not easy to understand their master. His observations were framed rather for those that were learning to write than for those that read only to talk.

An instructor like Addison was now wanting, whose remarks, being superficial, might be easily understood, and being just, might prepare the mind for more attainments. Had he presented *Paradise Lost* to the public with all the pomp of system and severity of science, the criticism would perhaps have been admired, and the poem still have been neglected; but by the blandishments of gentleness and facility he has made Milton a universal favorite, with whom readers of every class think it necessary to be pleased.

He descended now and then to lower disquisitions; and by a

serious display of the beauties of *Chevy Chase*[9] exposed himself to
the ridicule of Wagstaff, who bestowed a like pompous character
on Tom Thumb;[1] and to the contempt of Dennis who, considering
the fundamental position of his criticism, that *Chevy Chase* pleases
and ought to please because it is natural, observes "that there is a
way of deviating from nature, by bombast or tumor, which soars
above nature and enlarges images beyond their real bulk; by affectation, which foresakes nature in quest of something unsuitable;
and by imbecility, which degrades nature by faintness and diminution, by obscuring its appearances and weakening its effects." [2] In
Chevy Chase there is not much of either bombast or affectation,
but there is chill and lifeless imbecility. The story cannot possibly
be told in a manner that shall make less impression on the mind.

Before the profound observers of the present race repose too
securely on the consciousness of their superiority to Addison, let
them consider his *Remarks on Ovid*,[3] in which may be found
specimens of criticism sufficiently subtle and refined; let them peruse
likewise his *Essays on Wit*,[4] and on *The Pleasures of Imagination*,[5]
in which he founds art on the base of nature, and draws the principles of invention from dispositions inherent in the mind of man,
with skill and elegance such as his contemners will not easily attain.

As a describer of life and manners he must be allowed to stand
perhaps the first of the first rank. His humor, which, as Steele observes, is peculiar to himself, is so happily diffused as to give the
grace of novelty to domestic scenes and daily occurrences. He never
"outsteps the modesty of nature" [6] nor raises merriment or wonder
by the violation of truth. His figures neither divert by distortion
nor amaze by aggravation. He copies life with so much fidelity that
he can be hardly said to invent; yet his exhibitions have an air so
much original that it is difficult to suppose them not merely the
product of imagination.

As a teacher of wisdom he may be confidently followed. His
religion has nothing in it enthusiastic or superstitious: he appears
neither weakly credulous nor wantonly skeptical; his morality is
neither dangerously lax nor impracticably rigid. All the enchant-

---

[9] *Spectator* Nos. 70 and 74.
[1] William Wagstaffe, A *Comment Upon the History of Tom Thumb* (1711).
[2] *Cf.* Dennis, *Of Simplicity in Pastoral Compositions* (pub. 1721).
[3] Notes to Addison's translation, in which he first develops his concept of
mixed wit.
[4] *Spectator* Nos. 58–63.
[5] *Ibid.*, 411–21.
[6] *Cf. Hamlet*, III, ii, 21.

ment of fancy and all the cogency of argument are employed to recommend to the reader his real interest, the care of pleasing the Author of his being. Truth is shown sometimes as the phantom of a vision, sometimes appears half-veiled in an allegory, sometimes attracts regard in the robes of fancy, and sometimes steps forth in the confidence of reason. She wears a thousand dresses and in all is pleasing:

Mille habet ornatus, mille decenter habet.[7]

His prose is the model of the middle style; on grave subjects not formal, on light occasions not groveling; pure without scrupulosity, and exact without apparent elaboration; always equable and always easy, without glowing words or pointed sentences. Addison never deviates from his track to snatch a grace; he seeks no ambitious ornaments, and tries no hazardous innovations. His page is always luminous, but never blazes in unexpected splendor.

It was apparently his principal endeavor to avoid all harshness and severity of diction; he is therefore sometimes verbose in his transitions and connections, and sometimes descends too much to the language of conversation. Yet if his language had been less idiomatical, it might have lost somewhat of its genuine Anglicism. What he attempted he performed; he is never feeble, and he did not wish to be energetic; he is never rapid, and he never stagnates. His sentences have neither studied amplitude nor affected brevity; his periods, though not diligently rounded, are voluble and easy. Whoever wishes to attain an English style, familiar but not coarse, and elegant but not ostentatious, must give his days and nights to the volumes of Addison.

from Alexander Pope

It cannot be unwelcome to literary curiosity that I deduce thus minutely the history of the English *Iliad*. It is certainly the noblest version[8] of poetry which the world has ever seen; and its publication must therefore be considered as one of the great events in the annals of learning.

To those who have skill to estimate the excellence and difficulty of this great work, it must be very desirable to know how it was performed and by what gradations it advanced to correctness. Of such an intellectual process, the knowledge has very rarely been

---

[7] Tibullus, IV, ii, 14.
[8] translation.

attainable; but happily there remains the original copy of the *Iliad*, which, being obtained by Bolingbroke as a curiosity, descended from him to Mallet, and is now, by the solicitation of the late Dr. Maty,[9] reposited in the Museum. . . .

From the first copy I have procured a few transcripts, and shall exhibit first the printed lines, then, in a smaller print, those of the manuscripts with all their variations. Those words in the small print which are given in roman are canceled in the copy, and the words placed under them adopted in their stead.

The beginning of the first book stands thus:

> *The wrath of Peleus' son, the direful spring*
> *Of all the Grecian woes, O Goddess, sing!*
> *That wrath which hurl'd to Pluto's gloomy reign*
> *The souls of mighty chiefs untimely slain.*

> *The stern Pelides' rage, O Goddess, sing!*
> wrath
> *Of all the woes* of Greece *the fatal spring,*
> Grecian
> *That strew'd with* warriors *dead the Phrygian plain,*
> heroes
> *And* peopled the dark shades with heroes slain;
> fill'd the shady hell with chiefs untimely. . . .

Of these specimens every man who has cultivated poetry, or who delights to trace the mind from the rudeness of its first conceptions to the elegance of its last, will naturally desire a greater number; but most other readers are already tired, and I am not writing only to poets and philosophers. . . .

The person of Pope is well known not to have been formed by the nicest model. He has, in his account of the "Little Club," [1] compared himself to a spider, and by another is described as protuberant behind and before. He is said to have been beautiful in his infancy; but he was of a constitution originally feeble and weak, and as bodies of a tender frame are easily distorted, his deformity was probably in part the effect of his application. His stature was so low that, to bring him to a level with common tables, it was necessary to raise his seat. But his face was not displeasing, and his eyes were animated and vivid.

---

[9] Librarian of the British Museum.
[1] *Guardian* 92.

By natural deformity or accidental distortion, his vital functions were so much disordered that his life was a "long disease." [2] His most frequent assailant was the headache, which he used to relieve by inhaling the steam of coffee, which he very frequently required.

Most of what can be told concerning his petty peculiarities was communicated by a female domestic of the Earl of Oxford, who knew him perhaps after the middle of life. He was then so weak as to stand in perpetual need of female attendance; extremely sensible of cold, so that he wore a kind of fur doublet, under a shirt of very coarse warm linen with fine sleeves. When he rose he was invested in bodice made of stiff canvass, being scarce able to hold himself erect till they were laced; and he then put on a flannel waistcoat. One side was contracted. His legs were so slender that he enlarged their bulk with three pair of stockings, which were drawn on and off by the maid; for he was not able to dress or undress himself, and neither went to bed nor rose without help. His weakness made it very difficult for him to be clean.

His hair had fallen almost all away, and he used to dine some times with Lord Oxford, privately, in a velvet cap. His dress of ceremony was black, with a tye-wig and a little sword.

The indulgence and accommodation which his sickness required had taught him all the unpleasing and unsocial qualities of a valetudinary man. He expected that everything should give way to his ease or humor, as a child whose parents will not hear her cry has an unresisted dominion in the nursery.

> *C'est que l'enfant toujours est homme,*
> *C'est que l'homme est toujours enfant.*

When he wanted to sleep he "nodded in company," [3] and once slumbered at his own table while the Prince of Wales was talking of poetry.

The reputation which his friendship gave procured him many invitations, but he was a very troublesome inmate. He brought no servant, and had so many wants that a numerous attendance was scarcely able to supply them. Wherever he was he left no room for another, because he exacted the attention and employed the activity of the whole family. His errands were so frequent and frivolous that the footmen in time avoided and neglected him, and the Earl of Oxford discharged some of the servants for their resolute refusal of

---

[2] *Epistle to Arbuthnot*, 131.
[3] *Imitations of Horace*, II, i, 13.

his messages. The maids, when they had neglected their business, alleged that they had been employed by Mr. Pope. One of his constant demands was of coffee in the night, and to the woman that waited on him in his chamber he was very burthensome; but he was careful to recompense her want of sleep; and Lord Oxford's servant declared that in a house where her business was to answer his call, she would not ask for wages.

He had another fault, easily incident to those who, suffering much pain, think themselves entitled to whatever pleasures they can snatch. He was too indulgent to his appetite: he loved meat highly seasoned and of strong taste, and at the intervals of the table, amused himself with biscuits and dry conserves. If he sat down to a variety of dishes, he would oppress his stomach with repletion, and though he seemed angry when a dram was offered him, did not forbear to drink it. His friends, who knew the avenues to his heart, pampered him with presents of luxury, which he did not suffer to stand neglected. The death of great men is not always proportioned to the lustre of their lives. Hannibal, says Juvenal,[4] did not perish by a javelin or a sword; the slaughters of Cannae were revenged by a ring. The death of Pope was imputed by some of his friends to a silver saucepan, in which it was his delight to heat potted lampreys.

That he loved too well to eat is certain; but that his sensuality shortened his life will not be hastily concluded, when it is remembered that a conformation so irregular lasted six and fifty years, notwithstanding such pertinacious diligence of study and meditation.

In all his intercourse with mankind he had great delight in artifice, and endeavored to attain all his purposes by indirect and unsuspected methods. "He hardly drank tea without a stratagem."[5] If at the house of his friends he wanted any accommodation, he was not willing to ask for it in plain terms, but would mention it remotely, as something convenient, though when it was procured he soon made it appear for whose sake it had been recommended. Thus he teased Lord Orrery till he obtained a screen. He practiced his arts on such small occasions that Lady Bolingbroke used to say, in a French phrase, that "he played the politician about cabbages and turnips." His unjustifiable impression[6] of *The Patriot*

---

[4] *Satires*, X, 163 ff.
[5] *Cf.* Edward Young, *Satires*, VI, 188.
[6] printing. Pope secretly had printed 1500 copies of Bolingbroke's political treatise, from the manuscripts entrusted to him.

King, as it can be imputed to no particular motive, must have proceeded from his general habit of secrecy and cunning: he caught an opportunity of a sly trick and pleased himself with the thought of outwitting Bolingbroke.

In familiar or convivial conversation it does not appear that he excelled. He may be said to have resembled Dryden, as being not one that was distinguished by vivacity in company. It is remarkable that, so near his time, so much should be known of what he has written and so little of what he has said. . . .

He was fretful and easily displeased, and allowed himself to be capriciously resentful. He would sometimes leave Lord Oxford silently, no one could tell why, and was to be courted back by more letters and messages than the footmen were willing to carry. The table was indeed infested by Lady Mary Wortley, who was the friend of Lady Oxford, and who, knowing his peevishness, could by no entreaties be restrained from contradicting him, till their disputes were sharpened to such asperity that one or the other quitted the house.

He sometimes condescended to be jocular with servants or inferiors; but by no merriment, either of others or his own, was he ever seen excited to laughter.

Of his domestic character, frugality was a part eminently remarkable. Having determined not to be dependent, he determined not to be in want, and therefore wisely and magnanimously rejected all temptations to expense unsuitable to his fortune. This general care must be universally approved; but it sometimes appeared in petty artifices of parsimony, such as the practice of writing his compositions on the back of letters, as may be seen in the remaining copy of the *Iliad*, by which perhaps in five years five shillings were saved; or in a niggardly reception of his friends and scantiness of entertainment, as, when he had two guests in his house, he would set at supper a single pint upon the table, and having himself taken two small glasses would retire and say, "Gentlemen, I leave you to your wine." Yet he tells his friends that "he has a heart for all, a house for all, and, whatever they may think, a fortune for all." [7]

He sometimes, however, made a splendid dinner, and is said to have wanted no part of the skill or elegance which such performances require. That this magnificence should be often displayed, that obstinate prudence with which he conducted his affairs would

---

[7] Letter to Swift, March 23, 1737.

not permit; for his revenue, certain and casual, amounted only to about eight hundred pounds a year, of which, however, he declares himself able to assign one hundred to charity.

Of this fortune, which, as it arose from public approbation, was very honorably obtained, his imagination seems to have been too full. it would be hard to find a man, so well entitled to notice by his wit, that ever delighted so much in talking of his money. In his letters and in his poems, his garden and his grotto, his quincunx and his vines, or some hints of his opulence, are always to be found. The great topic of his ridicule is poverty: the crimes with which he reproaches his antagonists are their debts, their habitation in the Mint,[8] and their want of a dinner. He seems to be of an opinion, not very uncommon in the world, that to want money is to want everything.

Next to the pleasure of contemplating his possessions seems to be that of enumerating the men of high rank with whom he was acquainted, and whose notice he loudly proclaims not to have been obtained by any practices of meanness or servility—a boast which was never denied to be true, and to which very few poets have ever aspired. Pope never set genius to sale: he never flattered those whom he did not love or praised those whom he did not esteem. . . .

Of his social qualities, if an estimate be made from his letters, an opinion too favorable cannot easily be formed; they exhibit a perpetual and unclouded effulgence of general benevolence and particular fondness. There is nothing but liberality, gratitude, constancy, and tenderness. It has been so long said as to be commonly believed that the true characters of men may be found in their letters, and that he who writes to his friend lays his heart open before him. But the truth is that such were the simple friendships of the Golden Age, and are now the friendships only of children. Very few can boast of hearts which they dare lay open to themselves, and of which, by whatever accident exposed, they do not shun a distinct and continued view; and certainly what we hide from ourselves we do not show to our friends. There is, indeed, no transaction which offers stronger temptations to fallacy and sophistication than epistolary intercourse. In the eagerness of conversation, the first emotions of the mind often burst out before they are considered; in the tumult of business, interest and passion have their genuine effect; but a friendly letter is a calm and deliberate performance in the cool of leisure, in the stillness of solitude, and

---

[8] A debtors' sanctuary.

surely no man sits down to depreciate by design his own character. . . .

One of his favorite topics is contempt of his own poetry. For this, if it had been real, he would deserve no commendation, and in this he was certainly not sincere; for his high value of himself was sufficiently observed, and of what could he be proud but of his poetry? He writes, he says, when "he has just nothing else to do";[9] yet Swift complains that he was never at leisure for conversation because he "had always some poetical scheme in his head." [1] It was punctually required that his writing-box should be set upon his bed before he rose; and Lord Oxford's domestic related that, in the dreadful winter of Forty, she was called from her bed by him four times in one night to supply him with paper, lest he should lose a thought.

He pretends insensibility to censure and criticism, though it was observed by all who knew him that every pamphlet disturbed his quiet, and that his extreme irritability laid him open to perpetual vexation; but he wished to despise his critics, and therefore hoped that he did despise them. . . .

He very frequently professes contempt of the world, and represents himself as looking on mankind, sometimes with gay indifference, as on emmets of a hillock below his serious attention, and sometimes with gloomy indignation, as on monsters more worthy of hatred than of pity. These were dispositions apparently counterfeited. How could he despise those whom he lived by pleasing, and on whose approbation his esteem of himself was superstructed? Why should he hate those to whose favor he owed his honor and his ease? Of things that terminate in human life, the world is the proper judge: to despise its sentence, if it were possible, is not just, and if it were just, is not possible. Pope was far enough from this unreasonable temper; he was sufficiently "a fool to Fame," [2] and his fault was that he pretended to neglect it. His levity and his sullenness were only in his letters; he passed through common life, sometimes vexed and sometimes pleased, with the natural emotions of common men.

His scorn of the Great is repeated too often to be real: no man thinks much of that which he despises; and as falsehood is always in danger of inconsistency, he makes it his boast at another time that he lives among them.

---

[9] Preface to *Works* (1717).
[1] Letter in 1733.
[2] *Epistle to Arbuthnot*, 127.

It is evident that his own importance swells often in his mind. He is afraid of writing lest the clerks of the Post Office should know his secrets; he has many enemies; he considers himself as surrounded by universal jealousy; "after many deaths and many dispersions, two or three of us," says he, "may still be brought together, not to plot, but to divert ourselves, and the world too, if it pleases";[3] and they can live together and "show what friends wits may be, in spite of all the fools in the world." [4] All this while, it was likely that the clerks did not know his hand: he certainly had no more enemies than a public character like his inevitably excites, and with what degree of friendship the wits might live, very few were so much fools as ever to inquire.

Some part of this pretended discontent he learned from Swift, and expresses it, I think, most frequently in his correspondence with him. Swift's resentment was unreasonable, but it was sincere; Pope's was the mere mimicry of his friend, a fictitious part which he began to play before it became him. . . .

In the letters both of Swift and Pope there appears such narrowness of mind as makes them insensible of any excellence that has not some affinity with their own, and confines their esteem and approbation to so small a number, that whoever should form his opinion of the age from their representation would suppose them to have lived amidst ignorance and barbarity, unable to find among their contemporaries either virtue or intelligence, and persecuted by those that could not understand them.

When Pope murmurs at the world, when he professes contempt of fame, when he speaks of riches and poverty, of success and disappointment, with negligent indifference, he certainly does not express his habitual and settled sentiments, but either willfully disguises his own character, or, what is more likely, invests himself with temporary qualities, and sallies out in the colors of the present moment. His hopes and fears, his joys and sorrows, acted strongly upon his mind, and if he differed from others it was not by carelessness. . . .

The virtues which seem to have had most of his affection were liberality and fidelity of friendship, in which it does not appear that he was other than he describes himself. His fortune did not suffer his charity to be splendid and conspicuous, but he assisted Dodsley with a hundred pounds that he might open a shop; and of the subscription of forty pounds a year that he raised for Savage, twenty

<hr>

³ Letter to Swift, Sept. 14, 1725.
⁴ Letter to Swift, March 23, 1737.

were paid by himself. He was accused of loving money, but his love was eagerness to gain, not solicitude to keep it.

In the duties of friendship he was zealous and constant: his early maturity of mind commonly united him with men older than himself, and therefore, without attaining any considerable length of life, he saw many companions of his youth sink into the grave; but it does not appear that he lost a single friend by coldness or by injury: those who loved him once continued their kindness. . . .

The religion in which he lived and died was that of the Church of Rome, to which, in his correspondence with Racine, he professes himself a sincere adherent. That he was not scrupulously pious in some part of his life is known by many idle and indecent applications of sentences taken from the Scriptures—a mode of merriment which a good man dreads for its profaneness, and a witty man disdains for its easiness and vulgarity. But to whatever levities he has been betrayed, it does not appear that his principles were ever corrupted, or that he ever lost his belief of Revelation. The positions which he transmitted from Bolingbroke he seems not to have understood, and was pleased with an interpretation that made them orthodox.[5]

A man of such exalted superiority and so little moderation would naturally have all his delinquences observed and aggravated: those who could not deny that he was excellent would rejoice to find that he was not perfect.

Perhaps it may be imputed to the unwillingness with which the same man is allowed to possess many advantages that his learning has been depreciated. He certainly was in his early life a man of great literary curiosity, and when he wrote his *Essay on Criticism* had for his age a very wide acquaintance with books. When he entered into the living world, it seems to have happened to him, as to many others, that he was less attentive to dead masters: he studied in the academy of Paracelsus, and made the universe his favorite volume. He gathered his notions fresh from reality, not from the copies of authors, but the originals of nature. Yet there is no reason to believe that literature ever lost his esteem; he always professed to love reading, and Dobson, who spent some time at his house translating his *Essay on Man*, when I asked him what learning he found him to possess, answered, "More than I expected." His frequent references to history, his allusions to various kinds of knowledge, and his images selected from art and nature, with his

---

[5] Johnson alludes to *An Essay on Man* and the defense of its orthodoxy by Bishop Warburton.

observations on the operations of the mind and the modes of life, show an intelligence perpetually on the wing, excursive, vigorous, and diligent, eager to pursue knowledge and attentive to retain it.

From this curiosity arose the desire of travelling, to which he alludes in his verses to Jervas,[6] and which, though he never found an opportunity to gratify it, did not leave him till his life declined.

Of his intellectual character the constituent and fundamental principle was good sense, a prompt and intuitive perception of consonance and propriety. He saw immediately, of his own conceptions, what was to be chosen and what to be rejected; and in the works of others, what was to be shunned and what to be copied.

But good sense alone is a sedate and quiescent quality, which manages its possessions well, but does not increase them; it collects few materials for its own operations, and preserves safety, but never gains supremacy. Pope had likewise genius—a mind active, ambitious, and adventurous, always investigating, always aspiring; in its widest searches still longing to go forward, in its highest flights still wishing to be higher; always imagining something greater than it knows, always endeavoring more than it can do.

To assist these powers he is said to have had great strength and exactness of memory. That which he had heard or read was not easily lost; and he had before him not only what his own meditation suggested, but what he had found in other writers that might be accommodated to his present purpose.

These benefits of nature he improved by incessant and unwearied diligence; he had recourse to every source of intelligence, and lost no opportunity of information; he consulted the living as well as the dead; he read his compositions to his friends, and was never content with mediocrity when excellence could be attained. He considered poetry as the business of his life, and however he might seem to lament his occupation, he followed it with constancy: to make verses was his first labor, and to mend them was his last.

From his attention to poetry he was never diverted. If conversation offered anything that could be improved, he committed it to paper; if a thought, or perhaps an expression more happy than was common, rose to his mind, he was careful to write it; an independent distich was preserved for an opportunity of insertion, and some little fragments have been found containing lines or parts of lines to be wrought upon at some other time.

He was one of those few whose labor is their pleasure; he was never elevated to negligence, nor wearied to impatience; he never

---

* See *Epistle to Mr. Jervas* (1717), 23 ff.

passed a fault unamended by indifference, nor quitted it by despair. He labored his works first to gain reputation, and afterwards to keep it.

Of composition there are different methods. Some employ at once memory and invention, and with little intermediate use of the pen, form and polish large masses by continued meditation, and write their productions only when, in their own opinion, they have completed them. It is related of Virgil that his custom was to pour out a great number of verses in the morning, and pass the day in retrenching exuberances and correcting inaccuracies. The method of Pope, as may be collected from his translation, was to write his first thoughts in his first words, and gradually to amplify, decorate, rectify, and refine them.

With such faculties and such dispositions he excelled every other writer in *poetical prudence*; he wrote in such a manner as might expose him to few hazards. He used almost always the same fabric of verse;[7] and, indeed, by those few essays which he made of any other, he did not enlarge his reputation. Of this uniformity the certain consequence was readiness and dexterity. By perpetual practice, language had in his mind a systematical arrangement; having always the same use for words, he had words so selected and combined as to be ready at his call. This increase of facility he confessed himself to have perceived in the progress of his translation.

But what was yet of more importance, his effusions were always voluntary, and his subjects chosen by himself. His independence secured him from drudging at a task and laboring upon a barren topic: he never exchanged praise for money, nor opened a shop of condolence or congratulation. His poems, therefore, were scarce ever temporary. He suffered coronations and royal marriages to pass without a song, and derived no opportunities from recent events, nor any popularity from the accidental disposition of his readers. He was never reduced to the necessity of soliciting the sun to shine upon a birthday, of calling the Graces and Virtues to a wedding, or of saying what multitudes have said before him. When he could produce nothing new, he was at liberty to be silent.

His publications were for the same reason never hasty. He is said to have sent nothing to the press till it had lain two years under his inspection: it is at least certain that he ventured nothing without nice examination. He suffered the tumult of imagination to subside, and the novelties of invention to grow familiar. He knew that the mind is always enamored of its own productions, and did not trust

---

[7] That is, heroic couplet.

his first fondness. He consulted his friends, and listened with great willingness to criticism; and what was of more importance, he consulted himself, and let nothing pass against his own judgment.

He professed to have learned his poetry from Dryden, whom, whenever an opportunity was presented, he praised through his whole life with unvaried liberality; and perhaps his character may receive some illustration if he be compared with his master.

Integrity of understanding and nicety of discernment were not allotted in a less proportion to Dryden than to Pope. The rectitude of Dryden's mind was sufficiently shown by the dismission of his poetical prejudices, and the rejection of unnatural thoughts and rugged numbers. But Dryden never desired to apply all the judgment that he had. He wrote, and professed to write, merely for the people; and when he pleased others, he contented himself. He spent no time in struggles to rouse latent powers; he never attempted to make that better which was already good, nor often to mend what he must have known to be faulty. He wrote, as he tells us, with very little consideration; when occasion or necessity called upon him, he poured out what the present moment happened to supply, and when once it had passed the press, ejected it from his mind; for when he had no pecuniary interest, he had no further solicitude.

Pope was not content to satisfy; he desired to excel, and therefore always endeavored to do his best; he did not court the candor, but dared the judgment of his reader, and expecting no indulgence from others, he showed none to himself. He examined lines and words with minute and punctilious observation, and retouched every part with indefatigable diligence, till he had left nothing to be forgiven. . . .

His declaration that his care for his works ceased at their publication was not strictly true. His parental attention never abandoned them; what he found amiss in the first edition, he silently corrected in those that followed. He appears to have revised the *Iliad* and freed it from some of its imperfections, and the *Essay on Criticism* received many improvements after its first appearance. It will seldom be found that he altered without adding clearness, elegance, or vigor. Pope had perhaps the judgment of Dryden, but Dryden certainly wanted the diligence of Pope.

In acquired knowledge the superiority must be allowed to Dryden, whose education was more scholastic, and who before he became an author had been allowed more time for study, with better means of information. His mind has a larger range, and he collects his images and illustrations from a more extensive circumference of science. Dryden knew more of man in his general nature, and Pope in his local manners. The notions of Dryden were formed by comprehensive speculation, and those of Pope by minute attention. There is more dignity in the knowledge of Dryden, and more certainty in that of Pope.

Poetry was not the sole praise of either, for both excelled likewise in prose; but Pope did not borrow his prose from his predecessor. The style of Dryden is capricious and varied, that of Pope is cautious and uniform; Dryden obeys the motions of his own mind, Pope constrains his mind to his own rules of composition. Dryden is sometimes vehement and rapid; Pope is always smooth, uniform, and gentle. Dryden's page is a natural field, rising into inequalities, and diversified by the varied exuberance of abundant vegetation; Pope's is a velvet lawn, shaven by the scythe and leveled by the roller.

Of genius, that power which constitutes a poet; that quality without which judgment is cold and knowledge is inert; that energy which collects, combines, amplifies, and animates—the superiority must, with some hesitation, be allowed to Dryden. It is not to be inferred that of this poetical vigor Pope had only a little because Dryden had more, for every other writer since Milton must give place to Pope; and even of Dryden it must be said that if he has brighter paragraphs, he has not better poems. Dryden's performances were always hasty, either excited by some external occasion or extorted by domestic necessity; he composed without consideration and published without correction. What his mind could supply at call, or gather in one excursion, was all that he sought, and all that he gave. The dilatory caution of Pope enabled him to condense his sentiments, to multiply his images, and to accumulate all that study might produce, or chance might supply. If the flights of Dryden therefore are higher, Pope continues longer on the wing. If of Dryden's fire the blaze is brighter, of Pope's the heat is more regular and constant. Dryden often surpasses expectation, and Pope never falls below it. Dryden is read with frequent astonishment, and Pope with perpetual delight.

This parallel will, I hope, when it is well considered, be found just; and if the reader should suspect me, as I suspect myself, of some partial fondness for the memory of Dryden, let him not too hastily condemn me; for meditation and inquiry may, perhaps, show him the reasonableness of my determination.

The works of Pope are now to be distinctly examined, not so much with attention to slight faults or petty beauties, as to the general character and effect of each performance. . . .

One of his greatest though of his earliest works is the *Essay on Criticism*, which if he had written nothing else would have placed him among the first critics and the first poets, as it exhibits every mode of excellence that can embellish or dignify didactic composition—selection of matter, novelty of arrangement, justness of precept, splendor of illustration, and propriety of digression. I know not whether it be pleasing to consider that he produced this piece at twenty and never afterwards excelled it: he that delights himself with observing that such powers may be soon attained cannot but grieve to think that life was ever after at a stand.

To mention the particular beauties of the *Essay* would be unprofitably tedious, but I cannot forbear to observe that the comparison of a student's progress in the sciences with the journey of a traveller in the Alps[8] is perhaps the best that English poetry can show. A simile, to be perfect, must both illustrate and ennoble the subject, must show it to the understanding in a clearer view, and display it to the fancy with greater dignity. But either of these qualities may be sufficient to recommend it. In didactic poetry, of which the great purpose is instruction, a simile may be praised which illustrates, though it does not ennoble; in heroics, that may be admitted which ennobles, though it does not illustrate. That it may be complete, it is required to exhibit, independently of its references, a pleasing image; for a simile is said to be a short episode. To this, antiquity was so attentive that circumstances were sometimes added which, having no parallels, served only to fill the imagination and produced what Perrault ludicrously called "comparisons with a long tail." In their similes the greatest writers have sometimes failed: the ship-race, compared with the chariot-race, is neither illustrated nor aggrandised;[9] land and water make all the difference: when Apollo running after Daphne is likened to a greyhound chasing a hare,[1] there is nothing gained; the ideas of pursuit and flight are too plain to be made plainer, and a god and the daughter of a god are not represented much to their advantage by a hare and dog. The simile of the Alps has no useless parts, yet affords a striking picture by itself: it makes the foregoing position

[8] ll. 219 ff.
[9] *Aeneid*, V, 144–47.
[1] Ovid, *Metamorphoses*, I, 533–38.

better understood and enables it to take faster hold on the attention; it assists the apprehension and elevates the fancy.

Let me likewise dwell a little on the celebrated paragraph, in which it is directed that "the sound should seem an echo to the sense",[2] a precept which Pope is allowed to have observed beyond any other English poet.

This notion of representative meter,[3] and the desire of discovering frequent adaptations of the sound to the sense, have produced, in my opinion, many wild conceits and imaginary beauties. All that can furnish this representation are the sounds of the words considered singly, and the time in which they are pronounced. Every language has some words framed to exhibit the noises which they express, as *thump, rattle, growl, hiss*. These, however, are but few, and the poet cannot make them more, nor can they be of any use but when sound is to be mentioned. The time of pronunciation was in the dactylic measures of the learned language capable of considerable variety; but that variety could be accommodated only to motion or duration, and different degrees of motion were perhaps expressed by verses rapid or slow, without much attention of the writer, when the image had full possession of his fancy. But our language having little flexibility, our verses can differ very little in their cadence. The fancied resemblances, I fear, arise sometimes merely from the ambiguity of words; there is supposed to be some relation between a *soft* line and a *soft* couch, or between *hard* syllables and *hard* fortune.

Motion, however, may be in some sort exemplified; and yet it may be suspected that even in such resemblances, the mind often governs the ear and the sounds are estimated by their meaning. One of the most successful attempts has been to describe the labor of Sisyphus:

With many a weary step, and many a groan,
Up a high hill he heaves a huge round stone;
The huge round stone, resulting with a bound,
Thunders impetuous down, and smokes along the ground.[4]

Who does not perceive the stone to move slowly upward and roll violently back? But set the same numbers to another sense;

[2] ll. 337 ff.
[3] Cf. *Rambler* Nos. 92 and 94.
[4] Pope's *Odyssey*, XI, 735–38.

> *While many a merry tale, and many a song,*
> *Cheer'd the rough road, we wish'd the rough road long.*
> *The rough road then, returning in a round,*
> *Mock'd our impatient steps, for all was fairy ground.*

We have now surely lost much of the delay and much of the rapidity.

But to show how little the greatest master of numbers can fix the principles of representative harmony, it will be sufficient to remark that the poet, who tells us that

> *When Ajax strives some rock's vast weight to throw,*
> *The line too labors and the words move slow:*
> *Not so when swift Camilla scours the plain,*
> *Flies o'er th' unbending corn, and skims along the main;*[5]

when he had enjoyed for about thirty years the praise of Camilla's lightness of foot, tried another experiment upon *sound* and *time* and produced this memorable triplet:

> *Waller was smooth; but Dryden taught to join*
> *The varying verse, the full resounding line,*
> *The long majestick march, and energy divine.*[6]

Here are the swiftness of the rapid race and the march of slow-paced majesty exhibited by the same poet in the same sequence of syllables, except that the exact prosodist will find the line of *swiftness* by one time longer than that of *tardiness*.

Beauties of this kind are commonly fancied, and when real, are technical and nugatory, not to be rejected and not to be solicited.

To the praises which have been accumulated on *The Rape of the Lock* by readers of every class, from the critic to the waiting-maid, it is difficult to make any addition. Of that which is universally allowed to be the most attractive of all ludicrous compositions, let it rather be now inquired from what sources the power of pleasing is derived.

Dr. Warburton, who excelled in critical perspicacity, has remarked that the preternatural agents are very happily adapted to the purposes of the poem. The heathen deities can no longer gain attention: we should have turned away from a contest between Venus and Diana. The employment of allegorical persons always excites conviction of its own absurdity: they may produce effects but can-

---

[5] *Essay on Criticism,* 370–73.
[6] *Imitations of Horace,* II, i, 267–69.

not conduct actions; when the phantom is put in motion, it dissolves; thus Discord may raise a mutiny, but Discord cannot conduct a march, nor besiege a town. Pope brought into view a new race of Beings, with powers and passions proportionate to their operation. The sylphs and gnomes act at the toilet and the tea-table, what more terrific and more powerful phantoms perform on the stormy ocean or the field of battle; they give their proper help, and do their proper mischief.

Pope is said by an objector not to have been the inventor of this petty nation; a charge which might with more justice have been brought against the author of the *Iliad*, who doubtless adopted the religious system of his country; for what is there but the names of his agents which Pope has not invented? Has he not assigned them characters and operations never heard of before? Has he not, at least, given them their first poetical existence? If this is not sufficient to denominate his work original, nothing original ever can be written.

In this work are exhibited in a very high degree the two most engaging powers of an author: new things are made familiar, and familiar things are made new. A race of aerial people never heard of before is presented to us in a manner so clear and easy, that the reader seeks for no further information, but immediately mingles with his new acquaintance, adopts their interests, and attends their pursuits, loves a sylph and detests a gnome.

That familiar things are made new every paragraph will prove. The subject of the poem is an event below the common incidents of common life; nothing real is introduced that is not seen so often as to be no longer regarded; yet the whole detail of a female day is here brought before us invested with so much art of decoration that, though nothing is disguised, everything is striking, and we feel all the appetite of curiosity for that from which we have a thousand times turned fastidiously away.

The purpose of the poet is, as he tells us, to laugh at "the little unguarded follies of the female sex." [7] It is therefore without justice that Dennis charges *The Rape of the Lock* with the want of a moral,[8] and for that reason sets it below *The Lutrin*, which exposes the pride and discord of the clergy. Perhaps neither Pope nor Boileau has made the world much better than he found it; but if they had both succeeded, it were easy to tell who would have deserved most from public gratitude. The freaks and humors and

[7] See prefatory letter to the poem.
[8] See *Critical Works*, ed. Hooker, II, 330.

spleen and vanity of women, as they embroïl families in discord and fill houses with disquiet, do more to obstruct the happiness of life in a year than the ambition of the clergy in many centuries. It has been well observed that the misery of man proceeds not from any single crush of overwhelming evil, but from small vexations continually repeated. . . .

The epistle of *Eloisa to Abelard* is one of the most happy productions of human wit: the subject is so judiciously chosen that it would be difficult, in turning over the annals of the world, to find another which so many circumstances concur to recommend. We regularly interest ourselves most in the fortune of those who must deserve our notice. Abelard and Eloisa were conspicuous in their days for eminence of merit. The heart naturally loves truth. The adventures and misfortunes of this illustrious pair are known from undisputed history. Their fate does not leave the mind in hopeless dejection, for they both found quiet and consolation in retirement and piety. So new and so affecting is their story that it supersedes invention, and imagination ranges at full liberty without straggling into scenes of fable.

The story thus skillfully adopted has been diligently improved. Pope has left nothing behind him which seems more the effect of studious perseverance and laborious revisal. Here is particularly observable the *curiosa felicitas*,[9] a fruitful soil and careful cultivation. Here is no crudeness of sense nor asperity of language. . . .

The train of my disquisition has now conducted me to that poetical wonder, the translation of the *Iliad*, a performance which no age or nation can pretend to equal. To the Greeks, translation was almost unknown; it was totally unknown to the inhabitants of Greece. They had no recourse to the Barbarians for poetical beauties, but sought for everything in Homer, where, indeed, there is but little which they might not find. . . .

The chief help of Pope in this arduous undertaking was drawn from the versions of Dryden. Virgil had borrowed much of his imagery from Homer, and part of the debt was now paid by his translator. Pope searched the pages of Dryden for happy combinations of heroic diction, but it will not be denied that he added much to what he found. He cultivated our language with so much diligence and art that he has left in his *Homer* a treasure of poetical elegances to posterity. His version may be said to have tuned the English tongue, for since its appearance no writer, however de-

---

[9] Petronius, *Satyricon*, 118, 5, speaking of Horace's poetry; "labored richness."

ficient in other powers, has wanted melody. Such a series of lines so elaborately corrected and so sweetly modulated took possession of the public ear; the vulgar was enamored of the poem, and the learned wondered at the translation.

But in the most general applause, discordant voices will always be heard. It has been objected by some, who wish to be numbered among the sons of learning, that Pope's version of Homer is not Homerical; that it exhibits no resemblance of the original and characteristic manner of the father of poetry, as it wants his awful simplicity, his artless grandeur, his unaffected majesty.[1] This cannot be totally denied, but it must be remembered that *necessitas quod cogit defendit*, that may be lawfully done which cannot be forborne. Time and place will always enforce regard. In estimating this translation, consideration must be had of the nature of our language, the form of our meter, and, above all, of the change which two thousand years have made in the modes of life and the habits of thought. Virgil wrote in a language of the same general fabric with that of Homer, in verses of the same measure, and in an age nearer to Homer's time by eighteen hundred years; yet he found even then the state of the world so much altered, and the demand for elegance so much increased, that mere nature would be endured no longer; and perhaps, in the multitude of borrowed passages, very few can be shown which he has not embellished.

There is a time when nations emerging from barbarity and falling into regular subordination gain leisure to grow wise, and feel the shame of ignorance and the craving pain of unsatisfied curiosity. To this hunger of the mind, plain sense is grateful; that which fills the void removes uneasiness, and to be free from pain for a while is pleasure; but repletion generates fastidiousness, a saturated intellect soon becomes luxurious, and knowledge finds no willing reception till it is recommended by artificial diction. Thus it will be found in the progress of learning that in all nations the first writers are simple, and that every age improves in elegance. One refinement always makes way for another, and what was expedient to Virgil was necessary to Pope.

I suppose many readers of the English *Iliad*, when they have been touched with some unexpected beauty of the lighter kind, have tried to enjoy it in the original, where, alas! it was not to be found. Homer doubtless owes to his translator many Ovidian graces not exactly suitable to his character; but to have added can

---

[1] See Young, p. 368.

be no great crime if nothing be taken away. Elegance is surely to be desired if it be not gained at the expense of dignity. A hero would wish to be loved as well as to be reverenced.

To a thousand cavils, one answer is sufficient; the purpose of a writer is to be read, and the criticism which would destroy the power of pleasing must be blown aside. Pope wrote for his own age and his own nation: he knew that it was necessary to color the images and point the sentiments of his author; he therefore made him graceful, but lost him some of his sublimity. . . .

Of *The Dunciad* the hint is confessedly taken from Dryden's *Mac Flecknoe,* but the plan is so enlarged and diversified as justly to claim the praise of an original, and affords perhaps the best specimen that has yet appeared of personal satire ludicrously pompous.

That the design was moral, whatever the author might tell either his readers or himself, I am not convinced. The first motive was the desire of revenging the contempt with which Theobald had treated his Shakespeare,[2] and regaining the honor which he had lost, by crushing his opponent. Theobald was not of bulk enough to fill a poem, and therefore it was necessary to find other enemies with other names, at whose expense he might divert the public.

In this design there was petulance and malignity enough; but I cannot think it very criminal. An author places himself uncalled before the tribunal of criticism, and solicits fame at the hazard of disgrace. Dullness or deformity are not culpable in themselves, but may be very justly reproached when they pretend to the honor of wit or the influence of beauty. If bad writers were to pass without reprehension, what should restrain them? *impune diem consumpserit ingens Telephus;*[3] and upon bad writers only will censure have much effect. The satire which brought Theobald and Moore into contempt, dropped impotent from Bentley, like the javelin of Priam.[4]

All truth is valuable, and satirical criticism may be considered as useful when it rectifies error and improves judgment: he that refines the public taste is a public benefactor.

The beauties of this poem are well known; its chief fault is the grossness of its images. Pope and Swift had an unnatural delight in ideas physically impure, such as every other tongue utters with unwillingness, and of which every ear shrinks from the mention.

---

[2] Pope's edition of Shakespeare.
[3] Juvenal, *Satires,* I, 5: "Shall a monster like Telephus consume the whole day without impunity?"
[4] *Aeneid,* II, 544.

But even this fault, offensive as it is, may be forgiven for the excellence of other passages, such as the formation and dissolution of Moore,[5] the account of the Traveller,[6] the misfortune of the Florist,[7] and the crowded thoughts and stately numbers which dignify the concluding paragraph.

The alterations which have been made in *The Dunciad*, not always for the better, require that it should be published, as in the last collection, with all its variations. . . .

Pope had, in proportions very nicely adjusted to each other, all the qualities that constitute genius. He had Invention, by which new trains of events are formed and new scenes of imagery displayed, as in *The Rape of the Lock*, and by which extrinsic and adventitious embellishments and illustrations are connected with a known subject, as in the *Essay on Criticism*; he had Imagination, which strongly impresses on the writer's mind and enables him to convey to the reader the various forms of nature, incidents of life, and energies of passion, as in his *Eloisa, Windsor Forest*, and the *Ethic Epistles*; he had Judgment, which selects from life or nature what the present purpose requires, and by separating the essence of things from its concomitants, often makes the representation more powerful than the reality; and he had colors of language always before him ready to decorate his matter with every grace of elegant expression, as when he accommodates his diction to the wonderful multiplicity of Homer's sentiments and descriptions.

Poetical expression includes sound as well as meaning. "Music," says Dryden, "is inarticulate poetry";[8] among the excellences of Pope, therefore, must be mentioned the melody of his meter. By perusing the works of Dryden, he discovered the most perfect fabric of English verse, and habituated himself to that only which he found the best; in consequence of which restraint, his poetry has been censured as too uniformly musical, and as glutting the ear with unvaried sweetness. I suspect this objection to be the cant of those who judge by principles rather than perception, and who would even themselves have less pleasure in his works if he had tried to relieve attention by studied discords, or affected to break his lines and vary his pauses. . . .

New sentiments and new images others may produce, but to attempt any further improvements of versification will be danger-

---

[5] *Dunciad*, II, 35–50, 109–20.
[6] *Ibid.*, IV, 293–336.
[7] *Ibid.*, 405–36.
[8] Preface to *Tyrannic Love*.

ous. Art and diligence have now done their best, and what shall be added will be the effort of tedious toil and needless curiosity.

After all this it is surely superfluous to answer the question that has once been asked, Whether Pope was a poet? [9] otherwise than by asking in return, If Pope be not a poet, where is poetry to be found? To circumscribe poetry by a definition will only show the narrowness of the definer, though a definition which shall exclude Pope will not easily be made. Let us look around upon the present time and back upon the past; let us inquire to whom the voice of mankind has decreed the wreath of poetry; let their productions be examined and their claims stated, and the pretensions of Pope will be no more disputed. Had he given the world only his version, the name of poet must have been allowed him; if the writer of the *Iliad* were to class his successors, he would assign a very high place to his translator, without requiring any other evidence of genius.

from James Thomson

As a writer he is entitled to one praise of the highest kind: his mode of thinking and of expressing his thoughts is original. His blank verse is no more the blank verse of Milton or of any other poet than the rhymes of Prior are the rhymes of Cowley. His numbers, his pauses, his diction, are of his own growth, without transcription, without imitation. He thinks in a peculiar train, and he thinks always as a man of genius; he looks round on Nature and on Life with the eye which Nature bestows only on a poet, the eye that distinguishes in everything presented to its view whatever there is on which imagination can delight to be detained, and with a mind that at once comprehends the vast and attends to the minute. The reader of *The Seasons* wonders that he never saw before what Thomson shows him, and that he never yet has felt what Thomson impresses.

His is one of the works in which blank verse seems properly used; Thomson's wide expansion of general views, and his enumeration of circumstantial varieties, would have been obstructed and embarrassed by the frequent intersection of the sense which are the necessary effects of rhyme.

His descriptions of extended scenes and general effects bring before us the whole magnificence of Nature, whether pleasing or dreadful. The gaiety of *Spring*, the splendor of *Summer*, the tran-

---

[9] *Cf.* Warton, p. 203.

quillity of *Autumn,* and the horror of *Winter,* take in their turns possession of the mind. The poet leads us through the appearances of things as they are successively varied by the vicissitudes of the year, and imparts to us so much of his own enthusiasm that our thoughts expand with his imagery and kindle with his sentiments. Nor is the naturalist without his part in the entertainment; for he is assisted to recollect and to combine, to arrange his discoveries, and to amplify the sphere of his contemplation.

The great defect of *The Seasons* is want of method, but for this I know not that there was any remedy. Of many appearances subsisting all at once, no rule can be given why one should be mentioned before another; yet the memory wants the help of order, and the curiosity is not excited by suspense or expectation.

His diction is in the highest degree florid and luxuriant, such as may be said to be to his images and thoughts "both their lustre and their shade";[1] such as invests them with splendor through which perhaps they are not always easily discerned. It is too exuberant, and sometimes may be charged with filling the ear more than the mind.

from William Collins

He now, about 1744, came to London a literary adventurer, with many projects in his head and very little money in his pocket. He designed many works, but his great fault was irresolution; or the frequent calls of immediate necessity broke his schemes, and suffered him to pursue no settled purpose. A man doubtful of his dinner or trembling at a creditor is not much disposed to abstracted meditation or remote inquiries. He published proposals for a *History of the Revival of Learning,* and I have heard him speak with great kindness of Leo the Tenth and with keen resentment of his tasteless successor. But probably not a page of the *History* was ever written. He planned several tragedies, but he only planned them. He wrote now and then odes and other poems, and did something, however little. . . .

Mr. Collins was a man of extensive literature and of vigorous faculties. He was acquainted not only with the learned tongues but with the Italian, French, and Spanish languages. He had employed his mind chiefly upon works of fiction and subjects of fancy, and by indulging some peculiar habits of thought, was eminently delighted with those flights of imagination which pass the bounds of nature, and to which the mind is reconciled only by a passive

---

[1] *Hudibras,* II, i, 908.

531 - SAMUEL JOHNSON

---

acquiescence in popular traditions. He loved fairies, genii, giants, and monsters; he delighted to rove through the meanders of enchantment, to gaze on the magnificence of golden palaces, to repose by the waterfalls of Elysian gardens.

This was, however, the character rather of his inclination than his genius; the grandeur of wildness and the novelty of extravagance were always desired by him but were not always attained. Yet as diligence is never wholly lost, if his efforts sometimes caused harshness and obscurity, they likewise produced in happier moments sublimity and splendor. This idea which he had formed of excellence led him to Oriental fictions and allegorical imagery, and perhaps, while he was intent upon description, he did not sufficiently cultivate sentiment. His poems are the productions of a mind not deficient in fire, nor unfurnished with knowledge either of books or life, but somewhat obstructed in its progress by deviation in quest of mistaken beauties. . . .

The latter part of his life cannot be remembered but with pity and sadness. He languished some years under that depression of mind which enchains the faculties without destroying them, and leaves reason the knowledge of right without the power of pursuing it. These clouds which he perceived gathering on his intellects he endeavored to disperse by travel, and passed into France, but found himself constrained to yield to his malady, and returned. He was for some time confined in a house of lunatics, and afterwards retired to the care of his sister in Chichester, where death in 1756 came to his relief.

After his return from France the writer of this character paid him a visit at Islington, where he was waiting for his sister whom he had directed to meet him. There was then nothing of disorder discernible in his mind by any but himself; but he had withdrawn from study, and travelled with no other book than an English Testament, such as children carry to the school; when his friend took it into his hand, out of curiosity to see what companion a man of letters had chosen, "I have but one book," said Collins, "but that is the best."

Such was the fate of Collins, with whom I once delighted to converse, and whom I yet remember with tenderness. . . .

To what I have formerly said of his writings may be added that his diction was often harsh, unskillfully labored, and injudiciously selected. He affected the obsolete when it was not worthy of revival; and he puts his words out of the common order, seeming to think, with some later candidates for fame, that not to write prose is certainly to write poetry. His lines commonly are of slow motion, clogged and impeded with clusters of consonants. As men are often esteemed who cannot be loved, so the poetry of Collins may sometimes extort praise when it gives little pleasure.

Sir Joshua Reynolds

1723–1792

In his twenties, Reynolds educated himself in the art centers of Italy, especially Rome, where he recaptured the feel of Renaissance Neo-Platonism; first led into the Sistine Chapel, he records having spent the entire day walking up and down in a "paroxysm" of happiness and discovery. Though his forte was portrait-painting—an art of the particular, not the pure ideal—yet he would shape much of his criticism, and his ambitions for a national school of English painting, around the vision which he had gained during four years abroad.

Returning to England in 1753, he soon became the most fashionable painter of his day. When the Royal Academy was founded in 1768, he was knighted and elected president. In the following year he delivered the first of fifteen *Discourses* to students of the Academy, on which his reputation as a critic depends; thereafter, he produced one lecture a year—at the annual granting of prizes in December—then one every two years until 1790, when, almost blind, he retired from public life. Reynolds also wrote three papers for Johnson's *Idler* in 1759 (nos. 76, 79, and 82); notes to a translation of Du Fresnoy's Neo-Platonist *Art of Painting*; manuscript "characters" of Johnson, Goldsmith, and others; and miscellaneous notes or papers, including the draft of a sixteenth discourse. In a fragmentary apologia for tragicomedy, he observed that though Shakespeare's audience was ignorant of rules, its "sensibility was not subdued," and it was open to whatever honestly pleased, not what was supposed to please.

Though he dedicated himself to the studio not the study, yet the inspiration of his painting was often literary, and his most formative, lifelong friendships were with literary men—Johnson, Burke, and others of "the Club" which he first proposed at his fireplace one day in 1764. Johnson spoke of him proudly as "one of his literary school," a "thinking man," and no other critic so often sounds like Johnson while remaining independently himself. "He may be said to have formed my mind," Reynolds remarked, "and to have brushed off from it a deal of rubbish." From Johnson he learned his disposition to be critical and his humanistic practicality: he learned to despise "cant," to see through built-in trickeries of the human mind, and, with benign sophistication, to act upon his insights. In no way perhaps was he more like Johnson, or more authentically classical, than in his educative and practical stance. He would discuss the "theory" of art, he said, only as it related to a "method of studies" (no. II). He pitched his discourse at the level of practical help— which according to Longinus (I, 1) "it should be a writer's principal aim to give." His indebtedness to Johnson (and to Burke) is best explained by his advice to young painters in *Discourse* VII: above all else, they must draw and paint, but in off hours they should seek the conversation of savants, for thus "without formal training, they will insensibly come to feel and reason like those they live with, and find a rational and systematic taste imperceptibly formed in their minds." Yet, he added, they must always apply such "general truth to their own purposes."

After the twin peaks of Michelangelo (genius, energy, the sublime) and Raphael (taste, judgment, beauty), European painters abandoned the "great style" in an endeavor "to surprise and please by something uncommon and new" (no. V). Hence, despite cases of individual brilliance, post-Renaissance painting seemed to him marked by a general decline in imaginative power; he shaped his criticism to direct a reverse upward movement, hopefully to be centered in England. As "from the remains of the works of the ancients, the modern arts were revived," so "it is by their means that they must be restored a second time" (no. VI). As president of the Academy, he set himself to pass on an *idea* of humanistic classicism to young English painters. He borrowed eclectically, especially from literary critics, whom he considered more articulate than writers on painting (no. XV); yet, what he borrowed he weighed by his insights as a practicing artist, in a manner which may remind one of Dryden. The *Discourses* are the completest, one-volume synopsis of neoclassic tradition in the last half of the century. Yet they reach for the classic through contemporary English dilemmas such as genius and learning, the standard of taste, "rules" of authority and "principles" of nature, the Sublime and Beautiful (and Novelty), generality and particularity, reason and feeling. By assimilating neoclassicism to the psychology of feeling and imaginative response, Reynolds neared one threshold of Romantic theory; Hazlitt could read him with shocks of recognition.[1]

Like Johnson, he distinguished between "accidental blemishes and excrescences which are continually varying the surface of Nature's works, and the invariable general form which Nature most frequently produces, and always seems to intend in her productions" (*Idler* 82). To imitate nature is to express that which nature strives toward in particulars, but achieves only piecemeal and by degrees. Hence the "true," "great," or "liberal" artist converses with particulars—"particular customs and habits" or "the fluctuations of fashion" (no. IV), "local or accidental association of ideas" (no. VII), "local or temporary prejudices" (no. VII)—only to free himself from them and express the universal intended within them. As Reynolds realistically admitted, however, no artist can "supply the natural imperfection of things" *in vacuo* (no. XIII): "he that does not at all express particulars, expresses nothing" (no. XI). An imitation is not a mechanical or mirror copy, but of course the painter must have a skill in copying, must paint only one picture at a time, with one subject, and can never entirely escape the limits either of himself and his education, or of his nation and age. Yet he "imitates" by strength of his *mind*: he expresses with minimum particularity the idea or vision of nature which he has earned from long years of observation, thought, and labor, from the "accumulated experience" of his whole life (no. XIII). It follows, on classic ground, that "the great business of study is to form a *mind*" (no. XI), more especially "an artist-like mind" (no. XII). The *Discourses* are dedicated, above all else, to education of mind, which Reynolds conceived as a mutual process of individual human growth and "rational" knowledge of permanent realities. Neither is separable from the other: the uneducated and irrational painter cannot know what is permanent, but at the same time, the knowledge which matters artistically cannot be divorced "abstractly" from individual experience, vital energy and sensibility.

Until the last, Reynolds affirmed the primacy of *reason* in the

---

[1] See "Essay on Genius and Common Sense" in *Table Talk*.

mind, but in his later discourses especially, *imagination, feeling,* and *sensibility* competed for prominence. Traditional words like *reason,* as also *imitation* and *nature,* were being shorn by common usage of their older metaphysical and ethical meanings; he had to use the phraseology in fashion. All fine arts, he declared in *Discourse* XIII, "address themselves only to two faculties of the mind, its imagination and sensibility." Imagination is the residence of truth; the end of art—poetry, painting, music, sculpture, architecture, opera, gardening—is to strike the imagination and feelings. Yet he intended no ground-shift in his thinking. *Sensibility* or *feeling* includes that part of *reason* which belongs to art and the creative process; a "sagacity" which is the vestigial reservoir of all previous acts of reason, all previous knowledge, training, and experience.

His thought glided easily from education of an individual mind, or that in a single generation or country, to "progress of mind" in the history of civilization. The whole of *Discourse* IX is given over to "a short survey" of mankind in history, which is only a magnification of the life of an individual artist:

> The mind is continually laboring to advance, step by step, through successive gradations of excellence towards perfection, which is dimly seen at a great, though not hopeless distance, and which we must always follow because we can never attain; but the pursuit rewards itself. One truth teaches another, and our store is always increasing, though nature can never be exhausted.

Like a number of mid-century critics—Young, Johnson, Hume, Burke—Reynolds sometimes conceived of matters humanistic by analogy with "scientific" progress, Bacon's "advancement of learning." The artist inherits, or should inherit, "that idea of excellence which is the result of the accumulated experience of past ages" (no. I), in part to fulfill himself and keep from laboring out his life to rediscover what was already known, in part to enlarge his chance for advanced discovery. Reynolds conceived of "rules," for example, not as inflexible dogmas, but as discovered, "improved," and verifiable means of excellence, constantly enlarging by tradition. As criticism "advances," the powers of art are more and more articulated by "rules," but "genius," almost by definition, is always far ahead; both nature and invention are inexhaustible. Yet every artistic success, new or old, has its latent "rules," no matter how subtle and almost inexpressible they may be: "Unsubstantial, however, as these rules may seem, and difficult as it may be to convey them in writing, they are still seen and felt in the mind of the artist, and he works from them with as much certainty as if they were embodied, as I may say, upon paper" (no. VI). Their only foundation is "what is analogous to the mind of man," and what therefore will please in different ages and different countries (no. VII).

Obviously then, artistic gifts are not injured by rational learning, by laying in " a stock of materials"; by no other means, indeed, can they be "enlarged" or advanced to their highest pitch: "he who has the most materials has the greatest means of invention" (no. VI). Repeatedly, Reynolds attacked the superstition that something can come of nothing, and that works of art spring from "enthusiasm," "inspiration," or unassisted "genius." The mind without labor and learning is like a barren soil "which is soon exhausted, and will produce no crop, or only one" (no. VI). Even the greatest natural genius, if he ceases to "look out of himself" or "resolves never to ransack any mind but his own," soon lapses into self-parody and repetition. Reynolds thought of the mind under metaphors not only of growth, but of feeding and digestion of "materials." "Digestion" of art tends to be prior: one learns "the true art of seeing nature" by assimilating a tradition of masterworks. After passing through a mechanical first stage of rudiments, one's "business is to learn all that has been known and done before his own time," before passing into a third, emancipated stage in which inexhaustible nature lies open to the mind grown able to see and express it (no. II). Indeed, the study of masterworks of all kinds, the Longinian "habit of contemplating and brooding over the ideas of great geniuses," should be lifelong (no. XII):

> Labor to invent on their general principles and way of thinking. Possess yourself with their spirit. Consider with yourself how a Michelangelo or a Raphael would have treated this subject, and work yourself into a belief that your picture is to be seen and criticized by them when completed. Even an attempt of this kind will rouse your powers. (no. II)

For in feeding upon excellence, the mind realizes its own particular and vital identity. "Every seminary of learning," Reynolds remarked, "may be said to be surrounded with an atmosphere of floating knowledge, where every mind may imbibe somewhat congenial to its own original conceptions" (no. I). It is important gradually to try "what you can and what you cannot do," so that "instead of dissipating your natural facilities over the immense field of possible excellence, you may choose some particular walk in which you may exercise all your powers, in order that each of you may become the first in his way" (no. V).

He conceived all art as ranked along "a ladder of perfection"— a hierarchy of genres. Every excellence is vitally good and to be appreciated for so much as it is, but a distinction is still to be kept, by a cultivated mind, between low-level and high-level excellence. At the top is historical or Scriptural painting—"heroic action or heroic suffering" (no. IV); at the bottom is landscape, still life, drapery. As a corollary, Reynolds ranked the schools of European painting: at the top is "the Roman, the Florentine, the Bolognese schools . . . the three great schools of the world in the epic style"; below this, the "French school" of Poussin, Le Sueur, and Le Brun; finally, "the Venetian, together with the Flemish and the Dutch schools" (no. IV). His standard was partly dignity of subject and human "concern" for it, but more exactly, the degree of "mind" immanent in a work or kind of work. Portrait painting, for example —intermediate on the scale—advances in value insofar as it envelops the image of a particular man in an *idea* toward which his humanity has been striving.

In a manner of speaking, Reynolds spent his critical life trying to define *idea*; certainly he intended no mystification. By it he comprehended both "perfected" nature and "ideal" beauty. It is objectively real but subjectively known, and therefore for practical purposes may be said to exist only in the artist's mind:

> The beauty of which we are in quest is general and intellectual; it is an idea that subsists only in the mind; the sight never beheld it, nor has the hand expressed it. It is an idea residing in the breast of the artist, which he is always laboring to impart, and which he dies, at last, without imparting; but which he is yet so far able to communicate as to raise the thoughts and extend the views of the spectator, and which, by a succession of art, may be so far diffused that its effects may extend themselves imperceptibly into public benefits and be among the means of bestowing on whole nations refinement of taste. (no. IX)

Yet, he insisted, such an idea is neither supernatural nor fictitious: it is "assembled" empirically from shrewd and lifelong observation of deformed particulars, both in nature and art. "This great ideal perfection and beauty are not to be sought in the heavens, but upon earth. They are about us and upon every side of us" (no. III). Part of his ambiguity, one may think, was intrinsic in the history of neoclassicism itself, after its mixed origin in Plato and Aristotle. In addition, Reynolds found himself struggling personally to explain a Neo-Platonic vision of beauty on common-sense grounds: to locate an Italianate idealism within eighteenth-century English empirical psychology and sense of history.

* * * *

FROM

Discourses Delivered to the Students
of the Royal Academy [1769–1790]

from Discourse VI (December 10, 1774)

Imitation—Genius begins where rules end—Invention: acquired by being conversant with the inventions of others—The true method of imitating—Borrowing, how far allowable—Something to be gathered from every school.

The subject of this discourse will be *imitation*, as far as a painter is concerned in it. By imitation, I do not mean imitation in its largest sense, but simply the following of other masters, and the advantages to be drawn from the study of their works.

Those who have undertaken to write on our art and have represented it as a kind of *inspiration*, as a *gift* bestowed upon peculiar favorites at their birth, seem to insure a much more favorable disposition from their readers, and have a more captivating and liberal air, than he who attempts to examine, coldly, whether there are any means by which this art may be acquired, how the mind may be strengthened and expanded, and what guides will show the way to eminence.

It is very natural for those who are unacquainted with the *cause* of anything extraordinary to be astonished at the effect, and to consider it as a kind of magic. They who have never observed the gradation by which art is acquired, who see only what is the full result of long labor and application, of an infinite number and infinite variety of acts, are apt to conclude, from their entire inability to do the same at once, that it is not only inaccessible to themselves, but can be done by those only who have some gift of the nature of inspiration bestowed upon them.

The travellers into the East tell us that when the ignorant inhabitants of those countries are asked concerning the ruins of stately edifices yet remaining amongst them, the melancholy monuments of their former grandeur and long-lost science, they always answer that they were built by magicians. The untaught mind finds a vast gulf between its own powers and those works of complicated art which it is utterly unable to fathom, and it supposes that such a void can be passed only by supernatural powers.

And as for artists themselves, it is by no means their interest to undeceive such judges. . . .

But to bring us entirely to reason and sobriety, let it be observed that a painter must not only be of necessity an imitator of the works of nature, which alone is sufficient to dispel this phantom of inspiration, but he must be as necessarily an imitator of the works of other painters: this appears more humiliating, but is equally true; and no man can be an artist, whatever he may suppose, upon any other terms. . . .

What we now call "genius" begins not where rules, abstractedly taken, end, but where known vulgar and trite rules have no longer any place. It must of necessity be that even works of genius, like every other effect, as they must have their cause, must likewise have their rules: it cannot be by chance that excellences are produced with any constancy or any certainty, for this is not the nature of chance; but the rules which men of extraordinary parts, and such as are called men of genius, work, are either such as they discover by their own peculiar observations or of such a nice texture as not easily to admit being expressed in words, especially as artists are not very frequently skillful in that mode of communicating ideas. Unsubstantial, however, as these rules may seem, and difficult as it may be to convey them in writing, they are still seen and felt in the mind of the artist, and he works from them with as much certainty as if they were embodied, as I may say, upon paper. It is true, these refined principles cannot be always made palpable, like the more gross rules of art; yet it does not follow but that the mind may be put in such a train that it shall perceive, by a kind of scientific sense, that propriety, which words, particularly words of unpracticed writers, such as we are, can but very feebly suggest.

Invention is one of the great marks of genius; but if we consult experience, we shall find that it is by being conversant with the inventions of others that we learn to invent, as by reading the thoughts of others we learn to think.

Whoever has so far formed his taste as to be able to relish and feel the beauties of the great masters has gone a great way in his study; for, merely from a consciousness of this relish of the right, the mind swells with an inward pride, and is almost as powerfully affected as if it had itself produced what it admires. Our hearts, frequently warmed in this manner by the contact of those whom we wish to resemble, will undoubtedly catch something of their way of thinking, and we shall receive in our own bosoms some radiation at least of their fire and splendor. That disposition which is so strong in children still continues with us, of catching involuntarily the general air and manner of those with whom we are most conversant —with this difference only, that a young mind is naturally pliable and imitative, but in a more advanced state it grows rigid, and must be warmed and softened before it will receive a deep impression.

From these considerations, which a little of your own reflection will carry a great way further, it appears of what great consequence it is that our minds should be habituated to the contemplation of excellence, and that, far from being contented to make such habits the discipline of our youth only, we should, to the last moment of our lives, continue a settled intercourse with all the true examples of grandeur. Their inventions are not only the food of our infancy, but the substance which supplies the fullest maturity of our vigor.

The mind is but a barren soil, a soil which is soon exhausted, and will produce no crop, or only one, unless it be continually fertilized and enriched with foreign matter.

When we have had continually before us the great works of art, to impregnate our minds with kindred ideas, we are then, and not till then, fit to produce something of the same species. We behold all about us with the eyes of those penetrating observers whose works we contemplate; and our minds, accustomed to think the thoughts of the noblest and brightest intellects, are prepared for the discovery and selection of all that is great and noble in nature. The greatest natural genius cannot subsist on its own stock: he who resolves never to ransack any mind but his own will be soon reduced, from mere barrenness, to the poorest of all imitations: he will be obliged to imitate himself, and to repeat what he has before often repeated. When we know the subject designed by such men, it will never be difficult to guess what kind of work is to be produced.

It is vain for painters or poets to endeavor to invent without materials on which the mind may work and from which invention must originate. Nothing can come of nothing.

Homer is supposed to be possessed of all the learning of his time; and we are certain that Michelangelo and Raphael were equally possessed of all the knowledge in the art which had been discovered in the works of their predecessors.

A mind enriched by an assemblage of all the treasures of ancient and modern art will be more elevated and fruitful in resources, in proportion to the number of ideas which have been carefully collected and thoroughly digested. There can be no doubt but that he who has the most materials has the greatest means of invention, and if he has not the power of using them, it must proceed from a feebleness of intellect, or from the confused manner in which those collections have been laid up in his mind.

The addition of other men's judgment is so far from weakening our own, as is the opinion of many, that it will fashion and consolidate those ideas of excellence which lay in embryo, feeble, ill-shaped, and confused, but which are finished and put in order by the authority and practice of those whose works may be said to have been consecrated by having stood the test of ages. . . .

Nor whilst I recommend studying the art from artists can I be supposed to mean that Nature is to be neglected: I take this study in aid, and not in exclusion of the other. Nature is and must be the fountain, which alone is inexhaustible, and from which all excellences must originally flow.

The great use of studying our predecessors is to open the mind, to shorten our labor, and to give us the result of the selection made by those great minds of what is grand or beautiful in Nature; her rich stores are all spread out before us; but it is an art, and no easy art, to know how or what to choose, and how to attain and secure the object of our choice. Thus the highest beauty of form must be taken from Nature, but it is an art of long deduction and great experience to know how to find it. . . .

To find excellences however dispersed, to discover beauties however concealed by the multitude of defects with which they are surrounded, can be the work only of him who, having a mind always alive to his art, has extended his views to all ages and to all schools, and has acquired from that comprehensive mass, which he has thus gathered to himself, a well-digested and perfect idea of his art, to which everything is referred. Like a sovereign judge and arbiter of art, he is possessed of that presiding power which separates and attracts every excellence from every school, selects both from what is great and what is little, brings home knowledge from the East and from the West, making the universe tributary towards furnishing his mind and enriching his works with originality and variety of inventions. . . .

Study, therefore, the great works of the great masters, forever. Study, as nearly as you can, in the order, in the manner, and on the principles on which they studied. Study Nature attentively, but always with those masters in your company; consider them as models which you are to imitate, and at the same time, as rivals with whom you are to contend.

Discourse XIII (December 11, 1786)

Art not merely imitation, but under the direction of the imagination—In what manner poetry, painting, acting, gardening, and architecture depart from nature.

Gentlemen,

To discover beauties or to point out faults in the works of celebrated masters, and to compare the conduct of one artist with another, is certainly no mean or inconsiderable part of the criticism; but this is still no more than to know the art through the artist. This test of investigation must have two capital defects: it must be narrow, and it must be uncertain. To enlarge the boundaries of the art of painting, as well as to fix its principles, it will be necessary that *that* art and *those* principles should be considered in their correspondence with the principles of the other arts, which, like this, address themselves primarily and principally to the imagination. When those connected and kindred principles are brought together to be compared, another comparison will grow out of this, that is, the comparison of them all with those of human nature, from whence arts derive the materials upon which they are to produce their effects.

When this comparison of art with art, and of all arts with the nature of man, is once made with success, our guiding lines are as well ascertained and established as they can be in matters of this description.

This, as it is the highest style of criticism, is at the same time the soundest, for it refers to the eternal and immutable nature of things.

You are not to imagine that I mean to open to you at large, or to recommend to your research, the whole of this vast field of science. It is certainly much above my faculties to reach it; and though it may not be above yours to comprehend it fully, if it were fully and properly brought before you, yet perhaps the most perfect criticism requires habits of speculation and abstraction not very consistent with the employment which ought to occupy, and the habits of mind which ought to prevail in, a practical artist. I only point out to you these things, that when you do criticize (as all who work on a plan will criticize more or less), your criticism may be built on the foundation of true principles; and that though you may not always travel a great way, the way that you do travel may be the right road.

I observe, as a fundamental ground, common to all the arts with which we have any concern in this discourse, that they address themselves only to two faculties of the mind, its imagination and its sensibility.

All theories which attempt to direct or to control the art upon any principles falsely called rational, which we form to ourselves upon a supposition of what ought in reason to be the end or means of art, independent of the known first effect produced by objects on the imagination, must be false and delusive. For though it may appear bold to say it, the imagination is here the residence of truth. If the imagination be affected, the conclusion is fairly drawn; if it be not affected, the reasoning is erroneous, because the end is not obtained; the effect itself being the test, and the only test, of the truth and efficacy of the means.

There is in the commerce of life, as in art, a sagacity which is far from being contradictory to right reason, and is superior to any occasional exercise of that faculty; which supersedes it; and does not wait for the slow progress of deduction, but goes at once, by what appears a kind of intuition, to the conclusion. A man endowed with this faculty feels and acknowledges the truth, though it is not always in his power, perhaps, to give a reason for it; because he cannot recollect and bring before him all the materials that gave birth to his opinion; for very many and very intricate considerations may unite to form the principle, even of small and minute parts, involved in or dependent on a great system of things. Though these in process of time are forgotten, the right impression still remains fixed in his mind.

This impression is the result of the accumulated experience of our whole life, and has been collected, we do not always know how or when. But this mass of collective observation, however acquired, ought to prevail over that reason, which however powerfully exerted on any particular occasion, will probably comprehend but a partial view of the subject; and our conduct in life, as well as in the arts, is, or ought to be, generally governed by this habitual reason: it is our happiness that we are enabled to draw on such funds. If we were obliged to enter into a theoretical deliberation on every occasion before we act, life would be at a stand, and art would be impracticable.

It appears to me therefore that our first thoughts, that is, the effect which anything produces on our minds on its first appearance, is never to be forgotten; and it demands for that reason, because it is the first, to be laid up with care. If this be not done, the artist may happen to impose on himself by partial reasoning; by a cold consideration of those animated thoughts which proceed, not perhaps from caprice or rashness (as he may afterwards conceit), but from the fullness of his mind, enriched with the copious stores of all the various inventions which he had ever seen, or had ever passed in his mind. These ideas are infused into his design without any conscious effort; but if he be not on his guard, he may reconsider and correct them till the whole matter is reduced to a commonplace invention.

This is sometimes the effect of what I mean to caution you against—that is to say, an unfounded distrust of the imagination and feeling in favor of narrow, partial, confined, argumentative theories, and of principles that seem to apply to the design in hand, without considering those general impressions on the fancy in which real principles of *sound reason*, and of much more weight and importance, are involved, and as it were, lie hid under the appearance of a sort of vulgar sentiment.

Reason, without doubt, must ultimately determine everything; at this minute it is required to inform us when that very reason is to give way to feeling.

Though I have often spoken of that mean conception of our art which confines it to mere imitation, I must add that it may be narrowed to such a mere matter of experiment as to exclude from it the application of science, which alone gives dignity and compass to any art. But to find proper foundations for science is neither to narrow [n]or to vulgarize it; and this is sufficiently exemplified in the success of experimental philosophy. It is the false system of reasoning, grounded on a partial view of things, against which I would most earnestly guard you. And I do it the rather, because those narrow theories, so coincident with the poorest and most miserable practice, and which are adopted to give it countenance, have not had their origin in the poorest minds, but in the mistakes, or possibly in the mistaken interpretations, of great and commanding authorities. We are not, therefore, in this case misled by feeling, but by false speculation.

When such a man as Plato speaks of painting as only an imitative art, and that our pleasure proceeds from observing and acknowledging the truth of the imitation,[1] I think he misleads us by a partial theory. It is in this poor, partial, and, so far, false view of the art, that Cardinal Bembo[2] has chosen to distinguish even Raphael himself, whom our enthusiasm honors with the name of Divine. The same sentiment is adopted by Pope, in his epitaph on Sir Godfrey Kneller;[3] and he turns the panegyric solely on imitation as it is a sort of deception.

I shall not think my time misemployed if by any means I may contribute to confirm your opinion of what ought to be the object of your pursuit; because, though the best critics must always have exploded this strange idea, yet I know that there is a disposition towards a perpetual recurrence to it, on account of its simplicity and superficial plausibility. For this reason I shall beg leave to lay before you a few thoughts on this subject; to throw out some hints that may lead your minds to an opinion which I take to be the truth, that painting is not only to be considered as an imitation, operating by deception, but that it is, and ought to be, in many points of view, and strictly speaking, no imitation at all of external nature. Perhaps it ought to be as far removed from the vulgar idea of imitation as the refined civilized state in which we live is removed from a gross state of nature; and those who have not cultivated their imaginations, which the majority of mankind certainly have not, may be said, in regard to arts, to continue in this state of nature. Such men will always prefer imitation to that excellence which is addressed to another faculty that they do not possess; but these are not the persons to whom a painter is to look, any more than a judge of morals and manners ought to refer controverted points upon those subjects to the opinions of people taken from the banks of the Ohio or from New Holland.

It is the lowest style only of arts, whether of painting, poetry, or music, that may be said, in the vulgar sense, to be naturally pleas-

---

[1] *Republic,* X.

[2] See p. 285.

[3] "Living, great Nature fear'd he might outvie/Her works; and dying, fears herself may die." The couplet merely translates Cardinal Bembo's epitaph on Raphael. Kneller (1646–1723) was famous for his life-like portraits. *Cf.* Dryden, "To Sir Godfrey Kneller" (1694).

ing. The higher efforts of those arts, we know by experience, do not affect minds wholly uncultivated. This refined taste is the consequence of education and habit; we are born only with a capacity of entertaining this refinement, as we are born with a disposition to receive and obey all the rules and regulations of society; and so far it may be said to be natural to us, and no further.

What has been said may show the artist how necessary it is, when he looks about him for the advice and criticism of his friends, to make some distinction of the character, taste, experience, and observation in this art, of those from whom it is received. An ignorant, uneducated man may, like Apelles' critic,[4] be a competent judge of the truth of the representation of a sandal; or, to go somewhat higher, like Molière's old woman,[5] may decide upon what is nature, in regard to comic humor; but a critic in the higher style of art ought to possess the same refined taste which directed the artist in his work.

To illustrate this principle by a comparison with other arts, I shall now produce some instances to show that they, as well as our own art, renounce the narrow idea of nature and the narrow theories derived from that mistaken principle, and apply to that reason only which informs us not what imitation is—a natural representation of a given object—but what it is natural for the imagination to be delighted with. And perhaps there is no better way of acquiring this knowledge than by this kind of analogy: each art will corroborate and mutually reflect the truth on the other. Such a kind of juxtaposition may likewise have this use, that whilst the artist is amusing himself in the contemplation of other arts, he may habitually transfer the principles of those arts to that which he professes; which ought to be always present to his mind, and to which everything is to be referred.

So far is art from being derived from or having any immediate intercourse with particular nature as its model, that there are many arts that set out with a professed deviation from it.

This is certainly not so exactly true in regard to painting and sculpture. Our elements are laid in gross common nature, an exact imitation of what is before us; but when we advance to the higher state, we consider this power of imitation, though first in the order

---

[4] Pliny, *Natural History*, XXXV, 85: a shoemaker criticized Apelles's painting of a sandal. Pliny's chapter on painting popularized a belief that Greeks strove for naturalistic deception.

[5] According to Boileau, Molière tested whether his comedies were true or funny by reading them, first, to an old woman servant.

of acquisition, as by no means the highest in the scale of perfection.

Poetry addresses itself to the same faculties and the same dispositions as painting, though by different means. The object of both is to accommodate itself to all the natural propensities and inclinations of the mind. The very existence of poetry depends on the license it assumes of deviating from actual nature, in order to gratify natural propensities, by other means which are found by experience full as capable of affording such gratification. It sets out with a language in the highest degree artificial, a construction of measured words, such as never is nor ever was used by man. Let this measure be what it may, whether hexameter or any other meter used in Latin or Greek—or rhyme, or blank verse varied with pauses and accents, in modern languages—they are all equally removed from nature, and equally a violation of common speech. When this artificial mode has been established as the vehicle of sentiment, there is another principle in the human mind to which the work must be referred, which still renders it more artificial, carries it still further from common nature, and deviates only to render it more perfect. That principle is the sense of congruity, coherence, and consistency, which is a real existing principle in man; and it must be gratified. Therefore, having once adopted a style and a measure not found in common discourse, it is required that the sentiments also should be in the same proportion elevated above common nature, from the necessity of there being an agreement of the parts among themselves, that one uniform whole may be produced.

To correspond, therefore, with this general system of deviation from nature, the manner in which poetry is offered to the ear, the tone in which it is recited, should be as far removed from the tone of conversation as the words of which that poetry is composed. This naturally suggests the idea of modulating the voice by art, which I suppose may be considered as accomplished to the highest degree of excellence in the recitative of the Italian opera, as we may conjecture it was in the chorus that attended the ancient drama. And though the most violent passions, the highest distress, even death itself, are expressed in singing or recitative, I would not admit as sound criticism the condemnation of such exhibitions on account of their being unnatural.

If it is natural for our senses and our imaginations to be delighted with singing, with instrumental music, with poetry, and with graceful action, taken separately (none of them being in the vulgar sense natural, even in that separate state); it is conformable to experience, and therefore agreeable to reason as connected with and referred to experience, that we should also be delighted with this union of music, poetry, and graceful action, joined to every circumstance of pomp and magnificence calculated to strike the senses of the spectator. Shall reason stand in the way and tell us that we ought not to like what we know we do like, and prevent us from feeling the full effect of this complicated exertion of art? This is what I would understand by poets and painters being allowed to dare everything; for what can be more daring than accomplishing the purpose and end of art by a complication of means, none of which have their archetypes in actual nature?

So far therefore is servile imitation from being necessary, that whatever is familiar, or in any way reminds us of what we see and hear every day, perhaps does not belong to the higher provinces of art, either in poetry or painting. The mind is to be transported, as Shakespeare expresses it, "beyond the ignorant present," [6] to ages past. Another and a higher order of beings is supposed, and to those beings everything which is introduced into the work must correspond. Of this conduct, under these circumstances, the Roman and Florentine schools afford sufficient examples. Their style by this means is raised and elevated above all others, and by the same means the compass of art itself is enlarged.

We often see grave and great subjects attempted by artists of another school who—though excellent in the lower class of art, proceeding on the principles which regulate that class and not recollecting, or not knowing, that they were to address themselves to another faculty of the mind—have become perfectly ridiculous.

The picture which I have at present in my thoughts is a *Sacrifice of Iphigenia* painted by Jan Steen, a painter of whom I have formerly had occasion to speak with the highest approbation;[7] and even in this picture, the subject of which is by no means adapted to his genius, there is nature and expression; but it is such expression, and the countenances are so familiar and consequently so vulgar, and the whole accompanied with such finery of silks and velvets, that one would be almost tempted to doubt whether the artist did not purposely intend to burlesque his subject.

Instances of the same kind we frequently see in poetry. Parts of Hobbes's translation of Homer are remembered and repeated merely for the familiarity and meanness of their phraseology, so ill cor-

---

[6] *Macbeth*, I, v, 57.
[7] In *Discourse* VI, Reynolds praised his accuracy in delineating "vulgar" characters and passions.

responding with the ideas which ought to have been expressed, and, as I conceive, with the style of the original.

We may proceed in the same manner through the comparatively inferior branches of art. There are in works of that class the same distinction of a higher and a lower style; and they take their rank and degree in proportion as the artist departs more or less from common nature, and makes it an object of his attention to strike the imagination of the spectator by ways belonging specially to art—unobserved and untaught out of the school of its practice.

If our judgments are to be directed by narrow, vulgar, untaught, or rather ill-taught reason, we must prefer a portrait by Denner,[8] or any other high finisher, to those of Titian or Vandyck; and a landscape of Vanderheyden[9] to those of Titian or Rubens, for they are certainly more exact representations of nature.

If we suppose a view of nature represented with all the truth of the *camera obscura*,[1] and the same scene represented by a great artist, how little and mean will the one appear in comparison of the other, where no superiority is supposed from the choice of the subject. The scene shall be the same; the difference only will be in the manner in which it is presented to the eye. With what additional superiority then will the same artist appear when he has the power of selecting his materials, as well as elevating his style? Like Nicolas Poussin, he transports us to the environs of ancient Rome, with all the objects which a literary education makes so precious and interesting to man: or, like Sebastian Bourdon,[2] he leads us to the dark antiquity of the pyramids of Egypt; or like Claude Lorrain,[3] he conducts us to the tranquillity of Arcadian scenes and fairyland.

Like the history painter, a painter of landscapes in this style and with this conduct sends the imagination back into antiquity; and like the poet, he makes the elements sympathize with his subject: whether the clouds roll in volumes, like those of Titian or Salvator Rosa, or, like those of Claude, are gilded with the setting sun; whether the mountains have sudden and bold projections, or are gently sloped; whether the branches of his trees shoot out abruptly in right angles from their trunks, or follow each other with only

---

[8] Balthasar Denner (1685–1749), German portrait painter.
[9] Jan van der Heyden (1637–1712), Dutch painter of landscape and still life.
[1] See Addison, p. 248.
[2] French historical painter (1616–71).
[3] See p. 573.

a gentle inclination. All these circumstances contribute to the general character of the work, whether it be of the elegant or of the more sublime kind. If we add to this the powerful materials of lightness and darkness, over which the artist has complete dominion, to vary and dispose them as he pleases, to diminish or increase them as will best suit his purpose and correspond to the general idea of his work—a landscape thus conducted, under the influence of a poetical mind, will have the same superiority over the more ordinary and common views as Milton's *L'Allegro* and *Il Penseroso* have over a cold prosaic narration or description; and such a picture would make a more forcible impression on the mind than the real scenes, were they presented before us.

If we look abroad to other arts, we may observe the same distinction, the same division into two classes, each of them acting under the influence of two different principles, in which the one follows nature, the other varies it and sometimes departs from it.

The theatre, which is said "to hold the mirror up to nature," [4] comprehends both those ideas. The lower kind of comedy, or farce, like the inferior style of painting, the more naturally it is represented, the better; but the higher appears to me to aim no more at imitation, so far as it belongs to anything like deception, or to expect that the spectators should think that the events there represented are really passing before them, than Raphael in his Cartoons, or Poussin in his Sacraments expected it to be believed, even for a moment, that what they exhibited were real figures.

For want of this distinction, the world is filled with false criticism. Raphael is praised for naturalness and deception which he certainly has not accomplished, and as certainly never intended; and our late great actor, Garrick, has been as ignorantly praised by his friend Fielding, who doubtless imagined he had hit upon an ingenious device by introducing in one of his novels (otherwise a work of the highest merit) an ignorant man[5] mistaking Garrick's representation of a scene in *Hamlet* for reality. A very little reflection will convince us that there is not one circumstance in the whole scene that is of the nature of deception. The merit and excellence of Shakespeare, and of Garrick, when they were engaged in such scenes, is of a different and much higher kind. But what adds to the falsity of this intended compliment is that the best stage representation appears even more unnatural to a person of such a character, who is supposed never to have seen a play before, than it

---

[4] *Hamlet*, III, ii, 24.
[5] Partridge in *Tom Jones*, XVI, v.

does to those who have had a habit of allowing for those necessary deviations from nature which the art requires.

In theatric representation, great allowances must always be made for the place in which the exhibition is represented—for the surrounding company, the lighted candles, the scenes visibly shifted in your sight, and the language of blank verse, so different from common English, which merely as English must appear surprising in the mouths of Hamlet, and all the court and natives of Denmark. These allowances are made, but their being made puts an end to all manner of deception: and further, we know that the more low, illiterate, and vulgar any person is, the less he will be disposed to make these allowances, and of course to be deceived by any imitation, the things in which the trespass against nature and common probability is made in favor of the theatre being quite within the sphere of such uninformed men.

Though I have no intention of entering into all the circumstances of unnaturalness in theatrical representations, I must observe that even the expression of violent passion is not always the most excellent in proportion as it is the most natural; so, great terror and such disagreeable sensations may be communicated to the audience, that the balance may be destroyed by which pleasure is preserved and holds its predominancy in the mind: violent distortion of action, harsh screamings of the voice, however great the occasion, or however natural on such occasion, are therefore not admissible in the theatric art. Many of these allowed deviations from nature arise from the necessity which there is that everything should be raised and enlarged beyond its natural state, that the full effect may come home to the spectator, which otherwise would be lost in the comparatively extensive space of the theatre. Hence the deliberate and stately step, the studied grace of action, which seems to enlarge the dimensions of the actor and alone to fill the stage. All this unnaturalness, though right and proper in its place, would appear affected and ridiculous in a private room; *quid enim deformius quam scenam in vitam transferre?*[6]

And here I must observe, and I believe it may be considered as a general rule, that no art can be grafted with success on another art. For though they all profess the same origin, and to proceed from the same stock, yet each has its own peculiar modes both of imitating nature and of deviating from it, each for the accomplish-

---

[6] Apparently from Bacon's *Advancement of Learning* (see Hilles, *Literary Career of Sir Joshua Reynolds*, p. 110): "For what is more disgraceful than to carry over the stage into real life?"

ment of its own particular purpose. These deviations, more especialiy, will not bear transplantation to another soil.

If a painter should endeavor to copy the theatrical pomp and parade of dress and attitude, instead of that simplicity which is not a greater beauty in life than it is in painting, we should condemn such pictures as painted in the meanest style.

So also, gardening, as far as gardening is an art or entitled to that appellation, is a deviation from nature; for if the true taste consists, as many hold, in banishing every appearance of art, or any traces of the footsteps of man, it would then be no longer a garden. Even though we define it, *Nature to advantage dressed*,[7] and in some sense it is such, and much more beautiful and commodious for the recreation of man; it is however, when so dressed, no longer a subject for the pencil of a landscape painter, as all landscape painters know who love to have recourse to Nature herself and to dress her according to the principles of their own art; which are far different from those of gardening,[8] even when conducted according to the most approved principles, and such as a landscape painter himself would adopt in the disposition of his own grounds for his own private satisfaction.

I have brought together as many instances as appear necessary to make out the several points which I wished to suggest to your consideration in this discourse, that your own thoughts may lead you further in the use that may be made of the analogy of the arts, and of the restraint which a full understanding of the diversity of many of their principles ought to impose on the employment of that analogy.

The great end of all those arts is to make an impression on the imagination and the feeling. The imitation of nature frequently does this. Sometimes it fails, and something else succeeds. I think, therefore, the true test of all the arts is not solely whether the production is a true copy of nature, but whether it answers the end of art, which is to produce a pleasing effect upon the mind.

It remains only to speak a few words of architecture, which does not come under the denomination of an imitative art. It applies itself, like music (and I believe we may add poetry), directly to the imagination, without the intervention of any kind of imitation.

There is in architecture, as in painting, an inferior branch of art, in which the imagination appears to have no concern. It does not, however, acquire the name of a polite and liberal art from its use-

---

[7] Pope, *Essay on Criticism*, 297.
[8] *Cf.* Price, p. 593.

fulness, or administering to our wants or necessities, but from some higher principle: we are sure that, in the hands of a man of genius, it is capable of inspiring sentiment and of filling the mind with great and sublime ideas.

It may be worth the attention of artists to consider what materials are in their hands that may contribute to this end, and whether this art has it not in its power to address itself to the imagination with effect by more ways than are generally employed by architects.

To pass over the effect produced by that general symmetry and proportion by which the eye is delighted, as the ear is with music, architecture certainly possesses many principles in common with poetry and painting. Among those which may be reckoned as the first is that of affecting the imagination by means of association of ideas.[9] Thus, for instance, as we have naturally a veneration for antiquity, whatever building brings to our remembrance ancient customs and manners, such as the castles of the barons of ancient chivalry, is sure to give this delight. Hence it is that "towers and battlements" [1] are so often selected by the painter and the poet to make a part of the composition of their ideal landscape; and it is from hence, in a great degree, that in the buildings of Vanbrugh,[2] who was a poet as well as an architect, there is a greater display of imagination than we shall find perhaps in any other; and this is the ground of the effects we feel in many of his works, notwithstanding the faults with which many of them are justly charged. For this purpose, Vanbrugh appears to have had recourse to some of the principles of the Gothic architecture, which, though not so ancient as the Grecian, is more so to our imagination, with which the artist is more concerned than with absolute truth.

The barbaric splendor of those Asiatic buildings, which are now publishing by a member of this Academy,[3] may possibly, in the same manner, furnish an architect, not with models to copy, but with hints of composition and general effect which would not otherwise have occurred.

It is, I know, a delicate and hazardous thing, and as such I have already pointed it out, to carry the principles of one art to another, or even to reconcile in one object the various modes of the same

---

[9] *Cf.* Alison, p. 575.

[1] *L'Allegro,* l. 77.

[2] Sir John Vanbrugh (1664–1726), the playwright, also a baroque architect, "England's Michelangelo."

[3] William Hodges (1744–97) published aquatints, in 1786, of Indian buildings.

art when they proceed on different principles. The sound rules of the Grecian architecture are not to be lightly sacrificed. A deviation from them, or even an addition to them, is like a deviation or addition to or from the rules of other arts—fit only for a great master, who is thoroughly conversant in the nature of man as well as all combinations in his own art.

It may not be amiss for the architect to take advantage *sometimes* of that to which I am sure the painter ought always to have his eyes open, I mean the use of accidents: to follow when they lead, and to improve them rather than always to trust to a regular plan. It often happens that additions have been made to houses at various times, for use or pleasure. As such buildings depart from regularity, they now and then acquire something of scenery by this accident, which I should think might not unsuccessfully be adopted by an architect in an original plan if it does not too much interfere with convenience. Variety and intricacy are beauties and excellences in every other of the arts which address the imagination. And why not in architecture?

The forms and turnings of the streets of London and other old towns are produced by accident, without any original plan or design; but they are not always the less pleasant to the walker or spectator on that account. On the contrary, if the city had been built on the regular plan of Sir Christopher Wren,[4] the effect might have been, as we know it is in some new parts of the town, rather unpleasing; the uniformity might have produced weariness and a slight degree of disgust.

I can pretend to no skill in the detail of architecture. I judge now of the art merely as a painter. When I speak of Vanbrugh, I mean to speak of him in the language of our art. To speak then of Vanbrugh in the language of a painter: he had originality of invention, he understood light and shadow and had great skill in composition. To support his principal object, he produced his second and third groups or masses; he perfectly understood in *his* art what is the most difficult in ours, the conduct of the background, by which the design and invention is set off to the greatest advantage. What the background is in painting, in architecture is the real ground on which the building is erected; and no architect took greater care than he that his work should not appear crude and hard: that is, it

---

[4] English architect (1632–1723), professor of astronomy, and one of the founders of the Royal Society. After London burned in 1666, he drew plans for reconstructing the whole city, and completed fifty or more buildings, especially churches, including St. Paul's and Hampton Court.

did not abruptly start out of the ground without expectation or preparation.

This is a tribute which a painter owes to an architect who composed like a painter, and was defrauded of the due reward of his merit by the wits of his time,[5] who did not understand the principles of composition in poetry better than he, and who knew little or nothing of what he understood perfectly, the general ruling principles of architecture and painting. His fate was that of the great Perrault;[6] both were the objects of the petulant sarcasms of factious men of letters, and both have left some of the fairest ornaments which to this day decorate their several countries: the façade of the Louvre, Blenheim, and Castle Howard.

Upon the whole, it seems to me that the object and intention of all the arts is to supply the natural imperfection of things, and often to gratify the mind by realizing and embodying what never existed but in the imagination.

It is allowed on all hands that facts and events, however they may bind the historian, have no dominion over the poet or the painter. With us, history is made to bend and conform to this great idea of art. And why? Because these arts, in their highest province, are not addressed to the gross senses, but to the desires of the mind,[7] to that spark of divinity which we have within, impatient of being circumscribed and pent up by the world which is about us. Just so much as our art has of this, just so much of dignity, I had almost said of divinity, it exhibits; and those of our artists who possessed this mark of distinction in the highest degree acquired from thence the glorious appellation of *divine*.

---

[5] Swift and Pope ridiculed Vanbrugh, though Reynolds may allude to other wits.

[6] Claude Perrault (1613–88), French architect who designed the eastern façade of the Louvre.

[7] Bacon, *Advancement of Learning*, II, iv, 2. *Cf.* Hurd, p. 388.

NEW
DEVELOPMENTS

WHAT STRIKES one immediately at the end of the eighteenth century is a visible acceleration of change, a sudden gathering into shape of an unlikely world. Critics come on stage who seem more starkly "transitional" than their predecessors, whether or not they truly are, because so often in their criticism a *completed* past jams against the unprecedented and unassimilated. Examples have been chosen which are unmistakably developments from earlier criticism in this volume, which are consistent with it and dependent on it, in some respects unintelligible without it: by any definition, each one is "English eighteenth-century." Each of the four writers— Morgann, Alison, Whiter, and Price—self-consciously attempts the new, but only within a critical tradition long established in England or Scotland. Each "improves," works out new implications or new uses for old and familiar ideas. Yet each concludes at a shadowy threshold where a next improvement, already latent and forming, must tip over into the alien.

All four are associationists, historically conscious, deeply attracted to the particular, to irrational processes of the mind, and to the "characters" strangely emergent from nature. All four still have some twentieth-century relevance.

Maurice Morgann (1726–1802). Critics after Dryden often commented on the startling lifelikeness of Shakespeare's characters. "His

characters are so much nature herself that it is a sort of injury to call
them by so distant a name as copies of her," Pope said; "every
single character in Shakespeare is as much an individual as those
in life itself." [1] In the last half of the century, critics gradually
forged a technique of character analysis equal to their intuitions.
Joseph Warton pioneered in *The Adventurer* (1753–54) with two
essays on *The Tempest* (nos. 93 and 97) in which he analyzed
Ariel and Caliban, and three essays on *King Lear* (nos. 113, 116,
and 122). "General criticism," he announced, "is on all subjects
useless and unentertaining, but it is more than commonly absurd
with respect to Shakespeare, who must be accompanied step by
step, and scene by scene, in his gradual developments of characters
and passions." Warton struggled, by a kind of running paraphrase,
"to exhibit perfect pictures of the secret workings and changes in
Lear's mind, which vary in each succeeding passage, and which
render an allegation of each particular sentiment absolutely necessary." One finds still other tributaries to the new criticism in individualistic and real-life humor theory like that of Morris (see p.
200), in Johnson's notes (see p. 471), in the use of Shakespeare by
associationist critics to illustrate psychology (see Kames, p. 308;
Gerard, p. 323). Gradually, Shakespeare's characters came to be
studied in isolation, as if they were real-life beings—for example,
in William Richardson whose *Philosophical Analysis and Illustration of Some of Shakespeare's Remarkable Characters* (1774) explained tragic heroes by their "ruling passion" (e.g., love of power
in Richard III) and moralized over them as though they were
figures of history. In 1780, Henry Mackenzie constructed an essay-
portrait of Hamlet which clearly anticipates Romantic theories of
the sensitive idealist, whose jests reveal his depth of melancholy
(*The Mirror*, nos. 99 and 100).

   Morgann's essay on Falstaff (1777, written in 1774) is the
eighteenth-century peak of the movement; at the same time, in its
fusion of character analysis with theory, it reaches into the next
century. Morgann anticipates the manner of Lamb and Hazlitt and
the bardolatry of Coleridge (that is, the belief that Shakespeare
somehow transcends the humanly comprehensible). In his patient
massing of detail and his concentrated study of a whole, he brings
to sudden crystallization the method of the great Victorian critic
A. C. Bradley. Most of the "heavier part," that is, his theory, Morgann drops into long footnotes, and promises that if he ever publishes another edition, he will demote still more text to the bottom

---

[1] Preface to Shakespeare (1725), par. 4.

of the page. Evidently, he began with a simple intention, to argue that Falstaff is not a coward, but as the subject grew on his hands, he discovered in himself essentially Romantic premises of organic nature and sympathetic feeling, which he expresses with a mixed air of surprise, defiance, and apology.

In a character created by Shakespeare—and Shakespeare alone— we feel a history whose depth and coherence we cannot exhaust by analysis. We take an "impression" of the character from all the minute circumstances and interrelations of his life as a whole—the whole is implicit in every part—but the character eludes our reason, which can deal only in "abstractions and general propositions." Falstaff, for example, is not a type such as the *miles gloriosus*, which reason could quickly classify; he is not a static agent of the plot, the sum of "motives" which we infer from his actions. He is a unique individual, with a secret background of being, who has been formed what he is by a process like that of organic growth and assimilation. He has "a certain roundness and integrity," full of coalesced incongruities which steal secretly upon our feelings as he is progressively revealed. He is "struck out *whole*" as it were from the block of nature itself, by a comprehensive energy of mind which has "felt from within," as by magic, all the "seeds of things" and the principles of their unfolding in a given dramatic world.

Morgann's organicism dissolves every aspect of the play in Shakespeare's genius for realizing character. Plot, moral decorum, and greatness of subject—all cease to be important because they are abstract requirements, imposed from without. Plot disappears in the "grouping" of characters and the "process" of their revelation. In language, puns are justifiable because they reveal complications of passion and incongruities of character. A chorus would be an abstract piece of machinery; in place of it, Shakespeare, the organic artist, builds into the play internal commentary and mutual interpretation of one character by another. The audience "feels" its way through the play by a "certain mental sense" for which Morgann has no name.

The *organic* is an extremely elastic concept, which receives its fullest elaboration in later philosophy and criticism, especially in Germany—a dark house of many dark mansions and interconnecting passageways. No eighteenth-century Englishman explores it with systematic precision: it presupposes metaphysical inquiry of a sort which was unlikely in a country and century whose intellectual life was dominantly rational-empirical, legal, and practical. There are scattered and fragmentary anticipations, to be sure: in

Shaftesbury's "plastic Nature" (see p. 209), in the increasing frequency of biological analogies (*cf.* Young, p. 358; Gerard, p. 276), in the use of the word *spirit*—as in "spirit of romance," "spirit of liberty," or the later "spirit of the age"—by history-minded empiricists like Hurd or Burke. *Spirit* named the "character" of a thing emerging from its total relationships—a quality of wholeness greater than the sum of its parts. At the same time, the very success of rational empiricism in England, with its latent threat of suffocation in the mechanistic and abstract, encouraged sporadic protests in behalf of particularity, process, the unrational, which might at any time edge into organic analogies, and as quickly edge out again.

Morgann ventured into criticism only once, though he published pamphlets on practical subjects such as the slave trade, the prevention of adultery, and the post-Revolutionary state of France. Among papers which he had destroyed at his death were reportedly some on metaphysics, politics, and criticism. He was at one time Under-Secretary of State in charge of American affairs. Three years after publishing his essay he went to New York as an aide to General Carleton, to help negotiate American peace. Thus, though it has been called the first Romantic criticism of Shakespeare, Morgann's essay on Falstaff is equally one more example of gentleman-amateur criticism by a man of state responsibilities and broad practical experience. He belonged to the generation of Burke, Hurd, and the Wartons.

Archibald Alison (1757–1839). A recognizably "eighteenth-century English" stream of aesthetic theory dwindles through minor tracts, essays, and inquiries until almost the middle of the nineteenth century, but in his two *Essays on the Nature and Principles of Taste* (1790), Alison closes off what is best in it. Even as he restates what has gone before, he joins it to a radically separate future. His descent from earlier theorists on taste or imagination shows everywhere; here a resemblance to Addison or Shaftesbury, there a bit of Hutcheson, Hume, Kames, Gerard, Beattie, or Burke. But he is not a slack-minded eclectic; what he says is rigorously logical and his own. On balance, he ranks, or should rank, among the handful of original theorists in the history of English aesthetics. The fullest recognition of his *Essays*, which went into numerous nineteenth-century reprints, dates from the second edition of 1810, the subsequent notice by Francis Jeffrey (May, 1811) in the *Edinburgh Review* and article on Beauty in the 1824 *Encyclopaedia Britannica*. Understandably, Alison was better appreciated by a generation still grappling with Romantic poets. Gradually, he joined Lord Kames on the throne of public, textbookish authority, and reigned until the early 1840's when Ruskin began publishing *Modern Painters.*

A kinship with Wordsworth and Keats, who may have learned from him, is obvious in several passages, especially those on association. And yet, Alison should be imagined in the context of an eighteenth-century culture which, by 1790, was fading behind him with violent rapidity.

He claimed descent from a "Platonic school" so-called, represented by "Lord Shaftesbury, Dr. Hutcheson, Dr. Akenside, and Dr. Spence," and especially the Scottish common-sense philosopher Thomas Reid, under whom Alison studied at Glasgow. All had asserted, in one way or another, that "matter is not beautiful in itself but derives its beauty from the expression of *mind.*" Thus, Alison continued the long quarrel which Shaftesbury had begun with dead matter and with the near-solipsistic and skeptical implications of "modern philosophy." Like Addison and Hutcheson, he revived "final causes" in Nature: Providence has put imagination, emotion, and sympathy into the mind to free us from the miserable dullness of matter, and by their tasteful exercise, to intensify joy and benevolence. And yet, it is only "through the medium of matter that, in the present condition of our being, the qualities of mind are known to us." Alison was a Scottish Episcopalian minister who ended his *Essays* with praise to "the LIVING GOD," and some parts of his theory suggest a sacramental vision of Nature, intrinsic to his faith. Yet he was neither a propagandist of his faith nor a simple-minded debtor to earlier English and Scottish theorists. For example, he rejected the fiction of an "inner sense" or of various "inner senses," which, he argued, must be "resolved into more general principles of our constitution." And only by a curious eighteenth-century stretch of the term is he a "Platonist." Alison cannot be understood apart from empiricist models of the mind and empirical terminology. When he spoke of "ideas," he was closer to Locke than to Plato; he assumed a divorce of "imagination" and "judgment"; and he assumed, though less rigidly than Hume or Burke, that certain "qualities of objects" affect the mind by pre-established, mechanical linkages, that we know only "effects" in ordinary experience and advance to knowledge of "causes" only by the most patient, scientific induction. Furthermore, he relied heavily on a psychology of "customary" association which is still vaguely Lockian—though the associations established in childhood, which Locke considered odd and abnormal, have become for Alison a precious, if not sacred part of sensibility.

His strategy, typical in British aesthetics after Addison, was not to deny outright the empiricist model of mind and nature, but to build into it another dimension—to erect on its grounds a superstructure of ideal values.

Perhaps what is newest in his thought and most significant for literature is his fencing off the "emotion of taste" from experiences which are merely practical or "animal," and his theory of symbolism. Each is tightly implicated with the other.

Ordinary life, busied with duties and problems, is a state of practical attention and relative lack of emotion: our senses present us with objects in which we take only feeble or random "pleasure," if any at all. Unfortunately, many men of business never escape this stage; they harden in practical habit. The "emotion of taste," which may be called "delight" instead of "pleasure," occurs only when the mind is unbusied, open, and free to imagine. For when we experience beauty or sublimity, an object presented by the senses has triggered a free, spontaneous activity of imagination, which, as it were, envelops our perception of the object in a train of associated emotions and images, welling up from the reservoir in us which has been filling since childhood. We are in a state of emotion in which imagination creates alongside and around the object. Thus each aesthetic experience is individually subjective.

Alison saves himself from total subjectivism, however, by his doctrine of association. He assumes that in growing up, people will have responded to some qualities in objects with the same emotions— such is Nature—and therefore some stored associations of emotion will be universal. Still others may be shared by common experiences, by fortune, accident, or education. All men with a classical education, for example, who see the Tiber river winding through the ruins of Rome, will probably respond more intensely to it than other men, for ancient Rome will fill their imagination, not the paltry, stagnating stream which the senses present. Some associations, however, are inescapably private and unique, and therefore aesthetic response is always a "complex" emotion "peculiar" to one man at a given moment. Yet unlike ordinary experience, dissipated in formless practicalities, an aesthetic emotion has unity of "character," or in the work of art, unity of "expression." No matter how different men may be in the detailed peculiarities of their response, it is still possible to communicate, to share in the same *character* of experience, each man in his manner and degree.

Alison's next and logical step is into symbolism. *Any* quality of *any* material object may suggest[2] or trigger the complex chain of images and emotions for which it is the natural or created "sign." Such "signs" are wholly imaginative-emotional in character, and require no effort of reason. They "mean" non-rationally. Professor Tuveson rightly connects such a theory with the beginnings of nineteenth-century symbolist poetry and with Yeats.[3]

Alison prided himself on having solved a problem which had haunted neoclassicists for better than a century—the possibility of artistic exhaustion. The felt possibility of exhaustion lay behind the eighteenth-century dialect of originality and imitation, genius and learning, and to some extent Ancient and Modern. By 1790, the classical concept of Nature had shrunk so unrecognizably into "forms or proportions or combinations of matter," and was so completely divorced from all else which gives value, dignity, and meaning to human life, that "imitation" of it could promise only sterility and sameness. "It is not for imitation we look," Alison once remarked of painting, "but for character. It is not the art but the genius of the painter which now gives value to his compositions." A theory of art as "significant" self-expression opened, or seemed to open, upon an unbounded field of valuable human experiences. Both artist and public, instead of finding themselves chained to "a few forms which the superstition of early taste had canonized," were freed, or seemed to be freed, for endless creative and individual responses.

However, Alison's theory, as stated, encourages an emotionalistic art which, if carried to its end, splits off one part of the mind from the rest—an art to which classical reason and rhetoric are irrelevant, and which carries within itself its own seeds of exhaustion.

As so often with Scottish critics, his tastes seem strangely conservative alongside a theory so far-reaching if not revolutionary. For example, tragicomedy seemed to Alison "utterly indefensible"; he regretted that Shakespeare lacked knowledge of the laws of drama equal to his genius; and he praised Corneille as the first tragedian of modern Europe who understood the aesthetic necessity of unity of emotion. He believed in a normative human nature, probably in a standard of taste, in the centrality of education in the classics, and in the theatre as a school of virtue. Finally, "it ought to be the increasing study of the artist," he remarked, "to disengage his mind from the accidental associations of his age as

---

[2] *Cf.* Addison, p. 239.
[3] *The Imagination as a Means of Grace*, pp. 190 ff.

well as the common prejudices of his art, to labor to distinguish his productions by that pure and permanent expression which may be felt in every age." Dr. Johnson had believed no less.

Walter Whiter (1758–1832). Whiter's career follows a common pattern, as in Young and Hurd—classical training at the university for half one's life, in this instance Cambridge where Whiter was a fellow until 1797 and intimate friend of the great classical scholar Richard Porson; after that, appointment, for the other half of one's life, to a church parish. The *Specimen of a Commentary on Shakespeare* (1794) was his sole work of criticism, though he mentions having studied Milton's corrections of *Comus* in the Trinity College manuscript. The consuming efforts of his life were two etymological dictionaries, the *Etymologicon Magnum* (1800) and *Etymologicon Universale* (1811–25). According to one report, not necessarily reliable, he had mastered some twenty languages. The *Specimen* went virtually ignored, or undiscussed, until the 1930's when the flurry of image- and symbol-criticism of Shakespeare, as in Caroline Spurgeon, Wolfgang Clemen, and G. Wilson Knight, led a writer for the *Times Literary Supplement* (Sept. 5, 1936) to discover precedent for it in Whiter. "I may be permitted, on this occasion," Whiter remarked in his preface, "to adopt the language of science and to assume the merit of DISCOVERY." One can only regret that the work which he promised toward the end of his life, a new approach to mythology, was never finished.

Like Spurgeon, he found in the associational patterns of Shakespeare's language an unconscious residue of "the age in which he lived," the "employments in which he was engaged," and "the various objects which excited his passions or arrested his attention." Whether he glimpsed the rich possibilities of his discovery is doubtful: Whiter argued merely its usefulness to editors. And even in this, he must have doubted himself: when he examined Chatterton's Rowley poems, which he knew might be forgeries, he found "all the effects of an *ancient mind,* which my theory had brought me to expect." There is no doubt, however, that his reading of Shakespeare was historical-imaginative as well as philological, that he distinguished between the validity of his principles and the narrowness of his proofs, and spoke of "opening a new path to the researches of the critic and of supplying a future theme of investigation to a more sagacious or a more diligent inquirer." His remark on the pun *color, colors* in *Julius Caesar* springs from a mind responsive to created context as well as to the isolated meaning of

words. In a passage that suggests Gerard, he spoke of the genius of
the poet "which passes rapidly through a variety of successive
images, which discovers with so wonderful an acuteness their relations and dependencies, and which combines them with such exquisite effect in all the pleasing forms of fiction and invention."
Yet Whiter clearly divorced unconscious associations which he had
discovered—accidental, chance, or customary—from artistic form
and value, which he assumed to be altogether conscious and intended. Perhaps it is still an open question whether Shakespeare
"intended" all the amazing complications in his language.

Whiter deserves study on at least two other scores. He illustrates
with unusual clarity the long-lived relevance of Locke, and the
subtle ease with which Locke's doctrine of association could issue
in a limited concept of the unconscious. Fundamentally Whiter
is still a Johnsonian believer in general nature. Yet, at the same
time, in his attraction to the "peculiarities" of Shakespeare's imagery and language, and to "those impressions which are peculiar
to the country, the age, and the situation of the writer," he illustrates a general fascination with the particular in end-of-the-century
criticism.

Sir Uvedale Price (1747–1829). The aesthetic category—or craze
or attitude—of the *picturesque* was as much a native English invention as that of *humor*, with which it has some likenesses; and like
humor, it was so deeply implicated in late eighteenth-century culture as to make a precise, single definition almost impossible. Yet
it is felt easily enough in examples. As an attitude or elected way
of seeing, it is still defensible; as a craze, it engulfed English and
Scottish manners far into the nineteenth century. As a category of
formal aesthetics, it owed most perhaps, if only by omission, to
Burke: it named a *character* or mode of aesthetic experience, in
gardening, painting, poetry, music, and architecture, in all the fine
arts, which was felt as distinct from either the sublime or the
beautiful, though often mixed with both.

Its "efficient causes," as Price explains, are "the two opposite
qualities of roughness and of sudden variation, joined to that of
irregularity." At other times one hears of "ruggedness," "intricacy,"
"rich variety," and "destroyed symmetry"; qualities of the "broken,"
"abrupt," "agitated," "dishevelled," "shaggy," "ruffled," "wild,"
"confused," "angular," "capricious"—and strangely, both the "playful" and the "ruined." Its characteristic effect, according to Price,
is not the astonishment and tension of the sublime, not the pleasing

languor of beauty, but active curiosity, a drawing in of the *eye* by partial and uncertain concealments; "it is the coquetry of nature." Price's examples are sometimes helpful, sometimes startling: a Gothic cathedral with its capricious and shaggy angles is more picturesque than a Grecian temple, unless the temple has crumbled into ruined vistas overgrown with wild, irregular vegetation; so is an old mill with its intricate wheels, a tumbling waterfall, waves dashing against rocks, huge trees shattered by lightning, wandering gypsies or beggars, the rough penciling of Salvator Rosa, the inside of a barn, a winding lane enclosed by wind-torn banks of foliage, many descriptions in Milton, Virgil, Ariosto—the capriccio in a Scarlatti sonata, and tragicomedy!

The common denominator, so far as there is one, seems to be landscape and ruin. The picturesque is a category for appreciating both the actualities of a green world and the presentness of tradition, of objects complicated, in Burke's phrase, by "the silent touches of time."

Price was a wealthy baronet, the lifelong friend of Sheridan and Charles Fox, Oxford-trained, who, after a Grand Tour of the continent, returned to his first love of landscaping his inherited estate, Foxley. Parts of his *Essay on the Picturesque* (1794) are thick with technicalities of gardening, expounded still further in a *Letter to Humphrey Repton, Esq.* (1795) and, the following year, in three essays "On Artificial Water," "On Decorations Near the House," and "On Architecture and Buildings." In 1801 he published a *Dialogue on the Distinct Characters of the Picturesque and Beautiful.* Price soon found himself swept into a paper war with more traditional gardeners like Repton and with other aesthetic theorists, including his neighbor and one-time supporter Richard Payne Knight. Knight had published *The Landscape, a Didactic Poem* (1794), embodying reformist ideas congenial to Price, but they fell to internecine, if good-natured squabbling, especially after Knight's *Analytical Enquiry into the Principles of Taste* (1805), which attacked Burke and proposed a new, less empirical approach to beauty. Price answered in his 1810 enlarged edition of the *Essay.* But the War of the Picturesque, as Price knew, was only an episode; his cherished ambition was not just to reform gardening, but "to point out the best method of forming our taste and judgment in regard to the effect of all visible objects, universally." The method, as his preface explains, was learning to see with a painter's eye. Sir Walter Scott is reported to have remarked that Price "converted the age to his views."

The word *picturesque* first entered the language, apparently, in Steele's *The Tender Husband* (1705), where it meant no more than "picture-like," and despite Price's late attempt to enlarge its applicability, it has never lost a silent reference to painting and drawing, especially landscape-painting, and more especially still, in the eighteenth century, the landscapes of Poussin, Claude, and Rosa. Though the word itself was questionable usage until the 1780's and 1790's—Johnson omitted it from his *Dictionary*—its acceptance was made almost inevitable by coalescing facts of eighteenth-century taste. In fact, to explicate the concept by its evolution would lead one deep into the history of almost the whole of early and mid-eighteenth-century culture, including most of the writers represented in this volume. One would observe the growing sense of interrelation among the arts, as in Shaftesbury, and the *ut pictura poesis* tradition; the picture-making imagination and *camera obscura* aesthetic of Addison, as of empiricism generally; the descriptive poetry of Thomson, Dyer, Collins, and Gray, and the discovered precedent of Milton; the new public interest in painting and prints and the gradual evolution of a native school; new fashions in irregularity such as the Gothic and Chinese; and most important perhaps, the English school of gardening which, in general, set itself against geometrically trim ornamentality and favored more "naturalness"—gardens artfully suggestive of the irregular variety of the countryside, and indeed, by open vistas, continuous with it. Walking trips to observe the picturesque became fashionable about mid-century, as they still are, sometimes with a Claude-glass—a convex reflector which "framed" live scenes, with a slight mellowness of tinting like that in a painting by Claude.

If one man more than another established and popularized the late-century meaning of the picturesque, it was William Gilpin (1724–1804), rector and schoolmaster, who spent his school vacation on various walking trips throughout England—to the southern coast, Wales, the Wye Valley, and the Lakes region. His widely read volumes of "observations," starting in 1782, described the actualities of wild and rural scenery in England with a picture-consciousness and an accuracy almost botanical; they included aquatint sketches drawn after the life, and reflections on seeing with a painter's eye. Gilpin established by practice the aesthetic concept which Price struggled to define, and had the same general aims of cultivating a new order of sharply precise, visualizing taste for particulars of the natural world. From Gilpin it is a short and easy step to early Wordsworth, who published his own *Guide to the*

English Lakes, or indeed, later in the century, to Thoreau, with whom Gilpin was a favorite. Almost every Romantic poet owed something, however indirect, to picturesque stylization of the natural world. As it rested on no single emotion, but was a practique for seeing, the picturesque lent itself, as indeed it still does, to a vast variety of temperaments. Many tourists still sketch or photograph the picturesque, unaware of why they have singled out some "qualities of objects" instead of others.

* * * *

MAURICE MORGANN (1726–1802)

FROM

An Essay on the Dramatic Character of Sir John Falstaff [1777]

The following sheets were written in consequence of a friendly conversation, turning by some chance upon the character of Falstaff, wherein the writer, maintaining contrary to the general opinion, that this character was not intended to be shown as a coward, he was challenged to deliver and support that opinion from the press, with an engagement—now he fears forgotten, for it was three years ago—that he should be answered through same channel. Thus stimulated, these papers were almost wholly written in a very short time. . . . The impulse of the occasion, however, being passed, the papers were thrown by and almost forgotten. But having been looked into of late by some friends, who observing that the writer had not enlarged so far for the sake of Falstaff alone, but that the argument was made subservient to critical amusement, persuaded him to revise and convey it to the press. . . . The vindication of Falstaff's courage is truly no otherwise the object than some old fantastic oak or grotesque rock may be the object of a morning's ride; yet, being proposed as such, may serve to limit the distance and shape the course. The real object is exercise, and the delight which a rich, beautiful, picturesque, and perhaps unknown country may excite from every side. Such an exercise may admit of some little excursion, keeping however the road in view, but seems to exclude every appearance of labor and of toil. Under the impressions of such feelings, the writer has endeavored to preserve to his text a certain lightness of air and cheerfulness of tone, but is sensible, however, that the manner of discussion does not everywhere, particularly near the commencement, sufficiently correspond with his design. . . . The whole is a mere experiment, and the writer considers it as such. It may have the advantages, but it is likewise attended with all the difficulties and dangers of novelty. . . .

I am to avow then that I do not clearly discern that Sir John Falstaff deserves to bear the character so generally given him of an absolute coward, or, in other words, that I do not conceive Shakespeare ever meant to make cowardice an essential part of his constitution. . . .

What there is to the contrary of this, it is my business to discover. Much, I think, will presently appear, but it lies so dispersed, is so latent and so purposely obscured, that the reader must have some patience whilst I collect it into one body and make it the object of a steady and regular contemplation.

But what have we to do, may my readers exclaim, with principles *so latent, so obscured?* In dramatic composition the *impression* is the *fact,* and the writer who, meaning to impress one thing, has impressed another, is unworthy of observation.

It is a very unpleasant thing to have, in the first setting out, so many and so strong prejudices to contend with. All that one can do in such case is to pray the reader to have a little patience in the commencement, and to reserve his censure, if it must pass, for the conclusion. Under his gracious allowance, therefore, I presume to declare it as my opinion that cowardice is not the *impression* which the *whole* character of Falstaff is calculated to make on the minds of an unprejudiced audience, though there be, I confess, a great deal of something in the *composition* likely enough to puzzle, and consequently to mislead the understanding. (The reader will perceive that I distinguish between *mental impressions* and the *understanding.*[1] I wish to avoid everything that looks like subtlety and refinement, but this is a distinction which we all comprehend.) There are none of us unconscious of certain feelings or sensations of mind which do not seem to have passed through the understanding—the effects, I suppose, of some secret influences from without, acting upon a certain mental sense, and producing feelings and passions in just correspondence to the force and variety of those influences, on the one hand, and to the quickness of our sensibility, on the other. Be the cause, however, what it may, the fact is undoubtedly so; which is all I am concerned in. And it is

---

[1] "feelings" and "rational consciousness."

equally a fact, which every man's experience may avouch, that the understanding and those feelings are frequently at variance. The latter often arise from the most minute circumstances, and frequently from such as the understanding cannot estimate or even recognize; whereas the understanding delights in abstraction and in general propositions; which, however true considered as such, are very seldom, I had like to have said *never*, perfectly applicable to any particular case. And hence, among other causes, it is, that we often condemn or applaud characters and actions on the credit of some logical process, while our hearts revolt and would fain lead us to a very different conclusion.

The understanding seems for the most part to take cognizance of *actions* only, and from these to infer motives and character; but the sense we have been speaking of proceeds in a contrary course, and determines of actions from certain *first principles of character* which seem wholly out of the reach of the understanding. We cannot indeed do otherwise than admit that there must be distinct principles of character in every distinct individual: the manifest variety even in the minds of infants will oblige us to this. But what *are* these first principles of character? Not the objects, I am persuaded, of the understanding; and yet we take as strong impressions of them as if we could compare and assort them in a syllogism. We often love or hate at first sight; and indeed, in general, dislike or approve by some secret reference to these *principles*; and we judge even of conduct, not from any idea of abstract good or evil in the nature of actions, but by referring those actions to a supposed original character in the man himself. I do not mean that we *talk* thus; we could not indeed, if we would, explain ourselves in detail on this head; we can neither account for impressions and passions nor communicate them to others by words. Tones and looks will sometimes convey the *passion* strangely, but the *impression* is incommunicable. The same causes may produce it indeed at the same time in many, but it is the separate possession of each, and not in its nature transferable: it is an imperfect sort of instinct, and proportionably dumb. We might indeed, if we chose it, candidly confess to one another that we are greatly swayed by these feelings, and are by no means so *rational* in all points as we could wish; but this would be a betraying of the interests of that high faculty, the understanding, which we so value ourselves upon and which we more peculiarly call our own. This, we think, must not be; and so we huddle up the matter, concealing it as much as possible, both from ourselves and others. In books indeed, wherein character, motive, and action are all alike subjected to the understanding, it is generally a very clear case, and we make decisions compounded of them all. And thus we are willing to approve of Candide, though he kills my Lord the Inquisitor and runs through the body the Baron of Thunder-ten-tronchk, the son of his patron, and the brother of his beloved Cunégonde.[2] But in real life, I believe, my Lords the Judges would be apt to inform the Gentlemen of the Jury, that my Lord the Inquisitor was *ill killed*, as Candide did not proceed on the urgency of the moment, but on the speculation only of future evil. And indeed this clear perception, in novels and plays, of the union of character and action not seen in nature, is the principal defect of such compositions, and what renders them but ill pictures of human life, and wretched guides of conduct.

But if there was *one man* in the world who could make a more perfect draught of real nature, and steal such impressions on his audience, without their special notice, as should keep their hold in spite of any error of their understanding, and should thereupon venture to introduce an apparent incongruity of character and action, for ends which I shall presently endeavour to explain— such an imitation would be worth our nicest curiosity and attention. . . .

The reader will not need to be told that this inquiry will resolve itself of course into a critique on the genius, the arts, and the conduct of Shakespeare. For what is "Falstaff," what "Lear," what "Hamlet" or "Othello" but different modifications of Shakespeare's thought? It is true that this inquiry is narrowed almost to a single point. But general criticism is as uninstructive as it is easy: Shakespeare deserves to be considered in detail—a task hitherto unattempted. . . .

The reader must be sensible of something in the composition of Shakespeare's characters which renders them essentially different from those drawn by other writers. The characters of every drama must indeed be grouped, but in the groups of other poets, the parts which are not seen do not in fact exist. But there is a certain roundness and integrity in the forms of Shakespeare which give them an independence as well as a relation, insomuch that we often meet with passages which, though perfectly felt, cannot be sufficiently explained in words without unfolding the whole character of the speaker. And this I may be obliged to do in respect to that of Lancaster, in order to account for some words spoken by him in censure of Falstaff. Something which may be thought too heavy

---

[2] See Voltaire, *Candide*, chs. 9 and 15.

for the text I shall add here,[3] as a conjecture concerning the composition of Shakespeare's characters: not that they were the effect, I believe, so much of a minute and laborious attention, as of a certain comprehensive energy of mind, involving within itself all the effects of system and of labor.

Bodies of all kinds, whether of metals, plants, or animals, are supposed to possess certain first principles of *being*, and to have an existence independent of the accidents which form their magnitude or growth. Those accidents are supposed to be drawn in from the surrounding elements, but not indiscriminately: each plant and each animal imbibes those things only which are proper to its own distinct nature, and which have besides such a secret relation to each other as to be capable of forming a perfect union and coalescence. But so variously are the surrounding elements mingled and disposed that each particular body, even of those under the same species, has yet some *peculiar* of its own. Shakespeare appears to have considered the being and growth of the human mind as analogous to this system. There are certain qualities and capacities which he seems to have considered as first principles, the chief of which are certain energies of courage and activity, according to their degrees; together with different degrees and sorts of sensibilities, and a capacity, varying likewise in the *degree*, of discernment and intelligence. The rest of the composition is drawn in from an atmosphere of surrounding things; that is, from the various influences of the different laws, religions, and governments in the world; and from those of the different ranks and inequalities in society; and from the different professions of men, encouraging or repressing passions of particular sorts, and inducing different modes of thinking and habits of life. And he seems to have known intuitively what those influences in particular were which this or that original constitution would most freely imbibe, and which would most easily associate and coalesce. But all these things being, in different situations, very differently disposed, and those differences exactly discerned by him, he found no difficulty in marking every individual, even among characters of the same sort, with something peculiar and distinct. Climate and complexion demand their influence: "Be thus when thou art dead, and I will kill thee, and love thee after," [4] is a sentiment characteristic of, and fit only to be uttered by, a Moor.

But it was not enough for Shakespeare to have formed his char-

---

[3] In a footnote.
[4] *Othello*, V, ii, 18.

acters with the most perfect truth and coherence; it was further
necessary that he should possess a wonderful facility of compressing,
as it were, his own spirit into these images, and of giving alternate
animation to the forms. This was not to be done *from without*; he
must have *felt* every varied situation, and have spoken through the
organ he had formed. Such an intuitive comprehension of things
and such a facility must unite to produce a Shakespeare. The reader
will not now be surprised if I affirm that those characters in
Shakespeare, which are seen only in part, are yet capable of being
unfolded and understood in the whole; every part being in fact
relative and inferring all the rest. It is true that the point of action
or sentiment, which we are most concerned in, is always held out
for our special notice. But who does not perceive that there is a
peculiarity about it which conveys a relish of the whole? And very
frequently, when no particular point presses, he boldly makes a
character act and speak from those parts of the composition which
are *inferred* only, and not distinctly shown. This produces a wonderful effect; it seems to carry us beyond the poet to nature itself,
and gives an integrity and truth to facts and character, which they
could not otherwise obtain. And this is in reality that art in
Shakespeare which, being withdrawn from our notice, we more
emphatically call *nature*. A felt propriety and truth from causes unseen, I take to be the highest point of poetic composition. If the
characters of Shakespeare are thus *whole*, and as it were original,
while those of almost all other writers are mere imitation, it may
be fit to consider them rather as historic than dramatic beings; and,
when occasion requires, to account for their conduct from the
whole of character, from general principles, from latent motives,
and from policies not avowed. . . .

Shakespeare is a name so interesting that it is excusable to stop
a moment; nay, it would be indecent to pass him without the
tribute of some admiration. He differs essentially from all other
writers. Him we may profess rather to feel than to understand; and
it is safer to say, on many occasions, that we are possessed by him
than that we possess him. And no wonder: he scatters the seeds of
things, the principles of character and action, with so cunning a
hand yet with so careless an air, and, master of our feelings, submits himself so little to our judgment, that everything seems superior. We discern not his course, we see no connection of cause
and effect, we are rapt in ignorant admiration, and claim no kindred with his abilities. All the incidents, all the parts, look like
chance, whilst we feel and are sensible that the whole is design.

His characters not only act and speak in strict conformity to nature, but in strict relation to us; just so much is shown as is requisite, just so much is impressed; he commands every passage to our heads and to our hearts, and molds us as he pleases, and that with so much ease that he never betrays his own exertions. We see these characters act from the mingled motives of passion, reason, interest, habit, and complexion, in all their proportions, when they are supposed to know it not themselves; and we are made to acknowledge that their actions and sentiments are, from those motives, the necessary result. He at once blends and distinguishes everything: everything is complicated, everything is plain. I restrain the further expressions of my admiration lest they should not seem applicable to man; but it is really astonishing that a mere human being, a part of humanity only, should so perfectly comprehend the whole; and that he should possess such exquisite art, that, whilst every woman and every child shall feel the whole effect, his learned editors and commentators should yet so very frequently mistake or seem ignorant of the cause. A scepter or a straw are in his hands of equal efficacy; he needs no selection; he converts everything into excellence; nothing is too great, nothing is too base. Is a character efficient like Richard, it is everything we can wish; is it otherwise, like Hamlet, it is productive of equal admiration: action produces one mode of excellence and inaction another. The chronicle, the novel, or the ballad, the king or the beggar, the hero, the madman, the sot or the fool—it is all one; nothing is worse, nothing is better. The same genius pervades and is equally admirable in all. Or, is a character to be shown in progressive change, and the events of years comprised within the hour—with what a magic hand does he prepare and scatter his spells! The understanding must, in the first place, be subdued; and lo! how the rooted prejudices of the child spring up to confound the man! The Weird Sisters rise, and order is extinguished. The laws of nature give way, and leave nothing in our minds but wildness and horror. No pause is allowed us for reflection. Horrid sentiment, furious guilt and compunction, airdrawn daggers, murders, ghosts, and enchantment shake and *possess us wholly.* In the meantime, the *process* is completed. Macbeth changes under our eye—*the milk of human kindness is converted to gall;*[5] *he has supped full of horrors,*[6] and his *May of life is fallen into the sear, the yellow leaf* [7]—whilst we, the fools of amazement,

---

[5] I, v, 18, 49.
[6] V, v, 13.
[7] V, 14, 22–23. *May* is Dr. Johnson's emendation for *way*.

are insensible to the shifting of place and the lapse of time, and till the curtain drops, never once wake to the truth of things or recognize the laws of existence.—On such an occasion, a fellow like Rymer, waking from his trance, shall lift up his constable's staff and charge this great magician, this daring *practicer of arts inhibited,* in the name of Aristotle, to surrender; whilst Aristotle himself, disowning his wretched officer, would fall prostrate at his[8] feet and acknowledge his supremacy. "O supreme of dramatic excellence!" might he[9] say, "not to me be imputed the insolence of fools. The bards of Greece were confined within the narrow circle of the chorus, and hence they found themselves constrained to practice, for the most part, the precision, and copy the details of, nature. I followed them, and knew not that a larger circle might be drawn, and the drama extended to the whole reach of human genius. Convinced, I see that a more compendious *nature* may be obtained, a nature of *effects* only, to which neither the relations of place [n]or continuity of time are always essential. Nature, condescending to the faculties and apprehensions of man, has drawn through human life a regular chain of visible causes and effects; but poetry delights in surprise, conceals her steps, seizes at once upon the heart, and obtains the sublime of things without betraying the rounds of her ascent. True poesy is *magic,* not *nature*—an effect from causes hidden or unknown. To the magician, I prescribed no laws; his law and his power are one; his power is his law. Him, who neither imitates nor is within the reach of imitation, no precedent can or ought to bind, no limits to contain. If his end is obtained, who shall question his course? Means, whether apparent or hidden, are justified in poesy by success; but then most perfect and most admirable when most concealed. . . ."

I have now gone through the examination of all the persons of the drama from whose mouths anything can be drawn relative to the courage of Falstaff, excepting the Prince and Poins, whose evidence I have begged leave to reserve, and excepting a very severe censure passed on him by Lord John of Lancaster, which I shall presently consider. But I must first observe that, setting aside the jests of the Prince and Poins and this censure of Lancaster, there is not one expression uttered by any character in the drama that can be construed into any impeachment of Falstaff's courage—an observation made before as respecting some of the witnesses; it is now

---

[8] Shakespeare's, not Rymer's.
[9] Aristotle.

extended to all. And though this silence be a negative proof only, it cannot, in my opinion, under the circumstances of the case, and whilst uncontradicted by facts, be too much relied on. If Falstaff had been intended for the character of a *miles gloriosus*, his behavior ought, and therefore would have been commented upon by others Shakespeare seldom trusts to the apprehensions of his audience; his characters interpret for one another continually, and when we least suspect such artful and secret management. The conduct of Shakespeare in this respect is admirable, and I could point out a thousand passages which might put to shame the advocates of a formal chorus, and prove that there is as little of necessity as grace in so mechanic a contrivance.[1] But I confine my censure of the chorus to its supposed use of comment and interpretation only. . . .

The censure commonly passed on Shakespeare's puns is, I think, not well founded. I remember but very few which are undoubtedly his that may not be justified, and if so, a greater instance cannot be given of the art which he so peculiarly possessed of converting base things into excellence.

> *For if the Jew do cut but deep enough,*
> *I'll pay the forfeiture* with all my heart.[2]

A play upon words is the most that can be expected from one who affects gaiety under the pressure of severe misfortunes, but so imperfect, so broken a gleam can only serve more plainly to disclose the gloom and darkness of the mind; it is an effort of fortitude which, failing in its operation, becomes the truest, because the most unaffected pathos; and a skillful actor, well managing his tone and action, might with this miserable pun steep a whole audience suddenly in tears. . . .

Though I have considered Falstaff's character as relative only to one single quality, yet so much has been said that it cannot escape the reader's notice that he is a character made up by Shakespeare wholly of incongruities—a man at once young and old, enterprising and fat, a dupe and a wit, harmless and wicked, weak in principle and resolute by constitution, cowardly in appearance and brave in reality, a knave without malice, a liar without deceit, and a knight, a gentleman, and a soldier, without either dignity, decency, or honor. This is a character which, though it may be decompounded, could not, I believe, have been formed, nor the ingredients

---

[1] "Enobarbus in *Antony and Cleopatra* is in effect the chorus of the play, as Menenius Agrippa is of *Coriolanus*." (Morgann's note.)

[2] *The Merchant of Venice*, IV, i, 280–81.

of it duly mingled upon any receipt[3] whatever. It required the hand of Shakespeare himself to give to every particular part a relish of the whole, and of the whole to every particular part. . . .

But if vice, divested of disgust and terror, is thus in its own nature ridiculous, we ought not to be surprised if the very same vices which spread horror and desolation through the tragic scene should yet furnish the comic with its highest laughter and delight, and that tears and mirth and even humor and wit itself should grow from the same root of incongruity. For what is humor in the humorist but incongruity, whether of sentiment, conduct, or manners? what in the man of humor, but a quick discernment and keen sensibility of these incongruities? And what is wit itself, without presuming however to give a complete definition where so many have failed, but a talent for the most part of marking, with force and vivacity, unexpected points of likeness in things supposed incongruous, and points of incongruity in things supposed alike? And hence it is that wit and humor, though always distinguished, are so often coupled together, it being very possible, I suppose, to be a man of humor without wit, but I think not a man of wit without humor.

* * * *

ARCHIBALD ALISON [1757–1839]
FROM
Essays on the Nature and Principles of Taste [1790]

Essay I.
Of the Nature of the Emotions
of Sublimity and Beauty

FROM CHAPTER 1, SECTION 1
*Of the Effect Produced Upon the Imagination
by Objects of Sublimity and Beauty*

The emotions of sublimity and beauty are uniformly ascribed, both in popular and in philosophical language, to the imagination. The fine arts are considered as the arts which are addressed to the imagi-

---

[3] recipe, formula.

nation, and the pleasures they afford are described, by way of distinction, as the "pleasures of the imagination." The nature of any person's taste is, in common life, generally determined by the nature or character of his imagination, and the expression of any deficiency in this power of mind is considered as synonymous with the expression of a similar deficiency in point of taste.

Although, however, this connection is so generally acknowledged, it is not perhaps as generally understood in what it consists, or what is the nature of that effect which is produced upon the imagination by objects of sublimity and beauty. I shall endeavor, therefore, in the first place, to state what seems to me the nature of this *effect*, or in what that exercise of imagination consists which is so generally supposed to take place when these emotions are felt.

When any object, either of sublimity or beauty, is presented to the mind, I believe every man is conscious of a train of thought being immediately awakened in his imagination, analogous to the character or expression of the original object. The simple perception of the object, we frequently find, is insufficient to excite these emotions unless it is accompanied with this operation of mind—unless, according to common expression, our imagination is seized, and our fancy busied in the pursuit of all those trains of thought which are allied to this character or expression.

Thus, when we feel either the beauty or sublimity of natural scenery—the gay lustre of a morning in spring, or the mild radiance of a summer evening, the savage majesty of a wintry storm, or the wild magnificence of a tempestuous ocean—we are conscious of a variety of images in our minds very different from those which the objects themselves can present to the eye. Trains of pleasing or solemn thought arise spontaneously within our minds: our hearts swell with emotions of which the objects before us seem to afford no adequate cause; and we are never so much satiated with delight as when, in recalling our attention, we are unable to trace either the progress or the connection of those thoughts which have passed with so much rapidity through our imagination.

The effect of the different arts of taste is similar. The landscapes of Claude Lorrain,[1] the music of Handel, the poetry of Milton excite feeble emotions in our minds when our attention is confined to the qualities they present to our senses, or when it is to such qualities of their composition that we turn our regard. It is then

[1] French painter (1600–82) whose poetic landscapes, diffused with mild glimmering light and a mood of immense space, often illustrated "beauty" to eighteenth-century taste as distinct from the "sublimity" of Salvator Rosa.

only we feel the sublimity or beauty of their productions when our imaginations are kindled by their power, when we lose ourselves amid the number of images that pass before our minds, and when we waken at last from this play of fancy as from the charm of a romantic dream.

FROM CHAPTER 1, SECTION 3

There are many other instances equally familiar which are sufficient to show that whatever increases this exercise or employment of imagination, increases also the emotion of beauty or sublimity.

This is very obviously the effect of all associations. There is no man who has not some interesting associations with particular scenes, or airs, or books, and who does not feel their beauty or sublimity enhanced to him by such connections. The view of the house where one was born, of the school where one was educated, and where the gay years of infancy were passed, is indifferent to no man. They recall so many images of past happiness and past affections, they are connected with so many strong or interesting emotions, and lead altogether to so long a train of feelings and recollections, that there is hardly any scene which one ever beholds with so much rapture. There are songs also that we have heard in our infancy, which, when brought to our remembrance in after years, raise emotions for which we cannot well account, and which, though perhaps very indifferent in themselves, still continue from this association, and from the variety of conceptions which they kindle in our minds, to be our favorites through life. The scenes which have been distinguished by the residence of any person whose memory we admire produce a similar effect. *Movemur enim, nescio quo pacto, locis ipsis, in quibus eorum, quos diligimus, aut admiramur adsunt vestigia.*[2] The scenes themselves may be little beautiful, but the delight with which we recollect the traces of their lives blends itself insensibly with the emotions which the scenery excites, and the admiration which these recollections afford seems to give a kind of sanctity to the place where they dwelt, and converts everything into beauty which appears to have been connected with them. . . .

The delight which most men of education receive from the consideration of antiquity, and the beauty that they discover in every object which is connected with ancient times, is in a great measure to be ascribed to the same cause [of associative imagination]. The

---

[2] Cicero, *De Legibus*, II, iv: "For we are moved, I know not in what way, by those places in which traces remain of those we love or admire."

antiquarian in his cabinet, surrounded by the relics of former ages, seems to himself to be removed to periods that are long since past, and indulges in the imagination of living in a world which, by a very natural kind of prejudice, we are always willing to believe was both wiser and better than the present. All that is venerable or laudable in the history of those times present themselves to his memory. The gallantry, the heroism, the patriotism of antiquity rise again before his view, softened by the obscurity in which they are involved, and rendered more seducing to the imagination by that obscurity itself, which, while it mingles a sentiment of regret amid his pursuits, serves at the same time to stimulate his fancy to fill up, by its own creation, those long intervals of time of which history has preserved no record. The relics he contemplates seem to approach him still nearer to the ages of his regard. The dress, the furniture, the arms of the times are so many assistances to his imagination, in guiding or directing its exercise, and offering him a thousand sources of imagery, provide him with an almost inexhaustible field in which his memory and his fancy may expatiate. . . . Even the peasant, whose knowledge of former years extends but to a few generations, has yet in his village some monument of the deeds or virtues of his forefathers, and cherishes with a fond veneration the memorial of those good old times, to which his imagination returns with delight and of which he loves to recount the simple tales that tradition has brought him.

And what is it that constitutes that emotion of sublime delight which every man of common sensibility feels upon the first prospect of Rome? It is not the scene of destruction which is before him. It is not the Tiber, diminished in his imagination to a paltry stream and stagnating amid the ruins of that magnificence which it once adorned. It is not the triumph of superstition over the wreck of human greatness, and its monuments erected upon the very spot where the first honors of humanity have been gained. It is ancient Rome which fills his imagination. It is the country of Caesar, and Cicero, and Virgil, which is before him. It is the mistress of the world which he sees, and who seems to him to rise again from her tomb to give laws to the universe. All that the labors of his youth or the studies of his maturer age have acquired, with regard to the history of this great people, open at once before his imagination, and present him with a field of high and solemn imagery which can never be exhausted. Take from him these associations, conceal from him that it is Rome that he sees, and how different would be his emotion!

The effect which is thus produced by associations, in increasing the emotions of sublimity or beauty, is produced also, either in nature or in description, by what are generally termed "picturesque objects." Instances of such objects are familiar to every one's observation: an old tower in the middle of a deep wood, a bridge flung across a chasm between rocks, a cottage on a precipice, are common examples. If I am not mistaken, the effect which such objects have on every one's mind is to suggest an additional train of conceptions beside what the scene or description itself would have suggested, for it is very obvious that not objects are remarked as picturesque which do no strike the imagination by themselves. They are, in general, such circumstances as coincide but are not necessarily connected with the character of the scene or description, and which, at first affecting the mind with an emotion of surprise, produce afterwards an increased or additional train of imagery. . . .

The influence of such additional trains of imagery in increasing the emotions of sublimity or beauty might be illustrated from many other circumstances equally familiar. I am induced to mention only the following, because it is one of the most striking that I know, and because it is probable that most men of education have at least in some degree been conscious of it—the influence, I mean, of an acquaintance with poetry in our earlier years in increasing our sensibility to the beauties of Nature. . . . In most men at least, the first appearance of poetical imagination is at school, when their imaginations begin to be warmed by the descriptions of ancient poetry and when they have acquired a new sense, as it were, with which they behold the face of Nature.

How different from this period become the sentiments with which the scenery of Nature is contemplated by those who have any imagination! The beautiful forms of ancient mythology, with which the fancy of poets peopled every element, are now ready to appear to their minds upon the prospect of every scene. The descriptions of ancient authors, so long admired and so deserving of admiration, occur to them at every moment, and with them all those enthusiastic ideas of ancient genius and glory, which the study of so many years of youth so naturally leads them to form. Or, if the study of modern poetry has succeeded to that of the ancient, a thousand other beautiful associations are acquired, which, instead of destroying, serve easily to unite with the former and to afford a new source of delight. The awful forms of Gothic superstition, the wild and romantic imagery which the turbulence of the Middle Ages, the Crusades, and the institution of chivalry have spread over every country of Europe, arise to the imagination in every scene, accompanied with all those pleasing recollections of prowess and adventure and courteous manners which distinguished those memorable times. With such images in their minds, it is not common nature that appears to surround them. It is nature embellished. . . .

Nor is it only in providing so many sources of association that the influence of an acquaintance with poetry consists. It is yet still more powerful in giving *character*[3] to the different appearances of nature, in connecting them with various emotions and affections of our hearts, and in thus providing an almost inexhaustible source of solemn or cheerful meditation. . . .

Associations of this kind, when acquired in early life, are seldom altogether lost, and whatever inconveniences they may sometimes have with regard to the general character, or however much they may be ridiculed by those who do not experience them, they are yet productive to those who possess them of a perpetual and innocent delight.

FROM CHAPTER 2, SECTION 1
Analysis of This Exercise of Imagination

The illustrations in the preceding chapter seem to show that whenever the emotions of sublimity or beauty are felt, that exercise of imagination is produced which consists in the indulgence of a train of thought; that when this exercise is prevented, these emotions are unfelt or unperceived; and that whatever tends to increase this exercise of mind tends in the same proportion to increase these emotions. If these illustrations are just, it seems reasonable to conclude that the effect produced upon the mind by objects of sublimity and beauty consists in the production of this exercise of imagination.

Although, however, this conclusion seems to me both just and consonant to experience, yet it is in itself too general to be considered as a sufficient account of the nature of that operation of mind which takes place in the case of such emotions. There are many trains of ideas, of which we are conscious, which are unattended with any kind of pleasure. . . . The prospect of the house, for instance, where one has formerly lived excites very naturally a train of conceptions in the mind; yet it is by no means true that such an exercise of imagination is necessarily accompanied with

---

[3] "Some amiable or interesting quality of Mind." *Cf.* Shaftesbury's *Characteristics*.

pleasure, for these conceptions not only may be, but very often are of a kind extremely indifferent, and sometimes also simply painful. . . .

The greater part of such objects are simply indifferent or, at least, are regarded as indifferent in our common hours, either of occupation or amusement; the conceptions which they produce, by the laws of association, partake of the nature or character of the object which originally excited them, and the whole train passes through our mind without leaving any further emotion than perhaps that general emotion of pleasure which accompanies the exercise of our faculties. . . . The indifference with which such trains are either pursued or deserted is a sufficient evidence that the ideas of which they are composed are, in general, of a kind unfitted to produce any emotion, either of pleasure or pain.

In the case of those trains of thought, on the contrary, which are suggested by objects either of sublimity or beauty, I apprehend it will be found that they are in all cases composed of ideas capable of exciting some affection or emotion, and that not only the whole succession is accompanied with that peculiar emotion which we call the "emotion of beauty or sublimity," but that every individual idea of such a succession is in itself productive of some simple emotion or other. Thus the ideas suggested by the scenery of spring, are ideas productive of emotions of Cheerfulness, of Gladness, and of Tenderness. The images suggested by the prospect of ruins are images belonging to Pity, to Melancholy, and to Admiration. The ideas, in the same manner, awakened by the view of the ocean in a storm are ideas of Power, of Majesty, and of Terror. In every case where the emotions of taste are felt, I conceive it will be found that the train of thought which is excited is distinguished by some character of emotion, and that it is by this means distinguished from our common or ordinary successions of thought. To prevent a very tedious and unnecessary circumlocution, such ideas may perhaps, without any impropriety, be termed "ideas of emotion." . . .

In our ordinary trains of thought there seldom appears any general principle of connection among the ideas which compose them. Each idea indeed is related, by an established law of nature, to that which immediately preceded and that which immediately follows it, but in the whole series there is no predominant relation or bond of connection. . . . Of this irregularity I think every man will be convinced who chooses to attend to it.

In those trains, on the contrary, which are suggested by objects of sublimity or beauty, however slight the connection between individual thoughts may be, I believe it will be found that there is always some general principle of connection which pervades the whole and gives them some certain and definite character. . . . The sight of a torrent or of a storm . . . impresses us first with sentiments of awe, or solemnity, or terror, and then awakens in our minds a series of conceptions allied to this peculiar emotion. Whatever may be the character of the original emotion, the images which succeed seem all to have a relation to this character, and if we trace them back, we shall discover not only a connection between the individual thoughts of the train, but also a general relation among the whole and a conformity to that peculiar emotion which first excited them.

The train of thought, therefore, which takes place in the mind upon the prospect of objects of sublimity and beauty may be considered as consisting in a regular or consistent train of ideas of emotion, and as distinguished from our ordinary trains of thought: first, in respect of the nature of the ideas of which it is composed, by their being ideas productive of emotion: and secondly, in respect of their succession, by their being distinguished by some general principle of connection which subsists through the whole extent of the train.

FROM CHAPTER 2, SECTION 3

In the former section, I have endeavored to show that no objects are in themselves fitted to produce the emotions of sublimity or beauty which are not productive of some simple emotion. In this, I have attempted to show that no composition of objects or qualities is in fact productive of such emotions in which a unity of character is not preserved. The slight illustrations which I have now offered are probably sufficient to point out the truth of the general principle, but the application of it to the different arts of taste, and the explanation of the great rules of composition from this constitution of our nature, are objects far beyond the limits of these *Essays*. I must satisfy myself, therefore, with observing in general that, in the fine arts, that composition is most excellent in which the different parts most fully unite in the production of one unmingled emotion, and that taste the most perfect where the perception of this relation of objects, in point of expression, is most delicate and precise.

FROM CONCLUSION

The pleasure, therefore, which accompanies the emotions of taste may be considered not as a simple but as a complex pleasure, and as arising, not from any separate and peculiar sense, but from the union of the pleasure of *simple emotion* with that which is annexed by the constitution of the human mind to the exercise of *imagination.* . . .

If it were permitted me therefore, I should wish to appropriate the term *delight* to signify the peculiar pleasure which attends the emotions of *taste,* or which is felt *when the imagination is employed in the prosecution of a regular train of ideas of emotion.*

*

Essay II
Of the Sublimity and Beauty of the Material World

FROM CHAPTER 6, SECTION 6
*Conclusion of This Essay. Of the Final Cause
of This Constitution of Our Nature*

The illustrations that have been offered in the course of this *Essay* upon the origin of the *sublimity* and *beauty* of some of the principal qualities of *matter* seem to afford sufficient evidence for the following conclusions.

I. That each of these qualities is, either from nature, from experience, or from accident, the sign of some quality capable of producing emotion, or the exercise of some moral affection. And,

II. That when these associations are dissolved, or in other words when the material qualities cease to be significant of the associated qualities, they cease also to produce the emotions either of sublimity or beauty.

If these conclusions are admitted, it appears necessarily to follow that the beauty and sublimity of such objects is to be ascribed not to the material qualities themselves, but to the qualities they signify, and, of consequence, that the qualities of matter are not to be considered as sublime or beautiful in themselves, but as being the *signs* or *expressions* of such qualities as, by the constitution of our nature, are fitted to produce pleasing or interesting emotion.

The opinion I have now stated coincides in a great degree with a doctrine that appears very early to have distinguished the Platonic school; which is to be traced perhaps (amid their dark and figurative language) in all the philosophical systems of the East, and which has been maintained in this country by several writers of eminence, by Lord Shaftesbury, Dr. Hutcheson, Dr. Akenside,[4] and Dr. Spence,[5] but which has nowhere so firmly and so philosophically been maintained as by Dr. Reid in his invaluable work *On the Intellectual Powers of Man.* The doctrine to which I allude is that matter is not beautiful in itself but derives its beauty from the expression of *mind.*

As this doctrine, however, when stated in general terms, has somewhat the air of paradox, I shall beg leave, in a few words, to explain in what sense I understand and adopt it, by enumerating what appear to me the principal classes of this expression, or the principal means by which the qualities of matter become significant to us of those qualities of mind which are destined to affect us with pleasing or interesting emotion.

The qualities of *mind* which are capable of producing emotion are either its *active* or its *passive* qualities; either its *powers* and capacities, as beneficence, wisdom, fortitude, invention, fancy, etc., or its feelings and *affections,* as love, joy, hope, gratitude, purity, fidelity, innocence, etc. In the observation or belief of these qualities of mind, we are formed, by the original and moral constitution of our nature, to experience various and powerful emotions.

As it is only, however, through the medium of matter that, in the present condition of our being, the qualities of mind are known to us, the qualities of matter become necessarily expressive to us of all the qualities of mind they signify. They may be the signs, therefore, or expressions of these mental qualities in the following ways.

I. As the immediate signs of the *powers* or capacities of mind. It is thus that all the works of human art or design are directly significant to us of the wisdom, the invention, the taste, or the benevolence of the artist, and the works of Nature of the power, the wisdom, and the beneficence of the Divine Artist.

II. As the signs of all those *affections* or dispositions of mind which we love or with which we are formed to sympathize. It

---

[4] Mark Akenside (1721–70), physician and poet, whose *Pleasures of the Imagination* (1744), a didactic poem in aesthetics, mingled ideas from Addison, Shaftesbury, and Hutcheson. On "mind" *cf.* I, 481 ff. in the poem.

[5] See p. 498, n. 4.

is thus that the notes and motions of animals are expressive to us of their happiness and joy; that the tones of the human voice are significant of the various emotions by which it is animated; and that all the affections which we either love or admire in the human mind are directly signified to us by the various appearances of the countenance and form.

These may be called the *direct* expressions of mind, and the material qualities which signify such powers or affections produce in us immediately the peculiar emotions which, by the laws of our nature, the mental qualities are fitted to produce. But besides these, there are other means by which the qualities of matter may be significant to us of the qualities of mind *indirectly* or by means of less universal and less permanent relations.

1. From experience, when peculiar forms or appearances of matter are considered as the *means* or *instruments* by which those feelings or affections of mind are produced with which we sympathize or in which we are interested. It is thus that the productions of art are in so many various ways significant to us of the conveniences, the pleasures, or the happiness they bestow upon human life, and, as the signs of happiness, affect us with the emotion this happiness itself is destined to produce. It is thus also that the scenes of Nature acquire such an accession of beauty when we consider them as fitted, with such exquisite wisdom, for the habitation of so many classes of sentient being, and when they become thus expressive to us of all the varied happiness they produce, and contain, and conceal.

2. From analogy or resemblance—from that resemblance which has everywhere been felt between the qualities of matter and of mind, and by which the former becomes so powerfully expressive to us of the latter. It is thus that the colors, the sounds, the forms, and above all, perhaps, the motions of inanimate objects are so universally felt as resembling peculiar qualities or affections of mind, and when thus felt, are so productive of the analogous emotion; that the personification of matter is so strongly marked in every period of the history of human thought; and that the poet, while he gives life and animation to everything around him, is not displaying his own invention, but only obeying one of the most powerful laws which regulate the imagination of man.

3. From association (in the proper sense of that term[6]), when by

---

[6] Alison is disavowing philosophies of mind as totally built up by association (the Hobbes-Hume-Hartley tradition). *Cf.* Whiter's similar distinctions, p. 587.

means of education, of fortune, or of accident, material objects are connected with pleasing or interesting qualities of mind, and from this connection become forever afterwards expressive of them. It is thus that colors, forms, etc., derive their temporary beauty from fashion: that the objects which have been devoted to religion, to patriotism, or to honor, affect us with all the emotions of the qualities of which they become significant; that the beauty of natural scenery is so often exalted by the record of the events it has witnessed: and that in every country, the scenes which have the deepest effect upon the admiration of the people are those which have become sacred by the memory of ancient virtue or ancient glory.

4. From *individual* association, when certain qualities or appearances of matter are connected with our own private affections or remembrances, and when they give to these material qualities or appearances a character of interest which is solely the result of our own memory and affections.

Of the reality of these expressions I believe no person can doubt; and whoever will attend to the power and extent of their influence will, I think, soon be persuaded that they are sufficient to account for all beauty or sublimity we discover in the qualities of matter.

The conclusion, therefore, in which I wish to rest is *that the beauty and sublimity which is felt in the various appearances of matter are finally to be ascribed to their expression of mind, or to their being, either directly or indirectly, the signs of those qualities of mind which are fitted, by the constitution of our nature, to affect us with pleasing or interesting emotion.* . . .

This dependence of the beauty of matter upon the qualities of which it is significant is (in a very obvious manner) the great source of the progress and improvement of human *art* in every department, whether mechanical or liberal. Were there any original and positive beauty in *certain* forms or proportions or combinations of matter, and were it to these alone that the sentiment of beauty was constitutionally restricted, a very obvious barrier would be imposed to the progress of every art that was conversant in material form, and the sense of taste would of necessity operate to oppose every new improvement.

As the peculiar forms or combinations of form which nature had thus prescribed could alone be beautiful, the common artist would hardly dare to deviate from them, even when he felt the propriety of it; and whenever any strong motive of usefulness induced him to deviate from them, the spectator would feel that sentiment of

dissatisfaction which attends vulgar and unenlightened workmanship. The sense of beauty would thus be opposed to the sense of
utility; the rude but beautiful form would become as permanent in
the productions of art as we now see it in those cases where the
ideas of sanctity are attached to it: and thus, at once, an additional
influence would be given to the rude inventions of antiquity, and an
additional obstacle imposed to those progressive inventions which
are so necessarily demanded by the progress of society.

In the fine arts, still more, or in those arts which are directed
solely to the production of beauty, this obstacle would soon be
permanent and invincible. As no forms or combinations of form
could, in such a constitution of our nature, be beautiful but those
which this law of our nature prescribed, then the period of their
discovery must have been the final period of every art of taste. The
exertions of the artist must of necessity have been confined to strict
imitation; the demand of the spectator could alone have been
satisfied when accuracy and fidelity, in this respect, were attained;
and the names of genius, of fancy, or of invention, must either have
altogether been unknown or known only to be contemned.

By the dependence of our sense of beauty, on the other hand,
upon the qualities of which material forms are significant, and may
be made significant . . . a field is thus opened to the dignified
ambition of the artist, not only unbounded in its extent, but in
which, even in the lowest of the mechanical arts, the highest honors
of genius or of benevolence may be won. Instead of a few forms
which the superstition of early taste had canonized, every variety and
every possible combination of forms is thus brought within the pale
of cultivated taste; the mind of the spectator follows with joy the
invention of the artist. . . . The sensibility of imagination thus
follows the progress of genius. . . . Destined as they are to the
production of beauty, the field in which [the fine arts] are to labor
is not narrowed by the prescriptions of vulgar men or of vulgar
nature, nor are they chained, like the Egyptian artists of old, to the
servile accuracy of imitating those forms or compositions of form
alone which some irresistible law has prescribed. The forms and the
scenery of Material Nature are around them, not to govern but to
awaken their genius; to invite them to investigate the sources of their
beauty; and from this investigation, to exalt their conceptions to the
imagination of forms, and of compositions of form, more pure and
more perfect than any that Nature herself ever presents to them. It
is in this pursuit that that Ideal Beauty is at last perceived, which it

is the loftiest ambition of the artist to feel and to express, and which
. . . is capable of producing emotions of a more exquisite and profound delight than Nature itself is ever destined to awaken. . . .

It may not be our fortune, perhaps, to be born amid its nobler
scenes. But wander where we will, trees wave, rivers flow, mountains
ascend, clouds darken, or winds animate the face of Heaven, and
over the whole scenery the sun sheds the cheerfulness of his morning, the splendor of his noonday, or the tenderness of his evening
light. There is not one of these features of scenery which is not
fitted to awaken us to moral emotion; to lead us, when once the
key of our imagination is struck, to trains of fascinating and of endless imagery, and in the indulgence of them, to make our bosoms
either glow with conceptions of mental excellence or melt in the
dreams of moral good. Even upon the man of the most uncultivated
taste, the scenes of Nature have some inexplicable charm. There is
not a chord perhaps of the human heart which may not be awakened by their influence; and I believe there is no man of genuine
taste who has not often felt, in the lone majesty of Nature, some
unseen spirit to dwell, which, in his happier hours, touched as if
with magic hand all the springs of his moral sensibility, and re-
kindled in his heart those original conceptions of the moral or
intellectual excellence of his nature, which it is the melancholy
tendency of the vulgar pursuits of life to diminish if not altogether
to destroy. . . .

But it is chiefly in the beauty *of the human countenance and
form* that the great purpose of Nature is most apparent. When we
feel these, it is not a mere organic[7] or animal effect we experience.
Whatever is lovely or beloved in the character of *mind*, whatever in
the powers or dispositions of man can awaken admiration or excite
sensibility—the loveliness of innocence, the charms of opening
genius, the varied tenderness of domestic affection, the dignity of
heroic or the majesty of patriotic virtue—all these are expressed to
us in the features of the countenance or in the positions and movements of the form. While we behold them, we feel not only a
feeling of temporary pleasure, but what Lord Kames has profoundly
and emphatically called the "sympathetic emotion of virtue";[8] we
share in some measure in those high dispositions the expressions of
which we contemplate; our own bosoms glow with kindred sensi-

---

[7] physical.
[8] *Elements of Criticism*, II, i, 4.

bilities; and we return to life and tu its duties with minds either softened to a wider benevolence, or awakened to a higher tone of morality.

* * * *

WALTER WHITER [1758–1832]
FROM
A Specimen of a Commentary on Shakespeare [1794]

FROM II
An Attempt to Explain and Illustrate
Various Passages of Shakespeare,
on a New Principle of Criticism, Derived from
Mr. Locke's Doctrine of the Association of Ideas

The *association of ideas* is a fruitful and popular theme in the writings of metaphysicians, and they have supplied us with innumerable examples which prove at once the extent and the activity of its influence. They have taught us that our modes of reasoning, our habits of life, and even the motions of our body are affected by its energy, and that it operates on the faculties by a kind of fascinating control,[1] which we sometimes cannot discover, and which generally we are unable to counteract. The consideration, however, of this doctrine, curious and extensive as it may appear, has commonly been confined to the admirers of metaphysical researches; nor has the theory, I believe, ever been systematically discussed as a point of taste, or as a subject of criticism. We have seen the question totally exhausted as it refers to the general powers of the understanding and the habitual exercise of the reasoning faculty; but we may justly be astonished that the effects of this principle should never have been investigated as it operates on the *writer in the ardor of invention,* by imposing on his mind [2] some remote and peculiar vein

---

[1] by a kind of enchantment.

[2] "Ideas that in themselves are not at all of kin come to be so united in some men's minds that it is very hard to separate them; they always *keep in company,* and the one no sooner at any time comes into the understanding but its *associate* appears with it; and if they are more than two which are thus united, the *whole gang* always inseparably shows themselves together." Locke's *Essay,* II, 33, par. 5. (Whiter's note.)

of language or of imagery. If, in the ordinary exertions of the understanding, the force of such an association has been found so powerful and extensive, it may surely be concluded that its influence would predominate with absolute authority over the vigorous workings of a wild and fertile imagination. In the pages of the poet, therefore, may we expect to be supplied with the most curious and abundant materials for the discussion of this principle, and in none can we hope to find such frequent and singular examples of its effect as may probably be discovered by the diligent reader in the writings of Shakespeare.

By the *associating principle* I do not mean (as it appears to be understood by some metaphysicians) that faculty of the understanding by which, on all occasions, the chain of our ideas is generated and preserved;[3] nor, as referred to the genius of the poet, do I mean that active power which passes rapidly through a variety of successive images, which discovers with so wonderful an acuteness their relations and dependencies, and which combines them with such exquisite effect in all the pleasing forms of fiction and invention.[4] In this indefinite and unlimited sense, the *association of ideas*, when applied to the general operations of the mind, expresses little less than the whole arrangement of the reasoning principle, and as referred to the workings of imagination must signify all the embellishments of eloquence and all the graces of poetry.

In the theory of Mr. Locke, by the term *association* is not understood the combination of ideas *naturally* connected with each other; for these, as he observes, "it is the office and the excellency of our reason to form and preserve in that union and correspondence which is founded on their peculiar beings." On the contrary, it is understood to express the combination of those ideas which have *no* natural alliance or relation to each other, but which have been united only by chance or by custom. Now it is observable that no task can be imposed on the understanding of greater difficulty than to separate ideas thus accidentally combined, as the mind is commonly passive in admitting their original formation, and often totally unconscious of the force and principle of their union. . . .

I define, therefore, the power of this *association* over the genius of the poet to consist in supplying him with words and with ideas, which have been suggested to the mind by a principle of union unperceived by himself, and independent of the subject to which they are applied. . . .

---

[3] Total association, as in Hume or Hartley.

[4] *Cf.* Gerard, p. 319.

1. It will often happen that a certain word, expression, sentiment, circumstance, or metaphor will lead the writer to the use of that appropriate language by which they are each of them distinguished, even on occasions where the metaphor is no longer continued, where there is no allusion intended to the circumstance, nor is there any sense conveyed under this language which bears a peculiar reference to the words or sentiments that excited it. It is merely accidental that the imagery, in whose service the language thus suggested is employed, has any affinity to the subject from which it is borrowed. Now, as it is the business of the critic to discover and establish the original language of the author and to reject what is sometimes called the "improved" text of an "ingenious" commentator, we shall instantly perceive that from this principle may probably be derived a very important canon for the confirmation of disputed readings, which have perhaps been too hastily condemned as quaint, remote, or unintelligible. If the discerning critic should discover that the train of thought which had just occupied the attention of the writer would naturally conduct him to the use of this controverted expression, we should certainly have little difficulty in admitting the reading to be genuine, even though it had before appeared to us under a questionable shape, from the singular mode in which it was applied. On an art not capable of demonstration, surely no principle can be engrafted more sure and infallible than that which is derived from some acknowledged powers in the understanding, roused and controlled as they are by an active and a regular influence.

2. Certain terms containing an equivocal meaning, or sounds suggesting such a meaning, will often serve to introduce other words and expressions of a similar nature. This similarity is formed by having in some cases a coincidence in sense, or an affinity arising from sound, though the signification in which they are really applied has never any reference and often no similitude to that which caused their association.

3. The remembrance of a similar phraseology, of a known metaphor, or of a circumstance, *not* apparent in the text, will often lead the writer into language or imagery derived from these sources, though the application may be sometimes totally different from the meaning and spirit of the original.

4. An impression on the mind of the writer, arising from something which is frequently presented to his senses, or which passes within the sphere of his ordinary observation, will supply him with the union of words and sentiments which are not necessarily con-

nected with each other and which are combined only from the powerful influence of external impressions on the faculties of the understanding

These objects may be general and therefore equally apparent to the observers of every period, but the more curious examples of this nature will be derived from those impressions which are peculiar to the country, the age, and the situation of the writer. Here, likewise, we are still to understand that as these combinations were not formed by the invention, but forced on the fancy of the poet, he is totally unconscious of the effect and principle of their union. This then is a portion of criticism to which the diligence of commentators has never, I believe, been systematically applied. They have exhausted the abundance of their knowledge in discovering the *direct*, though sometimes perhaps obscure allusions which the poet has *intentionally* made to the customs of his own age, and to the various vices, follies, passions, and prejudices which are the pointed objects of his satire or his praise. But the commentators have not marked those *indirect* and *tacit* references which are produced by the writer with *no* intentional allusion, or rather, they have not unfolded those trains of thought, alike pregnant with the materials *peculiar* to his age, which often prompt the combinations of the poet in the wildest exertions of his fancy, and which conduct him, unconscious of the effect, to the various *peculiarities* of his imagery or his language. To illustrate passages which are dictated by a train of thoughts abounding with these materials, the critic must exert the same knowledge in the phraseology and customs belonging to the age of his author which he employed in the explanation of direct and intentional allusions, as they alike contain the forgotten circumstances of a remote period and differ only in the mode by which these circumstances are presented. As the poet indeed rises in genius, as he advances to the rank of that select and exalted band "who are not for an age, but for all time," [5] it is certain that his attention will be proportionally abstracted from the fleeting topics of his own period and the minute concerns of his peculiar situation. He will perhaps studiously avoid all occasions of satire on the characters of his age, and all *direct* allusions to the occurrences before him. His pictures of nature and of life will be drawn from broad and general views of our condition, from scenes to which the eye of every age is witness, and from those passions and affections of men which have been perpetually found to amuse or agitate our

---

[5] *Cf.* Ben Jonson, "To the Memory of my Beloved The Author Master William Shakespeare," preface to *Folio* (1623), l. 43.

being. Still, however, the secret energy of local influence will continue to operate on his mind: his modes of conception will be still affected by the ideas which were most familiar to the habits of his life. In the fictions, the thoughts, and the language of the poet, you may ever mark the deep and unequivocal traces of the age in which he lived, of the employments in which he was engaged, and of the various objects which excited his passions or arrested his attention. . . .

Among the various circumstances which might be selected on this occasion, there are two particulars eminently distinguishing the present time from the age of Shakespeare and the periods preceding, which must operate with singular effect on the genius of the poet as they are connected with the great resources of his art, with the colorings of description and the variety of invention: I mean the universal custom in those days of covering the walls of their chambers with arras or tapestry hangings, which represented the celebrated stories of ancient or modern times, and the frequent exhibition of masques, pageants, and processions.[6] In these wild and motley spectacles, the illustrious personages of history, romance, and mythology; the tales and fictions of every period, whether they were of Grecian, Gothic, Roman, Saracen, or Christian origin; the creatures of the imagination and the living characters of the world, were all blended and confounded by the licentious fancy or the ignorance of the inventor. The reader will instantly perceive that these must influence with considerable energy the imagination of the poet, as the former will impart to his descriptions certain traits of a precise and definite coloring, which are adventitious and accidental rather than general and characteristic, which belong rather to the impressions of the eye than to those abstract and universal conceptions that are formed by the contemplation of the mind. The latter will enrich the stores of his fancy with wild and original combinations, with a splendid train of lively and various imagery, and above all with the most ample materials for allegorical fictions and personified agencies. . . .

I shall now proceed to the examples themselves, which are intended to illustrate or confirm the theory of this associating principle. I have only to request the reader that they may not be hastily perused, but diligently studied; as the traces of so subtle an influence will often be invisible to the hasty glance of a superficial observer, though they will be apparent to a more careful view in

---

[6] There is no reader of taste who will not on this occasion be reminded of the *Dialogue on the Age of Elizabeth*. (Whiter's note.) See p. 374.

distinct and unequivocal characters. I must again suggest to the reader that he will be frequently induced to wonder or to smile at the minute and even ridiculous combinations which have been thus imposed on the mind of the poet, and which are able to deceive and control the most acute and powerful understanding. I have been desirous from various motives to confine within these narrow limits the present dissertation, which might easily have been extended to a more ample form and connected with other branches of critical inquiry; and I have only to add that if the ensuing pages should not convey to the reader all the conviction which they might be expected to afford, he has only to object that the author has been unfortunate in the proofs, not unfounded in the principles. It is universally acknowledged that such an influence exists, nor can it be doubted that it must thus operate on the composition of the poet. I may therefore at least assume the merit of opening a new path to the researches of the critic, and of supplying a future theme of investigation to a more sagacious or a more diligent inquirer.

The first example which I shall produce is the very passage which originally led me to the present inquiry. In *Timon of Athens*, when Timon has retired into the woods, Apemantus thus upbraids him with the contrast of his past and present condition:

> *What, think'st*
> *That the bleak air, thy boisterous chamberlain,*
> *Will put thy shirt on warm? Will these moist trees,*
> *That have outlived the eagle, page thy heels*
> *And skip when thou point'st out?* [7]

Sir Thomas Hanmer for *moist* reads very elegantly, says Dr. Johnson, *moss'd*. Mr. Steevens confirms the emendation by examples; and Mr. Malone believes it to be the true reading. I agree with our commentators that *moss'd* is a more elegant epithet, and at the same time better calculated to express the antiquity of trees "that have outlived the eagle." It is certain however that *moist* is not altogether destitute of force and propriety, as in many parts of old and rotten trees a kind of moist exudation is often to be seen, though perhaps other parts may be dry and withered by age. If, therefore, I can show with extreme probability, from some acknowledged principle in the mind, why this peculiar word might be suggested to our poet, it surely ought to be considered as a valuable touchstone in the art of criticism, of which it is certainly the busi-

---

[7] IV, iii, 221.

ness to discover and ascertain what the author really *has* written, and not what he *ought* to have done. The reader then is to be informed that *warm* and *moist* were the appropriate terms in the days of Shakespeare for what we should now call an *air'd* and a *damp* shirt. So John Florio (*Second Fruits*, 1591) in a dialogue between the master Torquato and his servant Ruspa.

> *T. Dispatch and give me a* shirt?
> *R. Here is one with ruffles.*
> *T. Thou dolte, seest thou not how* moist *it is?*
> *R. Pardon me, good sir, I was not aware of it.*
> *T. Go into the kitchen and* warme *it.*

Can the reader doubt (though he may perhaps smile at the association) that the image of the *chamberlain* putting the *shirt* on *warm* impressed the opposite word *moist* on the imagination of the poet? Though he was himself unconscious how he came by it, and certainly never would have applied it as an epithet to trees if it had not been fixed on his mind by a kind of fascinating power, which concealed from him not only the origin but the effect likewise of so strange an association. . . .

It will readily be understood and acknowledged that this propensity in the mind to associate subjects so remote in their meaning, and so heterogeneous in their nature, must of necessity sometimes deceive the ardor of the writer into whimsical or ridiculous combinations. As the reader, however, is not blinded by this fascinating principle, which, while it creates the association, conceals likewise its effect, he is instantly impressed with the quaintness or the absurdity of the imagery and is inclined to charge the writer with the intention of a foolish quibble or an impertinent allusion. I shall now therefore produce some passages of Shakespeare which have fallen under suspicions of this nature, and which I think may be completely defended by the application of the present theory. Our bard has so many grievous and undoubted quibbles of his own to answer for that it is surely unreasonable, as Mr. Steevens has somewhere observed, to censure him for those which exist only in the imagination of others.

> *He had a fever when he was in Spain,*
> *And when the fit was on him, I did mark*
> *How he did shake. 'Tis true this god did shake:*
> *His* coward *lips did from their* color *fly.*[8]

---

[8] *Julius Caesar*, I, ii, 119.

"A plain man," says Warburton, "would have said 'the color fled from his lips,' and not his 'lips from their color.' But the false expression was for the sake of as false a piece of wit: a poor quibble, alluding to a coward flying from his colors." The critic has discovered the association, which had escaped the author, who indeed intended no quibble, but was himself entangled by the similitude of *color* and *colors*. This introduced to him the appropriate terms of *coward* and *fly*, and thus, under the influence of such an embarrassment, it was scarcely possible to express the sentiment in a form less equivocal than the present. Let me add likewise another circumstance which might operate in suggesting this *military* metaphor—that the cowardice of a *soldier* is the subject of the narrative.

* * * *

SIR UVEDALE PRICE [1747–1829]

FROM

An Essay on the Picturesque as Compared with the Sublime and Beautiful, and on the Use of Studying Pictures for the Purpose of Improving Real Landscape [1794]

from the Preface [1796]

That painters do see effects in nature which men in general do not see, we have, in the motto prefixed to this *Essay*, the testimony of no common observer, of one who was sufficiently vain of his own talents and discernment in every way, and not likely to acknowledge a superiority in other men without strong conviction. It is not a mere observation of Cicero, it is an exclamation: *Quam multa vident pictores!* [1] It marks his surprise at the extreme difference which the study of nature, by means of the art of painting, seems to make almost in the sight itself. It may likewise be observed that his remark does not extend to form, in which the ancient painters are acknowledged to be our superiors; not to color, in which they are also conceived to be at least our rivals; but to light

---

[1] *Academica*, II, vii, 20: "how much painters see [in shadows and prominences, which we do not see]!"

and shadow, the supposed triumph of modern over ancient art. On which account, the professors of painting since its revival have a still better right to the compliment of so illustrious a panegyrist than those of his own age.

If there were no other means of seeing with the eyes of painters than by acquiring the practical skill of their hands, the generality of mankind must of course give up the point; but luckily, we may gain no little insight into their method of considering nature, and no inconsiderable share of their relish for her beauties, by an easier process—by studying their works. This study has one great advantage over most others: there are no dry elements to struggle with. Pictures, as likewise drawings and prints, have in them what is suited to all ages and capacities; many of them, like Swift's *Gulliver's Travels*, display the most fertile and brilliant imagination, joined to the most accurate judgment and selection, and the deepest knowledge of nature; like that extraordinary work, they are at once the amusement of childhood and ignorance, and the delight, instruction, and admiration of the highest and most cultivated minds.

It is not, however, to be supposed that theory and observation alone will enable us to judge either of pictures or of nature with the same skill as those who join, to the practical knowledge of their art, habitual reflection on its principles and its productions. Between such artists and the mere lover of painting, there will always be a sufficient difference to justify the remark of Cicero; but by means of the study which I have so earnestly recommended, we may greatly diminish the immense distance that exists between the eye of a first-rate painter and that of a man who has never thought on the subject. Were it indeed possible that a painter of great and general excellence could at once bestow on such a man not his power of imitating, but of distinguishing and feeling the effects and combinations of form, color, and light and shadow, it would hardly be too much to assert that a new appearance of things, a new world, would suddenly be opened to him, and the bestower might preface the miraculous gift with the words in which Venus addresses her son when she removes the mortal film from his eyes:

Aspice, namque omnem quae nunc obducta tuenti
Mortales hebetat visus tibi, et humida circum
Caligat, nubem eripiam.[2]

---

[2] *Aeneid*, II, 604–6: "Behold, for every cloud which now closes over and dulls your mortal sight, casting a humid mist on all sides of your vision, I shall tear away."

FROM CHAPTER III [1810]

There are few words whose meaning has been less accurately determined than that of the word *picturesque*.

In general, I believe, it is applied to every object and every kind of scenery which has been or might be represented with good effect in painting, just as the word *beautiful*, when we speak of visible nature, is applied to every object and every kind of scenery that in any way give pleasure to the eye; and these seem to be the significations of both words taken in their most extended and popular sense. A more precise and distinct idea of beauty has been given in an essay[3] the early splendor of which not even the full meridian blaze of its illustrious author has been able to extinguish; but the picturesque, considered as a separate character, has never yet been accurately distinguished from the sublime and the beautiful; though as no one has ever pretended that they are synonymous (for it is sometimes used in contradistinction to them), such a distinction must exist.

Mr. Gilpin, from whose very ingenious and extensive observations on this subject I have received great pleasure and instruction, appears to have adopted this common acceptation, not merely as such, but as giving an exact and determinate idea of the word, for he defines picturesque objects to be those "which please from some quality capable of being illustrated in painting;" [4] or, as he again defines it in his letter to Sir Joshua Reynolds, "such objects as are proper subjects for painting." [5] Both these definitions seem to me—what may perhaps appear a contradiction—at once too vague and too confined; for though we are not to expect any definition to be so accurate and comprehensive as both to supply the place and stand the test of investigation, yet if it do not in some degree separate the thing defined from all others, it differs little from any general truth on the same subject. For instance, it is very true that picturesque objects do please from some quality capable of being illustrated in painting, but so also does every object that is represented in painting, if it please at all; otherwise it would not have been painted; and hence we ought to conclude, what certainly is not meant, that all objects which please in pictures are therefore picturesque—for no distinction or exclusion is made. Were any other person to define picturesque objects to be those which please from some striking effect of form, color, or light and shadow, such

---

[3] Burke's *Sublime and the Beautiful.*
[4] Essay "On Picturesque Beauty," p. 1. (Price's note.)
[5] End of essay "On Picturesque Beauty." (Price's note.)

a definition would indeed give but a very indistinct idea of the thing defined; but it would be hardly more vague, and at the same time much less confined, than the others, for it would not have an exclusive reference to a particular art.

I hope to show in the course of this work that the picturesque has a character not less separate and distinct than either the sublime or the beautiful, nor less independent of the art of painting. . . .

But there is one circumstance particularly adverse to this part of my essay: I mean the manifest derivation of the word *picturesque*. The Italian *pittoresco* is, I imagine, of earlier date than either the English or the French word, the latter of which, *pittoresque*, is clearly taken from it, having no analogy to its own tongue. *Pittoresco* is derived, not like *picturesque* from the thing painted, but from the painter; and this difference is not wholly immaterial. The English word refers to the performance and the objects most suited to it; the Italian and French words have a reference to the turn of mind common to painters, who, from the constant habit of examining all the peculiar effects and combinations, as well as the general appearance, of nature, are struck with numberless circumstances, even where they are incapable of being represented, to which an unpracticed eye pays little or no attention. The English word naturally draws the reader's mind towards pictures, and from that partial and confined view of the subject, what is in truth only an illustration of picturesqueness becomes the foundation of it. The words *sublime* and *beautiful* have not the same etymological reference to any one visible art, and therefore are applied to objects of the other senses: *sublime*, indeed, in the language from which it is taken, and in its plain sense, means "high," and therefore, perhaps, in strictness should relate to objects of sight only; yet we no more scruple to call one of Handel's choruses sublime than Corelli's famous *Pastorale* beautiful. But should any person simply, and without any qualifying expressions, call a capricious movement of Scarlatti or Haydn *picturesque*, he would, with great reason, be laughed at, for it is not a term applied to sounds; yet such a movement, from its sudden, unexpected, and abrupt transitions, from a certain playful wildness of character and appearance of irregularity, is no less analogous to similar scenery in nature than the concerto or the chorus to what is grand or beautiful to the eye. . . .

I must here observe, and I wish the reader to keep it in his mind, that the inquiry is not in what sense certain words are used in the best authors, still less what is their common and vulgar use and abuse, but whether there be certain qualities which uniformly produce the same effects in all visible objects, and according to the same analogy, in objects of hearing and of all the other senses; and which qualities, though frequently blonded and united with others in the same object or set of objects, may be separated from them and assigned to the class to which they belong.

If it can be shown that a character composed of these qualities, and distinct from all others, does universally prevail; if it can be traced in the different objects of art and of nature, and appears consistent throughout, it surely deserves a distinct title; but with respect to the real ground of inquiry, it matters little whether such a character or the set of objects belonging to it be called beautiful, sublime, or picturesque, or by any other name, or by no name at all. . . .

I am therefore persuaded that the two opposite qualities of roughness[6] and of sudden variation, joined to that of irregularity, are the most efficient causes of the picturesque.

This, I think, will appear very clearly, if we take a view of those objects, both natural and artificial, that are allowed to be picturesque, and compare them with those which are as generally allowed to be beautiful.

A temple or palace of Grecian architecture, in its perfect entire state and with its surface and color smooth and even, either in painting or reality, is beautiful; in ruin it is picturesque. Observe the process by which Time, the great author of such changes, converts a beautiful object into a picturesque one: First, by means of weather stains, partial incrustations, mosses, etc., it at the same time takes off from the uniformity of the surface and of the color, that is, gives a degree of roughness and variety of tint. Next, the various accidents of weather loosen the stones themselves; they tumble in irregular masses upon what was perhaps smooth turf or pavement or nicely-trimmed walks and shrubberies—now mixed and overgrown with wild plants and creepers that crawl over and shoot among the fallen ruins. Sedums, wall-flowers, and other vegetables that bear drought find nourishment in the decayed cement from which the stones have been detached; birds convey their food into the chinks,

---

[6] I have followed Mr. Gilpin's example in using roughness as a general term. He observes, however, that "properly speaking, *roughness* relates only to the surface of bodies, and that when we speak of their delineation, we use the word *ruggedness*." In making roughness, in this general sense, a very principal distinction between the beautiful and the picturesque, I believe I am supported by the general opinion of all who have considered the subject, as well as by Mr. Gilpin's authority. (Price's note.)

and yew, elder, and other berried plants project from the sides; while the ivy mantles over other parts and crowns the top. The even, regular lines of the doors and windows are broken, and through their ivy-fringed openings is displayed, in a more broken and picturesque manner, that striking image in Virgil,

> Apparet domus intus, et atria longa patescunt;
> Apparent Priami et veterum penetralia regum.[7]

Gothic architecture is generally considered as more picturesque, though less beautiful, than Grecian, and upon the same principle that a ruin is more so than a new edifice. The first thing that strikes the eye in approaching any building is the general outline and the effect of the openings. In Grecian buildings, the general lines of the roof are straight, and even when varied and adorned by a dome or a pediment, the whole has a character of symmetry and regularity.[8] But symmetry, which in works of art particularly accords with the beautiful, is in the same degree adverse to the picturesque; and among the various causes of the superior picturesqueness of ruins, compared with entire buildings, the destruction of symmetry is by no means the least powerful.

In Gothic buildings, the outline of the summit presents such a variety of forms, of turrets and pinnacles, some open, some fretted and variously enriched, that even where there is an exact correspondence of parts, it is often disguised by an appearance of splendid confusion and irregularity. There is a line in Dryden's *Palamon and Arcite* which might be interpreted according to this idea, though I do not suppose he intended to convey any such meaning:

> And all appear'd irregularly great.

In the doors and windows of Gothic churches, the pointed arch has as much variety as any regular figure can well have; the eye too is less strongly conducted than by the parallel lines in the Grecian style, from the top of one aperture to that of another; and every person must be struck with the extreme richness and intricacy of

---

[7] *Aeneid*, II, 483–84: "The palace within is disclosed, and its long galleries stretch out; the inmost chambers are visible of Priam and of ancient kings."

[8] I hope it will not be supposed, that by admiring the picturesque circumstances of the Gothic, I mean to undervalue the symmetry and beauty of Grecian buildings: whatever comes to us from the Greeks has an irresistible claim to our admiration; that distinguished people seized on the true points both of beauty and grandeur in all the arts, and their architecture has justly obtained the same high pre-eminence as their sculpture, poetry, and eloquence. (Price's note, 1794.)

some of the principal windows of our cathedrals and ruined abbeys. In these last is displayed the triumph of the picturesque, and their charms to a painter's eye are often so great as to rival those which arise from the chaste ornaments and the noble and elegant simplicity of Grecian architecture.

Some people may, perhaps, be unwilling to allow that in ruins of Grecian and Gothic architecture any considerable part of the spectator's pleasure arises from the picturesque circumstances, and may choose to attribute the whole to—what may justly claim a great share in that pleasure—the elegance or grandeur of their forms, the veneration of high antiquity, or the solemnity of religious awe; in a word, to the mixture of the two other characters. But were this true, yet there are many buildings, highly interesting to all who have united the study of art with that of nature, in which beauty and grandeur are equally out of the question, such as hovels, cottages, mills, insides of old barns, stables, etc., whenever they have any marked and peculiar effect of form, tint, or light and shadow. In mills particularly, such is the extreme intricacy of the wheels and the wood work, such the singular variety of forms and of lights and shadows, of mosses and weather stains from the constant moisture, of plants springing from the rough joints of the stones—such the assemblage of everything which most conduces to picturesqueness that, even without the addition of water, an old mill has the greatest charm for a painter.

It is owing to the same causes that a building with scaffolding has often a more picturesque appearance than the building itself when the scaffolding is taken away; that old, mossy, rough-hewn park pales of unequal heights are an ornament to landscape, especially when they are partially concealed by thickets, while a neat post and rail regularly continued round a field, and seen without any interruption, is one of the most unpicturesque, as being one of the most uniform of all boundaries.

But among all the objects of nature, there is none in which roughness and smoothness more strongly mark the distinction between the two characters than in water. A calm, clear lake, with the reflections of all that surrounds it, viewed under the influence of a setting sun at the close of an evening clear and serene as its own surface, is perhaps, of all scenes, the most congenial to our ideas of beauty in its strictest and in its most general acceptation.

Nay, though the scenery around should be the most wild and picturesque—I might almost say the most savage—everything is so softened and melted together by the reflection of such a mirror that the prevailing idea, even then, might possibly be that of beauty, so long as the water itself was chiefly regarded. On the other hand, all water of which the surface is broken and the motion abrupt and irregular, as universally accords with our ideas of the picturesque; and whenever the word is mentioned, rapid and stony torrents and waterfalls and waves dashing against rocks are among the first objects that present themselves to our imagination. The two characters also approach and balance each other as roughness or smoothness, as gentle undulation or abruptness, prevail.

Among trees, it is not the smooth young beech nor the fresh and tender ash, but the rugged old oak or knotty wych elm that are picturesque; nor is it necessary they should be of great bulk—it is sufficient if they are rough, mossy, with a character of age, and with sudden variations in their forms. The limbs of huge trees shattered by lightning or tempestuous winds are in the highest degree picturesque; but whatever is caused by those dreaded powers of destruction, must always have a tincture of the sublime. . . .

In our own species, objects merely picturesque are to be found among the wandering tribes of gypsies and beggars, who, in all the qualities which give them that character, bear a close analogy to the wild forester and the worn-out cart horse, and again to old mills, hovels, and other inanimate objects of the same kind. More dignified characters, such as a Belisarius or a Marius in age and exile,[9] have the same mixture of picturesqueness and of decayed grandeur, as the venerable remains of the magnificence of past ages.

If we ascend to the highest order of created beings, as painted by the grandest of our poets, they, in their state of glory and happiness, raise no ideas but those of beauty and sublimity; the picturesque, as in earthly objects, only shows itself when they are in a state of ruin—

> Nor appeared
> Less than Archangel ruined, and the excess
> Of glory obscured—

when shadows have obscured their original brightness, and that uniform, though angelic expression of pure love and joy has been destroyed by a variety of warring passions:

---

[9] The noble picture of Salvator Rosa at Lord Townshend's which in the print is called Belisarius, has been thought to be a Marius among the ruins of Carthage. (Price's note.)

> *Darkened so, yet shone*
> *Above them all the Archangel; but his face*
> *Deep scars of thunder had intrenched, and care*
> *Sat on his faded cheek, but under brows*
> *Of dauntless courage and considerate pride*
> *Waiting revenge; cruel his eye, but cast*
> *Signs of remorse and passion.*[1]

If from nature we turn to that art from which the expression itself is taken, we shall find all the principles of picturesqueness confirmed. Among painters, Salvator Rosa is one of the most remarkable for his picturesque effects; in no other master are seen such abrupt and rugged forms, such sudden deviations both in his figures and his landscapes; and the roughness and broken touches of his penciling admirably accord with the objects they characterize.

Guido,[2] on the other hand, was as eminent for beauty: in his celestial countenances are the happiest examples of gradual variation, of lines that melt and flow into each other—no sudden break, nothing that can disturb that pleasing languor which the union of all that constitutes beauty impresses on the soul. The style of his hair is as smooth as its own character and its effect in accompanying the face will allow; the flow of his drapery, the sweetness and equality of his penciling, and the silvery clearness and purity of his tints, are all examples of the justness of Mr. Burke's principles of beauty. But we may learn from the works even of this great master how unavoidably an attention to mere beauty and flow of outline will lead towards sameness and insipidity. If this has happened to a painter of such high excellence, who so well knew the value of all that belongs to his art, and whose touch, when he painted a St. Peter or a St. Jerome, was as much admired for its spirited and characteristic roughness as for its equality and smoothness in his angels and madonnas—what must be the case with men who have been tethered all their lives in a clump or a belt?[3]

FROM CHAPTER IV [1810]

In pursuing the same train of ideas, I may add that the effect of the picturesque is curiosity—an effect which, though less splendid

---

[1] *Paradise Lost,* I, 592–605.
[2] Guido Reni (1575–1642), Bolognese religious painter of the Carracci School, much admired in England until the attack by Ruskin.
[3] Technical terms from ornamental gardening.

and powerful, has a more general influence. Those who have felt the excitement produced by the intricacies of wild romantic mountainous scenes can tell how curiosity, while it prompts us to scale every rocky promontory, to explore every new recess, by its active agency keeps the fibers to their full tone; and thus picturesqueness, when mixed with either of the other characters, corrects the languor of beauty or the tension of sublimity. But as the nature of every corrective must be to take off from the peculiar effect of what it is to correct, so does the picturesque when united to either of the others. It is the coquetry of nature: it makes beauty more amusing, more varied, more playful, but also

Less winning soft, less amiably mild.[4]

Again, by its variety, its intricacy, its partial concealments, it excites that active curiosity which gives play to the mind, loosening these iron bonds with which astonishment chains up its faculties. This seems to be perfectly applicable to tragicomedy, and is at once its apology and condemnation. Whatever relieves the mind from a strong impression, of course weakens that impression.

Where characters, however distinct in their nature, are perpetually mixed together in such various degrees and manners, it is not always easy to draw the exact line of separation; I think, however, we may conclude that where an object or a set of objects are without smoothness or grandeur, but from their intricacy, their sudden and irregular deviations, their variety of forms, tints, and lights and shadows, are interesting to a cultivated eye, they are simply picturesque. Such, for instance, are the rough banks that often enclose a byroad or a hollow lane. Imagine the *size* of these banks and the *space* between them to be increased, till the lane becomes a deep dell, the coves large caverns, the peeping stones hanging rocks, so that the whole may impress an idea of awe and grandeur: the sublime will then be mixed with the picturesque, though the *scale* only, not the *style* of the scenery would be changed. On the other hand, if parts of the banks were smooth and gently sloping, or if in the middle space the turf were soft and close-bitten, or if a gentle stream passed between them, whose clear unbroken surface reflected all their varieties—the beautiful and the picturesque, by means of that softness and smoothness, would then be united.

---

[4] *Paradise Lost*, IV, 479.

—◦◦❦❦◦◦—

Selected Bibliographies

Abbreviations:

ELH: A Journal of English Literary History
HLQ: Huntington Library Quarterly
JAAC: Journal of Aesthetics and Art Criticism
JEGP: Journal of English and Germanic Philology
JHI: Journal of the History of Ideas
MLN: Modern Language Notes
MLQ: Modern Language Quarterly
MLR: Modern Language Review
MP: Modern Philology
PLMA: Publication of the Modern Language Association
PQ: Philological Quarterly
RES: The Review of English Studies
SP: Studies in Philology
TLS: The Times Literary Supplement

COLLECTIONS

Dramatic Essays of the Neoclassical Age, Henry Hitch Adams and B. Hathaway, eds. (New York: Columbia University Press, 1950). *Critical Essays of the Eighteenth Century, 1700–1725*, Willard H. Durham, ed. (New Haven, Conn.: Yale University Press, 1915). *Eighteenth-Century Critical Essays*, Scott Elledge, ed. (Ithaca: Cornell University Press, 1961), 2 vols. *English Literary Criticism: Restoration and 18th Century*, Samuel Hynes, ed. (New York: Appleton-Century-Crofts, 1963). *English Critical Essays (Sixteenth, Seventeenth, and Eighteenth Centuries)*, Edmund D. Jones, ed. (Oxford: World's Classics, 1922). *Taste and Criticism in the Eighteenth Century*, H. A. Needham, ed. (London: Harrap, 1952). *Eighteenth Century Essays on Shakespeare*, D. Nichol Smith, ed. (Glasgow, 1903; reprinted New York: Russell and Russell, 1962). *Shakespeare Criticism, 1623–1840*, D. Nichol Smith, ed. (Oxford: World's Classics, 1916). *Critical Essays of the Seventeenth Century*, Joel E. Spingarn, ed. (Oxford: The Clarendon Press, 1909), Vols. 2 and 3.

HISTORIES AND GENERAL STUDIES

Meyer H. Abrams, *The Mirror and the Lamp: Romantic Theory and the Critical Tradition* (New York: Oxford University Press, 1953). J. W. H. Atkins, *English Literary Criticism: 17th and 18th Centuries* (London: Methuen & Co., Ltd., 1951). Walter Jackson Bate, *From Classic to Romantic, Premises of Taste in Eighteenth-Century England* (Cambridge, Mass.: Harvard University Press, 1946); and *Criticism: the Major Texts* (New York: Harcourt, Brace and Company, 1952), reprinted as *Prefaces to Criticism* (Garden City, N.Y.: Doubleday Anchor Books, 1959). A. Bosker, *Literary Criticism in the Age of Johnson* (Groningen: J. B. Wolters, 1930; rev. ed., New York: Hafner Publishing Company, 1953). Alexander F. B. Clark, *Boileau and the French Classical Critics in England* (1660–1830) (Paris: Librairie Ancienne Édouard Champion, 1925). R. S. Crane, "English Neoclassical Criticism: an Outline Sketch," in *Dictionary of World Literature*, J. T. Shipley, ed. (New York: The Philosophical Library, 1941), reprinted in *Critics and Criticism Ancient and Modern* (Chicago: University of Chicago Press, 1952); and "On Writing the History of English Criticism, 1650–1800," *University of Toronto Quarterly*, XXII (1953). Bonamy Dobree, *English Literature in the Early Eighteenth Century, 1700–1740* (New York and London: Oxford University Press, 1959), ch. 9. Francis Galaway, *Reason, Rule, and Revolt in English Classicism* (New York: Charles Scribner's Sons, 1940). Walter John Hipple, Jr., *The Beautiful, the Sublime, and the Picturesque in Eighteenth-Century British Aesthetic Theory* (Carbondale: Southern Illinois University Press, 1957). Gordon McKenzie, *Critical Responsiveness: a Study of the Psychological Current in Later Eighteenth-Century Criticism* (Berkeley: University of California Press, 1949). Samuel H. Monk, *The Sublime: a Study of Critical Theories in XVIII-Century England* (New York: Modern Language Association, 1935; reprinted Ann Arbor Paperbacks, University of Michigan Press, 1960). Marjorie H. Nicolson, *Mountain Gloom and Mountain Glory: The Development of the Aesthetics of the Infinite* (Ithaca, N.Y.: Cornell University Press, 1959). George Saintsbury, *A History of English Criticism* (Edinburgh and London: William Blackwood & Sons, Ltd., 1911). George Sherburn, "The Restoration and Eighteenth Century" in *A Literary History of England*, A. C. Baugh, ed. (New York: Appleton-Century-Crofts, 1948). Ernest L. Tuveson, *The Imagination as a Means of Grace: Locke and the Aesthetics of Romanticism* (Berkeley and Los Angeles: University of California Press, 1960). René Wellek, *A History of Modern Criticism: 1750–1950*; Vol. 1, *The Later Eighteenth Century* (New Haven, Conn.: Yale University Press, 1955). W. K. Wimsatt, Jr., and Cleanth Brooks, *Literary Criticism: a Short History* (New York: Alfred A. Knopf, 1957).

SPECIAL TOPICS AND STUDIES

Dwight L. Durling, *Georgic Tradition in English Poetry* (New York: Columbia University Press, 1935). Paul Fussell, Jr., *Theory of Prosody in Eighteenth-Century England* (1954), Connecticut College Monograph No. 5. C. C. Green, *The Neo-Classic Theory of Tragedy in England during the Eighteenth Century* (Cambridge, Mass.: Harvard University Press, 1934). J. H. Hagstrum, *The Sister Arts: the Tradition of Literary Pictorialism and English Poetry from Dryden to Gray* (Chicago: University of Chicago Press, 1958). R. D. Havens, *The Influence of Milton on English Poetry* (Cambridge, Mass.: Harvard University Press, 1922). J. B. Heidler, *The History, from 1700 to 1800, of English Criticism of Prose Fiction* (Urbana: Illinois Studies in Language and Literature, 1928). M. T. Herrick, *The Poetics of Aristotle in England* (New Haven, Conn.: Yale University Press, 1930). Sigurd Bernhard Hustvedt, *Ballad Criticism in Scandinavia and Great Britain during the Eighteenth Century* (New York: The American-Scandinavian Foundation, 1916). Norman MacLean, "From Action to Image: Theories of the Lyric in the Eighteenth Century," in *Critics and Criticism*, R. S. Crane, ed. (Chicago: University of Chicago Press, 1952). J. G. Robertson, *Studies in the Genesis of Romantic Theory in the Eighteenth Century* (Cambridge, Eng.: Bowes, 1925). David Nichol Smith, *Shakespeare in the Eighteenth Century* (Oxford: The Clarendon Press, 1928). L. P. Smith, *Four Words: Romantic, Originality, Creative, Genius* (Oxford: The Clarendon Press, 1924). D. A. Stauffer, *The Art of Biography in Eighteenth Century England* (Princeton, N.J.: Princeton University Press, 1941). H. T. Swedenberg, *The Theory of the Epic in England, 1650–1800* (Berkeley: University of California Press, 1944). René Wellek, *The Rise of English Literary History* (Chapel Hill: University of North Carolina Press, 1941). Lois Whitney, *Primitivism and the Idea of Progress in English Popular Literature of the Eighteenth Century* (Baltimore: Johns Hopkins Press, 1934).

R. W. Babcock, "The Idea of Taste in the Eighteenth Century," *PMLA*, L (1935). W. J. Bate, "The Sympathetic Imagination in Eighteenth-Century English Criticism," *ELH*, XII (1945). Donald F. Bond, "Distrust of Imagination in English Neo-classicism," *PQ*, XIV (1935). Louis Bredvold, "The Tendency toward Platonism in Neo-classical Esthetics," *ELH*, I (1934). J. Bullitt and W. J. Bate, "The Distinctions between Fancy and Imagination in Eighteenth-Century English Criticism," *MLN*, LX (1945). R. L. Brett, "The Aesthetic Sense and Taste in the Literary Criticism of the Early Eighteenth Century," *RES*, XX (1944). Wilson O. Clough, "Reason and Genius —an Eighteenth Century Dilemma," *PQ*, XXIII (1944). J. E. Congleton, "Theories of Pastoral Poetry in England, 1684–1717," *SP*, XLI

(1944). J. W. Draper, "The Theory of the Comic in Eighteenth-Century England," *JEGP*, XXXVII (1938). Scott Elledge, "The Background and Development in English Criticism of the Theories of Generality and Particularity," *PMLA*, LXII (1947). Baxter Hathaway, "The Lucretian 'Return upon Ourselves' in Eighteenth-Century Theories of Tragedy," *PMLA*, LXII (1947). R. D. Havens, "Thomas Warton and the Eighteenth Century Dilemma," *SP*, XXV (1928). E. N. Hooker, "The Discussion of Taste, from 1750 to 1770, and the New Trends in Literary Criticism," *PMLA*, XLIX (1934). A. C. Howell, "*Res et Verba*: Words and Things," *ELH*, XIII (1946). A. R. Humphreys, " 'The Eternal Fitness of Things': an Aspect of Eighteenth-Century Thought," *MLR*, XLII (1947). Paul O. Kristeller, "The Modern System of the Arts: a Study in the History of Aesthetics," *JHI*, XII, XIII (1951, 1952). R. W. Lee, "*Ut pictura poesis*: the Humanistic Theory of Painting," *Art Bulletin*, XXII (1940). E. L. Mann, "The Problem of Originality in English Literary Criticism, 1750–1800," *PQ*, XVIII (1939). R. McKeon, "Literary Criticism and the Concept of Imitation in Antiquity," *MP*, XXXIV (1936). A. O. Lovejoy, "The Parallel of Deism and Classicism," *MP*, XXIX (1932), and " 'Nature' as Aesthetic Norm," *MLN*, XLII (1927). E. Nitchie, "Longinus and the Theory of Poetic Imitation in Seventeenth and Eighteenth Century England," *SP*, XXXII (1935). H. V. S. Ogden, "The Principles of Variety and Contrast in Seventeenth Century Aesthetics, and Milton, and Poetry," *JHI*, X (1949). W. J. Ong, "Psyche and the Geometers: Aspects of the Associationist Critical Theory," *MP*, XLVIII (1951). Eugene R. Purpus, "The 'Plain, Easy, and Familiar Way': the Dialogue in English Literature, 1660–1725," *ELH*, XVII (1950). J. D. Scheffer, "The Idea of Decline in Literature and the Fine Arts in Eighteenth-Century England," *MP*, XXXIII (1936). Earl R. Wasserman, "The Pleasures of Tragedy," *ELH*, XIV (1947). George Williamson, "The Restoration Revolt against Enthusiasm," *SP*, XXX (1933). Paul S. Wood, "Native Elements in English Neo-classicism," *MP*, XXIV (1926). A. S. P. Woodhouse, "Collins and the Creative Imagination," in *Studies in English by Members of University College Toronto* (Toronto: University of Toronto Press, 1931).

THE ANGLO-SCOTS INQUIRY

Gladys Bryson, *Man and Society: the Scottish Inquiry of the Eighteenth Century* (Princeton, N.Y.: Princeton University Press, 1945). H. G. Graham, *Scottish Men of Letters in the Eighteenth Century* (London: Black and New York: The Macmillan Company, 1901). Michael Joyce, *Edinburgh: the Golden Age, 1769–1832* (New York: Longmans, Green, 1951). James McCosh, *The Scottish Philosophy, Biographical, Expository, Critical, from Hutcheson to Hamilton* (London: Macmillan and Co., 1875).

WIT AND HUMOR

Under General Studies, see Wimsatt *passim*, but especially ch. 12. "Rhetoric and Neo-Classic Wit." Under Johnson, see ch. i of Hagstrum: "True Wit"; and article by Perkins. In 1946 the Augustan Reprint Society initiated a series of facsimile *Essays on Wit* which reproduce scarce eighteenth-century pamphlets and items from periodicals. Richmond P. Bond, *English Burlesque Poetry, 1700–1750* (Cambridge, Mass.: Harvard University Press, 1932). Maurice O. Johnson, *The Sin of Wit* (Syracuse: Syracuse University Press, 1950), centered on Swift. Stuart M. Tave, *The Amiable Humorist: a Study in the Comic Theory and Criticism of the Eighteenth and Early Nineteenth Centuries* (Chicago: University of Chicago Press, 1960), the major book on humor-tradition. Geoffrey Walton, "Seventeenth-Century Ideas of Wit," in *Metaphysical to Augustan* (London: Bowes & Bowes, 1955). Scott Elledge, "Cowley's Ode *Of Wit* and Longinus on the Sublime: a Study of One Definition of the Word *Wit*," *MLQ*, IX (1948). William Empson, " 'Wit' in the *Essay of Criticism*," *Hudson Review*, II (1950). Virgil B. Heltzel, "Chesterfield and the Anti-Laughter Tradition," *MP*, XXVI (1928). E. N. Hooker, introduction to *Critical Works of Dennis* (see Dennis); "Humour in the Age of Pope," *HLQ*, XI (1948); and "Pope on Wit: the *Essay on Criticism*," in *The Seventeenth Century* by R. F. Jones, *et al.* (Palo Alto, Calif.: Stanford University Press, 1951). Richard E. Hughes, " 'Wit': the Genealogy of a Theory," *CLA Journal*, V (1961). Samuel Kliger, "Whig Aesthetics: a Phase of Eighteenth-Century Taste," *ELH*, XVI (1949). Maynard Mack, " 'Wit and Poetry and Pope': Some Observations on his Imagery," in *Essays Presented to George Sherburn* (Oxford: The Clarendon Press, 1949). A. H. Nethercot, "The Term 'Metaphysical Poets' before Johnson," *MLN*, XXXVII (1922); "The Reputation of the Metaphysical Poets during the Age of Pope," *PQ*, IV (1925); and "The Reputation of the Metaphysical Poets during the Age of Johnson and the Romantic Revival," *SP*, XXII (1925). Henry L. Snuggs, "The Comic Humours: a New Interpretation," *PMLA*, LXII (1947). W. L. Ustick and H. H. Hudson, "Wit, 'Mixt Wit,' and the Bee in Amber," *Huntington Library Bulletin*, VIII (1935). George Williamson, "The Rhetorical Pattern of Neo-Classical Wit," *MP*, XXXIII (1935).

JOSEPH ADDISON

Text: *The Spectator* (London, 1712–15). Biography: Peter Smithers, *The Life of Joseph Addison* (Oxford: The Clarendon Press, 1954). Commentary: Under General Studies, see discussions in Bosker, Hipple, Monk, Tuveson, and Wimsatt; under Hobbes, see chapter in Thorpe. E. K. Broadus, "Addison's Influence on the Development of Interest in Folk-Poetry of the Eighteenth Century," *MP*, VIII (1910). C. S. Lewis, "Addison," in *Essays Presented to David Nichol Smith* (Oxford: The Clarendon Press, 1945). J. H. Neumann, "Shakespearean Criticism in *The Tatler* and *The Spectator*," *PMLA*, XXXIX (1924). C. D. Thorpe, "Addison's Theory of Imagination as 'Perceptive Response,'" *Papers of the Michigan Academy*, XXI (1936); "Addison and Some of His Predecessors on 'Novelty,'" *PMLA*, LII (1937); and "Addison's Contribution to Criticism," in *The Seventeenth Century*, R. F. Jones, ed. (Palo Alto, Calif.: Stanford University Press, 1951).

ARCHIBALD ALISON

Text: Fifth edition (Edinburgh, 1817). Commentary: Under General Studies, see discussions in Hipple, Monk, and Tuveson; under Price, see Sir Thomas Dick Lauder. Francis Jeffrey, review of the *Essays on Taste* in *Edinburgh Review* (May, 1811), later enlarged and inserted, under the heading "Beauty," in *Encyclopedia Britannica* (1824 and 1841). Martin Kallich, "The Meaning of Archibald Alison's *Essays on Taste*," *PQ*, XXVII (1948). Jerome Stolnitz, " 'Beauty': Some Stages in the History of an Idea," *JHI*, XXII (1961); and "On the Origins of 'Aesthetic Disinterestedness,'" *JAAC*, XX (1961).

ISAAC BARROW

Text: *Works*, John Tillotson, ed. (London, 1716). Biography: Tillotson's Preface. P. H. Osmond, *Barrow: His Life and Times* (London, 1944). Commentary: Under Wit and Humor, see Tave. Useful for background is W. Fraser Mitchell, *English Pulpit Oratory from Andrews to Tillotson: a Study of Its Literary Aspects* (London: Society for Promoting Christian Knowledge, 1932). *Cf.* Martin C. Battestin, *The Moral Basis of Fielding's Art* (Middletown, Conn.: Wesleyan University Press, 1959).

SIR RICHARD BLACKMORE

Text: *Essays upon Several Subjects* (London, 1716). Biography: A. Rosenberg, *Sir Richard Blackmore* (Lincoln: University of Nebraska Press, 1953). Commentary: R. C. Boys, Introduction to *Series One: Essays on Wit*, No. 1, Augustan Reprint Society (Ann Arbor, Mich.:

Edwards Brothers, 1946); and *Sir Richard Blackmore and the Wits* (Ann Arbor: University of Michigan Press, 1949). L. Douglas, "A Severe Animadversion on Bossu," *PMLA*, LXII (1947). Robert M. Krapp, "Class Analysis of a Literary Controversy, Wit and Sense in Seventeenth-Century English Literature," *Science and Society*, X (1946).

THOMAS BLACKWELL

Text: Second edition (London, 1736). Commentary: Donald Foerster, *Homer in English Criticism: the Historical Approach in the Eighteenth Century* (New Haven, Conn.: Yale University Press, 1947); and "Scottish Primitivism and the Historical Approach," *PQ*, XXIX (1950). R. H. Pearce, "The Eighteenth-Century Scottish Primitivists: Some Reconsiderations," *ELH*, XII (1945). Lois Whitney, "Eighteenth-Century Primitivistic Theories of the Epic," *MP*, XXI (1924); and "Thomas Blackwell, a Disciple of Shaftesbury," *PQ*, V (1926).

EDMUND BURKE

Text: *Works*, F. Laurence and W. King, eds. (London, 1803). Biography and general study: W. J. Bate, Introduction to *Selected Writings of Edmund Burke* (New York: Modern Library, 1960). Donald Cross Bryant, *Edmund Burke and His Literary Friends* (1939), Washington University Studies in Language and Literature, No. 9. Alfred Cobban, *Edmund Burke and the Revolt Against the Eighteenth Century* (London: Allen, 1929). Sir Philip Magnus, *Edmund Burke* (London: J. Murray, 1939). Charles Parkin, *The Moral Basis of Burke's Political Thought* (Cambridge, Eng.: Cambridge University Press, 1956). Commentary: Under General Studies, see discussions in Hipple, Monk, and Tuveson. J. T. Boulton, Introduction to his edition of *The Sublime* (London: Routledge and Kegan Paul, 1958). Erika von Erhardt-Siebold, "Harmony of the Senses in English, German, and French Romanticism," *PMLA*, XLVII (1932). W. G. Howard, "Burke Among the Forerunners of Lessing," *PMLA*, XXII (1907). T. M. Moore, *The Backgrounds of Burke's Theory of the Sublime, 1660–1759* (Ithaca, N.Y.: Cornell University Press, 1933). Dixon Wecter, "Burke's Theory concerning Words, Images, and Emotion," *PMLA*, LV (1940). H. A. Wichelns, "Burke's Essay on the Sublime and Its Reviewers," *JEGP*, XXI (1922).

WILLIAM CONGREVE

Text: *Letters Upon Several Occasions*, John Dennis, ed. (London, 1696). Biography: John C. Hodges, *William Congreve the Man: a*

610 SELECTED BIBLIOGRAPHIES

Biography from New Sources (London: Oxford University Press, 1941). D. Crane Taylor, *William Congreve* (Oxford: The Clarendon Press, 1931). Commentary: Under Wit and Humor, see Tave. T. H. Fujimura, *The Restoration Comedy of Wit* (Princeton, N.J.: Princeton University Press, 1953). Samuel Johnson, *Lives of the Poets*, G. B. Hill, ed. (Oxford: Clarendon Press, 1905), Vol. II. Joseph Wood Krutch, *Comedy and Conscience after the Restoration*, second edition (New York: Columbia University Press, 1949).

ANTHONY ASHLEY COOPER, THIRD EARL OF SHAFTESBURY

Text: Second edition (London, 1714), which embodies final revisions, as reprinted in *The Characteristics*, J. M. Robertson, ed. (London: Grant Richards, 1900). *Second Characters, or the Language of Forms*, Benjamin Rand, ed. (Cambridge, Eng.: Cambridge University Press, 1914). Biography: R. L. Brett, *The Third Earl of Shaftesbury: a Study in Eighteenth-Century Literary Theory* (London: Hutchinson's University Library, 1951). Commentary: For influence on Herder, Winckelmann, Goethe, and Kant, see Ernst Cassirer, *The Platonic Renaissance in England*, James P. Pettegrove, trans. (Austin: University of Texas Press, 1953). For influence on Voltaire, Montesquieu, Diderot, and Rousseau, see Dorothy B. Schlegel, *Shaftesbury and the French Deists* (Chapel Hill: University of North Carolina Press, 1956). The controversy over "ridicule" in Anthony Collins, Akenside, Berkeley, Warburton, and others is reviewed in A. O. Aldridge, "Lord Shaftesbury and the Test of Truth," *PMLA*, LX (1945), and W. D. Templeman, "Warburton and Brown Continue the Battle over Ridicule," *HLQ*, XVII (1953). W. E. Alderman, "Shaftesbury and the Doctrine of Moral Sense in the Eighteenth Century," *PMLA*, XLVI (1931); and "Shaftesbury and the Doctrine of Benevolence in the Eighteenth Century," *Transactions of the Wisconsin Academy of Science, Arts, and Letters*, XXVI (1931). A. O. Aldridge, "Lord Shaftesbury's Literary Theories," *PQ*, XXIV (1945). R. L. Brett, "The Third Earl of Shaftesbury as a Literary Critic," *MLR*, XXXVII (1942). R. S. Crane, "Suggestions Toward a Genealogy of the Man of Feeling," *ELH*, I (1934). Thomas Fowler, *Shaftesbury and Hutcheson* (London, 1882). Cecil A. Moore, "Shaftesbury and the Ethical Poets in England, 1700–1760," *PMLA*, XXXI (1916); and "The Return to Nature in English Poetry of the Eighteenth Century," *SP*, XIV (1917). Ernest Tuveson, "The Importance of Shaftesbury," *ELH*, XX (1953); and "The Origins of the 'Moral Sense,' " *HLQ*, XI (1948).

SIR WILLIAM DAVENANT

Text: *Works* (London, 1673). Biography: Alfred Harbage, *Sir William Davenant, Poet-Venturer* (Philadelphia: University of Pennsylvania

Press, 1935). Arthur H. Nethercot, *Sir William D'Avenant, Poet Laureate and Playwright-Manager* (Chicago: University of Chicago Press, 1938). Commentary: C. M. Dowlin's study of Preface to *Gondibert* (see Hobbes).

JOHN DENNIS

Text: *The Critical Works of John Dennis*, Edward Niles Hooker, ed. (Baltimore: Johns Hopkins University Press, 1939–43). The introduction in Volume II is superb commentary not only on Dennis, but on his entire critical milieu. Biography: H. G. Paul, *John Dennis: His Life and Criticism* (New York: Columbia University Press, 1911). Commentary: Under General Studies, see Monk; under Hobbes, see Thorpe. E. N. Hooker, "Pope and Dennis," *ELH*, VII (1940). C. D. Thorpe, "Two Augustans Cross the Alps: Dennis and Addison on Mountain Scenery," *SP*, XXXII (1935).

JOHN DRYDEN

Texts: *An Essay of Dramatic Poesy* from the revised, second edition (London, 1684); "To the Reader" is from the first edition of 1668, however, because of its interesting last sentence. Other texts from *Essays of John Dryden*, W. P. Ker, ed. (Oxford: The Clarendon Press, 1900). Ker's introduction is still valuable criticism. Biography and general study: Louis I. Bredvold, *The Intellectual Milieu of John Dryden* (Ann Arbor: University of Michigan Press, 1934). George Saintsbury, *Dryden* (New York: Harper & Brothers, 1881). Kenneth Young, *John Dryden: a Critical Biography* (London: Sylvan Press, 1954). Commentary: Under Hobbes, see discussion in Thorpe. Reuben A. Brower, "An Allusion to Europe: Dryden and Tradition," *ELH*, XIX (1952). David Daiches, *Critical Approaches to Literature* (Englewood Cliffs, N.J.: Prentice-Hall, 1956), ch. 11. J. O. Edison, "Dryden's Criticism of Shakespeare," *SP*, XXXIII (1936). T. S. Eliot, *Homage to John Dryden* (London: L. and Virginia Woolf, 1924); *John Dryden: the Poet, the Dramatist, the Critic* (New York: T. & Elsa Holliday, 1932); and *The Use of Poetry & the Use of Criticism* (London: Faber and Faber, 1933), ch. 3. Prosser Hall Frye, "Dryden and the Critical Canons of the Eighteenth Century," *University of Nebraska Studies*, VII (1907). Baxter Hathaway, "John Dryden and the Function of Tragedy," *PMLA*, LVIII (1943). Frank L. Huntley, "Dryden's Discovery of Boileau," *MP*, XLV (1947); and *On Dryden's "Essay of Dramatic Poesy"* (Ann Arbor: University of Michigan Press, 1951). Richard Foster Jones, "Science and Criticism in the Neo-Classical Age of English Literature," *JHI*, I (1940). John H.

Smith, "Dryden's Critical Temper," *Washington University Studies, Humanistic Series*, XII (1925). Hoyt Trowbridge, "Dryden's *Essay on the Dramatic Poetry of the Last Age*," PQ, XXII (1943); and "The Place of the Rules in Dryden's Criticism," MP, XLIV (1946). A. W. Verrall, *Lectures on Dryden* (Cambridge, Eng.: Cambridge University Press, 1914).

ALEXANDER GERARD

Text: First edition (Edinburgh, 1774). Commentary: Under General Studies, see discussions in Hipple, McKenzie, and Monk. Marjorie Greene, "Gerard's *Essay on Taste*," MP, XLI (1943). Walter J. Hipple, Introduction to his edition of *An Essay on Taste* (Gainesville: Scholars' Facsimiles & Reprints, 1963). Margaret Lee Wiley, "Gerard and the Scots Societies," *The University of Texas Studies in English* (Austin, 1940).

THOMAS HOBBES

Texts: *Leviathan* (London, 1651). "Answer to Davenant" from the folio edition of Davenant's *Works* (1673), where normally it was read. Biography and general study: Richard Peters, *Hobbes* (London: Penguin Books Ltd., 1956). D. G. James, *The Life of Reason: Hobbes, Locke, Bolingbroke* (New York: Longmans, Green, 1949). Commentary: C. M. Dowlin, *Sir William Davenant's Gondibert, Its Preface, and Hobbes' Answer: a Study in English Neo-classicism* (Philadelphia, 1934). Martin Kallich, "The Association of Ideas and Critical Theory: Hobbes, Locke, and Addison," ELH, XII (1945). H. T. Swedenberg, Jr., "Rules and English Critics of the Epic, 1650–1800," SP, XXXV (1938). Clarence DeWitt Thorpe, *The Aesthetic Theory of Thomas Hobbes With Special Reference to His Contribution to the Psychological Approach in English Literary Criticism*, University of Michigan Publications in Language and Literature, XVIII (1940).

HENRY HOME, LORD KAMES

Text: Fourth edition (Edinburgh, 1785), which embodies final revisions. Biography: A. F. Tytler, *Memoirs* (Edinburgh, 1807). Commentary: Under General Studies, see chapters in Bosker and Hipple. Helen W. Randall, *The Critical Theory of Lord Kames* (Northampton, Mass.: Smith College Studies in Modern Languages, 1944). I. A. Richards, *The Philosophy of Rhetoric* (New York: Oxford University

Press, 1936). M. W. Bundy, "Lord Kames and the Maggots in Amber," *JEGP*, XLV (1946). Gordon McKenzie, "Lord Kames and the Mechanist Tradition," in *Essays and Studies*, University of California Publications in English, XIV (1942). Thomas M. Raysor, "The Downfall of the Three Unities," *MLN*, XLII (1927). On "moral Newtonianism," see Basil Willey, *The Eighteenth Century Background: Studies on the Idea of Nature in the Thought of the Period* (New York: Columbia University Press, 1941).

DAVID HUME

Text: *Essays and Treatises on Several Subjects* (Edinburgh, 1777), which embodies final revisions. Biography: Ernest Campbell Mossner, *The Life of David Hume* (Austin: University of Texas Press, 1954). Commentary: Under Hutcheson, see article by Kallich. Teddy Brunius, *David Hume on Criticism*, Studies Edited by the Institute of Art History, University of Uppsala (Stockholm: Almqvist & Wiksell, 1952). Ralph Cohen, "David Hume's Experimental Method and the Theory of Taste," *ELH*, XXV (1958). Frederick J. Doering, "Hume and the Theory of Tragedy," *PMLA*, XXXVI (1921). Walter J. Hipple, "The Logic of Hume's Essay 'Of Tragedy,'" *Philosophical Quarterly*, VI (1956). E. C. Mossner, "Hume and the Ancient-Modern Controversy, 1725–52: a Study in Creative Skepticism," *The University of Texas Studies in English*, XXVIII (1949). James Noxon, "Hume's Opinions of Critics," *JAAC*, XX (1961). Harold Taylor, "Hume's Theory of Imagination," *University of Toronto Quarterly*, XII (1943).

RICHARD HURD

Texts: *Letters on Chivalry*, second edition (1762); "Dissertation" from *Works* (London, 1811). Biography: F. Kilvert, *Memoirs* (London: Bentley, 1860). A. W. Evans, *Warburton and the Warburtonians* (London: Oxford University Press, 1932). Commentary: Victor M. Hamm, "A Seventeenth-Century French Source for Hurd's Letters on Chivalry and Romance," *PMLA*, LII (1937). Edwine Montague, "Bishop Hurd's Association with Thomas Warton," *Stanford Studies in Language and Literature* (1941). Audley L. Smith, "Richard Hurd's Letters on Chivalry and Romance," *ELH*, VI (1939). Hoyt Trowbridge, "Bishop Hurd: a Reinterpretation," *PMLA*, LVIII (1943).

FRANCIS HUTCHESON

Text: *Hibernicus's Letters: Or a Philosophical Miscellany* (1734), second edition of a London reprint from the *Dublin Journal*. Biography: W. R. Scott, *Francis Hutcheson* (Cambridge, Eng.: Cambridge University Press, 1900). Commentary: Under General Studies, see Hipple; under Wit and Humor, see Tave; under Shaftesbury, see Fowler. Martin Kallich, "The Associationist Criticism of Francis Hutcheson and David Hume," *SP*, XLIII (1946). Clarence DeWitt Thorpe, "Addison and Hutcheson on the Imagination," *ELH*, II (1935).

SAMUEL JOHNSON

Texts: *The Rambler*, twelfth edition (1793); *The Idler*, third edition (1767); Preface to the *Dictionary*, the revised fourth edition (1773); *Rasselas*, second edition (1759); Preface to Shakespeare, first edition (1765); Shakespeare notes follow the format which has become conventional since Sir Walter Raleigh's *Johnson on Shakespeare* (Oxford, 1908); *Lives of the English Poets*, George Birkbeck Hill, ed. (Oxford: The Clarendon Press, 1905), the standard scholarly edition. Biography and general study: Boswell's *Life* (1791) and *Tour to the Hebrides* (1785). *Johnsonian Miscellanies*, G. B. Hill, ed. (Oxford: The Clarendon Press, 1897). James L. Clifford, *Young Sam Johnson* (New York: McGraw-Hill Book Company, 1955). Joseph Wood Krutch, *Samuel Johnson* (New York: Holt, 1944). W. B. C. Watkins, *Perilous Balance* (Princeton, N.J.: Princeton University Press, 1939). Commentary: Walter Jackson Bate, *The Achievement of Samuel Johnson* (New York: Oxford University Press, 1955), by far the most brilliant and comprehensive study. Bertrand H. Bronson, *Johnson Agonistes and Other Essays* (Berkeley and Los Angeles: University of California Press, 1946). *The Critical Opinions of Samuel Johnson*, J. E. Brown, ed. (Princeton, N.J.: Princeton University Press, 1926). J. H. Hagstrum, *Samuel Johnson's Literary Criticism* (Minneapolis: University of Minnesota Press, 1952). Arthur Sherbo, *Samuel Johnson, Editor of Shakespeare*, Illinois Studies in Language and Literature, XLII (1956). W. B. C. Watkins, *Johnson and English Poetry Before 1660* (Princeton, N.J.: Princeton University Press, 1936). W. K. Wimsatt, Jr., *The Prose Style of Samuel Johnson* (New Haven, Conn.: Yale University Press, 1941); and *Philosophic Words* (New Haven, Conn.: Yale University Press, 1948). T. S. Eliot, "Johnson as Critic and Poet," in *On Poetry and Poets* (London: Faber & Faber, 1957). R. D. Havens, "Johnson's Distrust of Imagination," *ELH*, X (1943). W. R. Keast, "Johnson's Criticism of the Metaphysical Poets," *ELH*, XVII (1950); and "The Theoretical Foundations of Johnson's Criticism," in *Critics and Criticism Ancient and Modern*, R. S. Crane, ed. (Chicago: University of Chicago Press, 1952). F. R. Leavis, "Johnson and Augustanism" in *The Common Pursuit* (New York: George W. Stewart, Publisher, 1952); and "Johnson as Critic," *Scrutiny*, XII (1944). David Perkins, "Johnson on Wit and Metaphysical Poetry," *ELH*,

XX (1953). W. B. C. Watkins, "Dr. Johnson on the Imagination: a Note," *RES*, XXII (1946).

JOHN LOCKE

Text: *Works* (London, 1714), the first collected edition. Biography: Maurice Cranston, *John Locke* (New York: The Macmillan Company, 1957). Commentary: Under Hobbes, see article by Kallich; under General Studies, see Tuveson, whose imaginative study of Locke ranges down the entire eighteenth century. Kenneth MacLean, *John Locke and English Literature of the Eighteenth Century* (New Haven, Conn.: Yale University Press, 1936). G. G. Pahl, "Locke as Literary Critic and Biblical Interpreter," in *Essays Dedicated to Lily B. Campbell* (Berkeley: University of California Press, 1950). Basil Willey, *The Seventeenth Century Background* (London: Chatto & Windus, 1934).

MAURICE MORGANN

Text: The edition of 1777, as reprinted by William Arthur Gill (London: Henry Frowde, 1912). There is also an edition by David Nichol Smith, *Eighteenth Century Essays on Shakespeare* (Glasgow, 1903). Commentary: Under General Studies, see Bosker and Tuveson. R. W. Babcock, *The Genesis of Shakespeare Idolatry, 1766–1799* (Chapel Hill: University of North Carolina Press, 1931). Stuart M. Tave, "Notes on the Influence of Morgann's *Essay on Falstaff*," *RES*, New Series, III (1952).

CORBYN MORRIS

Text: First edition (London, 1744), from the facsimile version introduced by James L. Clifford for The Augustan Reprint Society, *Series One, No. 4: Essays on Wit* (Nov., 1947). Commentary: Stuart M. Tave, "Corbyn Morris: Falstaff, Humor and Comic Theory in the Eighteenth Century," *MP*, L (1952).

SIR UVEDALE PRICE

Text: First edition (London, 1794), and revised editions of 1796 and 1810, as indicated. Commentary: Under General Studies, see Hipple and Monk. Christopher Hussey, *The Picturesque. Studies in a Point of View* (London, 1927). Elizabeth W. Manwaring, *Italian Landscape in Eighteenth Century England* (New York: Oxford University Press, 1925). William D. Templeman, "Sir Joshua Reynolds on the Picturesque," *MLN*, XLVII (1932); "Thoreau, Moralist of the Picturesque," *PMLA*, XLVII (1932); and chs. VI and VII of *The Life and Work of William Gilpin*, XXIV, 3–4 (Urbana: University of Illinois Studies in Language and Literature, 1939). *Sir Uvedale Price on the Picturesque*, Sir Thomas Dick Lauder, ed. (Edinburgh: Caldwell, Lloyd, and Co., 1842), precedes selections by a long introduction, "On the Origin of Taste," which shows the influence of Alison.

SIR JOSHUA REYNOLDS

Text: *Works*, Edmund Malone, ed. (London, 1801), the revised third edition. Biography and general study: James Northcote, *Memoirs of Sir Joshua Reynolds* (London, 1818). F. W. Hilles, *The Literary Career of Sir Joshua Reynolds* (Cambridge, Eng.: Cambridge University Press, 1936); and "Sir Joshua's Prose" in *The Age of Johnson* (New Haven, Conn.: Yale University Press, 1949). Commentary: Under General Studies, see discussions in Bate, Bosker, Hipple, and Monk. Eugene Clinton Elliott, "Reynolds and Hazlitt," *JAAC*, XXI (1962). W. J. Hipple, "General and Particular in the *Discourses* of Sir Joshua Reynolds: a Study in Method," *JAAC*, XI (1953). Michael Macklem, "Reynolds and the Ambiguities of Neo-Classical Criticism," *PQ*, XXI (1952). Elder Olson, Introduction to joint edition of *Longinus . . . and Reynolds's Discourses* (Chicago: Packard, 1945). E. M. S. Thompson, "The *Discourses* of Sir Joshua Reynolds," *PMLA*, XXXII (1917). Hoyt Trowbridge, "Platonism and Sir Joshua Reynolds," *English Studies*, XXI (1939). Robert R. Wark's Introduction to his edition of the *Discourses* (San Marino: Huntington Library, 1959). Blake's famous annotations of the *Discourses* may be studied in *Complete Writings of William Blake*, Geoffrey Keynes, ed. (London: Nonesuch Press, 1957).

THOMAS RYMER

Text: *The Critical Works of Thomas Rymer*, Curt A. Zimansky, ed. (New Haven, Conn.: Yale University Press, 1956), whose introduction is the most reliable short biography and commentary. Commentary: For two interesting contemporary attacks, see John Dennis, *The Impartial Critic* (1693), and Samuel Butler, "Upon Critics Who Judge of Modern Plays precisely by the Rules of the Ancients," in *Critical Essays*, Spingarn, ed. (see Collections). Spingarn's introduction is still helpful. G. B. Dutton, "The French Aristotelian Formalists and

Thomas Rymer," *PMLA*, XXIX (1914). E. E. Stoll, *"Oedipus* and *Othello:* Corneille, Rymer, and Voltaire," *Revue anglo-américaine*, XII (1945). Fred G. Walcott, "John Dryden's Answer to Thomas Rymer's *The Tragedies of the Last Age*," *PQ*, XV (1936).

JOSEPH WARTON

Text: Second, corrected edition (London, 1762), a sample of mid-century taste preceding Warton's later changes and additions. Biography and general study: John Wooll, *Biographical Memoirs* (London, 1806). See J. Dennis, "The Wartons," *Studies in English Literature* (London: Stanford, 1876); Sir Edmund Gosse, "Two Pioneers of Romanticism, Joseph and Thomas Warton," *Proceedings of the British Academy* (1915); Eric Partridge, *The Three Wartons. A Choice of Their Verse* (London: The Scholartis Press, 1927). Commentary: J. Allison, "Joseph Warton's Reply to Dr. Johnson's *Lives*," *JEGP*, LI (1952). Paul F. Leedy, "Genre Criticism and the Significance of Warton's *Essay on Pope*," *JEGP*, XLV (1946); reviewed by W. J. Bate, *PQ*, XXVI (1947). W. D. MacClintock, *Joseph Warton's "Essay on Pope": A History of the Five Editions* (Chapel Hill: University of North Carolina Press, 1933). Edith J. Morley, "Joseph Warton: a Comparison of His *Essay on the Genius and Writings of Pope* with His Edition of Pope's Works," *Essays and Studies*, IX (1924). Hoyt Trowbridge, "Joseph Warton on the Imagination," *MP*, XXXV (1937), excellent; and "Joseph Warton's Classification of English Poets," *MLN* (1936).

WALTER WHITER

Text: First edition (London, 1794). Commentary: Under General Studies, see Tuveson. "The Imagery of Shakespeare: Dr. Clemen and Walter Whiter," *TLS* (Sept. 5, 1936).

EDWARD YOUNG

Text: Second edition (London, 1759). Biography and general study: Margery Bailey, "Edward Young," in *The Age of Johnson* (New Haven, Conn.: Yale University Press, 1949). Isabel St.-John Bliss, "Young's *Night Thoughts* in Relation to Contemporary Christian Apologetics," *PMLA*, XLIX (1934). Henry Pettit, *The English Rejection of Young's Night-Thoughts* (1957), University of Colorado Studies in Language and Literature, No. 6. H. C. Shelley, *The Life and Letters of Edward Young* (London: Isaac Pitman & Sons, 1914). W. Thomas, *Le Poète Edward Young* (Paris: Hachette, 1901). Commentary: Under General Studies, see discussions in Abrams, Bate, Bosker, and Monk. P. Kaufman, "Heralds of Original Genius," in *Essays in Memory of Barrett Wendell* (Cambridge, Mass.: Harvard University Press, 1926). A. D. McKillop, "Richardson, Young, and the *Conjectures*," MP, XXII (1925). Edition of the *Conjectures* by Edith J. Morley (Manchester University Press, 1918). Lawrence Marsden Price, *The Reception of English Literature in Germany* (Berkeley: University of California Press, 1932), chs. 9 and 17. M. W. Steinke, *Edward Young's "Conjectures on Original Composition" in England and Germany* (New York: F. C. Stechert Co., 1917).

Selective Index

Page numbers of significant introductions and of
bibliography are set in italics

ABOUT THE AUTHOR

GERALD WESTER CHAPMAN is *Chairman of the Department of English at the University of Denver and associate editor of* The Denver Quarterly: A Journal of Modern Culture. *He received his A.B. and M.A. from Southern Methodist University and his Ph.D. from Harvard University. Before going to the University of Denver in 1962, he taught at Southern Methodist, Harvard, Northwestern, and the University of Texas. Professor Chapman has edited* Essays on Shakespeare *and is the author of a forthcoming book entitled* Edmund Burke: The Practical Imagination.